Private Troubles and Public Issues
Social Problems in the Postmodern Era

Private Troubles and Public Issues
Social Problems in the Postmodern Era

University of California, Berkeley

Joel H. Henderson
School of Public Administration and Urban Studies, San Diego

Harcourt Brace College Publishers

Fort Worth Philadelphia San Diego New York Orlando Austin San Antonio
Toronto London Montreal Sydney Tokyo

Publisher	Christopher P. Klein
Senior Acquisitions Editor	Stephen T. Jordan
Developmental Editor	Roz Sackoff
Project Editor	Betsy Cummings
Production Manager	Diane Gray
Art Director	Lora Knox
Picture Editor	Sandra Lord
Photo Researcher	Sue C. Howard

ISBN: 0-15-501368-8

Library of Congress Catalog Card Number: 96-76139

Harcourt Brace College Publishers may provide complimentary instructional aids and supplements or supplement packages to those adopters qualified under our adoption policy. Please contact your sales representative for more information. If as an adopter or potential user you receive supplements you do not need, please return them to your sales representative or send them to:

Attn: Returns Department
Troy Warehouse
465 South Lincoln Drive
Troy, MO 63379

Address for Editorial Correspondence: Harcourt Brace College Publishers, 301 Commerce Street, Suite 3700, Fort Worth, Texas 76102.

Address for Orders: Harcourt Brace & Company, 6277 Sea Harbor Drive, Orlando, Florida 32887-6777, 1-800-782-4479, or 1-800-433-0001 (in Florida).

Printed in the United States of America

6 7 8 9 0 1 2 3 4 5 039 0 9 8 7 6 5 4 3 2 1

Dedication

David Simon dedicates this book to two beloved people, his brother, Stephen Isaac Simon, who died tragically and suddenly during the writing of this book. Steve, you were a wonderful and loving brother, and I will miss you always. David also dedicates this book to his wife, Judy Corrine Simon, whose love and inspiration made finishing this work a mission instead of a task. Thank you, darling, I hope we write many books together from now on.

Joel Henderson dedicates this book to Anne and Eddie Henderson with love and appreciation.

Preface

Every new book represents an opportunity to state one's beliefs in a new form, to enhance one's message, and to argue for one's position. This book represents the continuation of an intellectual journey begun nearly seventeen years ago with the publication of *Elite Deviance* (fifth edition, 1996), which represents the first effort in utilizing C. Wright Mills' sociological imagination paradigm (and its offshoots) to analyze elite crime. That effort led to a number of other books—specifically *Crimes of the Criminal Justice System* (Anderson, 1994), with Joel Henderson), and, most recently, *Social Problems and the Sociological Imagination* (McGraw-Hill, 1995).

Now, with *Private Troubles and Public Issues: Social Problems in the Postmodern Era,* a full-blown application of the paradigm Mills set nearly forty years ago has come to fruition. As I look at most other social problems texts, what I notice is the lack of a "holistic" approach, a paradigm that could be used to:

1. define social problems,
2. explain their causes,
3. point out the defects in other approaches, and
4. point to solutions that logically follow from the causal analysis.

I have always felt that Mills's paradigm, properly interpreted, offers the best hope for a critical approach to social problems. This is because:

- In contrast to constructionist views, social problems generate great physical, financial, and moral/psychological harms, whether they are officially recognized as problems or not. Thus, before John Kennedy's election in 1960, poverty was widespread in America, but officially unrecognized by the federal government in many of its forms. Yet America's poor suffered from the effects of poverty no matter what any politician did or did not recognize as poverty.

- Social problems are sociological conditions that are caused by other sociological conditions. Specifically, social problems constitute harms that are socially patterned; they are not random occurrences.

As our first chapter explains, the causes of social problems are sociological in that they are not found within the personalities of individuals (although their consequences certainly are) but rather in the conflict and contradictions within and between various societal institutions. The chief contradiction of postmodern capitalistic societies involves the great inequalities between the haves and have-nots in wealth and income, political power, and the ability to define cultural values. The lack of these scarce resources creates numerous micro social problems for the have-nots. It also requires that the haves devote more and more resources to attempting to control the powerless.

To meet the goals involved in demonstrating the sociological imagination perspective, we have employed a number of unique features. For example, in Chapter 2, there is a detailed description of some current and former members of the power elite, complete with names and affiliations. There are also detailed examples of the "higher immorality" in many chapters, including, for example, the CIA's record in drug trafficking. Chapters 5 through 14 contain "Private Troubles/Public Issues" features designed to inform students how the social problems under discussion directly affect them, and what they personally can do about them. For example, our discussion of racism contains the following "Private Troubles/Public Issues: Treating Hate Crimes on Campus" and what all students can do to reduce them:

- During the 1991 Gulf War, a large number of Arab and Jewish students were targets of hate crimes.
- Chinese student reporters at the University of California at Davis received threatening phone calls after an effort failed by some student government members to cut off the funding of the campus' minority-oriented newspaper, *The Third World*.

There have been a disturbing number of bigotry incidents in college fraternities around the nation:

- Members of the Zeta Beta Tau fraternity at the University of Wisconsin put on a mock slave auction for which they painted their faces black, wore Afro wigs, and lip-synched Jackson Five tunes.
- At Oklahoma State University, one fraternity put on a "plantation party" during which members dressed as slaves and sang songs to sorority members.
- At the University of Cincinnati, one fraternity held a Martin Luther King "trash party," where guests were asked to wear KKK hoods, carry boom boxes, and welfare checks, and identify "your father if you know who he is."
- One fraternity at Brown University issued party invitations announcing that only heterosexuals could attend.

Finally, we believe that it is grossly unfair to students to offer an analysis of the causes and consequences of social problems without pointing to some suggested solutions. Consequently, the final chapter is devoted to our personal views on resolving social problems. While we do not expect most students, or even most instructors, to agree with our views, this chapter can at least offer a starting point for dialogue, debate, and discussion.

Because of the use of the sociological imagination paradigm throughout this book, you will find additional unique features in virtually every chapter. For example, Chapter 4 is devoted to a discussion of ideological analysis and the shortcomings of conservative and liberal public policies, Chapter 14 addresses the social problems of everyday life (i.e., family, school, religion, and work) and the alienation that is a basic cause of them. We sincerely hope that you enjoy our approach to social problems, and would very much like to hear your comments.

Acknowledgments

We wish to express our gratitude to our two wonderful editors, Chris Klein and Stephen T. Jordan. We thank them for their patience, their tolerance of the views of two "contrary" graduate students of the seventies, and their willingness to take a chance on a new approach to social problems. We also wish to thank our production editor Roz Sackoff, as well as our book team at Harcourt Brace, project editor, Betsy Cummings, production manager, Diane Gray, and art director, Lora Knox.

Finally, we wish to thank all those who reviewed the manuscript in its various stages of production. Frank E. Hagan, Mercyhurst College; James M. Fendrich, Florida State University; John L. Boies; Texas A&M University; Jim Messerschmidt, University of Southern Maine; Sue Hammons-Bryner, Abraham Baldwin Agricultural College; James Bradford Powers, Dean College; Jackie Eller, Middle Tennessee State University.

Brief Contents

Contents

Part
ONE

The Sociological Imagination: A Paradigm for Studying Social Problems

•   •   •   •   •

Social Problems in the Postmodern Era

America's Crises in the 1990s

There are times in the life of every civilization when it must either honestly confront the realities or face its decline (Phillips, 1990, 1993; Ehrenreich, 1989:196–207). During such moments

- Myths created by the mass media must be separated from realities.
- Political rhetoric must be divorced from forthright evaluation of the political process.
- Myths about family, education, religion, and community must be distinguished from the actual events occurring in those institutions.

These times also require that the origins of the crises of personal life be properly attributed to the social problems from which they stem. We live in an era of crises and confusion.

America's "main drift" (master trend) today is toward economic, political, social, and ethical crisis, and the nation is "declining at an alarming rate" (Schaef, 1988:3). This decline is the subject of daily headlines. Consider what now occurs on an average day among American youth.[1]

- 2738 unmarried teenagers bear children.
- 2000 teens attempt suicide.
- 4.4 million youths consume illegal drugs or alcohol.
- 5200 children aged 10 to 17 are arrested.
- 5500 adolescents run away from home, and 14,000 drop out of school.
- Children 13 and under collectively watch 192 million hours of TV, yet the average mother spends eleven minutes per day with her offspring, the average father eight minutes per day with his.
- 700,000–800,000 high school seniors are unable to read.

Consider the dimensions of an average day's crime and drug problem:

- Employees steal $34 million from employers.
- Organized crime reaps nearly $250 million.
- Arsonists torch 225 buildings.
- Street criminals steal nearly $11 million from victims while engaging in about 82,000 criminal acts against property.
- Criminals assault 12,000 people and rape 2430 women.
- Americans smoke 87,000 bales of marijuana, snort 380 pounds of cocaine, and pay drug dealers $123 million.
- More than 1000 Americans die from the effects of cigarette smoking, the single most preventable cause of death in America.

[1]The following lists are based on information in *Scandal Annual* (1989).

Meanwhile, at the highest stratum of society,

- Corporations illegally take in $550 million.
- Individual white-collar criminals steal $110 million.
- Prosecutors indict five public officials on corruption charges.
- Industry produces 15 billion pounds of hazardous waste.

America's crime problem has become a focus of special concern:

- Violent crime in American cities is ten times higher than in European democracies, three times higher than in Canada. Even if all minority crime were subtracted from these statistics, America's rate of violent crime would still be four times higher than that of all industrial democracies combined (Messner & Rosenfeld, 1994).
- The rate of imprisoning people in the United States doubled between 1980 and 1990 and is expected to double again by the year 2000. America's incarceration rate is now the highest in the world and growing.

Finally, episodes of wrongdoing spread cynicism and pessimism throughout the land (Kanter & Mirvis, 1989; Goldfarb, 1991; Garment, 1991). Terrorist and hate crimes make headlines almost daily. Among the recent incidents, consider:

- The April 1995 bombing of the federal building in Oklahoma City, Oklahoma, by individuals connected with self-styled militia groups in Michigan.
- In 1994, arsonists set off firestorms in Southern California, forcing the rich and famous to evacuate or risk death, and teens in San Francisco set a sleeping homeless person afire for fun.
- U.S. officials indict the Panamanian dictator for taking drug smugglers' payoffs while in the employ of the CIA.
- The State Department dismisses an employee for searching the passport file of a presidential candidate's mother.
- The savings and loan scandal is the largest financial crisis in the nation's history, with costs estimated to run as high as $1 trillion. About 40 percent of the savings and loan failures were due to fraud and corruption.
- The nation is emerging from its longest economic slump since the Great Depression while American corporations export jobs to Third World nations. Meanwhile, American executives are paid almost 300 times more than the average worker.

In 1992, Oliver Stone's movie *JFK* sparked renewed interest in the 1963 assassination of President John F. Kennedy. A poll taken at the time of the movie's release indicated that nearly 70 percent of the public believed that either the Central Intelligence Agency or the U.S. military, or both, murdered their own commander-in-chief (*Time*, January 13, 1992: 56). The willingness of the public to doubt the government's version of events underscores the increasing loss of the government legitimacy in the eyes of its citizens. Many Americans doubt that even the release of all classified files in the case will reveal the truth behind the crime.

Social critic Christopher Lasch (1978/1992:259–60) prophetically described the nature of the current crisis:

> Today almost everyone lives in a dangerous world from which there is little escape. International terrorism and . . . bombings . . . arbitrarily effect the rich and poor alike. Crime, violence, and gang wars make cities unsafe and threaten to spread to the suburbs. Racial violence on the streets and in the schools creates an atmosphere of chronic tension and threatens to erupt at any time into full-scale racial conflict. Unemployment spreads from the poor to the white-collar class, while inflation eats away the savings of those who hope to retire in comfort . . . Many white-collar jobs require no more skill and pay even less than blue-collar jobs, conferring little status or security. The propaganda of death and destruction, emanating ceaselessly from the mass media, adds to the prevailing atmosphere of insecurity . . . [adding to] the sense of living in a world in which the past holds out no guidance to the present and the future has become completely unpredictable.

What are the public attitudes regarding the causes and solutions of such conditions? What, in this nation that considers itself the greatest experiment in democracy in world history, are the people's reactions to these multiple crises? What impact have these conditions had on the public mind?

Public Perceptions

In late 1990, two advertising researchers, James Patterson and Peter Kim, asked a representative sample of 2000 American adults 1800 questions regarding what they really believed about their lives. They asked people about a wide range of individual beliefs and behaviors, as well as about leading economic, political, and social problems. The results (1991) were so startling that they made headlines in newspapers across the nation. The findings reveal that the majority of Americans suffer a crisis of belief.

A Crisis of Morality
Few, if any, stable values exist on which to base decisions about daily life or social issues. Only 13 percent of Americans believe in all of the Ten Commandments. People now choose which rules they will obey.

There is no longer a moral consensus in the United States, as there was in the 1950s, and "there is very little respect for any rule of law" (Patterson & Kim, 1991:6). Many of the results of their survey support this notion:

- The official crime statistics underestimate crime by at least 200 percent. Sixty percent of Americans report being crime victims; over half of those report being victimized twice.
- Twenty-five percent of Americans say they would abandon their families for $10 million.
- Sixty-six percent believe there is nothing wrong with lying, and lie regularly.
- Thirty percent of employees have personally witnessed violations of criminal or ethical codes by their bosses, and 43 percent say they cannot trust their co-workers.

- Eighty percent of Americans want morals and ethics taught in public schools, and a majority believe that the leading cause of America's economic decline is "unethical behavior by [business] executives" (Patterson & Kim, 1991:237).

A Crisis of Confidence in Authority

Public confidence in America's institutions is at an all-time low, and 80 percent of Americans say there are no living heroes. Among the lowest rated occupations for honesty and integrity are congressional representative and local politician; lawyer; TV evangelist; stockbroker; oil executives, network television; labor unions; and car and insurance salespeople.

Studies in 1987 and 1991 detailed what Americans feel about their political system. Americans are deeply alienated from the political life of their nation. When the pollster Lou Harris asked a national sample in 1987 if their interests were represented by politicians, 60 percent said they were not—the highest percentage since Harris first asked the question in 1966 (Harris, 1987:35–37).

A 1991 Kettering Foundation study found that most Americans believe there is no point to voting and that money has overwhelming influence in political campaigns, with millions being spent to secure jobs paying $100,000 a year. This sample of respondents believed that media coverage of campaigns alienates voters, partly because of reliance on "sound bites," politicians' practice of reducing complex public problems to empty slogans (Seattle *Post Intelligencer,* June 11, 1991:A-3).

Polls taken in 1992 and 1993 reveal that the average American believes that the federal government wastes 48 cents of every dollar, and only 20 percent of the public trust Washington to do the right thing most of the time, down from 76 percent in 1963 (Gore, 1993:1).

Pessimism about the
Future of the Nation

Americans feel their nation has become "colder, greedier, meaner, more selfish, and less caring" (Patterson & Kim, 1991:213) and they are markedly pessimistic about the future. How do Americans picture their world in the year 2000?

- Fifty-two percent believe that Japan will be the world's economic world leader.
- Seventy seven percent believe the rich will be richer and the poor poorer.
- Seventy-two percent believe that crime rates will have risen and 71 percent believe there will be more violence in the streets.
- Sixty-two percent believe the homeless rate will have risen and 60 percent feel AIDS will have become epidemic—and 60 percent believe that no cure will have been found.
- Fifty-eight percent feel drug and alcohol abuse will have worsened.
- Sixty-two percent see pollution as worse, and 43 percent believe it will be so bad that life will become unbearable.
- Item: A majority believe that such social problems as poverty and racism will outlast their children's lifetimes.

A Crisis of Ideology

A major reason for these pessimistic attitudes is that Americans have little confidence in either the political parties or the dominant schools of ideological thought.

- More Americans now identify themselves as environmentalists (39 percent) than as either Democrats (31 percent) or Republicans (20 percent).
- Only 27 percent of Americans describe themselves as ideologically conservative.
- A mere 9 percent of Americans identify themselves as liberals. Even the 1992 nominee of the Democratic party, Bill Clinton, claimed he was a "centrist."

Contradictory Beliefs about Individualism and Community

Although most Americans believe that social problems will worsen, they think their private lives will get better. This means that they have become increasingly alienated from what happens to other people and the nation, yet they believe they are patriotic. People believe they are "little islands, that they don't really belong to any larger unit" (Patterson & Kim, 1991:217). They have withdrawn from public issues. Thus from 1965 to 1990, the percentage of Americans who read a daily newspaper fell from 67 percent to 30 percent, and the percentage of people who watched television news fell from 52 percent to 41 percent.

Yet the Patterson and Kim study also revealed that Americans want to do the right thing to resolve the crises of our age. Half say they would volunteer to help prevent child abuse. Forty-one percent say they would volunteer to help others learn to read. Twenty-nine percent say they would volunteer to clean up the environment, and 66 percent say they would pay more taxes to do so.

Clearly, Americans are troubled and confused about their own values, and about the future of the nation. This confusion was recently depicted in a Broadway play that aroused considerable attention—*Twilight of the Golds*. Every Sunday, Mrs. Gold tells the audience, she sits down with the week's issues of the New York *Times* and spends all day reading them. When she finishes, she feels overwhelmed by all the information she has absorbed; she has no way to sort out what it all means. She feels that Americans are so overwhelmed by facts that continually keeping up with the news is of questionable value. What Mrs. Gold lacks is a perspective that would allow her to make sense of the news and enable her to relate what she reads to her own life.

The sociologist C. Wright Mills described the nature of Mrs. Gold's confusion decades before the play was written. Mills once remarked that ours is an era of uneasiness and indifference, a time when people experience their personal lives as a series of traps (Mills, 1959:3). In the 1950s and 1960s Mills warned against the dangers inherent in celebrity worship and mass media addiction, militarism and criminal and unethical behaviors among the nation's leaders, conformity, status seeking, bureaucracy, and alienation (Mills' work is profiled in Box 1.1).

Mills believed that ordinary people lack a **sociological imagination**—an ability, or quality of mind, to see the interrelationship of their own lives and the historical period and institutional arrangements (society) in which they live. A sociological imagination allows one to conceive of the relationship between seemingly private troubles and public issues. It encourages its possessor to resolve both personal problems and societal crises. One goal of this book is to stimulate a sociological imagination that can serve as a tool for help with personal problems and for an analysis of societal ills. The sociological imagination is a mode of critical thinking that will help you to understand how social problems affect you personally.

Box 1.1 • C. Wright Mills: Perspective and Paradigm

C. Wright Mills (1917–1962) was a professor of sociology at Columbia University. In an assortment of influential books in the 1950s and early 1960s he openly criticized American society, its foreign policy, and many of his fellow sociologists. Yet some people consider Mills "the greatest sociologist the United States has ever produced" (Horowitz, 1963: 20). In *Character and Social Structure* (1953), written with Hans Gerth, Mills developed the sociological model he used to analyze postmodern America. Gerth and Mills argued that institutions select and shape social character (Eldridge, 1983:14; Scimecca, 1977:37).

Mills applied the model in *White Collar* (1951), where he examined the character of white-collar workers and their social structure (the organizations that employed them). The white-collar employees of impersonal business and government bureaucracies, Mills found, were bored at work and lacked satisfying leisure activities.

White Collar is a portrait of the worker as victim. Controlled by bosses, white-collar workers are "cheerful robots." Outwardly they are pleasant, courteous, and helpful to customers and bosses. Psychologically, they suffer self-alienation because their resentment and anger remain hidden. Politicians fail to keep their promises and regularly lie to them, and they are at the mercy of advertisers' appeals. White-collar workers are unaware of their membership in a distinctive class (a potential interest group) and lack an understanding of the larger economic and political institutions that shape their lives. In *The Power Elite* (1956), a bestseller, Mills gave Americans a horrifying view of America's dominant institutions. Corporations and communications media, portions of the federal government, and the military are interlocked in a "military-industrial complex." The power elites who head these key institutions undemocratically make decisions about war and peace, where to locate factories, how many people to hire for what jobs. Collectively, these elites lack morals. Scandals (flouting of antitrust laws, political corruption) are commonplace. In *The Causes of World War III* (1958) Mills warned of the power elite's preparation for war and their "crackpot realism" (a nuclear war, they determined, was "winnable"). Mills also preached a "pagan sermon" to the clergy, urging them to protest the preparation for a war that could end civilization.

In *The Sociological Imagination* (1959) Mills noted that sociologists (wrongly) attributed social problems to individual deviance. Mills argued that social problems are caused by institutional contradictions, not by deviant individuals.

Mills criticized sociologists' fascination with "grand theories" that are politically conservative and scientifically untestable. He also objected to sociologists' obsession with methodology and measurement, and their neglect of moral issues.

All of Mills' concepts are explored in this book. We hope this discussion will motivate you to read these and other works by Mills.

Private Troubles and Public Issues

Mills argued that people's personal troubles, their feelings of being trapped and manipulated, their marital and career fortunes, and their goals and ways of achieving those goals are sociological in both origin and consequences. To use the sociological imagination we must be able to interrelate the structural causes of social problems, major trends, private troubles, and public (social) issues that occupy our everyday existence.

Private troubles "occur within the character of the individual and within the range of . . . immediate relations with others; they have to do with [the] self and with those limited areas of social life of which [one] is directly and personally aware" (Mills, 1959:8). Perceptions of and solutions to personal troubles lie within one's immediate environment: one's family, workplace, school, religious organization, or neighborhood. Accordingly, if two college roommates quarrel and decide they no longer wish to room together, each can resolve the problem by finding a more compatible partner, and most college campuses have a place to post "seeking roommate" notices. Thus the "private trouble" is resolvable within the immediate environment of the college campus. Social problems, on the other hand, are of a dramatically different nature.

Public issues (social problems) transcend the local environments of work, family, and community. Social problems involve a genuine crisis in institutional arrangements. Crises are genuine only when they demand that choices be made about situations that confront a society. Troubles become issues when they become widespread. Consider:

Unemployment

If, in a society of over 100 million workers, the only people who are unemployed are those who refuse to work, that is a private trouble. The cause is within the characters of individuals who are either mentally challenged or morally wanting. If, however, that society suffers massive layoffs as businesses downsize and move factories overseas in search of cheap labor and other financial advantages, sociological forces are clearly at work. No amount of counseling or punishment of errant workers will resolve a crisis of permanent recession.

Education

If a few hundred high school students of various backgrounds drop out annually, one can point to various personal deficiencies that inhibit learning. However, when almost 30 percent of the nation's secondary students withdraw before graduation and another 700,000 graduate despite their inability to read and write, then clearly some institutional factors are at work. Insufficient educational achievement is a great financial harm because high school and college graduates' earnings greatly exceed those of high school dropouts.

Marriage and the Family

Observe those venerable institutions our politicians never tire of telling us are the backbone of American life. If only a few thousand divorces and cases of abuse took place annually, one could conclude that a few dysfunctional personalities needed therapy. However, when half of first-time marriages end in divorce and 4000 spouses and significant others murder each other every year, something is clearly wrong with the institutions of courtship and the family.

Street Crime

If only a hundred or so murders took place annually, the problem would obviously be a matter of violence-prone individuals. Unfortunately, the United States' homicide rate is ten times higher than that of the entire continent of Europe. Clearly, patterned violence is at work.

Corruption

If a few ward politicians in a few cities were on the take, their corruption could be attributed to a deficiency in personal integrity. But what if prosecutors indict five public officials each day, and the nation regularly experiences scandal after scandal? The resolution of recurrent scandal lies within the political process and within the institutions in and outside of government that influence that process.

Mental Illness

Finally, if a minute proportion of the population exhibited neurotic symptoms or psychotic episodes, then hormonal imbalances or childhood traumas would be the relevant issues. But when one in five persons is mentally impaired, societal stresses and cultural strains merit examination.

Mills believed that many social problems indicate a "crisis in institutional arrangements" (Mills, 1959:9). Such crises involve what sociologists term macro social problems. Macro-level problems involve "certain economic, political, social, and technological arrangements that have come to prevail [and] are problematic because these arrangements harm millions of people" (Neubeck, 1991:12). Such problems include the maldistribution of global and national resources, global and national environmental pollution, economic inequalities and poverty, political corruption, business fraud, war, unequal access to health

This picture of Tokyo Bay, Japan, symbolizes a number of important aspects about postmodern social problems. Social problems, like pollution, plague rich and poor nations alike and often most directly affect those living closest to the source of such pollution. Very frequently, such victims are among the world's poorest, most powerless people.

care and the justice system, and such constant economic harms as unemployment, inflation, and indebtedness. Another set of macro problems consists of the exploitation of groups of people on the basis of sexual preference, age, race, gender, or handicap.

Micro social problems, in contrast, consist of "the troublesome and troubled behavior of individual societal members" (Neubeck, 1991:13)—such behaviors as drug and alcohol abuse, suicide, mental illness, street crime (including violent crimes inside and outside families), and sexual deviance (child pornography, child molestation, incest). An essential aspect of both macro and micro social problems is that they are harmful. Social problems are objectively harmful conditions. In other words, the harms involved can be measured or counted. These measurable harms are of three types (Schrager & Short, 1978):

1. **Physical harms:** physical injury, illness, death. Many social problems cause physical harm in the forms of injury and/or death. Some of these include crime (including murder and assault), environmental pollution, cigarette smoking, and war.

2. **Financial harms:** robbery, fraud, and various scams that are not legally defined as fraud but that nevertheless cause consumers and investors to be deprived of their funds without receiving the goods or services for which they contracted. There are many social problems that are financially harmful to either groups of individuals, organizations, or the public at large. Price-fixing by corporations, for example, costs the public some $60 billion per year. The Catholic Church has paid out over $400 million in the last decade in lawsuits for victims of child abuse by priests. Crimes, such as robbery and burglary, cost additional billions per year.

3. **Moral harms:** deviant behaviors by elites (people who head governmental and corporate institutions) that encourage deviance, distrust, cynicism, or alienation among the rest of the population. Before Richard Nixon resigned from the presidency in 1974, for example, his administration had been involved in a broad range of deviant acts: burglarizing the headquarters of the Democratic National Committee, attempting to rig elections, lying to Congress and the American people about the secret illegal bombing of Cambodia, bribery, and tax evasion (Simon, 1992; Simon & Eitzen, 1993). After the Watergate scandal and Nixon's resignation, confidence in government fell dramatically, and it has never recovered (Simon & Eitzen, 1993: 3–7).

Not all harmful conditions are social problems. Harms become social problems only if they are socially patterned. Socially patterned harms are traits, characteristics, or behaviors exhibited by groups of people or institutions. Émile Durkheim described one such pattern when he studied suicide in European countries. He found the highest suicide rates among people of certain characteristics: unmarried civilian Protestant males with a high level of education who lived in cities. Durkheim also found that the suicide rate rose in times of economic recession and times of dramatically increasing prosperity (Durkheim, 1960; Walton, 1993:68–69).

If harms are suffered at high rates with regularity by groups of people with certain characteristics and in specific historical circumstances, they may be said to be socially patterned. If harms are socially patterned, they must, it follows, be caused by social conditions. A recognition of such conditions is a key element of the sociological imagination.

The idea that social problems are conditions that are measurably harmful is not shared by all schools of thought. Among contemporary liberals the notion that social problems are value-relative social constructions is popular. According to this view, social problems are "real" only if they are publicly recognized as problems (Thio, 1988; Manis, 1974; Gusfield, 1984, 1989). The problem with this approach is that it ignores the fact that harm often exists whether a problem is acknowledged or not.

Before John F. Kennedy won the presidential election in 1960, for example, poverty was not publicly defined as a social problem, but many poor people were hidden in America's rural areas and urban ghettos. Once Kennedy drew attention to the issue, congressional hearings were held and legislation was passed as part of a "war" on poverty. By 1980, concern over poverty and the expectation that government could solve the problem had drastically waned. Yet there were more poor people in the United States in the 1980s than there had been in the 1960s. This is why it is important to view social problems as harms that exist regardless of public recognition. Social problems have "careers" (Blumer, 1971; Spector & Kitsuse, 1973), over the course of which public concern about them and the resources devoted to their resolution wax and wane. If left unresolved, the problems merely reappear later, and when they do, they tend to worsen.

What then is a social problem? A **social problem** is a socially patterned condition involving widespread physical, financial, and/or moral harm that is caused by contradictions (permanent conflicts) stemming from the institutional arrangement of a given society. Such harms exist whether or not they have gained the attention of the mass media and politicians.

Social Problem Interrelationships

Modern society is characterized by a series of interrelationships. We depend on supermarkets for food, letter carriers to deliver mail, lawyers, doctors, dentists, and countless others to provide us with the goods and services necessary for our well-being. These people in turn are dependent on us to buy their products and services so that they, too, may buy what they need.

Given societal interdependence, it is understandable that social problems are interrelated as well. Harvey Brenner (1973) did a unique study of what takes place when unemployment increases for a time. He discovered that for every 1.4 percent rise in the unemployment rate that lasts for eighteen months or longer, numerous social problems become worse. The rates of homicide and property crime, deaths from alcoholism and suicide, deaths from cardiovascular and kidney disease, new cases of mental illness—all increased. So do rates of admission to state mental hospitals and prisons. What is true for unemployment is true of virtually all types of social harms. There are often vital and unrecognized interrelations between various social problems.

In this regard, consider the nation's crime and drug problems. The United States' crime problem resembles a factory in which a different type of crime is manufactured on each floor. The floors in the factory are connected by distribution systems of money and drugs. The first floor of the factory is inhabited by street criminals—the robbers and burglars. They commit the vast majority of their crimes to obtain money to support their drug addiction. Drug-related crime accounts for over half of urban homicides. It is also associated with prostitution, shoplifting, arson, and vehicle theft.

The second floor of the plant is inhabited by criminal gangs, such as the Bloods and Crips of Los Angeles. These gangs now flourish in virtually every state, selling drugs to the criminal addicts. The gangs are largely the retailers of the drug trade. Their suppliers and processors are located on the third floor of the factory. The suppliers are people of various nations who have organized criminal syndicates to engage in international drug trafficking: the American and Sicilian Mafia and criminal syndicates in Latin America, the Far East, and various Caribbean nations. Each syndicate is involved in a different trade route by which drugs are imported into the United States.

The next floor of the factory belongs to money handlers. The world's drug traffickers launder $750 billion to $1 trillion a year (J. Mills, 1986). The gangs and syndicates deal strictly for cash. Banks, investment firms, jewelry and gold exchanges, and check-cashing services launder (disguise) this money. Large sums of cash are deposited in accounts and then electronically transferred to secret bank accounts in Switzerland and other banking havens. These transactions are made in exchange for a commission (about 2 percent of the amount deposited). In this way, corporate crime is related to both organized crime and street crime.

Finally, the top floor of the crime factory is occupied by representatives of the political system, including the criminal justice system. The illegal drug trade is an important source of bribes for police and judicial and correctional personnel. Organized criminal syndicates also bribe politicians in various nations around the world. In some countries, such as Haiti, political and military leaders are deeply involved in drug trafficking as suppliers. U.S. intelligence organizations, especially the Central Intelligence Agency, have helped give rise to narcotics syndicates for the last forty years (Simon & Eitzen, 1993:82; Henderson & Simon, 1994:17–18) as part of its anti-Communist covert operations. (The details are spelled out in Box 1.2.)

The link with other social problems does not stop here. Drug addiction itself is related to a host of additional harms. Drug addicts are the source of one-third of all AIDS cases. They account for over a million visits to hospital emergency rooms each year. The public cost of treating the gunshot wounds resulting from street and gang crime is currently estimated at $13 billion annually (Los Angeles *Times*, November 11, 1993, p. A-1). The drug problem in the nation's schools has prompted the hiring of numerous security guards and the installation of metal detectors, thereby eating into already strained public school budgets. Drug-related crime cases have clogged the nation's court dockets and overcrowded the prisons of more than thirty states, thereby increasing the indebtedness of state and local governments. All social problems, both domestic and international, are interrelated.

The sociological imagination is a paradigm, an orientation for looking at reality. It is also much more. Virtually all schools of thought advocate policies for the resolutions of social problems. The sociological imagination is no exception, and its relation to solutions to social problems is discussed in this book's final chapter.

Like any paradigm, the sociological imagination defines "what should be studied, what questions should be asked, and what rules should be followed in interpreting the answers

Box 1.2 • The CIA and Drug Trafficking

When most people think about drug abuse, images of the needles that transmit AIDS and vials of crack cocaine come to mind. The idea that the Central Intelligence Agency (CIA) has been a major force in international drug trafficking is difficult to believe, yet the evidence to support this claim is overwhelming.

- In France in 1950 the CIA recruited Corsican gangsters, the Ferri-Pisani family, to break a strike by dock workers. The workers had refused to ship arms to Vietnam (where France was then at war). Corsican gangsters assaulted picket lines of Communist union members and harassed union officials. In return for stopping the strike, the Ferri-Pisani family was allowed to use Marseilles as a shipping center for heroin (Simon & Eitzen, 1993:82).

- For over thirty years the U.S. government supported opium production in Southeast Asia's Golden Triangle by providing arms, military support, and protection to corrupt officials—all in the name of anti-Communism, of course. This relationship began in the 1950s, after the Chinese Communists defeated Chiang Kai-shek's Nationalist Chinese army (the Kuomintang) in 1949. The CIA helped the Kuomintang regroup and settle in Burma's Shan states, bordering on China. The Shan area is a rich source of opium poppies. The CIA even helped smuggle the heroin out of Laos on its own airline, Air America. The CIA was aided in this project by American Mafia members whose lucrative Cuban market had increased after Fidel Castro ousted the corrupt dictator Fulgencio Batista (Simon & Eitzen, 1993:82). The story of Air America was made into a movie titled *Air America* starring Mel Gibson in the 1980s.

  In the 1970s the Kuomintang's Cholon triad (Chinese Mafia) began producing injectable heroin and importing it into Vietnam. It has been estimated that 100,000 American soldiers in Vietnam had become addicted to heroin by 1974 (Posner, 1988:69-70).

- The CIA also aided its Southeast Asian drug producers by establishing money-laundering facilities for them in Australia. The Nugen Hand bank was established by a number of ex-CIA agents and U.S. military officers. William Colby, former director of the CIA, was hired as the bank's lawyer. The bank was involved in a host of illegal activities, including a scheme to defraud U.S. oil workers in Saudi Arabia of their wages (Henderson & Simon, 1994:18; Kwitney, 1987).

- Other incidents link U.S. government agencies to drug trafficking by the Nicaraguan Contras in the 1980s. The Medellin cocaine cartel paid the Contras $10 million to allow its agents safe passage through Contra-held territory, with the full knowledge of the CIA. The Enterprise operation established by Lieutenant Colonel Oliver North and Admiral John Poindexter provided airplanes to the Medellin cartel in 1984–85. The cartel paid the Enterprise for

Continued on next page

Box 1.2 •   Continued

use of planes, landing strips, and labor to load drug shipments. The proceeds were allegedly used to buy arms for the Contras (Simon & Eitzen, 1993:320).

• In 1985, the CIA supplied arms to the Afghans under General Hekmatyar. The CIA aided the Mujahedin (holy war fighters) after the Soviet army invaded Afghanistan to prop up the Communist regime it had installed there. Hekmatyar and his army promptly went into the heroin business, and by 1988 they had 100 to 200 heroin refineries just across the border in Pakistan. By the late 1980s, heroin from these Southwest Asian nations accounted for about 50 percent of the European and American heroin supplies (McCoy, 1991a, 1991b:12).

obtained" (Ritzer, 1980:7). At its heart, a paradigm is "a fundamental model that organizes our view" (Babbie, 1989:47) of issues related to the sociological analysis of social problems. These key issues include:

1. A criticism of other paradigms or ideologies, especially their contradictions (Rosenau, 1992:xi). This critique is sometimes termed **deconstruction**.

2. The relationship between personal troubles and social problems.

3. A model for analyzing the relationships between (a) the structure of society, (b) the historical epoch (period) in which that society is located, and (c) the social character (human nature) being produced.

4. A model for the analysis of social problems.

The sociological imagination paradigm is also eclectic; it was constructed from the various insights provided by different schools of sociological thought. Likewise, Mills' perspective evolved from a critique of traditional approaches to the study of social problems. Many of these theoretical viewpoints remain with us today, and, therefore, it is important to understand their influence, strengths, and perceived shortcomings.

Mills' Critique of Social Problem Perspectives

The Social Pathology Perspective

In the 1940s, when Mills was a college student, both conservative and liberal scholars concerned with social problems unquestioningly accepted the prevailing structure of private property (capitalism) and the American political system as normal and untroubled.

The conservatives of Mills' day called themselves **social pathologists**. They were "straightforward moralists, staunch supporters of the virtues of thrift, hard work, sexual purity, and personal discipline" (Skolnick & Currie, 1994:2). Since the early nineteenth century, conservative social scientists had concentrated on the "social pathology" of the lower ("dangerous") classes, whose *personal* defects, either biological or moral, caused their poverty, sexual deviance, drug and alcohol abuse, crime, delinquency, mental illness, and suicide. Their analysis focused on nonwhite, non-Protestant, newly arrived immigrant groups from Southern Europe. The social pathologists' view of these "nuts, sluts, and 'preverts'" (Liazos, 1993) was colored by the fear that lower-class deviance and crime might throw society into total chaos (anarchy). In fact, many people feared that if newly arrived immigrant factory workers were allowed to congregate in saloons, they would soon be plotting revolution.

Not only were these groups viewed as dangerous to society, they were also viewed as racially inferior, as less worthy than white Protestant Americans. Strict social control of these inferior groups was advocated. In the 1920s and 1930s this meant policies designed to let only racially superior white people have children. Known as eugenics, this policy involved sexual sterilization for everything from stealing chickens to insanity, and limited the immigration of nonwhite, non-Protestant groups into the United States (Simon, 1977, 1981). The sterilization laws passed in the United States became the basis for the laws passed by Hitler's Nazis that were eventually used systematically to murder millions of Jews, gypsies, homosexuals, and mentally ill people during World War II.

Today the social pathology approach, while less popular, still has its advocates. The bestseller *The Bell Curve*, by Charles Murray and the late Richard Hernstein (1994) insists that crime is caused primarily by the low intelligence (low IQ scores) of criminals. Moreover, the authors argue, the IQs of African Americans are several points lower than those of white Americans, and this difference is genetic (biological, and, therefore, racial). There is a good amount of evidence that contradicts the *Bell Curve* theory concerning the association between race, intelligence, and crime, but this has not stopped bigoted people from believing these myths.

The Social Disorganizationists

A second group of scholars, the liberal reformers, emerged in the 1920s and their views remained influential until the mid-1960s. The social pathologists believed that a society was like a body (organism) made up of various parts (organs), each of which had a valuable function. As long as each of the parts performs its function, the body runs smoothly. If one of the parts becomes ill, the functioning of the entire body is affected. The **social disorganizationists** believed that society's smooth functioning was made possible by agreed upon rules (norms) which provided guidelines for appropriate behavior for people in the performance of their various social roles (family members, workers, teachers, clergy, students, and so on). Social problems were caused by deviations from these rules (Mills, 1963:532). Such deviance included crime, drug addiction, delinquency, prostitution and other lower-class behaviors.

Why did such deviations occur? Different disorganizationists provided different answers. Some believed that immigrant groups possessed cultural norms that were in conflict with the standard rules of American life. Thus, in a number of other cultures prostitution is an accepted means for women to make money. In American society, prostitution is against the law in all states except Nevada, where it is legal in some counties and illegal in others. Clearly there are different norms at work here.

Still other disorganizationists viewed the cause of deviant behavior as stemming from a lack of opportunity in American life. Robert Merton (1938) claimed that America places a heavy emphasis on achieving material success (making money), but does not provide equal opportunity to the means (access to education and good jobs) of achieving monetary success. People who suffer from such lack of opportunity, Merton argued, have four basic choices (adaptation modes) that may be exercised. These include the following:

1. *Innovation* is an option for those persons who lack such means and wish to become successful, yet have not the means of achieving material wealth. The result is often unapproved means (innovation). Innovation includes all manner of illegal money-making deviance: property crime, fraud, con games, and white-collar and corporate crimes (such as antitrust violations).

2. *Ritualism* is characteristic of people who have reduced somewhat the expectation of becoming successful but retain commitment to the available means of honest work. The classic ritualist is the bureaucratic clerk who pushes papers day in and day out, with no hope of promotion or advancement.

3. *Retreatism* takes place when both the goals of material success and the means of hard work are renounced. People making this choice are literally society's dropouts, and include skid row alcoholics, drug addicts, the seriously mentally afflicted, and various nonconformists (hippies, beatniks, and other bohemians).

4. *Rebellion* appeals to those attempting to change both the goals related to material success and the means available to achieve those goals. Included would be people dedicated to revolutionary social movements designed to alter both cultural values and dominant social institutions.

Other social disorganizationists blame, not society's opportunity structure, but everyday environments, especially dysfunctional families and socially disorganized (pathological) neighborhoods for causing social problems (Horton, 1968). Disorganizationists took pity on the lower classes, however, and advocated a series of social welfare measures. These measures included counseling and joining various neighborhood groups dedicated to clean living, such as the Boy Scouts and the Girl Scouts (Mills, 1963:544). These reforms reached their zenith during the Johnson administration's war on poverty in the mid-1960s. The goal of such reforms was to influence the lower classes to adjust to middle-class norms. While there was a major improvement in the lives of some 8 million poor people during this period, deteriorating economic conditions in the United States have reversed virtually all gains made against poverty in the past thirty years.

Aside from its bias concerning which norms are normal, the disorganization perspective suffered from a major contradiction: If social problems are caused by a defect in the social structure (lack of equal opportunity), then shouldn't the reasons for this lack of legitimate means be assessed? Why aren't there more good-paying jobs? Why are there relatively so few slots in graduate, medical, and law schools considering the large number of applicants? Why is all this scarcity perceived as natural? Instead, as we've seen, Merton and others focused on the people who lacked such means, not on the social structure itself. Accordingly, the war on poverty was aimed at aiding the poor, in helping them compete for the relatively scarce number of positions available for those seeking success by honest means.

The failure of the war on poverty marked the decline of the social disorganization school's influence on public policy, and the perspective was eclipsed by a new liberal view, that of symbolic interaction.

Symbolic Interactionism

The interactionist school marked, not only the end of the era of liberal reforms, but the beginning of the postmodern view of society. Interactionists insist that social problems are simply conditions that a significant number of people or a number of significant people perceive as problematic conditions. In this view, social problems are merely **social constructions,** widely agreed upon definitions of wrongful conditions within society. The interactionists, or social constructionists, have focused their attention on the processes by which conditions come to be defined as social problems. Indeed, Blumer (1971) and Spector and Kitsuse (1973) contend that social problems possess careers consisting of recognizable stages. These stages include:

1. A complaining group, like Mothers Against Drunk Driving, attempts to define some condition as a social problem, such as the killing and or injury of victims by drunk drivers. Complaining groups include concerned citizens, social workers, or public interest lobbies. They may begin by calling a press conference. If ignored by the press, groups may change their tactics. This may lead to hunger strikes, protest demonstrations, and other efforts to capture the attention of media, the public, and policy makers. Failure to do so means the issue will not become a social problem.

2. An official agency of government recognizes the problem as "real" (Blumer, 1971). Government reactions may range from acceptance of the group's demands and investigation of the problem to arresting the complainants.

3. The complainants may lose faith in the slowness of government action and come to regard investigating bodies as defenders of the status quo who are out to whitewash the problem.

4. Complainants refuse to work with official agencies and attempt their own solutions. For example, neighborhood watch groups attempt to reduce local street crimes. Ross Perot began an alternative political organization for voters fed up with the Washington "gridlock." If successful, these efforts may be coopted (taken over) by corporate or government elites. Finally, the cause may become part of a larger revolutionary movement.

The interactionist view is not so much a scientific theory about causes of troubling conditions as it is a *description of a political process*. There is no cause given for why the problem initially began. Thus, the interactionist perspective is not a theory in the scientific sense precisely because it contains no causal (independent) variable. An additional problem with the interactionist perspective concerns a lack of proposed solutions to social problems.

Supporters of this perspective have sometimes advocated that their political stance should be one of being on the side of not proposing solutions to social problems but merely studying them (Gusfield, 1984).

None of this is to say that the above perspectives are "wrong" in any literal sense of the word. All seek to make the world a better place by analyzing social problems from their respective worldviews, and advocating certain solutions based on those views. The pathologists and disorganizationists alert us to the fact that some schools of thought view social problems as objectively harmful conditions that exist independent of whether or not they have been publicized by the media and politicians. These schools of thought also satisfy conservatives' need for basic definitions of right and wrong ("traditional values").

The social constructionists, on the other hand, alert us to the importance of public recognition of social problems as a precondition for social action. The constructionists also rightly point out that some so-called social problems, such as homosexuality, or drinking on Sunday, are defined as harmful in some places merely because they offend some influential people's sense of morality, and not because they are physically, financially, or morally harmful in and of themselves.

This book also advocates an identifiable perspective, one that seeks to utilize the strengths of the perspectives just discussed, as well as go beyond these more traditional views in an effort to create a social problems paradigm that is truly sociological in nature.

The Sociological Imagination Perspective

In *The Sociological Imagination* (1959) Mills recognized three basic levels of analysis in sociological research: (1) the conservative focus on individual personalities, (2) the liberal focus on immediate environments (such as family and neighborhood), and (3) a larger (macro) sociological environment, which included both cultural values and larger sociological units such as the nation-state, the political economy and other institutions, and groups of nations. Much of what passed for a "sociological" analysis of social problems, Mills argued, was merely the study of individual personalities, or an analysis of the immediate environment of the family or neighborhood. A study conducted more than thirty years later (Gregg et al., 1980) confirmed that Mills' critique was still valid. Theodore Gregg and his colleagues examined about five hundred articles in social problems journals published in 1936, 1956, and 1976 and recorded the unit of analysis used in each study. They found that 60 percent of the studies used the individual as the unit of analysis, 30 percent focused on the immediate environment, and only 10 percent involved macro-level variables. Thus the pattern that Mills observed over fifty years ago continues.

A *genuine* sociological analysis of social problems is one that appreciates and interrelates all three levels of analysis. A recent important example of this approach to social problems is sociologist William Julius Wilson's analysis of the new poverty in the American inner city. Professor Wilson defines the new poverty as poverty that has emerged in the United States since 1970, and that is concentrated in older industrial cities with highly segregated black and Hispanic residents (Wilson, 1995:2). The analysis carefully takes into account activity on the macro, neighborhood, and individual levels to form a complete sociological picture of the new poverty and its devastating consequences.

On the macrological level, manufacturing corporations have transferred some 2.5 million jobs out of the older cities in the midwest and northeast since 1970. Thus between 1967 and 1987, the cities of Philadelphia, New York, Chicago, and Detroit all lost between 50 and 64 percent of their manufacturing jobs (Wilson, 1995:8). Loss of these jobs reflects important trends in the new global economy: the comparatively low cost of labor in poor nations outside the United States, America's growing trade deficit (less demand for American-made products overseas), and government policies encouraging overseas investment. Likewise, during the 1980s, the amount of federal aid for America's inner cities was drastically slashed by the Reagan-Bush administrations. Consequently, in 1980 the federal contribution to city budgets was 18 percent; by 1990 it had dropped to 6.4 percent (Wilson, 1994:1).

Wilson then analyzes the effects of these changes on a particular set of neighborhoods in Chicago. The consequences of high-paying jobs lost and cuts in federal aid were devastating: The percentage of Chicago inner city black fathers employed in manufacturing fell from 57 percent in 1974 to only 27 percent in 1987. Many nonpoor working-class and middle-class families left the neighborhoods for the suburbs, with its better job opportunities, better schools, lower crime rates, and more stable property values. Many neighborhood stores, credit institutions, banks, restaurants, cleaning establishments, and other businesses lost patrons. Churches lost parishioners, neighborhood block clubs and community associations lost significant membership. Without these usual organizations to provide social control (including social activities for young people), crime, street violence, and crack-cocaine dealing and abuse skyrocketed. The result was overall deterioration of inner city neighborhoods populated by minorities.

On the individual level, the decline of employment prospects and the accompanying neighborhood deterioration produced devastating effects on the relationships between community members and reduced the self-esteem of many inner city residents. This blow to the self-confidence of young inner city dwellers took a number of forms:

- Job losses often caused increased family tensions and resultant family breakups (separations and divorces), depriving many children of fathers.

- The exiting of many middle-class residents from the inner city meant an absence of middle-class role models (such as doctors, dentists, ministers, and business people) for the young.

- Some of the behavior of residents of inner city ghetto neighborhoods—like watching a movie and simultaneously engaging in a running conversation or reacting in a loud manner to what appears on the screen—offends both black and white middle-class people. Expressions of disapproval by middle-class patrons tend only to trigger angry responses of those doing the talking. As a result, offended patrons often take their business elsewhere, thus further isolating ghetto dwellers, and feelings of racial and/or class resentment are intensified (Wilson, 1995:8).

- Unemployed ghetto residents going into other neighborhoods to find jobs were frequently perceived with suspicion and hostility by a representative sample of greater Chicago area employers. One suburban electrical business owner stated that any ghetto resident applying for a position with his company would be immediately suspect because "A, if you give him a job, he's going to be

under unbelievable pressure to give information to his peer group in the ghetto
. . . about the security system, and the value of what's at work that could be
ripped off" (Wilson, 1995:11).

An inner city factory president stated that hiring ghetto residents is risky because they
are frequently unable to get to work on time, and need to be watched more carefully, lest
they steal from the workplace (Wilson, 1995:12).

Wilson's study demonstrates how changes at the macro level (decreased job opportunities and lower levels of federal aid) can have a devastating impact on inner city neighborhoods (rising crime rates, decreased community cohesion). Likewise, these macro and
neighborhood changes have a devastating impact on inner city residents. Unemployment
contributes to family breakup, absentee fathers, poverty among single-parent families and
discrimination against ghetto dwellers outside their neighborhoods when seeking employment. All of this signals lower self-confidence among ghetto-dwelling children, who must
contend with increased family tensions, crime in and out of school, increased likelihood of
dropping out of school, and bleak future job prospects. Wilson's study carefully documents
how a host of seemingly personal troubles are intimately related to economic and political
changes in the larger society.

A key reason for the lack of sociological imagination can be found in Americans'
belief in individualism (Bellah et al., 1986: 10). Our notions of sin, of legal responsibility,
and of rights focus on individuals. In a less complex era, perhaps, these ideas seemed progressive. Today they function largely to mask the workings of a society that is primarily
corporate and bureaucratic. The lone individual is somewhat at the mercy of these organizational forces. One reason for this state of affairs is that organizations (the mass media
make up the prime example) try to define reality for mass audiences. Official views of reality often mystify the causes and solutions of social problems.

Mystification of Social Problems

Contradictions are often hidden from public view because the actual values, processes,
and goals of organizations are discussed behind closed doors and in classified documents. These actualities are submerged beneath the ideologies of free enterprise, democracy, community, and traditional values. Organizations mystify contradictions and the social
problems they engender by denying the structural causes of public issues. Thus, layoffs are
blamed on greedy workers who refuse to take pay cuts, not the will of corporations to find
cheap labor in foreign countries. Massive government indebtedness is said to result, not
from huge increases in defense spending, but from the greedy demands of recipients of
"entitlement" programs (which categorically never include the large corporations that
receive government subsidies). Social problems are frequently blamed on individuals by
those in power; thus their true causes remain clouded by an ideology of personal (individual) responsibility.

A sociological imagination sometimes invites the charge that one has lost sight of
individual responsibility. One responsibility that needs to be emphasized is not the individual's but the organization's and the elite's (a distinction we shall explore in depth later). The
power elite's National Advertising Council, for example, used to produce public service

messages starring the cartoon character Woodsy Owl. Woodsy informed Americans of a "great" pollution problem. Picnickers were failing to dispose of their litter in garbage cans. Woodsy never bothered to inform us, though, that American corporations generate half of the world's industrial pollution. Polluting firms are a major cause of our fouled waters, dirty air, threatened water supplies, and toxic waste crisis. The environmental crisis is difficult for Americans to confront precisely because their culture lacks a notion of organizational wrongdoing and has created no institutions to counter organizational propaganda concerning the cause of this and numerous other problems.

The National Advertising Council has done its best to convince the public that pollution is the fault of irresponsible picnickers who fail to dispose of their litter properly. A focus on individuals serves to mask the underlying causes of many social problems. Moreover, many individuals suffering from problems that spring from their society remain convinced that their troubles are strictly personal. The relationship between seemingly personal troubles and social problems is a key aspect of the sociological imagination.

Causal Analysis

Which social conditions cause social problems? Mills believed that social problems were caused by *contradictions (antagonisms)* within the structure of society. Structural contradictions are conflicts that are virtually built into societal institutions (Worsley, 1982:28). One contradiction within the economic institution concerns workers' demands for increased wages versus owners' need to hold down labor costs. The two sides react to this contradiction in many ways: Unions and management engage in collective bargaining, management relocates factories in places where labor is cheaper, workers purchase their companies, and so forth. Still the conflict between business and labor over wages goes on.

A basic assumption of the sociological imagination is that much human history is about the conflict between the few who have control over scarce resources and the many who do not. These resources include *wealth* (property), *income* (wages and salaries), *power* (the ability to make economic and political decisions that affect the entire society), and *cultural values* (standards of right and wrong, beautiful and ugly).

Where do such contradictions originate? Mills believed that the way to locate contradictions was to begin by asking key questions. These questions, which form the elements of the sociological imagination paradigm, are listed in Table 1.1. Central to these questions are three issues:

1. Social structure.

2. The master trend ("main drift") of the current historical period.

3. Biography, or social character, and the degree of alienation it exhibits (Mills, 1959:7, 171).

Structure

The **social structure** is an interrelated set of societal institutions. **Institutions** are collections of social roles, norms, and social organizations that are organized to meet some societal need (Messner & Rosenfeld, 1994: 72). Among these institutions are:

1. The economy, which produces and distributes goods and services.

2. The polity (political system), which functions to resolve conflict and protect society from internal and external threats to stability.

3. The family, which functions to regulate the sex drive, produce and rear children, and serve as the emotional center of people's private lives.

4. Education, which imparts skills necessary for playing roles in the economy and other institutions, and socializes the young to accept the values of the society.

Table 1.1

**Key Questions of
the Sociological Imagination**

Structure What is the particular structure of the entire society and what are its essential component parts? How do the parts relate to one another? How does this society differ from others?

The historical era's main drift Where does the society stand in history? Is it on the ascendant or in decline? How does social change happen? What are the essential features of the historical epoch? How is history made? What master trends of the current era will soon cause contradictions and social problems?

Biography (social character) Mills believed it is important to answer the following questions about social character:

- What kinds of men and women characterize the society?
- What kinds of "human nature" are evolving?
- In what ways are social characteristics shaped?
- Which characteristics are encouraged and which are repressed?
- What types of "human nature" are revealed in the character we observe in the society of this period?
- How is human nature shaped by the society's dominant institutions?

For Mills a feature of social character that must be addressed is *alienation*.

- What are the institutional conditions responsible for feelings of alienation and low self-esteem in individuals?
- How are these alienating conditions within institutions related to various macro and micro social problems?
- What can be done to overcome alienating conditions and the feelings they engender in individuals?
- Why are people confused about (mystified by) the causes of their alienation? Mills' questions concerning structure, history, and biography provide a road map with which sociological inquiry can be undertaken.

5. Religion, which functions to meet spiritual needs and provide answers to life's fundamental questions: What is life's purpose? How did we get here? Why do we die? Why do some people escape punishment for evil acts? Why do the innocent often suffer victimization?

6. The aesthetic institution, which functions to produce and distribute works in the arts and humanities (art, music, literature, opera, plays, movies, television shows).

History's Main Drift

The **master trends**, or the **main drift**, consist of the means by which social change takes place within the social structure. Almost all the founders of sociology—those who wrote in what Mills termed "the classic tradition" (Mills, 1960)—assessed modern society for its main drift. Here are a few of their concerns.

Karl Marx: Class Struggle and Alienation

Karl Marx (1818–1883) viewed the main drift of industrial capitalism as another chapter in the history of conflict. This conflict took place between the class that owned the society's economic base (the mode of production) and the class that toiled for the owners (the proletariat). For Marx, the coming of modern society meant that the working class had engaged in joyless, alienating work. Factory jobs reduced work to meaningless monotony and separated (alienated) workers from the products they produced, from the process of work, from other workers (all of whom constituted a potential revolutionary class), and from the workers' own (human) nature, which Marx viewed as free and creative (Roberts, 1978:85–86).

Further, Marx saw the owning class (the bourgeoisie) as controlling the government, religion, and education as well as all dominant ideas (values, ideologies, ethics, and laws) by which society was ruled. However, Marx was an optimist. He believed the workers would in time realize that their labor was exploited, used only to profit the owners, while they themselves barely survived economically (Worsley, 1982:90). Marx believed that social change would be accomplished by a revolution in which the workers would seize the economic base of society from the owners.

Émile Durkheim: Mechanical Solidarity and Anomie

Émile Durkheim (1858–1917), a leading French sociologist, focused on the social bonds (emotional and moral) that held societies together. In more traditional societies these ties were formed by strong traditions based on customs, ceremonies (weddings, for example), religious beliefs, and values. These bonds made for what he called *organic solidarity.* The coming of modern society, Durkheim argued, had resulted in a marked decline in these traditional ties. Whatever societal glue was left seemed to make for *mechanical solidarity,* a

Émile Durkheim (1858–1917), like the other founders of sociology, was greatly concerned about the moral condition of modern life. Durkheim feared the growth of what he termed anomie (normlessness; social situations without rules).

Karl Marx (1818–1883), described well some of the most contradictory aspects of capitalist societies, especially the class conflicts that take place between working and owning classes, and the alienation bred by the degrading working conditions of factory life. Much of what Marx said still possesses great value for the analysis of postmodern social problems.

Max Weber (1864–1920), another founder of sociological theory and method, described the growth and nature of modern bureaucracy. Weber was especially concerned about the corrupt and alienating nature of bureaucratic institutions and their negative effects on the consciousness of individuals.

functional set of social relationships based on a specialized division of labor (different jobs or careers). Thus people in modern societies use the money they earn to purchase goods and services from various others who occupy specialized posts in the economic order.

Durkheim lamented the passing of traditional norms (accepted rules of right and wrong) and expressed fear that the result would be a form of institutionalized moral chaos that he termed *anomie*. **Anomie** (literally lawlessness) is a structural alienation that occurs when rapid social change causes large numbers of people to recognize no rules to guide their behavior. They lose faith in both major social institutions and the rules they seek to enforce. The result is a high rate of crime and deviant behavior (such as suicide), which in turn further weakens people's belief in the legitimacy of major institutions and laws. Durkheim believed that social change could come about when people formed institutions (such as workers' cooperatives) that would lead to the establishment of moral and emotional bonds.

Max Weber: Iron Cages and Disenchantment

Max Weber (1864–1920), a leading German sociologist, wrote on an incredible number of topics. Some of Weber's most influential writings concern the coming of bureaucracy and what he termed the rationalization of the world. Weber described the great shift from a society in which people looked to the traditions of their ancestors to guide their decision making to a mass society in which decision making was based on impersonal rules that had been codified into laws. This rationalization of the world takes many forms, among them the rise of science and dependence on experts in various fields; modern democratic government, with its rights and laws as the bases for the conduct of both organizations and citizens; and the modern corporation, with its focus on efficiency and the bottom line.

Weber deeply lamented the expansion of bureaucracy into every area of social life. He feared that the oppression of serfdom would be replaced by new "iron cages" in which all forms of value-oriented social conduct (feelings and creativity) would be suffocated by bureaucratic organizations and their rational laws and regulations. The result would be a generalized malaise in which individuals would suffer disenchantment with "official tasks" that excluded love, hate, and virtually all other human feelings (Josephson & Josephson, 1962:23). Weber believed that the only alternative to increasing regulation by bureaucracies was the emergence of charismatic individuals. A charismatic leader is one to whom followers have a strong emotional attachment. When such individuals manage to exert control over systems of bureaucratic administration, they inspire their followers and society in general to grow and develop (Denhardt, 1984:31-32).

Biography and Alienation

Biography, or **social character**, consists of personality traits and behaviors that are widely shared by members of a culture. The concept of social character is central to both the sociological imagination paradigm and our study of social problems. Social character consists of widely shared cultural values, beliefs, goals, attitudes, and norms. This is what Mills refers to when he asks in what ways men and women are "formed, liberated, and repressed, made sensitive and blunted" (1959:7).

Self-alienation involves such feelings as powerlessness, meaninglessness, loneliness, isolation, normlessness, and estrangement from oneself, from other people, from society at large. Alienation has both a sociological and an individual (emotional) component. That is, *alienating social conditions cause feelings associated with self-alienation in individuals.* Alienation also involves a lack of self-esteem. When feelings of alienation and low self-esteem are widespread, macro and micro social problems ensue.

Power Elites, Mass Society, and Cheerful Robots

One purpose of this book is to answer questions regarding structure and historical drift, social character, and alienation. As you explore these answers, please keep in mind that structure, history, and biography constantly intersect and affect one another. Take Weber's view of bureaucracy as the main drift of modern society, for example. Bureaucracy is as much a structure (a form of social organization) as it is a trend. Bureaucratic organizations are constantly shaping the social characters of the people they employ and the publics they supposedly serve. Thus one cannot point to a simplistic cause-and-effect relationship here.

Second, the answers to the questions posed by the sociological imagination are not eternal. Social structures, historical drift, and social character vary with the society and period of history under study. The America of the 1990s is not the America of the 1790s. The America of the 2290s will not be the America of the 1990s. The questions that make up the sociological imagination are constant, but the answers are always evolving.

What is the social structure of the United States today? What is its main drift? What sort of social character does it have?

The Structure of American Society

The *structure* of American society is that of a mass society. A *mass society* is characterized by:

1. A capitalistic economy dominated by huge multinational corporations. Corporate elites (owners and managers) frequently take temporary positions in government and its military establishment.

2. A centralized government that has the power to make the big decisions about war and peace, inflation and unemployment, and the production of cultural values. There is increased coordination and cooperation between large corporations and the federal government on matters of domestic and foreign policy that affect large corporations. (These policies are discussed in Chapter 2.) The power structure of mass society is not monolithic. There are influences that compete with the elite for dominance. Among them are competitive interest groups and middle-class voters. Important decisions, however, are increasingly made in secret by such organizations as the Central Intelligence Agency, which are not effectively regulated by democratic forces.

3. Mass media owned by corporate institutions and influenced by government. The danger is that the media can manipulate the masses of people who lack such power. Such manipulation takes the forms of advertising, public relations, government propaganda, and other media fare (Kornhauser, 1968).

4. A highly mobile population of nonelites.

A **mass society** is one in which small, intimate (primary) groups, such as extended families and communities, have lost their substance. People still spend time with their friends and family members, but interaction in the social world is impersonal. People interact impersonally with bureaucratic organizations (large corporations, political parties, government bureaus, television networks, universities) and have superficial (secondary) contacts with clerks and auto mechanics—people with whom they have no real friendship (Mills, 1951:161–286).

Families no longer grow their own food, make their own clothing, or construct their own shelter, so people in mass societies are increasingly dependent on one another for goods and services. Likewise, there is great emphasis on expertise in such fields as medicine, law, journalism, dentistry, tax preparation, show business and sports, and religion. These and many other fields have become the monopolies of various professionals, on whom nonprofessionals depend for help. As a result, much of life in mass society revolves around the various organizations and institutions that have taken over functions that in earlier eras were performed by families and communities—care of the sick and the elderly, child welfare, criminal justice, mental health. Consequently, the family, religion, the schools, and the local community have lost importance as sources of morality and relationships. People in mass societies move in and out of communities at will. They marry, divorce, and remarry with bewildering speed, and switch religions as if they were test-driving cars.

These changes generate numerous contradictions and, as a result, social problems. People are crowded close together in cities and suburbs, yet are largely strangers to one another. Millions of people have migrated to cities only to experience endless traffic snarls, delinquent gangs and high crime rates, AIDS, environmental pollution, and unaffordable housing.

A central vulnerability in mass societies is manipulation of masses of people "from above," by a bureaucratic elite. Entire populations are presented with the same products, "news," candidates, sports, and popular culture idols. People select between carefully structured alternatives: The next president will be either a Republican or a Democrat. What is "right" or "good" becomes what sells, wins elections, or becomes popular. This state of affairs gives mass societies a strange form of egalitarianism, in which all consumers or voters are equally valued as objects of manipulation. This manipulation makes for a major form of societal alienation.

Mass societies are also prone to spontaneous behavior "from below." Such collective behaviors as riots, protests, and labor strikes threaten to disrupt society. Mass societies are economically and politically linked, so disruptions in one area of life, such as the rail system, can adversely affect all economic activity. Mass behavior at its extreme—rioting, looting, burning—poses the threat of chaos or anarchy. When such behavior occurred in Los Angeles in 1992, more than fifty people were killed and $1 billion in damage was done.

People who engage in mass behavior are usually among the least rooted in their communities and least incorporated in workplace organizations. This is especially the case among the younger and poorer members of society. The vulnerabilities of mass societies have been viewed from a variety of vantage points (Kornhauser, 1959, 1968: 62–65), as Box 1.3 makes clear.

Box 1.3 • Mass Society Theory and Its Origins

Mass society theory consists of four distinct yet interrelated views on the meaning of modern life. Mass theory has been referred to as the "kitchen sink" because new ideas continue to be added to the theory and nothing is ever removed. Postmodern theory is a continuation of mass society theory.

The Aristocratic Conservative View
Aristocratic conservative theorists worry about the decline of morality, authority, and order in modern society. They also decry the decline of cultural standards in art, music, literature, and entertainment. The original aristocratic writers were Catholic conservatives who feared the rise of mass rule with the French Revolution of 1789. To conservative critics, the masses (not usually specifically defined by these writers) are morally, intellectually, emotionally, and culturally inferior to the elites. The elites are people who occupy social roles as the heads of such wealthy, powerful, and culturally influential institutions (as corporations, government agencies, and the communications media).

Continued on next page

Box 1.3   •   Continued

Today this view of the masses continues in the writings of Thomas Dye and Harmon Zeigler (1993:14–16). In their eyes, the irony of democracy in America is that elites, not masses, are committed to democratic values. "Despite a superficial commitment to the symbols of democracy, the American people have a surprisingly weak commitment to individual liberty, toleration of diversity, and freedom of expression. . . . Democratic values have survived because elites, not masses govern. . . . Unchecked mass influence could threaten democratic values. . . . Occasionally the masses mobilize, and their activism is extremist, unstable, and unpredictable . . . is usually an expression of resentment against the established order, and . . . usually occurs in times of crisis when a 'counterelite' (dema-gogue) emerges from the masses. . . . Democracies can survive only if the masses are absorbed In the problems of everyday life, and are involved in groups that distract their attention from mass publics. . . . The masses define politics in simplistic terms. They want simple answers to society's problems, regardless of how complex those problems may be."

The Democratic View

Democratic critics of mass society worry about the domination of the masses by elites, and view elites as the real threat to democracy (Mills, 1956). As Daniel Hellinger and Dennis Judd (1991:v, 5–7) argue, "America's elites have evinced chronic anxiety about their posi-tion. . . . They have employed a panoply of strategies to manipulate democratic processes . . . controlled the compositions of the electorate and restricted political discourse, with the consequences that elections concern 'safe' political issues and voters are able to decide only between candidates who represent elite preferences. . . . In the past decades they have taken decisive steps to insulate government policy making from elections altogether. . . . The elites that have governed in America have shown little attachment to democracy except as a device to legitimate their political control. . . . From time to time they have resorted to [violent] repression . . . and elites have made much more liberal use of it . . . than the mainstream textbooks will ever reveal."

The ultimate fear of democratic theorists is the imposition of a totalitarian state on the masses, as in Germany under the Nazis and in Russia under the Soviet regime.

Mass Psychology

Many writings about mass collective behavior are elitist in tone. Such early theorists as Sigmund Freud and Gustav Le Bon viewed the masses as highly suggestible and easily manipulated, especially when they are together in crowds. Crowd behavior is viewed as unrestrained by conscious thought. Crowds are dangerous because they are suggestible. They can be manipulated by unscrupulous demagogues at public rallies.

The Rural-Urban Continua

Virtually all the founders of sociology agonized over the consequences of the transition from a close-knit rural society to an impersonal urban one. Each of them analyzed a dif-ferent aspect of the decline of social attachment and the rise of the alienation, loneliness, impersonality, and disenchantment that characterize the mass society.

To summarize, a mass society is a modern society that is characterized to various degrees by:

1. Centralized power in the hands of bureaucratic elites.

2. Manipulation of the masses by elites in undemocratic ways by such means as mass culture and government propaganda.

3. The creation of alienated masses, groups of people who no longer feel attachment to their community or to society.

4. Disruptive mass behavior (e.g., riots, demonstrations, revolts, strikes).

Overall, the mass society is one in which the many without power are vulnerable to manipulation and control by the elites, and the elites are vulnerable to disruptive behavior by the powerless masses. Such a society is prone to disruption from both ruling elites and unintegrated masses.

The Postmodern Era

Much of this book focuses on the structural conditions and cultural characteristics of the postmodern era. The modern era is characterized chiefly by the processes of urbanization and industrialization, and reached its zenith between the 1830s and 1945. The modern era, which is dominated by a manufacturing economic base, has given way to a postmodern age, dominated by services, and the culture of the mass media.

The term **postmodern** is loaded with meanings, and can refer to a variety of institutional and cultural phenomena within the postmodern era. As Denzin (1991:ix–x) has noted, it is four things at the same time:

First, postmodern describes a sequence of historical events from World War II to the present. These include: "the Vietnam War; the worldwide economic recessions of the 1970s and 1980s; the rise to power of conservative political regimes in Europe and America; the failure of the Left to mount an effective attack against these regimes; the collapse in the inter-national labor movement; the emergence of a new, conservative politics of health and morality centering on sexuality and the family; totalitarian regimes in Europe, Asia, Latin America, and South Africa; the breakdown of the cold war and the emergence of *glasnost*; increased worldwide racism" (Denzin, 1991:ix).

Second, the postmodern references the multinational forms of *late* capitalism which have introduced new cultural products and new forms of communication into the world economic and cultural systems.

Third, it describes a movement in the visual arts, architecture, cinema, popular music, and social theory which goes against the grain of classic realist and modernist formations.

Fourth, it *refers to a form of theorizing and writing about* the social. Postmodern theorizing is preoccupied with the visual society, its representations (symbols), and their meanings, or, more frequently, their lack of meaning. Many postmodernists subscribe to the notion that symbols hide the fact that there is no such thing as reality, merely the symbolic messages coming from corporate and political image makers that pretend to portray reality. Postmodern theorizing is also concerned with the new types of personal troubles (AIDS, homelessness, drug addiction, family and public violence) and public problems that define the current age.

In this book, postmodern refers to those institutional and cultural changes that have taken place since the end of World War II. Concerning social structure, the postmodern era is dominated by a capitalistic global economy. This structure consists of groups of nations whose wealth and power are grossly unequal. The end of the Cold War and the collapse of the Soviet empire have ensured the ascendancy of the richest capitalist countries—the United States, Canada, Japan, and the leading democracies of Western Europe. Within these nations and within the global economy as well, huge multinational corporations dominate both economies and governments. Most of the so-called Third World nations of Asia, Africa, and Latin America (accounting for 60 percent of the world's population) are very poor. This great inequality of wealth and power is a major cause of the world's social problems—its political instability and wars, its environmental pollution, its terrorism, even its uncontrolled population growth. The Third World has experienced either a war or a revolution every month since the postmodern world system emerged in 1945. The nations of the former Soviet empire also face a future clouded by the threat of civil wars, economic collapse, and massive scandals involving elite corruption.

The postmodern era is also characterized by a global popular culture that is spread throughout the world by multinational corporations who produce and distribute television programs, movies, advertising, popular music, plays, newspapers and magazines, and consumer goods. Postmodern culture contains some disturbing tendencies that are making many social problems worse:

1. Preoccupation with sex and the separation of sex and love.

2. Increasing reliance on violence as a solution to conflict.

3. Commodification, that is, the turning of virtually every human impulse, moral principle, and sacred belief into a commodity.

4. Endless advertising of commodities and the cultivation of conspicuous consumption.

5. Lifestyles of mass consumption centering on the fast-food restaurant, the theme park, the shopping mall, and the mass media.

6. This lifestyle promotes a confusing culture that lacks stable values and makes it difficult to separate fantasy from reality.

7. A disbelief in traditional values, political ideologies, and faiths by many, and a radical adherence to traditional beliefs by extremist groups (e.g., fundamentalists and cults) (Denzin, 1991:1-20; W. Anderson, 1990).

Finally, the unstable global society and its popular culture have had a profound effect on the nature of social character in the postmodern era. The sense of self, who one is and where one fits into the world, is not only unclear, some writers on the postmodern condition believe the self is threatened with extinction. Kenneth Gergen (1991) believes people's sense of self has reached a point of social saturation. Gergen argues that the individual is continually bombarded with messages about the self from advertising, self-help books, movies, and other cultural sources of the postmodern era. The effect of these various messages is to make people confused about who they are, what they are supposed to believe,

This photograph of Honduras (a Central American nation) demonstrates the absolute and desperate poverty in which roughly two-thirds of the world's peoples live. Most often, the world's poor are nonwhite minority populations.

and how they are supposed to behave. Old values concerning patriotism, belief in the superiority of one's own group or religion, have given way to relativism, the notion that all values and beliefs are valid. Thus what people believe about themselves and the choices they have made in life is true only for a limited period of time and in a limited set of relationships. Morality is now totally situational, with no stable standards existing to guide a person's behavior in multiple situations.

Another source of confusion is the fact that people in postmodern societies must now play multiple roles, each one of which demands different sets of skills. Thus, one is a parent, a spouse, a worker, a consumer, a voter, and conflicts between such roles are common. Many people are torn between devoting time to their careers and to raising their children.

Any stable sense of self is therefore lost. People in the postmodern era go through life in their gender, class, and racially related social identities, not knowing what to believe about themselves or about the world in which they live. Theirs is an age of confusion and self-doubt (Scimecca, 1995: 94; Denzin, 1991: vii), one that contains within it some alarming tendencies for the future of social character.

The Antisocial Social Character

The postmodern era is also characterized by the antisocial character and he or she is typified by the following:

1. A "cheerful robot" mentality at work and in private life (Mills, 1959:171; 1951:182–88): People display a false pleasantness to customers, co-workers, and bosses for purposes of personal gain. In private life, they often manipulate personal relationships to gain sexual favors.

2. An unhealthy self-centeredness, or narcissism, which makes one unable to empathize with other people or to form emotional or moral bonds with them.

3. A disturbing tendency toward "wilding" (Derber, 1992:29–32), the commission of deviant or criminal activity without guilt or concern for its effects on others. A well publicized case of wilding occurred on August 20, 1989, when Lyle and Erik Menendez killed their father, the multimillionaire head of the company that produced the movie *Rambo II*, and their mother. José Menendez had wanted his sons to become successful and rich, as he had done. After they received the first shares of their inheritance, the boys went on a spending spree. One bought a new Porsche, a Rolex watch, and expensive clothes. Lyle Menendez had told a friend that he did not want to struggle for success the way his father had had to do. He wanted things quick and easy, and he had a better way in mind. His "better way" turned out to be the murder of his parents (Derber, 1992:31–37).

Underlying the antisocial character are two alienating conditions: inauthenticity and dehumanization. **Inauthenticity** is characterized by the presence of *positive overt appearances* coupled with *negative underlying (hidden) realities* (Simon & Eitzen, 1993:340ff). Inauthenticity can be seen in advertisements for cigarettes, liquor, cosmetics, cars, deodorants, clothing products of every sort. Nearly all of these so-called lifestyle ads (those picturing people) have a common theme in the form of *implied promises*. The implied promise in each ad constitutes the positive overt appearances that are a hallmark of inauthenticity. We are promised that if we drink the whiskey or smoke the cigarettes, we will find sex, romance, or love; we will become successful or powerful (note that all such ads picture the trappings of affluence); and we will be popular and have friends.

What are the consequences of smoking and drinking? Tobacco and alcohol combined kill about 500,000 Americans each year. They cause a variety of diseases, and cost billions of dollars in medical bills and lost workdays. These harms—death, disease, and financial loss—are the negative underlying realities of lifestyles based on the consumption of alcohol and tobacco. In our personal lives, too, we are subjected to the inauthenticity of lies and manipulation as people put on a false front for financial or sexual purposes.

Object-directed dehumanization is an alienating condition of the social structure that occurs when people are labeled less than human for purposes of profit, exploitation, and manipulation. We see this form of dehumanization in mass media stereotypes (the dumb blonde, for example). Racial, gender, ethnic, and age stereotypes are common in corporate and governmental institutions, too. Bureaucracies tend to treat people as undifferentiated items in nonhuman categories. Employees, once valued, become "labor costs" when the time comes to "restructure" and "downsize" the "organization." Accordingly, real people suffering the pain and trauma of job loss are no longer involved, only "units" in organizations. (By the way, I am not a human being, according to my university. As a member of the faculty, I am a "Unit 3 element.")

Self-directed dehumanization is a form of self-alienation. It involves turning oneself into a "cog in a wheel," a dehumanized machine. The workaholic is subject to such stress-related diseases as ulcers and heart attacks and to job burnout (feelings of intense dislike of one's job).

The natures of mass society, the postmodern era, and the antisocial character and alienation are explored in depth throughout this book.

A Paradigm for Analysis

The sociological imagination is a paradigm designed for the analysis of social problems. A starting point concerns the definition of social problems, socially patterned harms that cause physical, financial, or moral harm. These harms are problems whether or not they are identified as such by media and governmental elites. The remainder of the paradigm consists of elements that either cause or are harmful consequences of social problems. These include:

1. Structure and Contradiction:
The Power Elite and
Massive Inequality

The power elite dominates the American social structure. This elite consists of large corporations, the executive and legislative branches of the federal government, and that group of organizations that make up what we have described as the military-industrial complex and its "secret government."

Contradictions within the structure of society are the cause of social problems. The power elite constitutes a structure that has amassed an undemocratic amount of wealth and political power, as well as the power to define cultural values. Such values include the unlimited accumulation of private property, consumerism and materialism, celebrity worship, and a belief in "rugged" individualism in an organizational society.

The Higher Immorality is an institutionalized set of deviant and criminal practices that take place within corporate and governmental institutions. These practices involve deception and manipulation of the public, corruption, corporate crime, and, occasionally, cooperation with organized criminal syndicates. All the practices associated with the higher immorality are in and of themselves major social problems and they, in turn, cause further problems.

2. Historical Epoch:
The Postmodern Era

The economies of these nations are divided into modern, (First World), semi-modern (old Soviet Bloc states/Second World), and Third World (poor and struggling to modernize nations). First World multinational firms increasingly extract raw materials, cheap labor, and surplus profits from Third World nations, whose international debts continue to mount. The capitalist world system tends toward instability at numerous "flashpoints," and wars, revolutions, and terrorism are common in the face of massive international inequalities.

3. Mass Society and
Postmodern Culture

Below the power elite structure is an evolving mass society composed of unorganized, relatively powerless masses of people, who lack a sense of community concerning their neighborhoods and society. A power elite prevents the masses from capturing democratic power. Elements of postmodern culture, especially advertising, make it difficult to separate fantasy and reality.

4. Social Character:
The Antisocial Social Character

The dominant social character in mass society is a person who dislikes or is indifferent to work, is politically, societally, and self-alienated, and is prone to engage in various degrees and types of "wilding" (deviant acts). The antisocial social character tends to escape into mass culture, and engages in personal relationships through interpersonal manipulation and self-deception. The inauthentic and dehumanizing contents of postmodern culture reinforce various forms of personal alienation.

5. Master Trends: The Descendancy
of American Civilization

While it is difficult to predict the future's crises and their causes, some elements of trouble down the road seem clear. Massive inequalities of wealth and power within and between nations, and environmental and population growth problems constitute genuine harms. The spread of postmodern culture worldwide is contributing to a crisis of democracy in which manipulated masses of people react passively to media propaganda by corporate and governmental elites. Democracy itself is at risk.

A final word: Many students who study social problems find the experience grounds for cynicism and doubt. The sociological imagination focuses on the idea of social harm precisely because such harms must be ended. To acquire a sociological imagination is also to acquire a set of beliefs about the dignity and worth of all human beings, the promise of genuine democracy, and the ability to think critically and independently of dominant ideologies and forms of mystification.

This book is written in hope, not despair.

Suggested Readings:
A Brief Bibliographic Essay

The works of C. Wright Mills are the most important source of knowledge about the sociological imagination. The best survey of Mills' works is *Power, Politics, and People: The Collected Essays of C. Wright Mills,* edited by Irving Louis Horowitz (New York: Ballantine, 1962). Horowitz also edited a book of essays in Mills' honor titled *The New Sociology* (New York: Oxford University Press, 1964). The most important of Mills' works are *The Sociological Imagination* (1959), *The Power Elite* (1956), and *White Collar* (1951), all published by Oxford University Press. Mills also wrote *Character and Social Structure* (with Hans Gerth) (New York: Harcourt, Brace & World, 1953), an important source of the model that would become the sociological imagination. Mills also wrote an interesting book on Marxism, *The Marxists* (1962), published by Dell Books. Finally, Mills' anthology in sociological theory, *Images of Man: The Classic Tradition in Sociological Theory* (New York: Braziller, 1960), is a magnificent collection of works on the classic tradition.

There are also some interesting works about Mills' thought and life. Joseph Scimecca's *Sociological Theory of C. Wright Mills* (Port Washington, NY: Kennikat Press, 1978) is an excellent survey of Mills' thought. A good brief introduction to Mills is John Eldridge's *C. Wright Mills* (London: Tavistock, 1983).

Works in the Tradition of C. Wright Mills

Two works inspired by Mills' view of power and crime are David R. Simon, *Elite Deviance,* 5th ed. (Needham Heights, MA: Allyn & Bacon, forthcoming), and Joel H. Henderson and David R. Simon, *Crimes of the Criminal Justice System* (Cincinnati: Anderson, 1994). A fine study influenced by Mills' view of white-collar workers is Arlie Hochschild, *The Managed Heart* (Berkeley: University of California Press, 1984).

Finally, the most important works inspired by Mills' political sociology are those by G. William Domhoff. *Who Rules America?* (Englewood Cliffs, NJ: Prentice-Hall, 1967), *The Higher Circles* (New York: Random House, 1970); *Fat Cats and Democrats* (Englewood Cliffs, NJ: Prentice-Hall, 1972); *The Bohemian Grove and Other Retreats* (New York: Harper & Row, 1974); *The Powers That Be* (New York: Random House, 1979); *Who Rules America Now?* (Englewood Cliffs, NJ: Prentice-Hall, 1983); and *The Power Elite and the State: How Policy Is Made in America* (New York: DeGruyter, 1990).

Exercises

Critical Thinking Exercise 1.1	**Personal Troubles, Social Issues, and You**

Write a short paper (three to five pages, double-spaced) stating your opinion in response to the following questions. Be sure to make a copy of your paper. *What's important now is your impressions of the issues raised here.*

1. *Social problem* Select a magazine or newspaper article about a topic currently in the news—a murder in a high school, say, or an indictment of a politician on corruption charges, a kidnapping, a terrorist bombing incident, or a shoot-out between rival drug gangs. Does the article's topic indicate a more widespread problem in America? What types of harm result from this socially patterned problem? Consider the following dimensions of the sociological imagination.

Continued on next page

Exercise 1.1 Continued

2. *Contradiction* What are the institutional contradictions surrounding the problem? For example, do some institutions in American society approve of drug use, either legal or illegal, while other institutions condemn it? What contradictions are inherent in American institutions that may cause the problem you selected?

3. *Historical epoch* What events in the recent past have raised concern about this problem?

4. *Immediate milieu* To what extent is this problem a part of your immediate environment? For example, do you know other students who abuse alcohol or illegal drugs? Has anyone ever attempted to sell you illegal drugs? Have you experienced any direct contact with the problem you chose to analyze?

5. *Personal troubles* Have you or have members of your family experienced problems with the issue you chose? Are any of your friends experiencing problems with it? If so, what sorts of trauma have you experienced because of this social problem? Is the problem resolvable within your immediate environment, or do you believe that some larger effort is necessary—perhaps a private effort in your local community, or government legislation, or public service education by the mass media? If so, what kinds of efforts do you believe are necessary to rid your everyday life of this problem?

Critical Thinking Exercise 1.2	Personal Troubles and Social Issues

Ron Kovic and Vietnam

The United States' involvement in Vietnam from 1964 to 1975 became a social issue when the public perceived that the government was lying about many aspects of the conflict. Critics argued that the war was not a crusade against communism but a long-standing civil conflict between factions of the Vietnamese. It was also perceived that the government was lying about the competence of the South Vietnamese government to fight the war, about the ability of the United States to "win" the war, about the numbers of enemy troops that were overrunning South Vietnam. Some important institutional contradictions were also involved. The U.S. government accused communists of using chemical weapons, yet the United States had embarked on a massive defoliation campaign with Agent Orange. The South Vietnamese were officially praised as democratic allies, yet their government violated human rights by imprisoning enemy soldiers in tiger cages, and many South Vietnamese officials engaged in corruption on a wide scale.

America's military behaved in a contradictory fashion. While the Pentagon charged that the enemy did not value human life, U.S. soldiers were raping, torturing, and massacring innocent civilians. The army professed high morale, yet a disturbing number of American soldiers either returned home as drug addicts or deserted the military altogether.

The Historical Epoch

Once these realities reached public awareness, the war's continuation became a social issue. Antiwar demonstrators and their critics clashed in public demonstrations. The public's opposition to the war after 1968 clearly challenged the ability of the military to motivate troops. Social change was being attempted from below as hundreds of thousands of people confronted their government in massive street demonstrations.

Personal Troubles and the Immediate Milieu

Ron Kovic was a young man from Long Island, New York, who graduated from high school just as a large troop buildup was taking place in Vietnam. Kovic had been socialized to believe in the necessity and rightness of fighting for one's country. His childhood movie idols were such stars as Audie Murphy and John Wayne, who played brave war heroes. His family and school stressed participation in sports, which reinforced the importance of winning. His toys were guns, and he and his friends regularly played at war. He joined the Cub Scouts and marched in Memorial Day parades. Since 1957, when the Soviet Union launched the first space satellite, Ron had been taught the importance of beating the Soviets at everything. Ron wanted to be a hero, and this very shy guy also dreamed of having a girlfriend. Everything in his immediate environment led him to join the Marines and go to Vietnam.

Once he was in Vietnam, Ron's striving for heroism resulted in his being seriously wounded and paralyzed. This trauma, along with others from his Vietnam tour, led to a great personal change. The social and personal contradictions he experienced resulted in a profound personal transformation. He became enraged over the lies the government was telling the public about the war, and about the bad treatment he received at the Veterans Administration hospital where he recovered from his wounds. Rats gnawed on his bedding, and machines vital to his treatment were not kept in proper repair.

For the first time, Ron challenged the basic values of blind patriotism, obedience to authority, and the rightness of American foreign and defense policy. He turned against the war and became active in the antiwar movement. The contradiction between the government's proclaimed reason for pursuing the war (communism) and the reason Ron perceived (protection of multinational corporations and the military-industrial complex) was glaring. Another contradiction lay in the demeaning treatment of veterans by a nation that professed to care about them.

Ron Kovic's experiences show clearly how institutional contradictions can result in both social problems and personal troubles. The contradictions surrounding our involvement in Vietnam divided the nation politically, plunged many families into crisis as the war separated them both physically and emotionally, and brought severe personal trauma to returning veterans.

A film based on Ron Kovic's book about his experiences, *Born on the Fourth of July* (1976), was nominated for an Oscar. It has been released on videotape. See the film, then collect a sample of reviews of it published in various newspapers and national magazines. Analyze the reviews by answering the following questions:

Continued on next page

Exercise 1.2 Continued

1. Did the critics point out any connections relating to Vietnam or Kovic's experiences, such as maltreatment of veterans by the Veterans Administration?

2. Did reviewers notice any symptoms of inauthenticity or dehumanization, such as perceptions of the enemy as barbarians?

3. Did reviewers mention any mystification of social problems, such as deliberate lying by the government to the American people about the war?

Ron Kovic (seated) was the subject of an Oliver Stone film, *Born on the Fourth of July*, which traced his evolution from unquestioning belief in his country's military and foreign policy to antiwar activist during the Vietnam era. Kovic's experiences offer an excellent case study in how social structure, historical epoch, and social character interact to form a world in which seemingly private troubles and social issues often overlap.

Social Structure and Contradiction: The Mass Society and the American Dream

Chapter · Chapter · Chapter · Chapter · Chapter

2

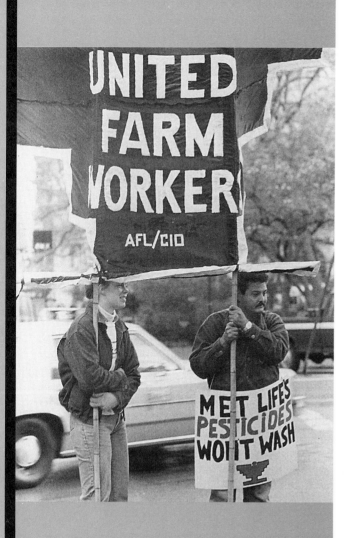

Social Problems and the American Dream

In the United States, the economic institution has always taken precedence over other institutions. This has immense implications for the nature of America's social problems.

America is the only nation in the history of the world whose founding creed involved the inalienable right to pursue happiness. The American concept of happiness has always involved the unlimited accumulation of profit and property. The goal of making money has been widely accepted as the main component of happiness and success, a central feature of what is called the American Dream.

So important has become the goal of accumulating wealth, of achieving the American Dream, that profit in America has frequently accrued without the restraints placed on capitalist economies in other nations. In the United States, attempts to regulate the excesses of business have been criticized as government interference, or "socialism."

The goal of money making is so central to American culture that noneconomic forms of success have been devalued. Accordingly, as Messner and Rosenfeld (1994:79–81) point out, people who are wonderful teachers, mothers, child care workers, or nurses are not paid very much in America. In fact, bartenders make more money here than people who work with children. Why? Because there are few profits to be made from raising good children. Profits come largely from products and services that people are willing to pay a lot of money to secure.

Second, other institutions in American life have had to accommodate the needs of business. Most people go to college, not because they are fascinated by learning, but because it leads to a middle-class occupation afterwards. America has always been the most antiintellectual nation in the Western world precisely because its primary definition of success involves making money. Colleges and universities offer evening and weekend programs, many of them in business, because people's jobs take precedence over the needs of educational and other institutions. The requirements of work also take precedence over the needs of family life. The United States remains the only advanced industrial democracy without paid family leave, without national health care, without an extended family vacation policy—precisely because the needs of business are given precedence over everything else in the American institutional order.

Government, too, has historically been subservient to the needs of business. Now the government is a central part of the economy. The primary responsibility of modern government is not to provide for the needs of its citizens, but to assure economic growth. Much of American foreign and defense policy is about protecting the holdings of multinational corporations, as opposed to assuring that human rights and democracy are encouraged in other nations. As will be discussed, the United States has a long history of supporting oppressive regimes that are friendly to American business interests. Moreover, American government at all levels grants generous subsidies, tax breaks, loans and loan guarantees, as well as government contracts, to American businesses in the hope of stimulating economic growth. This is one reason why the U.S. federal government has spent over $4 trillion on defense since 1947, much of it on expensive weapons systems.

Finally, other institutions in American life have been penetrated by the language, ethics, and requirements of American business. Terms like "bottom line" and "cash flow" have become part of everyday language. Many politicians believe the way to solve the problems of government is to run government like a business. In 1992 Ross Perot ran for president promising to bring the principles that had made him a billionaire businessman to bear on government problems. Moreover, many individuals from the private sector are appointed to cabinet level positions in America.

All of this is part and parcel of a central contradiction in American life. American culture places so much emphasis on the *goal* of success, of achieving the American Dream, that it neglects the *means* by which success is to be achieved. The result is a lack of social control that motivates many people and organizations to strive for winning by any means. Thus a central contradiction of American life is that the value of making money is stressed, while the social structure does not provide the equal opportunity necessary for all to achieve such a monetary goal. America has thus managed to create a structural form of **anomie**, a lack of rules concerning how that goal of success is to be achieved. Table 2.1 depicts the causes of America's anomie.

The result of this major contradiction is that Americans and American institutions (like corporations and government organizations) come to value goals related to success

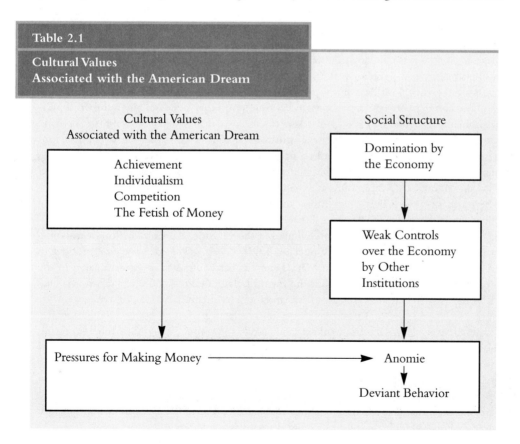

Table 2.1

**Cultural Values
Associated with the American Dream**

over the legitimate means prescribed to reach such goals. Thus, a great deal of harmful behavior takes place in the name of achieving the goals associated with the American Dream. It is this contradiction that is responsible for virtually all of the social problems discussed in this book.

Steven Messner and Richard Rosenfeld (1994:6) argue that the causes of social problems lie within the same values and behaviors that are usually viewed as part of the American version of success. They define the American Dream as a "broad cultural ethos that entails a commitment to the goal of material success, to be pursued by everyone in society, under conditions of open individual competition." The power of the **American Dream** comes from the widely shared values that it includes:

1. *An achievement orientation*: This includes pressure to "make something" of oneself, to set goals and achieve them. Achieving material success is one way personal

Box 2.1 • The Debate over Contradictions

Contradictions are inherent conflicts within the social structure that cannot be resolved without modification of the system (Mills, 1962:83; Worsley, 1982:10). The contradictions within a social structure vary over time. As social structures (that is, institutions and societies) change, the nature of contradictions likewise changes, as does the nature of the social problems they create. One economic contradiction can be seen in the idea that the way to make a profit is to hold down labor costs (wages and salaries). The conflict here is that businesses also want people (workers) to consume the goods they produce. Before people can consume, they must have money to spend.

The conflict between labor costs and consumption may generate any number of public problems. When a firm lays off workers to cut costs, it may decrease consumer demand for its products, thus creating the conditions that lead to recession or depression. Unemployment itself is linked to a host of personal troubles and social problems, including increased rates of suicide, mental illness, divorce, crime, and imprisonment. Unemployment may also devastate communities, as when a single-industry town is virtually shut down when a plant closes. Thus institutional contradictions generate public issues, and these public issues directly parallel personal troubles suffered by ordinary people.

Such contradictions may seem obvious, but the very idea of contradictions is troubling to many social scientists (Knapp & Spector, 1991: 319–24). The idea was first brought to sociological analysis by Karl Marx. Marx believed that contradictions were located in the economic substructure of societies in the form of class conflict. Under capitalism, the class of property owners (the bourgeoisie) was in conflict with the class of propertyless factory workers (the proletariat). These two classes form relations of production in which owners pay wages in exchange for the workers' labor (skills and time). The conflict inherent in this relationship is that workers end up exploited: The wages they are paid are disproportionately low in relation to the wealth they create. Marx believed that the labor it takes to create (manufacture) a product accounts for the entire worth of that product beyond the costs of raw materials and tools. Of course, the difference between those costs plus what workers are paid and the price that the products they manufacture sell for is called profit by capitalists. Marxists, however, call it surplus value; profit is merely exploitation.

worth is measured in America. While this is a shaky basis for self-esteem, it is nevertheless true that Americans view their personal worth much like a stock, one that rises or falls with the realization of money making.

2. *Individualism*: Americans not only possess autonomy, but basic individual rights. Americans make individualistic decisions regarding marriage and career choices, religion, political outlook, and probably thousands of other life choices. The result is that individualism and achievement combine to produce anomie and this is because fellow Americans often become rivals and competitors for rewards and status. Intense personal competition increases pressure to succeed. Often this means that rules about the means by which success is obtained are disregarded when they threaten to interfere with personal goals. The case of Charles Stuart offers an extreme example of anomie and the American Dream.

This situation does not represent a social problem unless it results in demonstrable harm. Marx insisted that real harm was being inflicted on workers. As he and his colleague Friedrich Engels repeatedly demonstrated, workers were so poorly paid that they were barely able to afford basic necessities, and lacked adequate medical care.

Workers labored under very dangerous conditions that often resulted in injury or death. Workers were injured by machines and by breathing in toxic chemicals and coal dust. In his *Das Kapital* Marx describes one supervisor's testimony at an investigation into the death of one of her employees. The employee died after working "26 1/2 hours, with 60 other kids, 30 in one room, that afforded only one third of the cubic feet of air required for them" (Marx, 1952:123). The supervisor describes her disappointment that the worker failed to finish the dress she was sewing before she died.

Work was not only poorly paid and physically dangerous, it was stressful and alienating. Workers had no voice in the quality of the products they produced, their prices, or the work process itself. Laborers were simply required to keep up with the pace of production, or they were fired and replaced by other workers, who were competing for the same jobs. Marx termed these working conditions that psychically and physically harmed workers alienating, and related how they contributed to workers' feelings of isolation, loneliness, powerlessness, and self-estrangement. In short, working conditions under capitalism did not allow workers to exercise their own human nature, to be creative.

Much of what Marx saw as problematic in nineteenth-century capitalism was of concern to Charles Dickens and many other writers. Contradictions exist and cause problems in all social structures, not just economic institutions. Some of Marx's observations about capitalism's structure and contradictions still seem relevant, yet capitalism's structure and its contradictions have changed dramatically since Marx died in 1883. Consequently, Marx's insights have limited utility today, and they are made more limited still by "vulgar" Marxists, who believe that every aspect of society is economically determined. One problem with such reductionism is that it overlooks other social structures that also generate contradictions, which in turn cause social problems.

On October 23, 1989, Charles and Carol Stuart were on their way home from a Boston hospital childbirth class. When Charles pulled the car over to allegedly check some problem, he pulled a gun on his wife (who was eight months pregnant) and shot her at point blank range. Initially, Stuart told police his wife had been killed by a black gunman. Two months later, Charles confessed that he shot his wife because he stood to collect hundreds of thousands of dollars in life insurance, with which he could realize his American Dream of owning a restaurant (Derber, 1992:8).

3. *Universalism:* The American Dream is open to all. Universalism means the chances of success and failure are possibilities that are open to everyone. Fear of failure is intense in America and increases pressure to abandon conformity to rules governing proper conduct in favor of expedience.

4. *The "Fetishism" of Money:* Money has attained an almost sacred quality in American life. It is the way Americans keep score in the game of success, and, as noted, there are no rules that tell us when enough is enough. What is stressed in the American Dream are ends over means. As Elliott Currie (1991:255) notes in his discussion of a market society, the pursuit of private gain has become the organizing principle for all of social life. Charles Derber (1992) argues that during the Reagan-Bush era, increasing inequality, along with an ethic of "greed is good," combined to give the American character an element of narcissism. Narcissism is a personality disorder, a mental illness, characterized by distorted self-love and, most important, selfishness coupled with a

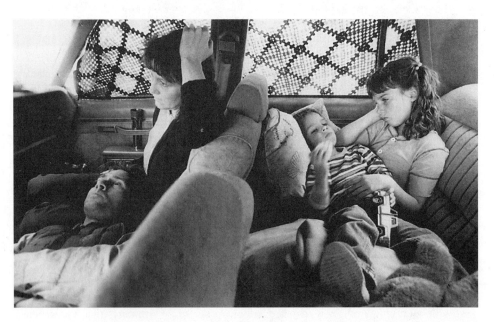

This family now sleeps in its car because it has fallen out of the middle class and faces the prospect of poverty. Many social commentators now argue that the American Dream of home ownership and a better life for one's children is no longer a realistic goal in the postmodern global economy.

lack of guilt. The Reagan-Bush ideology of self-reliance stimulated large numbers of upperworld crooks to engage in a quest for power, status, and attention in a "money culture." The result was an unrestrained quest for personal gain.

Between 1971 and 1991, the top 1 percent of Americans experienced an 85 percent increase in their pretax incomes and a 23 percent decline in their tax burden. The bottom 20 percent of the population, in contrast, endured a decline of 12 percent in their real income and a 3 percent increase in their tax burden. Real income of families headed by single parents under 25 years of age dropped by over 23 percent during this period.

These increasing inequalities mean that the poor are much poorer. There are ten million more people living in poverty in the 1990s than there were in the 1980s. They are also increasingly desperate, so desperate that few people in the United States seem to feel safe from criminal victimization. A 1993 poll by the Harvard School of Public Health reported that 94 percent of Americans fear criminal victimization (New York *Times,* October 24, 1993: D-1).

The Crimogenic Society

Sociologist Robert Merton pointed out over a half century ago that one great contradiction of American culture was its emphasis on winning and success, yet without opportunity necessarily to achieve such success. A portion of this contradiction is due to what sociologist Émile Durkheim (1950) described as *anomie,* a social situation where norms are unclear. Success in America has no official limits, the private accumulation of wealth is without "a final stopping point" (Merton, 1938/1994:119). No matter what their income level, people want about 50 percent more money (which, of course, becomes 50 percent more once it is achieved).

Merton (1938/1994:119) noted that crime "is a very common phenomenon" among all social classes in the United States. A study of 1700 middle-class New Yorkers in 1937 indicted that 99 percent of them admitted to committing crimes violating one of New York's forty-nine criminal offenses for which they could have been imprisoned for at least a year. Moreover, 64 percent of the men and 29 percent of the women reported committing felonies. A 1991 survey by Patterson and Kim also showed a high percentage of Americans engaging in criminal behavior. Yet one of our persistent myths about crime is that America is divided into two populations, one law-abiding, the other criminal.

Social critic James Adams, who coined the term "The American Dream," once remarked that many people coming to America's shores were relatively law-abiding before they arrived here. People "were made lawless by America, rather than America being made lawless by them." It has been American elites that have served as role models to ordinary people. Thus elite deviance provides an excuse for nonelites to engage in crime without feeling guilty. Elite deviance also sends the message that it is stupid not to commit crime if one has the opportunity. Many a drug dealer and street gang member has remarked that they are just doing what the Rockefellers, Carnegies, and other robber barons did in the nineteenth century—establishing monopolies.

The same ideology is found among organized crime figures. When Peter Lupsha (1981) investigated the life stories of these people, he found that none of them embarked on a criminal career because there were no jobs to be had ("blocked opportunities"), as some theorists of organized crime suppose. American gangsters, Lupsha discovered, tend to divide the world into "suckers" and "wiseguys." Suckers are working-class people who toil at legal jobs and struggle to make ends meet. Wiseguys are gangsters who do what they want and have plenty of money to show for it.

It is not just Mafia figures who think this way. Achieving success via force and fraud has always been considered smart, so smart that for a number of decades our culture has lionized gangsters. Beginning with Al Capone, we have come to admire Mafia dons who do not hesitate to take shortcuts to success. In 1994, Oliver Stone's film *Natural Born Killers* demonstrated the American penchant for making heroes out of serial killers, again noting the American admiration for people who take what they want.

Likewise, *People* magazine's 1989 cover story on Gambino family godfather John Gotti pictured the don as so tough that he could punch his way through a cement block. A multimillionaire, with plenty of charisma, *People* noted, Gotti is also a loyal family man, who has never cheated on his wife. The fact that he personally has murdered a number of rivals is largely talked of as being an occupational requirement. What all of this means is that America is disturbingly tolerant of certain forms of deviant behavior that stem from the American value of success and making money. Our emphasis on the goal of accumulating wealth and ignoring the means to achieve that goal hits hardest those groups that have the least opportunity to accumulate wealth. This is one reason why the poor commit so much street (violent) crime. When other opportunities to make money are lacking, turning to crime becomes a viable choice for people who feel they have nothing to lose.

Former Mafia boss John Gotti (right) pictured here with his lawyer (Bruce Cutler) represents one of the least understood aspects of celebrity in American life.

More important, the poor do not possess a monopoly on deviant behavior. Crime and the other harms that cause social problems are rampant at all class levels in American society, as shall be explored throughout this text.

The Political Economy and the Power Elite

In 1956, C. Wright Mills warned the American people of a growing centralization and coordination of wealth and power in the United States. He wrote (1956:7–8):

> The economy . . . has become dominated by two or three hundred giant corporations, and politically integrated, which together hold the keys to economic decisions. The political [system] has become a centralized, executive establishment which has taken unto itself many powers previously scattered, and now enters into each and every cranny of the social structure. The military . . . has become the largest and most expensive feature of government, and, although well versed in smiling public relations, now has all the grim and clumsy efficiency of a sprawling [bureaucracy]. . . . There is no longer, on the one hand, an economy, and, on the other hand, a political order containing a military establishment unimportant to politics and to money making. There is a political order linked, in a thousand ways, with military institutions and decisions. . . . If there is government intervention in the corporate economy, so there is corporate intervention in the governmental process.

Collectively the people who head these institutions of great power (large corporations, the executive branch of the government, and the military apparatus) form what Mills termed the *power elite*. Six years later, in 1961, President Dwight D. Eisenhower called them the *military-industrial complex*. These two terms are interchangeable.

The Corporate Sector

The **corporate component** of the power elite's structure is made up of the largest hundred to two hundred industrial corporations in the nation and the insurance companies, banks, and other financial entities (such as mutual funds) that own stock in them. The largest hundred firms are usually awarded about 75 percent of the contracts for major weapons systems by the Department of Defense (the Pentagon). Weapons systems account for about 30 percent of the nation's military budget.

The hundred largest industrial corporations dominate the entire corporate sector of the American economy. They control more industrial assets than the next 199,900 corporations combined (about 60 percent of such assets are controlled by the hundred largest firms). The five largest industrial corporations (General Motors, Exxon, Ford Motor Company, IBM, and General Electric) alone control 15 percent of the nation's industrial assets (Dye & Zeigler, 1993:98).

The largest hundred corporations are also multinational: They own factories and contract for labor and raw materials in many nations throughout the world. They also tend to be interlocked. The Clayton Antitrust Act of 1914 forbids any company to own stock in

Former Reagan cabinet officers James Baker and George Schultz now are employed by prestigious law firms that represent wealthy and powerful clients in Washington, D.C. They also serve on the boards of large corporations. Such positions are very common for former cabinet officers of both Republican and Democratic administrations.

another company in the same industry. Thus General Motors (GM), for example, cannot own stock in Ford. However, if a large bank buys a 5 percent interest in GM and a 5 percent interest in Ford, the bank can sit on both boards of directors. This practice is known as an *interlocking directorate*. This is the story of much corporate ownership:

One study of the two hundred fifty largest American corporations found that all but seventeen of them have at least one chief executive sitting on the board of another corporation. Over two hundred fifty directors of the top five hundred American corporations hold seats on the boards of competing firms. Much of this interlocking stems from the fact that the fifty largest banks (which control 66 percent of all banking assets) hold seats on the boards of America's five hundred largest firms. As of the late 1970s, one large New York bank, Morgan Guaranty Trust, was the single largest stockholder in 122 of the largest American corporations. The Rockefeller-owned Chase Manhattan Bank is interlocked with the nation's hundred largest corporations. Finally, large banks and financial institutions own blocks of one another's stock. Citibank and Chase Manhattan are the largest owners of Morgan Guaranty Trust (Simon & Eitzen, 1993:16).

What all this means is that the two hundred or so largest corporations and some fifty financial institutions control about two-thirds of all business income and half of all bank deposits. These firms are interlocked by directorships controlled by less than one-half of 1 percent of the nation's population (Simon & Eitzen, 1993:16–17). This great concentration of corporate ownership and the immense political influence corporations exercise have enabled corporate America to escape effective regulation by government.

The nation's five hundred largest corporations account for 90 percent of all prime-time television advertising. These large firms also hire the nation's largest and most prestigious law firms, many of which employ former members of the president's cabinet. Finally, the defense contractors have hired over 4500 high-ranking retired military officers and three hundred fifty retired civilian Pentagon employees.

Defense contractors employ almost 16 percent of the civilian workforce, including nearly 20 percent of all U.S. corporate managers and administrators (Simon & Eitzen, 1993:167).

The Military Sector

The military component of the military-industrial complex consists of the major branches of the military services (army, navy, and air force), as well as the nation's intelligence community (the National Security Council, the Central Intelligence Agency, the Defense Intelligence Agency, and the intelligence arms of the various branches of the military). Involved as well are the Veterans Administration and organizations representing the nation's veterans (the Veterans of Foreign Wars, the American Legion). The secrecy of the intelligence apparatus and its web of affiliations with the military services have created something of a "secret government" (Moyers, 1988). Since 1945, the actions of this secret government have had immense consequences for the nation's foreign and defense policies.

The Political Sector

The **political sector** of the power elite includes defense contracting lobbies, members of Congress who sit on the appropriations committees of the U.S. Senate and House of Representatives, the Joint Chiefs of Staff, and the civilian administrators (the secretary of defense and the secretaries of the various armed services) who oversee the nation's military establishment. Two-thirds of all the nation's congressional districts either contain or border on military installations or defense plants (Simon & Eitzen, 1993:172).

The Research and Policy-Formulating Sector

The military-industrial complex also possesses a research and policy-formulating sector. The lion's share of Pentagon-funded research goes to twelve elite universities and to a series of think tanks (private research firms, such as the Rand Corporation and the Stanford Research Institute) that do research, much of it highly classified. Through private foundations the nation's largest corporations have also set up a series of policy-formulating associations that publish journals and issue white papers on various policy questions.

Many Americans wonder if there is still a military-industrial complex in the post–Cold War world. While the Pentagon's budget has been cut somewhat, weapons are still being produced in significant numbers and varieties. Domestic orders for weapons are declining, yet the United States' defense budget is still "larger than most national economies" (Evans, 1993:14). Moreover, 60 percent of all weapons purchased by foreign nations are produced by U.S. corporations.

Many of these sales are paid for by your tax dollars as part of foreign aid. In 1994 Israel alone received $1.8 billion in foreign aid to purchase military aircraft. Thus the export arm of the defense industry is thriving. In short, there is no evidence that the arms complex has disappeared or will do so any time soon. The 1994 defense budget, in 1994 dollars, is $33 billion more than it was in 1975, at the end of the Vietnam War (Evans, 1993:18).

The Power Elite

The power elite is dominated by a group of people that compose a significant segment of America's national upper class. One can spot members of the **upper class** by a few characteristic indicators:

1. Their names and addresses appear in the *Social Register,* a list of socially influential people published in major U.S. cities. About 138,000 Americans are listed in the various editions of the *Social Register.*

2. They have attended elite private preparatory schools and universities. Among the favored preparatory schools are St. Paul's in New Hampshire, Hotchkiss in Connecticut, Foxcroft in Virginia, and Chapin in New York (Gilbert & Kahl, 1993:211). (The elite universities are listed in Figure 2.1.)

3. They belong to exclusive social clubs and attend upper-class vacation retreats (Bohemian Grove, Knickerbocker Club, Pacific Union).

4. They sit on the boards of directors of the nation's largest corporations (Domhoff, 1967: 87–96).

5. Their annual income is typically in the millions of dollars and their wealth typically totals tens of millions of dollars. These 0.5 percent of Americans possess 25 to 30 percent of all privately held wealth (Domhoff, 1993:174), an increase of 6.7 percent between 1979 and 1989 (Dowd, 1993:223). The ramifications of this increasing inequality are explored in Chapter 4.

- A study of the president's cabinet from 1897 to 1973 found that the percentage of cabinet members coming from big business increased from 60 percent during William McKinley's administration to 95.5 percent during Richard Nixon's administration (Freitag, 1975).

- Another study found that 63 percent of the secretaries of state, 62 percent of the secretaries of defense, and 63 percent of the secretaries of the treasury have been members of the national upper class (Kerbo, 1993:227). Among the members of the power elite we find:

- John Foster Dulles, secretary of state from 1953 to 1960. Before his appointment he was senior partner in a prestigious law firm, Sullivan & Cromwell, and sat on the boards of numerous corporations: Bank of New York, American Bank Note Company, United Railroad, International Nickel of Canada, American Cotton Oil Company, and European Textile Corporation. Dulles was also a trustee of leading civic organizations: the New York Public Library, the

Figure 2.1

The Capitalist Elite—
Links among the Ruling Elite

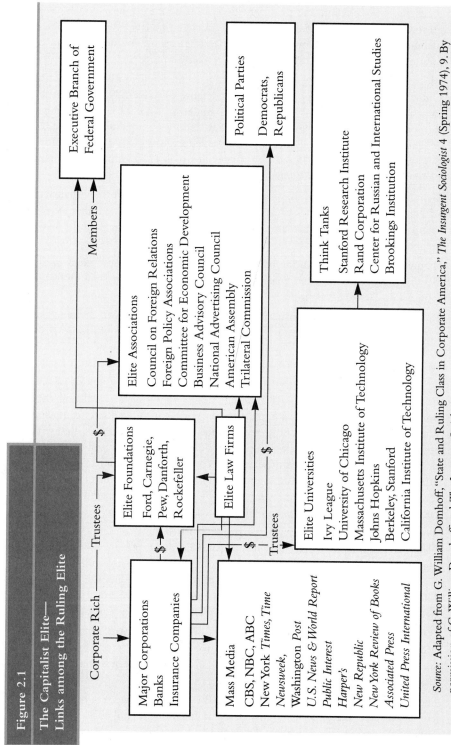

Corporate Rich —— Trustees ——

Executive Branch of Federal Government

Members

Elite Associations

Council on Foreign Relations
Foreign Policy Associations
Committee for Economic Development
Business Advisory Council
National Advertising Council
American Assembly
Trilateral Commission

Political Parties

Democrats,
Republicans

Think Tanks

Stanford Research Institute
Rand Corporation
Center for Russian and International Studies
Brookings Institution

Elite Foundations

Ford, Carnegie,
Pew, Danforth,
Rockefeller

Elite Law Firms

Elite Universities

Ivy League
University of Chicago
Massachusetts Institute of Technology
Johns Hopkins
Berkeley, Stanford
California Institute of Technology

Trustees

Major Corporations
Banks
Insurance Companies

Mass Media

CBS, NBC, ABC
New York Times, Time
Newsweek,
Washington Post
U.S. News & World Report
Public Interest
Harper's
New Republic
New York Review of Books
Associated Press
United Press International

Source: Adapted from G. William Domhoff, "State and Ruling Class in Corporate America," *The Insurgent Sociologist* 4 (Spring 1974), 9. By permission of G. William Domhoff and *The Insurgent Sociologist.*

Rockefeller Foundation, and the Carnegie Endowment for International Peace. His brother, Allen, was director of Central Intelligence (1953–1961) and was a member of the Warren Commission, the panel set up by President Lyndon B. Johnson to investigate the assassination of President Kennedy.

- Alexander Haig, secretary of state in 1981–1982, is currently president of United Technologies Corporation, a major defense contractor. Haig is a former four-star general and former supreme commander of NATO forces in Europe; former assistant to President Nixon; former deputy commander of the U.S. Military Academy at West Point; and former deputy secretary of defense. He is the man most responsible for the terms set down in the pardon of President Nixon after the Watergate scandal.

- George Bush's secretary of the treasury, Nicholas Brady, was a former chairman of Dillon Read, a major Wall Street investment firm, and a member of the boards of directors of Purolator, NCR, Georgia International, and Media General.

- Jimmy Carter's secretary of the treasury, Michael Blumenthal, is president of the Bendix Corporation, former vice president of Crown Cork, and trustee of the Council on Foreign Relations.

- Bill Clinton promised the American people a cabinet that would "look like America," with women and minorities represented; but he did not promise us a cabinet that would look like America in social class makeup. President Clinton has appointed more millionaires to cabinet posts than Reagan and Bush (Savio, 1993: 24–26). Among them:

- Former Treasury Secretary Lloyd Bentsen was champion of tax breaks for corporations during his Senate career. Of the $2.5 million in Bentsen's campaign fund for his last Senate bid, 89 percent came from corporate PACs. Bentsen's personal worth exceeds $10 million, and his holdings include a number of businesses in Texas. Former deputy secretary, Roger Altman, comes from a Wall Street investment firm, the Blackstone Group, which has been involved in the four largest acquisitions of American firms by Japanese firms, including Sony's takeover of Columbia Pictures and CBS Records.

- The late Commerce Secretary Ron Brown, former head of the Democratic National Committee, represented many major corporations as a partner in an elite law firm, Patton, Boggs, & Blow, including Japan Air Lines and American Express, and his firm represents such clients as Mutual Life Insurance, New York Life, and the former dictator of Haiti, "Baby Doc" Duvalier.

- U.S. Trade Representative Mickey Kantor is a law partner in Manatt, Phelps, Phillips, & Kantor, which has represented Occidental Petroleum, ARCO, Martin Marietta, and Philip Morris. Kantor represented tobacco industry groups in their efforts to prevent passage of a smoke-free restaurant bill in Beverly Hills, California.

- Secretary of State Warren Christopher is a lawyer from O'Melveny & Meyers. He represented Exxon in the lawsuits stemming from its pollution of Prince William Sound, Alaska. He also represented E. F. Hutton when it was revealed that Hutton had regularly taken advantage of the lag between the time checks were written and the time they actually cleared, thus giving themselves millions in interest-free loans. Christopher has also served on the board of Southern California Edison, Lockheed, United Airlines, Banker's Trust (New York), Occidental Petroleum, and Japan's Fuji Bank and Mitsubishi Corporation.

It makes little difference, then, whether the White House is occupied by a Republican or a Democrat. Most of the people who run the government have corporate backgrounds and share remarkably similar educational and cultural experiences and affiliations. Numerous additional studies support the finding that the upper class not only is overrepresented in governmental circles but runs corporate America as well.

- Fifty-four percent of members of boards of directors of the twenty largest American corporations are from the upper class.

- Sixty-two percent of members of the boards of directors of the nation's fifteen largest banks are from the upper class.

- Forty-four percent of members of boards of directors of the nation's fifteen largest insurance companies are from the upper class.

- Fifty-three percent of members of boards of directors of the nation's fifteen largest transportation companies are from the upper class. (Kerbo, 1993:225)

The power elite makes certain its wishes are given every consideration in Washington and in other governmental circles by exerting an influence on the policy-making process (Domhoff, 1974; Kerbo, 1993; Greenberg, 1985; Greider, 1992). The policy-making process is composed of a series of interrelated practices engaged in on an ongoing basis by corporate, political, and military elites. The corporate rich exert their political influence by: donating substantial sums of money to political candidates; occasionally running for office; holding posts in the executive branch of the federal government; establishing private foundations and elite associations and sponsoring university research. The policy position statements that issue from these activities are readily given to politicians the corporate elites wish to influence. Finally, they exert their influence by spending billions of dollars in "institutional" advertising and "charitable" ventures in an effort to create a favorable public image and socialize the public in the ideology of free enterprise.

Major corporations are not the only institutional players in the policy-making process.

1. Twenty-five elite universities and colleges annually garner half of all educational endowment funds, and some 656 corporate elites sit on their boards of trustees. A mere fifty foundations (out of over 1200) control 40 percent of all foundation assets. Foundations account for a large proportion of funds devoted to university and foundation research. Foundation executives usually have experience in either corporate America or the federal government.

2. Elite civic associations (such as the Council on Foreign Relations) bring together national (and sometimes international) elites from the corporate, educational, legal, and governmental worlds. The political scientist Thomas Dye (1990) views these associations as coordinators of national policy. These organizations typically issue white papers on domestic and international policy matters. Membership in them is often a prerequisite for a high-ranking cabinet

post. Twenty of the last twenty-one secretaries of state, for example, have been members of the Council on Foreign Relations (Simon & Eitzen, 1993:20–23).

3. The mass media are central to the policy-making process because they set limits on the breadth of ideological views that will enter the policy-making debate in the United States. The media also choose which stories to emphasize and which to ignore. The major media almost completely ignored the savings and loan scandal, for example, until the industry's losses became so overwhelming that Congress had to vote billions of dollars to bail it out. Finally, the media are merely a group of corporations that are owned by other corporations and financial institutions. Controlling shares in the three major television networks are owned by five large New York banks (Citibank, Chase, Morgan Guaranty, Bank of New York, and Banker's Trust). The five hundred largest American corporations account for 90 percent of all prime-time television network advertising revenues.

4. Twenty-eight large law firms do much of the legal work for corporations and the upper class. Ninety percent of all the legal work in the United States is done for a mere 10 percent of the population. These law firms are also heavily involved in the lobbying process in Washington, and many of their partners are former members of the president's cabinet, as we have seen.

5. The research institutes known as think tanks typically receive money from corporate and governmental sources. The Rand Corporation and the Stanford Research Institute (owned by Stanford University until 1970) are annually awarded about 5 percent of the Pentagon's research and development budget (Simon & Eitzen, 1993:23). The process by which the power elite makes public policy is described in Figure 2.1.

Numerous studies have confirmed the power of elite networks in America and other modern democracies (Olsen & Marger, 1993:153–249; Greenberg, 1985; Domhoff, 1990). No one has described the current policy-making process better than the journalist William Greider (1992), who notes a fundamental contradiction in American political and economic life: The public has great contempt for its politicians and politicians are contemptuous of the public. The two are locked in a dance of mutual distrust, cynicism, and alienation. Politicians know full well that "the people" are not their constituents. The elites who finance elections are their real constituents. Democracy has become a ritual dance in which politicians profess to care about the common people and their needs (jobs, health care, homelessness), but behind the scenes the interests of organized money groups call the tune.

What has emerged in Washington is a shadow government made up of public relations firms, think tanks, and polling organizations, all funded by corporate interests. The results are staggering:

- Fifty-one U.S. senators and 146 members of the House of Representatives are either founders or officers of tax-exempt organizations that produce either research statistics or corporate propaganda for lobbying purposes (Greider, 1992:51).

- In 1960 fewer than four hundred lobbyists were registered with the U.S. Congress. By 1992, 40,000 were so registered (Perot, 1993:120). Those 40,000 people represent mostly American and foreign corporations. Much of this growth came in the 1970s and 1980s, when the capitalist class decided it was underrepresented in the nation's capital. Eighty percent of the *Fortune* 500 corporations established "public affairs offices" (lobbies) in Washington.

- In the 1970s, new think tanks were established and richly endowed by corporate money. The right-wing Heritage Foundation was started with a $250,000 donation from the Colorado beer tycoon Joseph Coors (Gilbert & Kahl, 1993:224–25). The patrons of the American Enterprise Institute include AT&T ($125,000), Chase Manhattan Bank ($125,000), Exxon ($130,000), General Electric ($65,000), General Motors ($100,000), and Procter & Gamble ($165,000). The "institute" quickly became a "primary source of Washington opinion," shaping the policy positions of Washington politicians and the mass media (Greider, 1992:48).

Elite rule has not only made the United States less democratic by converting American democracy into what Greider terms "a busy commerce in deal making" (1992:112); it has also converted much of American society into what C. Wright Mills described as "a network of rackets" (1960:17).

The Capitalist World System

The world's societies are interdependent economically, politically, culturally, and environmentally. Consequently, conflict anywhere on the globe affects conditions in other nations. A fundamentalist religious sect in Egypt can now easily bomb the World Trade Center in New York. Starving Somalis can appear on U.S. network news programs and soon spur the mobilization of U.S. troops.

The contemporary capitalist world system—Bush's "new world order"—began in 1989 with the fall of the Berlin Wall and the disintegration of the Communist bloc. The Soviet Union itself fragmented into a fluid alliance of regions that barely hang together as a "commonwealth of independent states." The American news media remain fixated on the old Soviet Union in an effort to convince the American public that the Cold War was worth the sacrifices of Vietnam and $4 trillion in military spending. In consequence, inordinate attention has been paid to the various crises in the nations of the former USSR since 1989: the 1992 military coup that toppled the government of General Secretary Mikhail Gorbachev; the 1993 revolt against Russian president Boris Yeltsin that culminated in an assault by Russian troops on the parliament building (the "White House") and purged Yeltsin's critics four months before new elections were to be held; and the civil wars raging in Georgia, Azerbaijan, and other remnants of the old Soviet empire.

The real power blocs of the new world order, however, gain their strength more from economic prowess than from military might. These blocs are composed of three groups of nations, popularly known as the First, Second, and Third Worlds (Perdue, 1993; Russell, 1992:52).

This is the Tokyo office of the IBM corporation. Such multinational corporations no longer know any national boundaries, and their power is thought to surpass those of governments.

The First World

The First World includes the advanced capitalist democracies of North America, Western Europe, and Japan. Economically, politically, and culturally the world system is dominated by the First World. While First World nations often come in conflict (witness Japan's "invasion" of the American automobile market), they also cooperate. There is now essentially one international capitalist economy, which is the basis on which all national economies function. Countries in the Second and Third Worlds have progressively lost sovereignty over their own economies. The more powerful the capitalist world system grows, the more that system and the international corporations that dominate it, rather than any national economy, become the focus of economic and class conflicts.

Inequalities of wealth and power within and between the three groups of nations cause numerous social problems. Within the First World are actually three formidable economic alliances in Europe, Asia, and North America.

The European Communities (EC)

In 1967 the European Common Market was created by the merger of three organizations: the European Coal and Steel Community, the European Atomic Energy Commission (Euratom), and the European Economic Community. Today the European Communities consist of Belgium, Denmark, France, Germany, Greece, Ireland, Italy, Luxembourg, the Netherlands, Portugal, Spain, and the United Kingdom. The European

Act of 1987 committed these nations to form a single European market by the end of 1992, eliminating all barriers to trade and the free movement of people, and investment capital. The EC is composed of 340 million potential consumers. The nations that have become independent with the collapse of the Soviet empire (Hungary, Romania, Poland, and so on) have also expressed an interest in joining the EC.

The Asian Pacific Bloc

A second bloc of advanced capitalist powers is found among the rapidly developing nations of the Pacific. Popularly known as "the flying geese," they are Japan, South Korea, Singapore, Thailand, Taiwan, and Malaysia. These nations have achieved huge trade surpluses since 1980. Each year from 1984 to 1993 the United States imported goods worth over $100 billion more than those it exported, and most of these imports come from Japan. The Asian "geese" nations all trade with one another and have developed extensive joint ventures. They are also economically active with the People's Republic of China, the nation with the fastest growing economy in the world.

The Americas

A free trade agreement signed by the United States and Canada in 1988 created a potential $6 trillion consumer and manufacturing zone. Mexico joined the North American Free Trade Agreement (NAFTA) in 1993. The potential of this alliance rivals that of the EC and the Asian Pacific nations.

Together these two dozen nations generate almost four-fifths of all of the economic activity on earth (Barnet & Cavanagh, 1994:284).

The Second World

The Second World of nations consists of the formerly communist nations of Eastern Europe and the old Soviet Union. Russia is now in turmoil. The other Eastern European nations are struggling to make the transition to a market economy with varying degrees of success, but there is every chance that at least some of them will be integrated into the EC in future decades.

Economically, most of the former communist nations of Eastern Europe are having a difficult time in the transition to capitalism. With the exception of former East Germany, now merged with West Germany, there is no appreciable foreign investment flowing into these nations. For the first two years following the collapse of communism, Hungary attracted nearly half of all foreign investment in Eastern Europe, including: a General Electric lightbulb plant, a Schwinn bicycle factory, and a Levi blue jeans factory.

Foreign investment has come to Hungary because it had gone further toward establishing a "free market" than any other Eastern Bloc nation during the communist era, and now labor costs are very low and labor strikes are almost nonexistent (Barnet & Cavanagh, 1994: 285).

The Third World

The Third World is composed of the poorest nations of Asia, Africa, and Latin America. The Third World is desperately poor, and much of it is starving. About 14,000 people die of starvation each day and 1.5 billion people lack medical care (Babbie, 1993:2). The average per capita income in 1991 ranged from less than $350 a year in Ethiopia and Kenya to under $3000 a year in Mexico, Turkey, and Chile (the average U.S. per capita income in 1991 was nearly $22,000) (*World Almanac,* 1993:742, 752, 778, 811).

What this means is that life in some Third World nations is much better than others. China, Indonesia, Thailand and Malaysia, for example, have already achieved limited degrees of industrialization, and massive famines are a thing of the past in China. Eight additional nations, still poor in many ways, have become global manufacturers of many consumer products. These nations include Brazil, Mexico, Argentina, and India. Technologically, all of these nations remain dependent on the technology of First World corporations of America, Europe, and Japan.

Another dozen nations, who are members of the Organization of Petroleum Exporting Countries (OPEC), play a special role in the global economy. Oil-rich desert kingdoms in the Middle East, these nations are able to import entire factories and any products needed by their affluent populations. What they lack are the engineering and scientific skills to develop their own industrial bases. What manual labor is required is imported from poor nations, and First World corporations continue to provide technological expertise in these rich, but nonindustrial monarchies (Barnet & Cavanagh, 1994:286).

In some forty other Third World nations, however, about 3 percent of the population own 60 to 90 percent of all private wealth, and military dictatorships attempt to keep the poor masses from making revolutions that might bring a better life. These dictatorships are kept in power in part with military and other aid from the United States and other advanced capitalist nations. Collectively, Third World nations owe First World governments and banks over $1.3 trillion (Dowd, 1993:391). This debt makes them vulnerable to First World demands regarding wage levels, trade practices, and a host of other policies. Meanwhile, multinational corporations make substantial returns on investments in Third World nations, but do not reinvest their profits in these poor lands. Instead, profits tend to be paid to stockholders or invested in other overseas ventures in First and Second World nations.

As a result, the Third World is plagued by numerous social problems, many with global consequences: overpopulation, illegal emigration to First World nations, pollution, wars, violations of human rights, famines. Moreover, American elites have at times supported Third World governments that have engaged in serious violations of human rights. Human rights are defined in two treaties of which the United States is a signatory, the United Nations Declaration of Human Rights of the 1940s and the Helsinki Agreement of 1975. Among these rights are freedom from arrest without probable cause, freedom from kidnapping and torture, and freedom of speech and of the press. In yet another contradiction of American life, the United States has played an important role in supporting regimes that violate human rights, all in the name of anticommunism.

Guatemala

In 1954 the CIA directed a coup that toppled the government of Jacobo Arbenz in Guatemala. After it was learned that Arbenz planned to implement a land reform program by requiring the United Fruit Company to sell land not under cultivation at the low valuation it had claimed for tax purposes, the Eisenhower administration recklessly branded Arbenz a communist, and replaced him with a U.S. Army–trained officer, Carlos Castillo

Armas. Castillo Armas issued a decree giving himself all executive and legislative functions, halted the land reform program, canceled the registration of more than five hundred labor unions, and required that all unions be certified free of communist influence by a government committee. He was assassinated in 1957, but his policies lived on. Between 1963 and 1993 his U.S.-backed successors tortured and killed 150,000 of their own citizens and kidnapped 50,000 more. Guatemala's human rights record was so grotesque that in 1990 the Bush administration was forced to suspend aid under congressional pressure (Johnson et al., 1993:13; Simon & Eitzen, 1993: 201).

The Bush administration claimed in 1991 that the Guatemalan human rights record was improving, but the evidence contradicted this assertion. Human rights groups documented 730 assassinations and one hundred disappearances (an average of three a day) between January and September 1991. A Guatemalan Indian woman, Rigoberta Menched, was awarded the Nobel Peace Prize in 1992 for her efforts to get the government to stop relocating and killing her people (the government forcibly relocated a million Indians between 1982 and 1991). The Reagan and Bush administrations provided Guatemala with over $77 million in aid during this period.

Chile

In 1973 the CIA supported a coup that ousted the democratically elected government of the Marxist Salvador Allende. Allende was murdered in the overthrow and replaced by a brutal dictator, General Augusto Pinochet. Two years later, one of every 125 Chilean citizens had been arrested and detained for more than a day. People were routinely held for twenty days or more without notification of their families. A wide range of torture methods were reported: rape, shocks applied through electrodes on knees and genitals, sleep deprivation, mock execution, submersion in water, live rats shoved into victims' mouths. Pinochet built himself a 15,000-square-foot house with an infrared security system at a cost of between $10 and $13 million, and secured it with a private force of eighty guards. He finally left office in 1989 after losing a plebiscite (Neier & Brown, 1987; Simon & Eitzen, 1993:202–203).

El Salvador

Between 1978 and 1993 more than 40,000 people were killed in El Salvador by government-supported right-wing death squads, and 800,000 people (20 percent of the population) became refugees. Between 1979 and 1984 the Reagan administration gave El Salvador six times more aid than it had received in the previous thirty years. In 1980 the government's death squads raped and murdered four American nuns, and Amnesty International declared the death squads' activities a gross abuse of human rights. Over the years such multinational corporations as Chevron, Kimberly-Clark, and Texaco have invested over $100 million in El Salvador (Kwitney, 1984:10–11; Caldicott, 1984:160). Human rights abuses in El Salvador continue in the 1990s. A United Nations observer mission reported 105 assassinations, fifteen kidnappings, and 281 illegal captures by security forces in 1992. In January 1993 the widow and children of a former head of the Salvadoran Human Rights Commission were fired on by government troops. The children had personally witnessed their father's murder by the government in 1987 (Johnson et al., 1993: 54–55).

Foreign Aid

The U.S. government still supplies some of the world's most oppressive regimes with foreign aid and weapons. Much of this aid is obtained with the help of highly paid Washington lobbyists.

In 1991, Guatemala received $91 million in American aid, even though arms sales to that nation had been ordered suspended because of human rights abuses. The Guatemalan government paid $680,000 to public relations firms (one of which was the late Commerce Secretary Brown's law firm).

Turkey receives about $800 million annually in U.S. aid. It spends $3.8 million on lobbying efforts in Washington. Political killings in Turkey increased 600 percent between 1991 and 1992, many of them committed by government security forces (Gozan, 1993:6–7).

Bureaucracy and the Higher Immorality

U.S. support for regimes that violate human rights is an indication of a much more fundamental problem both inside and outside the United States. The power elite have become the most dominant force in American life and in the lives of other advanced capitalist nations. As we have seen, their influence holds Third World nations in a tight grip. These institutions are shapers of social character. Their ethical and moral priorities have become the central values of American culture. Indeed, a central contradiction among the members of the power elite is that they frequently violate the very laws they are sworn to uphold. This set of deviant practices has been termed the *higher immorality* (Mills, 1956:343–61; Simon & Eitzen, 1993:49–90). These violations take place in part because of the way corporate, political, and military intelligence institutions are structured: They are bureaucracies. Bureaucratic organizations are structured in ways that regularize crime and deviance.

Forms of the Higher Immorality

Bureaucratic organizations are goal-oriented. They exist to make money or to expand their power. This means that bureaucracies are amoral entities: They recognize no moral constraints, only goals, and there is often nothing moral about their goals. From time to time most organizations want to achieve goals they cannot pursue within the limits imposed by existing rules, laws, or ethical codes. When this happens, organizations secretly engage in illegal or unethical behaviors. Power in bureaucracies is concentrated at the top. The people who head the organizations are shielded from their workers and from the public by layers of secretaries, public relations departments, and lawyers. It is this hierarchical structure that makes secrecy a central characteristic of bureaucratic life. This combination of goal orientation and secrecy makes scandal a frequent occurrence.

- *Item:* In the 1970s, Ford rushed its Pinto automobile into production. This car contained an unprotected gas tank that would explode if the car was hit from the rear at speeds as low as five miles per hour. Ford executives wrote a secret memo (subsequently leaked to the press) comparing the estimated amount of money the company would have to pay out in wrongful death claims with the estimated amount it would have to pay to fix the gas tanks in all the vehicles. The memo clearly demonstrated that it would be more profitable to let people die or be seriously injured than to insert an $11.80 rubber bladder inside the gas tank. The result: Ford let the unsafe Pinto roll off the assembly line and hundreds of people were either killed or maimed.

- *Item:* After the Nicaraguan Contras mined the harbor in Managua in 1982, the U.S. Congress voted to cut off all military aid to them. The Reagan administration, determined to continue sending aid to the Contras, set up a secret operation that sold arms to Iran and funneled part of the profits to the Contras. As a result of the Iran-Contra scandal, several members of the Reagan administration resigned from office or were sent to prison.

These are not the only instances of the higher immorality. Socially patterned deviant and criminal acts among the power elite take many forms.

Violations of Antitrust, Advertising, and Pollution Laws

Corporate crime in the form of violation of antitrust, advertising, and pollution laws costs American consumers an estimated $200 billion a year, forty times more than estimated losses from street crime (Donahue, 1992:16). Studies reveal that only about 2 percent of corporate crime cases result in imprisonment. Moreover, a study conducted in the 1970s (Clinard, 1979) revealed that:

- Sixty percent of the 582 largest American corporations committed at least one crime in a twenty-four-month period (a rate confirmed by subsequent studies described below).

- Nearly half of the crimes were committed in just three industries: autos, petroleum, and drugs. These industries comprise some of the largest and most politically active firms in the nation.

- Of those firms charged with at least one crime, the average number of crimes charged was 4.2 per firm—a rate approaching habitual criminality.

Amitai Etzioni (1990:3) found that between 1975 and 1984, 62 percent of the *Fortune* 500 companies were involved in one or more incidents of corrupt behavior (bribery, price-fixing, tax fraud, or violations of environmental regulations). A study of the twenty-five largest *Fortune* 500 corporations found that all were either found guilty of criminal behavior or fined for civil violations between 1977 and 1990 (Donahue, 1992:17–18).

Corruption, Violations of Civil Liberties, and Unethical Campaign Practices: The Watergate Era

The Watergate scandal of 1972–74 is the classic example of political corruption. Watergate was actually an endless series of miniscandals.

Burglars, bankrolled by the Committee to Reelect the President, broke into the headquarters of the Democratic National Committee in the Watergate complex in Washington, DC, and planted eavesdropping devices for reasons still unknown. The burglars, all former CIA agents, some associated with the 1961 Bay of Pigs fiasco, were promised executive clemency and hush money by the White House.

Another burglary was committed at the office of Daniel Ellsberg's psychiatrist. Ellsberg, who had leaked the Pentagon Papers to the New York *Times*, was standing trial at the time. While the trial was in progress, the judge in the case was approached with an offer of the directorship of the FBI. The judge declared a mistrial.

President Nixon had placed microphones in his own office and in the offices of his top aides to record every conversation.

Nixon's vice-president, Spiro Agnew, confessed to accepting kickbacks on government contracts from Maryland contractors, and resigned from office as part of a plea bargain.

A White House secret intelligence unit, called "the plumbers" because they were intended to stop leaks to the press, engaged in a host of dirty tricks aimed at discrediting potential Democratic presidential candidates. They wrote and distributed letters that allegedly came from Senator Edmund Muskie's campaign charging that Senator Henry Jackson was a homosexual. They hired prostitutes and planted them at campaign rallies to embarrass opposition candidates.

Nixon's administration generated an "enemy list" of its critics inside and outside government, and illegally misused the Internal Revenue Service by requesting tax audits of those critics. The FBI and CIA were manipulated into cutting short the investigation into Watergate, and the head of the FBI even destroyed vital evidence in the case by burning files along with Christmas wrappings.

Nixon lied repeatedly to Congress concerning both his involvement in the case and his possession of evidence that would reveal his involvement. Nixon offered his two top aides, John Ehrlichman and H. R. Haldeman, money in exchange for their silence. He had his personal attorney solicit illegal campaign contributions in exchange for promises of ambassadorships. Money from these contributions was illegally laundered to conceal the donors' identities.

Attorney General John Mitchell helped plan the bugging of the Democratic National Committee. Mitchell and numerous other Nixon administration officials were convicted of perjury and other crimes and sent to prison.

Unfair Compensation, Tax Advantages, and Subsidies: The Savings and Loan Debacle

American corporate executives make three hundred times more on average than do their employees, and some of the special benefits they receive have caused major scandals. This is especially the case with regard to the $500 billion savings and loan scandal of the 1980s.

Several S&Ls paid their executives fabulous sums while they were losing considerable amounts of money. During the period when the Lincoln S&L was losing $300 million, its owner, Charles Keating, paid himself and his staff (which included several members of his family) some $4 million in salaries.

Under the charter of the Resolution Trust Corporation, formed by Congress to bail out ailing S&Ls, all S&L assets are guaranteed profitable for ten years by direct federal subsidy. Among the big winners:

- Arizona businessman James Fall received $1.5 billion in government subsidies to buy fifteen failed S&Ls while putting up only $1000 of his own money.

- Trammel Crow, a Texas billionaire, and his partners invested $128 million in 1989 and received $3.2 billion in thrift assets and $1.49 billion in federal aid. Crow donated $128,000 to the 1988 Bush campaign.

- Robert Bass invested $550 million in American Savings and Loan and in return received ownership of a $30 billion S&L, along with $2.5 billion in cash for a profit of $31.95 billion. Bass promptly created a separate S&L branch for the institution's bad loans, and used $1.5 billion in S&L deposits to finance corporate mergers (San Diego *Times Union*, September 1, 1991: A–2).

The Creation of Phony Crises and the Manipulation of Public Opinion

The power elite are adept at creating "crises" and manipulating public opinion for financial and political advantage.

- In the 1970s, American oil companies used the excuse of an embargo by the Organization of Petroleum Exporting Countries (OPEC) to quadruple the price of gasoline, even though there was no evidence of a shortage of gasoline in the United States.

- After a televised speech on Vietnam, President Nixon claimed his views were shared by an overwhelming majority of Americans and substantiated his claim by holding up some of the 10,000 telegrams he said he had received in support. Actually, Nixon had his staff send the messages in order to deceive the public.

- In the late 1980s President Bush portrayed Iraq's Saddam Hussein as an evil dictator who was creating a huge military machine that threatened the peace of the Middle East and the world. In truth, the United States had been selling weapons to Iraq for years, in violation of its own laws. Just before Hussein marched into Kuwait, the U.S. ambassador to Iraq told Hussein that the United States would not object if he invaded Kuwait.

The Hiring of Prostitutes to Close Business and Political Deals

Corporations and politicians are highly appreciative of the efforts of prostitutes to make their clients happy. Karen Wilkening of San Diego, the notorious Rolodex madam, supplied Don Dixon, head of Vernon S&L, with prostitutes for the S&L's "staff meetings" in

San Diego County. The S&L paid the bill. In April 1991 Dixon was sentenced to three consecutive five-year prison terms. He was also fined $611,000 for using depositors' money to hire Ms. Wilkening's call girls and to build the house where he and his staff partied with them (Simon & Eitzen, 1993: chap. 2).

Cooperation with Elements of Organized Crime

The crime syndicates are often happy to cooperate with corporations and governments. It has frequently been claimed that the CIA laundered drug money through Mafia-linked S&Ls in order to buy arms for the Contras. Much of the information regarding CIA/Mafia activity in the S&L crisis was uncorked by the Houston *Post* reporter Pete Brewton. Brewton almost single-handedly discovered that the failure of at least twenty-two S&Ls was linked to a small group of operatives, men such as Herman Bebe, a former casino owner with ties to the New Orleans crime boss Vincent Marcello, and Mario Renda, a financier with ties to Bebe.

Bebe had ties to Neil Bush, son of the president and board member of Silverado Savings of Denver. Silverado lent money to Bebe and to Howard Corson, Houston developer and CIA operative. Some of the funds lent to Corson may have been used to pay for the CIA's covert operations in Nicaragua.

Renda and the CIA were involved in the 1984 failure of the Indian Springs State Bank of Kansas City, Kansas. Indian Springs hired Anthony Russo, attorney for the Civella Mafia family of Kansas City. Russo was also a consultant to Global International Airways, whose owner, Farhad Azima, was loaned $600,000 by Indian Springs, in violation of a $349,000 borrower limit. Global flew missions under contract to the CIA. Indian Springs also lent $400,000 to Morris Shenker, owner of the Dunes casino in Las Vegas, former attorney to Teamster president Jimmy Hoffa, and associate of the Civella family. At the time loans were being made to the Civellas, the family was under indictment for skimming $280,000 from Las Vegas' Tropicana casino.

Renda also brokered deposits to S&Ls that agreed to lend them to phony companies. In return, Renda and his business associates, men with ties to New York's Lucchese family, received "finders' fees" of from 2 to 6 percent of the loans. Most of the borrowers with Mafia ties defaulted on the loans, hastening the demise of the S&Ls.

In one trial involving a former Mafia stockbroker, it was revealed that the broker's partner was a CIA pilot. The pilot confessed that the CIA had laundered drug money through unsuspecting S&Ls, and obtained S&L loans just before it sent money to the Contras in violation of the Boland Amendment (Simon & Eitzen, 1993: chap. 2).

The Evils of Modern Bureaucracy

In their efforts to amass profits from military and nonmilitary spending and to secure access to overseas markets, the corporate elite have created a permanent war economy that is always either fighting or preparing to engage in armed conflict. This structure is not a conspiracy. It evolved from the nation's triumph in World War II and has grown ever since. These elites have increasingly centralized wealth and power. Less than one ten-thousandth of 1 percent of the nation's population now controls corporate America and the executive branch of the federal government (Dye, 1990:30ff.).

The elites have become so powerful that they now undemocratically make the major decisions regarding war and peace, inflation and unemployment. By employing what Mills termed "enveloping techniques of political domination" (1959:13)—ideological persuasion, propaganda, advertising, and a host of media distractions—they keep the masses of people from resisting either the maldistribution of resources or their undemocratic government. When these noncoercive forms of social control fail, a host of control institutions (jails, prisons, mental hospitals) await those who threaten the status quo. If repressive institutions are unable to handle disruption of the system, armed force by the police (or the military if necessary) remains a last resort (Hellinger & Judd, 1991). Thus, in Los Angeles in 1992, the National Guard was brought in to quell the rioting that followed the acquittal of police officers in the first Rodney King police brutality trial.

Inside these huge corporate, political, and military organizations people without much power are easily manipulated and mobilized to realize the goals of the organization. Workers in large organizations tend to feel powerless. One of the first lessons corporate and governmental bureaucracies teach workers is that they are replaceable (Coleman, 1986).

I experienced powerlessness most dramatically during a tour of duty in the U.S. Air Force. Upon reaching my first post, I was shown to my office. On the desk was the base phone book. The names in it were not of people but of positions within the various squadrons: squadron commander, administrative officer, first sergeant, and so on. According to the phone book, people did not exist, only positions and offices. The feeling of powerlessness engendered by the very structure of bureaucracy also represents a social problem that manifests itself in various forms of work alienation and mental illness.

No bureaucracy openly admits that it treats people with indifference or cruelty. All bureaucracies constantly issue official pronouncements about morale, compassion, concern, and so on. As we shall see, these public relations efforts are a part of the distortion that characterizes mass societies.

The Symbiosis of Social Problems

The inequalities of wealth and power, and the higher immorality to which they give rise, cause many types of social problems. The macro social problems caused by corporations and centralized government and the micro social problems of the powerless are symbiotic; that is, they are interdependent. The powerless—the poor and the working classes, nonwhite minorities, women, gays, the elderly, and children of the lower classes—suffer the most from the inequalities inherent in our social system.

Physical Harm

The power elite can directly inflict harm on the powerless: For example, the war that began secretly with the CIA's training of the South Vietnamese police resulted in the deaths of 58,000 American men and women and cost nearly $160 billion to fight. Many people who served in Vietnam thought the war was immoral and did not want to serve, but were forced to do so (Thio, 1988:96). Money needed to alleviate poverty went instead to conduct the war.

More than 40,000 Vietnamese civilians were murdered in the CIA-sponsored Phoenix program, most of them without trial.

More than 5 million acres of South Vietnam were sprayed with defoliating chemicals. Agent Orange caused high incidences of cancer, birth defects, and other diseases in American service personnel. The government withheld information on the dangers of Agent Orange until 1993 (Simon & Eitzen, 1993:6–7).

Physical harm caused by the power elite is not confined to military activities. The National Commission on Product Safety estimates that dangerous products injure 20 million Americans each year in home accidents, resulting in 10,000 permanent disabilities and 30,000 deaths. One dangerous drug alone, Eli Lilly's Darvon, has been associated with 11,000 deaths and 79,000 emergency room visits (Simon & Eitzen, 1993:126).

Approximately 100,000 American workers die each year from diseases attributable to exposure to dangerous chemicals at work. An additional 3.3 million workers suffer work-related injuries that require medical treatment, and almost 400,000 workers suffer occupational diseases.

The American food supply contains more than 1500 chemical additives, only a few of which have been tested for their carcinogenic properties. One slice of white bread can contain up to 93 chemicals. Unfortunately, it takes twenty to thirty years to learn which additives can cause cancer and what level of ingestion is safe.

The largest industry in America is the food industry, in which fifty of 20,000 firms make 60 percent of all the profits. Much of the industry consists of fast-food restaurants, which currently serve about 50 percent of restaurant meals in the United States. Much fast food contains high levels of saturated fat, sodium, and sugar. These substances are associated with the most common causes of death in America: heart disease, cancer, and high blood pressure. After Americans became enamored of fast food in the 1950s, consumption of saturated fats in the United States went from 45.1 pounds per person per year in 1960 to 60.7 pounds in 1989.

Another serious form of physical harm is industrial pollution. This nation, with a mere 5 percent of the world's population, is responsible for 50 percent of the world's industrial pollutants. The results are increasingly serious:

In 1993 the Environmental Protection Agency (EPA) and the Harvard School of Public Health estimated that particle pollution from factories causes 50,000 to 60,000 deaths each year. Most vulnerable are children with respiratory diseases, asthmatics of all ages, and elderly people with such ailments as bronchitis. It is the poor and the working class that tend to live close to chemical factories, and they suffer the highest rates of pollution-caused cancer. Indoor pollution from cigarette smoke and radon gas causes 5000 or more cases of cancer annually (Hilts, 1993:A–1).

In response to a congressional inquiry in 1990, the EPA identified 149 industrial plants in thirty-three states where the surrounding air was known to be "quite dangerous" (Greider, 1992:124). At one facility in Port Neches, Texas, the lifetime risk of contracting cancer was one in ten. A risk of one in a million is unacceptable by EPA standards. Yet at forty-five other plants the risk of contracting cancer was one in less than one hundred, and at all the others the risk was greater than one in 10,000.

Financial Harm

Some harms caused by the power elite are less physical but no less far-reaching.

Price-fixing, a criminal act in which two or more firms conspire to rig prices, costs American consumers about $60 billion a year.

Price gouging is especially common in the prescription drug industry. For example, 100 tablets of Abbot's brand of the antibiotic erythromycin wholesales for $15.50, but the generic tablets wholesale for $6.20 (Simon & Eitzen, 1993:100–102).

Fraud, the crime of inducing people to part with valuables or money by lies, deception, and misrepresentation, is the most common nonviolent crime in the United States. It costs American consumers tens of billions of dollars every year. Repair fraud alone costs consumers approximately $20 billion a year (Simon & Eitzen, 1993:99).

Perhaps the largest fraud in American history is the savings and loan scandal. Investigators estimate that 60 percent of the $500 billion to $1 trillion lost in the scandal is due to fraud. Since late 1990 the FBI has been investigating some 7000 of these cases, one hundred of which were selected for priority prosecution. The scandal could cost each American taxpaying family about $5000 (Simon & Eitzen, 1993:53).

Moral Harm

Another contradictory aspect of mass society is that wrongdoing by the powerful may serve as a model of behavior for the powerless. Scandal in high places provides a rationalization for powerless people that neutralizes any guilt that may arise from the victimization of other people. This moral harm causes citizens at all levels of society to become distrustful of their political and corporate leaders. They don't care about me, they think, so why should I care about them? This attitude makes it more likely that people will cheat on their taxes, especially if they believe the government wastes their money or spends it only to benefit the wealthy and powerful. People who work for corporations are more likely to steal from them if they do not trust them. Moreover, the homicide rate generally increases after an execution has been publicized, thereby forming a link between the actions of political elites, who promote capital punishment, and those nonelites who commit capital crimes (Thio, 1988:96).

Immorality and Power

Many aspects of the higher immorality, especially subsidies, tax breaks for the wealthy, and excessive corporate salaries, have only worsened inequality in the United States, and a great degree of inequality makes many micro social problems into macro problems. During the 1980s, the poorest 40 percent of Americans saw a decline of $256 billion in their wealth. The wealth of African Americans declined from 24 to 19 percent of the wealth held by white Americans (Gozan, 1993:8). From 1973 to 1993, the number of young people living in poverty increased by 51 percent. Between 1983 and 1993, crime among youth increased 50 percent (Males, 1993:18).

Great inequalities of wealth and income also worsen social problems of relative deprivation. That is, people who are not so destitute that they are forced to steal for food or rent may steal to obtain consumer goods they cannot afford. In the 1980s, gold jewelry, hundred-dollar sneakers, and Mercedes cars were status symbols of the "lifestyle" of the rich and famous. The more the rich and powerful parade their possessions, the more their showy ways will be copied by the less powerful. This points to one of the unfortunate equations current in America: The more the powerful emphasize the American dream of material success, the more crime the powerless commit. In other words, by displaying wealth and material goods, especially through advertising and movies, the powerful can intensify the social problems suffered and played out by the powerless.

The behavior of the powerful not only influences that of the powerless but also is influenced by it. And to extend the circle, the social problems caused by the powerless also influence the social problems caused by the powerful. First, the problems of the powerless "help to deflect, weaken, or nullify the social control over the powerful, thus freeing the powerful to engage in their own deviant pursuits" (Thio, 1988:97). For example, street crime is defined as "the crime problem." The vast majority of the resources of the criminal justice system are devoted to apprehending, prosecuting, and incarcerating street criminals. The powerful believe that the "real" criminals are muggers, rapists, and burglars, not the corporate executives who fix prices or the politicians who lie to the public. To wit, the powerful judge the acts of the powerless as morally wrong and rationalize their own wrongdoing.

When the powerful are caught, their punishment pales in comparison to that of the powerless. Between 1987 and 1992, for example, 75 percent of the cases of criminal fraud referred by federal regulators to the Justice Department in connection with the savings and loan scandal were dropped. In those cases that were prosecuted, the average prison sentence was 2.4 years. The average prison sentence for bank robbery in the United States is 7.8 years (Pizzo & Muolo, 1993:56). The powerful thus have little incentive not to do wrong. The chance of getting away with a crime is good. If they are apprehended, the punishment is often a small fine or a brief stint in a federal minimum-security country club–like facility, with golf course and tennis courts.

Finally, most victims of street crimes are poor people. This risk is part of what sociologists term their "life chances"—their opportunities for the good things in life. Acts of victimization reflect the culture and social institutions in which they occur. The likely victims are not merely people who happen to be in the wrong place at the wrong time. They are, tragically, members of victimization-prone groups whose life chances are adversely affected by their social statuses—their lower class position, their minority racial makeup, and gender. (Over 90 percent of rape victims are women, but the rate is three times higher among minority women.) People at the bottom of the class structure in the United States (and nearly everywhere else) are "more frequently the victims (and perpetrators) of violent crime, less likely to be in good health, and more likely to feel lonely. Those at the top [of the class structure] are healthier, safer, and more likely to send their children to college" (Gilbert & Kahl, 1993:2).

Indeed, people at the bottom of the class system have an even greater risk of being victims of so-called "natural disasters that presumably threaten all alike." In 1912 the ocean liner *Titanic* sank on its first crossing of the Atlantic. Among the ship's female passengers (who were expected to be given priority in the few lifeboats available) only 3 percent of first-class passengers drowned, in comparison with 16 percent of the second-class and 45 percent of the third-class passengers. Sadly, these differential rates of victimization were no accident. The third-class passengers were ordered to stay below decks, some at gunpoint, and were kept away from the lifeboats (Lord, 1955:8).

All of the life-enhancing opportunities in a society may be viewed as lifeboats. When opportunities to enter society's lifeboats are perceived as unequal and in fact are unequal, social problems occur. Victimization by elites, street criminals, and organized crime syndicates reinforces inequality by keeping the poor poor (or making them poorer), thus diminishing their life chances.

Summary

Our lack of sociological imagination has created an age of confusion, characterized by forms of alienation that blind the public to the causes and solutions of social problems. This deficiency of knowledge also keeps individuals from seeing that the sources of many of their troubles, including feelings of inferiority and insecurity, are sociological rather than personal. People lack the ability to relate the policies of large corporations and governmental agencies to what takes place in their own communities and inside their own heads.

In this chapter we have explored the aspects of postmodern mass society that cause social problems and mystify their causes and solutions. Social problems are caused by conflicts over the distribution of wealth, political power, and the power to determine the nature of culture. Postmodern life is structured by impersonal institutions:

1. a world system composed of capitalist economies and competing nation-states;

2. mass societies in which wealth is concentrated in the hands of elites and power is exercised through bureaucratic organizations; and

3. impersonal local communities in which people feel no sense of belonging, of values, or of order.

The centralization of wealth and power in the hands of a fortunate few who own much of corporate America and have inordinate influence over government policy has given rise to a host of social problems. The most important of these problems is a set of institutionalized deviant and criminal practices that can be called the "higher immorality." The people most adversely affected by these acts tend to be the poorest members of their societies.

In a variety of ways the social problems created by the powerful and those caused by the powerless are interdependent and mutually reinforcing. The powerful can sometimes order or manipulate the powerless into victimization. The powerful's definition of morality tends to create an ethic that emphasizes the wrongdoing of the powerless and lessens the social control over acts of powerful individuals and organizations. The wrongdoing of the powerful creates a role model for the powerless whereby powerless people become cynical about elite behavior and desirous of the materialism of elite lifestyles. Crime and other deviant acts by the powerless become easy to rationalize. The wrongdoing of the powerful increases inequality by victimizing the powerless. Many deviant acts of the powerless also victimize other powerless people.

Suggested Readings

Douglas Dowd (1993) *Capitalist Development since 1776* (Armonk, NY: M. E. Sharpe). An excellent and well written historical analysis of the American political economy by a passionate radical historian.

William Greider (1992) *Who Will Tell the People?: The Betrayal of American Democracy* (New York: Simon & Schuster). The most readable and sensible analysis of the crisis of confidence of the American political system.

Steve F. Messner and Richard Rosenfeld (1994) *Crime and the American Dream.* (Belmont, CA: Wadsworth). A significant work that successfully links the values of the American dream to deviant behavior.

Exercises

Critical Thinking Exercise 2.1	The Higher Immorality

Look up the categories having to do with corporate crime in the latest complete New York *Times Index* or the *Wall Street Journal Index*. These categories include:

1. Antitrust violations.
2. Pollution law violations.
3. False advertising.
4. Fraud.
5. Sexual harassment.

Do you notice any patterns in respect to which industries have the most violations? Many violations take place in the petroleum, automobile, and drug industries. Do these firms serve as models of corporate behavior for others? Were any specific corporations involved in more than one violation?

Critical Thinking Exercise 2.2	Examining Contradictions: A Term Project

America's value system is loaded with contradictions. Polls indicate that a majority of Americans

- Favor a woman's right to an abortion, but do not want women to actually have abortions.

- Think democracy is the greatest political system in the world, but do not trust the politicians who run that system.

- Believe free enterprise capitalism is the best economic system, but distrust the large multinational corporations that dominate that system.

- Frown on criminal activity, but admire characters such as J. R. Ewing of TV's "Dallas," who can get away with breaking the rules.

There are numerous other contradictions in the values Americans espouse. Write a paper that explores Americans' contradictory beliefs concerning any of our major institutions:

the economy	the military
the polity	the family
the mass media	the educational system
the criminal justice system	religion

The Mass Media, Alienation, and Micro Social Problems

STEPS ALREADY TAKEN

☐ Conducting Counter-Drug Operations

☐ Reducing and Reconfiguring Inventories of Supplies

☐ Improved Joint Oversight of Materiel Requirements

☐ More and Better Joint Doctrine and Training

The All-American Lie

Among the most fascinating and least appreciated social problems in American life are lying and deception. A recent survey indicates that 91 percent of Americans tell lies regularly, and two-thirds of Americans see nothing "wrong in telling a lie" (Patterson & Kim, 1991:45, 49). Most important to the sociological imagination paradigm, lying is "*an integral part of American culture, a trait of the American (social) character*" (Patterson & Kim, 1991:7).

Lying and deception are social problems because they often result in a wide variety of physical, financial, or moral harms:

- It is now estimated that there may be as many as 500,000 Americans who possess fraudulent credentials and diplomas, including 10,000 questionable medical degrees. As many as one in three employed Americans may have been hired with credentials that had been altered in some way.

Box 3.1 • Social Character as a Sociological Concept

The concept of social character is central to both the sociological imagination paradigm and our study of social problems. This is because the notion of social character is crucial to the understanding of a society's assumptions about human nature. Objectively, there is no given "human nature." This means that there is no evidence to suggest that specific character traits, such as greed, aggression, or "sin," are inborn in humans. Instead, one can speak of various values, beliefs, goals, attitudes, and norms prescribed by various cultures for their members (role players). This is what Mills refers to when he asks in what ways men and women are "formed, liberated, and repressed, made sensitive and blunted" (1959:7).

Social character then consists of those character traits that are widely "shared among significant social groups and . . . [are] a product of the experience of those groups" (Riesman, 1950:3–4). Social character can be thought of as those parts of our personalities we have in common with most other members of our society. In diverse, multicultural nations, like the United States, there are also social characters specific to genders (also known as gender roles), regional groups (e.g., southerners), ethnic groups (e.g., Italians, Irish, Swedes, etc.), and other influential group memberships (e.g., Republicans and Democrats).

Within this view, two components of character are crucial. These include: (1) the structure of selfhood in question, and (2) the nature of the value system embraced by a given social character. It is within the realms of self and values that social character interrelates with social problems. The notion of selfhood is difficult to grasp because it is so taken for granted. If I asked you what is your "self," you would probably say, "Well, myself is me. It's who I am," and in the psychological sense this is true. Sociologically, however, selves are more complex. What you are telling me by noting that your self is you is that you possess what is termed an individualized sense of selfhood. That is, you are aware of your existence as both psychologically and physically separate from other people. Moreover, you probably think all people conceive of themselves in the same way, but they do not.

- An FBI undercover investigation, DIPSCAM (Diploma Scam) involved one agent who was able to obtain seventeen advanced degrees (by mail) for little or no work. The late Florida congressman, Claude Pepper, cooperating with the investigation, obtained a Ph.D. from Union University (Los Angeles) by paying $1,780 and mailing in four book reviews.

- A college professor, Paul A. Crafton, acquired thirty-four aliases, seventy credit cards (including four American Express Gold Cards) and five drivers' licenses. He was arrested because he taught at three different colleges under different names.

- In 1975, the management of the Equity Life Insurance Company defrauded its investors of between $2 and $3 billion by literally inventing thousands of nonexistent insurance policies, thereby inflating the company's assets.

There are many cultures in the world that exhibit what is called a collectivized sense of self. People in these societies conceive of themselves as part of some group—their family (including ancestors), a clan, tribe, or nation. People in such cultures see themselves as both psychologically and physically connected to other people (Guttman & Wrong, 1968).

In the United States, there are few subjects more written about than the self. Go into any bookstore and you will find an entire section titled "self-help," literally help for the self. The vast majority of these books are written by psychologists and other members of the so-called "helping" professions. Of interest to students of social problems is just why do so many selves in America need help and what with?

Another important aspect of social character is values in which a given culture believes. A value is "an abstract concept which determines for a person or some social groups the relative worth of various ends or goals"[1] Values are merely general ideas that are widely shared by a social group about what is desirable or undesirable, good or bad, beautiful or ugly, and so on. Value systems are interrelated collections of such beliefs. Such systems come in two broad categories. Sets of values tend to be either stable and relatively unchanging over the centuries, or fluid and prone to relatively rapid change. American culture is characterized by rapid social change, and values change with astonishing rapidity. For example, just a few years ago, premarital sex was considered the norm in America. But since the AIDS crisis began in the mid-1980s, people's values and behavior about premarital sex have become more conservative. Doubtless when a vaccine for AIDS finally becomes a reality, sexual norms will once again undergo a rapid change.

Because American values constantly come in and out of fashion, uncertainty about values creates a number of issues.

[1]Benjamin J. Wolman, *Dictionary of Behavioral Science*. 2nd Edition (New York: Academic Press, 1989):359.

- In 1981, Robert Cranberg was on a fishing boat with two companions. Mr. Cranberg was subsequently reported to have fallen into the ocean. His wife then filed insurance claims totaling $6 million. Cranberg had jumped overboard, swum ashore, and escaped to England. He was finally indicted for fraud.

- Ever since actor Tony Curtis played Waldo Demara in the movie *The Great Impostor* (1960) (a true story), the film has become a template for other impostors. Demara was a man who successfully passed himself off as a monk, teacher, assistant warden of a Texas prison, and Royal Canadian Navy physician and surgeon. (Yes, he actually performed surgery on sailors.) Following the movie, one woman, Dorothy Woods, who lived in an eighteen-room mansion and owned a Rolls-Royce, successfully bilked the government out of $377,500 in welfare, medical, payments, and food stamps. Ms. Woods opened twelve different welfare claims (files) under phony names, claiming a total of forty-nine children. One San Francisco man posed as a game warden for three months, issuing citations and confiscating fish. Upon being caught, the man told police that he had always wanted to be a game warden, and thought he would see what it was like. A Miami novelty shop owner, pretending to be a flight attendant, obtained $40,000 worth of trips on Pan American airlines (Marx, 1988:1–2).

Alienation: Structural and Personal

To the above examples could be added numerous others about lying and deception by individuals and organizations. Indeed "deception regarding (individual) identity and biography . . . (is a) common, but little commented upon feature of American life" (Marx, 1988:1). Many people now believe that "if honesty counts for something, it counts for very little" (Ehrhart, 1993:A-23). Lying and deception are deeply embedded in American culture and are institutionalized behaviors among the America's power elite (i.e., major corporations, government, and, above all, the mass media).

The English language, as used by these dominant institutions, has become thoroughly perverted by the use of a deceptive tongue termed *doublespeak*. The concept was first coined by George Orwell in his novel about a future totalitarian state, *1984*. Doublespeak involves language that is incongruous, and has conflicting elements. To date, Rutgers University English professor William Lutz (1989) has identified five kinds of doublespeak:

1. A *euphemism* is "an inoffensive or positive word or phrase used to avoid a harsh, unpleasant, or distasteful reality" (Lutz, 1989:2). Euphemisms are often used by corporate and government organizations to deceive, mislead, and/or otherwise alter the public's perception of reality. Euphemisms designed to deny the morally wrong are used constantly:

    For example, in 1984, the U.S. State Department decided that the word "killing" would no longer be used in reports about nations that violated human rights. Instead, the phrase "unlawful or arbitrary deprivation of life" was employed when the nations involved were those supported by U.S. military aid (a potentially embarrassing situation) (Lutz, 1989:3).

Similarly, euphemisms pour out of the Pentagon. Killing civilians has been termed "pacification." Assassination has been dubbed "termination with extreme prejudice."

Euphemisms are a lingua franca in advertising. "Boxes of pudding announce four generous portions but neglect to mention that this applies only to people no larger than hamsters" (Ehrhart, 1993:A-23).

2. *Jargon* is specialized language used in a trade or profession. When used to communicate with other members of the same profession, jargon can be a useful shorthand, but often it is used to deceive people negatively affected by organizations. Employees are nowadays often termed "associates," and when they are fired ("laid off") "their former employers call it downsizing (or restructuring), and speak boldly of the company's bright future while voting themselves bonuses" (Ehrhart 1993:A-23).

Several years ago, a scandal occurred when it was learned that the Defense Department paid $400 apiece for ordinary hardware store hammers (Simon & Eitzen, 1993:170). Rather than call these items hammers, they were termed "multidirectional impact devices" (Nader, 1986) in an attempt to deceive the public into believing a fancy machine had been purchased.

During the Gulf War of 1991 the Pentagon used the term "smart bombs" to describe what were really (in 92 percent of the cases) the same kinds of ordinances that were used against Germany in 1944, thus deceiving the public concerning the existence of a new weapon.

3. *Gobbledygook (bureaucratese)* consists of words and sentences designed to overwhelm audiences or impress them with the speaker's apparent competence and expertise. Former Vice President Quayle, explaining the need for the "Star Wars" weapons system, noted: "Why wouldn't an enhanced deterrent, a more stable peace, a better prospect to denying the ones who enter the conflict in the first place to have a reduction of offensive systems and an introduction to defensive capability?" (Lutz, 1989:5). Bureaucratese is commonly mixed with euphemisms and jargon of all kinds.

4. *Puffery*—inflated language, usually in the form of unprovable superlatives and overgeneralizations—is used endlessly in advertising and sales. We encounter puffery every day:

"Every kid in America loves Jell-O brand gelatin."

"Pepsi, the only cola with 'Uh-Huh.' "

"Ford gives you better ideas."

"Coke is it!" (Simon & Eitzen, 1993:111)

Automobile dealers are fond of claiming to be "number one" in their area, but they often do not define what "number one" means.

5. *Weasel Words* are words that appear to be making a claim, but in reality make no claim at all. They get their name from the fact that a weasel is an animal that sucks the insides out of eggs by making a small hole therein, and then replacing the egg in the raided nest. The egg still looks whole, but has no substance.

The most commonly used of such words is "helps," as in our cold medicine helps relieve your cold symptoms. Since "helps" does not mean cures, stops, or ends, the word is practically meaningless. Nor does the claim specify how much the medicine "helps." Another such word is "virtually." A dishwasher soap can be advertised as leaving dishes "virtually spotless," leave plenty of spots, and yet, the advertiser can escape any responsibility for the spots because "virtually" means almost, but not quite 100 percent. Other weasel words and phrases include "new and improved," "acts fast," and "works like magic." In most cases, such claims are so unspecified as to be meaningless (Lutz, 1989:85–94).

These examples of individual and organizational deception, interesting as they are in their own right, are merely symptomatic of a much more serious condition. Doublespeak is a dangerous weapon of social control, manipulation, and exploitation (Lutz, 1989:xiii). In his novel *1984*, Orwell described an official state language called "Newspeak." Newspeak is about limiting the way people critically view their government and its activities. It involves getting people to believe in things that are inherently contradictory such as:

"Nuclear war is winnable."

"We had to destroy the village in order to save it."

"Peace through war."

"Capital punishment enhances life."

Newspeak results in a type of illogic called *doublethink*. Doublethink is the ability to have two contradictory ideas in your mind at the same time, and believe both are true. The only way one can persist in believing both ideas are true is to never put them side by side, which would reveal the contradiction.

C. Wright Mills (1951:viii) believed that one of the great tasks of modern social science was to describe the effects of economic and political institutions (social structures) on people's inner feelings values, goals, and behaviors. Indeed, the sociological imagination involves the ability to shift from one perspective to another, "from the political to the psychological . . . [the sociological imagination] is the capacity to range from the most impersonal and remote . . . to the most intimate features of the human self" (Mills, 1959:7). Moreover, Mills believed that "it may well be that the most radical discovery [of] psychology and social science is the discovery of how so many intimate features of the person are socially patterned and even implanted" (Mills, 1959:161). This means that many of the personality traits that most people consider to be individual characteristics are actually widely shared products of mass socialization by the communications media and other bureaucratic institutions that dominate postmodern life.

Alienating Conditions and the Macro-Micro Link

There is a link between societal institutions and micro social problems, between alienating conditions of social structure and feelings of alienation experienced by individuals.

Such connections are often described as the macro-micro link, implying a relationship between the most intimate of feelings and the most important structural features of modern life. It is crucial to understand that dominant societal institutions mold character, but they do not mold it by themselves. Often their influence is indirect (Wilkinson, 1992:12). However, the character molded within families, and by schools, religious institutions, and such community organizations as the Boy Scouts, Girl Scouts, and Little League reinforces those traits that economic and political institutions require of us. Finally, in a nation as diverse as the United States, character traits differ widely among various social classes, racial and ethnic groups, and geographic regions. Thus, it is not easy to speak of a "national character," a set of traits that applies equally to all Americans. It is reasonable, however, to describe traits for which there is solid empirical evidence, such as the highest levels of crime in the Western world, the highest percentage of people who believe in God of any industrial democracy, and so on.

The issue is not which institutions have the most influence, but what kinds of social character the society as a whole is producing, and what sort of social problems are experienced by individuals within postmodern culture. One central theme in the writing on American character has dominated the literature since the 1940s. It is the picture of a lonely individual wishing to be liked by other people, with a "marketing personality," who packaged and sold him/herself like a "handbag" on the job market. Life in postmodern society has become an act wherein people's real (authentic) needs are suppressed in reaction to social pressures to conform and to achieve (Fromm, 1955; Riesman, 1950; Lasch, 1978, 1984; Wilkinson, 1992:12).

If members of American society are encouraged to develop certain personality traits, like chronic lying, then a condition of *alienation* may be said to exist. Alienation is directly related to a host of micro- (individual behavior) level social problems, including suicide, drug abuse, delinquency, sexual deviance, and, most central to this discussion, mental illness. To be sure, alienation is not the only cause of these maladies, anymore than any human behavior is caused by a single variable. To think in such terms is to engage in reductionism. Nevertheless, the more a group or groups of people are alienated, the more likely they are to suffer from micro social problems. And if alienation is socially patterned in various groups, it is, by definition, structurally caused. We then need to ask what is there about the social structure that produces feelings of alienation in groups of people? This theory requires a basic knowledge of notions regarding (1) basic human needs, (2) alienating conditions within the social structure, and (3) feelings of alienation.

There are good reasons to suggest that a basic human nature exists in the form of *basic human needs* (Breed, 1971:203–204; Fromm, 1955:37–39, 61–64; Mecca, Smelser, & Vasconcellos, eds., 1989). Evidence suggests that people in every type of social structure have a need for:

1. *Love*—including physical affection, and emotional cohesion with other people.

2. *Self-esteem*—including recognition of achievement, approval, encouragement, and affirmation that result in a positive concept of oneself and one's abilities (a sense of "power, confidence, agency" that is positive as measured against some standard that may be either absolute or relative) (Smelser, 1989:10).

3. *Identity*—including context or wholeness, organizing principles that define who one is and where and how one fits into the social roles that make up one's environment. An identity gives one the ability to organize one's perceptions, emotions, and beliefs into a coherent picture of one's self and place in the world.

When these three emotional needs are met, they result in people feeling (1) secure, and (2) that life possesses meaningful purpose(s). Gratification of these needs is ongoing, and demands frequent repetition. However, people are to some extent unique in both interests and personality. The more a social structure allows for social roles to satisfy these basic needs, the lower the alienation in that society (Breed, 1971:204).

The Nature of Alienation

Alienation is the result of basic human needs for love, self-esteem, and identity not being met. If societies do not allow all members to meet these basic needs, excluded individuals and groups will feel resentment and confusion. Confusion and resentment are both subjective and reactions to an objective condition which exposes people to forces beyond their control and understanding. Thus, the negative feelings of the alienated individual are rooted in a societal (institutional) base. "The roots of alienation do not reside in either intrapsychic (individual personality) processes or in interpersonal relationships, but in societal structures" (Breed, 1971:197–198; Schmidt, 1983:2–18).

Alienation is characterized by feelings of estrangement from either society or from oneself—often from both. Specific emotions are associated with alienation (Seeman, 1972; Israel, 1971:208–215). They include:

1. *Powerlessness*—a "person's expectation or belief that his or her behavior will not determine or affect his or her future" (Rogers & Mays, 1987:167). Such feelings result in people perceiving they are helpless to achieve their goals or roles in life. People who experience powerlessness often see their future as shaped by forces that are beyond their control.

2. *Meaninglessness* involves "confusion or vagueness about what one ought to believe or the criteria for making important decisions" (Rogers & Mays, 1987:168). To experience meaninglessness is to lack an understanding of the environment of which one is a part (Israel, 1971:210). To experience life as meaningless is to live in the present, and with a sense of optimism about one's future.

3. *Normlessness (anomie)* is a social situation by which people strive to achieve culturally prescribed goals (e.g., becoming "successful" by acquiring money and status) but can no longer influence their behavior, and lack access to honest means to achieve these goals. This can result in an "adaptation mode" (choice) (Merton, 1938) in which deviant or criminal behavior is chosen over legal or societally approved behavior as a means of achieving goals.

4. *Cultural estrangement (value isolation)* involves rejecting widely shared societal values, such as wealth and success. When people become "cheerful robots," they put in their eight hours of work each day, go home and engage in mass culture,

Many people now work in jobs where they constantly have to put on false faces, pretend they are happy to be working with their coworkers, customers, and clients, when they often are not. Such impression management is not only part of the postmodern workplace in a service-oriented economy, it has also become part of human relationships in general in the postmodern age.

such as watching television; mass leisure, such as going on a picnic in a public park; and mass consumption, such as going to the shopping mall.

5. *Loneliness* results from a lack of social acceptance by people within one's environment, with resultant feelings of estrangement from others, and rejection. Since loneliness is a feeling experienced by individuals, it is possible to feel lonely even in crowds (Riesman, 1950).

6. *Self-estrangement* is the experiencing of oneself as alien, with resultant feelings of resentment, and confusion. Self-estrangement often opens people to the possibility of self-deception (Schmidt, 1983:65). Self-estranged people often feel fragmented, and feel guilty for feeling this way. Self-estranged people often hide these feelings by putting on masks (called "impression management," "image construction," acting, selling of the self, etc.). Being strangers to themselves, they lack a stable identity, and often feel like frauds. Not trusting themselves, self-estranged people tend to be distrustful of other people, and society as well.

The Mass Media and
Alienating Conditions

Perhaps the best way to view alienating conditions within the American social structure is to study the mass media. The mass media are everywhere in postmodern society. The very structure of the mass media is alienating because the average person is so far removed from their ownership and control. The dominant media institutions—television networks, major newspapers, recording companies, book and magazine publishing houses, movie studios—are huge multinational corporations that either own or are owned by other corporations, banks, and insurance companies: In 1936, and for several decades thereafter, most movie studios were owned by New York investment banks controlled by superrich families like the Rockefellers and the Morgans (Parenti, 1991:181).

Since the mid–1980s, forty-four corporations have controlled "half or more of all media output" in the United States (Asa Berger, 1991:388). This is down from fifty companies in 1982, so concentration of media ownership is increasing. The three major television networks combined own over 1000 local stations, as well as considerable portions of the cable television industry (e.g., NBC owns the CNBC network).

For example, one firm, Time-Warner, possesses over $15 billion in assets, and owns media outlets that include major magazines (*Time, Sports Illustrated, Fortune, Mad, Money, People,* and *Life*), movies (Warner Brothers), recording (Warner Records), book publishing (Warner Books), cable television (HBO and Showtime).

Fewer than one hundred corporate executives now control the majority of each medium. Twenty corporations control 52 percent of all newspaper circulation. Twenty firms control 50 percent of all periodical sales. Twenty publishing houses control 52 percent of book sales, and another twenty control 76 percent of all compact disc and cassette tape sales. "If one counts the three (television) networks and the ten corporations whose sponsorship dominates prime time, thirteen corporations control two-thirds of the audience in television, and radio" (Bagdikian, 1991:389). A mere seven companies control 75 percent of all movie distribution.

What all of this means is that media ownership and control are approaching monopolistic proportions. Competition among newspapers, for example, is nearly dead. Ninety-seven percent of all chain-owned newspapers have no competition from other newspapers. Moreover, by the year 2000 a mere ten multinational firms will control most of the world's mass media (Hewitt, 1991:396). The concern most observers have about increased concentration of ownership is that it restricts the content of news and political opinion allowed in the media. While this is a serious concern, there is also a concern about the content of media programming, movies, and advertising, and the effects of that content on audiences.

Recent polls concerning public attitudes do indeed reveal a deeply felt alienation. Fully 65 percent of the public in a 1993 poll stated that the news media look out for the interests of powerful people more than the interests of ordinary people. Many people in the news media, such as Dan Rather and Peter Jennings, are now viewed as celebrities in their own right, and are shown attending presidential inaugurals, gracing the covers of national magazines, guesting on talk shows, and keeping company with other celebrities. In consequence, nearly two-thirds of the public feel the news media have little in common with ordinary people, and the public has come to distrust the news media in large numbers

(Shaw, 1993: A-18–19). Unfortunately, no poll questions were asked concerning the non-news portions of television programming, with its rampant violence, gratuitous sexual imagery, and manipulative advertising. The effects of these aspects of the media on social character are assessed below.

Media Socialization Effects

C. Wright Mills once observed that no one knows all of the functions served by the mass media. Today, the mass media not only keep us informed of what's going on in the world, but they dramatically shape our perceptions of that world. Indeed, mass communications professor Arthur Asa Berger (1991:328) believes that America has evolved into a "teleculture" wherein television "has become the most powerful socializing . . . force in society." Its influence has replaced traditional sources of socialization and ethics: parents, priests, teachers, and peers. There is also a raging debate over the media's effects on people's values and behavior. To be sure, the way in which the media influence people is often subtle and indirect, and people's perceptions of media messages are filtered through a number of lenses, including social class, age, gender, race and ethnicity, and earlier socialization experiences with media. Nevertheless, there is enough evidence to indicate that Asa Berger's notion of the media as the dominant socializing force in America is realistic.

- Ninety-eight percent of American households own television sets, 30 percent of households have two or more (Parenti, 1991:10). Even homes that lack hot running water or indoor toilets have a television in America.

- Since the mid-1980s Americans have been spending fifty-two hours per week in front of the TV. Homes with three or more people have a TV on sixty-one hours per week.

- The average American is exposed to one hundred television commercials, sixty radio commercials, and thirty print ads per day; 90,000 ads per year of various types. The ads equate happiness with materialism, present sexist portrayals of women (see below), and contribute to dependency, anxiety, and low self-esteem (Asa Berger, 1991:330).

There are some interesting links between certain media themes and various character traits that are relatively undisputed:

There is a tremendous amount of violence in the American media and in American life, and there is a relationship between the two. Virtually thousands of studies have demonstrated that media violence can motivate individuals who are predisposed to commit violence to do so. For example, after the movie *The Deer Hunter* opened in theaters in 1979, at least twenty-five people in the United States committed suicide by imitating the movie's Russian roulette scene. Suicides also increase significantly in the United States after a famous person, like Marilyn Monroe, is reported to have committed suicide. Homicide rates also increase immediately after heavyweight boxing matches (Parenti, 1991:7), but this is the tip of a very ugly iceberg: America is the most violent industrial democracy in the world, with a homicide rate ten times higher than the entire continent of Europe. Half of the American public reports having violent urges, and one-fourth of the population has acted on those impulses (Patterson & Kim, 1991:120). One-third of the entire American adult population now owns at least one gun, and, most frighteningly, *26 million Americans now carry guns with them when they leave home!* Media violence outpaces even the real violence in society:

- *Item*: Children's television is the most violent of all, averaging twenty-five violent acts per hour. Ninety-five percent of children's programs feature violent acts (Patterson & Kim, 1991:123). Moreover, studies reveal that children often believe what they see on television is real.

- *Item*: The more time people spend watching television, the more they are likely to overestimate the actual amount of violent crime in American life, and the number of police.

- *Item*: The mass media shape some key sexual traits, including the link between sex and violence. Eroticization (assigning of sexual symbols) pervades postmodern culture. Sexual symbols are now attached to virtually every product and service that is the subject of media advertising. Sex has become a commodity in itself, and in ads it is associated with youth, power, and success. Even children in ads have become sexual beings "thrusting their pelvises in suggestive ways to sell jeans, kiddie cosmetics" (Davis & Stasz, 1990:251).

Television violence is an important part of postmodern culture, but such violent presentations tend to distort the true nature of the violence in postmodern life. Evidence strongly indicates that heavy viewers of such violence believe that the violent crime rate is much higher than it is, believe there are more police than is actually the case, and are more likely to vote for larger and larger increases in spending for new prison construction.

Sexual presentations in contemporary ads and in movies and television shows are an ever-present feature of postmodern life. Sex has become a mere commodity in postmodern culture, and women (and sometimes men) featured in such ads are often dehumanized into mere body parts.

- *Item*: Studies of movies and television, men's magazines, and pornography all indicate "increased depictions of violence against women" (Malamuth, 1984; Davis & Stasz, 1990:251). The main effect of such presentations is to forge a link between sex and violence. Such images also reinforce myths about women and rape (e.g., they like it and want it, or they deserve it).

- *Item*: In movies, magazines, and television shows, sex is frequently separated from emotions and relationships. Sex is depicted as unrelated to personal responsibility for consequences, affection, intimacy, or commitment. Many movie heroes remain single and seduce multiple partners without ever becoming emotionally attached to a woman. Recent movies have also involved the rise of the sexually aggressive female who is incapable of love, such as the character recently played by Demi Moore in *Disclosure*.

- *Item*: In May, 1995, ABC's "Prime-Time Live" aired a segment revealing how sexually charged entertainment and advertising was being watched by young children, and making them far more aware of and eager for sex than many parents suspect. Hidden cameras showed seven-year-old girls "ogling photos of half naked male models. Teachers showed pictures drawn by first- and second-graders—Cinderellas with breasts and nipples" (Saunders, 1995:A25). Six-year-old girls stated that girls should be sexually assertive in order to attract boys. Both little boys and girls told interviewers that the job of being sexually aggressive now belongs to girls. Children just over five years of age were shown simulating intercourse during recess in schools. America's obsession with sexual gratification has now filtered down to the youngest members of the society, and results may be extremely dangerous, increasing incidents of sexually transmitted diseases, illegitimate births, and other forms of sexual deviance, such as rape.

- Much of the content of media's sexual presentations is mirrored in the sexual crime statistics. The United States has twenty times the number of reported rapes in Japan, Spain, and England combined. Moreover, 20 percent of American women report being victims of date rape (Patterson & Kim, 1991:120, 129).

There are several important issues here:

1. Advertising is not just a set of messages for products. It is a medium that social-izes people to be consumers. Much of the time[2] it does so in a deceitful way.

2. Most advertising is based on appeals to people's fears about not being loved or on low self-esteem. The ad appeals testify to the recognition that these basic human needs are widely unmet in American culture. Drugs of all types are very heavily advertised on television (about once every eleven minutes) and in mag-azines. These ads attempt to increase feelings of insecurity and low self-esteem in consumers, and, obviously, the people who feel most insecure are the most vulnerable to such appeals. The overall message is: If you want to be confident, loved, successful, know who you are, where you are going in life and how to get there, you need us. In short, one trait the media attempt to instill in con-sumers is dependency.

3. Many people who read about the themes in lifestyle ads respond by saying something like, "Well, those may be the themes, but I don't take such appeals seriously, and neither does anyone else I know." Jeffrey Schrank has pointed out that 90 percent of America's television viewers consider themselves "personally immune" to commercial appeals, yet these viewers account for 90 percent of all sales of advertised products (Schrank, 1977:84).

Moreover, there is evidence that ad claims are believed much more than most of us would like to think:

- Research supports the notion that people perceive more content in ads than the ads contain. Additional values are perceived by consumers and are attached to products. For example, in one study of sweater ads, when sweaters were shown with belts and captioned with a Scottish accent, consumers were twice as likely to perceive the sweaters as imported (Rotfeld & Preston, 1981).

---

[2]Warning labels in cigarette ads were placed there with the permission of the tobacco companies only after a protracted political struggle—the outcome of which was to relieve cigarette makers of legal responsibility for the harm done by tobacco in exchange for placing the labels on cigarette packs. The tobacco industry kept evidence of the harms of smoking secret for thirty years, and has been successfully sued by people who suffered the ill effects of tobacco prior to the placement of warning labels on the packages.

- Research further supports the notion that implied deceptions (puffery claims) are believed more than outright lies. In one study of seventeen puff claims, 70 percent of respondents felt the claims were either wholly or partially true (Kuel & Dyer, 1976).

- There is also evidence that puffery claims are often indistinguishable from factual claims. Rotfeld and Rotzall (1980) placed a sample of one hundred people in a room and presented them with both puff claims (e.g., St. Joseph's aspirin for children is the best children's aspirin), and factual claims (e.g., St. Joseph's aspirin for children lowers children's fevers). The researchers found that "many of the puff claims were believed by a large proportion of the respondents," and "that the subjects could not tell that these puffs might not be literally true" (Rotfeld & Rotzall, 1980:19–20). What these researchers found was that the factual claims were believed just as often as the puff claims used in their survey. This is one indication that postmodern culture confuses people's perception of the difference between fantasy and reality.

- A review of puffery research states that puffery "has the potential to deceive consumers, and as well, injure the credibility of advertising." Research indicates that a "large proportion of the sample interpret the claim [puff] to suggest superiority [of the product being advertised]" (Wyckham, 1987:55).

Consumers fed a constant diet of puffery ads may confuse factual and puffery claims and actually come to distrust advertising on the one hand, yet be manipulated by it on an unconscious level on the other (Hemmelstein, 1984: 68, 271; Rotfeld & Preston, 1981:10)

Advertisers spend over $130 billion per year to get their deceptive messages across. Would you spend this gigantic amount of money on something that did not work? Indeed, the most problematic and profound aspect of all media may be their constantly mixing fantasy and reality. There is evidence that mixing fantasy and reality causes confusion in vulnerable groups, especially in teenagers (Calabrese, 1987:935). Inauthenticity is more than themes about unmet emotional needs; it is based on the logic of doublespeak: It requires us to believe in two contradictory things at once.

Individual Inauthenticity

Over forty years ago, C. Wright Mills (1951) described the inauthenticity that takes place among the "cheerful robots," white-collar workers. At work, they must smile and be personable, courteous, and helpful. White-collar employees sell not only their energy and time to their organization, but their personalities as well. They repress their resentment and anger over having to interact with people they do not like behind a carefully cultivated good humor.

Sociologists who study the sociology of emotions have found some interesting evidence supporting Mills' claims. Arlie Hochschild (1983:234–41) estimates that one-third of American jobs now involve "emotional labor," positions that require inauthentic behavior in the form of acting. Hochschild differentiates between superficial (surface) acting (i.e., pleasant facial expressions and gestures) and deep acting (expressions of feelings). Superficial acting requires putting on a pleasant expression and repeating the same pat phrases over and over.

George Ritzer (1993:134–35) has described the superficial acting by fast-food restaurant employees. Rule Number 17 for Burger King workers is "smile at all times." The Roy Rogers employees who used to say "Happy Trails" when I paid for my food really had no interest in what happened to me in the future, on the trail. (In fact, they were really saying, in a polite way, "get lost!") This phenomenon has been generalized to many workers who say "Have a nice day" as one is departing. They have no interest in, or concern for, how the rest of your day goes. Again, in a ritualized way they are really telling us to "get lost," to move on so someone else can be served.

Deep acting (expressions of feelings) is required in jobs that place people in more prolonged public contact. Flight attendants, for example, are supposed to project a friendly image no matter what the passenger may do. Hochschild (1983:55) quotes a flight attendant who describes the deep acting she does to keep from expressing feelings of personal anger: "If I pretend I am feeling really up, I actually get into it. The passenger responds to me as though I were friendly. Sometimes I purposely take some deep breaths. I try to relax my neck muscles. I try to remember that if he's drinking too much, he's probably scared of flying. I think to myself, 'He's like a little child' . . . And when I see him that way, I don't get mad that he's yelling at me. He's like a child yelling at me then."

Approximately one-half of the positions requiring impression management are in service sector jobs occupied by women (e.g., airline attendants, clerks, nurses, social and recreational workers, radio and television announcers, and—no insult intended—college professors).

Most important, Hochschild reports that both men and women who must engage in selling their emotions as commodities experience feelings of powerlessness, an important form of alienation, in reaction to the constant pressure to perform. The language, clothes, and "look" that make up these roles are provided by the inauthentic role models in the media. The "look" for women is typified by a *Good Housekeeping* story describing Mary Tyler Moore's different "faces." One is her "business face" which uses "golden, toasty" colors that are flattering, even in harsh fluorescent office lighting. Ms. Moore's "evening face" highlights her "flawless skin," smoldering dark eyes, and glistening, molded mouth, all worthy of a "round of applause" (Papson, 1985:225–26).

Unfortunately, life in mass organizations is increasingly concerned with impression management and emotional acting (Lasch, 1984; Hochschild, 1983). Some students of bureaucracy (Kanungo, 1982:157) have noted that certain types of cynical and successful people at the top of organizational hierarchies exude charisma via a superficial sense of warmth and charm, yet make decisions based on an object-directed dehumanization (see below) that converts people into subhuman categories. Such leaders have few problems in making decisions because of their abilities to think in nonhuman, black-and-white terms regarding plant closings, layoffs, manipulative advertising campaigns, or organizational deviance. Thus inauthenticity and dehumanization are causes of social problems because these behaviors are, at times, handsomely rewarded.

Such "impression management" (pseudo-identity) often becomes an important part of private life. "What began as the public and commercial relations of business have become deeply personal: there is a public relations aspect to private relations of all sorts, including even relations with oneself" (Mills, 1951:187). Young cheerful robots often spend much of private life in singles bars and other "meat markets" projecting false images (fronts) about their personalities and statuses. They manipulate each other for monetary and/or sexual purposes, and many use cocaine in order to be "accepted" by others and/or to escape feelings of alienation they harbor. Their relationships, whether sexual or friendly in nature, tend to be shallow because they keep so many of their true feelings hidden from others, and, most sadly, from themselves as well (Bellah et al., 1986).

We live in a postmodern culture in which reason and freedom have become increasingly weakened; it is a time of indifference, uneasiness, and cynicism among people. The social character of American life is dominated by a "cheerful robot" (Mills, 1959) who puts in an eight-hour workday (mostly in a white-collar position in a bureaucratic organization as a salesperson or manager), and engages in the escapist entertainment of television and alienated consumption during his or her "leisure time." The cheerful robot is a product of mass society, urban life, with its emphasis on status seeking, consumption, competition, and dependence on bureaucratic organizations for employment, goods, and services.

Dehumanization

Because of the impersonal nature of bureaucratic structures, values centering on materialism and status, and the decline of community, mass societies are prone to another form of alienation termed dehumanization. **Dehumanization** exists in two interrelated forms, *object-directed* and *self-directed*.

Object-directed dehumanization occurs when people are labeled less than human for purposes of profit, exploitation, and manipulation. The mass media, both as to programming and advertising, are loaded with this type of dehumanization in the form of stereotypes. Numerous studies of television and movies have documented how women and minorities are negatively portrayed. Michael Parenti (1991) notes that the mass media have constructed an unreal world in which minorities and women are continually stereotyped as a part of a greater set of ideological messages:

- Italian Americans are featured in media either as members of the Mafia, or as dumb gluttons incapable of speaking correct English. Italian women are portrayed as shrieking hysterics.

- Working-class people, both on television and in movies, are pictured as stupid and slovenly in speech and appearance, and the work that they do is almost never shown. Labor unions are depicted as corrupt. Individual heroism is nearly always preferable to collective action (teamwork).

- American Indians are portrayed as savages, barbarians, and "devils" (Parenti, 1991:14), who aren't defending their homeland against invaders and colonizers, but are possessed of a lust for killing, destruction, and a disregard for human life, including their own.

- Women in movies were for years portrayed as either seductive spies who endangered lone, individual heroes, or passive accessories who kept male heroes company.

Self-directed dehumanization is a symptom of self-alienation. It involves turning oneself into a "cog in a wheel," a dehumanized machine. The results are symptoms of high stress (Harris, 1987) and burnout on the job. It is thought that people who dehumanize themselves by perceiving themselves as parts of machines also tend to stereotype other people negatively (Bernard et al., 1971). Thus self-directed and object-directed dehumanization are interrelated on the individual level. Moreover, both dehumanization and inauthenticity are an integral part of the social character of postmodern mass society (Montagu & Matson, 1985; Shrader, 1992).

The Individualized Self

America's concept of the individualized self is so extreme as to be unrealistic. It is a notion loaded with myths and contradictions, and a major cause of many micro social problems. The United States was long ago proclaimed the land of individual rights, individual cases, individual personalities, and individual egos. As we have seen, all these notions are constantly reinforced in the mass media, especially with their focus on celebrities and individual heroes.

Box 3.2 • Rugged Individualism or Pseudo-Individualism: The Making of a Social Problem

Pseudo-Individualism

Much of what people would like to believe is rugged individualism is really pseudo-individualization (Adorno, 1974), a mass-produced notion of the self that is sold to individuals through the media to make people feel cared about as individuals in a society controlled by impersonal, mass institutions. For example, buy a newspaper and turn to the astrology column. Under your sign is some advice that is supposedly directed at you. My horoscope for yesterday said that I was to receive a long distance communication revealing a project was underway. This project could mean an opportunity for travel, including travel overseas. The column also noted that I was to focus on my ability to rise above obstacles (Omar, 1993:E-11). The astrologist implies that he knows what the reader is or was like. The references are, of course, so general that they can be made to fit nearly anyone's situation all the time (Adorno, 1974:29).

The idea that this column was written just for me is irrational, and indeed, scientific tests of astrology's validity have revealed no evidence supporting the claims of astrologers. Researchers tested the claim that the planet Mars influenced military careers, and found that being born under the sign of Mars, or any other sign, bore no relationship to a career in the armed services (Jerome, 1975:15).

That astrology columns are nearly always about individuals, their success, and luck is part of a socialization process that reinforces a particular concept of the self, namely, that we are all "rugged individuals" who are responsible for our own successes or failures. The great contradiction here, of course, is that astrology actually represents a gigantic collective exercise in mass conformity, not individualism. Individualism as a belief system may be unrelated to individuality of tastes and style, but individualism as a widespread belief (character trait) has enormous ramifications for how people perceive the actual causes of social problems. Individualism is a key element in American social character, and it is widely per-

Americans are probably the only people on earth who believe in something they call "rugged individualism." This belief holds that people are imbued with a near unlimited freedom in the form of free will, and that the exercise of this freedom requires that individuals become self-sufficient and psychologically secure so that they may compete against other individuals in seeking life's material rewards. This ideology is not only mythical, it is downright dangerous.

America's extreme view of individualism causes us great problems when it comes to establishing intimate relations with others. The psychologist Karen Horney wrote on this subject, noting, in 1938, that one of the great problems Americans face is deciding whom they can trust. As she noted, American "culture is economically based on the principle of competition . . . the psychic result of this situation is a diffuse hostile tension between individuals . . . competitiveness and the potential hostility that accompanies it, pervades all human relationships . . . between men and men, between women and women and men

ceived as a positive value. But taken to an extreme, it can become, not freedom, but selfishness, greed, and narcissism.

There are additional contradictions related to individualized selfhood. There is a real tension between success and competition, on one side, and humility and love, on the other. Careers often require Americans to become assertive, even ruthless and aggressive in reaching the top. Yet, the Christian ethic is loaded with admonishments about loving thy neighbor, and turning the other cheek. The culture itself alternates between periods stressing teamwork or community, and others emphasizing individual recognition, self-gain, and greed.

Mills, of course, would have none of the myth of individualism. He criticized it when it was perhaps at the height of its popularity. In 1951, Mills published an in-depth view of the American middle classes. Titled *White Collar*, the volume began with the premise of profound alienation among white-collar employees. "Whatever their future," Mills wrote, "it will not be of their own making" (1951:ix). At work, they were individuals, but not rugged. They were, to Mills, lost souls within the bureaucracies for which they toiled, living life out in "slow misery . . . yearning for the quick American climb (to success)" (1951:xi).

As we saw in Chapter 2, American society is dominated by massive institutions, where resources and power are heavily centralized. Within bureaucratic organizations, decision making takes place far away from the influence of the average person. Being removed from key economic and political decisions tends to obscure the nature of reality, and makes a significant number of people feel they are alone and relatively insignificant. The horoscope fills a number of needs for insecure, alienated, and lonely individuals. It is a pseudo-solution for the social insecurity that permeates mass society. The horoscope creates the illusion that someone out there cares about me. It also provides advice about making personal decisions,

Continued on next page

Box 3.2 • Continued

something sorely lacking in a rapidly changing society with few stable values and even fewer moral principles that may serve as a guide for making the decisions of daily life.

As one self-help bestseller puts it, we must constantly make decisions for which we have no guideline:

"Demands are made for decisions from the moment we awake until our final weary retreat under the covers. Shall we drink coffee or decaffeinated? (But decaffeinated *is* coffee says the kindly TV doctor who is not a doctor.) Shall we drink it black or with cream? Or with nondairy creamer? Artificial sweetener or sugar? Shall we have eggs or Egg Beaters? Is bacon carcinogenic or is that just another laboratory rat exaggeration?"

Having struggled through these decisions we unfold the morning paper. Does the murderer have "diminished capacity" or is he responsible? Shall we sell the silverware or hide it? Shall we enroll in Weight Watchers or Slim Gym? Shall we put the kids in private school or impeach the school board? Shall we move or buy better locks?

The kids sit at the breakfast table, listless. In response to a parental inquiry about their well-being this fine morning we are told they don't feel like talking. Shall we admonish them or give them a pep talk? Shall we keep quiet or sit on our feelings? Do repressed feelings cause cancer? Doesn't everything? (Harris & Harris, 1985:92–93).

Second, individualism as a belief system is an illusion, and a dangerous one at that. First of all, human beings are among the most social creatures on the face of the earth. There are few other species where most children live with their parents for the first eighteen years of life. Moreover, human social organization guarantees that people will be dependent upon and interdependent with other people for securing their basic material needs for food, clothing, and shelter, as well as their basic social psychological needs.

and women, and whether the point of competition be popularity, competence, attractiveness, or any other social value it greatly impairs the possibilities of reliable friendship" (Horney, 1938:284).

One result of the potential hostility between individuals is fear. This includes the potential fear of the anger of others, the fear of failure, and lowered self-esteem. Together, competitiveness, the potential hostility it engenders between individual selves, fear, and lowered self-esteem result in individuals feeling lonely (i.e., psychologically isolated). One reaction to loneliness is an intensified need for love and affection. Because it meets such vital needs, romantic love is overvalued in American culture, reaching mythical proportions as a cure to all ills. Because we have come to expect more than it can possibly deliver, romantic love has become an illusion, an illusion that serves to cover up the destructive factors that created the exaggerated need for it in the first place (i.e., extreme individualism and competition).

The result is genuine contradiction. America's individualized selves need a great deal of affection, but America's extreme individualism and competition have made love difficult to acquire. Because love is both highly cherished and surprisingly scarce, this contradiction causes people to become neurotically possessed with low self-esteem, destructiveness, anxiety, and an excessive need for attention, approval, and affection from others.

A second contradiction of the American self concerns a tension between the alleged freedom we enjoy and all of the factual limitations placed on that freedom. Our myths teach that anyone can grow up to be president of the nation, or become a millionaire. Yet, in reality, America has only one president at a time, and fewer than one person in a million acquires millionaire status. The result is that individuals constantly drift between feeling great power in determining their own destiny, and feeling powerless to accomplish much of anything by themselves. From a sociological perspective, living in a culture that promises individual happiness and success, but fails to provide the means for the vast majority to achieve it, causes a great many social problems including crime (at all social class levels), alcoholism, and drug addiction. Choosing such deviant activities has been described as an adaptation to the reality of living in a society that prescribes the goal of material success, but fails to provide the means to achieve it. This structural anomie is now playing an important role in shaping both social character and social problems.[3]

Far from being individualistic, Americans are a living contradiction. They live in a homogeneous culture, are constantly propagandized as a mass, frequently engage in the same spectator behavior (especially television, movies, sports, pop music), yet persist in the belief that they are a nation of nonconformists. As demonstrated in this chapter, it is the nature of that conformity that is at issue.

Box 3.3 • Minorities and Social Character: The Case of African Americans

African Americans occupy a unique place in American culture. They are the only group of immigrants whose members were kidnapped, and brought to these shores against their will. To one degree or another, the descendants of this group all share this heritage, a legacy of oppression and domination by the larger white culture. Social scientist Andrew Hacker (1992:31–49) has described what "Being Black in America" is like:

- In the eyes of the dominant culture, being black characterizes your identity in an all-pervasive and unique way. No matter your social class, gender, or occupation. If you write a book on Euclidean geometry or the Renaissance, you are still described as a "black author" (1992:32).

- African Americans are torn between being members of white America and seeking their own identity. Most blacks feel they are different than whites. No other ethnic group refers to its own people as "folks,. . . brothers and sisters,. . . in ways whites never can" (1992:34). When famous blacks change their names, they frequently adopt Muslim titles: Cassius Clay to Mohammed Ali, Lew Alcindor to Kareem Abdul-Jabbar, and so on. But even this is telling. White America prefers that blacks be "performers who divert them as athletes, musicians, and comedians" (1992:34).

Continued on next page

[3]This is precisely the argument made by Robert Merton, 1938/1994.

Box 3.3 • Continued

- The preferences of African Americans are at odds with the realities of American life. Polls indicate that 85 percent of blacks would prefer to live in racially mixed neighborhoods, yet 85 percent of American neighborhoods are racially segregated. When white neighborhoods reach about 8 percent black population, whites begin moving out (they cannot even accept a 12 percent mix, the percentage of blacks in America's population) (1993:36). Thus blacks, no matter what their status in life, are seen as contaminating American neighborhoods in many places in the United States, opening wounds and leaving psychological scars that never heal, that constantly serve to remind African Americans how far away they remain from full American citizenship.

  When in the company of whites, blacks feel constantly on display. Tokenism frequently makes them the only black jurors, corporate board members, college classroom members. The presence of one black frequently makes whites uncomfortable and blacks know it. When present, whites prefer that blacks smile. That way whites can be assured blacks are well treated. So blacks feel they must constantly be upbeat, never show anger, exasperation, or rage. But most people can not keep such control over these powerful feelings, and the news is dotted with outbursts of black celebrities and the collective anger of ghetto dwellers.

- Even when they are not with whites, blacks know they are the subject of white conversation. No other group has been so intensely studied, pitied, deplored, reduced to data, and dehumanized. Yet most of the culture available to blacks (books, television, movies, music) are cultural works blacks have adapted to the

Summary

The discussion has centered on the nature of social character in American life. Social character consists of widely shared traits within a culture. This chapter focused on some specific attitudes and behaviors: lying and deception and sexual and nonsexual violence. These traits are caused by two alienating conditions within the larger culture, namely, inauthenticity and dehumanization. These two conditions are built into the structure of the mass media and the nature of bureaucratic life in postmodern mass society. On a personal level, self-directed dehumanization and personal inauthenticity are also symptoms of a lack of self-esteem often associated with drug abuse, mental illness, alcoholism, and a host of other social problems of everyday life.

The social character of our age is overly sensitive to the opinions of others due to insecurity regarding our personal identity and status. This sensitivity to the judgments and values of other people is often termed other-directedness. All of these themes fly in the face of the American myth of rugged individualism.

tastes of white audiences. And one of America's great cultural contradictions is that despite white ravings about black inferiority, whites have long admired and adopted black slang, black music, and black sexuality. These days white television and movies present more black doctors and lawyers than have ever existed in real life, and blacks appear in commercials, as long as they are not "too" black and look pleased to be among whites. And in most history books, if mentioned at all, blacks appear as passive, faceless victims.

- No other group has ever had a word like "nigger" thrown at it to keep it in line. The word reminds blacks of their history of inferiorization by whites, and blacks' long history of being divided and conquered. Today, blacks find themselves in a confusing and contradictory position in America, and their attitudes reflect this no-win situation.

- Much of African-American life, especially working- and lower-class life, is loaded with a variety of social problems, from birth to death: The majority of black families are affected by divorce, and many black women never marry. Black women live five fewer years than white, black men live seven years less. Indeed, a black man living in Harlem is less likely to reach sixty-five than a male in Bangladesh, one of the world's poorest nations. Black males have three times the greater risk of contracting AIDS; a seven times greater risk of being murdered, of having their civil rights violated by the police; twice the risk of being a crime victim; and a higher risk of insomnia, obesity, and hypertension than whites. These odds are not merely a result of poverty, but stem from all of the rage, distrust, and anxiety that comes from being an African American.

Suggested Readings

Arthur Asa Berger (ed.) (1991) *Media U.S.A.,* 2nd ed. (New York: Longman). A wonderful collection of readings dealing with all problematic aspects of the American mass media.

Andrew Hacker (1992) *Two Nations: Black and White, Separate, Hostile, and Unequal* (New York: Scribner's). One of the most interesting and important books on American racism in a long time.

George Ritzer (1993) *The McDonaldization of Society* (Thousand Oaks. CA: Pine Forge Press). A provocative study of inauthentic and dehumanizing trends in the processes of franchising and mass consumption in the postmodern economy. Ritzer's book is a profound analysis of the contradictions of mass consumerism.

Rupert Wilkinson (ed.) (1992) *American Social Character* (New York: HarperCollins). The most important reader on American character in a generation. It contains classic articles and a superb set of bibliographic essays.

Exercises

Critical Thinking Exercise 3.1	The Dehumanization of Women and Crime

Two excellent videos concerning the dehumanization of women in ads are *Killing Us Softly* and *Still Killing Us Softly*. These are available in most college video collections, and are also owned by a number of public libraries. Each is about thirty minutes long. Write a brief paper (two to four pages) concerning your reactions to these videos.

You may wish to focus your paper on the following issues:

1. What is the relationship suggested by the video between how women are presented in ads and the victimization of women in crimes like rape and murder?

2. What messages does advertising send women regarding their independence, beauty, and ability to love their families?

3. What messages does advertising send to men concerning what women want from them?

4. How are men depicted in ads, and what messages do you think men are given by such images?

Critical Thinking Exercise 3.2	Alienation in Media

One way to study inauthenticity and dehumanization is by doing content analysis of magazine ads. This may be done using the following directions.

Select a series of full-page ads at random from current issues of three types of magazines:

General interest magazines: *Time, Newsweek, U.S. News & World Report*

Men's magazines: *GQ, M, Playboy, Penthouse, Esquire*

Women's magazines: *Cosmopolitan, Vanity Fair, Redbook, Vogue*

Select ads from one issue of one magazine in each category (e.g., the current issues of *Time, Esquire,* and *Cosmopolitan*). Use only full-page ads that feature pictures of people (i.e., no "tombstone" ads that show just products).

Analyze both the pictures and words in each ad for the following:

1. Inauthenticity as noted in words or phrases containing any of the following implied promises:

> sexuality and sexual intercourse
>
> success, power, status, wealth
>
> personal popularity, friendship
>
> love, romance, marriage
>
> a happy family life, successful parenting
>
> other implied promises

2. The implied promises pictured in advertisements. These include promises of:

> sexual intercourse
>
> monetary success
>
> popularity/friendship
>
> love, romance, marriage
>
> a happy family life
>
> pleasurable experience(s)—feeling good
>
> other implied promises

3. Dehumanization as expressed in words or phrases. Search for two types of dehumanizing phrases:

> *Sexual dehumanization:* mention of sex, nudity, or body parts associated with sex (e.g., breasts, hips)
>
> *Nonsexual dehumanization,* in which men and women are described as objects that are less than human (e.g., "resources," machine comparisons, weapons, animals and/or plants)

4. Pictured dehumanization involves presenting people as sex objects as expressed by:

> (a) The degree of undress found in pictured models in ads:
>
> > scantily dressed: clothed but revealing contours or genitalia
> >
> > partially clad
> >
> > naked
>
> (b) Degree of physical contact found among couples pictured in ads:
>
> > holding hands
> >
> > arms around one or both partners
> >
> > kissing
> >
> > sexual or erotic poses (e.g., simulated intercourse)
> >
> > other dehumanizing poses

Coding Sheet

Use a separate coding sheet for each ad. A coding sheet is a kind of scorecard used to count the number of themes in each item (i.e., advertisement) in your sample:

1. Magazine name:

2. Issue date (Optional):

3. Page # (Optional):

4–9. Inauthenticity code(s): words/phrases

4. Sexuality and sexual intercourse _____

5. Success, power, status, wealth, _____

6. Personal popularity, friendship _____

7. Love, romance, marriage _____

8. A happy family life, successful parenting _____

9. Other implied promises _____

10–16: The implied promises pictured in advertisements. These included promises of:

10. Sexual intercourse _____

11. Monetary success _____

12. Popularity/friendship _____

13. Love, romance, marriage _____

14. A happy family life _____

15. Pleasurable experience(s)—feeling good _____

16. Other implied promises (Specify): _____

17–18: Dehumanization as expressed in words or phrases. Search for two types of dehumanizing phrases:

17–18. *Nonsexual dehumanization* in which men and women are described as objects that are less than human (e.g., "resources," machine comparisons, weapons, animals, and/or plants). _____

19–20: Pictured dehumanization involves presenting people as sex objects as expressed by:

19. The *degree of undress* found in pictured models in ads:

a) scantily dressed: clothed but revealing contours or sex organs _____

b) partially clad: _____

c) naked: _____

20. *Degree of physical contact* found among couples pictured in ads:

a) holding hands: _____

b) arms around one or both partners: _____

c) kissing: _____

d) sexual or erotic poses (e.g., simulated intercourse): _____

e) other dehumanizing poses: _____

Now observe and record either (1) the dehumanization and inauthenticity themes in each ad, (2) the presence or absence of such themes (depending on the instructions of your professor). You may want to total the results for all your ads in a table like the following:

Table 1

Alienation in Advertising (in percent)

		Magazine	
	Time	*GQ*	*Cosmopolitan*
Verbal inauthenticity:	75	85	95
Pictured inauthenticity:	60	85	95
Verbal dehumanization:	75	85	95
Pictured dehumanization:	60	85	95

In each cell, the percentage of ads in each magazine where such themes were present is recorded.

You might want to compare ads from the 1950s and 1960s with the ads of the 1990s. This will reveal whether ads are becoming more or less inauthentic and/or dehumanizing.

The Sociological Imagination and the Analysis of Social Problems

Chapter 4

An Age of Crises

The world has become a mysterious place to many people. Values and relationships once thought permanent now easily fall by the wayside. The American dream of home ownership, enduring affluence, and U.S. economic and military power are now in question. A myriad of social problems, from huge government deficits and a declining middle class to crime, poverty, racism, sexism, ageism, overpopulation, permanent recession, and creeping inflation, now seem insoluble.

On a more personal level, the social character of our age now seems dominated by unique and insidious forms of alienation. As the Josephsons (1962:10) noted over thirty years ago,

> The alienation of our age is not found merely in statistics on crime, drug abuse, mental illness and suicide, but in "untold lives of quiet desperation that mark our age—the multitudes of factory and white-collar workers who find their jobs monotonous and degrading; the voters and nonvoters who feel hopeless or "don't care"; the juveniles who commit senseless acts of violence; the growing army of idle and lonely old people; . . . the stupefied audiences of the mass media."

> Indeed, the very nature of modern life is contradictory and schizoid: "Unparalleled economic growth has occurred side by side with the profoundest human misery; and struggles for freedom and enlightenment side by side with continuing social injustice." (Josephson & Josephson, 1962:9)

All these problems and many others have made our age one in which many people have adopted a stance of cynicism about other people and the future. The one great difference between America and the European nations from which most Americans initially emigrated was America's optimism. For nearly two centuries, people came to America's shores believing they would find a better life, and that belief persisted through wars, depressions, mass poverty, and violent repression of labor unions. For the first time in the nation's history the optimism of young and old, conservative and liberal, white and nonwhite is waning. The brilliant psychiatrist Kenneth Keniston (1965:1) described the decline in a positive future vision over three decades ago:

> Our age inspires scant enthusiasm . . . ardor is lacking, instead (people) talk, growing distant from each other, from their social order, from their work and play, and from values and heroes which in perhaps a romanticized past seem to have given meaning and coherence to their lives . . . . Alienation, once seen as imposed on (people) by an unjust economic system, is increasingly chosen . . . as their basic stance toward society . . . there has seldom been so much confusion about what is valid and good . . . more and more people question what their society offers and asks in return: hopeful visions of the future are increasingly rare.

The reaction of most Americans to their troubled world is to ignore it and deny it until it comes crashing in on them. A son is sent to war, a daughter is raped or becomes pregnant out of wedlock and obtains an abortion, a father is among millions of workers being laid off, a mother develops breast cancer—and soon the family learns that each of their private troubles is merely a symptom of a more widespread condition. The awareness of the sociological usually stops at this point. The skill that would allow these people to

Many Americans believe that the United States is a totally middle-class nation, and that sharp class distinctions do not exist here. However, social class is a major reality of American life. Currently the United States is the most inequitable of modern democracies regarding the distribution of wealth and income. Working-class people, like the blue-collar workers pictured above, are steadily becoming less well off, and many of their ranks are now composed of members of the working poor. Upper-middle and upper-class people, in contrast, are becoming steadily better off.

perceive the relationship between their personal biographies, the historical period in which they live, and the contradictory social structures responsible for their various crises remains undeveloped. Is it possible for the public to achieve an understanding of how society functions, and their place in it? Yes, it is.

If there is to be a better future, the development of a sociological imagination is essential. Only by relating seemingly personal troubles to social issues will social problems ever be resolved. Only by realizing that the social structure does impact one's personality traits and life choices can an opportunity for true freedom emerge. Only by realizing that the social structure and the dominant values thereof are the ultimate source of social problems can we begin to resolve the crises of our age.

How does one stay informed in such a world? Perhaps the greatest understanding of public issues can come from an appreciation of the differing dominant ideological viewpoints. Ideology is something Americans do not like to think about. However, ideology is a crucial aspect of the analysis of social problems, as well as an important feature of the sociological imagination.

The Quilt of Ideology and Policy

The resolution of social problems begins with a critique (deconstruction) of the dominant ideological groups within a society. A first myth of ideological analysis is the notion that social science and social policy are an objective enterprise. Nothing could be further from the truth. Social scientists "are influenced in their definition of what a social problem is by their own backgrounds and values," and ideologies (Roberts, 1978:4). It is often difficult, if not impossible, to separate ideology from science. As anthropologist Clifford Geertz notes, "Where, if anywhere, (values) leaves off and science begins has been the Sphinx's Riddle of much of modern sociological thought and the ruthless weapon of its enemies" (Geertz, 1964:48). Indeed, "ideology is the permanent hidden agenda" of the study of social problems (Miller, 1974:21).

Karl Marx noted that dominant ideologies are those that support the interests of dominant groups. Because they are backed by those in power, they are taken to be accurate accounts and explanations of social events. On closer analysis, however, dominant ideologies are at best half-truths based on "misleading arguments, incomplete analyses, unsupported assertions, and implausible premises that cast a veil over clear thinking" (Ferrante, 1992:289–290) and allow social problems to persist. Accordingly, to some degree, dominant ideologies mystify the causes of social problems (see below), and this is one reason why it is important to deconstruct them and reveal their shortcomings and contradictions.

Ideologies "form a . . . logically interrelated system" (Ladd, 1986:6). An ideology is like a quilt, with each position (stance) being a patch. Like quilt patches, an ideology is more than the sum of its patches (Ladd, 1986:7–8). The patches of the ideological quilt include beliefs about

1. the definition of a social problem;

2. what social problems are "serious" (i.e., crises) and which are less serious;

3. the causes of social problems;

4. the solution(s) to social problems;

5. the consequences to society various social problems will have if they go unresolved. Underlying ideological statements are assumptions about (1) the nature of human nature, and (2) the relationship between the individual and society, meaning whose rights should take precedence when a conflict occurs, those of the individual or the society's (Simon, 1977; 1981)?

Marx was the first to argue that "ideologies are ideas that do not hold up to the rigors of scientific investigation" (Ferrante, 1992:289). They tend to be more like articles of faith (theologies) (Walker, 1994:3–5), and may be far removed from the actual workings of societal institutions. Most ideological causal theories suffer from some unscientific dimension, and thus, such "theories" usually are scientifically untestable. This means they lack measurable independent and dependent variables. For example, one early criminological theory held that crime was caused by brain abnormalities that could be detected by studying the lumps and bumps on the skulls of criminals. At times, plaster casts were made of the heads of criminals, and head shapes were classified as "wolfmen," and "lionmen," reflecting assumptions about the animal nature of such criminals. These skull-shape classifications were used by prison personnel in determining how dangerous certain prisoners were. A more unreliable basis for crime policy is hardly imaginable, but the facts never got in the way of those who believed in the relationship between skull shapes and criminal activity.

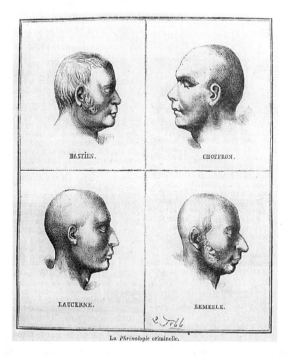

La *Phrénologie* criminelle.

Nineteenth-century conservative criminologists were convinced that criminals were biologic physically different than "normal" people, so much so that criminal minds could be recogr the "lump and bump" patterns on their skulls.

Sometimes these theories have been disconfirmed by scientific testing, yet the belief in them persists. For example, another early crime policy called *eugenics* was based on the causal theory that criminal traits were genetically inherited. The plan derived from eugenics called for the sterilization of many categories of criminals, including car thieves, people who stole chickens, and other robbers and burglars. Street criminals, along with other lower-class people, were considered biologically inferior because they had lost the great race for material success in America.

Despite scientific proof that there was no biological basis for crime or poverty, belief in this notion persisted long after proof challenging it was made public. What finally caused the belief that the poor were biologically inferior to go out of vogue was the Great Depression of the 1930s. Once the Depression hit, previously rich people and poor people stood in the same soup kitchen lines and benefitted from the same social programs. Since many of the previously rich were made poor by the 1929 stock market crash, they were in no position to advance theories about the biological inferiority of the poor. Again, policy and the ideological beliefs underlying it are loaded with values, biases, and frequently resemble religious faith much more than they do science.

The two dominant ideologies in American social science and politics are conservatism and liberalism. Both of these approaches have some elements in common:

1. Both accept the basic institutions of corporate capitalism and American democracy.
2. Both have failed to resolve the many social problems discussed above. This is because neither approach is sociological in nature. They do not understand the actual workings of most institutions and the contradictions contained therein.

These members of Mothers Against Drunk Driving (MADD) are involved in a public demonstration designed to bring their cause to the public attention, and, consequently, help get their concern officially defined as a social problem.

3. Albeit for different reasons, both have lost their vision of a positive future. One tragedy of American politics is that most of the criticisms conservatives and liberals have about each other are largely true.

The news media constantly reinforce conservative and liberal views of social problems and policy by the way they "frame" the causes and solutions of problems. As Wendy Griswold (1994:96–97) has noted, American culture emphasizes individual responsibility and personal control. No matter what the social problem, fault is always traced to individuals. A problem like drunk driving, for example, has been carefully constructed by interest groups like Mothers Against Drunk Driving (MADD) as the fault of "killer drunks." Powerful corporate interests, such as liquor companies and auto manufacturers, support this view of drunk driving as "poor judgment" by individuals, rather than pointing to advertising's encouraging people to drink or suggesting that drunk driving is unsafe or that there are too many automobiles. Likewise, villainization of individual drunk drivers forecloses many policy debates ("Who would be for drunk driving?"), and reinforces the notion that nonindividual solutions, like high taxes on gasoline or a better mass transit system, are unthinkable. Within MADD itself, high prestige is given to women whose children have been killed by drunk drivers. Mothers grieving for their dead children make powerful media images in a society where the *Pietà*—the Virgin Mary holding her dead son—is a respected idol (Griswold, 1994:96–97). In this way, social problems are molded so they are perceived within the framework of the culture's dominant value system. That value system is also reflected in the conservative and liberal ideologies that dominate American political life. The rightness of these ideologies, and the basic values on which they are based, are simply taken for granted. This position of dominance ensures that the numerous shortcomings and contradictions are rarely examined. The result is two failed ideologies.

Conservatism in Crisis

Conservatism is the oldest approach to defining and analyzing social problems. The main beliefs of conservatives include: (1) an emphasis on anomie, social pathology, and social disorganization as causes of deviance and social problems, and a preference for studying lower-class deviants as statistical categories, not as human beings; (2) a distrust of human nature (anti-egalitarianism) and a strong belief in the primacy of traditional institutions and established authority over individual freedom.

Conservative solutions include: (1) rejecting government intervention to improve the welfare of the poor, but approval of subsidies, and tax concessions for corporations and the wealthy; (2) emphasizing punishment and other forms of social control by government to reduce crime and other threats to established institutions of wealth and power (economic and political systems).

Conservative outcomes perceive a fear of a breakdown of moral order (anarchy). Conservatives define social problems as violations of what they perceive as absolute values. They believe social problems are caused by the failure of deviant individuals to conform to societal rules. Deviants are people who are "out of adjustment" to society because of some biological, psychological, and/or sociological (socialization) defect (Thio, 1988:13–15). Deviance consists of acts committed by members of certain lower orders of society (variously termed the lower classes, the masses, or deviant subcultures). This "dangerous class" exhibits "defective self-control, self-indulgence, limited time horizons (i.e., an inability to delay gratification) and an underdeveloped moral conscience" (Miller, 1973:35). Conservatives regard human nature as "the secular version of original sin" (Etzioni, 1977:1). Put bluntly, conservatives do not trust lower-class people, or people with values that conservatives oppose, like hippies, liberal intellectuals, and Hollywood leftists.

Conservatives call this supposed lack of moral rules among lower-class deviants anomie, and such individuals are labeled anomic. To conservatives, most social problems involve acts of lower-class deviance. Such problems include juvenile delinquency, "street" crime, prostitution, mental illness, drug addiction, and welfare cheating. These and other "nuts, sluts, and 'preverts' " (Liazos, 1972/1993:165) type deviants are considered the most serious of social problems.

Conservatives also fear that too much anomic behavior by deviant people will produce "social disorganization—a lack or breakdown in social organization reflected in weakened social control . . . inadequate socialization" (Horton, 1966: 598). If extreme, this lack of social control (law and order) might result in anarchy. Anarchy is complete breakdown of social order (variously described as chaos, riots, disorder, the breakdown of authority, and the end of civilization as we know it).

Elite deviance, whether it's scandals caused by the actions of corporations, political parties, or individual corporate executives and politicians, is dismissed as the overblown estimations of a liberal press (Garment, 1991). Conservatism is thus elitist. It favors the values of people occupying key posts in the nation's most wealthy corporations and governmental agencies and elites.

The problems with the conservative approach are considerable:

C. Wright Mills described some important biases of conservatism. First, conservatives regard as pathological or abnormal what is simply a lifestyle differing from "the norms of independent middle-class persons verbally living out Protestant ideals in small town America" (1943:87). Second, conservatives accept the structure of society as "at root, just" (Roberts, 1978:4), and consider institutions moral and unproblematic. Left unconsidered is the notion that the institution may be oppressive to the point of practically driving individuals crazy, or may contain other contradictions that cause serious social problems whose root causes are never addressed by policies.

This ignoring of institutional results is perhaps the most contradictory aspect of American conservatism. Conservatives laud the free enterprise system and the magic of the market, with its law of supply and demand. However, what if the free enterprise system produces X-rated movies, media violence, addicting drugs, and encourages gambling addiction? Conservatives blame the popularity of these problematic products on permissive liberals, or morally deficient (addictive) personalities. The free enterprise system's role in making a profit off the availability of such products is never mentioned. Moreover, it does not occur to conservatives that the entire basis of American capitalism is gambling with invested money in the form of venture capital, stocks, and bonds.

This is in part what C. Wright Mills meant when he noted that conservatism is an ideology trying to uphold a liberal tradition (1956:335). What is liberal here is the freedom of expression and creativity required to create the very products that conservatives feel are so decadent. Contradictory beliefs haunt American conservatism. Conservatives favor the government's staying out of people's private lives, yet favor government regulation (even banning) of abortions. They claim to favor the right to life, yet support capital punishment, and freely eat animal meat. They favor the First Amendment, yet believe political protest will lead to anarchy. In short, conservatism is an ideology loaded with contradictions.

There is mounting evidence that most conservative policies are failures. For example, conservatives for twelve years advocated a "get tough" approach on street crime. The number of Americans in prisons more than doubled between 1980 and 1990, but America's crime rate went up, not down, during those years (Walker, 1994). The rich accumulated greater wealth, but the economy did not prosper. Between 1982 and 1992 America experienced the longest recession since World War II, and millions of middle-class Americans experienced a decline in their living standards (Phillips, 1993). The defense budget quadrupled and tax cuts for the rich were enacted. Instead of the promised balanced budget, a quadrupling of the national debt occurred, the largest such increase in the two hundred–year history of the nation (Phillips, 1990). In short, conservatism is an ideology in crisis and disrepute largely because it has failed in practice.

Conservatism is contradictory in that its positive vision of the future is about idealizing the past. President Reagan was elected in 1980 by promising to bring America back to the year 1955. In 1955, inflation and unemployment were both running at 1 percent, and there were no apparent problems with AIDS, drug addiction, racism, child and spouse abuse, or many other crises haunting contemporary American life. Conservatism is a failed ideology of, by, and for the wealthy and powerful.

Liberalism in Disrepute

According to Sargent (1993), liberal beliefs about causes of social problems include: (1) ambivalence about human nature. People possess both good and bad characteristics, and are capable for changing for the better; (2) seeing social problems as merely social constructions, competing definitions of reality (not based on absolute values).

Liberal beliefs about solutions center on a faith in government intervention and limited reform to increase human welfare.

The liberal view of outcomes shows a lack of a positive future vision and fear of abuse of governmental power resulting in a totalitarian state like that described by George Orwell (in *1984*) (Simon, 1977, 1981). This is an all encompassing dictatorship based on government spying ("Big brother is watching you"), illogical propaganda (doublespeak and doublethink), and the constant preparation for and engaging in armed conflict (i.e., a permanent warfare state).

For liberals, social problems are not violations of absolute definitions of right and wrong, but are the outcomes of political contests between conflicting definitions of morality (values). Social problems are merely products of collective definition and actions by special interest groups who have successfully pressed their demands in the political arena.

Winners in this process have their "values embodied in . . . law . . . deviations from these standards (are) labeled as crimes" (Gibbons & Garabedian, 1974:51). Social problems are conditions recognized by either a significant number of people, or a number of significant people (Roberts, 1978:5; Manis, 1974; Rose, 1957). This is the height of value relativism.

Liberals believe that institutions in charge of punishing or rehabilitating deviants are "screwed up" (Gibbons & Garabedian, 1974:52), that the elites who run them must lie about what goes on there. This is because institutions do not function properly (Becker, 1967). Liberals advocate whistle blowing as a solution to the problems of defective total institutions. Liberalism displays a distinct lack of solutions to the social problems that are its concern.

There are a number of strengths and weaknesses of the liberal position:

1. The liberal view of social problems as social construction is valuable. It sheds light on the process by which officials recognize and act upon social problems. Yet, this view of social problems goes too far in emphasizing the value-relative nature of reality. There are certain conditions, such as homicide, incest, theft, torture, of which most cultures have disapproved throughout history.

2. Another problem with the social construction approach is that it is not much of a causal theory. It says very little about why groups of people become upset about social conditions initially. There is no concept of socially patterned harm in liberal thought.

3. Liberals tend to favor endless piecemeal reforms. Liberals accept as relatively unproblematic the basic structure of corporate capitalism and a political system that heavily favors the wealthy and powerful. Occasionally there may be certain structural pockets of unemployment, crime, slight structural defects, pockets of poverty (like rural poverty), but overall the system is thought to provide equal opportunities for most. In short, liberalism as an ideology is in crisis, but the reasons for its woes are not the same as the problems of conservatism.

   Liberalism is in crisis for two interrelated reasons. First, the perceived failure of the Great Society programs of the 1960s resulted in many liberals becoming cynical about the possibility of social experimentation by government. For a number of years thereafter, liberal sociologists advocated that liberals merely critique the workings of institutions and remain "on the side" (Gusfield, 1984) when it came to advocating institutional reform. This is one reason why President Clinton ran as "the man from Hope," and portrayed himself as a "centrist," not a liberal. Liberalism is an ideology without a firm agenda of solutions aimed at repairing the nation's ills and is, therefore, an ideology without direction.

   Second, the failure of the reforms of the 1960s together with a number of major scandals (like Vietnam, Watergate, Iran-Contra, the savings and loan "crisis") made liberals cynical regarding the future. Liberalism, in short, experienced "the decline of utopia" (Keniston, 1965). This means that liberalism lost a view of a positive future for America and the world. An ideology without a positive vision of the future is an ideology in decline. George Bush learned this lesson when he failed to master "the vision thing," as he termed it. Liberalism is an ideology not even advocated by liberals anymore.

4. As C. Wright Mills (1963) noted, liberalism was born in the Enlightenment, an eighteenth-century philosophical movement stressing the rational and perfectible side of human nature. The notion that human nature is rational is questionable. Writers like Karl Marx, Sigmund Freud, Max Weber, and Karl Mannheim all pointed out the irrational influences on rational thought by the unconscious mind, one's position in the social class system, and how large-scale bureaucracies dominated the world. Many historical events of the twentieth century (the death of over 50 million people in wars, Hitler's genocide of Europe's Jews, the atom bomb) have caused liberals to question seriously the

rational human nature. In the process, they have lost hope in a positive future vision. Liberals fear the "police-state methods of totalitarianism" (Wise, 1976:412) adopted by even supposedly democratic governments.

Studying Policy: The Critique of Conventional Wisdom

One of the most important dimensions of critiquing ideologies is exposing the myths and realities upon which policies are based. Such a critique begins with a clear understanding of the nature of policies. Policies are "more or less clearly articulated sets of ideas about what should be done about" a particular social problem or set of social problems (Marshall, 1994:492). Such policies are often set down in writing, and usually require formal adoption by a decision-making body, such as the U.S. Congress or various state legislatures.

Policies are often confused with plans, but they are not the same things. Plans specify in detail the way certain objectives are to be reached. Policies, in contrast, are stated in more general terms, and often involve only objectives and intended directions for change, not detailed instructions on how to implement specific programs. For example, both Republicans, and Democrats have announced a policy to balance the federal budget within several years' time, but they differ substantially in their specific plans for budget balancing. Republicans want drastic reductions in social programs and large tax cuts. In contrast, Democrats are opposed to cuts in many of the social programs, such as Medicare. One particular problem, however, demonstrates the lack of realism regarding dominant schools of ideological thought. This is the issue of violent crime.

Policy Deconstruction and the Sociological Imagination: Crime as a Case Study

Both conservative and liberal solutions to the crime problem have failed to accomplish their objective—reducing rates of crime. This is because both ideologies are based on mythical notions concerning what causes crime, and the way the criminal justice system works. The conservative model of crime control resembles that of the patriarchal family. Crime, for conservatives, is caused by anomic individuals who make freely willed, rational choices to commit criminal acts. Thus crime is viewed as a failure of individuals to exercise personal responsibility (Walker, 1994:17).

The solution to the crime problem is to deter criminals and would-be criminals from committing crime by inflicting appropriate punishment—swift, severe, and certain—on guilty parties. Punishment is meted out in degrees that match the severity of the offense committed. The more severe the punishment, the more likely it is thought to have a deterrent effect (Walker, 1994:17–19).

The great failure in their approach lies in the fact that criminal reality bears little resemblance to family discipline. Punishment within families works best when it is meted out by a loved and trusted parent in an informal manner, and involves a certain amount of shaming behavior. The family analogy breaks down in the real world of crime and street criminals. This is because the society in which we live is one where the bonds of attachment and mutual trust between family members have to an alarming degree broken down. But conservatives insist that the failure of punishment is the fault of the criminal justice system, with its numerous loopholes that protect criminals more than victims. What is needed, conservatives insist, is to close legal loopholes that grant rights to accused people, and mete out swifter and more severe punishment. Only then, conservatives argue, will crime rates be reduced.

Much of this reasoning is just plain wrong, yet conservatives and the mass media have convinced the public that the criminal justice system's policies actually have some effect on the crime rate. A 1989 poll revealed that 80 percent of the public continues to believe the courts are too lenient, but the facts belie this notion (Kappeler et al., 1993:194). Yet, the rate of imprisoning people in the United States doubled between 1980 and 1990, and is expected to double again by the year 2000 (Irwin & Austin, 1994:1–5). America's incarceration rate is now the highest in the world and growing (see Table 4.1).

One in every four black males, ages twenty to twenty-nine, in 1989 was either in prison, on probation, or on parole. On a given day over 1.4 million Americans are either in jail or prison, and another 3.1 million are either on probation or parole. Accordingly, some five million Americans are under correctional supervision in this country (Irwin & Austin, 1994:3–5). According to the Brookings Institution, if imprisonment continues at its current rate, by the year 2054 half of the U.S. population will have been incarcerated (*The Progressive*, 1994:8).

And what has the "lock 'em up and throw the key away" binge accomplished over the last decade? For one thing, it has gotten many conservative politicians elected on this basis of simplistic, quick-fix promises. These conservatives are extremely good at making wild

Table 4.1		
World Incarceration **Rates per 100,000 Citizens, 1990–1991**		
United States	455	
South Africa	311	
Canada	111	
Australia	79	
Denmark	71	
Japan	42	
India	34	
Source: Bureau of Criminal Justice Statistics; Skolnick, 1995:3.		

claims in favor of building new prisons, but woefully neglectful in telling voters how they intend to pay for them. Between 1973 and 1994, the United States spent $42 billion on prison construction. (This does not include the $23,500 average cost of maintaining each prisoner per year.) So the first result of this failed policy has been to increase the cost of government and further fuel the fires of government indebtedness.

Has the cost been worth it? Has the crime rate declined? As Table 4.2 indicates, the doubling of the prison population was accompanied by a 22 percent increase in the crime rate between 1980 and 1993. In other words, increasing incarceration is not only *not* a deterrent to crime, but there is increasing evidence that it actually results in more crime. Why is this so?

Well, the "lock 'em up" binge has produced overcrowded prison conditions in nearly forty states. It is now the case that many states can not build new facilities fast enough to keep pace with their prison populations. As a result, the "lock 'em up" policy ends up causing the conservative's worst nightmare—namely, the early release of prisoners. Nationwide, the average prisoner now serves only one-third of his/her original sentence. This is one reason why the new "three strikes and you're out" initiative will have little effect on crime rates. Criminals are rarely convicted of their third offenses until late in their criminal careers (after age twenty-three). The three-time losers are thus likely to occupy prison space that needs occupying by younger, more aggressive criminals, who, by necessity, will be granted early release (Skolnick, 1995:5).

Second, contrary to some people's beliefs, prisons that hold street criminals are not resorts. They offer some genuinely degrading conditions, including assault, rape, drugs, beatings, and stabbings. It is not difficult to see why many convicts leave prison feeling angrier, meaner, and worse about themselves and their society than when they entered prison.

Third, many prisons have become classrooms for teaching prisoners how to commit more serious types of crime. Nearly two-thirds of all federal prisoners and almost the same number of state prison inmates have been incarcerated for drug-related offenses (Irwin & Austin, 1994:32–34). In prison, they learn how to commit property and violent crimes.

What should be clear to all but the most diehard of conservative ideologues is that the policies of the criminal justice system do not cause crime, and, hence, do not reduce it. Indeed, the entire point here is that if we really want to find out what causes crime, we must look outside the criminal justice system, beyond the crime policy myths and misconceptions, and into those aspects of American life that really do cause crime. For example, both conservatives and liberals begin with the premise that the policies of the criminal justice system can lower crime rates. There is not now, nor has there ever been, the slightest proof that this is the case. Neither conservatives nor liberals possess a realistic picture of either what causes crime or how the criminal justice system actually functions. One reason why this is true is that both sides refuse to consider facts that contradict whatever ideological biases they hold. Unfortunately the assumptions and biases of both groups are constantly perpetuated by the mass media, whose owners and employees share these same wrongheaded notions. Media messages are translated into stereotypical pictures and scripts concerning what America's "good" values are and how power in America is structured. The picture that emerges is one of a black-and-white (right and wrong) world in which live only criminals and honest folk, good institutions and some bad apples who are responsible for corrupting government and business. All of this is a gigantic distortion of the way the crime problem works.

Table 4.2

Crime Rates and Punishment, 1980–1993

	CHANGE IN RATES OF VIOLENT CRIME	PERCENT INCREASE IN FEDERAL AND STATE PRISON POPULATIONS
1980	0	0
1985	−1	60
1990	20	140
1993	22	180

Source: Bureau of Criminal Justice Statistics.

All of these wrongheaded policies are perpetuated by a series of myths about the criminal justice system (Walker, 1994). Some of the leading crime policy myths might include the following:

- *Myth:* A survey made in Illinois in the 1980s found that most people believe the insanity defense is used in about 40 percent of all criminal trials.

- *Fact:* The insanity defense is used in less than 2 percent of all criminal trials; almost all of its uses are in murder trials. Of those cases where it is employed, it is successfully accepted in less than .1 of 1 percent of all felony cases. Eliminating the insanity defense would thus have virtually no effect on crime rates, including homicide rates. In those rare instances where the insanity defense is accepted, it is permitted because all parties (defense attorneys, prosecuting attorneys, expert witnesses, and judges) agree that the defendant is legally insane.

- *Myth:* The exclusionary rule, which excludes illegally seized evidence from being used in court (established in *Mapp* v. *Ohio,* (1961), allows thousands of would-be criminals to go free each year.

- *Fact:* The *Mapp* rule concerning the inadmissibility of illegally gathered evidence was already in use by about half of the states before the *Mapp* ruling. The exclusionary rule is actually used in less than 5 percent of all court cases; almost none of these cases are robberies or burglaries (serious felonies). Moreover, in those cases where the exclusionary rule is requested, it is successful in only .69 of 1 percent of the time on the federal and state levels. Looking just at the federal level, the General Accounting Office of the U. S. Government found that the exclusionary rule is requested in about 11 percent of all federal cases, but is permitted in only 1.3 percent of all cases. The rule is actually good for the criminal justice system because it keeps the police honest, and maintains the integrity of the judiciary.

- *Myth*: *Miranda* v. *Arizona* (1966), which mandates that suspects be apprised of their rights upon arrest, results in the dismissal of thousands of cases each year merely because the police forget or didn't have time to read someone's rights to him or her.

- *Fact*: *Miranda* warning failures make up only a minuscule percentage of the cases that are dismissed each year. Between 40 and 50 percent of all suspects still confess voluntarily, and another one-third don't exercise their right to counsel at all. Since nearly 60 percent of street crime suspects haven't finished high school, a surprising number of them don't even understand *Miranda* rights when read to them. It is also a myth that police must read suspects their rights at the point of arrest. These rights do not have to be communicated to suspects until questioning begins, but Hollywood almost always portrays the rights being imparted directly after a fierce struggle to subdue the criminal.

- *Myth*: Eliminating plea bargaining would reduce crime.

- *Fact*: Plea bargaining, pleading guilty in exchange for a reduced sentence, is an integral part of the criminal justice system. Without it, many time-consuming trials might take place, and the already overcrowded courts would become clogged with cases. In the one place where the practice was abolished, Alaska, the charges brought against suspects remained the same in nearly two-thirds of all cases. Moreover, the elimination of plea bargaining had no measurable effect on the overall Alaskan crime rate. One of the main reasons plea bargaining is not an important element in crime policy is that arrests are made in only 21 percent of all crimes reported to police.

- *Myth*: Closing other legal loopholes would drastically reduce the crime rate.

- *Fact*: Closing whatever loopholes remain would do precious little good because there are virtually no loopholes left. In San Diego, California, a program to target repeat offenders raised the conviction rate from 89.5 to 91.5 percent. These results were modest because convictions rates were already very high. And San Diego is not exceptional at all in this regard. The United States has one of the highest conviction rates in the world for stranger-on-stranger felony offenses. This is the reason why jail and prison populations shot up so dramatically in the 1980s, and are expected to double again by the year 2000.

Liberal Myths and Crime Policies

Like conservatives, liberals too possess time-honored and dead wrong assumptions about crime being caused by the policies of the criminal justice system. If conservative crime policy is based on the notion that the criminal justice system can reduce crime by functioning as a punishing father figure, liberals tend to reduce the criminal justice system to a huge classroom. The prison is viewed as an institution capable of rehabilitating criminals. A major problem here is that little agreement exists about what the term *rehabilitation* means, and even if a definition could be agreed upon, there is little credible evidence that rehab programs have much success. One important reason why this is true is that some criminals are incorrigible, crime is the only way of life they know. Some have been in prison for so long, they do not know how to function outside prison walls. This fact has not stopped liberal reformers from continuing to seek the correct magic rehabilitation policy.

In consequence, when prisons had obviously failed to alter criminal behavior, various experiments in rehabilitation, such as probation, parole, individual diagnosis and group counseling, and intensive supervision of parolees, were attempted. "None of these changes seem to make the correctional process work" (Walker, 1994:18).

The one reform convict program that has proven effective is giving ex-cons a job on release from prison. The problem here is that the tragic state of the American economy prohibits the full employment of many honest folk, let alone former convicts.

Second, the liberal approach to crime policy is contradictory regarding the issue and nature of individual responsibility. Liberals do emphasize the role of certain social conditions, such as family breakup, domestic abuse, racism, poverty, and unemployment, in contributing to the crime problem. Yet their prescribed rehabilitation policies are aimed at changing individual behavior, getting criminals to change their decision to commit a crime.

The recently passed Clinton crime law is designed to deter crime by putting more police on the streets. The Clinton program advocated 100,000 new police officers, but the actual number of new officers may end up at around 20,000. In any case, there is no hard evidence that increasing the number of police actually lowers crime rates. In the famous Kansas City experiments, three zones were established. One zone had twice the usual number of police patrols. Another zone had the normal number of police. A third zone had all police patrols removed. The police still entered this "empty" zone when requested by citizen phone calls. Surprisingly, crime remained at normal levels in all the zones in the experiment. More police, the usual number of police, or no police, the effects were all the

Many liberals used to believe that inmate therapy programs and other forms of rehabilitation could be effective in reducing recidivism rates.

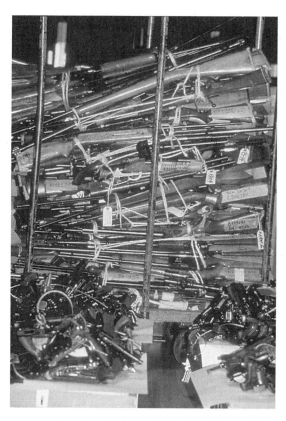

This cache of guns represents only a few of the over 215 million firearms that are in private hands in the United States. One reason for the failure of most gun control legislation is that it neglects the fact that the gun ownership problem is already profoundly out of control, that in many respects there is nothing left to control.

same. Similar real-life experiments have produced similar results. Some good might be done if when police were added to a city's force, they were proactive in their approach to crime. Actively patrolling, asking questions, and stopping suspects do seem to help a little. The dirty little secret of police work, however, is that many murders and assaults do not take place on the streets, but indoors. The police don't learn of these crimes until after they've happened. In addition, it is doubtful that more police will act as a deterrent to crime. Interviews with robbers confirm that only 22 percent of them bothered to check for police patrols before committing their robberies.

Another individual choice liberals wish to influence concerns the choice to purchase a gun. Gun control laws with real teeth, liberals argue, will reduce crime rates. Gun control laws, however, come in a wide variety of forms, from outright bans on guns within city limits, to waiting periods and registration involving gun owners. The problem with all gun control legislation is that there are already over 215 million firearms in private hands in the United States. There is simply almost nothing left to control. The ownership of guns is profoundly out of control in America. What about controlling ammunition?

This would provide organized crime with one more illegal monopoly to establish that would net them very big bucks.

We have also noted the liberal belief in social construction/labeling theory as a cause of social problems. Liberals argue that un-labeling (legalizing) prostitution and gambling would reduce the crime rate. Yet legalizing these vices would have almost no effect on the violent crime rate. Most clients of prostitutes and most gamblers are not violent criminals. They are rather ordinary people afflicted with ordinary vices.

What should be clear from our discussion is that the policies of the criminal justice system do not cause crime. If we really want to find out what causes street crime we must look outside the criminal justice system, and into those aspects of American life that really do cause crime: illegal drug abuse, poverty, unemployment, family breakup, child abuse, lack of educational and economic opportunity, the transfer of manufacturing jobs outside the United States by multinational corporations, violence in the media, and the constant advertising inducements to buy the latest products. These causes are discussed in depth throughout this book.

What should also be clear is that conservative and liberal approaches to crime have resulted in wasting billions of dollars in building prisons and experimenting with questionable rehabilitation programs. None of these policies have perceptively altered crime rates, and, in many instances, they have probably increased them. The example of crime policy points up the importance of being able to recognize the myths and misconceptions regarding solutions to social problems proposed by dominant ideological groups. This is why critiquing conventional ideological wisdom is an important element of the sociological imagination.

This critique of the policies advanced by dominant ideological groups concludes our examination of the elements of the sociological imagination paradigm. The next step in using the sociological imagination is to analyze various macro and micro social problems using the various elements of the paradigm.

Applying the Sociological Imagination: The Analysis of Social Problems

The sociological imagination rests on basic concepts and definitions regarding social problems. Social problems are conditions involving socially patterned harms. In examining the major macro and micro social problems that confront the postmodern world, we shall utilize the key analytical elements of the sociological imagination paradigm:

1. *Social Structures and Institutional Contradictions: The Power Elite, Global Capitalism, and Massive Inequality*

    The power elite dominates the social structure of mass society in the postmodern era. This elite consists of large corporations, the executive and legislative branches of the federal government, and that group of organizations that make up what we have described as the military-industrial complex and its "secret government."

The power elite functions within the environment of the postmodern system of global capitalism. The economies of the global capitalist system are divided into modern (First World), semi-modern (old Soviet Bloc states/Second World), and Third World (poor and struggling to modernize nations). First World multinational firms increasingly extract raw materials, cheap labor, and surplus profits from Third World Nations, whose international debts continue to mount.

Contradictions within the structure of society, as well as the global political economy, are the cause of social problems. The capitalist world system tends toward instability at numerous "flashpoints," and wars, revolutions, and terrorism are common in the face of massive international inequalities. Likewise, the central contradiction of American life is the built-in conflict between the power elite that has amassed an undemocratic amount of wealth, political power, and the power to define cultural values, and the many who lack such power, wealth, and ability to define values. Such values include the unlimited accumulation of private property, consumerism and materialism, celebrity worship, and a belief in "rugged" individualism in an organizational society. Many of these values constitute alienating conditions of inauthenticity and dehumanization that, in turn, cause feelings of alienation in masses of individuals.

2. *Social Problems as Socially Patterned Harms and the Higher Immorality*

Social problems consist of physical, financial, and/or moral harms that result from great inequalities of wealth, political power, and the ability of one group to define cultural values. Among the most important types of socially patterned harms in the global economy and contemporary American society are a set of institutionalized deviant and/or criminal behaviors among the power elite. Collectively, these deviant practices are termed the higher immorality. These practices involve deception and manipulation of the public, corruption, corporate crime, and, occasionally, cooperation with organized crime syndicates. All the practices associated with the higher immorality are in and of themselves major social problems and they, in turn, cause further problems, especially micro social problems among nonelites.

3. *Social Character and Alienation: The Antisocial Social Character, Inauthenticity, and Dehumanization*

The dominant social character in mass society is a person who dislikes or is indifferent to work; is politically, societally, and self-alienated; and is prone to be engaged in various degrees and types of "wilding" (deviant acts). The antisocial social character tends to escape into mass culture, and engages in personal relationships through interpersonal manipulation and self-deception. The inauthentic and dehumanizing contents of postmodern culture reinforce various forms of personal alienation.

The inauthentic and/or dehumanizing forms of alienation within postmodern culture constitute a special cause of social problems, one that contributes to a host of micro social problems, including drug abuse, nonelite crime, mental illness, dysfunctional families, and domestic abuse, as well as racism, sexism, and ageism.

4. *Critiquing Conventional Wisdom—Analyzing Policy Failure Among Dominant Ideological Groups: The Failure of Conservatism and Liberalism*

The policies advanced by conservatives and liberals have failed to resolve the major socially patterned harms of the postmodern era. The underlying assumptions and myths that justify these policies are part of a "conventional wisdom" that must be exposed if the root causes of social problems are to be exposed, and viable solutions are to be introduced.

These elements of the sociological imagination paradigm are used in analyzing the macro and micro social problems in Parts II and III of this book. This analysis of social problems will also produce a portrait of the master trends of the postmodern era. The specific nature of socially patterned harms, the forms of social character and alienation produced within a given social structure, and the conventional wisdom that functions to limit human liberation provide valuable clues for how meaningful social change can be accomplished in the future.

To this end, each of the chapters that follows contains "Private Troubles/ Public Issues" forums, that demonstrate ways in which the social problems under discussion personally affect your life, and what you can do about them. Some of these discussions are guides for personal change (such as enhancing your self-esteem, improving your nutrition, or making wise consumer choices). Others deal with how you can personally get involved with resolving social problems (like what you can do to help homeless people). The sociological imagination is not just a paradigm; it is a way of life that can be used as a basis for personal decisions regarding the challenges of daily life. At its best, sociology is a healing art, and these forums are presented in the hope that they will enrich your personal life, as well as your life as a citizen of a democracy.

Summary

The postmodern world is a source of confusion to many people. Citizens lack a set of tools that can be used to analyze the causes and solutions of social problems. Part of the sociological imagination involves the ability to critique the dominant ideological schools of thought whose beliefs dramatically influence the making of public policy. Ideological writing involves assumptions about:

1. the definition of a social problem;

2. what social problems are "serious" (i.e., crises) and which are less serious;

3. the causes of social problems;

4. the solution(s) of social problems; and

5. the consequences to society that various social problems will have if they go unresolved. Underlying ideological statements are assumptions about the nature of human nature, and the relationship between the individual and society (meaning whose rights should take precedence when a conflict occurs, those of the individual or society's?).

The two dominant ideologies in American life are conservatism and liberalism. Conservatives view social problems as caused by deviant (anomic) individuals. They believe that imposing social control, such as imprisonment, upon deviant individuals will resolve major social problems.

Liberals tend to view social problems as being caused by certain power imbalances that result in the undemocratic possession of power by special interest groups. Liberals believe in the modest changing of individuals (rehabilitation) and institutions (reform and regulation by government) in resolving social problems.

Both conservative and liberal approaches have failed to resolve the nation's leading social problems. The conservative "lock 'em up and throw the key away" approach of the last two decades, and its emphasis on increased imprisonment, has not reduced the crime rate. The liberal approach to crime, involving rehabilitation of criminals, has similarly failed to reduce crime. Neither the conservative nor the liberal approach will work because both fail to address the sociological causes of crime, and, instead remain focused on the wrongheaded notion that the policies of the criminal justice system cause crime. The failure of both conservative and liberal approaches to public policy underscores the importance of critiquing dominant ideological schools of thought as a key element of the sociological imagination.

The critique of dominant ideologies completes the sociological imagination paradigm that is used in the analysis of social problems throughout the remainder of this book. These elements include:

1. Social structures and institutional contradictions, including the global capitalist system and the American power elite, with its massive inequalities in wealth, political power, and the ability to shape cultural values.

2. The social problems, physical, financial, and/or moral harms resulting from the above contradictions, including a set of institutionalized deviant practices among elites collectively termed the higher immorality.

3. The inauthentic and/or dehumanizing forms of alienation involved in such harms.

4. The policy failures of the conservative and liberal ideological perspectives to resolve socially patterned harms.

Taken together, these analytical elements of the sociological imagination provide valuable insights regarding the "main drift" of the postmodern era.

Suggested Readings

Gerald Posner (1993) *Case Closed* (New York: Random House). This book represents perhaps the best defense of the Warren Commission in the three-decade-long debate over the assassination of President Kennedy.

Oliver Stone and Zachary Sklar (1991) *JFK: The Book of the Film* (New York: Audience Press). The screenplay to Stone's *JFK*, plus over ninety reactions to the movie. A solid introduction to the JFK assassination debate and the radical position therein.

Samuel Walker (1994) *Sense and Nonsense About Crime and Drugs: A Policy Guide,* 3rd ed. (Belmont, CA: Wadsworth). This is the best treatment of the failure of conservative and liberal crime policy. The book exposes numerous myths about the effect of various criminal justice system policies on the violent crime problem.

Exercises

Critical Thinking Exercise 4.1	Ideological Content Analysis

The following is an exercise in ideological content analysis. Doing this exercise will accomplish several ends:

1. The exercise introduces students to the world of social critics. Many social critics, like Senator Daniel Moynihan, have become influential in the policy-making process.

2. Examining the ideologies of others will also give you an opportunity to examine your own ideological beliefs and values. This can be a meaningful experience in self-reflection.

3. The methodology you will use in this exercise, content analysis, is a research tool useful in studying any form of communication. The method itself can serve you well in undergraduate or graduate classes. Content analysis has the great advantage of being easily learned by undergraduate students. Moreover, representative, random probability samples of data are as far away as the local college library, video store, or television set/VCR. Few other methods offer these advantages for research.

4. Finally, the periodicals recommended in this exercise constitute elite journals of social criticism. Reading one or more of them on a regular basis constitutes a first-rate way to stay informed about important social issues that are either not covered by the press, or covered, but from a "mainstream" perspective only.

    In short, learning ideological content analysis can have a utility far beyond a simple research exercise.

The Ideologies of American Social Critics

An expanded version of this exercise appeared in *Teaching Political Science* in July 1981. Three of the periodicals listed in Figure 4.1 are new additions: *American Prospect, Foreign Policy,* and *Tikkun.* Instructors, of course, may add others of their own choosing. I allow students to use such periodicals as *Esquire* and *GQ* when their articles are appropriate.

    I see no significant changes in the content of either conservatism or liberalism since 1981, with the possible exception of the so-called neoliberalism championed by President Clinton and the Democratic Leadership Council. Frankly, the only difference between this new liberalism and old-style liberalism is that the neoliberals want to cut government spending and reduce the deficit. I know of no ideological group that does not want to reduce the deficit, so this issue does not make for much of a distinction.

While this exercise is rewarding, it does require a fair amount of instruction, and I suggest that you do a pilot study on one or two articles before you attempt to analyze a sample of a dozen or more. Feel free to alter the size of the sample and the number of periodicals to suit your needs. I suggest students and instructors go through the instructions together, slowly, to clear up any uncertainties that may arise.

Ideology Awareness Project: An Exercise in Item Unit Content Analysis

This is an exercise in the analysis of the ideological content of writings in journals of social criticism. This will be most students' introduction to such periodicals. Thus the exercise not only teaches you to use content analysis as a research method but introduces you to the ideological statements of America's leading social critics.

Undergraduates often complain about the necessity of writing term papers, most of which end up being merely exercises in regurgitation. The ideological content analysis exercise is a response to this group. Familiarity with the various ideological perspectives among American social critics also allows you to analyze virtually any unit of communication that has some ideological content (newspaper editorials and political columns, commentary on television news programs, television interviews with people holding strong political opinions, and so on).

The phases of the project parallel the phases of most research projects. The sampling universe from which articles may be drawn is taken from Charles Kadushin's (1974) list of the top periodicals of social criticism in the United States. The list of periodicals and the initial choices of samples from which you may draw are described in Figure 4.1.

After selecting articles at random from the journals listed or selected, code each article for its ideological content. Enter the relevant codes on a coding sheet modeled on Figure 4.2, using the codes in Figure 4.3. Use the entire article as the unit of analysis. The coding categories used to determine the ideological orientation of each article consist of causal codes (which refer to the cause or causes of a given problem), solution codes (which refer to the policy or policies proposed to resolve a given problem or set of problems), and outcome codes (which refer to the predicted consequences of a given problem or set of problems if the solution or solutions proposed are not put into effect).

Give each article an overall ideological rating (9 on the coding sheet, Fig. 4.2) in accordance with the following rules:

1. Assign the overall ideological rating of the article on the basis of the *causal* and *solution* codes only; outcome codes at times tend to cut across ideological borders. (All causal, solution, and outcome codes are listed in Figure 4.3).

2. If an article discusses a cause but suggests no solution, determine the ideological rating of the article on the basis of the causal code only. Though it is possible for an article to discuss only solutions or only outcomes, with no reference whatever to a cause, this is almost never the case. Even pieces that are concerned primarily with prediction tend to begin with a causal analysis as a reference point.

3. Should discussions of either causes, solutions, or outcomes fall outside the categories used here, code them as "Other" (codes 4d, 5d, and 7d, respectively).

4. In any case, when an article both analyzes a cause and proposes a solution, the cause and solution must be of the same ideological type for the entire piece of writing to be classified as conservative, liberal, or socialist. Should the ideological content of a piece of writing be mixed or fall outside the various causes and solutions outlined in Figure 4.3, code the entire piece as 7d ("Mixed"). This tends to happen in about six of every one hundred cases.

5. No specific list of social problem codes is given here because such a list is virtually endless, and the rules for coding various categories of social problems, crime, and deviance are extremely complicated. (See Simon, 1975, 1977; Funkhouser, 1973.) However, I recommend that instructors keep such codes as simple as possible: Assign an article or other piece of writing a social problem/crime/deviance code on the basis of its major theme; don't assign a separate code for every social problem mentioned in it.

After you have coded each article, select examples of causes, solutions, and/or outcomes in the form of either direct quotes from the materials read or summaries of such passages in your own words. Write your examples on the appropriate lines on the coding sheet.

This exercise often provokes students to examine their own ideological beliefs. Students often report that the exercise has made them much more aware of the ideological content of newspaper editorials, television commentaries, and the like. It is here that the lasting value of this exercise may be found.

Figure 4.1

Exercise in Ideological Content Analysis

1. Select ten articles for analysis. You may divide your sample in any of the following ways:

   (a) Select ten articles from any one periodical published in 1994.

   (b) Select ten articles from any two periodicals published in 1994.

   (c) Select ten articles from a single periodical, five published in 1993 and five in 1994. This option will allow you to gain an understanding of a change in ideological orientation over time.

   (d) Select ten articles written on a *single topic* that have appeared in any of the periodicals listed below since 1980.

2. Select articles at random; that is, all articles (other than book reviews and editorials) should have an equal chance of being selected. The articles may deal with any of the topics covered in this course.

3. Code all articles for cause(s), solution(s), and outcome(s), in accordance with the codes listed in Figure 4.3. Not all articles will contain examples of all

Figure 4.2

Coding Sheet

1. Periodical no. _____ 2. Article no. _____ 3. Year _____ 4. Page no. _____

5. Topic(s) _____

6. Causal code _____ Example★ _____

_____

_____

_____

7. Solution code _____ Example★ _____

_____

_____

8. Outcome code _____ Example★ _____

_____

_____

9. Ideological rating of article _____

_____

categories listed. If a category is not represented, simply write "none" after that category on the coding sheet.

Periodicals and codes★

01 *American Scholar*	11 *Public Interest*
02 *Atlantic Monthly*	12 *Progressive*
03 *Dissent*	13 *Saturday Review*
04 *Harper's*	14 *Social Policy*
05 *Mother Jones*	15 *Society*
06 *Nation*	16 *Village Voice*
07 *New Republic*	17 *Washington Monthly*
08 *New Yorker* (especially "Letter from Washington")	18 *Yale Review*
09 *New York Review of Books*	19 *American Prospect*
10 *Partisan Review*	20 *Foreign Policy*
	21 *Tikkun*

★Instructors may of course use other periodicals of their choosing.

Figure 4.3

Codes

1. Periodical no. (01–21) (see list of periodicals in Fig. 4.1)

2. Article no. (01 to 10).

3. Social problem or problems (to be coded by instructor).

4. *Causal codes*

   (a) Conservative: anomie/bureaucracy. As used by contemporary conservatives, "anomie" refers both to the behavior of individuals who, because of biological abnormality, mental or psychological deficiency, or improper socialization, do not conform to societal (accepted; "normal") rules and values, and to collective behavior involving anomic individuals (e.g., riots, lootings, panics) (see Banfield, 1974; Etzkowitz, 1980: xviii–xxi). "Bureaucracy" refers to the growth of the size of government, "overregulation" of business by government, government waste, and the like.

   (b) Liberal: democracy out of control (special interests). Problems are attributed to undemocratic accumulations of power in the hands of special-interest groups, especially large corporations, law enforcement bureaucracies (e.g., the CIA, the Pentagon), organized crime, etc.

   (c) Socialist: capitalism. Problems are attributed to the political economy of American "monopoly" capitalism; the values of capitalist culture (e.g., militarism, materialism, exploitation, domination, alienation); the contradictions of capitalist society (e.g., "the fiscal crisis of the state").

   (d) Other.

5. *Solution codes*

   (a) Conservative.

      i. Streamline/redefine bureaucracy. Make cutbacks in government spending, bureaucrats, programs; reorganize certain social problems so that they appear less serious (e.g., raise the poverty-level income ceiling so that fewer people qualify as poor).

References

Banfield, Edward C. 1974. *The Unheavenly City Revisited*. Boston: Little, Brown.

Etzkowitz, H., ed. 1980. *Is America Possible?* Mineola, NY: West.

Funkhouser, Ralph. 1973. "The Issues of the Sixties: An Exploratory Study in the Dynamics of Public Opinion." *Public Opinion Quarterly* 37 (Spring): 62–75.

Kadushin, Charles. 1974. *The American Intellectual Elite*. Boston: Little, Brown.

ii. Extend social control: take measures to ensure conformity of "deviant" individuals to prevailing societal norms (e.g., mandatory prison sentences, capital punishment).

(b) Liberal: legislative reform. Effect modest redistributions of power and resources in order to overcome the effects of poverty, discrimination, and powerlessness among various minorities (the young, nonwhites, women, the poor); enforce government regulation of powerful interests (e.g., corporate polluters, manufacturers of unsafe products); break up monopolistic economic concentrations; "delabel" certain acts now considered criminal (e.g., prostitution, gambling, status offenses).

(c) Socialist: Socialism. Lessen the amount of property in private hands, either by nationalization of basic industries or by collective ownership and control of the means of production by the workers.

(d) Other.

6. *Outcomes*

(a) Benign/automatic solution (no negative consequences).

(b) Anarchy.

(c) Problem will get worse.

(d) Apocalypse (e.g., nuclear war, famine, ecocide).

(e) Problems will worsen, causing collapse of capitalist order.

(f) None mentioned.

7. *Article ideological rating*

(a) Conservative.

(b) Liberal.

(c) Socialist.

(d) Mixed/other.

Simon, David R. 1975. "Ideology and Sociology." Ph.D. dissertation, Rutgers University.
———. 1977. *Ideology and Sociology. Perspectives in Contemporary Social Criticism.* Washington, DC: University Press of America.
Source: Adapted from *Teaching Political Science* 8, no. 4 (July 1981): 487–92. © 1981. Reprinted with permission of the Hellen Dwight Reed Foundation. Published by Heldret Publications, 1319 18th St., N.W., Washington, D.C. 20036-1802.

Critical Thinking Exercise 4.2	The Kennedy Assassination

Introduction

The assassination of President Kennedy remains, after thirty years, one of the most hotly debated events in modern American history. The killing's profound impact on the minds and hearts of the public has not ceased. Just as polls at the time indicated, the "crime of the century" (Groden & Livingston, 1989) remains a source of profound "grief, loss, sorrow, shame, and anger" (Light, 1988:167). It was a seminal event that marked the beginning of an entire generation's political alienation that continues to this day (Dionne, 1991).

Three decades later these disturbing questions remain: (1) Who murdered the president, and (2) is there a conspiracy to hide the identity of the killers from the American public? The Warren Commission has been challenged on several grounds, including the "single-bullet theory," its refusal to interview (or ignoring) an entire series of witnesses who claim they heard and saw shots from the grassy knoll area, and its refusal to investigate carefully the backgrounds of many of the principal suspects. These criticisms have served as the basis for over six hundred books challenging and, a few defending, the Warren Commission (Grunwald, 1991). A second investigation into the assassination concluded that President Kennedy "was probably assassinated as a result of a conspiracy" (Summers, 1980:14). Probable suspects included members of organized crime (Select Committee on Assassinations of the U.S. House of Representatives, Volume IX, 1979:53). Moreover, the public remains skeptical: As of 1988, only 13 percent of a nationwide poll believed the Warren Commission's version, and 66 percent believed there was a conspiracy (*The Economist*, 1988:25). In 1993, 90 percent of the American public expressed belief in a conspiracy.

This exercise uses the categories involving ideological thought developed in this chapter, including, as well, a third, nondominant, radical ideology. The categories include:

(a) the causes of a social problem, in this case who caused the president's death;

(b) the solution of the problem in question; and

(c) the consequences (outcomes) society will incur by not invoking the solution prescribed.

The Conservative View: Oswald Alone

Conservatives are critics of the critics of the Warren Commission. They insist that Lee Harvey Oswald was a lone assassin. The single-bullet theory, the notion that one bullet inflicted seven wounds on President Kennedy and Governor Connally and emerged merely slightly flattened (as opposed to fragmented), they insist, is true. Further, conservatives (Belin, 1988; Moore, 1990) are firmly convinced that Oswald shot officer Tippit following the assassination. Belin views the Tippit murder (by Oswald) as "the Rosetta Stone"

(1988:17–21) confirming Oswald's guilt. Both authors insist that Oswald attempted to murder General Walker, a noted right-wing extremist and alleged CIA contract agent, several months before the assassination.

Conservative Solution: Social Control of JFK Assassination Writers

Conservatives are angry with the Warren Commission's critics for what they perceive as distortions and omissions concerning eyewitnesses, fingerprints, and ballistic evidence regarding Oswald's involvement in these killings. For the conservatives, the solution to the problem in this case is for the critics of the Warren Commission to stop distorting the record to enrich themselves.

Conservative Outcome: Anarchy

The outcome of what the Warren Commission's critics are doing is to cause the public to lose faith in America's governmental institutions, a step toward anarchy. Moore (1990:208, 211) states:

> . . . the critics (of the Warren Commission) need to be bashed by somebody who knows what he's talking about . . . why should we continue to believe . . . a handful of greedy individuals intent on destroying the credibility of a system many obviously detest.

For conservatives, it is not the assassination's causes that are any longer a problem. What upsets conservatives are the lies and distortions of critics. They believe there is conclusive evidence that Oswald killed officer Tippit, and that Ruby killed Oswald to spare Mrs. Kennedy the trauma of having to testify at Oswald's trial. Belin claims that Ruby passed a lie detector test proving this motive, and denying his participation in a conspiracy (1989:40–43).

The Liberal Position: The Mafia Conspiracy

The House Committee on Assassinations concluded that Mafia bosses Marcello of New Orleans and Trafficante of Florida, and/or anti-Castro Cubans had the "means, motive, and opportunity" to assassinate the president. These sentiments have been echoed in five books. The authors of these works claim the Mafia killed the president for a number of reasons:

1. Carlos Marcello was angered over his illegal deportation to Latin America by Attorney General Robert Kennedy;

2. Jimmy Hoffa was angered over his imprisonment by the Kennedy administration;

3. Sam Giancana was angered over the Kennedy war on organized crime (116 Mafia indictments by RFK's Justice Department) (Magnuson, 1988:43) after

the Chicago Mafia boss had "delivered" Illinois, especially Chicago's north wards, to Kennedy in the 1960 election;

4. Numerous Mafiosi were incensed over the Kennedy decision not to reinvade Cuba after the Bay of Pigs disaster; and

5. Castro, angered over CIA plots to kill him, enlisted the aid of Santos Trafficante, after jailing Trafficante, who, in turn, enlisted Giancana and Marcello. The latter two dons hated Kennedy because of his administration's crackdown on organized crime (Anderson & Spear, 1988a; 1988b).

Liberals also insist that Oswald, while not the lone assassin, did participate in the assassination (Kaiser, 1983):

1. The House Committee found that four shots, not three, were fired in Dealey Plaza, including one from the grassy knoll. Moreover, Oswald's wife had discovered a picture of General Walker's home among Oswald's personal effects. The committee, like the Warren Commission, believed Oswald had tried to kill General Walker.

2. Then there was the Sylvia Odio incident, in which Ms. Odio, a wealthy Cuban refugee, told the FBI in December 1963 that she visited with three men in September 1963, two Cubans and a third man introduced as Leon Oswald. These visitors were allegedly raising money for their anti-Castro activities. Oswald was then supposedly traveling from Mexico City to New Orleans, where he would form the Fair Play for Cuba Committee. The Warren Commission did not believe Mrs. Odio, but subsequent investigations by the 1979 House Committee, and journalists Epstein and Summers, support her story. Specifically, the two Cubans, who were trying to get Ms. Odio's father out of Castro's prison, described Oswald as a former Marine, excellent marksman, and a man who would do anything (including kill Castro).

3. The CIA recruited mobster Johnny Roselli who told columnist Jack Anderson in the early 1970s that Santos Trafficante hired Oswald to kill the president. Roselli related that another gunman also fired at JFK from the front (Kaiser, 1983:F-3).

   The most recent evidence of Mafia involvement in the assassination pointed to by liberal critics concerns the 1988 documentary by British director Nigel Turner, aired the week of November 22, 1993, on Bill Kurtis' "Investigative Report" series. Two witnesses support investigator Steve Rivele's claims—former French drug smugglers Christian David and Michel Nikoli. He said that three Marseilles-Corsican Mafia members, Lucien Sarti (known as "Badgeman" because he was disguised as a Dallas police officer behind the picket fence on the grassy knoll), Roger Bocognani, and Sauveur Pironti killed Kennedy. U.S. Mafia members Marcello, Giancana, and/or Trafficante recruited the trio. Davis (1989:122–126) also cites evidence that Marcello predicted in some detail the assassination, and Moldea (1986: 234–235) claims that Marcello later confessed to an associate his involvement in the assassination.

Liberal Solution:
Reinvestigation

The liberal solution to the mysteries of the Kennedy assassination is in keeping with the liberal emphasis on reform. There are numerous liberal calls for further investigations and even trials for the accused Mafia-linked assassins and their employers (Investigative Report, 1991; Marrs, 1989; Scheim, 1989; Davis, 1989; Lifton, 1988:708; Summers, 1980:522–523). Liberals claim that the Mafia may have also murdered Robert Kennedy and Martin Luther King (Davis, 1988:260–261, 307 ff.). Robert Blakey (Kurtis, 1993), former HSCA chair, wants to establish a permanent special prosecutor to look into all the assassinations of the 1960s.

Liberal Outcomes:
Mob Corruption

Regarding outcomes, the liberals point out that Mafia fortunes increased considerably following the assassination. (1) Government drastically reduced its crackdown on organized crime between 1964 and 1981. (2) President Nixon commuted Jimmy Hoffa's sentence. (3) Mafia influence over the heroin trade and cooperation with Latin American drug lords increased. (4) Organized crime influence in the Nixon administration was substantial. Nixon and Bebe Rebozo jointly invested in the Mafia-dominated Keyes Realty Company (of which Watergate burglar Eugene Martinez was vice president). There is speculation that organized crime may have provided the "hush money" used by Nixon to buy the silence of the Watergate plumbers.

There was also considerable alleged Mafia influence in the Reagan White House. Reagan ally and Nevada Senator Paul Laxalt intervened on Jimmy Hoffa's behalf to get President Nixon to commute Hoffa's sentence. In return, the Mafia allegedly funneled casino profits to the Nixon reelection campaign. Liberals see the outcome of the Kennedy assassination as increased Mafia power and increased corruption within the American government.

Radical Cause: A Coup D'État
by the National Security State

The radical position begins with the premise that the Mafia may have indeed supplied the killers for the assassination, but that organized crime could not have possibly covered up the evidence, including medical evidence in the case. Radicals postulate a JFK assassination alliance growing out of the CIA-Mafia ties established in the early 1960s. The CIA recruited organized crime figures Roselli, Giancana, and Trafficante to assassinate Castro. Anthony Summers (1980) claimed that JFK was a victim of a right-wing conspiracy made up of anti-Castro Cubans and dissident elements within the CIA. The killing was in retaliation for the Bay of Pigs failure and Kennedy's subsequent pledge not to invade Cuba (Kaiser, 1983:F2–F3).

Radicals insist on government, including CIA, involvement in the cover-up of the assassination. They believe that the Mafia is neither influential enough to suppress government-gathered evidence, nor was it influential enough to solicit the cooperation of government agencies in carrying out the actual assassination. The likely scenarios, radicals insist, are either (1) an assassination by dissident CIA elements with Mafia assistance, or (2) a Mafia assassination, with mere complacency by government agencies and persons who stood to benefit from Kennedy's death. Finally, Lane (1991) believes the CIA alone, using its disaffected anti-Castro Cubans, committed the murder, and worked with the FBI to cover it up.

Most radicals believe the conspiracy began soon after the assassination with the transfer of all physical evidence, including Kennedy's body, out of Dallas to Washington. It included President Johnson's, Nicholas Katzenbach's, and J. Edgar Hoover's insistence that the public believe that Oswald acted alone. The cover-up climaxed by ignoring, suppressing, and/or destroying vital evidence. Such evidence includes government involvement in the assassination itself.

Radical Solutions: Revolution

Radicals believe that nothing less than a restructuring of the nation's institutions is in order (Marrs, 1989:590). As Weberman and Canfield (1992:357) state, " . . . former Communist Bloc nations are purging themselves of the secret police who violated their human rights during the Cold War . . . . We should purge ourselves of the antidemocratic elements who came to power during the Kennedy and Nixon administrations . . . . Rule by the intelligence community must come to an end."

Radical Outcomes: *1984* and *Brave New World* Combined

Aside from the continued prosperity of organized crime in America, 1963–1980, the death of the president also profited a host of other military-industrial complex related interests:

1. The CIA, stopped from engaging in covert operations in Cuba and Vietnam under Kennedy, began to engage in covert actions once again. Further, Oswald's murder spared the agency possible negative publicity regarding its ties to Oswald both during his Marine Corps days and his involvement in "anti-" or "pro-" Castro events on the CIA's behalf just before the assassination (Melanson, 1990)

2. The military-industrial complex undertook the war in Vietnam that Kennedy (perhaps) had planned to stop (Lardner, 1991:D-2).

3. Lyndon Johnson, whom Kennedy planned to drop from the 1964 Democratic ticket, became president, a long-cherished goal. Johnson may have had ties to Marcello, and possibly a history of having opponents physically injured and/or killed (Marrs, 1989:292–295)

4. Richard Nixon, present in Dallas on November 22, 1963, experienced a political revival and went on to become president.

5. FBI Director J. Edgar Hoover lost two of his most hated political enemies, the president and an effectual attorney general, and could continue with his obsession with dissidents and ignore the Mafia, with whom he reputedly had close ties (Scheim, 1988; Marrs, 1989). Oswald's murder also spared the FBI embarrassing possible revelations concerning Oswald's ties with the agency (a perhaps informant).

6. Congress allowed the oil industry to retain its oil depletion allowance, a deduction Kennedy wanted reduced.

In short, powerful undemocratic factions took a large step in establishing a military dictatorship in the United States.

Exercise Table 4.1

Summary of Ideological Views of the Kennedy Assassination

IDEOLOGY	CAUSE	SOLUTION	OUTCOME
Conservatism	Anomie: Oswald	Social Control	Anarchy
Liberalism	Mafia	Reform	Corruption
Radicalism	Military-Industrial Complex	Restructuring of Society	Dictatorship

Directions for Exercise 4.2:
Studying *Case Closed*

Gerald Posner's (1993) recent book on the assassination of president Kennedy, *Case Closed*, has received much attention from the mainstream mass media. Look up reviews of the book in the *Book Review Digest (BRD)* (usually found in the reference section of the library). Do a content analysis of the reviews abstracted in *BRD*. Use the categories listed in Exercise Table 4.1 above. Instructions for how to code each review are given in Exercise Table 4.2 below. Use a separate coding sheet for each review.

Present your results in a table like the one below:

Exercise Table 4.2	
Sample Ideological Analysis of Reviews of *Case Closed*	
CONSERVATIVE	60
LIBERAL	20
OTHER	20
Total	100

Part TWO

Institutional Contradiction: Problems of Social Structure

• • • • •

The Problems of the American Political Economy: Economy Contradiction and Political Crisis

The Crypto-Plutocracy
and the Contradictions
of Political Economy

In 1776, Adam Smith (1723–1790), a professor of moral philosophy, published his treatise *The Wealth of Nations*. The work, unexpectedly and, unintentionally, has become a foundation of the myth of "free enterprise" in the modern world. Smith argued that economic self-interest (consumers exercising freedom of choice in the marketplace) produces the ideal economic system. **Laissez-faire capitalism** was Smith's vision of a world where numerous businesses in the same industry, without government regulation, compete for consumer loyalty by producing the amount of product in demand at the price consumers are willing to pay. Smith theorized that if consumer demand for a product is high, investment dollars will flow into that market, and more goods will be produced. Competition will eliminate inefficient firms that make inferior products. Consumer demand will result in increased production and increased demand for workers, increasing wages as well. Thus, the law of supply and demand leads to an invisible hand (an unseen market mechanism) that regulates the marketplace (which is made up of numerous choices made by individual consumers, investors, and workers).

What most proponents of laissez-faire (French for "let do," meaning the government should not interfere in the marketplace) forget is that Smith also was aware that there were a number of conditions under which the magic of the law of supply and demand would *not* work. One of those conditions, monopoly or oligopoly, is exactly what characterizes an important aspect of America's economy today, and this condition is one of the most serious harm-causing contradictions of the postmodern political economy.

The structure of corporate life in America is now about *oligopolies*. An **oligopoly** occurs when fewer than four firms control 50 percent of a market for a given product. Oligopoly is one of the great contradictions of the capitalistic system. Oligopolies formed in the United States between 1865 and 1920.

For all the folklore about the wonders of competition, there is considerable evidence that firms will go to considerable lengths to eliminate competition at every opportunity. Table 5.1 describes the extent of oligopoly in major American industries. When four or fewer firms control 50 percent or more of a given market, the magic law of supply and demand ceases to function. For example, between 1970 and 1980, demand for American automobiles reached an all-time low in the postwar United States. Yet the price of American cars doubled during this period. Prices in oligopolistic markets are determined by price leadership wherein in one giant company will raise prices and the others will follow suit.

Oligopolization of the economy causes numerous additional harms, not the least of which is inflation. A study by the Federal Trade Commission concluded that prices in industries where four or fewer firms control 50 percent of market share would fall by at least 25 percent if market share shrank to just 40 percent. A second study by economist John Blair concluded that when four or fewer firms control 70 percent or more of sales, profits are 50 percent higher than in less-concentrated industries. Most corporate profits end up in the hands of the richest 16.7 percent of Americans (Simon & Eitzen, 1993:94).

Industry	Percent of Market Share
Razors and Blades	99
Lightbulbs	91
Cigarettes	90
Electric Calculators	90
Linoleum	90
Clocks and Watches	84
Refrigerators	82
Cereal	80
Roasted Coffee	66

TABLE 5.1

Degree of Oligopolization in Major Industries Held by Four or Fewer Firms

Thus corporate concentration enriches a relatively few people while costing the average consumer in buying power, power which has not increased since 1969.

There is another frightening consequence of concentrated corporate ownership and corporate-held political power; that is, corporate practices, unregulated by either government or effective political opposition by consumers and workers. This lack of control over corporations has contributed to the drastic economic decline of the United States over the last quarter century, and to numerous other social harms.

Harms of the Political Economy: The Distrusted Giants

Two sets of social problems result from the dominance of oligopolistic corporations. The first set of problems involves the notion of corporate deviance, physical, financial, and moral harms brought about by wealthy and powerful corporations no longer being constrained by government in their relentless pursuit of profits. These harms involve: (1) the frequent breaking of antitrust and other corporate laws; (2) physical harm inflicted on consumers (from dangerous products), and workers (from dangerous working conditions), and pollution of the environment; (3) financial harm stemming from monopolistic pricing practices (price leadership), and unemploying workers through plant closings and exporting jobs to Third World nations; and (4) undemocratic influence within the federal government, resulting in all manner of corporate subsidies and tax breaks at the expense of the average taxpayer.

These forms of physical and financial harms in turn cause moral harm (alienation) among consumers and workers. One way to grasp the enormity of these problems is to examine the activities of one large American corporation, General Electric (GE).

General Electric: A Symbolic Case Study

GE is a massive multinational conglomerate, with 107 factories in the United States and 103 overseas plants in 23 foreign nations. It employs 243,000 American workers and has about 500,000 stockholders. About three hundred major retail stores (e.g., Levitz furniture and Montgomery Ward) use its credit card system, and its NBC television network has about two hundred affiliate stations in the United States.

Also consider that GE is the third-largest defense contractor, and has been involved in developing most major weapons systems in the past two decades, including the MX missile, B-1 bomber, Stealth aircraft, and Star Wars program. GE is also a major builder of nuclear weapons. It has even received government contracts to estimate Soviet military strength. On GE's board of directors sit General David Jones, retired head of the Joint Chiefs of Staff, and William French Smith, former attorney general of the United States.

GE is the nation's second-largest plastics manufacturer, the owner of RCA, has its own cable television network, and is a stockbroker (it owns Kidder Peabody) and its own bank, GE Capital, which has $91 billion in assets (Greider, 1992:335).

Moreover, GE is a major Washington lobbyist because it sells many items to the government and is directly affected by government regulations in defense contracting, environmental law, securities oversight, and many other areas.

General Electric is also among the most lawless of American corporations:

Between 1981 and 1983, GE had net profits of $6.5 billion, but received a tax rebate of $283 million from the debt-ridden federal government due to favorable tax legislation. In fact, from 1981 until 1987, GE saved over a billion on its taxes, but created virtually no new American jobs. It was busy shrinking its American workforce by 50,000 employees, selling off its American subsidiaries, and aggressively buying other firms—Utah Construction, RCA, and NBC. In 1986 alone, GE spent $11.1 billion to buy 338 companies, while it closed 73 of its own plants and offices (Russell, 1987:44–45). As will be noted, such corporate "restructuring" has contributed mightily to the economic decline in the United States since 1970.

Since the repeal of the law that gave GE all those tax advantages, the company has been carrying a $3.5 billion tax deferment on its books. It does this legally because, as a defense contractor, it doesn't have to pay its taxes until some future date. This is not to argue that GE is a "tax cheat." To the contrary, the deductions that it claims are perfectly legal. The problem is that GE has the power to affect the writing of tax laws regarding corporations, something ordinary individuals can not do with regard to their taxes.

In 1988, GE was indicted on 317 counts of fraud in connection with a scheme to defraud the Army of $21 million on a logistics computer contract.

Moreover GE has a very long history of corporate crime:

- 1957–1961: GE was convicted of price-fixing and other charges for electrical equipment valued at $1.74 billion per year, the largest price-fixing case in the history of the Sherman Antitrust Act to that time.

- 1981: GE was convicted of paying a $1.25 million bribe to a Puerto Rican official to obtain an electrical plant contract. Three GE executives were imprisoned in the case.
- 1986: GE officials at a machine tool company were charged with providing kickbacks to three former GE purchasing employees to obtain Pentagon subcontracts.
- 1987: It was revealed that GE supplied thousands of defective military and civilian airplane engines to customers. The defects included cracks in tubing and brackets in the F-404 engine used in the F-18 Navy fighter, the T-700 helicopter, and the CT-7 for small commuter planes (Simon & Eitzen, 1993: 178–179).
- GE's stockbrokerage firm, Kidder Peabody, paid $25.3 million to settle an insider trading complaint with the Securities and Exchange Commission. GE Capital paid a $275,000 civil penalty in 1989 for discriminating against low-income consumers, the largest fine ever under the Equal Credit Opportunity Act. GE itself paid a $32 million settlement to women and minorities in an employment discrimination case, and its Canadian subsidiary was convicted (along with Westinghouse and other firms) of conspiring to fix prices on lightbulbs (Greider, 1992:350).

GE is also a major environmental polluter. Four of its factories are on the Environmental Protection Agency's list of the most dangerous industrial sources of toxic air pollution, and GE has been identified as responsible for contributing to the damage of forty-seven sites in need of environmental cleanup. The company has also paid tens of millions of dollars in out-of-court settlements for its toxic dumping of chemicals, which can cause cancer and other diseases (e.g., birth defects) in humans (Greider, 1992:351–352).

If GE were an individual, it would be considered a habitual criminal under American law. Instead it tries to undo laws and cultivate a favorable public image by engaging in a host of image-making activities: GE acts as a social philanthropist by giving away about $19 million per year through its tax-exempt foundations. Most of the money goes to scholarships for poor and minority college students. It also donates money to certain charities like the United Way. Even charitable contributions further GE's political and economic aims. Some of GE's tax-exempt contributions go Chris Walker's American Council for Capital Formation ("an 'educational' front group that campaigns against the corporate income tax and for a national sales tax"), the Institute for International Economics (a think tank "promoting procorporate positions on economic policy and trade"), and Americans for Generational Equity (which campaigns for issues like reducing Social Security entitlements) (Greider, 1992:338). GE also funds other causes promoting political socialization and propaganda, including:

- Sponsoring "The McLaughlin Group"—a right-wing TV talk show.
- Membership in the Business Roundtable—the policy formation activities of which disseminate the views of the largest five hundred American corporations.
- The Committee on Present Danger—a defense industry–financed group whose propaganda promoted the massive defense spending of the 1980s.
- Tripling its advertising budget to about $30 million per year in the mid-1980s after the firm came under attack for its production of nuclear weapons and its

involvement in various corporate scandals. GE cultivates the image of a company that cares about its employees and "brings good things to light" by making bulbs, makes jet engines, invented night baseball games, helped liberate Hungary from Communism. (GE got an exemption from U.S. antitrust laws so it could buy Hungary's state-owned Tungsram Company, Eastern Europe's major lightbulb maker.)

Many corporations make charitable gestures like underwriting programs on the Public Broadcasting System (PBS) or contributing funds to the Jerry Lewis Muscular Dystrophy Labor Day Telethon. Many of these public relations efforts begin after the corporation has been involved in an embarrassing scandal. Spending on public image advertising by major American firms runs about $1 billion (Greider, 1992:339). Evidence exists that confirms such public relations efforts do increase trust of individual companies seeking to reduce public distrust (Winters, 1988).

Many large corporations also cultivate political goodwill by greasing the campaigns of members of Congress. In 1988, GE's political action committees (PACs) gave $595,000 to various congressional campaigns. Before limitations were placed on outside income by congressional members, GE paid an additional $50,000 directly to representatives and senators as speaking fees before the practice was ended (with a huge congressional pay raise) in 1990. Most of these speeches are given to members of the armed services and other defense-related committees. The company has about two dozen permanent lobbyists and a large support staff in Washington overseeing such contributions. Indeed, in the 1970s there were about six hundred political action committees in Washington. By the 1992 election, there were 4585, and all but about 365 of these are corporate in nature. "Candidates have become so dependent on PAC money that they actually visit PAC offices and all but demand contributions" (*The World Almanac of U.S. Politics,* 1993:19). The beer distributors' PAC is called Six-PAC. There is also a Beef-PAC, and an Ice Cream–PAC. These PACs may donate up to $5000 to each congressional candidate in both primary and general election campaigns. During the 1991–1992 political campaign, all Democratic congressional candidates raised $360 million, while Republican candidates raised $293 million. And the GOP National Committee raised an additional $85.4 million, while the Democratic National Committee raised $65.7 million. The vast majority of these funds (about 80 percent) came from PACs.

The Higher Immorality and Corporate Harms

General Electric is not unique among U.S. corporations for its socially harmful activities. In fact, C. Wright Mills (1956:Chapter 13) argued that there is a set of deviant and criminal practices that are so common they are virtually institutionalized among the American power elite. These practices range from the employment of prostitutes to business and political deals that are close to criminal acts.

Corporate harm is frequently physical. For example, the National Commission on Product Safety estimates that dangerous products injure 20 million Americans each year in home accidents, resulting in 110,000 permanent disabilities and 30,000 deaths. One dangerous drug alone, Eli Lilly's Darvon, has been associated with 11,000 deaths and 79,000 emergency room visits (Simon & Eitzen, 1993:126).

- An estimated 100,000 American workers die each year from diseases contracted at work due to exposure to dangerous chemicals. An additional 3.3 million workers suffer work-related injuries that require medical treatment, and almost 400,000 workers suffer occupational diseases.

- The American food supply contains more than 1500 chemical additives, only a few of which have been tested for their carcinogenic properties. One slice of white bread can contain up to ninety-three different chemicals. Unfortunately, it takes twenty to thirty years to learn which additives are cancer causing and what level of chemical ingestion is safe.

- The largest industry in America is the food industry in which fifty firms out of 20,000 make 60 percent of all the profits. Much of the industry consists of fast-food restaurants which currently serve about 50 percent of the meals in the United States. Often fast food contains high levels of saturated fat, sodium, and

Millions of Americans still work in jobs where conditions are hazardous to worker health. Some 19 million Americans are exposed to cancer-causing and other dangerous chemicals on the job. Each year some 100,000 Americans die from diseases they contract at work.

sugar. These substances are associated with the most common causes of death in America: heart disease, cancer, and high blood pressure. Since Americans began ingesting fast food in the 1950s, saturated fat consumption in the United States has gone from 45.1 pounds (in 1960) to 60.7 pounds per person per year (1989 figures).

Another serious form of physical harm in America is industrial pollution. This nation, which contains a mere 5 percent of the world's population, is responsible for 50 percent of the world's industrial pollutants. The results are increasingly serious.

- In 1993, the EPA and Harvard School of Public Health estimated that particle pollution from factories causes 50,000 to 60,000 deaths each year. Most vulnerable are children with respiratory diseases, asthmatics of all ages, and elderly people with ailments like bronchitis. Indoor pollution, including secondhand cigarette smoke and radon gas, causes 5000 or more cancer cases annually (Hilts, 1993: A-1).

- Answering a congressional inquiry in 1990, the EPA identified 149 industrial plants in thirty-three states where the surrounding air was known to be "quite dangerous" (Greider, 1992:124). At one facility in Port Neches, Texas, the lifetime risk of contracting cancer was one in ten. A risk of one in one million is considered unacceptable by EPA standards. Yet at another forty-five of these plants, the risk of contracting cancer was less than one in one hundred, and at all the others the risk was greater than one in 10,000. In short, the corporate way of life is objectively dangerous to the health of many Americans.

A number of large corporations continue to violate America's environmental laws.

For millions of American workers, however, the greatest immediate social problem concerns having no job or a job at a salary that does not keep pace with inflation. These problems, too, stem from the structure of concentration of economic and political power. Corporate crime, which includes antitrust, advertising law, and pollution law violations, costs American consumers an estimated $200 billion per year, more than all other types of criminal activity combined. While there have been very few scientific studies of corporate crime, those that do exist indicate that only about 2 percent of corporate crime cases result in imprisonment. Moreover, the first corporate crime study ever funded by the Department of Justice by Clinard et al. (1979) revealed that: (1) 60 percent of the largest 582 American corporations committed at least one crime in a twenty-four-month period, (2) nearly half of these crimes occurred in just three industries—autos, petroleum, and drugs. These industries contain some of the largest and most politically active firms in the nation, and (3) of those firms charged with at least one crime, the average number was 4.2—a rate approaching habitual criminality.

Another study by Amitai Etzioni (1990:3) found that between 1975 and 1984, 62 percent of the *Fortune* 500 companies were involved in one or more incidents of corrupt behavior (bribery, price-fixing, tax fraud, or violations of environmental regulations). A study of the twenty-five largest *Fortune* 500 corporations found that all were either found guilty of criminal behavior or fined for civil violations between 1977 and 1990. In a third study in 1992 by *Multinational Monitor* of the 25 largest *Fortune* 500 corporations' activities between 1977 and 1990, all of the corporations were either found guilty of criminal behavior or fined and required to make payment for civil violations (Donahue, 1992: 17–18).

The fact that so few studies have been done on corporate crime rates is but one indication of how powerful corporate interests have succeeded in defining the American crime problem as a "street" (i.e., lower-class) problem. Those studies that have been done indicate that the penalties for corporate criminal violations are quite meager, and provide no deterrent to violating corporate criminal laws. Finally, it is important to understand that corporate crime is extremely harmful.

Price-fixing by corporations, a criminal act in which two or more firms conspire to rig prices, costs American consumers about $60 billion per year in lost purchasing power. Price gouging, charging high prices when cheaper versions of the same product are available, is another deviant practice. Gouging is especially common in the prescription drug industry. For example, one hundred tablets of Abbot's erythromycin wholesales for $15.50, but the generic brand wholesales for $6.20 per hundred tablets (Simon & Eitzen, 1993:100–102). The role of such practices in America's health care crisis is discussed below.

Fraud, a crime based on inducing people to part with their valuables or money via lies, deception, and misrepresentation, is the most common nonviolent crime in America. It costs American consumers tens of billions of dollars every year. Repair fraud alone costs consumers an estimated $20 billion per year (Simon & Eitzen, 1993:99). Some of the more serious examples in recent years include the following:

- Chrysler sold a number of 1987 automobiles as new when they actually had been used as demonstration models or as transportation for company executives. (The odometers had been turned back to zero.)

- In 1988, the Hertz Corporation pleaded guilty to defrauding 110,000 customers, motorists, and insurance companies from 1978 to 1985 by charging them inflated and sometimes fictitious collision repair costs. Hertz agreed to a fine of $6.85 million and to make full restitution of $13.7 million to the victims (Buder, 1988:A-1, A-10).

- In 1993, Prudential Securities paid a $371 million fine to settle charges that fraud permeated the sale of its limited partnerships and its retail branch agents' commissions. Many of its agents were not licensed to sell securities, but did so anyway. Securities brokers and agents illegally split commissions via use of computer programs which also involved senior Prudential executives (New York Times, 1993:C-1).

- Beech-Nut Nutrition Corporation, the nation's second-largest baby food maker, admitted to 215 counts of shipping mislabeled products purporting to be apple juice for babies with the intent to defraud and mislead the public. The bogus product, misrepresented as pure apple juice with no sugar added, was actually a concoction of beet sugar, cane sugar syrup, corn syrup, water, flavoring, and coloring. It contained little or no apple juice. The intended consumers were babies (Traub, 1988).

These examples also point up one of the key myths involving corporate crime. Corporate crime and other acts of the powerful are defended as mere oversights or accidents, lacking in the criminal intent exhibited by violent street criminals. Indeed, the argument that corporate offenders lack criminal intent is one of a series of guilt-neutralizing myths employed by white-collar criminals to excuse their conduct (Kappeler et al., 1993: 105).

Each of the incidents described above, and many others mentioned throughout this book, indicate exactly deliberate intent. Fraud is a crime that usually requires a good deal of advanced planning, even conspiracy (a form of criminal intent), and must, therefore, be deliberate.

Many fraudulent schemes are based on the classic perfected by Bostonian Charles Ponzi in the 1920s: the pyramid system, whereby early investors are paid off handsomely with proceeds from sales of later participants. The result is often a rush of new investors, greedy for easy profits. An example of the Pronzi scam was the Home-Stake swindle perpetrated by Robert Trippet, which consisted of selling participation rights in the drilling of sometimes hypothetical oil wells. The beauty of this plan was that, since oil exploration was involved, it provided a tax shelter for the investors. Thus, the plan especially appealed to the wealthy. As a result, many important persons were swindled of a good deal of money, including the chairman of Citibank, the head of United States Trust, the former chair of Morgan Guaranty Trust, the former chair of General Electric, and entertainers such as Jack Benny, Candice Bergen, Faye Dunaway, Bob Dylan, Liza Minnelli, and John Kenneth Galbraith, the noted economist (Galbraith, 1977).

In 1993, the U.S. Postal Service discovered that numerous businesses had learned to rig their postage meters, cheating the government out of over $100 million in postage fees annually. The Postal Service offered a $50,000 reward for information leading to the arrest and conviction of anyone altering one of the 1.4 million postage meters currently used by U.S. businesses (Ferrighett, 1994;60, 75).

Another important form of fraud is fraudulent advertising. This type of advertising differs from puffery advertising (discussed in Chapter 3) in that the claims made are demonstrably false, and, hence, illegal. Such advertising can be extremely harmful. For example, in 1994, Unocal oil company agreed to stop advertising claims concerning the performance of its high octane gasoline. Several studies have found that American motorists waste billions of dollars per year on higher octane fuels, which add nothing to a vehicle's performance.

Other recent advertising fraud cases have centered around two American obsessions, eating and weight loss.

- Coors Light beer had to stop advertising "A taste of the Rockies," as long as its water came from Virginia (Washington *Post,* 1992b).
- General Nutrition Centers paid $2.4 million for unsubstantiated health claims involving more than forty of their products (New York *Times,* 1994:C-2).
- Eggland's Best had to stop advertising their egg substitute as "better than real eggs." (*Wall Street Journal,* 1994:B-6).
- Diet Centers, Nutri/System, and Physicians Weight Loss Centers were forced to stop advertising their claims concerning losing weight and keeping it off. Studies demonstrate that over 90 percent of dieters gain back the weight they lose (Washington *Post,* 1993a:D-11).

Companies commonly use bait-and-switch advertising, although it is a clear violation of FTC rules. The bait involves advertising a product at an extremely low price. The switch is made when customers arrive to buy it; there is none available, so the salespersons pressure people to buy other more expensive articles.

- In 1979, the nation's largest toy maker, CPG Products, a subsidiary of General Mills, was found guilty of two deceptive acts: (1) use of a television commercial that showed a toy horse being able to stand on its own when in fact it could not through the use of special camera techniques and film editing; and (2) use of oversized boxes in model airplane kits that gave a misleading impression of the size of the contents.

    Products are sometimes advertised at exaggerated sizes. Lumber is uniformly shorter than advertised; a twelve-inch board really is eleven and one-quarter inches wide. The quarter-pounder advertised by McDonald's is really three and seven-eighths ounces. Nine-inch pies are in truth seven and three-quarter inches in diameter because the pie industry includes the rim of the pan in determining the stated size.

- When Libby-Owens-Ford Glass Company wanted to demonstrate the superiority of its automobile safety glass, it smeared a competing brand with streaks of Vaseline to create distortion and then photographed it at oblique camera angles to enhance the effect. The distortion-free marvels of the company's own glass were shown by taking photographs of a car with the windows rolled down (Preston, 1975: 220, 229–231).

- Nutritional labeling has been a major issue in the United States for years. Currently, the FDA is cracking down on companies advertising and labeling products as "cholesterol free" that are nevertheless made with high saturated fats. Many other examples of misleading labeling have yet to come to the FDA's attention. For instance, many products advertised as "sugar free," including Equal and Sweet 'n Low, contain dextrin (or corn syrup), which is made of calorie-containing carbohydrates, very similar to sugar in chemical makeup. These products are not safe for diabetics and/or mold allergy sufferers (Podolsky et al., 1991).

- Montgomery Ward paid a fine for false advertising in 1993. Ward claimed it was selling items at sales prices when it was really selling them at everyday prices (Washington *Post,* 1993b:D-10).

Perhaps the largest fraud in American history is the savings and loan (S&L) scandal. Investigators estimate that 60 percent of the $500 billion to $1 trillion lost in the scandal is due to fraud. Since late 1990, the FBI has been investigating some 7000 fraud cases, one hundred of which were selected for priority prosecution. The scandal could cost each American taxpaying family about $5000 (Simon & Eitzen, 1993:53). The S&L scandal, however, is only one way in which corporate greed robs the federal treasury. There is also an entire class of government expenditures that can be called corporate welfare that is likewise quite harmful.

Neil Bush, son of former President George Bush, was on the board of the Silverado Savings and Loan when it went bankrupt. Records indicate that Bush knew virtually nothing about the S&L business, and that he and his friends received preferential treatment from Silverado. Yet no criminal charges or other lawsuits were ever brought against Bush. Such incidents are typical of the ease with which the wealthy and powerful escape punishment for their wrongdoings in the United States.

Of Porkbarrels and Honey Bees: Corporate Welfare and Congressional Largesse

The federal government has made a disturbing practice of using public money to bolster private profit. The modern practice of subsidizing corporations began in the 1950s when the Eisenhower administration granted some $50 billion worth of offshore oil reserves, federally owned synthetic rubber factories, and various additional public facilities. A multibillion dollar interstate highway system was constructed, as was a national system of urban airports. These projects greatly benefited the automobile, trucking, and airline industries (Parenti, 1995:77).

By the 1990s, even mainstream publications, like *Time,* admitted that the welfare for the rich and corporations was much more costly than welfare for the poor (Goodgame, 1994:35). The federal government spends $25 billion annually for Aid to Families with Dependent Children (AFDC), what is commonly thought of as welfare for the poor (Donlan, 1995:50). Welfare for corporations, in contrast, costs the federal treasury about $80 billion per year in subsidies, special tax deductions and credits, and other programs (Grant & Black, 1995:38). Much of foreign aid, for example, is really a corporate subsidy. Monies voted to foreign countries by the federal government must be spent on American products and those products must be transported by American shippers. Agricultural subsidies, begun to aid small farmers during the Great Depression of the 1930s, have become welfare for the rich. Currently, about 50 percent of all agricultural subsidies go to farmers earning over $100,000 per year, many of them corporate (Goodgame, 1994: 38). Even conservative periodicals, like *Baron's,* now criticize corporate welfare on the grounds that it interferes with the competition and efficiency of the free market (Donlan, 1995: 50).

Because there is so much money to be had at the federal level, members of Congress and lobby groups usually cooperate with each other in various ways to obtain it. The results of this cooperation are some of the most bewildering, irrational, and debt-increasing programs imaginable:

- The Farmer's Home Administration (FMHA) has lent the nation's farmers $56 billion, but is continually unable to collect bad loans. In one instance, forty-three large borrowers owing $79 million ($1.8 million each) had their loans reduced to $64 million when they could not pay. The FMHA has already written off some $10 billion in bad loans, and some borrowers are paying as little as 1 percent interest due to government subsidies on loans.

- The General Services Administration owns some 15 million feet of vacant office space. Yet, in 1992 it leased an additional $2 billion in space, and spent an additional $5 billion on new construction (including $1.6 billion for a World Trade Center building). Most puzzling is the fact that 10 to 25 percent of federal office space is vacant. Vice-President Gore has recommended suspension of all new federal office space construction (Gore, 1993:98). The government also owns 340,000 nonpostal motor vehicles which cost $3 billion to buy and $915 million a year to maintain. Depreciation costs on these vehicles are estimated at about $600 million annually. The White House alone has a fleet of twenty-nine limousines.

- The government also operates a fleet of 1200 civilian aircraft at an annual cost of $800 million. But it spends another $100 million to lease an additional 5000 planes. The two presidential 747s alone cost $410 million.

- The federal government spends somewhere between $676 million and $2 billion a year for office furniture and decorations. The exact amount is not known.

- The Department of Interior spends $100,000 a year to train beagles in Hawaii to sniff for brown tree snakes (Gore, 1993:20).

The federal government subsidizes a variety of businesses and professions for little apparent reason. Government funds have been spent to build a $6.4 million ski resort in Idaho; perform $13 million worth of repairs on a privately owned dam in South Carolina; convert a ferryboat into a $3.1 million crab restaurant in Baltimore; refurbish a privately owned museum in Johnstown, Pennsylvania, at a cost of $4.3 million; buy a private pleasure boat harbor in Cleveland for $11 million; do a $6 million track repair job for the Soo Railroad; build a $10 million access ramp at a privately owned Milwaukee stadium; pump sand onto privately owned beaches of Miami hotels for $33 million; buy Vice-President Quayle gold-embossed playing cards for $57,000 (Gross, 1992:179–181).

- Beekeepers have been voted a special subsidy for producing honey. The law involved has resulted in the American government storing away 110 million pounds of honey at a cost of $1 billion while the United States imports 110 million pounds of expensive foreign honey.

- In 1990, Congress allocated $1 billion for the Department of Agriculture to aid in the advertising of American agricultural products overseas. The money was allegedly supposed to help farmers and small, struggling firms, but some of the funds went to the nation's largest corporations: Gallo Wines, Sunkist, Blue Diamond Almonds, McDonald's, Ralston-Purina, Dole, Pillsbury (a British-owned firm), Wesson, Campbell Soup, Kraft—and even Newman's Own received from $100,000 to $6.2 million to promote the sale of that company's products in what amounted to a grant in a strange "corporate welfare" program (Gross, 1992:136).

- The Small Business Administration (SBA) is supposed to aid America's 15 million small firms, many of whom are struggling to stave off bankruptcy. However, one government investigation revealed that many of the loans go to large businesses, firms worth up to $6 million with 1500 employees. Moreover, the SBA, as of 1990, had $10 billion in outstanding loans, and $1 billion in liquidations (i.e., loans in default) (Gross, 1992:206).

Then there's the 1993 federal Omnibus Budget Reconciliation Act. It gives corporations some of the most ridiculous deductions in American history:

A "potato chip" deduction clause allows merging corporations to depreciate their product names and intangible assets. Accordingly, over a fifteen-year period companies are allowed to deduct all manner of secret ingredients in product formulas (e.g., floor waxes, deodorant, and so on), as well as brand name depreciation for potato chips (e.g., Lay's), Doritos, Quaker, and Kellogg's.

Corporations now can also deduct executive salaries and interest payments on borrowed money, much of which has gone for mergers in recent years. Deductions on interest payments alone now total $200 billion a year.

Government tax policies substantially favor rich individuals and corporations. The amount of tax revenues collected by the federal treasury from major corporations fell from 50 percent in 1945 to 8 percent in 1994. The difference in lost revenues has been made up by higher taxes on the incomes of ordinary middle- and working-class citizens, and increased government borrowing. By 1983, a single mother with three children and a $10,500 salary paid more in taxes than Texaco, Mobil, Boeing, General Electric, DuPont, and AT&T combined (Parenti, 1995:81).

Officially the federal government owns the airwaves, meaning it sells licenses for radio, television, and cellular phone businesses. Recently, it let its cellular phone licenses go for a mere $200 each. These licenses are worth an estimated $232 million.

The Army Corps of Engineers has been providing services for commercial customers for a song. It has processed 15,000 applications for dredging various lakes, rivers, and streams costing $86 million, but collected only $400,000 in fees (Gore, 1993:106). The Food and Drug Administration inspects 1.5 million food products per year for labeling and safety standards. But the government, not food firms, pay for this service. Charging user fees could save an estimated $1.5 billion over a five-year period (Gore, 1993:105–106).

Corporate Dinosaurs and the Crisis of American Economic Life

The story of America's economic decline parallels the increase of corporate and governmental power in American life. For example, in 1984 International Business Machines (IBM) was the largest advanced technology firm on earth. Its after-tax profits stood at an astronomical $7 billion. A mere eight years later, IBM lost $5 billion, more than any other technological corporation on earth. By 1992, it had laid off half of its 400,000 employees, and more layoffs were announced in 1993. The company's market value declined from $75 billion to $36 billion, and its dividend had decreased from $4.84 per share per year to $2.16 (Bell, 1993:316).

What caused IBM's monumental decline? A number of factors were involved, but the most important concerned the company's inability to change its practices in order to compete with the new technologies and other developments brought about by rival firms. IBM became so dominant in its industry position that it assumed the rest of the computer industry would follow its lead. Instead, its competitors developed new computer architecture allowing for millions of pieces of data to be transferred in nanoseconds. The personal and laptop computers were developed, but IBM lost its dominant position by failing to match its competitors' prices for IBM clones, a shortcoming it just now is trying to remedy.

The same inability of an oligopolistic corporation to compete with its rivals has occurred in numerous industries. For example, in 1992, General Motors lost an estimated

$5.3 billion, and announced the layoffs of about 50,000 workers. In fact, the U.S. economy has entered a stage of more or less permanent recession with hundreds of thousands of lay-offs taking place each year, and steadily decreasing levels of economic growth.

- Between 1989 and 1993, the United States lost 1.6 million manufacturing jobs. Between 1979 and 1992, the largest five hundred American corporations fired 4.4 million of their employees, about 340,000 per year, and the losses continue to increase (Barnet, 1993:47–48). During the first seven months of 1993, anoth-er 400,000 Americans lost their jobs through layoffs, an increase of 20 percent over the first eight months of 1991 (when the recession was in full force). Sadly, over 60 percent of the jobs created between January and June, 1993 were part-time positions, further contributing to the decline of the middle-class and worker purchasing power that has so characterized the last fifteen years. In fact, the percentage of American households with incomes below the current poverty level is expected to increase from 34.1 percent in 1984 to 36 percent by 2000 (Phillips, 1993:200). Moreover, in 1993, the Clinton administration proposed eliminating 100,000–250,000 federal positions as government restruc-tures (Herbert, 1993:A-15). The result could be an even more serious recession than that taking place in the early 1990s, and, as a result, increased government indebtedness.

- The U.S. normal official unemployment rate seems stuck around 7 percent in the 1990s (a level that would have been considered recessionary in the 1960s), and economic growth in the United States has declined from a robust 6 percent in the 1960s to an anemic 2 percent in the 1990s (Perot, 1993:54–57). The actual unemployment rate (including people with part-time jobs who would like a full-time job) is estimated at about 12 to 13 percent, a depression level (Phillips, 1993:11–12).

What has happened to make the American dream become something of a nightmare for millions of laid-off workers and others desiring employment? Again, unregulated cor-porate behavior is partially to blame. (Activities of government contributing to this prob-lem are assessed in Chapter 6.) Corporations have contributed to American economic decline through a number of practices, including the following:

Mergers and Acquisitions

Corporate mergers and leveraged buyouts (LBOs) are a source of several economic prob-lems. From 1981 to 1988, spending on buying other firms by American corporations increased from $3.1 billion per year to $67.4 billion annually. In 1968, ninety-four large firms were purchased for $8 billion. From 1979 to 1988, the smallest acquisition of a single company cost $2.4 billion (the largest, RJR Nabisco by Kohlberg Kravis Roberts, cost nearly $25 billion) (Dowd, 1993:113; Simon & Eitzen, 1993:93). These transactions totaled $190 billion from 1980 to 1990. Corporate buyouts enrich the financiers handling the deal and the corporate executives and stockholders in on the deal. They do nothing to create new jobs. In fact, they end up unemploying people because the mergers of the 1980s and 1990 have left corporate America "with a heavy burden of debt and interest payments, and in some of the more extravagant cases, lapsed into bankruptcy" (Galbraith, 1992:157).

American corporate debt increased from $15,000 per employee in 1960 to $23,387 per employee in 1990. Moreover, corporate bankruptcies increased from 3700 per year in the late 1970s to 15,200 per year in the late 1980s. Between 1970 and 1980, only one in nine American businesses filed for bankruptcy. Between 1980 and 1990, one-third of all America businesses filed for bankruptcy (Bartlett & Steele, 1992:85). Many of these mergers were financed with "junk" bonds (bonds of inflated value), and figured heavily in the collapse of about seven hundred savings and loans during the 1980s and early 1990s (at a cost to taxpayers of between $500 billion and $1 trillion).

In 1994 alone, over $65 billion was spent on corporate mergers.

Table 5.2

Largest Corporate Mergers, 1994

Company	Acquirer	Dollars
Lockheed	Martin-Marietta	10.0 billion
Paramount	Viacom	9.7 billion
American Cyanamid	American Home Products	9.7 billion
Blockbuster Video	Viacom	7.7 billion
Syntex	Roche Holding	5.4 billion
PCS Health Systems	Eli Lilly	4.0 billion
Gerber	Sandoz	3.7 billion
Kemper	Conseco	3.0 billion
WilTel	LDDS Communications	2.5 billion
Times Mirror	Cox Enterprises	2.3 billion
BB&T Financial	Southern National	2.2 billion
Grumman	Northrop	2.1 billion
Borden	Kohlberg Kravis Roberts	2.0 billion

Source: **The World Almanac, 1995.**

Overseas Investments

American global corporations have expanded overseas investment dramatically in the last three decades, taking millions of jobs out of the United States, 900,000 between 1980 and 1985 alone (Parenti, 1989:75). In Mexico alone, the number of plants increased from 620 to 2200 between 1980 and 1992, and the number of jobs held by Mexican workers in those plants increased from 119,550 to nearly 600,000 (Perot & Choate, 1993:48–49). U.S. firms experience gross labor costs of only $1.15 to $1.50 per hour in Mexico (versus costs of $7–$10 per hour in the United States). It is estimated that by 1995, more than 2800 U.S. factories will have closed and 800,000 American jobs will have been transferred to Mexico since 1965 (Bartlett & Steele, 1992:31). The effects of the North American Free Trade Agreement (NAFTA) on the transfer of manufacturing jobs from the United States to Mexico remain uncertain and are hotly debated at this point.

As of 1990, U.S. corporations had invested $431.3 billion in foreign nations (up from $11.8 billion in 1950). Two-thirds of this amount is invested in advanced capitalist nations, especially European nations (Magdoff, 1992:54–55). However, the rate return on investments in Third World nations is two-thirds more than return on investments in advanced nations (Simon & Eitzen, 1993:185).

To illustrate the problem, fewer than one-tenth of 1 percent of American firms received half of all profits from overseas investments, and 90 percent of all foreign tax credits under American tax law. Although exact figures do not exist because reports underestimate the actual profits from abroad, somewhere around 30 percent of the profits made by these corporate giants stem from overseas activity (up from 10 percent in 1950). Foreign investment accounted for over half of all profits for thirteen of the largest corporations in the late 1980s. These included: Exxon (75 percent), Gillette (63 percent), Mobil Oil (61

During the 1980s, the United States spent over $2 trillion on defense, much of which was completely unnecessary in the face of a declining Soviet threat. This militarization of the American economy since the end of World War II has greatly contributed to America's inability to compete in the global economy.

percent), Colgate-Palmolive (56 percent), Dow Chemical (56 percent), Coca-Cola (55 percent), and IBM (54 percent) (Braun, 1993:102). Thus foreign investment is an increasingly important source of profitable investment outlets for corporate America.

The Militarized Economy

From 1945 to 1992, the United States spent over $4 trillion on national defense, $2 trillion of which was spent between 1980 and 1992 (Simon & Eitzen, 1993:166). In the 1980s and early 1990s, over 80 percent of U.S. research and development (R&D) was devoted to military hardware (i.e., weapons). The billions of dollars in government R&D money was accompanied by additional billions in capital investment in defense contracting firms. Seventy-five percent of the defense weapons systems contacts annually go to the largest hundred corporations in America. All of this money poured into defense "ate away at America's industrial competitiveness. The per capita investment in civilian research and development in America has been far lower, for many years, than in Japan and Western Europe. The result: American business, with the exception of perhaps space and satellite technology, is no longer leading the world as it did twenty years ago. For example, in 1975, the first 15 places on the Fortune 500 list of the world's largest companies included 11 American corporations. Now there are only seven. Further, in the early 1970s, America's computer industry controlled 90 percent of the U.S. market. By 1990, Japan had surpassed it in many areas" (Meyer-Larsen, 1991:25–26).

The militarization of the American economy has had a number of additional consequences for America's democratic form of government, and these are discussed in Chapter 6. With the Cold War over, it is estimated by the Bureau of Labor Statistics that 1.9 million defense-related jobs will be lost by 1997 (Barnet, 1993:49).

Economically, huge military expenditures have resulted in massive government deficits, which contribute to inflation and a decline in purchasing power for average families. Large defense expenditures have also diverted monies that could have been spent on pressing domestic social problems, including education, health care, public infrastructure, school dropouts, drugs, and so on (Hopkins, 1993:A-11).

Alienation and
Social Character in a
Contradictory Political Economy

In Chapter 3, the inauthentic nature of corporate advertising and government propaganda was discussed. It is also important to understand some of the ways in which these institutions of political economy dehumanize people. The federal government is a frequent ally in numerous acts of alienation. A key example of such dehumanization involves the various efforts by both government and corporations to place a monetary value on human life:

- *Item:* The Ford Motor Company asked the National Highway Traffic Safety Administration to estimate the monetary worth of a human life. What, Ford wanted to know, was the average wrongful death claim in a vehicle accident? About $200,000 was the government's reply. Ford used this figure in an internal company memo that argued it would be more profitable to produce a car that Ford knew would kill and seriously disfigure an estimated 360 people than it would be to spend $11.80 per vehicle to correct a defective gas tank. The result—Ford let the Pinto roll off the assembly line, and hundreds of people were victims of a crime Indiana prosecutors tried to label "corporate homicide" (Simon & Eitzen, 1993:123–124; Cullen, Maakestead and Cavender, 1987).

- *Item:* The federal government's various agencies routinely estimate the worth of a human life in ways that are both inauthentic and dehumanizing. Termed cost benefit analysis or regulatory impact analysis, these tools attempt to calculate the costs versus the savings as a result of governmental decisions.

The Federal Aviation Administration estimates the cost of human life lost in airplane crashes at about $650,000. The Occupational Health & Safety Administration claims dead construction workers are worth $3.5 million, but the Office of Management and Budget claims dead construction workers are only worth about $1 million. The deception associated with these estimates is that they appear "rational," (i.e., efficient), but they really are not. Human beings are reduced to mere producers of income (economic actors) and their worth is simply calculated based on their expected earnings over a lifetime. This makes some people's lives worth a great deal more than others (Greider, 1992:54).

During the 1970s, the Ford Motor Company marketed a car, the Pinto, that it knew would explode if its gas tank was hit at speeds as low as five miles per hour. Ford used the federal government's estimate of the worth of a human life to make its decision to leave the gas tank in dangerous condition, rather than fixing it for $11.80 per vehicle.

Another aspect of such dehumanization concerns government regulations that allow for the loss of human life. For example, the Clean Air Act of 1990 permits chemical, steel, and petroleum firms discharging poisonous materials into the atmosphere to kill as many as ten people in 100,000 in neighborhoods surrounding their plants. Moreover, the act gives companies twenty years to achieve these standards (Greider, 1992:56).

All of these examples point to yet another related problem, namely the failure of government to control corporate crime.

Policy Failure: Corporate Crime and Conventional Wisdom

As discussed, the conservative view of social problems is based on the notion that deviant individuals, who lack proper norms of a normal, middle-class culture, are in large part responsible for the nation's ills. So powerful and widespread has this myth become that it has given rise to a curious counter-myth. This counter-myth holds that the crimes of corporations are unimportant, not especially harmful, and not in need of law enforcement's resources and attention. The passage and enforcement of white-collar, especially corporate, crime laws are based on such unfortunate myths. Clinard (1979) found that in over five hundred corporate crime cases in which a firm was found guilty, prison terms were imposed in only 2 percent of cases. The average imprisonment term was only six months. Compare this with street crime imprisonment. In California, a "three-strike" felon was sentenced to life in prison for stealing a pizza (Skolnick, 1995:4)!

There is a great irony to corporate crime. Corporate criminals tend to be among the most rational criminals there are. They plan their crimes carefully. Criminologist Jay Albanese (1995:13) has argued that virtually all white-collar criminality, including corporate crime and political corruption, involves conspiracy, which requires an agreement to commit an illegal act between two or more persons. This implies that corporate criminals do think about the possible risks and rewards involved in their crimes.

Given this rationality, white-collar crooks of all stripes are likely to be deterred from committing crimes by the knowledge that (1) the likelihood of getting caught is great, and (2), if apprehended, a prison term and/or substantial fine, or other penalties (such as being fired without pension and stock option rights) is certain.

The great irony here is that the very criminals most likely to be deterred by threat of apprehension and punishment are the least likely to suffer either consequence. The sad truth is that enforcement meant to deter white-collar crime so often fails because the wealth and influence of the criminals enable them to avoid the full weight of the law (Coleman, 1994:173). For example, the Sherman Act prohibits unreasonable restraints upon and monopolization of trade (Vancise, 1979:7). The act also outlaws arrangements that result in price-fixing or limiting access to trade or commerce (e.g., dividing market). However, the act is loaded with exclusions and ambiguities. Thus, the Sherman Act applies only to monopolies in trade (commerce), not to monopolies in manufacturing. Moreover, under a series of cases in 1911 involving American Tobacco and Standard Oil, it was ruled that the act applied only to *unreasonable* trade combinations and did not exclude consolidation per se. The definition of a *reasonable* combination, of course, is a matter of judicial opinion. Under the Sherman Act's price-fixing definitions, businesses that are already regulated by the federal government (such as the Civil Aeronautics Board's regulation of the nation's airlines) are excluded from the law. This exclusion also applies to interstate water carriers, railroads, and trucks. Other loopholes are present in the act, as well. While the act specifies that it is illegal to fix the price of a product by agreement, this practice is legal in states that authorize it under so-called fair laws (Bequai, 1978:96).

In 1914, the **Federal Trade Commission Act** was passed, making it unlawful to restrict competition and to engage in unfair and deceptive trade practices. However, the power of the FTC is limited to issuing cease-and-desist orders, which it can do only upon securing the permission of a federal court. The FTC can recommend prosecution of criminal cases, but the Justice Department is specifically charged with this task.

In 1936, the **Robinson-Patman Act** made it illegal to discriminate among various buyers of products by charging different prices to different buyers. But the act has several limitations. First, it applies only to products, not to services, which are supposedly covered by other laws. In addition, the law specifically exempts U.S. companies that have joined together for purposes of export. The antitrust laws also exempt such items as bank mergers, agricultural cooperatives, and insurance companies, which are unregulated by state laws (Bequai, 1978: 100–101).

During the Reagan-Bush years, the enforcement of antitrust and other laws designed to control corporate crime became a very low priority. So lax was the enforcement that, by

Private Troubles   Public Issues

Consumerism and Corporate Crime: "Your Money or Your Life"

Given the prevalence of fraud and other corporate crimes, as well as the extremely high cost of living in the United States, the ability to consume wisely has never been more important. The savings rate among American consumers is 4.5 percent, lowest in the industrialized world. As of 1990, American consumer debt was about $800 billion, $3000 for every man, woman, and child in the nation (42 percent more than in 1985, and 146 percent more than in 1980) (Dominguez & Robin, 1990:6).

Joe Dominguez and Vicki Robin (1990) have written a wise book, with many useful suggestions for how people can get control over their money and also develop a philosophy about the role of material possessions in the pursuit of a contented life. The heart of these suggestions is a straightforward plan designed to end consumer indebtedness. The plan works as follows:

These steps are simple, commonsense practices. It is absolutely necessary that you do, diligently, *every* step. The steps build on each other, creating the "magic" of synergy—the whole is greater than the sum of its parts. You may not see this effect until you have been following the steps for a number of months.

Conscientiously applying all the steps automatically makes your personal finances an integrated whole; this is a whole-systems approach.

1982, 60 percent of corporations had failed to pay their fines following conviction or court settlement. As a result, there were $38 billion in fines outstanding (Sherrill, 1988:573). Moreover, the Reagan administration made clear its dislike of the very structure of antitrust laws. In 1986, it sent to Congress a package designed to, in effect, repeal some key provisions of the Clayton Act, especially those prohibiting mergers that reduce competition and hence create monopoly. It was proposed that the government prove the *significant probability*—not just the *possibility*—of monopoly before antitrust sanctions could be applied. Federal courts would have had to evaluate proposed mergers, considering not simply their effects on U.S. markets but world markets, as well. Most important, the Reagan proposal allowed a five-year exemption from antitrust laws for corporations found to be seriously injured by imports, especially shoes, steel, and textiles (*Newsweek*, 1986:46).

The Clinton administration, also showed the same reluctance to enforce the antitrust laws in a meaningful way. Its one great exception thus far concerns its threat to sue Microsoft, the computer software giant. Microsoft agreed to stop a number of licensing practices that would give computer manufacturers more freedom in installing programs from other companies. Microsoft used to receive a royalty for each computer sold, even if operating systems made by other manufacturers were installed on some computers by manufacturers who had a contract with Microsoft for Microsoft Windows or DOS operating systems. This discouraged the selling of other operating systems, like Novell's Dr. DOS, or IBM's OS/2. The agreement could give Microsoft more competition in its dominance over the personal computer (PC) market (San Francisco *Chronicle*, 1994: C-1, C-4).

Step 1: Making Peace with the Past

A: How much have you earned in your life? Find out your total lifetime earnings—the sum total of your *gross* income, from the first penny you ever earned to your most recent paycheck.

HOW:

- Social Security Administration—"Request for Statement of Earnings."
- Copies of federal or state income tax returns.
- Paycheck stubs; employers' records.

WHY:

- Gives a clear picture of how powerful you are in bringing money into your life.

Continued on next page

Private Troubles   Public Issues

Continued

- Eliminates vagueness or self-delusion in this arena.
- Instills confidence, facilitates goal-setting.
- This is a very basic, fundamental practice for any business—and *you* are a business.

B: What have you got to show for it? Find out your net worth by creating a personal balance sheet of assets and liabilities—everything you own and everything you owe.

HOW:

- List and give a current market value to everything you own.
- List everything you owe.
- Deduct your liabilities from your assets to get your net worth.

WHY:

- You can never know what is enough if you don't know what you have. You might find that you have a lot of material possessions that are not bringing you fulfillment, and you might want to convert them to cash.
- This is a very basic, fundamental practice for any business—and *you* are a business.

Step 2: Being in the Present—
Tracking Your Life Energy

A: How much are you trading your life energy for? Establish the actual costs in time and money required to maintain your job, and compute your *real* hourly wage.

HOW:

- Deduct from your gross weekly income the costs of commuting and job costuming; the extra cost of at-work meals; amounts spent for decompressing, recreating, escaping and vacating from work stress; job-related illness; and all other expenses associated with maintaining you on the job.
- Add to your work week the hours spent in preparing yourself for work, commuting, decompressing, recreating, escaping, vacating, shopping to make you feel better since your job feels lousy, and all other hours that are linked to maintaining your job.
- Divide the new, reduced weekly dollar figure by the new, increased weekly hour figure; **this is your real hourly wage.**

- Individuals with variable incomes can get creative—take monthly averages, a typical week, whatever works for you.

WHY:

- This is a very basic, fundamental practice for any business—and *you* are a business.
- You are in the business of selling the most precious resource in existence—your life energy. You had better know how much you are selling it for.
- The number that results from this step—your **real hourly wage**—will become a vital ingredient in transforming your relationship with money.

B: Keep track of every cent that comes into or goes out of your life.

HOW:

- Devise a record-keeping system that works for you (such as a pocket-sized memo book). Record daily expenditures accurately. Record all income.

WHY:

- This is a very basic, fundamental practice for any business—and *you* are a business.
- You are in the business of trading the most precious resource in existence—your life energy. This record book shows in detail what you are trading it for.

Step 3: Where Is It All Going?
(The Monthly Tabulation)

- Every month create a table of all income and all expenses within categories generated by your own unique spending pattern.
- Balance your monthly income and outgo totals.
- Convert "dollars" spent in each category to "hours of life energy," using your real hourly wage as computed in Step 2.

HOW:

- Simple grade-school arithmetic. A basic hand-held calculator is needed only if you have forgotten (or are young enough never to have learned) longhand addition and subtraction. A computer home accounting program is useful only if you are already computer-literate.

Continued on next page

Private Troubles   Public Issues

Continued

WHY:

- This is a very basic, fundamental practice for any business—and *you* are a business.
- You are in the business of trading the most precious resource in existence—your life energy. This Monthly Tabulation will be an accurate portrait of how you are actually living.
- This Monthly Tabulation will provide a foundation for the rest of this program.

Step 4: Three Questions That Will Transform Your Life

On your Monthly Tabulation, ask these three questions of each of your category totals expressed as hours of life energy and record your responses:

1. Did I receive fulfillment, satisfaction and value in proportion to life energy spent?
2. Is this expenditure of life energy in alignment with my values and life purpose?
3. How might this expenditure change if I didn't have to work for a living?

At the bottom of each category, make one of the following marks:

− Mark a minus sign (or a down arrow) if you did not receive fulfillment proportional to the hours of life energy you spent in acquiring the goods and services in that category, or if that expenditure was not in full alignment with your values and purpose or if you could see expenses in that category diminishing after Financial Independence.

+ Mark a plus sign (or an up arrow) if you believe that upping this expenditure would increase fulfillment, would demonstrate greater personal alignment or would increase after Financial Independence.

0 Mark a 0 if that category is just fine on all counts.

HOW:

- With total honesty.

WHY:

- This is the core of the program.
- These questions will clarify and integrate your earning, your spending, your values, your purpose, your sense of fulfillment and your integrity.
- This will help you discover what is enough for you.

Step 5: Making
Life Energy Visible

Create a large Wall Chart plotting the total monthly income and total monthly expenses from your Monthly Tabulation. Put it where you will see it every day.

HOW:

- Get a large sheet of graph paper, 18 by 22 inches to 24 by 36 inches with 10 squares to the centimeter or 10 squares to the inch. Choose a scale that allows plenty of room above your highest projected monthly expenses or monthly income. Use different-colored lines for monthly expenses and monthly income.

WHY:

- It will show you the trend in your financial situation and will give you a sense of progress over time, and the transformation of your relationship with money will be obvious.

- You will see your expense line go **down** as your fulfillment goes **up**—the result of "instinctive," automatic lowering of expenses in those categories you labeled with a minus.

- This Wall Chart will become the picture of your progress toward full Financial Independence, and you will use it for the rest of the program. It will provide inspiration, stimulus, support and gentle chiding.

Step 6: Valuing Your Life
Energy—Minimizing Spending

Learn and practice intelligent use of your life energy (money), which will result in lowering your expenses and increasing your savings. This will create greater fulfillment, integrity and alignment in your life.

HOW:

- Ask the three questions in Step 4 every month.
- Learn to define your true needs.
- Be conscious in your spending.
- Master the techniques of wise purchasing. Research value, quality and durability.

Continued on next page

Private Troubles	Public Issues

Continued

WHY:

- You are spending your most precious commodity—your life energy. You have only a finite amount left.
- You are consuming the planet's precious resources—there is only a finite amount left.
- You cannot expect your children—or your government—to "know the value of a buck" if *you* don't demonstrate it.
- "Quality of life" often goes down as "standard of living" goes up. There is a peak to the Fulfillment Curve—spending more after you've reached the peak will bring **less** fulfillment.

Step 7: Valuing Your Life Energy—Maximizing Income

Respect the life energy you are putting into your job. Money is simply something you trade your life energy for. Trade it with purpose and integrity for increased earnings.

HOW:

- Ask yourself: Am I making a living or making a dying?
- Examine your purposes for paid employment.
- Break the link between work and wages to open up your options for increased earnings.

WHY:

- You have only X number of hours left in your life. Determine how you want to spend those remaining hours.
- Breaking the robotic link between **who you are** and **what you do for a "living"** will free you to make more fulfilling choices.

Step 8: Capital and the Crossover Point

Each month apply the following equation to your total accumulated capital, and post the monthly independence income as a separate line on your Wall Chart:

$$\frac{\text{capital} \times \text{current long-term interest rate}}{12 \text{ months}} = \frac{\text{monthly investment}}{\text{income}}$$

HOW:

- Find the long-term interest rate by looking at the interest of the thirty-year treasury bonds in the treasury bond table of *The Wall Street Journal* or a big-city newspaper. After a number of months on the program, your total monthly expense line will have established a smaller zigzag pattern at a much lower level than when you started. With a light pencil line, project the total monthly expense line into the future on your chart.

- After a number of months on the program, your monthly investment income line will have begun to move up from the lower edge of the chart. (If you have actually been investing this money as outlined in Step 9, the line will be **curving** upward—the result of the magic of compound interest.) With a light pencil line, project the monthly investment income curve into the future. At some point in the future it will cross over the total monthly expenses line. That is the **Crossover Point.**

- You will gain inspiration and momentum when you can see that you need to work for pay for only **a finite period of time.**

WHY:

- At the Crossover Point you will be financially independent. The monthly income from your invested capital will be equal to your actual monthly expenses.

- You will have enough.

- Your options are now wide open.

- **Celebrate!**

Step 9: Managing Your Finances

The final step to financial independence: become knowledgeable and sophisticated about long-term income-producing investments. Invest your capital in such a way as to provide an absolutely safe income, sufficient to meet your basic needs for the rest of your life.

HOW:

- Empower yourself to make your own investment decisions by narrowing the focus to the safest, nonspeculative, long-duration fixed-income securities, such as U.S. treasury bonds and U.S. government agency bonds. Temper the prevailing irrational fears about inflation with clear thinking and increased consciousness.

Continued on next page

Private Troubles | **Public Issues**

continued

- Cut out the high expenses, fees and commissions of middlemen and popularly marketed investment "products."
- Set up your financial plan using the three pillars:

  Capital: The income-producing core of your Financial Independence.

  Cushion: Enough ready cash, earning bank interest, to cover six months of expenses.

  Cache: The surplus of funds resulting from your continued practice of the nine steps. May be used to finance your service work, reinvested to produce an endowment fund, used to replace high-cost items, used to compensate for occasional inroads of inflation, given away, etc.

WHY:

- There is more to life than nine-to-five.

Summary

The U.S. economy is almost nothing like the world described by Adam Smith in his *The Wealth of Nations* (1776). Multinational oligopolistic conglomerates now dominate the U.S. and global economy. Oligopoly is a structure in which four or fewer firms control at least 50 percent of a given product market. The existence of oligopoly also increases the likelihood of a host of harmful economic practices including:

- price-fixing
- fraud
- price-gouging
- false advertising
- mergers and acquisitions at the expense of job expansion
- transfer of plants to foreign (Third World) nations, such as Mexico, where labor costs are a fraction of their American counterparts, and many costly regulations can be easily evaded
- undemocratic influence within the federal government, resulting in all manner of corporate subsidies and tax breaks at the expense of the average taxpayer

Conventional wisdom is demonstrably false concerning the realities of corporate crime. Crimes by corporations are more harmful than street crime by any objective measure. Corporate crime takes at least five times as many lives as street crime, costs at least six times more money, and, along with other forms of elite deviance, contributes greatly to the mass distrust of institutions of political economy.

Many of these practices, as well as the militarization of the economy after World War II, have served to make the manufacturing sector of the American economy uncompetitive with products from such nations as Germany and Japan.

Moreover, giant corporations influence America's government in problematic ways. The government, far from being a neutral party in economic matters, is deeply involved in all aspects of economic life. The government hosts numerous subsidy, tax relief, and loan guarantee programs, all designed to aid in the accumulation of corporate profits. These programs are largely paid for by the heavily taxed American middle class.

These examples, together with the other facts examined in this chapter, point to the dangerousness of America's persistent myths about its economic and political systems. The relative lack of free market mechanisms, the harmful nature of corporate crime, and the undemocratic influence of wealthy individuals and corporations speak volumes about the most harmful macro problems facing the nation. The same is true for the harms committed by government, the subject of our next chapter.

Suggested Readings

D.L. Bartlett and J. Steele (1992) *America: What Went Wrong?* (Kansas City, MO: Andrews & McMeel). A wonderfully readable analysis of what went wrong with the economic dimensions of the American Dream in the 1980s and early 1990s.

D. Braun (1993) *The Rich Get Richer* (Chicago: Nelson-Hall). An excellent text regarding the inequitable distribution of wealth in various contemporary economies in the global marketplace.

N. Miller (1992) *Stealing From America* (New York: Paragon House). A fascinating history of political corruption on the federal level in American society, and the role corruption has played in American history.

Exercises

Critical Thinking Exercise 5.1	The Higher Immorality

Look up the categories having to do with corporate crime in the latest complete *New York Times Index* or the *Wall Street Journal Index*. These categories include:

1. Antitrust violations
2. Pollution law violations
3. False advertising
4. Fraud
5. Sexual harassment

Do you notice any patterns in respect to which industries have the most violations? Many violations take place in the petroleum, automobile, and drug industries. Do these firms serve as models of corporate behavior for others? Were any specific corporations involved in more than one violation?

Critical Thinking Exercise 5.2	Business Crime and Punishment in America

The *Wall Street Journal* calls itself "the daily diary of the American Dream." As argued in Chapter 2, the values connected with the American Dream, as well as a lack of opportunity, encourage a great deal of criminal behavior, including crimes among corporations. Using fifty recent issues of the *Wall Street Journal,* do a content analysis of the amount of corporate and employee crime. In your analysis, answer the following questions:

1. What is the most common crime committed by corporations?
2. What percentage of the articles mention prison as part of the sentence imposed on convicted executives and employees?
3. What is the average fine imposed on corporations? On employees?
4. Who are the most frequent victims of corporate criminals? The public? The government? Women? Children? Minorities?

What do the results of your study indicate about the way corporate and white-collar employees are treated by the criminal justice system?

The Politics of Postmodern Crises: The Scandalization of America

Chapter • Chapter • Chapter • Chapter • Chapter

6

Structure and Contradiction of American Government: The Unstoppable Expansion

There are two interrelated and disturbing trends in the structure of government that relate directly to social problems. The first is that the federal government has become "big government." Government in mass society has taken over many activities that individuals, families, local communities, and state and local governments used to manage for themselves. The federal government has expanded its authority into such areas as health care, education, crime prevention, and birth control. It regulates working conditions, the purity of the food supply, the safety of drugs, the quality of air and water, the money supply, and interest rates.

The federal government also encourages the arts and humanities, preserves historic structures, and ensures the rights of the handicapped. It spends hundreds of billions on national defense, oversees the design of automobile engines, the building of interstate highways and mass transit systems, and even operates two zoos and a host of museums. In short, "nearly all national issues are ultimately resolved in Washington. (Moreover) about half of all American families now receive some form of payment from the Treasury" (Caplow, 1991:108). In fact, government spending at all levels (federal, state, and local) now accounts for about one-third of the U.S. gross domestic product (GDP). Two-thirds of all monies spent by government is federal money. Despite all of this economic activity, the federal government is, many economists believe, "a root cause of America's unstable economy—that its $4 trillion debt creates high long term interest and home mortgage rates that hold back (economic) growth" (Gross, 1992:18).

This growth in the federal establishment has come about for a number of reasons. Among these are (1) the domestic programs created by the New Deal (Roosevelt) and Great Society (Kennedy-Johnson) administrations; (2) the decisions of the U.S. Supreme Court mandating the federal government to enforce various regulations concerning civil rights; (3) the creation and growth of a permanent military and intelligence establishment; and (4) the growth of various subsidies, porkbarrel projects, and loan programs in response to pressures from various lobbies and powerful members of Congress.

This great expansion of function has been accompanied by a great increase in the number of agencies, bureaus, and personnel, along with an enormous increase in the federal budget.

- *Item:* Congress' 535 members employ a supporting staff of over 25,000 at a cost of well over $1 billion. The House chaplain's salary is $115,300. Congressional pay costs taxpayers $55 million per year, plus $30 million to maintain up to three offices in their districts, and $78 million in free mailing privileges.

- *Item:* The executive office of the president is budgeted at over $300 million per year. The president's airplane alone costs $391 million because it is specially equipped. In fact, the federal budget has increased from $92 billion in 1960 to well over $1.515 trillion in 1995. There are now 2.2 million federal civilian

Senator Robert Packwood (R–Oregon) was forced to resign because of numerous complaints by his former female staff members and other women regarding sexual harassment.

employees, 800,000 postal workers, and 1.8 million military employees. There are 700,000 federal employees, one-third of all federal civilian workers, who control, manage, audit, or check up on other employees at a cost of $35 billion a year (Gore, 1993:14,121). Vice-President Gore estimates that 252,000 federal jobs could be cut with no loss of efficiency or function. Thus the structure of the modern federal government is in part a money machine, with the government cranking out over a trillion dollars each year for borrowing money, weapons, and nearly every conceivable good and service (e.g., food, medicines, toilet paper, paint, and so on).

"The Secret Government"

The second important trend in the structure of the federal government has been the growth of what is called the "national security state" (Moyers, 1988). In 1947, the National Security Act was passed. The act created a national intelligence apparatus composed of the National Security Council, the Central Intelligence Agency, and the various intelligence agencies of each of the armed services. Along with the national security apparatus came the growth of secrecy, including a "black" (secret) budget.

It was Max Weber who first called sociologists' attention to the most disturbing attributes of modern bureaucracy. Among its most disturbing features, Weber noted, was that as bureaucratic organizations become larger and more powerful, they tend to become more secretive. The secrecy and centralization of power are perhaps the greatest threat to democracy in America. And the massive growth in federal budget increases make this secrecy all the more dangerous.

These two tendencies, expansion of functions and secrecy, form the contradictions of the modern corporate state. The writers of the Constitution intended for government to be small in scope, very open in its business, and to benefit all its citizens. Instead, government has evolved into a mass institution that regulates a great many functions in modern life. Instead of being open to public scrutiny, secrecy, in the form of classifying information and conducting paramilitary operations hidden from public view, have become a way of life in the National Security State. Rather than benefiting the entire population, government has grown into an enterprise that directly benefits large corporations and rich individuals in amassing profits, sometimes at the expense of the welfare of the masses of citizens. Secrecy, along with the vast monetary and military resources of the government, has created a distinct set of social-patterned harms. These harms include:

- recurrent scandals within the executive branch of the federal government,
- waste, fraud, and abuse regarding contracting for defense weapons systems,
- welfare for rich individuals and corporations in the form of wasted monies and special tax privileges, all for the ultimate purpose of aiding corporations in amassing profits,
- support for undemocratic governments that sponsor terrorism and violate basic human rights, again, in large measure for supporting the expansion of economic activity by First World multinational corporations (Parenti, 1995).

The major scandals of the postmodern era provide a microcosm of virtually all of these problems.

America the Scandalized

Between 1860 and 1920, the United States suffered only two major crises involving corruption on the federal level: the Credit Mobilier Scandal of the Grant administration of the 1860s and the Teapot Dome oil lease scandal of the Harding administration in the 1920s. This amounts to about one scandal every fifty years. However, beginning in 1963 with the investigation into the assassination of President Kennedy, the American federal government has experienced repeated scandals. The scandals themselves are serious social problems, causing all manner of social harm.

When President Kennedy was assassinated in Dallas, Texas, on November 22, 1963, a cover-up of the investigation into the crime was personally ordered by President Johnson, Assistant Attorney General Katzenbach, and FBI Director Hoover. They allegedly felt that Communist elements from either Cuba or the Soviet Union (or both) might be involved, and feared a war would result. They agreed that the public must be convinced that Lee Harvey Oswald acted alone in killing the president (Simon, 1993). This was President Johnson's motive in setting up the Warren Commission in December, 1963. The FBI, CIA, and other government agencies all withheld valuable evidence from the Warren Commission. For example, the CIA never informed the commission that it had hired organized crime figures in an attempt to assassinate Cuban premier Castro. The FBI withheld information that it had received a handwritten note from Lee Harvey Oswald shortly before the assassination.

Moreover, the Warren Commission did indeed find that Oswald had acted alone in killing the president, and that Dallas nightclub owner Jack Ruby had acted alone in killing Oswald (who at the time was surrounded by nearly seventy armed law enforcement officers) in the Dallas police station.

Subsequent investigations into the crime by the House Special Committee on Assassinations (HSCA), 1975–1978, found numerous inconsistencies in the case. The HSCA found that President Kennedy "was probably assassinated as a result of a conspiracy" (Summers, 1980:14). Probable suspects included members of organized crime (Select Committee on Assassinations of the U.S. House of Representatives, Volume IX, 1979:53). The HSCA concluded that Mafia bosses Marcello of New Orleans and Trafficante of Florida had the "means, motive, and opportunity" to assassinate the president, and/or that anti-Castro activists may have been involved.

The precise nature of the conspiracy concerning actual assassination, and those persons or organizations that employed them were never determined, and, consequently, numerous theories have been advanced. Between 1966 and 1993, over six hundred books and 2000 articles were written about the Kennedy assassination. The dominant view in these writings is that government agencies killed their own president, theoretically because the president was going to make peace with the Soviet Union and end the Cold War. There is also speculation that Kennedy was going to disengage the United States from its involvement in Vietnam. The *investigation* of the JFK assassination is important in that it marks not only the first major postwar scandal, but the beginning of a drastic decline in public confidence in government agencies and politicians.

Following President Kennedy's death, the United States escalated its presence in Vietnam. The war that began secretly with the CIA's training of the South Vietnamese police lasted from 1964 until 1975. It resulted in the deaths of over 158,000 American men and women and cost nearly $160 billion to fight. During the war's course, numerous miniscandals resulted concerning the war's conduct and course. A classified secret history of the Vietnam War, the Pentagon Papers, revealed a number of scandalous incidents:

- President Johnson had manipulated Congress into passing the Gulf of Tonkin resolution, authorizing funds for the war. The president told the lawmakers that the U.S. ships in the Gulf had been the victims of unprovoked attacks. Yet, the evidence demonstrates that the ships had been warned by the North Vietnamese concerning their ships' activities in the Gulf, but refused to heed the warnings.

- More than 40,000 Vietnamese civilians were murdered in the Central Intelligence Agency–sponsored Phoenix program, mostly without trials.

- President Nixon told the American people that the United States was respecting the neutrality of Cambodia. Yet, evidence was unmasked that confirmed the

United States' conduct of secret bombing raids of enemy sanctuaries. The U.S. Air Force covered up knowledge of these targets by keeping two sets of books, one for the public and an internal set for Pentagon and White House reference.

- More than 5 million acres of South Vietnam was sprayed with defoliating chemicals. The most serious of these was Agent Orange, which caused a high incidence of cancer, birth defects, and other environmental disease in American service personnel. The government withheld information on the dangers of Agent Orange from the 1960s until 1993, when government scientists announced a link between the defoliant and cancer (Simon & Eitzen, 1993:6–7).

Near the end of the Vietnam War, the Nixon administration collapsed in the Watergate scandal. Watergate was actually an endless series of mini-scandals, the causes of which remain unknown (Simon, 1992):

- Burglars, bankrolled by the Committee to Reelect the President, burglarized and bugged the headquarters of the Democratic National Committee in the Watergate complex in Washington, DC, for reasons still unknown. The burglars, all former CIA agents, some associated with the 1961 Bay of Pigs fiasco, were promised executive clemency and hush money by the White House.

- Another burglary involved the office of Daniel Ellsberg's psychiatrist. Ellsberg, who had leaked the Pentagon Papers to various newspapers, was standing trial at the time. The judge in the case was contacted about becoming FBI director while the trial was in progress. The judge proceeded to declare a mistrial.

- President Nixon had secretly wiretapped his own offices and those of his top aides, and planted various microphones in White House offices to record every conversation.

- Nixon's vice-president, Spiro Agnew, confessed to accepting kickbacks on government contracts from a Maryland engineer, and resigned from office as part of a plea bargain.

- The White House secret intelligence unit, called "the plumbers" (to stop leaks to the press), engaged in a host of campaign dirty tricks aimed at discrediting potential Democratic presidential candidates. Letters were written and distributed that allegedly came from Senator Muskie's campaign charging that Senator Jackson was homosexual. Prostitutes were hired and planted at campaign rallies to embarrass opposition candidates.

- The Nixon administration generated an enemy list of its critics inside and outside government, and illegally misused the Internal Revenue Service by requesting tax audits of these critics. The FBI and CIA were manipulated into ceasing the investigation into Watergate, and the head of the FBI even destroyed vital evidence in the case by burning files along with Christmas present wrappings.

- President Nixon lied repeatedly to Congress concerning both his involvement in the case, and possession of evidence that would reveal his involvement. Nixon offered his two aides, John Ehrlichman and H. R. Haldeman, hush money in exchange for their silence. He had his personal attorney solicit illegal campaign contributions in exchange for the promise of ambassadorships. Monies from these contributions were illegally laundered to conceal donors' identities.

- Attorney General John Mitchell helped plan the bugging of the Democratic National Committee headquarters. Mitchell and numerous other Nixon administration officials were convicted of perjury and other crimes and sent to prison in record numbers.

Following the Watergate scandal in 1975, investigations into the postwar activities of the CIA and the FBI revealed that both agencies had engaged in systematic violations of the civil liberties of thousands of American citizens. Such violations have continued to this day:

- Since 1947, the FBI has committed over 1500 illegal break-ins of headquarters of American organizations and foreign embassies. During the Reagan administration (1981–1988) alone, the FBI spied on various citizens groups and citizens opposed to administration policy in Central America. Such groups included the United Auto Workers, the Maryknoll Sisters, and the Southern Christian Leadership Conference (Shenon, 1988:A-1, A-8; Simon & Eitzen, 1993:257).
- After Reverend Martin Luther King, Jr.'s 1963 "I have a dream" speech, the FBI illegally spied on Reverend King, bugging his house and hotel rooms. The FBI even tried to induce him to commit suicide by threatening to reveal evidence that he had carried on adulterous affairs.

The CIA has been involved in a variety of illegal activities both inside and outside the United States. The following examples are taken from the 1947-to-1975 period.

- The CIA illegally experimented on a variety of American citizens—scientists from the Army Chemical Corps, and some of its own agents (without their knowledge or consent)—with knockout drops, incapacitating chemicals, and LSD (a hallucinogenic drug). The CIA even hired San Francisco prostitutes to give their customers drugs.
- Abroad, the CIA has been involved in various assassination plots against foreign heads of state, including Cuba's Castro, Lamumba (Zaire), Trujillo (Dominican Republic), Diem (South Vietnam), and Allende (Chile) between 1950 and 1974. (This practice continued into the 1980s when, in 1985, CIA director Casey secretly arranged for the murder of Shiite Muslim leader Fadlallah in a deal with Saudi intelligence.) (Johnson, 1987; Corn, 1988; Simon & Eitzen, 1993:270–272)

In 1987, news broke concerning what was to be the most damaging scandal of the Reagan administration, the so-called Iran-Contra affair. The root of the scandal involved the diversion of funds from profits on missiles sold to the Iranian government to the Nicaraguan Contras, a counterrevolutionary force virtually created by the CIA (Moyers, 1988). At first, the entire episode was blamed on a marine, Lieutenant Colonel Oliver North, with virtually all high-ranking officials of the Reagan administration claiming they were "out of the loop" concerning any knowledge of the events. Subsequent investigations and trial testimony, however, pointed to a massive cover-up by White House aides and others:

- North's 1989 trial revealed that at a 1984 national security group meeting composed of Vice-President Bush, the Joint Chiefs of Staff, several cabinet officers, and President Reagan, a discussion of Contra aid based on solicitation of "third" parties (foreign governments) took place. This was adopted as a strategy of getting around the Boland Amendment which forbid further military aid to the Contras (Draper, 1989).

- President Reagan personally solicited the largest contributions for Contra aid from foreign nations, and a number of Latin American governments were requested to cooperate by falsifying arms sales transactions so that knowledge that the weapons were for the Contras could be hidden. Those nations agreeing to falsify such documents were promised increased U.S. foreign aid. Both illegal arms sales and illegal solicitation of funds were orchestrated by a secret group, the Enterprise, set up apart from the CIA and other governmental agencies to assure secrecy. The Enterprise was composed of retired military and intelligence personnel, arms dealers, and drug smugglers. Thus, in 1994, North's Iran-Contra activities were linked to drug trafficking by former Drug Enforcement Administration agent Celerino Castillo III. Mr. Castillo was the DEA's principal agent in El Salvador between 1985 and 1991. He claims that North smuggled both guns and drugs through a Salvadoran military airport with the help of over two dozen cocaine traffickers. The drug traffickers were even granted visas by the U.S. Embassy, even though their criminal records were documented by the DEA.

- Agent Castillo even informed Vice-President George Bush of North's smuggling activities at a 1986 cocktail party. Bush simply shook his hand and walked away. When Mr. Castillo pushed for an investigation of North's activities within the DEA, he was suspended and then transferred to San Francisco in 1991. He also tried to pass his documented information concerning North's activities on to an FBI agent working with special prosecutor Walsh's investigation. Castillo never heard from the agent again, and none of North's drug and arms smuggling on behalf of the Contras was ever investigated by either congressional committees or the special prosecutor (Bernstein & Levine, 1994:6).

According to *Webster's Third International Dictionary,* the term *scandal* has various meanings. One notion of scandal relates to religious faith, and involves the loss thereof, or violations of religious precepts (rules, sin). A second aspect of scandal refers to gossip of true or false details damaging to an individual's personal reputation. Another meaning of scandal concerns anger brought about by violations of morality. A final view of scandal relates to impertinent remarks or reproachful tactics used in a court of law (*Webster's International Dictionary,* 1986). While these definitions of scandal are suggestive, they bear little resemblance to the scandals plaguing American life since 1963.

What do these events tell us about (1) modern scandal as a social problem, and (2) the structure and contradictions of contemporary American government? All of the scandals listed above share common characteristics:

1. They were all the result of secret actions of government agencies (e.g., the FBI, CIA, executive office of the president) that were either illegal or unethical, and caused severe physical, financial, and or/moral harm to the nation.

 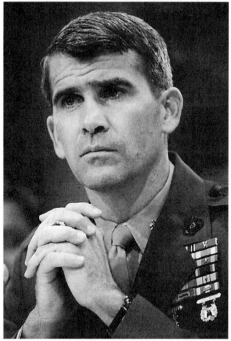

Left: While he was Vice-President, George Bush consistently denied that he had any knowledge of what took place during the Iran–Contra scandal. Documented evidence, however, demonstrates that Bush attended at least eleven meetings wherein the scandal was discussed.

Right: Lieutenant Colonial Oliver North made many of the key decisions that resulted in the Iran–Contral scandal of the 1980s. North admitted to lying to Congress, destroying vital documents, and personally benefitting from government monies. There is also evidence that North may have been involved in drug smuggling and other illegal activities. His punishment for these crimes was practically nil. He now has his own nationally syndicated radio show, has written a book, and (in 1994) ran for U.S. Senate from Virginia. Making heroes out of criminals is a long-time American tradition.

2. All the episodes discussed were the subject of official government hearings or investigations. The Watergate and Iran-Contra hearings were nationally televised.

3. The original causes of most of these episodes remain unknown. Thus motives for President Kennedy's assassination, the reason(s) for the Watergate break-in, and the possible involvement of Vice-President Bush, President Reagan, and CIA Director Casey in planning the Iranian arms sales and diversion of funds to the Contras remain matters of heated debate.

These scandals reveal that (1) immense sums of money and (2) great secrecy have combined to create a situation characterized by great physical harm and corruption of democratic processes, both at home and abroad, and increased governmental debt. These great harms are not limited to the major scandals of the postmodern era, however; they are also characteristic of American defense policy in general.

The Pentagon Waste Machine

Out of 30,000 firms engaged in weapons contracting, the top twenty-five are awarded more than 50 percent of all defense weapons business. Ten states received almost two-thirds of the prime contracts awarded for weapons procurement, with California receiving between one-fifth and one-quarter of all Pentagon monies each year throughout the 1980s. Moreover, ten states receive more than half of all funds spent on military bases and personnel. Finally, there are almost 3 million private sector employees who work in defense industries, making politicians representing such districts extremely sensitive to the tax bases and local incomes involved.

Among the firms garnering the lion's share of defense contracts are corporate giants like General Dynamics, McDonnell Douglas, Lockheed, Rockwell, General Electric, Boeing, United Technologies, Raytheon, Westinghouse, IBM, RCA, Ford, General Motors, Exxon. Moreover, eight of the top ten contractors in 1963 were still among the top ten in 1988, and two others persist in the top fifteen.

The weapons industry is notoriously noncompetitive. Inefficiency, cost overruns, waste, and corruption are rampant. At times, it is characterized by excessive secrecy, designed to hide mistakes and criminal behavior from Congress and the public (see Box 6.1). "Seven thousand dollar coffee pots, $900 Allen wrenches, $700 toilet seats, and $400 hammers, as well as government investigations of contract abuse by more than half of the Pentagon's top 100 contractors indicate the massive extent of deviance within the MIT-LAMP complex. During the 1980s nearly every major weapons system was plagued with performance shortcomings and cost overruns—including the Bradley fighting vehicle, the DIVAD gun, the Viper missile, the F-18 fighter and attack submarines, and the B-1B, Stealth, and F-15 aircraft" (Stubbing & Mendel, 1989:55).

Pentagon procurement is also riddled with a continuing pattern of fraud and other crimes among defense contractors. Here are recent scandals:

- In March 1989, an ex-Singer employee joined in a lawsuit brought by the Navy accusing the Singer company of fraud by overcharging the Pentagon $77 million for flight simulators sold between 1980 and 1988. The government is seeking $231 million, plus civil damages of $5000–$10,000, for each of six counts involving false claims, fraud, breach of contract, and unjust enrichment. Also in March 1989, Rockwell was fined $5.5 million for double-billing the Air Force on the NAVSTAR satellite program. The company was placed on five-years probation, and received the largest fine ever in a defense fraud case. Rockwell pleaded guilty to one fraud count and one criminal contempt count.

- In March 1991, a Unisys official pleaded guilty to conspiracy in attempting to obtain a $100 million Marine Corps communications contract. The official, Robert Elfering, also paid Pentagon consultants for insider information regarding the status of a radar command and control contract, and then tried to hide this illicit activity. The issue of whether other, higher ranking, Unisys officials knew of these activities is also under investigation.

- In March 1991, two Litton officials were indicted for using insider bidding information in an attempt to secure two defense contracts worth $150 million.

Charged with approving $96,000 in illegal payments to a defense consultant in return for information about Litton's competitors on marine and navy electronics work in the late 1980s, the consultant, Thomas Muldoon, and ten other industry and Pentagon officials have been convicted for attempting to influence the award of the two contracts.

- A McDonnell Douglas subsidiary received a $7.5 million civil fine for charging the government greatly inflated costs on a 1983 contract for the M-242 gun, used on the Bradley fighting vehicle. Douglas settled without having to admit falsifying any data, but received the largest fine in the history of defense fraud cases since the March 1989 Rockwell case.

- The exploits of one company, the Northrop Corporation, are a case in point. In May 1991, Northrop agreed to a unique $18 million settlement with its shareholders. The payments came in reaction to a suit by shareholders challenging the conduct of corporate officials who have become enmeshed in wrongdoing or controversy. Among the breach of duties cited:

    The advanced Cruise missile scandal in which Northrop pleaded guilty to criminal fraud for falsifying missile test results. The Cruise was a "black" item in the Pentagon budget (see Box 6.1 for details).

    Between 1988 and 1990, the investigation into the scandal, code named "Operation Ill Wind," resulted in almost thirty-six guilty pleas. Eleven Unisys officials pleaded guilty to a variety of crimes from tax evasion to bribery. Three United Technologies officials were convicted of fraud. Nine other defense contractors have also pleaded guilty to defense contracting fraud and received fines of $1 million to 5.8 million.

One problem with Pentagon-related waste and fraud is that there seems to be little penalty involved when it comes to the right of companies to continue to do business with the government. As William Greider (1992:112–113) notes, "exemptions to law are granted routinely to the major defense contractors . . . who committed criminal fraud against the government . . . twenty-five of the one hundred largest contractors have been found guilty of . . . fraud in recent years . . . . Typically they plead guilty and pay a fine. To appease the public, the Pentagon sometimes 'suspends' contractors, but the suspensions are always lifted in time for the company to participate in the next bidding for contracts." Another problem with Pentagon procurement is that contracts are let on a "cost–plus" basis, meaning that profit made by the company involved is always a fixed percentage (e.g., 10 percent) of the final cost of the project. If a contract is initially signed for a billion dollars, the cost will typically rise to, say, $3.2 billion due to alleged increases in various costs of production. The Pentagon rarely refuses increases like this because it has already sunk billions into such projects. The typical cost overrun from the 1960s to the early 1990s was about 230 to 320 percent of initial costs (Simon and Eitzen, 1993: 170–173).

There are additional harms associated with America's permanent war economy. First, the military is a major environmental polluter. It poisons groundwater, air, and soil with a host of toxic and radioactive chemicals in the United States and overseas in bombing exercises, and the production of nuclear, chemical, and biological weapons. Around the world, there are an estimated 21,000 contaminated sites on nuclear weapons plants and military bases (Parenti, 1995:88).

Second, military spending accumulates profits for corporations, but generates fewer jobs than any other form of government spending, except the space program. If research and development and defense-related expenditures by agencies outside the Defense Department are included, the actual military budget is really closer to $400 billion (Parenti, 1995:87). When government funds are spent on most domestic needs, such as scholarships for college students, schools, public building projects, and drug rehabilitation programs, these expenditures benefit the nonprofit sector of the economy. Sometimes income is redistributed to ordinary citizens, away from private corporate profits, by such expenditures. Weapons systems contracts, however, function to amass profits for the wealthy, redistribute income to upper middle- and upper-class individuals, make the society more economically unequal, and the nation less democratic by concentrating power in the hands of fewer people.

Meanwhile, the government giveaways to defense contractors continue to reach new heights. In 1995, for the first time since the corporate merger and acquisition binge began in the 1980s, tax dollars were being used to finance bonuses for corporate executives. The Clinton administration used $31 million to pay one-third of the $92 million in bonuses that top executives of Lockheed and Martin-Marietta granted themselves for staging the largest merger in defense-contracting history.

One result of the merger is the loss of 30,000 defense jobs (layoffs), most of them in still economically depressed California. The fact that Secretary of Defense Perry and his deputy, John Deutch, were consultants to Martin-Marietta before joining the Pentagon, and are close personal friends of Martin-Marietta's chairman may have played a role in the scheme.

The $31 million is part of an overall bonus package of $92 million that represents $10 million more than was claimed by Lockheed-Martin officials in December 1994. The bonus package comes on top of an estimated $1 billion subsidy given Lockheed-Martin that is part of a plan to preserve companies that build America's weapons systems.

"Bonusgate" may represent an all-time low in the ethical standards surrounding corporate welfare and mergers. It may be an entirely new form of corruption—legal bribery. Only this time it's not politicians who are being bribed by business executives; it is business executives who are being bribed by government (Sloyan, 1995:2-B). A second major set of policies that aid the rich and large corporations concerns corporate welfare.

More Congressional Porkbarrels

The federal government has made a disturbing practice of using public money to bolster private profit. The modern practice of subsidizing corporations began in the 1950s when the Eisenhower administration granted some $50 billion worth of offshore oil reserves, federally owned synthetic rubber factories, and various additional public facilities. A multibillion-dollar interstate highway system was constructed, as was a national system of urban airports. These projects greatly benefited the automobile, trucking, and airline industries. Today there are $651 billion in federal subsidies, loans, grants, and the like received annually by affluent individuals and corporations (Parenti, 1995:77).

Because there is so much money to be had at the federal level, members of Congress and lobby groups usually cooperate with each other in various ways to obtain it. The results of this cooperation are some of the most bewildering, irrational, and debt-increasing programs imaginable. For example, Uncle Sam owns power plants in Nevada which produce electricity for about one penny per kilowatt. As a result the citizens of Las Vegas (with its huge neon signs) pay 5.6 cents per kilowatt for electricity, while residents in the Northeast pay twelve cents per kilowatt for their unsubsidized electricity.

One of the long-cherished functions of members of Congress is to secure government facilities and contracts for their districts. The study of which districts are the recipients of government largesse is a reliable guide to who is in power in Washington. The champion in the U.S. Senate in securing government facilities is Senator Robert Byrd of West Virginia, former majority leader and current chair of the Senate Appropriations Committee. West Virginia is among the nation's poorest states, and in need of all the money and jobs it can get.

However, some of Senator Byrd's acquisitions of government funds make little sense. Here are some examples:

- A $4.5 million federal project to renovate a downtown movie theater in Huntington, West Virginia;

- The entire U.S. Coast Guard Computer Operation Center was relocated to Martinsburg, West Virginia, a landlocked city, and a NASA research center was relocated to Wheeling, West Virginia.

The Las Vegas gambling strip was literally built by a combination of Teamster Union Pension Fund loans to the American Mafia, corrupt politicians, and local business interests.

- The FBI Identification Unit, home of 190 million fingerprints, is situated in Clarksburg, West Virginia (population 18,000) in a new $185 million building that will engage the services of 2800 employees.
- Finally, Senator Byrd has won his battle to relocate up to 3000 CIA agents to Charles Town, a rural West Virginia village, at a cost of $1.4 billion (Gross, 1992:183–185).

What all of this means is that much of what the federal government spends is wasted, and, aside from increasing debt, incidents such as those mentioned above cause considerable moral harm. Public confidence in government in early 1993 was at an all-time low: The average American believed government wastes 48 cents of every tax dollar. Five of every six Americans said they wanted fundamental change in Washington (Gore, 1993:1).

There is good reason for such cynicism. The average citizen is done considerable financial harm by the government's financial favors to corporations. As taxpayers, we all pay for the costs of these subsidies, and we then pay again as consumers, because many subsidies keep the prices of the goods we buy, agricultural products for example, artificially high. Entire new technologies in such areas as biogenetics, computer systems, and aeronautics are developed at taxpayer expense, and then handed over to private corporations for profit. For example, in 1962 the entire satellite communications system was put under the control of AT&T after the government had spent $20 billion to develop it (Parenti, 1995:78).

Another harmful practice supporting the accumulation of profits by multinational corporations involves supporting regimes that violate the basic human rights of their citizens.

Human Rights, Terrorism, and Multinational Corporations

The United States is a signatory to two international agreements on human rights and the renunciation of terrorism. The first of these was the International Bill of Rights passed by the United Nations in 1948. The agreement endorses the protection of a range of both economic and civil liberties and specifically pledges signatories not to subject anyone to "torture or to cruel, inhuman or degrading treatment, or punishment" or to "arbitrary arrest, detention, or exile" (Joyce, 1978:239).

The United States is also a party to the Helsinki Agreement of 1975, which contains a detailed section of human rights–pledging signatories to "respect human rights and fundamental freedoms, including freedom of thought, conscience, religion, or belief, and without distinction to race, sex, language, or religion" (Buncher, 1977:11–17).

While the American government has committed itself to the safeguarding of human rights on paper, it has a disturbing record of supporting governments that engage in violent repression of these rights. The United States has in the postmodern era (1947–present) supported with military and foreign aid, as well as the training of police forces and death squads, some of the Third World's most repressive dictatorships. A number of these regimes, military dictatorships, have routinely engaged in murdering innocent civilians, kidnapping, arbitrary torture, terrorism, and arrest, as well as wanton murder by roaming death squads.

On the surface, much of the world's terrorism consists of the actions of nongovernmental, extremist individuals and groups, and seems present in every corner of the globe. Consider these examples over the last decade:

- In Corsica, separatists seeking autonomy from France have attacked the property of French mainlanders since the 1960s.

- On Cyprus, Turkish troops occupied the northern part of the island in 1974 following a Greek-backed coup, later creating an independent republic recognized only by Turkey. Thousands of Greeks and Turks have been expelled from each other's side of the island.

- In Northern Ireland, British troops and Protestant paramilitary groups battle Catholic nationalists seeking end to British rule and unification with the Irish Republic. More than 2500 people have been killed since 1969.

- In Spain's Basque region, separatists advocating independence in three northern provinces have caused over five hundred deaths since 1968.

- In Yugoslavia, ethnic Serbs and Muslims have clashed with disastrous results. Seeking to create an ethnically pure province, thousands of Serbs have been killed or forced to flee their homeland.

- In Angola in the 1980s, the Union for the Total Independence of Angola (UNITA), supported by South Africa (covertly by the United States as well), opposed the Cuban-backed Angolan government. UNITA leader Jonas Savimbi's power base is in the Ovambo tribe, of which he is a chief. Thousands were killed, 2000 in 1985 alone.

- In Ethiopia, four different rebel groups fight for independence. More than 45,000 have been killed since the conflict began in the early 1960s.

- Ethnic and religious violence has plagued India since its independence in 1947. Today the Punjab Sikhs, who seek autonomy, have the strongest movement. Approximately 5000 died in Sikh-Hindu violence in the 1980s.

- In the Philippines, Moslem insurgents began to battle government forces for a separate homeland on the southern islands of Mindanao and Sulu. Rebel leaders say 100,000 were killed in the 1980s; government estimates exceed 50,000.

In reality, however, the most harmful forms of terrorism are committed or sponsored by governments, and the United States has sponsored a good deal of it, sometimes unintentionally. Lest you doubt this claim, consider the following examples.

- In 1993, New York City's World Trade Center was bombed by a group of Moslem terrorists. The bomb killing six people. Assassination plots against New York Senator D'Amato, New York Assemblyman Hikind, and UN Secretary General Boutros-Ghali were uncovered. Most of those arrested for the bombing had Sudanese passports, and had come to the United States under tourist visas. All those arrested remained in America by marrying American citizens. These facts suggest a complex conspiracy extending far beyond a small band of extremists.

The terrorists responsible for the World Trade Center bombing were trained in two places, Sudan and Afghanistan (along with Islamic radicals from over forty nations) (Weiner, 1994:53; Krulak, 1993:B-6). In Sudan, members of Iran's elite Revolutionary Guard train terrorists. The Sudan training operation is financed by a world terror network backed by seven nations. These nations include not only Sudan and Iran, but Libya, Iraq, North Korea, Cuba, Syria, but also an Afghan group that has received extensive aid from the CIA.

- Between 1986 and 1991, the CIA secretly aided Afghan rebels headed by Gulbuddin Hekmatyar. The Afghan rebels were fighting Soviet troops until the collapse of the Soviet Union. After the Afghan war, Hekmatyar and his troops were left free to engage in whatever activities they liked. These included growing and selling heroin and training terrorists from around the Arab world.

- In 1991, the Haitian military, led by the Haitian intelligence service, overthrew democratically elected president Aristide, and quickly imposed a reign of state terror involving death squad assassinations, and drug trafficking. In 1994, the Clinton administration sent troops to Haiti to restore a democratically elected government after buying off Haiti's dictators with promises of amnesty and an affluent exile (complete with relocation at U.S. expense). What is less known is that the CIA created the Haitian intelligence service in the 1980s as part of the United States' war on drugs (San Diego Times Union, 1993).

- In 1991, the United States went to war with Saddam Hussein's army in order to prevent a takeover of Kuwait. What is less well known is that the Bush administration helped provide financing and arms to Saddam Hussein in an effort to win him over and then covered up the policy after he invaded Kuwait. Banca Nazionale del Lavoro is an Italian bank whose Atlanta branch was used by Iraq to finance its arms buildup. Billions in loans to Hussein to finance his military were guaranteed by the U.S. Department of Agriculture in a labyrinth of deceit. All of this began when George Bush first took office and after the Iran-Iraq War. Ironically Bush and his secretary of state, James Baker, had secretly built up the armed forces of the same Saddam Hussein that the United States would go to war with in Operation Desert Storm (Hagan and Simon, 1994). The powers that went to war with Iraq had sold $163.2 billion in arms to the Middle East nations involved in that war, including $52 billion in illegal arm sales from the United States to Iraq itself. Saddam Hussein was largely a threat created by the United States itself (Simon & Eitzen, 1993:164).

All of these examples confirm that terrorism is not primarily caused by crazed individuals, but by governmental organizations, most of them secret. William Chambliss has referred to such activities as state-organized crime. Chambliss traced the origins of state-organized crime to European nations' support for piracy between 1400 and 1800. In the modern era, state-organized crime involves institutionalized practices discussed in depth in this chapter: namely, state-sponsored drug and arms smuggling; assassinations of foreign leaders (with the cooperation of organized crime syndicates); illegal surveillance of U.S.

citizens; illegal drug experimentation on unsuspecting subjects by the CIA; and the illegal harassment of dissidents by the FBI.

State-organized crime and terrorism grow out of the same values that form the American Dream—the drive for money, power, and status. Accordingly, Chomsky and Hermann (1977) believe that there has been a pattern to this brutality involving U.S. economic and military aid, as well as loans, that has been positively related to the investment climate for U.S. multinational corporations and negatively associated with human rights and maintaining democratic processes. In other words, a pattern of U.S. aid to Third World nations precedes the granting of concessions to U.S. multinational firms, and continuance of such aid is contingent upon the continuance of a favorable investment climate.

Chomsky (1992:7–28) has recently argued that while the United States claims it wants nations in both former Communist and Third World areas to adopt democracy and free enterprise, its real goal is maintaining control of vital raw materials, access to cheap labor supplies, and access as well to potential markets for goods and services produced by U.S. multinational corporations.

- In 1948, State Department Policy Planning Study 23, written by diplomat George Kennan, declared that since the United States possessed 50 percent of the world's wealth, but only 6.3 percent of the world's population, "we cannot fail to be the object of envy and resentment." The real task of foreign policy, Kennan declared, was to find a way to hang on to American wealth. The real fear of the United States is that the poor of the world will find solace in revolutionary movements that seek to redress the imbalance in the world's distribution of wealth. As Secretary of State John Foster Dulles stated privately to his brother, the real threat of "communism" (very broadly defined in this case) is its ability "to get control of mass movements . . . something we (the United States) have little capacity to duplicate . . . . The poor people are the ones they appeal to, and they have always wanted to plunder the rich" (in Chomsky, 1992:78–79).

  In 1950, at a briefing for ambassadors, Kennan declared that the major concern of U.S. foreign policy must be "the protection of our (i.e., Latin America's) raw materials" (quoted in Chomsky, 1992:11).

- In 1949, a State Department memo declared that the major function of the Third World was to serve "as a source of raw materials and a market" for industrial capitalist societies (Chomsky, 1992:12).

Thus access to markets, raw materials, and cheap labor, not the promotion of democracy or free enterprise, has been the stated goal of U.S. foreign policy in the postmodern era. U.S. support for allegedly anti-Communist regimes, no matter how repressive, has been a consistent and tragic pattern and continues into the era of the post–Cold War New World Order. Indeed, the CIA has trained more police forces around the world than virtually any other agency of U.S. government, yet it is almost never mentioned in criminal justice and law enforcement texts. Obtaining a working knowledge of the motives for and depth of state-organized—and what Edward Herman and Gerry O'Sullivan (1989) term *the terrorism industry*—is essential to understanding both social problems, and the overall political economy of the nation functions.

For example, Chambliss claims that not all governmental agencies are likely to engage in state-organized crimes. Usually the more secretive ones, like the CIA, FBI, Drug

Enforcement Administration (DEA), and various intelligence agencies are in ideal positions to commit terrorist acts. Indeed, these agencies have repeatedly obstructed justice and used national security as their excuse to do so. For example, the CIA and FBI covered up the crimes of former employee and Cuban exile Ricardo Morales, who, on CIA orders, bombed a Cuban airliner in Venezuela, killing seventy-three people. Moreover, Honduran General José Buseco was indicted for plotting the murder of his nation's president, but Lieutenant Colonel Oliver North, along with Department of Defense and CIA officials, pressured Justice Department personnel to be lenient with the general. Finally, the Drug Enforcement Administration (DEA) paid Panamanian General Manuel Noriega $4.7 million to protect the Medellin drug cartel's cocaine shipments in Panama (Chambliss, 1989:185).

Likewise, the United States has made a tragic habit of supporting some of the world's most terroristic regimes, governments that regularly violate the human rights of their own people. The United States is a signatory to two human rights treaties, the United Nations Declaration of Human Rights of the 1940s and the Helsinki Agreement of 1975. Both documents emphasize freedom from arrest without probable cause, kidnapping, torture, and violations of freedom of speech and press.

However, the United States has played an important role in supporting regimes that violate human rights, all in the name of anti-Communism:

In 1954 the CIA directed a coup in Guatemala that toppled the government of Jacobo Guzman. After it was learned that Guzman planned to nationalize the holdings of the United Fruit Company, the Eisenhower administration, under the guise of anti-Communism, replaced Guzman with a U.S. Army–trained officer, Castilo Armis. Armis immediately halted the nationalization of United Fruit's holdings, abolished political parties and trade unions. Between 1963 and 1993, Armis' regime and its United States-backed successors tortured and killed 150,000 of its own citizens, and kidnapped another 50,000. Guatemala's human rights record was so grotesque that the Bush administration in 1990 was forced to suspend aid due to congressional pressure (Johnson et al., 1993:13; Simon & Eitzen, 1993:201).

While the Bush administration tried to claim the Guatemalan rights record was improving under a newly elected regime in 1991, the evidence contradicted this view. Between January and September, 1991, 730 assassinations and a hundred disappearances (an average of three per day) were documented by human rights groups. A Guatemalan Indian leader, Rigoberta Menchu, was awarded the Nobel Peace Prize in 1992 for her work in trying to get the government to stop forcibly relocating and killing her own people from 1982 to 1991 (when 1 million Indians were forcibly relocated by the government). The Reagan-Bush administration provided Guatemala with over $77 million in aid during this period.

In 1995, it was revealed that Guatemalan Colonel Julio Alpirez had been a paid secret operative of the CIA, and was linked to the murder of Michael DeVine and Effran Valasquez. Mr. DeVine was an American innkeeper, who worked and lived in the Guatemalan jungle. DeVine was murdered because he stumbled on Colonel Alpirez's illegal smuggling operation involving ancient mahogany trees. Mr. Valasquez's murder was made into a scandal by his crusading widow, American attorney Jennifer Harbury. Valasquez was a Mayan rebel leader who was captured, tortured, and murdered by the Guatemalan army. The State Department tried to cover up Ms. Harbury's revelations, accusing her of being stuck in a 1960s mentality. But the murder of DeVine and Valasquez is merely a symptom of a much more widespread Guatemalan program of repression, supported by the CIA. In the 1980s, Colonel Alpirez was in a special unit called the Cabalas. The outfit was responsible for the systematic murder of tens of thousands of Guatemalan Indians in the 1980s, a massacre so brutal that it left, by official government count, 40,000 widows and 150,000 orphans in its wake. The CIA ended its relationship with Alpirez in 1992 by giving him severance pay of $44,000 (Weiner, 1995; Manegold, 1995).

In El Salvador between 1978 and 1993, over 40,000 people were killed by government-supported right-wing death squads, and 800,000 people (20 percent of the population) became refugees. Between 1979 and 1984, the Reagan administration gave El Salvador six times more aid than it had received in the previous thirty years. In 1980, the government death squads raped and murdered four American nuns, and Amnesty International declared the death squads a gross abuse of human rights. Over the years, multinationals such as Chevron, Kimberly-Clark, and Texaco have invested over $100 million in El Salvador (Kwitney, 1984:10–11; Caldicott, 1984:160). Human rights abuses in El Salvador continued in the 1990s. A U.N. observer mission reported 105 assassinations in 1992, fifteen kidnappings, and 281 illegal captures by security forces. In January 1993, the widow and children of a former El Salvadoran Human Rights Commission head were fired on by government troops. The children had personally witnessed their father's murder by the government in 1987 (Johnson et al., 1993:54–55).

In Panama, the United States had aided the regime of General Noriega for nearly a decade in the 1980s. Noriega was even on the payroll of the CIA for $200,000 a year as an informant in the war on drugs. In 1989, the Bush administration claimed it had learned that Noriega was accepting payoffs from the Medellin cocaine cartel, and invaded Panama to have him arrested. An estimated 4000 people were killed in the invasion, many times the number the Pentagon was willing to acknowledge. Two American soldiers have been killed by the Panamanian police since 1990.

A new president, Guillermo Endara, was sworn in on a U.S. military base. Both Endara and his second vice-president have been involved in laundering drug money, according to U.S. Drug Enforcement Administration reports. Moreover, in 1991, two hundred fifty murders and 17,000 drug-related crimes were reported in Panama, and over two hundred fifty charges of corruption were filed against the Panamanian police. A law was passed in 1990 forbidding public employees from participating in public demonstrations (Johnson et al., 1993:12). Why did the United States really invade? One line of reasoning makes the connection that nearly 40 percent of the national budget of Panama is interest on its debt owed to American banks and the U.S. government (Steel, 1978:12). For a second factor consider that in 1990, partial administrative responsibility for the Panama Canal was due to pass into Panamanian hands, with complete control over the Canal scheduled to go to Panama in 2000. Noriega, whose drug dealing has been known about since the 1970s, was pursuing a course independent of the United States' wishes. Of the $1 billion of U.S. aid promised Panama after the invasion, $400 million consisted of incentives for U.S. multinationals to export products to Panama, $150 million went to pay off bank loans, "$65 million went to private sector loans and guarantees to U.S. investors" (Chomsky, 1992:55).

In Nicaragua, the United States backed the Samoza family's rule from 1929 to 1979, when it was overthrown by a popular revolution. Upon taking office in 1981, the Reagan administration helped former Samoza national guardsmen form a counterrevolutionary

Panamanian General Manuel Noriega was employed by the CIA at the same time as he was helping the Medellin cocaine cartel smuggle drugs into the United States. Noriega was arrested by U.S. troops after an invasion of Panama in which hundreds of Panamanian civilians were killed.

army, the Contras, and used the CIA to train them. The revolutionary Sandinista government, meanwhile, redistributed peasant land, eliminated malnutrition, and reduced the illiteracy rate from 50 to 12 percent. Oxfam America, a human rights groups, declared that Nicaragua was unique among Third World nations in having a government that was dedicated to the needs of its people (Chomsky, 1992:42; Simon & Eitzen, 1993:201–202). That the Sandinistas might provide a model of democratic development was a threat to U.S. interests readily acknowledged by Reagan administration officials. Secretary of State George Schultz declared that Nicaragua was a "cancer," and one State Department official openly declared that Nicaragua would be turned into a poor and isolated country—"the Albania of Central America" (in Chomsky, 1992:43).

When the Sandinista government turned to Cuba and the former Soviet Union for aid, the Reagan administration began a covert war against Nicaragua. The Nicaraguan Contras mined Managua's harbor, an action found illegal by the World Court. When Congress cut off military aid to the Contras in response to the World Court's decision, the Reagan administration undertook projects to aid the Contras privately, part of which was the diversion of funds from Iranian arms sales to the Contras. The Contras also received monies from the Medellin cocaine cartel, committed atrocities against the civilian population, and engaged in numerous acts of corruption (Moyers, 1988).

This same pattern of U.S. support for repression of democratic or revolutionary movements, accompanied by the most extreme types of physical and financial harm, has been repeated in numerous countries outside Latin America in the postmodern era.

After World War II, the CIA recruited ex-Nazis, including Klaus Barbie, "the Butcher of Leon," responsible for the deaths of thousands of French Jews during World War II. Barbie was transported to Latin America in the 1940s, where he was instrumental in establishing Latin American cocaine production (Linklater, 1984; Scott, 1988:30). The CIA also hired Mafia figures on numerous occasions to, among other things (1) assassinate Fidel Castro of Cuba, (2) break a strike on the docks of Marseilles, France, in 1948, and (3) set up a heroin-smuggling operation in Southeast Asia during the Vietnam War to finance a secret war in Laos (Pearce, 1976:149–151). All of these harms point to a massive policy failure to resolve the political crises of the postmodern era, and a profound alienation of the public from political life.

Conventional Wisdom and Continuing Failed Policies

Documents declassified in 1993 demonstrate that the military-industrial complex "systematically and repeatedly lied to Congress and the public to frighten them into an ever-larger military. The military has sucked away public investment, both dollars and talent, from many of the areas now so deeply in need—education, health care, public infrastructure, social services and research and development for civilian economic enterprise" (Johnson, 1993: A-8). Moreover, the National Security State created by the 1947 National Security Act resulted in many harmful practices by government agencies. These included forced loyalty oaths; classification of documents, even when there was no war; spying on innocent American citizens by government agencies; and the firing, blacklisting, and imprisoning of thousands of innocent citizens, all in the name of national security.

As harmful as secrecy, waste, fraud, abuse, and resultant violations of human rights of the military-industrial complex have been, there is no evidence that much has changed since the Cold War's end. The myth being perpetuated in the 1990s is that the United States is militarily threatened by numerous enemies and is not spending enough on defense. The facts, however, belie this conventional wisdom.

- There are now $90 billion in surplus equipment in Pentagon warehouses, about $30 billion in excess of what would be needed if World War III were to break out.

- The Air Force has $5 million in unneeded engine blades. The Army Corps of Engineers lost $1.3 billion worth of equipment in 1992, and an Air Force computer routinely misclassifies one-time orders as needed repeatedly. There were three hundred aircraft engines that had to be scrapped because of improper storage. The Army spent $35.9 million for replacement equipment of repairable items.

- Even the Pentagon admits that the Sea Wolf submarine ($2.8 billion) and a new aircraft carrier ($4.5 billion) are unneeded. The systems are being built just to keep defense workers employed (O'Conner, 1994).

Meanwhile, an additional $1.5 trillion will be spent on defense between 1995 and 2000, and the United States will maintain 1.4 million men and women on active duty. About 100,000 of these personnel and their dependents will be stationed in Germany alone, defending against a threat—East German and Soviet Communism—that no longer exists. The annual American defense budget, about $230 to $280 billion, costs more money than the defense budgets of the next ten nations combined. Thus England, with the world's second-highest defense outlay, will spend only $200 billion on defense between 1995 and 2000. The Defense Department will continue to employ seven out of every ten federal workers (Borosage, 1994:65).

Both former Republican and Democrat defense policy personnel, as well as the former head of the Joint Chiefs of Staff, General Colin Powell, have all acknowledged that there is no direct military threat to the United States anywhere in the world. Even its worst enemies, like North Korea and Iraq, annually spend, at most, about $40 billion on defense. Another danger of spending over $200 billion per year on the military is that the generals will find things to do, places to go, if only to look useful (Borosage, 1994:74).

Operation Desert Storm made it clear that the United States has the ability to create enemies like Saddam Hussein in the Third World. Some observers speculate that the villainization of Hussein was just the beginning of a process of fighting short wars in faraway places (Klare, 1991; Nossiter, 1991:26). U.S. military personnel will constantly be placed in harm's way, enforcing a UN embargo in the Persian Gulf, intervening in one or more of

Box 6.1 • The Pentagon's Black Budget

Perhaps the clearest example of the harms stemming from excessive secrecy has been revealed by Pulitzer Prize–winning journalist Tim Weiner. In his recent book, *Blank Check,* he describes a "black (secret) budget." The black funds had their origin in the World War II Manhattan Project, which created the atomic bomb used on Japan in 1945. The agencies created by the 1947 National Security Act justified the continuation of the secret budget by lying to Congress about the size of the Soviet's military spending. The net result was to hide control over the nation's nuclear strategy from Congress and the American people. The budget is controlled by only three people—the president, the secretary of defense, and the director of the CIA; it is hidden from public view under titles like "Special Programs" and "Selected Activities."

Since its beginnings, the "black budget" has continually expanded and in 1990 was estimated at $36 billion. Hidden within it are monies for a host of questionable weapons projects, as well as the cover-up of a variety of covert, sometimes criminal, operations (Korb, 1990:16). Among the examples chronicled by Weiner:

- *Item*: MILSTAR is a proposed $20 billion top secret satellite project designed to coordinate a six-month-long nuclear war with the Soviet Union. Since the U.S.S.R. is currently begging for American foreign aid, and the end of both the Soviet empire and the Cold War have been declared by the Bush administration, justification for this proposed overpriced system is puzzling. Now that the world's ethnic civil wars currently raging in Bosnia, Rwanda, the old Soviet Union, or any one of a dozen other places. Meanwhile, European nations and Japan have many of their defense needs paid for by the United States, as they continue to out-compete the United States economically.

Meantime, inside the United States, 58 percent of all research and development continues to be spent on defense. This means that great public needs for mass transit, education, job training, the development of alternative energy resources, and universal health care continue to be unmet. A recent study by Employment Research Associates estimated that a $70 billion diversion of defense funds into education, repair of roads and bridges, and other domestic needs would create 477,000 jobs over a four-year period and add $17.6 billion per year to the nation's output of goods and services (GDP) (Bischak, 1994:90).

In short, the United States stands at a historic crossroads: The choice is between creating enemies, due to massive military aid to dictatorships, and converting the United States to a peacetime economy, with the goal of reinvigorating the manufacturing sector. To continue a policy of massive military spending would clearly mean continuation of the influence of the military-industrial complex and its devious practices. This will prove an unfortunate choice. The best choice to embrace—peace—might allow the United States to stop the economic decline that has been so devastating in recent years. The continuation of the policies discussed above will also increase the already substantial alienation of American citizens from their democracy.

Congress has finally gotten wind of the system, perhaps some hard questions can be asked.

- *Item:* The B-2 Stealth bomber has become the costliest airplane in the history of the nation. The Stealth's initial costs was estimated at $22 billion in 1981 and was finally pegged at over $68 billion ($820 million per plane) in 1991. The B-2's history is also laced with incidents of crime:

1. In 1985, the Stealth's manufacturer, Northrop, hired William Reinke as chief engineer. Mr. Reinke promptly set up his own firm, R E Engineering, and awarded the company $600,000 in subcontracts. Before being sentenced to five years in prison for fraud, Reinke sold Northrop $20 Radio Shack headphones for $90, and $1.24 cables for $4.50.

2. Ron Brousseau was Northrop's buyer of Stealth parts. Concerned about his retirement funds, he demanded and received a 5 percent kickback from subcontractors, a practice so common in the defense industry that it has been nicknamed the "nickel job." Brousseau also assisted subcontractors in a courtesy bidding (price-fixing) scheme, wherein different firms take turns being

Continued on next page

Box 6.1 • Continued

low bidders on contracts, creating the illusion of competition. Finally, Brousseau was sentenced to a three-year prison term for fraud.

- *Item:* The Northrop Corporation itself was involved in a host of illegalities regarding the Stealth and other projects:

  Northrop overcharged the government $400 million for the Stealth, was indicted for fraud and conspiracy for the act, and its chairman, William Jones, resigned in disgrace.

  The company providing fasteners for the Stealth, Voi-shan, defrauded the government by providing defective parts "approved" by a fictitious inspector.

Aside from questionable and sometimes illegal projects, the black aspect of the Pentagon budget has also involved a host of covert operations, knowledge of which was unconstitutionally hidden from congressional oversight.

- *Item:* After the failed hostage rescue in Iran in 1981, a secret operations unit continued activities. The unit had a secret budget funneled from other projects approved by Congress. Funds totaling $320 million were utilized for these operations, named Yellow Fruit, but a great deal of the money was illegally misspent on a variety of activities, including: vacations, prostitutes' services, drugs, clothing, and a variety of high tech equipment. As a result of the fraud connected with operation Yellow Fruit, only 10 to 20 percent of the $320 million was actually spent on covert operations. Three U.S. Army officers responsible for the funds were sentenced to prison terms ranging from eighteen months to ten years with fines of $5000 to $50,000 in the first secret court-martial held by the U.S. Army since the Vietnam era (Weiner, 1990:187–188).

- *Item:* In another "black" operation between 1986 and 1991, the CIA secretly aided the Afghan rebels who were fighting Russian troops. The CIA also got China, Saudi Arabia, and Iran to aid the Afghan rebels. Some arms were sold to Pakistan in acts of self-enrichment. Some of the funds earmarked for the Afghans were diverted to the Contras in a violation of the Boland Amendment.

- *Item:* In 1984, the CIA received Palestinian arms captured by Israel. The arms were funneled illegally to the Nicaraguan Contras. In one of the CIA's deals, Israel received CIA weapons credits for sending captured arms to the Contras. Israel would then sell a like amount of arms to China, who promptly exported an equal sum of weapons to a CIA dummy corporation. In turn, the CIA would funnel the secret arsenal to Iran and/or the Contras. Other weapons were stockpiled for use, not against the Soviets, but in the bloody civil war that followed the Russian withdrawal of 1990. All of these examples are merely a small portion of the financial harm taking place as part of the Defense Department's weapons-contracting process.

Political Alienation in America

Political alienation is a special form of moral harm involving cynicism about and distrust of government. The various scandals discussed in this chapter, along with additional incidents, such as the secretive and divisive Vietnam War (1964–1975), have contributed greatly to a crisis of confidence in government.

Table 6.1		
Distrust in Government, 1964–1992		
YEAR	*TRUST IN WASHINGTON*	*PERCENT WHO BELIEVE SPECIAL INTERESTS DOMINATE*
1964	76.4	28.4
1968–Vietnam	59.4	38.2
1976–Watergate	33.1	65.6
1988–Iran-Contra	40.5	63.1
1992	28.9	74.7

Source: Craig, 1993:11.

In 1964, a National Elections Studies poll revealed that over 76 percent of the public believed that Washington could be trusted to do the right thing most of or part of the time. By 1992, the percentage of the public who trusted the federal government had fallen to less than 30 percent. Likewise, the percentage of people who believe Washington politics is undemocratic and dominated by a few large interests increased from nearly 29 percent in 1964 to 74.7 percent in 1992.

Why is such distrust so harmful? American government was set up with a particular view of citizenship in mind. It was assumed that elected bodies, such as Congress, would be composed of well educated farmers, who would care deeply about public affairs. Office holding was viewed as a civic duty that would be exercised by concerned citizens for a limited time period. Following their tenure in office, citizens would return to their farms where they would continue their interest in public affairs by staying well informed, and would participate in debates about public issues. This is one reason why nowhere in the Constitution is the profession politician, or the establishment of political parties, lobbyists, or other trappings of what has come to pass for democratic government mentioned.

What has evolved over two centuries is a system that bears scant resemblance to what America's founders envisioned. As C. Wright Mills pointed out in the 1950s, the advent of the mass media has transformed an active public into something of a passive, undifferentiated mass that mostly receives and filters information, and provides limited feedback to its leaders via public opinion polls, letters, and occasional demonstrations. There are a minority of citizens who are organized in interest groups, most of which are of narrow focus (e.g., gun ownership, abortion, concern for the elderly, and so on). Between the mindless mass audience open to manipulation and the special issue group, there is a void of apathetic voters.

Indeed, instead of an informed citizenry, there is now an ignorant one. This is not because most people do not try to follow public affairs, they do. What the public *is* is "selectively misinformed" (Cohen & Solomon, 1993:113).

- In 1992, nearly 90 percent of the public knew that Murphy Brown was the TV character criticized by Dan Quayle, but only 19 percent could identify the Reagan cabinet member indicted in the Iran-Contra scandal (Caspar Weinberger). One reason for this is that the press devoted great attention to Quayle's position of family values and his criticism of the Murphy Brown, but devoted more attention to Bill Clinton's draft status during the Vietnam War than to the role of Bush administration officials in the much more recent Iran-Contra scandal.

- Half of the public believed that President Bush imposed sanctions on China due to its human rights abuses, but, in fact, he vetoed such legislation, allowing China to retain most-favored-nation status.

- Nearly one-third of the public believed the Bush campaign's claim that taxes in Arkansas were among the nation's highest, when in fact they were among the lowest (which 21 percent knew).

- Two-thirds of the public believed that Congress spent more money in 1992 than President Bush's budget requested, when in fact Congress spent less than requested (only 22 percent knew). Nearly half of the public did not know how government money was spent. Forty-two percent believed that more was spent on foreign aid than defense or welfare. Nearly one-third chose welfare. In fact, only 1 percent was spent on foreign aid, and 5 percent on welfare, compared with over 20 percent spent on defense (which only 22 percent knew) (Cohen & Solomon, 1993:113–114).

The problem is not merely that television networks and print media are selective in their presentations of public issues. That indeed is true, and the list of major scandals unreported until they are well under way or over is long and disturbing. The press underreported the massive savings and loan scandal, it failed to report how many civilians were actually killed in the Panamanian invasion, and said nothing about the Pentagon's "black budget" until it was exposed by Tim Weiner. However, the press is only part of the problem of public ignorance and elite manipulation.

An additional factor contributing to public distrust involves the process of political campaigns, especially as to presidential politics. These campaigns have become increasingly about negative campaign advertising (involving personal attacks on the candidates themselves), manipulation, and deceit.

The public resents such manipulation and deceit. Following are a few examples of some of the more memorable incidents in the postmodern era:

- In the 1960 election campaign, Democrats John Kennedy and Lyndon Johnson faced Republicans Richard Nixon and Henry Cabot Lodge. Kennedy won his party's nomination (in part) when Mafia figures were hired to buy votes for Kennedy in the West Virginia primary. During the election, Mafia personnel from Sam Giancana's Chicago family were hired to rig votes on Chicago's North Side. Lyndon Johnson, Kennedy's vice-president, broke into politics by being elected to the Texas State Senate in 1948. Johnson won by portraying himself as a war hero (he actually was stationed in the States), buying votes outright, and having results miscounted and changed (Mitchell, 1992:95,99).

- In 1980, the Reagan campaign stole the briefing books that were used to prepare President Carter for his debates with Ronald Reagan. George Will, newspaper and media commentator, helped brief Reagan for the debate using documents he knew were stolen. Will then praised Reagan's performance while analyzing the debate for ABC News (Cohen & Solomon, 1993:145).

- In 1988, the Bush campaign accused rival Michael Dukakis of favoring early prison release of dangerous criminal murderers and rapists. Such ads were also racist in that they frequently featured a convicted African American, Willie Horton.

The results of such tactics are discussed in the following "Private Troubles/Public Issues" forum.

Private Troubles Public Issues

Voter Alienation

Democracy requires the active participation of informed and interested citizens, but the United States has the lowest rate of voter turnout of any modern democracy. Voter turnout has declined steadily in every presidential election in this century, except for the 1992 election, wherein a very slight increase took place. Presidential elections are now decided by less than half of the eligible voters. Political campaigns on the federal level increasingly feature two wealthy candidates running against each other, and millions in PAC money. More often, however, younger voters mimic the voting behavior of their parents. That is, if parents take voting seriously, so will their children. Likewise, nonvoting parents tend to raise nonvoting children.

Part of the sociological imagination must involve the realization that politics is not something that is out there some place far away, unrelated to your life. Political decisions vitally affect every aspect of your life. The military draft and its uses, the amount you pay for your college tuition, the presence or absence of family planning services and birth control on your campus, the funds available for scholarships and loans, whether or not you

Continued on next page

Private Troubles Public Issues

Continued

can drink liquor on campus, the quality of the food you eat, and the water you drink are just a few of the vital political issues affecting the quality of your life.

Many studies demonstrate that those citizens most likely to get involved in democratic processes are college educated and middle class. On most large college campuses, there are numerous political groups students can join—Democratic and Republican clubs, chapters of Ralph Nader's Public Interest Research Group, and other organizations supporting worthy political causes. Historically, less than 10 percent of the student population will involve themselves in such groups. Yet, as the student movement of the 1960s demonstrated, such groups can serve a vital role in creating progressive social change concerning stopping unjust wars, passing civil rights legislation, expanding birth control services, and aiding the poor and hungry.

What are your attitudes about joining student political groups? What are your attitudes about politics and voting? These are just a few of the questions involved in confronting the social issues that contribute to the private troubles of college students.

Summary

This chapter has explored the harmful results when a society is characterized by the principles of democratic government in combination with the ethos of capitalism. A major consequence of attempting democracy in a society dominated by the profit-making ethos of business is a multifaceted corruption of government.

Since the investigation of the assassination of President Kennedy in 1963, the executive branch has seen a parade of major scandals. These scandals have involved both personal enrichment on the part of some individuals, and gross abuses of power on the part of governmental organizations, especially the CIA. The CIA was created by the National Security Act of 1947, and, ever since, deviant behavior (both criminal and noncriminal) has been institutionalized in a Secret Government (a National Security State) that has demonstrated itself to be beyond democratic controls.

To wit, the CIA has attempted to assassinate foreign leaders, established narcotics routes in conjunction with organized crime, hired former Nazis, and illegally spent monies that were part of a black (secret) budget. The CIA has also played a major role in the cover-up of the Kennedy assassination, as well as the Watergate, Iran-Contra, and savings and loan scandals.

Another consequence of the National Security Act was the establishment of a permanent warfare state, with its high levels of military spending, especially on expensive weapons systems. Our examination of Pentagon contracting has revealed a long history of waste, fraud, abuse, and corruption within defense contracting circles. There is also a long history of revolving-door movement where personnel are easily exchanged between Pentagon and weapons manufacturers.

In addition to the growth of the military-industrial complex, the federal government, since the 1930s, has experienced a tremendous increase in various executive branch departments and congressional staffs. The result is that the federal government now spends over $1 billion per year just for congressional staffs. The great influence of corporate money in politics and the quest for political power in Washington among politicians have resulted in a gravy train mentality in which members of congresses secure subsidies and porkbarrel projects for their most influential constituents. These expenditures, along with the costs of the warfare state, have greatly increased the federal debt (which has nearly quintupled since 1980, and currently stands at over $4.5 trillion).

Finally, abroad, the influence of multinational corporations and the creation of the Secret Government have produced foreign and defense policies whose central priorities concern the protection of the overseas holdings of multinational corporations and the arms sales of the military-industrial complex and its Secret Government. Support for terroristic governments by the United States was all too common during the Cold War, and remains an important element of American foreign policy today.

Sociologically, the values associated with the American Dream (especially profit and power) are so embraced by governmental officials that the prescribed means for achieving such goals (living within the law) are ignored. Indeed, within the confines of the National Security State, illegal means have been institutionalized in the form of secrecy and the ideology of national security.

Suggested Readings

E.J. Dionne (1991) *Why Americans Hate Politics* (New York: Simon & Schuster). An interesting analysis concerning the reasons for widespread political alienation in America.

Dan Moldea (1986) *Dark Victory: Ronald Reagan, MCA, and the Mob* (New York: Viking). A fascinating study of the influence of organized crime in the career of President Reagan.

Bill Moyers (1988) *The Secret Government* (Berkeley: Seven Locks Press). The PBS host of many documentaries published the entire script of one of the most important of his programs. Moyers sounds the national alarm over the lack of democratic control of the nation's war powers. There is also included a good discussion of the causes of modern scandal.

Exercises

Critical Thinking Exercise 6.1	Subsidies Without Reason

Senator William Proxmire used to present a Golden Fleece award for the most ridiculous expenditures by the federal government. One of his awards spotlighted such funding research as to discover why monkeys fall in love. As you can tell from the above discussion of subsidies, the federal government continues to spend money on wasteful projects. Do a search of databases like *Infotrack, Proquest,* or the *Reader's Guide* for the past three years. Make a list of what newspapers and magazines consider the most questionable expenditures. On what basis are most of these grants and subsidies questioned? Who are the recipients of most such programs?

Critical Thinking Exercise 6.2	Scandal: The Hidden Dimensions

This chapter began with a discussion of some of the characteristics of modern scandal on the federal level. One of the most interesting aspects of contemporary scandal concerns lingering questions which remain the subject of controversy and debate. For example, after nearly twenty-five years, we still do not know why the Nixon administration decided to bug the Democratic National Committee headquarters in the Watergate Hotel. This and many other unanswered questions are the subject of this exercise.

Select one of the following scandals:

1. Watergate

2. Iran-Contra

3. Inslaw

4. The savings and loan scandal

5. Iraqgate

Utilizing the list of periodicals given at the end of Chapter 4, look up articles about any one of the above scandals. Then write a paper answering the following questions:

1. What remains unknown concerning the causes of the scandal?

2. What other scandalous events are speculated about by writers as occurring during the scandal? For example, some people have speculated that the Nixon administration hired Arthur Bremmer to assassinate George Wallace during the 1972 election campaign.

3. What reforms are proposed to prevent such scandals from taking place in the future?

Postmodern Environmental Crises: Alienation, Mass Consumption, and the Overpopulation Debate

Chapter · Chapter · Chapter · Chapter · Chapter

7

Clarifying the Pollution Debate

One of the most hotly debated social problems of the postmodern era concerns the destruction of the environment. A chief cause of such destruction is pollution. **Pollution** is defined as "the direct or indirect alteration of physical, thermal, biological, or radioactive properties of any part of the environment in such a way as to create a hazard or potential hazard to the health, safety, or welfare of any living species" (Allaby, 1989:309).

The term *pollution* is most often used to describe the changes brought about by the emission of industrial contaminants or by the careless discharge or disposal of human domestic waste products or sewage, excessive noise production, and the release of excessive heat (thermal pollution) (Allaby, 1989:309). Environmental problems are extremely hard to define for many reasons. First, consider **sustainability,** the efforts that meet the needs of the present generation without compromising the needs of future generations (Wright, 1994:H-1). These needs include available raw materials for manufacturing, as well as supplies of clean water, air, and other life-sustaining substances. No group of economists has fully determined earth's limits—or how sustainability can soon be achieved (Wright, 1994:H-4). Because of the above reasons and many others, policy makers find defining an environmental problem a difficult task. The line between a problem and something that is acceptable is arbitrary. An economist, for example, will draw the defining line at a very different point than would an ecologist. Very rarely will a consensus be reached. This allows for a weak, ambiguous definition or the lack of any at all. There is also no consensus concerning how many more people can be added to the earth's population without exhausting available resources and creating life-threatening levels of pollution.

From a sociological imagination perspective, it serves no use to debate the earth's capacity to absorb pollutants or accommodate additional billions of people. The real social problems regarding environment and harmful patterns of population growth are those that are physically, financially, and/or morally harmful, and, therefore, objectively measurable. Using the standard of objective harm, there is no question that various types of environmental pollution are extremely harmful.

Consider air pollution. The Clean Air Act of 1970 named seven major pollutants that are found in the air around us. These cause the largest volume of air quality degradation and are also considered the most threatening to human health and welfare. They include sulfur dioxide, photochemical oxidants, carbon monoxide, particulates, nitrogen oxides, hydrocarbons, and lead (Cunningham & Saigo, 1992:464–465). Air pollution has reached health-threatening levels in many cities around the world. Hundreds of thousands, possibly millions, of people suffer from pneumonia, asthma, bronchitis, cardiovascular complications, sinusitis, conjunctivitis, laryngitis, bloody noses, and allergies, which are all pollution-related illnesses. The numbers are not certain, but experts believe pollution-triggered deaths are somewhere around 5000 a year in Mexico City alone (Rodriguez, 1991:M-1; Brown, 1992).

About 70 percent of the earth's city dwellers—more than 1.5 billion people—breathe unhealthful air. At least 800 million people will die prematurely due to air pollution. Fifty-six million tons of carbon dioxide are spewed out into the atmosphere, largely because of the use of fossil fuels and the burning of rain forests. More than 1500 metric tons of ozone-depleting chlorofluorocarbons are discharged into the atmosphere from leaking refrigerators and air conditioners, aerosol spray cans, and some industrial processes (Fox &

Lutgen, 1992:H-6). Consequently, these chlorofluorocarbons are thinning the ozone layer that protects the planet from harmful sunlight. This raises the risk of cataracts and skin cancer and damages marine life at the most minute level (Fox & Lutgen, 1992:H-7).

Air pollutants are also acidifying many lakes in North America. Approximately 48,000 lakes in Canada are endangered. Nearly half of the high altitude lakes in the Adirondack mountains of New York are so acidified that they contain no fish (Cunningham & Saigo, 1992:480).

Consider a related form of pollution, global warming. **Global warming** potentially threatens the sustainability of life on earth by causing the average surface temperatures to rise three to eight degrees (Stevens, 1992:C-4). The rising temperature might result in the melting of polar ice caps, and sharp changes in weather patterns (Fox & Lutgen, 1992:H-7). Global warming occurs because gases such as carbon dioxide and methane form a barrier that traps heat. Sunlight is able to pass through this barrier to warm the earth, but "the resulting heat is unable to pass back into space" (Fox & Lutgen, 1992:H-7).

A wide variety of land spaces are threatened by global warming. For example, the Mississippi marshes make up 41 percent of the wetlands in the United States. Unfortunately, 130 square kilometers of marsh are washed away each year. Louisiana loses more land annually than any place on the planet. Like the Mississippi marshes, many other areas will be affected by land erosion. A rise in sea level of only 30 centimeters will result in hundreds of thousands of refugees from the Indian and Pacific Ocean basins alone (Hilbertz, 1991:234). Already suffering from poverty and overpopulation, Bangladesh will most likely lose more lives to increasingly numerous and intense tropical storms (Brown, 1991:26).

Another possibly catastrophic result of air pollution is ozone depletion. In 1985, ozone levels in the stratosphere over the South Pole dropped precipitously. By 1990, "stratospheric ozone was depleted by 70 percent over an area the size of the continental United States" (Cunningham & Saigo, 1992:470).

Ozone (in the upper atmosphere) is necessary for life on earth, screening out over 99 percent of the sun's dangerous ultraviolet rays (Cunningham & Saigo, 1992:470). The culprits in ozone depletion are a group of otherwise useful compounds called chlorofluorocarbons (CFCs). An estimated 2 billion pounds of CFCs are released into the atmosphere annually (Lipske, 1992:33). The destruction of the ozone layer is a major cause of life-threatening skin cancer, as well as eye cataracts. Ozone depletion can also bring about suppression of immune systems and an increase in infectious diseases. Moreover, scientists have tested some two hundred plant species, most of them crops, and found that two-thirds are harmed by increased ultraviolet radiation through ozone layer depletion. Likewise, in the Antarctic Ocean, located beneath the atmosphere's biggest ozone "hole" and the site of one of the world's most bountiful fisheries, the productivity of phytoplankton—tiny plants that form the basis of marine food chains—has already been reduced by 6 to 12 percent, thus posing a potential threat to the world's fish (Myers, 1994b:25).

Consider pesticides, chemicals used to kill insects. Currently, our soils, streams, rivers, and oceans are laced with chemicals, as are our bodies. Most everyone carries at least small traces of at least half a dozen pesticides in his or her tissue. Pesticides result in 25 million human poisonings a year, according to the World Health Organization (WHO) and in various parts of the Third World they kill more people than major diseases do (Matthiessen, 1992:49; Pimintel et al., 1991; 1992:750).

One problem that has surfaced in recent years has been a drastic increase in the number of cases of skin cancer. This increase is believed due to the depletion of the earth's ozone layer which protects us from the harmful ultraviolet rays of the sun.

Consider water pollution. There are various categories of water pollution. Those causing health problems include infectious agents, such as bacteria and viruses, which originate from areas harboring human excretion. Radioactive materials like uranium, cesium, and radon enter the water supply through the mining and processing of ores and from power plants, weapons production, and natural sources, ultimately causing health problems. The category of plant nutrients, such as nitrates and phosphates, originate from agricultural and urban fertilizers. Plant nutrient pollution can disrupt entire water-based ecosystems by killing fish, and affecting all other animals that feed on fish, including humans. A 1992 EPA study reported that agricultural runoff figured prominently in an EPA analysis that found nearly half of more than 500,000 miles of rivers tested to be too polluted for their intended uses. There was also bad news concerning U.S. coastal waters, where pollution had closed a third of all shellfish fisheries, and where there were more than 2000 beach closings because of sewage contamination in 1991. The beach closings included fourteen states; another ten coastal states did not regularly test for contamination (Famighetti, ed., 1993:172).

Related to water pollution is the environmental problem known as **acid rain.** Many ecosystems and works of architecture are suffering as a result of its prevalence. Places like the Parthenon in Athens, the Colosseum in Rome, the Taj Mahal in India, and Rheims Cathedral in France are victims of acid rain. These structures are being degraded due to its destructive force. Acid rain is caused by emissions of sulfur dioxide and nitrogen oxides from metal foundries and power plants, as well as from heating systems and vehicles. These particles are carried by the wind over long distances (Bequette, 1993:23–24).

The term *acid rain* may be inappropriate. *Acid deposits* would be more accurate. Drifting air pollutants are deposited not only by rainfall but also by snow, clouds, and fog (so-called "wet deposits") as well as by gases and dust ("dry deposits") during the dry season. Even normal rain is mildly acidic (Bequette, 1993:24).

Significant numbers of lakes and streams in eastern Canada and the northeastern United States are polluted. Some 350,000 lakes in eastern Canada are sensitive to acidification. About 14,000 of these lakes have become severely acidified, and 150,000 have experienced some polluting effects. In the United States, about 1000 lakes have been severely affected and 3000 or so are somewhat affected (French, 1990).

Part of the water pollution equation is the actual lack of water itself. Water shortages are plaguing many people, places, and natural environments around the globe. Only about one-third of the world's fresh water is actually available to humans for drinking and irrigating (water in lakes, rivers, and the accessible water table below the ground) (Myers, 1994b:23). Today more than 1 billion people around the globe suffer water shortages. The number of people who are expected to suffer water shortages twenty years from now is

The sad erosion of this statue is due to the effects of acid rain. This type of pollution is extremely harmful to the earth's soil and water, as well as many artificial objects. Acid rain is a special problem along the northeastern part of the U.S.–Canadian border.

approximately 3 billion. Diseases caused by water shortages include 300 million cases of roundworm and 200 million cases of diarrhea, a major cause of infant death in the Third World (Myers, 1994b:23). Some 15,000 people, mostly children, die from diseases caused by unsafe water each year (Fox & Lutgen, 1992:H-6).

Consider **biodepletion,** the mass extinction of species throughout the globe. Basically, between one-third and two-thirds of the earth's species, plus a similar proportion of subspecies, verge on extinction. This situation has the potential to be the greatest extinction spasm since the demise of the dinosaurs and associated creatures 65 million years ago. Biodepletion could result in a massive draining of the planetary gene pool. "The minimum length of time it will take evolution to come up with a replacement stock of species to match today's stock is 5 million years" (Myers, 1994b:5).

In the tropical rain forests alone, a conservative estimate tells us that we are losing several species to extinction every day. Since we do not even know what species are being destroyed in tropical forests, a more realistic estimate could be several species per hour. An animal that dies out this year might take with it a resistance to AIDS. Or, that animal may be essential to an insect that pollinates a flower that produces a chemical that kills human cancer (Sawhill, 1991:54).

Finally, consider desertification, the turning of agricultural lands into cropless deserts. A study done for the United Nations Environment Program indicates that a quarter of the world's irrigated land, half of its rain-fed cropland, and three-quarters of the range land are desertified (Dregne, 1993:33). Desertification also occurs because of overgrazing and wind and water erosion. The harms of tropical deforestation are numerous. It threatens a large share of the world's plant and animal species. Although tropical forests cover only about 7 percent of the globe, they are thought to contain more than half the world's species. On the most profound level, the benefit biodiversity confers is a healthy biosphere, for species are the agents of essential biological processes. Varied species help scientists answer evolutionary questions. They also provide valuable products. New medicines are constantly being sought, as well as fibers, species, oils, and lumber. Perhaps most immediately important to people, varied species insure vigorous crops and the resources for crop improvement (Stevens, 1992:C-6).

Often, clearing of forest for ranching is promoted by international development organizations (Fearnside, 1987) and by government incentive and subsidies, based on the legal definition of such action as "improvement" of the land (Hecht, 1989).

Deforestation could result in a loss of tropical forest plant species of between 5 and 15 percent between the years 1990 and 2020. If approximately 2.4 million species still exist in tropical forests, this translates into losses of 4000 to 12,000 species per year. Higher losses are projected if rates of forest destruction increase (Cox, 1992:66). Deforestation can also produce major changes in regional water supplies and climate. Deforestation tends to increase surface runoff into streams during rainy periods, for example, causing water pollution. Some evidence also indicates that deforestation in tropical areas leads to a decline in local precipitation (Myers, 1988).

Deforestation also reduces the rate of return of moisture to the atmosphere by transpiration and increases landscape albedo, or ratio of solar energy reflected to that absorbed. The result may be a shift to a new climate regime with longer dry seasons and drier overall conditions, such that even with protection from cutting, forests may be unable to recover (Cox, 1992:67).

This man was a resident of the Love Canal area of Niagara Falls, New York. He was forced to leave his home because toxic chemicals from a nearby dump, established by the Hooker Chemical Company, began seeping into his basement.

What this brief set of definitions and examples demonstrates is that environmental pollution is a major source of global harm, and much of that harm is measurable. It exists independently of any debate over how much pollution and resource depletion the earth can stand. What is crucial is that pollution is killing large numbers of human beings, animals, and plant life. Environmental pollution is also extremely expensive to remedy.

For example, from 1942 to 1953, the Hooker Chemical Company dumped more than 20,000 tons of toxic chemical waste into the Love Canal near Niagara Falls, New York. After Hooker sold the dumpsite to the Board of Education in 1953 for one dollar, an elementary school and playground were built on the site, followed by a working-class housing development. For at least twenty years prior to 1977, toxic chemicals had been seeping through to the land surface. However, in 1977, highly toxic black sludge began seeping into the cellars of the school and nearby residences. Tests showed the presence of eighty-two chemicals in the air, water, and soil of Love Canal, among them, twelve known carcinogens, including dioxin, one of the deadliest substances ever synthesized.

Once word of the contamination got out, the homes became worthless. But much more important, tests revealed that the inhabitants of this area had disproportionately high rates of birth defects, miscarriages, chromosomal abnormalities, liver disorders, respiratory and urinary disease, epilepsy, and suicide. In one neighborhood a few blocks from the Love Canal, a survey by the homeowners' association revealed that only one of the fifteen pregnancies begun in 1979 ended in the birth of a healthy baby; four ended in miscarriages, two babies were stillborn, and nine others were born deformed. A recent study disclosed that children who have spent three-fourths of their childhood living near Love Canal are experiencing subnormal growth as adolescents. The Love Canal case, finally settled in 1995, cost Hooker Chemical and other entities $120 million.

The costs of the 1989 Exxon Valdez oil spill, in which over 100,000 gallons of oil were discharged into Prince William Sound, Alaska, have reached over $5 billion in fines and clean-up costs.

The Office of Technology Assessment estimates that the cost of cleaning up hazardous waste sites over fifty years will run about $500 billion, roughly the initial costs of the savings and loan scandal, the worst financial scandal in American history (Commoner, 1994:144; Simon & Eitzen, 1993: 50–56).

There is, then, no question concerning the harms of pollution. What is sociologically significant about these harms is their structural origins, which lie within the contradictions of the global political economy, and the social patterns of victimization of global nonelites. These contradictions and patterns of victimization are the subject of this chapter.

Structure and Contradictions of Environmental Sustainability

Mass consumption is a major economic foundation of capitalist economies everywhere. The First World nations and the elites of developing nations all engage in mass consumption. The rates of consuming material goods are highest in First World nations. Mass advertising urges people the world over to buy the latest products produced by corporations in an effort to attain a satisfying life.

The great contradiction of mass consumption is that it uses up resources at an alarming rate, and in doing so, generates pollution on a global scale. Contemplate for a moment the following: A child born in a typical middle-class American home will go through 28,627 aluminum cans and 12,000 grocery bags, burn out 750 lightbulbs, eat 8486 pounds of red meat, and 17,591 eggs (equal to the lifetime production of thirty-five chickens), and wear and discard 250 shirts and 115 pairs of shoes. The United States contains only 5 percent of the world's population but consumes 25 percent of the fossil fuels used annually and a disproportional amount of other raw materials as well (Fox & Lutgen, 1992:H-6). The average American's energy use is equivalent to the consumption of 3 Japanese, 6 Mexicans, 12 Chinese, 33 Indians, 147 Bangladeshis, 281 Tanzanians, or 422 Ethiopians (During, 1992: 48–61).

To make matters worse, America's use of minerals since the 1940s equals the amount consumed by all humankind prior to that year. First World nations, such as the United

States, account for only a quarter of the world's human population, but intensively consume three-quarters of the planet's natural resources, inevitably contributing to three-quarters of its waste and pollution (Myers, 1994b:13).

- *Item:* The United States Bureau of Mines estimates that world consumption of aluminum will be twice today's level in nine years, that use of iron will double in a decade and a half, and that demand for zinc will double in seventeen years (Brown et al., 1976:58).

- *Item:* Western Europe must now import nearly all the copper, phosphate, tin, nickel, manganese, ore, and chrome ore it uses. In 1950, the United States depended on foreign sources for 50 percent or more of four of the thirteen basic minerals; by the year 2000, it is expected to rely on imports for at least 50 percent of twelve of these thirteen minerals. Except for coal, the major deposits of raw materials are found in the poor and developing nations of the world. Because these resources are rapidly diminishing (except for coal), severe shortages could occur. First World countries could raise prices and be able to trade their coal surpluses for scarce resources.

In regards to human population, consumption presents a grave problem. For example, Great Britain is increasing at only one-twelfth the rate of Bangladesh. But because each Briton consumes thirty times the commercial energy as a Bangladeshi, British population growth contributes 3.9 times as much carbon dioxide to the global atmosphere and hence more to global warming. Ironically, unplanned births account for all of Britain's population growth. Equally as shocking, the size of the average American family in terms of per capita pollution and consumption of critical resources is the equivalent of thirty citizens of the developing world (Myers, 1994b:13).

High energy use is a result of high consumption. Today nearly 90 percent of all commercial energy worldwide is provided by fossil fuels: coal, oil, and natural gases. The proven reserves of oil represent only about thirty-five years' supply at present rates of usage. Proven reserves of natural gas will last about sixty years at current usage rates, while coal in proven reserves could last three hundred years if usage remains constant. In the United States industry consumes about 37 percent of the energy used, primarily in manufacturing and processing. Residential and commercial space and water heating account for about 33 percent of our energy use. Transportation consumes almost all the remaining commercial energy (Cunningham & Saigo, 1992:343).

Why do we consume so much? Although there are many reasons, we shall focus on the major one: the global capitalist system, a system based on profits, the quest for which is never satiated. Companies must grow. More sales mean more profits. Sales are increased through advertising, product differentiation, new products, and creative packaging. Advertising creates previously nonexistent demand for products. The introduction of new products makes the old ones obsolete. Product differentiation (many models with different features) is redundant and wasteful, but it increases sales. The automobile industry is an excellent illustration of both product differentiation and planned obsolescence. Minor styling changes for each model year, with massive accompanying advertising campaigns, have the effect of making all older cars obsolete, at least in the minds of consumers.

Writing in 1960, Vance Packard warned of the waste demanded by our economic system. Progress through growth in profits is maximized by consumers who purchase products because they feel the need to replace old ones when they are used up or outmoded. This supposed need is promoted by manufacturers who produce goods that do not last long or who alter styles so that consumers actually discard useable items. These two marketing strategies create obsolescence through poor quality, and, through desirability, produce growing profits. But both strategies are fundamentally based on waste, a societal problem that cannot continue indefinitely.

One type of obsolescence is positive: the introduction of a new product that outperforms its predecessor. However, even this type can be orchestrated to increase waste and profit. The technology may exist for a major breakthrough, but the manufacturer or industry may choose to bring out a series of modifications that eventually lead to the state of the art. The rationale for this procedure is to saturate the potential market with the stepped-up technology, move to the next stage of development, and so on until the major breakthrough is attained. In this way, the consumer purchases a number of products rather than immediately purchasing the ultimate. The history of high-fidelity sound equipment provides a good illustration of this marketing principle (Packard, 1960:55–56).

The waste of our throwaway age is easy to see. Beverages are packaged in disposable cans. Meat can be purchased in disposable aluminum frying pans, to be thrown away after one use. TV dinners are warmed and eaten in the same containers. We can purchase disposable cigarette lighters, plastic razors with built-in blades, even throwaway cameras. We also junk 7 million cars annually, as well as 10 million tons of iron and steel. These are merely a small sample of the products that are quickly used and tossed out. Obviously, corporations are not only the major force in getting consumers to purchase the goods they advertise; they are also a major cause of environmental pollution. While this statement must seem obvious, it is not. There is a temptation to view pollution as an unintentional by-product of a mass consumption economy, and to view corporate pollution as an unfortunate consequence of manufacturing. The facts, however, point in a different direction. Evidence indicates that environmental pollution is concentrated among a few industries, and that these industries, in addition to pollution, are characterized by high levels of various types of corporate deviance.

Along these lines, *Mother Jones* (1993) magazine published a list titled "the toxic ten." The list contained the descriptions of the most environmentally destructive corporations in America. Here are five of them:

DuPont

The largest chemical company in the United States has given the world nylon, Teflon, Freon, and leaded gasoline (which it still makes for markets overseas); is the country's number-one emitter of toxins, releasing poisons at the rate of just under a million pounds a day, according to the EPA's 1989 data; is the world's largest producer of ozone-destroying chlorofluorocarbons (CFCs), and leads all other companies in domestic deep-well injection of toxic wastes (254.9 million pounds in 1989). Recently, DuPont was forced to pay $1.4 million in damages for concealing records showing that six employees had developed lung damage from asbestos exposure. Its operation of the government's Savannah River nuclear weapons complex (1950–1989) polluted water sources for the area and has been connected to elevated levels of leukemia, lung cancer, and other diseases.

Georgia Pacific

According to 1991 EPA data, Georgia Pacific has the worst air permit compliance record in the forest products industry, and has pulp and paper mills that were cited as out of compliance for a cumulative sixty-one quarters (fifteen-plus years!). It also has plants emitting dangerously high amounts of cancer-causing chloroform into the air of at least four states. Recently, GP was fined $5 million for tax evasion in a scheme that allegedly would have damaged a wetlands area, and lost two court decisions concerning its release of the fiendishly toxic pollutant dioxin.

Cargill

Although Cargill is one of the world's largest grain traders, meat packers, flour millers, seed companies, and also runs steel mills, this $49 billion company is able to operate in great secrecy because it is privately held. Nonetheless, Cargill has been cited for over 2000 OSHA violations since 1987; spilled 40,000 gallons of toxic phosphoric solution into the Alifia River in Florida in 1988, causing a massive fish kill; and since 1991 has had the worst air compliance record of any company in its industry. It is also one of the top two emitters of toxins in its industry, according to the EPA. In 1991, then-governor Bill Clinton criticized the company for releasing into Arkansas rivers animal waste comparable to the output of 21 million people, or about ten times the state's population.

USX

Formerly United States Steel Corporation, USX operates a notorious steelworks in Gary, Indiana, which has been fined $34 million in penalties and cleanup costs for dumping toxin-laden wastewater, and $1.6 million more for violating the Clean Air Act. USX has also been repeatedly cited for violating air standards for toxic emissions in Pennsylvania at its Fairless and Clairton works. Additionally, USX's Marathon subsidiary was responsible for a hydrofluoric acid leak that led to the evacuation of 4000 people in Texas City in 1987. USX owns Marathon and Speedway gas stations in the Midwest and Southeast.

Ciba-Geigy

Ciba-Geigy, Ltd., is a Swiss-based agrichemical and drug multinational, and represents a global problem. In behavior shocking by any standard, Ciba-Geigy tested herbicides on human subjects in the 1970s in Egypt and India.

These examples are symbolic of a more widespread condition. For example, in the United States, 100 percent of toxic waste is made by industrial corporations (Miller & Miller, 1991:3–4). The leading emitters of such waste are all petrochemical companies (Epstein, 1994:688), producing 80 percent of all hazardous waste (Landers, 1988:380). The petrochemical industry is a vital part of the corporate sector of the American political economy.

As economist Harold Barnett (1994:19) notes, "the fifty-one largest U.S. domestic chemical corporations (not including petroleum refineries) are (all) Fortune 500 companies with total sales" running over $170 billion annually, and after-tax profits of around $150 billion. The top eight companies (DuPont, Dow, Union Carbide, Monsanto, Hanson, W. R. Grace, Hoccst Celanese, and PPG Industries) account for over half of the sales and profits of these firms, while the two largest (DuPont and Dow) account for 30 percent of sales.

While the exact extent of petrochemical hazardous waste is difficult to determine, here are some suggestive statistics. There are some 1200 chemical firms operating some 11,500 production facilities. The fifty largest industrial organic chemical firms account for nearly 90 percent of all shipments, and the fifty largest agricultural chemical firms account for slightly over 90 percent of all shipments. The fifty largest inorganic chemical firms account for roughly three-fourths of all shipments. One study by Booz Allen concluded "that these three industrial segments are the major source of petrochemical industry hazardous waste" (Barnet, 1994: 19).

Three electronics firms, including General Electric and Westinghouse, were also identified in the EPA's Clean Water Project as Potentially Responsible Parties (PRPs) at Superfund sites (hazardous waste sites in need of cleanup). Westinghouse is identified as a PRP at ninety EPA Superfund sites. Ford and General Motors, two automotive firms, are identified as PRPs at nineteen and twenty-one Superfund sites, respectively (Barnett, 1994:21). Consistent with the higher immorality, there is evidence that major chemical corporations, including DuPont, Union Carbide, and others, have hired organized criminal syndicates to illegally dispose of hazardous waste in New York, New Jersey, and other locations (Rebovich, 1992: 64–76; ABC News, 1988). In a number of states, mob-connected garbage haulers have obtained permits and set themselves up as solid waste disposers. Landfill owners were then bribed to sign for shipments that were never received, while the actual shipments were dumped illegally in sewers, waterways, or into the ocean (Albanese & Pursley, 1993:325–326). The hiring of organized criminal syndicates to perform various services for corporations and the federal government, especially the CIA, has a long and sordid history in the United States (Simon & Eitzen, 1993:77–80, 292–296). As is evident, patterns of environmental abuse are also related to patterns of corporate crime in general (Simon, 1995). That is, corporations that are consistent violators of environmental laws also tend to be consistent violators of other corporate crime statutes as well. This fact is extremely important for a number of reasons: (1) Many firms in the petrochemical and related industries are characterized by what can be termed a *crimogenic organizational culture*. Corporate crimes of many varieties are now almost like rituals, part of a set of deeply imbedded customary practices. (2) Because such deviant practices are so well entrenched, they are more difficult to deter, and the reason for this is that the punishment for most corporate crimes rarely involves prison time for corporate executives, and the fines imposed are usually minuscule, compared to corporate cash flows and assets (Simon & Eitzen, 1993: 72–73). (3) One reason why corporate crimes of all types flourish within certain industries is because the mainstream press underreports both individual incidents of crime, and the seriousness of such violations. In 1994 alone, six of the top ten Project Censored stories were ecologically related (Curran, 1995:15–17), and this pattern has been consistent since Carl Jensen (1993) began the project. The following are among Project Censored's top ten underreported stories of 1994:

• The EPA learned in the late 1980s of the dangers involved in the incineration of dangerous chemicals, but declined to take actions to protect public health.

- The Clinton EPA asked DuPont to continue manufacturing CFCs for automobile air conditioners. The administration also gave research grants to large firms, rather than smaller, more progressive firms that were exploring alternatives to CFCs. Some were forced out of business after being rejected for such grants.

- Industrial fishing fleets routinely discard 60 billion pounds of fish per year, some of them members of endangered species. Millions of the fish are caught, thrown overboard, and left to die because they are too small to eat. Clinton backer Don Tyson is trying to convince the federal government to grant his $4 billion firm corporate rights to the Alaska fishery without having to pay a dime in royalties.

- Because companies like General Electric also own major media outlets, news stories of GE's criminal violations are consistently given short shrift by mainstream media.

What all this means is that corporate violators of ecological criminal laws are part of an entire political economy, a macro environment over which they exert considerable control. Part of this environment concerns the global political economy in which such transnational corporations operate. Often, corporate violations are international in scope, and involve, not just violations of hazardous waste laws, but corruption statutes as well.

The problem of environmental destruction thus represents one of the most dangerous contradictions of giving priority to the value of accumulating wealth without regard to the means of doing so. Environmental problems also represent the outgrowth of an international system of nations in which corporations have been allowed to set priorities without regard to the welfare of individuals, especially the poorest and most powerless individuals in Third World nations—Third World workers, and poor men, women, and children around the globe.

Patterns of Environmental Victimization

The victimization of nonelites by environmental harms is a global pattern, one that especially strikes people of color. **Environmental racism** is the term used to describe the victimization of people of color by corporate polluters. Various studies have established that minorities in the United States are at considerable risk from such victimization:

- By 1986, some two million tons of radioactive uranium tailings had been dumped on Native American lands, and cancer rates among Navajo teens have climbed to seventeen times the national average (Rosen, 1994:225).

- African Americans are 40 percent more likely to live in neighborhoods in which toxic waste dump sites are located than are nonminorities. In the American South, 60 percent of neighborhoods surrounding waste disposal sites are African-American (Bullard, 1994:6 ff). Nationally, 60 percent of African-American communities are endangered by abandoned toxic waste dumps, and

One tragic form of inner-city pollution involves the ingestion of lead particles by poor children. Lead is contained in paint, which chips and is then eaten by unsupervised children. Eating paint chips can cause mental retardation and even death from lead poisoning.

commercial hazardous waste landfills (Rosen, 1994:226). In the United States, the lower a family's income, the higher the lead content in children's blood (Parenti, 1995:112).

- Some communities are repeatedly victimized by toxic hazards. When North Richmond, California, experienced a fifteen-mile-long toxic cloud from a ruptured rail car at General Chemical's plant, it marked the fifteenth time a serious industrial accident occurred at a Contra Costa County chemical facility or refinery within the past five years. Within the county itself, there are at least thirty-eight industrial sites in which 94 million pounds of some forty-five industrial chemicals are stored (Rosen, 1994:223–224).

It is the poor and working class of all colors that tend to live the closest to chemical factories, toxic dump sites, incinerators, and suffer the highest rates of pollution-caused cancer (Hilts, 1993: A-1; Rosen, 1994:225–228).

Similarly, recent studies confirm that toxic cleanup programs under the Superfund law take longer and are less thorough in minority areas (Rosen, 1994:226). A related harm associated with ecological destruction can be termed *employee blackmail*. This occurs when corporate polluters threaten victims living near factories where they work with job losses, should the victims continue pressing claims for environmental justice (investigations and cleanups) (Rosen, 1994: 225). Moreover, violations of environmental justice cause moral harm in the form of decreased public confidence in corporate and/or governmental legitimacy. There is overwhelming public opinion data indicating that corporations that pollute the environment deepen public distrust of corporations (Simon & Eitzen, 1993:4–6), especially of those citizens living near pollution sites.

Finally, the most helpless victims of environmental pollution are animals, many of whom are endangered. In the last twenty years, the U.S. Department of Interior claims, over three hundred species of wildlife have become extinct, and another 850 are now considered endangered (1100 species if plants are included) (Frank & Lynch, 1992:84). There are a number of causes of this carnage, but toxic incidents, such as the Exxon Valdez oil spill, must be considered, as well. Thousands of mammals, fish, and birds in Alaska were killed as a result of the spill. Numerous other chemical accidents and hazardous waste incidents have collectively killed millions of fish and other wildlife the world over.

The above examples are paralleled by victimization statistics of both humans and other species in Third World nations. Populations who have suffered at the hands of polluting multinational corporations and lax, sometimes corrupt, governmental policies are overwhelmingly people of color, and among the poorest and most powerless of the world's population. From Bhopal, India (where a 1984 chemical accident at a Union Carbide plant killed 5000 and injured 30,000) (Frank & Lynch, 1992:73), to Mexican border towns near Maquiladora plants, the victims of hazardous toxic waste scandals are most frequently those with the least access to sanitation, health education, and health care. Third World women and children have frequently suffered the harmful effects of dangerous products banned for use in the United States and exported to Third World nations, including pesticides like DBCP. These incidents serve to further increase the distrust and alienation experienced by people of color, and people everywhere victimized by corporate pollution.

International Environmental Pollution

There are a large number of toxic waste problems that are exported to foreign countries, many of which have involved the illegal bribery of officials of foreign governments. The advanced nations of the world generate about 400 million tons of toxic waste annually; 60 percent comes from the United States. A shipment of toxic waste leaves the United States every five minutes, every day of the year. The vast majority of America's internationally exported toxic waste, 80 percent, is sent to Canada and Britain (Cass, 1994:2). The Environmental Protection Agency (EPA) requires U.S. companies to provide on-site disposal facilities for toxic waste that cost upwards of $30 million and take years to build. However, such waste can be dumped in Third World nations for a fraction of the cost, sometimes for as little as $20 a ton (Cass, 1994:7). In 1991, an internal memo written by one of the World Bank's chief economists advocated that the World Bank encourage "more migration of dirty industries to the Less Developed Countries" (Rosen, 1994:226), thus giving credence to those who believe that environmental racism is an intentional policy.

At times, multinational corporations have provided handsome financial rewards to the recipient nations. For example, Guinea-Bissau, which has a gross national product of $150 million, will make $150 to $600 million over a five-year period in a deal through which it will accept toxic waste from three European nations.

Third World participation in the waste dumping of advanced nations has generated a host of scandals (Brooks, 1988; Cass, 1994):

- In April 1988, five top government officials in the Congo were indicted after they concluded a deal to import 1 million tons of chemical waste and pesticide residue, receiving $4 million in commissions from a firm specializing in hazardous waste disposal. The total contract was worth $84 million.

- After dumping toxic waste in Nigeria and Lebanon, in 1988, Italy agreed to take back some 6400 tons. What's more, Nigeria recalled its Italian ambassador and arrested twenty-five people when it discovered some of the waste was radioactive. To complicate matters, Italian dockworkers in ten port cities refused to handle the waste: Italy pledged to ban further toxic exports to the developing world and plans to spend $7 billion a year to clean up its own toxic dumps at home. The Italian government also sued twenty-two waste-producing firms to force them to turn over $75 million to pay for transporting and treating incoming waste.

- In 1987, Weber, Ltd., a West German waste transporter, found a Turkish cement plant willing to accept 1500 tons of toxic waste–laden sawdust for about $70 a ton. Instead of being burned, the sawdust waste sat in the open air for nearly sixteen months, slowly leaking poison into the ground. A newspaper reported the sawdust contained lethal PCBs, and a scandal ensued. Under pressure from the governments of Turkey and West Germany, Weber finally agreed to transport the waste back to West Germany. Normally, Weber charges its customers $450 to $510 a ton to dispose of waste in Germany. With Third World costs of $110 per ton, the amount of profit involved is substantial (*Newsweek*, 1988).

Moreover, manufacturers, like Pepsi, who used to transport toxic waste to nations like India, are now building bottling plants in that country, exporting the plastic bottles, and leaving the toxic waste on the manufacturing site in New Delhi. Workers at the Pepsi plant are paid thirty cents per day to wash the bottles as they roll off the assembly line (Leonard, 1994:9).

Closer to home, there are currently about 1800 Maquiladora plants owned by multinational firms along the U.S.–Mexican border. Out of six hundred plants owned by America's *Fortune* 500 firms, only ninety-one have thus far complied with Mexican law requiring that waste generated by American corporations be transported to the United States for disposal (Kelly, 1993).

Currently, some 100 million gallons of untreated sewage are dumped into the Rio Grande River daily, 10 million gallons in El Paso alone (Kelly, 1993:15). Rather than pay for incineration of hazardous waste at licensed American facilities, some firms load wastes on American trucks that are then smuggled into Mexico for illegal dumping. It is currently estimated that the pollution caused by Maquiladoras will cost over $16 billion to clean up, but, thus far, the World Bank has committed itself to just $1.8 billion in loans to Mexico for this purpose.

On both sides of the U.S.–Mexican border, there have been reports of deformed fish, human birth defects, increased cancer rates, and a doubling of typhoid and infectious hepatitis (Wolkomir, 1994:27, 30). In towns like Matamoros, xylene levels in the drinking water behind the Stepan Chemical plant are 50,000 times higher than those considered safe in the United States. Xylene levels near Matamoros' General Motors plant are 6000 times greater than those considered safe in the United States. Moreover, 90 percent of the toxic waste generated there is being disposed of illegally and improperly.

One result of this pollution is a drastic rise in birth defects. Between 1990 and 1992, forty-two babies in Matamoros were born with underdeveloped brains. Mexico lacks the necessary financial resources either to enforce existing regulations or pay for the cleanup of toxic waste pollution sites along its border (Kelly, 1993:13, 16–17). Ironically, the greatest problem with toxic dumping in Third World nations is that much of the time it is perfectly legal. About all that concerned citizens in developing nations can do is publicize the dangers involved. What environmental disasters may befall such nations in the future is anyone's guess.

Third World dumping involves a series of related implications. For instance, some would suggest that deliberate racist and genocidal policies are being practiced by certain corporations and government agencies. Corporate dumping may well have such effects on the nonwhite people of the world. The same may be said concerning support by corporations and government for regimes that violate human rights. Taken collectively, all of this indicates that the waste industry is one of the most corrupt industries in the world (Jensen, 1993:57). Most disturbingly, many times the federal government has covered up, and at other times been a coconspirator in, the violation of environmental and other laws.

The Government as Polluter

According to Helen Caldicott (1992:7) the U.S. government is the nation's chief polluter. Federal facilities discharge almost 2.5 million tons of toxic and radioactive waste without reporting it annually. The General Accounting Office estimates that 95 percent of U.S. government toxic pollution is exempt from the government's own reporting procedures. At Department of Defense weapons plants alone, there are 14,401 potentially contaminated dump sites.

Many of these sites have been the focus of their own scandals. For example, in 1991, it was learned that the companies that operated the Department of Energy's Savannah River nuclear reactor, Westinghouse and Bechtel subsidiaries, hid huge cost overruns by illegally transferring tens of millions of dollars in and out of construction accounts. The illegal transfers also went to pay Bechtel's expensive management fees, to construct unauthorized new projects, and to hide other cost increases from both Congress and the Department of Energy. The scandal followed news by the General Accounting Office that the cleanup of the Department of Energy's radioactive poisons would cost $200 billion or more and would take up to fifty years. The department has spent $3 billion trying to repair three nuclear reactors at its Savannah River plant, only one of which will be reopened. Moreover, it has shut down its plutonium-machining and -processing plant in Colorado—and also a nuclear repository in New Mexico—because of safety and environmental problems.

Various agencies of the U.S. government are named as PRPs at 8 percent of the Superfund sites, but this estimate is considered very conservative because the federal government is exempt in over 90 percent of cases from EPA regulations. Likewise, more than half of the 10.5 billion pounds of toxic chemicals released into the air, soil, and water are not covered by EPA regulations (Caldicott, 1992:7). The environmental crime violations by corporations and government are also symbolic of a deeper problem, the relationship between alienation and mass consumption as a way of life.

Alienation and Mass Consumption

Perhaps no one has described the social character of the corporate rich as well as *Harper's* magazine editor Lewis Lapham. It is Lapham's contention that the attitudes of

Private Troubles   Public Issues

Happiness and Materialism

Are Americans happier for having used up as large a share of the earth's resources since 1940 than did everyone in the world before that date? A number of studies say no:

- Regular surveys by the National Opinion Research Center reveal that no more Americans state they are very happy in the 1990s than in 1957, despite a near doubling of the gross domestic product and of the amount spent for per capita personal consumption.

- A 1974 study of people in various cultures from Nigeria and Yugoslavia to Israel and Japan found that people in all places ranked themselves in the middle on the happiness scale. Confusingly, both low-income Cubans and upper middle-income Americans reported themselves considerably happier than most people. Thus, there seems little difference in the happiness levels found in either affluent or very poor nations. Even the upper classes in any given society report they are no more satisfied with their lives than the upper classes of the poorest nations—nor the upper classes in the less affluent past (Durning, 1992:39).

Mass consumption has actually become a treadmill, with consumers judging their own self-worth by who has more and who has less. Once consumption becomes a status game, a sort of psychological anomie sets in. The game becomes one of happiness as a the rich are mirrored by the rest of America. When it comes to money, the rich seem convinced that (1) they never have as much as they need, and (2) what they do have is always in danger of being taken away. "No matter what their income," states Lapham, "a depressing number of Americans believe that if they only had twice as much, they would inherit the estate of happiness promised them in the Declaration of Independence" (in Durning, 1992:38). Accordingly, during the rapid upper-income expansion of the 1980s, New York investment bankers earning $600,000 per year felt poor, and suffered from anxiety and self-doubt. As one of them told the New York *Times,* "I am nothing. You understand that, nothing. I earn $250,000 a year, but it's nothing. I am nobody" (Durning, 1992:40). The lack of self-esteem exhibited by this stockbroker alerts us to the notion that material goods do not make people satisfied with their lives, although many Americans do not believe it. (See the accompanying "Private Troubles/Public Issues.")

An entirely new field of study, **ecopsychology** (Rozak et al., 1995), studies the psyche of mass consumption and its relationship to environmental concerns. Psychologist Mary Gomes (1995) studied students in an undergraduate psychology class at Sonoma State University in California. One question asked students if they considered themselves ecologically conscious. Sixty percent said they did consider themselves concerned about the environment. Asked what they did to aid the environment, they reported that they

function of ever-rising levels of consumption, of outdoing your purchases from last year. Each new luxury item becomes a necessity, thus creating an ever-increasing need for new necessities. The definition of an adequate living standard among the affluent climbs ever higher. Children whose parents haven't bought the latest video games are embarrassed to invite other children to their homes. Teens without cars feel inferior to their auto-owning peers.

What is it, then, that makes for happiness? Ironically, the main factors revealed in studies on life satisfaction are completely unrelated to consumption. They include:

• a contented family life, especially marriage, followed by;

• a satisfying work life—doing work that one enjoys;

• leisure time to develop one's talents; and

• friendships.

These factors were all cited as more significant than income or buying material goods in achieving happiness. Even millionaire lottery winners frequently report feeling miserable. They often experience alienation from their network of friends, frequently feel their jobs have lost whatever meaning and structure they possessed, and even suffer estrangement from close friends and family members.

recycled cans, bottles, and newspapers. Not one of the ecologically concerned students, no matter what their income level, reported any plans to buy fewer things. In fact, Professor Gomes found that, at whatever the income level, all her students bought as many consumer goods as they possibly could.

Much mass consumption is directly related to the inauthenticity and narcissism of postmodern life. Ecopsychologists Allen Kanner and Mary Gomes (1995:78) see the consumer society as having created an increasingly isolated and individualistic American individual who bears the dual trademarks of narcissism and inauthenticity: appearing masterful on the outside, yet empty. American consumer habits reflect both the grandiosity and emptiness of narcissism. The inauthentic (false) self feels entitled to endless purchase of consumer goods, which also demonstrates the economic and political superiority of the United States.

Simultaneously, however, consumer spending often functions to relieve the pain of a lonely and empty life. Purchasing new products, especially *big ticket* consumer goods like automobiles and computers, often produces an immediate surge of pleasure, if not achievement. As the novelty wears off, the anguish threatens to reappear. The standard solution is to focus on the next large purchase, hoping that the next time satisfaction will be more meaningful and longer lasting.

Rather than being in touch with the environment, most consumers in advanced societies are alienated from the earth's ecosystems in profound ways. Traveling in an automobile, especially at high speed, does not allow one time for contemplation of the beauty of the outdoors. Passing by so quickly, the environment is perceived, not as an interrelated

Automobiles are not only a major source of air pollution in modern societies, they also serve to alienate people from nature. Many people who drive, watch natural settings go by at a rapid pace, rarely stopping to appreciate the wonders of the remaining plant and animal life with whom we share our natural environment.

system of living things, but as life devoid of categories such as time and space. The environment is merely something one must travel through to get where one is going.

Consumers in affluent societies are cut off not only from the environment, they are cut off from others and themselves as well. A 1978 study of English working-class people dealt with their rising levels of consumption. Despite dramatic increases in consumption levels and material goods compared to grandparents and parents, they were more dissatisfied than contented. One respondent remarked "People aren't satisfied, only they don't seem to know why they're not. The only chance of satisfaction we can imagine is getting more of what we've got now. But it's what we've got now that makes everybody dissatisfied." Elderly people interviewed in this study feared for their children, feared rapists, vandals, and muggers, who seemed strangely vicious, and expressed feelings of isolation from their neighbors. Instead of bonds of mutual attachment and cooperation, they reported living out their final days in isolation, each in front of his or her own television set. Studies of the United States suggest that informal visits between friends and neighbors, time spent with family members at meals, and family conversations have all dramatically declined since 1950. The average American now moves every five years or so, and 70 percent of Americans no longer even know their next-door neighbors (Durning, 1992:43, 46).

Another cost of the consumer society is the increased stress accompanying the self-dehumanization connected with the pace of daily life. One psychologist measured such items as the average walking speed on urban streets to the average conversational speed of postal workers in six different nations. He found that, as countries industrialize and develop consumer economies, the pace of life itself accelerates. In these ways, mass consumption is a major cause of the inauthentic and dehumanizing conditions of alienation that are the hallmarks of postmodern society. An additional problematic aspect of mass consumption is that it makes a number of global social problems much worse, especially the maldistribution of food and the increasing world population growth.

Environmental Destruction and the Overpopulation Debate

Aside from a serious set of environmental concerns, the world's resources are being pushed to new limits due to ever-increasing population growth. Currently planet earth is home to 5.6 billion people; this number is expected to double by the year 2050 (Myers, 1994a:6). In the next thirty years alone, 3 billion people will be added to the world's human population. Globally, population size grew by 93 million in 1992. If the current trends persist, the world's population is expected to grow by about 1 billion during the 1990s (Kennedy, 1993). The U.S. population alone (currently 259 million) is growing by approximately 3 million people each year. This makes the United States the world's fastest-growing industrialized nation. By the year 2050, the nation's population is projected to increase by 133 million people. This is the equivalent of adding more than thirty-eight cities the size of Los Angeles.

Many areas of society are already operating beyond their carrying capacity, their ability to feed and house their population. Plant breeders and agronomists, it appears, have run out of technological innovations. Meanwhile, the world population has grown by almost 13 percent, adding 625 million people to be fed. To put it another way, to adequately feed the 90 to 97 million new humans expected each year, and replace the farmland ruined by desertification, soil erosion, or acid rain, the world will need to clear about 15 million hectares per year (Nixon, 1994:18).

Population is a problem that is bound up with poverty, especially in Third World nations. It is this combination of poverty and high fertility rates that produces a variety of social harms, many of them global in scope:

Migration Tensions

Many First World nations, including the United States, Greece, Germany, and Japan, all experienced net increases in migrating populations in the 1980s. When the international economy suffered a worldwide recession in the late 1980s, immigrant populations were singled out as scapegoats. Most First World nations have, consequently, experienced an increase in hate crimes directed toward nonwhite immigrants from Third World nations (United Nations, 1994:109–110).

Refugees

Extreme poverty and near starvation conditions have produced a war or revolution in the Third World on a once-a-month average since 1945. It is not unusual for three or four civil and/or international conflicts to be taking place in the Third World at once. These conflicts, along with natural disasters, have produced a massive refugee problem, consisting of peoples who have lost their homes and homelands, and become international wanderers. There were 17 million refugees in 1990, compared to 8 million in 1980. The 1991 Gulf War produced 5 million more refugees, and by 1994, the civil war in the former Yugoslavia produced 2 million refugees (United Nations, 1994:111). Many of these people wander into other poor Third World nations, putting tremendous burdens on the meager resources, and, in some instances increasing starving populations. In nations like Kenya, refugees are placed in overcrowded camps, often with inadequate water and food supplies.

In developed nations, the cost of dealing with asylum seekers (political refugees) reached $7 to $8 billion, and the United States has spent additional billions trying to stem illegal immigration from countries like Mexico, Haiti, and Cuba. New restrictions in many developed nations have jeopardized the position of bona fide asylum seekers by making access to the host nation more difficult, and, once in the host nation, being denied the full range of legal protections afforded citizens of the host nation, divisive debates have occurred over teaching classes in languages other than English in public schools, and denying social services and welfare to illegal immigrants.

There are optimists who view the population growth problem as a series of potentials. Emphasized here is the earth's carrying capacity, the absolute number of people the earth could sustain without an environmental catastrophe. Estimates of the optimists are that the earth's basic resources are vastly greater than what are needed to feed even the 10 billion people who are almost certain to inhabit the planet by the end of the next century (Budiansky, 1994:58). The problem here is not the earth's capacity, but the capacity of the world's dominant institutions to pursue economic and social policies that will place an emphasis on producing more and cheaper food, family planning, basic medical care, and so on.

For example, while 13,000 to 18,000 people per day are dying of starvation in Third World nations, grain is in such surplus in the United States and Europe that 57 million acres have been deliberately taken out of production under government programs to increase farmers' incomes. Moreover, an additional 200 million acres in South America could be activated to produce food, if Third World peoples had money to buy it (Budiansky, 1994:58). Thus a good deal of the problem of overpopulation is not about numbers of people so much as it is about the contradictions inherent in economic arrangements based on accumulating wealth.

Regarding reproduction and fertility rates (the average number of children that a woman bears during her life) (Alper, 1992:13), the goal is to achieve zero population growth. Zero population growth (ZPG) refers to the number reached when the population is being replaced, but no net growth occurs. Zero population growth occurs in the United States at 1.8 or 1.9 children per woman. In 1976 the fertility rate was 1.7 in the United States. Today it has edged above 2.0 and is close to 2.1 percent (Alper, 1992:13). The conservative political climate of recent years, along with the strength of the religious right, have dealt a number of setbacks to population control policy. Most antiabortion groups do not take a position on the connection between overpopulation and environmental degradation. The Roman Catholic church dismisses the problem as irrelevant, suggesting that there is no overpopulation problem. At the 1994 Cairo conference on population, the Catholic church was in the forefront of the opposition to population control.

Mrs. Clinton is pictured here at the 1995 Women's Conference in China. One of the great problems faced by the world's women is that they are held responsible for preventing pregnancy, when, in truth, both men and women are equally responsible for conceiving children.

What can be done about overpopulation? Some 300–350 million Third World couples want to practice family planning, but they lack the means to do it. More important, adequate birth control could reduce the number of mothers dying in childbirth from its current 500,000 per year down to less than 150,000. In addition, adequate birth control could bring about a substantial decrease in the number of abortions performed each year (currently at 50 million worldwide). Abortions cause the deaths of 60,000 women each year (MacFarquhar, 1994:56). The developed world, via foreign aid, needs to help. A massive international effort could reduce future global population growth by more than 2 billion.

Second, the status of women in the developing nations must be upgraded. This means funding projects that will promote women's education, get them jobs, and enhance their social status. Such programs usually result in smaller family size (Nixon, 1994:15–16).

Third, poverty must be ended. As people become better educated (especially women) and more affluent, their fertility rates decline (United Nations, 1994:96–99).

Regarding individual action, one can avoid unwanted pregnancies, consider adopting or becoming a foster parent instead of having a child, or limit one's family to one or two children. If we cannot check our rate of reproduction on our own, more drastic methods of population control, especially famine, disease, and war, will set in (Alper, 1992:13, 15).

The increase in the world's population is only part of the story, however. Clearly First World nations do not experience the massive starvation that kills 13 to 18 million people per year in Third World nations (Babbie, 1994:1). The term **overpopulation** is extremely relative to a nation's ability—and most important its willingness—to devote resources to meeting survival needs and establishing humane policies of population control. Unfortunately, there is a tragic link between environmental pollution and a lack of concern for humane population control in many Third World nations.

This sad scenario works as follows:

1. Third World upper classes and the governments they control frequently take the form of military dictatorships. These repressive governments control the mass unrest born of poverty with brute force, often supplemented by large amounts of military aid and arms sales from First World nations, including the United States.

2. With so many resources devoted to the militarization of mass suffering, little is left for increased agricultural output, water purification, health care, and other massive needs, including population control.

Problems of environmental destruction and population growth are also intimately interconnected with those discussed in the last chapter: war and terrorism.

- During the 1991 Gulf War, Saddam Hussein ordered that hundreds of Kuwaiti oil wells be set afire. The wells burned for months, creating a huge toxic cloud which polluted the air as far away as India. The smoke and soot created by the fires resulted in the deaths of thousands of Persian Gulf fish and birds. In fact, 10 to 30 percent of all environmental degradation in the world is a direct result of the various militaries, and 6 to 10 percent of the world's air pollution is a result of the armed forces of the world (Lanier-Graham, 1992:xxix).

- The maldistribution of food has become a major cause of both famine and war in poor nations like Somalia. The recent United Nations mission to that country, headed largely by the United States, illustrates why lack of food and war are inseparable problems in the global economy. The mission's original purpose was merely humanitarian. Food and agricultural supplies and technology were to be distributed to Somalia's starving. No intervention in Somalia's civil war was to be allowed. However, between 1993 and 1994, UN troops were fired on, and some American soldiers were killed, and their dead bodies dragged through the streets of Somalia's capital. Before the American contingent departed Somalia in March, 1994, American pilots were flying air strikes under UN auspices against Somalia's most powerful warlord.

Policy Failure: The Politics of "Regulatory Capture"

Aside from the government's own abysmal record of polluting the environment, the EPA itself has demonstrated an alarming degree of corruption, misfeasance, and malfeasance. The Environmental Protection Agency (EPA) faces a daunting task in regulating an industry with a long criminal record. Given its past activities, it was inevitable that the waste industry would corrupt the EPA, and that is exactly what's happened.

In 1992, the Environmental Research Foundation issued a report on the EPA's failure to adequately regulate the waste industry. Among the report's findings, (1) the EPA, more frequently than not, opposes congressional attempts to pass tougher environmental regulations; (2) the EPA devotes more of its resources (time and money) to attempting to exempt corporations from its regulations than it does enforcing them; (3) the agency's efforts at enforcement are frequently so weak that environmental groups must bring it under court-ordered deadline before such efforts are considered for administrative signature.

For example, in the United States, corporate officers can not be convicted of polluting the environment unless their acts were committed knowingly (on purpose). Such knowledge is frequently difficult, if not impossible, to prove. Moreover, this knowledge and intent to violate the law must be shown by the government to have existed beyond a reasonable doubt (Albanese & Pursley, 1993:315–316). Thus if employees are caught dumping toxic waste, they can claim they were only following their bosses' orders. The corporate officers, in turn, can deny such instructions were given, as well as deny any knowledge of the dumping itself.

All this, however, is the tip of a dirty iceberg spanning much of the EPA's twenty-five-year history:

- The EPA's most important scandal, Sewergate, occurred in 1983, when the agency was accused by congressional critics of multiple violations of ethics and law. These violations included: having a cozy relationship with regulated firms, including personal assurances of nonenforcement of environmental laws; agreeing to sweetheart deals with firms that allowed polluting industries to avoid full payment of cleanup costs; and manipulation of site cleanup timetables to benefit Republican candidates in congressional districts (Szasz, 1986:205–206).

After EPA administrator Ann Gorsuch Burford refused to turn over Superfund files (because they were enforcement sensitive) the Justice Department refused to prosecute her, and asked a federal court to uphold its refusal. The federal judge ordered that the matter be resolved, and before a case could be brought Burford, Rita Lavelle, and dozens of other EPA officials resigned. Lavelle stood accused of harassment of a dissident employee, perjury, and conflict of interest. This scandal began a long history of EPA corruption.

- In 1983, Representative James Florio accused the EPA of awarding a cleanup contract to a company that had, one month earlier, been charged by EPA with cleanup violations. The company, Chem Waste Management, Inc., was represented by attorney James Sanderson, a former consultant to EPA administrator Ann Burford (Rebovich, 1992:6).

- In 1988, officials from industry met secretly with officials of the White House Office of Management and Budget to discuss pending EPA regulations. The OMB allowed the executives to suggest revisions in the regulations and the EPA subsequently made the necessary changes in those regulations (Jensen, 1993:57).

- In 1994, an EPA employee wrote an internal memo charging that Monsanto had lied to the EPA concerning the toxic effects of Agent Orange by falsifying scientific studies on the carcinogenicity of dioxin. The employee, rather than being praised for exposing a scandal, was harassed by the EPA, and was threatened with termination. The EPA quietly closed the case on the issue of Monsanto's falsification of findings (Freeman, 1994:5).

- Today, there are twenty high-ranking former EPA administrators who have left the agency and become millionaire waste industry executives, giving rise to charges of a revolving door between the EPA and the hazardous waste management industry.

Taken together, these incidents constitute evidence of what Harold Barnet (1994:45ff) terms **regulatory capture,** meaning that the EPA is now dominated by the very industries it is supposed to be regulating. According to the Environmental Research Foundation, the EPA, like many federal regulatory agencies, is more concerned with the interests of the parties it is supposed to be regulating than it is with the public interest (Jensen, 1993:56).

The toxic waste disposal companies not infrequently work with the federal government in making waste problems worse. In 1992, David Leroy, head of the Federal Office of the Nuclear Waste Negotiator, offered various Native American tribes at a National Congress of American Indians $100,000 each, no strings attached, just to consider storing hundreds of canisters of highly radioactive waste on their reservations.

Summary

This chapter has shown the fundamental flaw of the American political economy. Corporations are formed to seek and maximize profits. All too often, the result is a blatant disregard for human and humane considerations. Government also contributes to environmental deregulation by (1) permitting corporations to unduly influence environmental law and policy, and (2) sometimes polluting the environment around its own facilities.

The dangers pointed to in this chapter demonstrate one of the great contradictions of consumer capitalism. Profits are made at the expense of the health of workers and consumers. Corporate decisions often encourage waste of precious resources and environmental destruction. As a result, the materialistic way of life in First World societies could be in some jeopardy in the years ahead.

Suggested Readings

Alan Durning (1992) *How Much Is Enough?* (New York: Norton). The most readable statement of the ills of mass consumption in a decade.

Michael Allaby (1989) *Dictionary of the Environment,* 3rd ed. (New York: New York University Press). This is a first-rate reference work on all aspects of environment and population. It is found in most college and many public libraries.

Worldwatch Magazine. This very readable publication contains articles on every aspect of global environmental and population crises. If your library does not subscribe, you can order it from The Worldwatch Institute.

Vance Packard (1960) *The Waste Makers* (New York: David McKay). This is one of the first books on the ills of mass consumption, and it is still one of the best. Packard writes eloquently concerning the harms associated with planned obsolescence, resource depletion, and consumer debt.

Exercises

Critical Thinking Exercise 7.1	**Ideology and Environment**

Using the conservative, liberal, and radical categories discussed in depth in Chapter 4, do a content analysis of recent articles on the environment. Your sample of articles can come from those social-critical periodicals listed in Critical Thinking Exercise 4.1, or from newspaper editorials. If desired, your instructor may want you to work in groups.

Critical Thinking Exercise 7.2	The Overpopulation Debate

The 1995 Cairo population conference stimulated the writing of hundreds of articles and editorials in newspapers and magazines around the nation. Using the ideological categories given in Chapter 4, do a content analysis of fifty articles and editorials from weekly news magazines, newspapers, and/or social-critical periodicals. Present your results in a table like the one given in Critical Thinking Exercise 4.1 on the Kennedy assassination. Which ideological group is most pessimistic concerning the outcome of the population problem? Pessimistic indicators involve predicting various catastrophes as a result of population growth. Such catastrophes usually include:

- the ecological destruction of the earth
- massive famine
- world war between First and Third World nations over scarce resources, including food

Which ideological group is the most optimistic? Optimistic indicators concern the idea that the above catastrophes are simply the exaggerated ravings of social critics, and a population crisis does not really exist. Optimism also involves the notion that the earth can support and feed billions of additional people without environmental harm taking place.

Why do you think the respective groups hold these opinions?

The American Crime Factory: The Crime-Drug Nexus

Crimogenic Structures and Contradictions: The Crime-Drug Nexus

From a sociological imagination perspective, the causes of crime and drug problems are located within the institutional and cultural contradictions of American society and social character. Crime, and to a substantial degree drug abuse, can be traced to the nature of America's social structure with its competitive capitalism, immense inequalities of wealth and power, and culture of mass consumption. As noted (Chapters 2, 3, 5, and 6), one of the "master trends" of the postmodern era, one from which many harmful patterns flow, has been the unprecedented increase of economic and political power in the hands of a small group of elites. The consequences of this increased concentration of ownership are important:

Between 1982 and 1992, percentage of wealth owned by the wealthiest 1 percent of Americans increased from 31 to 37 percent, an all-time high. More important, it is now estimated that the top 10 percent of wealth holders own as much wealth as the bottom 90 percent of the population.

Income distribution has also become more concentrated since the 1970s. During the twenty years between 1970 and 1990, only the top 20 percent of income earners saw their earnings increase. The other 80 percent of families lost ground. The United States now has the most inequitable income distribution of any industrial democracy.

This maldistribution of wealth and income is a major cause of the increase in violent crime in America's cities. As discussed (Chapter 1), manufacturing corporations have transferred some 2.5 million jobs out of the older cities in the Midwest and Northeast since 1970 (Wilson, 1995:8). Federal aid for America's inner cities was drastically slashed by the Reagan-Bush administrations. Job losses often caused increased family tensions and resultant family breakups (separations and divorces), depriving many children of fathers. Without the usual community organizations to provide social control (including social activities for young people), crime, street violence, and crack-cocaine dealing and abuse skyrocketed from 1985 to 1990, when they leveled off at high annual rates. The result was overall deterioration of inner-city neighborhoods populated by minorities. (The alienation created by these dehumanizing conditions is discussed in depth below.)

A second structural condition involves the importance of drugs as a commodity within American capitalism. Drugs of all sorts are an important part of American capitalism, advertising, and consumer culture. The products advertised in commercials and various lifestyle magazines are constantly depicted in soap operas, prime-time shows, and movies as composing a lifestyle to be emulated. Many of the same products are given away as prizes on game shows and in mail order contests (Barnouw, 1978).

Aside from continually urging people to purchase items they do not need with money they do not have (Inkeles, 1983), advertising is extremely drug oriented.

In fact, modern advertising began in the late nineteenth century with the advertising of drugs (Inciardi, 1986). This fact speaks volumes about the relationship between America's material culture and addiction. Today, legal drugs remain among the most heavily advertised items, and, as discussed in Chapter 9, pharmaceuticals are one of the most profitable industries in America. We Americans are constantly being asked to consume legal drugs. If we can't sleep, or can't stay awake, when we want to celebrate, mourn, lose or gain weight, raise our spirits, kill our pain, or deal with hundreds of additional psycho-physiological conditions, we are told, there is an over-the-counter drug we can purchase. In this regard, "Drugs . . . symbolize the larger and thoroughly legal consumer culture with its addictive appeal and harsh consequences for those who cannot keep up or default on their debts" (Ehrenreich, 1989:247).

Moreover, America's media advertising and government propaganda are loaded with mixed messages concerning drug use. Advertisers constantly encourage use of various drugs for an entire variety of purposes. The public is now informed, via public service messages, that the nation suffers from a serious substance abuse problem. One of the best known of these announcements shows eggs being cooked in a frying pan as the macho-sounding announcer states, "This is your brain on drugs. Any questions?" Another of these anti-drug use announcements is done by actor Bruce Willis, who also does commercials for Budweiser, urging viewers to drink alcohol. Alcohol ads, in general, are loaded with implied promises of popularity, friendship, sexual attractiveness, and success (Strickland et al., 1982a, 1982b). For all the lip service paid to discouraging people from consuming drugs, there is an even greater emphasis on consuming drugs for all sorts of reasons.

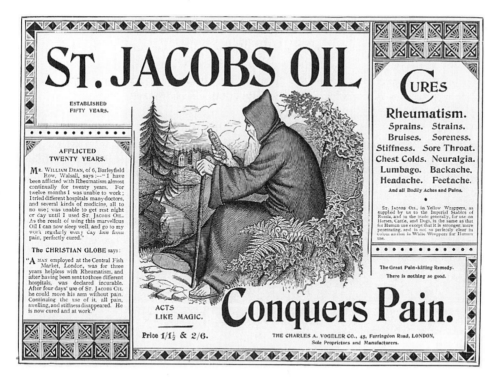

This ad for St. Jacobs oil is typical of many patent medicines sold between 1865 and the early 1900s. Most of these remedies were useless in either preventing pain or curing disease, yet they were touted as beneficial for a host of illnesses. Much of American advertising began with advertisements for patent medicines.

Indeed, there is a relationship between legal and illegal drug use that is both subtle and profound. Studies demonstrate that people who begin smoking cigarettes in their teens are one hundred times more likely to encounter an abuse problem with illegal substances than nonsmokers. Likewise, in fact, this study found that children who come from homes where alcohol was abused by parents were 70 percent more likely to use illegal narcotics than children coming from homes where there was no alcohol abuse (Inciardi, 1986:128). More to the point, the cultural emphasis on consuming legal drugs gives rise to a contradiction whereby both illegal and legal substances are abused.

For example, in the late 1970s and early 1980s, one of the largest studies of "street" criminals who were also drug abusers was conducted in Florida (Inciardi, 1986). More than 3000 people were interviewed, including one group of 576 Miami narcotics users. Of these 576 users 83 percent (476) were actively committing crimes and using drugs at the time of their interviews. All had used illegal narcotics at least once within the ninety days prior to being interviewed. Half of the respondents were under 26.9 years of age, accurately mirroring the fact that half of all street crime is committed by people between fourteen and twenty-six years of age. Concerning ethnicity, 52 percent of those interviewed were white, 36 percent African-American, and 12 percent Hispanic. Thus minorities were overrepresented in this criminal population, and this is also true in America in general. Thus street criminals and their victims are overwhelmingly young, urban, minority members, who are poor, high school dropouts who are either unemployed or underemployed, and reside in America's urban ghettos.

The results of the study were surprising. Virtually all of the drug abusers began their drug use at young ages, between thirteen and fourteen, and by abusing a *legal* drug, alcohol. In other words, the contradiction involving the cultural encouragement to take drugs of all types results in high levels of drug addiction, *especially among the poorest and most oppressed and dehumanized groups in inner cities.*

Together these two structural conditions, (1) the emphasis placed on accumulating wealth, and (2) the cultural encouragement to take drugs, have spawned an entire range of illegal organizations involved in the manufacture and sale of various illegal drugs, including marijuana, heroin, and crack cocaine. At times the illegal organizations make political alliances or business deals with legitimate entities, such as the Central Intelligence Agency, or banks and other financial institutions who, for a fee, will launder profits made from drug trafficking. The entire structure resembles a large factory that produces illegal drugs and crime at all levels of society. These organizations and individual criminal addicts commit an immense amount of physical, financial, and moral harm.

The Crimogenic Factory

One way to conceive of the interrelated nature of the crime and drug use problem is to view it as a factory with different floors. Drug users who commit street crimes are only the factory's front display window, the tip of a very large and dirty iceberg. In essence, street criminals who use drugs are part of the demand side of the drug abuse problem. It is their crimes that pay for their drug cravings, and the street addicts form the first floor of this crime factory.

Several years ago, the Miller Brewing Company brought out a book that pictured all the celebrities in their "tastes great, less-filling" Lite Beer commercials. The book was dedicated to the 20 percent of beer drinkers who consume 80 percent of all the beer sold in America. What is true for beer, is also true for street crime and drugs—a tiny percentage of criminals commit an immense amount of the street crime, and also consume a disproportionate amount of illegal drugs.

For example, Inciardi (1986) found that drug addicts who commit street crimes begin their drug abuse at about fifteen years of age, by moving from alcohol to marijuana. This was followed at about age seventeen with sedatives, and at age nineteen with heroin. Accordingly, the vast majority of drug users who are street criminals are what are termed **polydrug users,** meaning they are addicted to more than one drug, some of which, like

Box 8.1 • The Social Reality of Drug Abuse

Drug abuse is always a matter of debate in part because the terms "drug" and "abuse" are subjective notions. Their definitions are sociological in nature. As sociologist Erich Goode (1993:30–35) notes, there is no precise way to define what is or is not a drug, and this imprecision has important social consequences. In modern societies, the term *drug* has two connotations, a positive one associated with its role in medicine as therapeutic, and a negative one based, not on the chemical makeup of the drug itself, but on the self-destructive and socially harmful patterns caused by drug abuse. In this discussion, the term *drug* refers to any chemical substance that has psychoactive or mood-altering effects. Drug *addiction*, from the Latin word *addicere,* meaning to bind someone to something, refers to chronic physical or psychological dependence. Psychological dependence means that use of a drug is a habit, although the strength of some drug habits can be as strong as physical addictions. As Figure 8.1 describes, caffeine (found in coffee, colas, and chocolate) is among the easiest drugs to which one may become addicted. Physiological dependence involves a measurable and objective set of withdrawal symptoms. Once physiological dependence occurs, regular doses of the drug must be taken or withdrawal symptoms will take place (Abadinsky, 1989:5–6). Withdrawal symptoms from various addictive drugs are listed below.

The drugs below fall into four categories, relative to their effects on the body's central nervous system (CNS). These include depressants, stimulants, hallucinogens, and cannabis (marijuana). Depressants, especially alcohol and heroin, reduce pain by depressing the CNS, and are physiologically addicting. Stimulants stimulate the CNS and produce feelings of well-being in proper doses. Most common here are caffeine and nicotine among legal drugs, while cocaine is the favorite illegal stimulant on American society. These drugs produce profound psychological dependence. Hallucinogens, like LSD or PCP, are psychologically habituating, and alter people's perceptions, producing illusions (fantasies).

Finally, cannabis can produce characteristics of all 4 of the above drug categories (fantasies, well-being, stimulation, or depression). The actual effects depend on a host of factors associated with an individual's personality, mood, and the environment in which the drug is ingested. Drug abuse is similar to addiction but it is different. Drug abuse refers to drug use that is considered "excessive," to the extent that it produces effects that are hazardous to the individual or community (Goode, 1993:238).

Figure 8.1

Controlled Substances of Abuse

Class	Drugs	Prescribed Brand Names	Medical Uses	Other Names	Dependence Potential: Physical	Psychological
Narcotics	Opium	Dover's Powder, Paregoric	Analgesic, antidiarrheal	Parepectolin	High	High
	Morphine	Morphine	Analgesic	Pectoral syrup	High	High
	Codeine	Codeine	Analgesic, antitussive	Robitussin A-C Empirin compound with codeine	Moderate	Moderate
	Heroin	None	None	Horse; Smack		
	Meperidine (Pethidine)	Demerol, Pethadol	Analgesic		High	High
					High	High
	Methadone	Dolophine, Methadone, Methadose	Analgesic, heroin substitute		High	High
	Fentanyl			China white		
	Other Narcotics	Dilaudid, Leritine, Numorphan, Percodan	Analgesic, antidiarrheal, antitussive		High	High
Depressants	Alcohol	None	None	Liquor; Beer; Wine	High	High
	Chloral Hydrate	Noctec, Somnos	Hypnotic		Moderate	Moderate
	Barbiturates	Amytal, Butisol, Nembutal, Phenobarbital, Seconal, Tuinal	Anesthetic anticonvulsant, sedation, sleep	High	High	High
	Glutethimide	Doriden	Sedation, sleep		High	High
	Methaqualone	Optimil, Parest, Quaalude, Somnafac, Sopor	Sedation, sleep		High	High
	Tranquilizers	Equanil, Librium, Miltown, Serax, Tranxene, Valium	Anti-anxiety, muscle relaxant, sedation		Moderate	Moderate
	Other Depressants	Clonopin, Dalmane, Dormate, Noludar, Placydil, Valmid	Anti-anxiety, sedation, sleep		Possible	Possible
Inhalants	Nitrous Oxide	None	Anesthetic	Laughing gas; Whippets	Possible	Unknown
	Butyl Nitrite		None	Locker room; Rush		
	Amyl Nitrite		Heart stimulant	Poppers; Snappers		
	Chlorohydrocarbons		None	Aerosol paints; cleaning fluid		
	Hydrocarbons		None	Gasoline; glue; paint thinner		

sedatives, are legal substances. Virtually all of these drug users were heavily involved with legal and illegal substances. The average user took five different drugs, and over 90 percent of these users consumed narcotics on either a daily basis, or three or more times per week. Most commonly used were marijuana, alcohol, cocaine, heroin, and sedatives. Other studies have found similar patterns (Abadinsky, 1989:7–8). The New York State Division of Substance Abuse Services found that heroin and cocaine were commonly used because one drug alleviates the undesired side effects of the other. Another study in San Antonio, Texas, found that in 70 percent of cases where heroin was a cause of death, cocaine was also present in body tissue (Texas Commission on Alcohol & Drug Abuse, 1987). Other studies report widespread alcohol use, coupled with other drugs (Minnesota Department of Human Services, 1987).

Tolerance	Duration of Effects (in hours)	Usual Methods of Administration	Possible Effects	Effects of Overdose	Antidote	Withdrawal Syndrome
Yes	3 to 6	Oral, smoked				
Yes	3 to 6	Injected, smoked				
Yes	3 to 6	Oral, injected	Euphoria; drowsiness; respiratory depression; constricted pupils; nausea	Slow and shallow breathing; clammy skin; convulsions; coma; possible death	Maintain body heat; artificial respiration	Watery eyes; runny nose; yawning; loss of appetite; irritability; tremors, panic; chills and sweating, cramps; nausea
Yes	3 to 6	Injected, sniffed				
Yes	3 to 6	Oral, injected				
Yes	12 to 24	Oral, injected				
Yes	3 to 6	Oral, injected				
Yes	1 to 12	Oral				
Probable	5 to 8	Oral				
Yes	1 to 16	Oral, injected				
Yes	4 to 8	Oral	Slurred speech; disorientation; drunken behavior; loss of coordination, impaired reactions	Shallow respiration; cold and clammy skin; dilated pupils; weak and rapid pulse; coma; possible death	Empty stomach; maintain body heat; artificial respiration	Anxiety; insomnia, tremors, delirium; convulsions; possible death
Yes	4 to 8	Oral				
Yes	4 to 8	Oral				
Yes	4 to 8	Oral				
Probable	Up to .5	Inhaled	Excitement; euphoria; giddiness; loss of inhibitions; aggressiveness; delusions; depression; drowsiness; headache; nausea	Loss of memory; confusion; unsteady gait; erratic heartbeat and pulse; possible death	Artificial respiration	Insomnia; decreased appetite; depression; irritability; headache

Continued on next page

The results concerning crime were even more dramatic. Inciardi (1986) found that about half of the 576 drug users committed their first crimes at about age fifteen. This was usually a property crime, most commonly larceny, vehicle theft, burglary, or shoplifting. This is representative of American street crime in general, with 90 percent of all crimes being property crimes, and a considerable portion of violent crime (no one is sure exactly how much) being committed in the course of the commission of property crime.

Of the 186 female narcotics users in this study, twenty-four of them began their criminal careers with acts of prostitution. Most typical among first offenses by female criminal addicts were property crimes like shoplifting.

Almost all of the 576 narcotics users had been arrested at least once by age seventeen, and by age twenty-six, almost all of them had been in jail or prison at least once. This, too,

Figure 8.1

Continued

Drugs	Prescribed Brand Names	Medical Uses	Other Names	Dependence Potential:	
				Physical	Psychological
Stimulants					
Nicotine	None	None	Tobacco; cigars; cigarettes; snuff	High	High
Caffeine	None	None	Coffee; tea; soft drinks; No–Doz	Low	Low
Cocaine*	Cocaine	Local anesthetic	Coke; flake; snow	Possible	High
Amphetamines	Benzedrine, Biphetamine, Desoxyn, Dexedrine	Hyperkinesis, narco–lepsy, weight control		Possible	High
Phenmetrazine	Preludin	Weight control		Possible	High
Methylphenidate	Ritalin	Hyperkinesis		Possible	High
Other Stimulants	Bacarate, Cylert, Didrex, Ionamin, Plegine, Pondimin, Pre-Sate, Sanorex, Voranil	Weight control		Possible	Possible
Hallucinogens					
LSD	None	None	Acid	None	Degree unknown
Mescaline and Peyote	None	None	—	None	Degree unknown
Psilocybin– Psilocyn	None	None	Mushrooms	None	Degree unknown
MDA	None	None		None	Degree unknown
Phencyclidine†	Sernylan	Veterinary anesthetic	PCP; Angel Dust	None	Degree unknown
Other Hallucinogens	None	None		None	Degree unknown
Cannabis					
Marijuana Hashish Hashish Oil Tetrahydrocanna-binol	None	None‡	Pot; grass; reefer; sinsemilla; THC	Degree unknown	Moderate

Source: "Controlled Substances: Uses and Effects," U.S. Department of Justice, Drug Enforcement Administration; "Common Drugs of Abuse," Maine Department of Educational and Cultural Services; Drug Enforcement Administration.

is quite typical of street criminals in general. As David Greenberg (1993) has pointed out, street criminals are usually viewed as children who have made mistakes when they are arrested in their early teens. As they reappear before judges reaching their late teens and early twenties, they are perceived less and less as children. Thus as street criminals reach young adulthood, they are more likely to be labeled adult criminals by enforcement and judicial personnel, more likely to be arrested and sentenced to do time. Hence as they age and appear before judges on a repeat basis, they are more likely to be sent to jail or prison.

Most importantly concerning crime, during the twelve-month period prior to being interviewed, these 576 drug users reported committing a staggering 215,105 crimes, an average of 373 each (more than one per day). Of these 215,000-plus offenses, over half were non-felonies, including 82,000 cases of drug peddling and 43,000 "victimless" offenses, such as

Tolerance	Duration of Effects (in hours)	Usual Methods of Administration	Possible Effects	Effects of Overdose	Antidote	Withdrawal Syndrome
Yes	2 to 4	Smoked, chewed	Increased alertness; excitation; euphoria; dilated pupils; increased pulse rate and blood pressure; insomnia; loss of appetite	Agitation; increase in pulse rate and blood pressure, loss of appetite; insomnia	Supportive care; medical attention; check for shock	Apathy, long periods of sleep, irritability, depression, disorientation
Probable	2 to 4	Oral				
Yes	2	Injected, sniffed		Agitation, increase in body temperature; hallucinations; convulsions; possible death; tremors		
Yes	2 to 4	Oral, injected				
Yes	2 to 4	Oral				
Yes	2 to 4	Oral				
Yes	2 to 4	Oral				
Yes	Variable	Oral				
Yes	Variable	Oral, injected	Illusions and hallucinations (with exception of MDA); poor perception of time and distance	Longer, more intense "trip" episodes; psychosis; possible death	Emotional support; quiet; darkened room; protect from self-injury	Withdrawal syndrome not reported
Yes	Variable	Oral				
Yes	Variable	Oral, injected, sniffed				
Yes	Variable	Oral, injected, smoked				
Yes	Variable	Oral, injected, sniffed				
Yes	2 to 4	Oral, smoked	Euphoria; relaxed inhibitions; increased appetite; disoriented behavior; increased heart and pulse rate	Fatigue; paranoia; possible psychosis; time disorientation; slowed movements	Emotional support; quiet; darkened room; avoid threatening behavior	Insomnia, hyperactivity, and decreased appetite reported in a limited number of individuals

*Designated a narcotic under the Controlled Substances Act.
†Designated a depressant under the Controlled Substances Act.
‡Synthetic THC, marketed under several trade names (e.g., Dronabinol, Maronal), is used medically in the treatment of glaucoma and to alleviate the side effects of cancer chemotherapy.

prostitution. Nevertheless, there was a substantial amount of felony crime, including 6000 robberies and assaults, 6700 burglaries, nine hundred vehicle thefts, 46,000 larceny and fraud cases, and 25,000 incidents of shoplifting. Of all 215,105 occurrences, arrests were made in only three-tenths of 1 percent of the cases, underscoring the notion that one reason people commit property crime is because it usually "pays" (i.e., they get away with it and it's tax free).

Lest you think the above pattern was atypical, another 429 nonnarcotic-using criminals were also interviewed in the Florida study. This group committed 137,036 offenses within the year prior to being interviewed (about 320 offenses per person, a little less than one per day). Again, arrests were made in only one-half of 1 percent of the cases. The importance of this is that drug-using street criminals commit more crimes and more serious crimes than do nondrug-using street criminals.

This fact is confirmed by several years' worth of "weekend" studies conducted by the Department of Justice in major American cities during the past dozen years. During fourteen weekends each year, all arrestees in fourteen major cities received urine tests. These studies have consistently shown that between 60 and 90 percent of people arrested for felony crimes test positive for illegal drugs. It has never been completely clear if drug users who commit street crimes begin using drugs first and then begin committing crimes, or start with criminal activity, and then enter into drug use as part of a criminal subculture (street scene).

Most often, criminals who begin their drug abuse with alcohol are alcoholics first and then engage in crime. Criminals addicted to heroin or cocaine largely begin by committing crimes and then become addicted to drugs. A recent survey of U.S. prisoners found that 60 percent of the prison population who had ever abused drugs did not do so until after their first arrest (Currie, 1993:70). However, there is little doubt that drug use makes the crime problem in America much worse than it would be otherwise. Estimates are that there are currently 600,000 to 750,000 criminals addicted to heroin in the United States, about 300,000 in New York City alone. These heroin users commit an astounding three-fourths of all urban street crime in America (Posner, 1988:20–21). Most of it is petty property crime (involving around $35 per incident) and drug selling. A very small percentage of these users, as the Florida study and others confirm, commit a large number of crimes involving considerable amounts of money and violence. Collectively, heroin users commit an estimated $6.8 to $10 billion per year in property crime to support their addiction (Reiman, 1990:28; Witkin & Griffin, 1994:40).

There are an additional 1.7 million crack users and 5.7 million users of inhalants and hallucinogens. Altogether, there are about 2 million "hard core" addicts of heroin and cocaine, and it is this group that accounts for the vast majority of the street crime in America. The victims of this crime are largely other lower-class people, and a large number of them also use illegal drugs.

The relationship between drugs and crime does not stop at the street crime level. That is only where it is most visible to the news media, the public, and politicians seeking office. All of the emphasis placed on individual criminal addicts by the news media masks the overwhelmingly organizational nature of the crime-drug nexus. The crimogenic organizations begin with gangs of criminals who distribute drugs to individual criminal addicts.

First Floor: Street Gangs and Guns

At the street level of distribution to individual drug users there are street gangs made up of youthful offenders. These gangs are often involved in the manufacture and distribution of crack cocaine. Crack cocaine made its debut in America in 1985 and 1986, and has been a staple product of many street gangs throughout the United States ever since. Crack cocaine is merely cocaine hydrochloride powder mixed with water, baking soda, and ammonia. The mixture is then dried and subsequently smoked. With regular cocaine going for $100 or more a gram in the mid-1980s, crack provided a cheap alternative (about $5–$10 per dose). After crack was introduced, cocaine-related deaths increased fourfold in the United States (Kappeler et al., 1993:165).

The great increase in crack use in the mid-1980s created a huge market for street gangs in large urban areas, especially Los Angeles. Substantial increases in the number of Crips and Bloods followed the introduction of crack. Between 1985 and 1988, the L.A. Police Department noted a 71 percent increase in the number of gangs in L.A. Recent studies have reported the presence of over one hundred gangs in Chicago, fifteen to twenty in Cleveland, fifteen in Columbus, Ohio, thirty-one in Phoenix, sixty-six in New York City, eighty in Dade County, Florida, and thirty-five in San Diego, California. The gangs are about 90 percent male, although the percentage of female members of male gangs and the number of female gangs are reported growing. Ethnically, the gangs are homogeneous, reflecting the ethnic composition of the segregated neighborhoods from which they evolve. Thus, African-American neighborhoods such as South Central L.A. give rise to African-American gangs; Asian neighborhoods (heavily concentrated on the West Coast) give rise to Asian gangs; and so on.

The Drug Enforcement Administration claims that members of L.A.'s gangs have branched out into virtually every state in the United States, and members of the Crips have been arrested for drug-related shootings as far away as Buffalo, New York (Albanese & Pursley, 1993:206). By 1991, the Crips had about 30,000 members and the Bloods about 9000 (Witkin, 1991:53).

Contemporary street gangs operate with all the bureaucratic efficiency of McDonald's franchise owners. They often possess powerful weapons, such as Uzi submachine guns, and use state-of-the-art technology, such as cellular phones and pagers. The L.A. gangs quickly spread their operations to major cities on the West Coast, and then inland to places like Denver, before heading east. Miami-based gangs have also branched out to cities in the South like Atlanta and Savannah, Georgia, and Mobile and Montgomery, Alabama. Their spread was not necessarily conspiratorial. Often they went where there was a perception of less law enforcement and cheaper drug product available for purchase.

Crime rates in these cities have increased, especially weapons offenses and drug-related homicides from battles over territory. Many innocent people, including children, have been gunned down in the crossfire in these wars. In 1991, after crack-dealing gangs entered Chicago neighborhoods, there were 623 drug-related murders by August of that year (New York *Times,* September 24, 1991:A-1). This example is typical of the relationship between drugs and violent crime, especially homicide. Goldstein et al. (1990) noted that at the height of New York City's crack epidemic, 1988, murders there reached an all-time high (1896 in a single year). A sample of 414 of these homicides was studied in depth. The results: over half, 52.7 percent, of these murders were "primarily drug related" (Goldstein et al., 1990:6). Moreover, 34 percent of the victims of these 414 homicides were drug dealers. In the vast majority of the cases, those committing the murders were not high on drugs. These homicides were about the struggle for neighborhoods (territory) in which drugs could be sold to street users. It is now estimated that between one-third and one-half of the murders in America are drug related, and they are largely a gang phenomenon.

Finally, 86 percent of the murders studied were committed with a handgun, either a .38 caliber or nine millimeter. Only 20 percent were committed with knives or cutting instruments. This, too, is typical of America's violent crime problem. An estimated sixty-five Americans are killed by handguns every day, a rate ten times higher than that of the entire continent of Europe. There are already an estimated 215 million guns in private hands in the United States, with 4 million new guns bought each year (Yoachum, 1993:A-1). Street gangs also buy illegally imported weapons, such as assault rifles. That is to say, gangs tied into drug distribution are a "threatening trend for the future" of crime in America (Albanese & Pursley, 1993:208).

Second Floor: Organized Crime

While street gangs are a vital link in the drug manufacture and distribution processes, they do not grow or import drugs into the United States. That floor of the crimogenic department store belongs to members of organized criminal syndicates. The definition of organized crime has always been controversial, and the exact structure of organized crime itself is steeped in myth and heated debate. One study (Hagan, 1983:52–57) found that organized crime was given eleven different characteristics by thirteen different authors, only five of which were cited by most authors. These common traits were:

1. an organized hierarchy (an organization);
2. making profits through criminal activity (criminal enterprise);
3. uses the threat of or actual use of force;
4. engages in corruption of public officials (law enforcement and politicians); and
5. provides illegal goods and services that are in high public demand (e.g., drugs, prostitution, illegal gambling, loan sharking, dumping illegal toxic waste, arson, securities fraud, and so on).

Taken together these attributes constitute a definition of organized crime as an ongoing criminal enterprise engaged in profit making from illegal activities that are in high demand. Its survival is maintained by the threat of or use of force and the corruption of public officials (Albanese, 1989). It is also important to understand that organized crime syndicates frequently engage in a host of legitimate business activities. These include everything from owning car dealerships and pizza parlors to real estate development (Abadinsky, 1990). Many of these businesses serve as fronts which are used to hide profits and criminal acts connected with illegal enterprises.

Unlike street gangs, whose members tend to be teens or young adults and eventually quit gang life, members of organized crime tend to be adults, and their membership is for life. There is an important link here, however, with many street gang members tending to join organized crime syndicates upon reaching adulthood. New York's former Gambino family godfather John Gotti (convicted of murder in 1992) and his brother began their organized crime careers with membership in a street gang that specialized in robbery. In January, 1992, a two-year federal investigation found that L.A.'s Crips gang had direct ties to the Medellin cocaine cartel, a leading organized crime syndicate (New York *Times,* January 12, 1992:A-12).

While organized criminal syndicates engage in a host of illegal activities, none are more profitable than the importation and selling of illegal drugs. It is estimated that the American Mafia realizes an annual profit of $78 billion from the drug trade. Compare this to the $200 million income it receives from bootlegged cigarettes, and you have some idea of the immense profits to be made by keeping drugs illegal (Kappeler et al., 1993:168). These criminal syndicates include the traditional Italo-American Mafia, as well as numerous crime families of both Asian and Hispanic origin.

Different crime syndicates sometimes specialize in different drug sales. Italo-Sicilian crime families got into the heroin trade in the 1950s, and still import heroin into the United States from Europe, especially Italy, and have concentrated primarily on the East Coast market. In the 1980s, the Mafia also began selling cocaine. The United States supposedly has about twenty-four traditional Mafia families, composed of a boss (godfather), underboss, a counselor (who is sometimes a lawyer), lieutenants (capi), and their employees (soldati). The American Mafia is linked to the modern-day Sicilian Mafia (a new urban Mafia) via the Sicilian Zips. The Zips are Sicilian Mafia sent to the United States as transporters of heroin and cocaine, and supply the New York–New Jersey Mafia families. The Zips are linked to the American Mafia by blood, and include two of the Gambino brothers, relatives of the heads of one of New York's most powerful crime families.

The American Mafia in recent years has suffered over 1200 convictions, including, as we have noted, that of New York's Gambino family head John Gotti. Consequently, the traditional American Mafia has been weakened and forced to cede or share power with non-Sicilian organized crime groups:

A Mexican organized crime syndicate, the Herrera Family, has operations in cocaine and Mexican brown heroin. The Herrera Family consists of six interrelated familial groups, about 2000 of whose members are related by marriage or blood, and is centered in the Mexican state of Durango. In the United States, the Herrera are headquartered in Chicago, where they have now allied with the Colombian cocaine cartel. The Herrera illustrate well the "organized" aspect of organized crime. In 1985, 135 of their members were indicted in Chicago. Over eighty Herreras were convicted and dozens became fugitives. By 1988, all those convicted or on the run had been replaced (Abadinsky, 1990:231). This ability of organized criminal syndicates to guarantee succession is a major reason why they are so difficult to eliminate completely.

A Japanese crime syndicate, the Yakuza (meaning "good for nothing," and stemming from a Japanese card game), specializes in methamphetamine production in Korea, Japan, and the Philippines. This group has origins that are three hundred years old, and lives by a code established in feudal times by Japan's Samurai warriors. Yakuza are famous for rituals involving cutting off fingers, and tattooing their bodies from ankle to neck to demonstrate their loyalty to the group. In Japan, the Yakuza are very influential with the police and politicians at highest levels of government. Their relationship with Japan's police involves an arrangement whereby the Yakuza escape prosecution in exchange for literally policing Japan's street criminals. As a result, Japan's street crime rate is very low, and its organized crime syndicates are so open that some of them even have phone book listings, published newsletters for members, and office buildings that display the organizations' logos.

Jamaican gangs (posses) are composed of thirty different groups with an estimated 10,000 members. The posses operate fifty-five crack-cocaine houses in fifty-five American cities, some of which bring in $9 million a month (McGuire, 1988:22). There are organized crime syndicates in America's prisons (e.g., the Mexican Mafia, La Nuestra Familia, the Aryan Brotherhood, Black Guerilla Family, and the Texas Syndicate) that distribute drugs, especially heroin, in some of the largest prisons in the United States. There are also

Russian-organized crime groups in the United States that smuggle narcotics into the country from the old Soviet bloc. Finally, there are motorcycle gangs (e.g., Hell's Angels, Outlaws, Pagans, and Bandidos) that deal in methamphetamine and phencyclidine (PCP, "Angel Dust").

A Cuban-organized crime group grew out of the failed invasion of Cuba's Bay of Pigs in 1961. Trained by the CIA, some of their members went into cocaine trafficking after the failed invasion, but they were taken over in 1976 after a bloody war with the Colombian cartel. The famous Colombian cartel is actually a combination of three different crime families from Medellin—the Escobars, Ochoas, and Lehders—and a group centered in Cali. These families are related by blood and marriage, and are structured like Italian crime families. That is, there are bosses, underbosses, lieutenants, and soldiers. The lieutenants oversee soldiers in various departments that specialize in various activities (drugs, security, payoffs to politicians and police, and other illegal goods and services).

African-American organized crime began when American black soldiers in Vietnam experienced the Southeast Asian heroin market firsthand in the early 1970s. That experience taught them they could purchase heroin directly from Asian suppliers, bypassing the Italo-American Mafia. The most prominent African-American crime organization is the El Rukins. The El Rukins were founded by Jeff Fort in 1970 while serving a prison sentence for contempt of Congress and embezzling funds from an Office of Economic Opportunity (federal) grant. The El Rukins have been involved in cocaine smuggling, assisting Libya's Mu'ammar Gadhafi in terrorist activities, and have been employed by Chicago's Cook County Democratic Organization to campaign in black wards, and serve as poll watchers in the 1983 Chicago mayoral election (Abadinsky, 1990:259). Other African organized crime families are of Nigerian and Haitian origin, and are usually suppliers of heroin to cities in the East and Midwest. There are additional organized crime groups in drug trafficking that have been heavily allied with the CIA, and these we shall discuss below.

The reason that there are so many criminal syndicates involved in drugs is because the international drug market is so huge. The worldwide illicit drug market is estimated at $500 to $750 billion per year, larger than the entire gross national product of many of the world's nations (J. Mills, 1986:1130ff). This estimate is probably conservative, with the real figure around $1 trillion in the 1990s. The vast majority of these profits are made by organized crime syndicates, with the assistance of corrupt government officials. In some cases, the syndicate and the government are the same organization.

While there are many theories about both the structure and causes of organized crime, as well as many myths about it, there is empirical evidence that in America's crimogenic department store, organized crime occupies a unique position. Organized criminal syndicates are the bridge, a vital link between "underworld" crime conducted by drug gangs and "street" addicts, and so-called "upper world" crime (Geis, 1974) engaged in by white-collar professionals and legitimate corporate and governmental organizations.

Third Floor:
White-Collar Criminals
and Organized Crime

It is the relationship between the white-collar professional, corporations, and government organizations that is probably most shrouded in myth. The media presentations in films like

The Godfather portray a super secret conspiratorial group of organized crime families who, through force and threat, bully their way into legal and illegal endeavors alike. That is how the expression "I'll make you an offer you can't refuse" came to be known as the modus operandi of the Mafia. There is much empirical evidence that points in another direction, however.

At times, businesspeople and corporations agree to launder drug money for criminal syndicates. Money laundering involves the acceptance of huge amounts of cash, typically in small denominations ($5s, $10s, and $20s) in exchange for cashier's checks or other liquid assets (e.g., bonds, stocks, money orders).

- In 1992, James Boulder, an associate of basketball superstar Michael Jordan, was indicted on drug and money-laundering charges, and was found guilty of trying to hide the drug money he had laundered (New York *Times,* October 9, 1992:B-11; October 24, 1992:B-1).

- In Freeport, New York, an owner of a liquor store and delicatessen bought a thirty-seven-foot yacht with profits he had made dealing drugs. Under federal law, properties purchased with money obtained illegally can be seized by criminal justice officials and sold. The New York district attorney confiscated the yacht (New York *Times,* October 9, 1991:B-4).

- An estimated $1 billion in cash was laundered by Colombian drug traffickers through wholesale jewelry markets in New York, Los Angeles, and Houston. Those convicted in the scheme included two gold traders (New York *Times,* December 28, 1990:A-14).

Check-cashing establishments are frequently used to launder drug money so its origins cannot be traced. Large banks, investment houses, and wholesale jewelry stores are also favorite outlets of drug traffickers to launder their cash. Current estimates are that about $300 billion in cash is laundered in the United States each year.

- In 1993, a federal grand jury indicted the Rosenthal car dealership in Washington, DC, one of the nation's largest auto dealers, on money-laundering charges. Federal agents posed as Colombian drug traffickers in the operation, buying dozens of cars there. Nineteen managers and salespeople were arrested (New York *Times,* January 15, 1993:A-3).

Organized crime, and the illegal drug business, could not exist without the cooperation of legitimate government officials, the criminal justice system, and business. In fact, there is much evidence that organized criminal syndicates, corporations, and government agencies have cooperated with each other throughout the postmodern era, and this is especially true where drug trafficking is concerned.

Fourth Floor: Government Agencies and Organized Crime

The Central Intelligence Agency's (CIA) long history of "accepting assistance from and providing logistical support to some of the largest drug-trafficking (and arms-smuggling) syndicates in the world" (Kappeler et al., 1993:163) is an integral part of the higher immorality:

- In France, in 1950, the CIA recruited Corsican gangsters, the Ferri-Pisani family, to form an elite terror squad for use on the Marseilles docks in order to break a strike by dock workers. The workers had refused to ship arms to Vietnam in support of the French military there. Corsican gangsters assaulted picket lines of Communist union members, and harassed union officials. In return for stopping the strike, the Ferri-Pisani family was allowed to use Marseilles as a shipping center for Corsican heroin on route to the United States (Simon & Eitzen, 1993:82). In Frank Pearce's words, "The CIA helped build (what became known as) the French connection" (Pearce, 1976:150), the enterprise primarily responsible for the postmodern heroin market in the United States from the 1950s to the 1970s.

- For over thirty years, the U.S. government supported opium production in Southeast Asia's Golden Triangle. It did this by providing arms, military support, and protection of corrupt officials, all in the name of anti-Communism, of course. This relationship began in the 1950s after the Chinese Communists defeated Chiang Kai Shek's Nationalist Chinese army (KMT) in 1949. The CIA helped the KMT regroup and settle in Burma's Shan states (bordering on China). The Shan area is one of the richest sources of opium poppies in the world. The KMT tried military invasions of China in 1951 and 1952, but these efforts failed. In 1952, the KMT seized all lands in the Shan states, and took over opium production there. By 1959, opium production in the region had increased nearly tenfold, and the leading Chinese organized crime operation, the Cholon Triad, was born. The CIA helped the KMT ferry opium to Laos, where the CIA taught farmers to grow opium poppies there.

- Between 1964 and 1975, the CIA–funded Laotian tribe members were used to process opium into heroin. The CIA even helped smuggle the heroin out of

Laos on its own airline, Air America. The CIA was aided in this project by American Mafia members whose lucrative Cuban market had dried up because of Fidel Castro's antisyndicate activities following a successful revolution that ousted corrupt dictator Batista (Simon & Eitzen, 1993:82). The story of Air America was made into a movie in the 1980s that starred Mel Gibson.

- In Thailand in the 1950s, the CIA aided Chinese organized crime by bribing the head of the Thai police, General Phao. Phao went into partnership with Cholon Triad in vice operations, extorted money from wealthy citizens, rigged Bangkok's gold exchange, and became the largest drug-trafficking organization in the country. Phao was ousted in 1957 by a revolution. Those taking over the government gave exclusive drug-trafficking rights to the KMT, now, thanks to the CIA, the world's largest heroin trafficking army (Posner, 1988:77). The CIA also aided its Southeast Asian drug producers by establishing money-laundering facilities for them in Australia. The Nugen Hand bank was established by a number of ex-CIA agents and U.S. military officers. Former CIA Director William Colby was hired as the bank's lawyer (Kwitney, 1987).

Other incidents link U.S. government agencies to drug trafficking by the Nicaraguan Contras in the 1980s. The Contras were paid $10 million by the Medellin cocaine cartel for being allowed safe passage through Contra-held territory with the full knowledge of the CIA. The Enterprise operation established by Lieutenant Colonel Oliver North and Admiral John Poindexter also provided airplanes to the Medellin cocaine cartel in 1984–1985. The cartel paid the Enterprise for use of planes, landing strips, and labor in loading drug shipments. The proceeds went allegedly to buy arms for the Contras. In other cases, the Contras smuggled drugs directly, swapping them for arms. U.S. government agencies have also been linked to drug-trafficking operations by the governments of Chile and Guatemala (Simon & Eitzen, 1993:320).

- In 1985, in Afghanistan, the CIA supplied arms to the Afghan General Hekmatyar after the Communists took over Afghanistan and the Russian army subsequently invaded it to prop up the Communist regime there. Hekmatyar and his army promptly went into the heroin business, and by 1988 had one hundred to two hundred heroin refineries just across the border in Pakistan. By the late 1980s, heroin from these Southwest Asian nations accounted for about 50 percent of the European and American heroin supplies. They went into partnership with America's ally, General Zia in Pakistan, where the heroin market reached $8 to $10 billion in value, a sum greater than Pakistan's national budget. Today the Russian army is gone, but the Communists still rule Afghanistan, despite $2 billion in CIA aid (McCoy, 1991a; 1991b:12).

- The CIA effectively blocked a major DEA investigation into the activities of General Noriega of Panama, a corrupt drug trafficker who was in the pay of the CIA for $200,000 a year. The State Department blocked an investigation into the government of the Bahamas' relationship with drug traffickers. The Bahamas was used as a safe haven for money laundering and drug shipments.

Aside from a persistent pattern of cooperation with U.S. federal agencies, organized crime syndicates are a chief source of corruption among federal, state, and local criminal justice personnel. There is a long history of police corruption in the United States, so long that every source investigating the problems since the 1890s has consistently revealed serious forms of police bribery. About one hundred drug-related bribery cases involving police at all levels of the criminal justice system now come before American courts each year. A partial list of 1988 cases includes:

- Seven Boston police detectives were convicted on fifty-seven bribery counts involving $18,000 over eight years.
- Sheriffs in several rural Georgia counties accepted bribes of $50,000 each to permit drug smugglers to land airplanes on abandoned roads.
- A member of the Justice Department's Organized Crime Strike Force received $210,000, for which he revealed the identity of government informants to drug smugglers.
- A federal customs agent received $50,000 for each marijuana-ladened vehicle allowed to cross the U.S.–Mexican border without examination.

In 1990, sheriffs in four Kentucky counties were arrested by federal agents for taking money from cocaine traffickers in exchange for safe passage through their state (New York *Times,* August 17, 1990:A-15).

In 1991, a Los Angeles grand jury indicted seven members of an elite police narcotics squad unit for stealing tens of thousands of dollars from drug seizure money and for falsely accusing defendants. The seven deputies from the Narcotics Division of the L.A. County Sheriff's Department were ultimately convicted of skimming $1.4 million from drug seizures (New York *Times,* November 22, 1990:A-25; December 11, 1990:B-3).

In 1992, New York City police officer Michael Dowd was indicted for cocaine trafficking. Dowd reportedly received $5000 to $8000 per week in payments from drug gangs. Four other officers were also arrested. Reportedly, the U.S. Attorney had obtained evidence necessary for indictment in 1988, but delayed the arrest for four years for unexplained reasons (New York *Times,* July 7, 1992:B-1).

At the federal level, the Drug Enforcement Administration (DEA) has also exhibited corrupt tendencies. Michael Levine personally accounted for the prosecution of at least 3000 persons serving some 15,000 years of incarceration. Then in 1979, Levine notified the DEA that he had an opportunity to arrest Roberto Suarez, termed by CBS's "60 Minutes" as "the biggest drug dealer alive." To Levine's astonishment, the DEA had never even heard of Suarez, and didn't believe Levine's story. Levine went on to uncover a virtual coup d'état in Colombia involving Suarez and an ex-Nazi war criminal, Klaus Barbie, a man smuggled into Colombia by the American Central Intelligence Agency. Levine would later write a best-selling book, *Deep Cover,* which relates how the DEA failed to pursue prosecution of many of the most significant drug dealers involved in the Latin American cocaine trade. Levine learned that many of the people most closely tied to the Latin American drug trade were the same personnel the CIA was attempting to put into positions of power in Argentina and Colombia. Levine also insists that the South Florida Drug Task Force lied to the press and the public concerning drug seizures by counting each major bust two or three times in their statistics, and that the drug economy in the United States, some $200 billion a year, is being used to "finance political operations, pay international debts . . . all sorts of things." In other words, drugs are a major source of corruption within the criminal justice system and in politics as well. Aside from political corruption, the crime factory is also characterized by corporate criminality.

Fifth Floor: Banks, Corporations, and Money Laundering

Federal law requires that banks report all cash deposits of $10,000 or more to the Internal Revenue Service (IRS). In 1975, there were only 3000 such activities reported. By 1988, there were 5.5 million reported annually. A number of major American banks have been more than willing to overlook the IRS's reporting requirement, sometimes receiving a 1.5 to 2 percent commission from drug trafficking depositors for doing so.

Other sources of money laundering are investment firms, like Shearson/American Express and Merrill Lynch, and jewelry wholesalers.

It is now estimated that the total amount of drug money laundered each year is an immense $300 billion, about half of all monies involved in the worldwide drug market. Of this amount, $100 billion is laundered in the United States. Nine-tenths of this amount ends up overseas, often in secret Swiss accounts, where it can then be moved freely. This outflow of money contributes substantially to the nation's foreign trade deficit (Harris, 1991:52–53).

The largest money-laundering operation ever uncovered took place in 1989. U.S. banks were used to ship $1 billion a year to cocaine traffickers. The drug profits were disguised as stemming from phony front businesses—wholesale gold and jewelry—run largely out of Los Angeles. Another money-laundering investigation in 1990, Operation Polar Cap, resulted in the freezing of hundreds of bank accounts in 173 American banks, more than half of which were in New York and Florida. The accounts contained some $400 million in Colombian drug profits. Another channel of laundered money is the storefront check-cashing and money-transmitting service, most of which are unlicensed and run by newly arrived or illegal immigrants. The better part of these are in states with few regulators, who are consequently unable to keep up with the growth of such businesses. This is especially true in Florida, Texas, New York, and California. Each year such operations take billions in cash from drug dealers and send it overseas. These storefront operations defraud honest customers by failing to send their money to requested addresses. Many customers can not complain because they are either newly arrived immigrants ignorant of the law or illegals (Harris, 1991:60–61).

- In the 1980s, the famous "Pizza Connection" case resulted in the conviction of over four hundred Mafia members in Sicily and the United States on numerous charges, including heroin trafficking. The Pizza Connection cons laundered tens of millions of dollars in cash through a number of New York City banks. The banks would then electronically wire the millions of dollars into secret accounts in Swiss banks so they could not be traced. The Pizza Connection traffickers also deposited $5 million in cash with the Merrill Lynch brokerage firm in $5, $10, and $20 bills over a six-week period. Merrill Lynch not only accepted these dubious deposits, it provided the couriers transporting the money with extra security. The same couriers also laundered $13.5 million through accounts at the E.F. Hutton & Co. investment firm, which also provided security for them (Keppeler et al., 1993:85).

- In 1991, the National Mortgage Bank of Greece was fined a record $1.8 million by a Brooklyn, New York, federal judge because the bank's American branch engaged in one of the largest money-laundering schemes in U.S. history (New York *Times,* March 23, 1991:I-40).

- CIA associates used Florida's Castle Bank to launder drug money for organized crime figures. Another Florida bank with CIA ties, the Bank of Perrine, was purchased by the Colombian cocaine cartel to launder drug money.

- The CIA and the Mafia played an important role in establishing the World Finance Corporation. This Florida company laundered drug money and supported terrorist activities in the early 1970s.

What all of these examples indicate is that corporations and banks are not pawns in the hands of organized criminal syndicates, but part of its fabric (Keppeler et al., 1993:85). The illegal drug business, both domestically and internationally, can not exist without the willing participation of money-laundering banks and corrupt public officials, and these legitimate entities are a major part of America's crime and drug problems.

Drugs, Crime, and Social Harm

Aside from their link with crime, drugs, both legal and illicit, are the cause of much social harm:

- Drug abuse in the American workplace, in lost workdays and disabilities alone, is estimated to cost American business $166 billion a year. Hospital treatment for the victims of crimes by street-level drug dealers is estimated at $1 billion. Court costs for illicit drug trafficking cases runs $30 billion. All tolled, costs of substance abuse are now estimated at about $500 billion (*Forbes,* 1994:94).

- The most seriously addicting illegal drugs in America are heroin and cocaine. These two drugs kill between 2000 to 3000 people per year. Alcohol, a legal drug, is implicated in 100,000 deaths a year, and cigarettes kill an estimated 400,000 people a year (Lazare, 1990:24). Indeed, one surprise in the war on drugs comes with knowledge that the legal drugs kill thousands of times more people than the illegal ones do. And, as we shall see, there is a link between the abuse of alcohol and/or tobacco and the illegal drug abuse. Injectable drugs are held responsible for about one-third of the nation's acquired immune deficiency syndrome (AIDS) cases, due to unsanitary needles.

- In 1991, it was estimated that one-fifth of all children in Oakland, California, were being raised by their grandparents. This was due to their parents' drug involvement. Another study found that thousands of grandparents in New York City were also raising their grandchildren because their mothers were either drug addicts, in prison, or dead from AIDS (New York Times, July 23, 1990:A-1; May 12, 1991:IV-6).

As we can see, drugs in all their forms are an immensely harmful problem in and of themselves. Couple drugs with crime, and the effect is devastating. Street crime, as measured in the FBI's Uniform Crime Reports (UCR) (issued annually), consists of serious felony offenses that include criminal homicide, assault, forcible rape, robbery, burglary, arson, motor vehicle theft, and larceny. Felony offenses are punishable by one or more years in prison or death (Inciardi & Rothman, 1990:G-5). The UCR statistics may underestimate the true crime rate by as much as 200 percent in some categories. Street crime and related violence now cost America between $425 billion and $647 billion, including the costs of running the criminal justice system, constructing new prisons and jails, private security measures, violence-related health costs, and other expenses (*Forbes,* 1994:94; *Dissent,* 1991). Drugs are also a major cause of violations of civil liberties at all levels of government.

Private Troubles | Public Issues

Preventing Crime Victimization

While at Home:

Have your door key in your hand so that you can open the door immediately when you return home.

When you are arriving home by a private auto or taxi, ask the driver to wait until you are inside.

Always leave your headlights on when arriving home until you have opened the garage door or unlocked your front door.

If you are a woman alone, list only your last name and initials on your mailbox or in the phone directory.

If you just moved into a new apartment or residence, re-key or change all locks. You never know who might have a key.

Know who is at your door before opening it. A wide-angle door viewer (180°–190°) enables you to identify the visitor. You can see him, he can't see you.

Don't rely on chain locks. They are a great privacy lock but they are not a security lock.

Continued on next page

Private Troubles   Public Issues

Never dress in front of windows; always close the drapes.

Never let anyone—repairmen, police officers, etc.—into your home without proper identification. Don't be afraid to ask for identification.

Never let strangers in to use your telephone. If necessary, you may call the police for them.

Always leave outside lights on after dark.

If you receive wrong number phone calls, don't give out your name or phone number.

If you receive obscene phone calls, quietly hang up and call the police.

In an apartment building, try never to be alone in the laundry room.

If you suspect someone is in your home, don't go in or call out. Call the police from your neighbor's house.

If you see or hear something or someone suspicious, call the police.

Prevention Tips While You Are Out:

These are the best prevention methods to deter attacks while you are out. Naturally, you won't be able to follow them to the letter but use them as a guideline.

Try not to go out at night alone.

Avoid unfamiliar areas, if possible.

Don't take shortcuts.

Don't walk in or near alleys.

Don't walk on deserted streets.

Use caution in parking lots.

Don't walk in poorly lighted areas.

Don't accept rides with strangers.

Don't respond to comments from strangers on the street.

It is better to wait for an empty elevator than to get in one with a stranger.

If you ride an elevator with another person, stand near the control panel if possible. If you are attacked, press the alarm button and as many of the other control buttons as possible.

Don't walk near dark doorways or shrubbery.

Don't hitchhike.

Cross the street if you see someone suspicious following you.

Call the police if you feel that someone is following you or acting suspicious.

Walk into an open business if you become suspicious of someone while walking.

Walk with a friend.

Watch your surroundings. Be alert for suspicious persons especially around banks, stores, streets, and your car or home.

If you are alone at work before or after normal business hours, keep the door locked if possible.

If you work late, ask a coworker or security guard to walk out to your car with you.

When meeting a new friend, exchange phone numbers only, not addresses.

When going on a first date, let a family member or friend know where you are going. Consider a daytime meeting rather than night for a first date.

It is a good idea to take a friend with you when going to a nightclub. If you go to a club alone, provide your own transportation.

Don't allow alcohol or drugs to impair your judgement.

If you haven't already, set a few personal social standards and stick to them. Don't allow an overly aggressive pursuer to change your mind.

While in Your Automobile:

Never pick up hitchhikers.

Don't park in the dark.

Never leave your keys in your car.

Always lock your car.

Never allow another vehicle to follow you home. Drive to the nearest open business and call the police.

Have your keys in your hand so that you can open your car door without delay.

Always keep your car in gear while stopped for traffic signals or signs. If threatened, simply drive away.

Always check the back seat of your car before getting in.

If you stop to aid others, don't get out of your car. Ask what the problem is and drive to the nearest phone and call the police.

Continued on next page

Private Troubles   Public Issues

Always park in well-lighted areas, if possible.

Always lock your doors while driving.

Prearrange meetings so that you don't have to wait alone.

Riding the Bus or Trolley:

During off hours, ride as near to the operator as possible.

If you are going to be out late, make sure you have cab fare.

If someone bothers you on the bus, change seats or tell the operator.

Have your fare or pass ready in your hand when boarding the bus.

At night, avoid dark/isolated intersections or stops.

Look around when getting off the bus or trolley and be aware of people around you.

If You Are Attacked:

The course of action you take if you choose to act is strictly up to you. Keep in mind that not all cases are alike. Each attacker is different and is motivated by a different set of circumstances. Therefore, what may deter one attacker may only aggravate another.

There is no sure answer. If you are attacked, DON'T PANIC. Some options available to you are:

Use common sense.

Try to talk your way out of it.

Scream (loudly).

Run (towards people, open businesses).

Hide (if you get the opportunity).

Bide your time.

Notify the police immediately if you are attacked and if there are witnesses, ask them to stay until the police arrive.

Whatever Your Decision Is:

When an attacker threatens your life with a deadly weapon and you come out of the attack alive, you took the proper course of action.

During an armed attack, if you feel your life is about to be taken, you must decide what course of action you should take. There is no hard and fast rule when it comes to self-defense. You must consider such things as the location, your own physical capabilities, your perceived chance of success, and whether a weapon is involved. If you cannot escape, bide your time and look for another opportunity. Remember, a half-hearted attempt could be worse than no resistance at all.

What About Judo and Karate?

This type of training is great for physical conditioning, but it takes years of training and continual practice to develop usable skills.

Don't substitute self-defense training for common sense, alertness, and caution.

What About Carrying a Weapon?

It is not advisable to carry guns, knives, clubs, or chemical sprays. It would be illegal to carry some of these weapons, and all of them could be used against you. It is advisable *not* to carry weapons.

Purse Protection:

The crime of purse snatching has increased and will continue to rise until people take precautionary measures. It is a problem that all women, especially the elderly, should be aware of. In addition to property loss, serious physical injury can result. Like most crimes, it is a crime of opportunity. Frequently it occurs because so many women, through lack of awareness, provide the thief with the opportunity.

The purse snatcher is usually a young male under eighteen years of age. He usually approaches his victim from behind, catching her off guard in a hit-run manner. The culprit(s) usually strike a person who is walking home, to or from her car, or who is waiting for transportation while standing in public. He might even ask for the time or directions to make you feel more at ease, drop your guard, or preoccupy you.

Women can reduce the risk of being victimized by using a few simple precautions.

Tips for Protection:

Do's:

Carry shoulder strap purses with the strap over the shoulder, flap nearest your body, and keep your hand on the strap.

Carry clutch purses upside down with your hand on the clasp so that everything will fall out if grabbed.

Keep your purse under physical control at all times.

When possible, carry your wallet, keys, and other valuables on your person in an inside pocket or other suitable place other than your purse.

Credit cards and checks should be carried instead of cash. Maintain a record of the account numbers at home.

Carry only those credit cards you will be using.

If you are wearing a coat, carry a purse worn over the shoulder, but under the coat.

Continued on next page

Private Troubles   **Public Issues**

When shopping, place your purse in a shopping bag.

Practice "buddy shopping." Shop with a friend when possible.

It is not advisable to leave your purse in your car but if you must, hide it in the trunk or under the seat.

Don'ts:

Don't let your purse hang loosely in your hand.

Don't carry large amounts of money.

Don't carry unnecessary valuables in your purse.

Don't fight for your purse.

While at the office, never leave your purse in plain view.

If at all possible, don't carry a purse.

If You Are a Victim:

CALL THE POLICE and report the crime immediately.

- For crimes in progress or life-threatening situations—Call 911 *IMMEDIATELY*
- For suspicious activity, to give information concerning a crime, or for general business call your campus or local police department.

When you call the police, the communications operator will ask several questions of you. The operator will ask questions similar to those listed below. The questions are to ensure that the police will be able to respond to your call in an efficient manner. Remain calm and answer the operator's questions to the best of your ability.

What Will Be Asked and What to Say:

I. WHY ARE YOU CALLING?

    A. Crime:

        1. In progress
        2. Happened earlier

II. WHAT IS THE LOCATION?

    A. Exact address

    B. Hundred block

    C. Cross street

III. WHAT IS YOUR NAME?

IV. WHAT TELEPHONE NUMBER ARE YOU CALLING FROM?

V. SUSPECTS AND THEIR DESCRIPTIONS?

A. Was a weapon used?

B. Was there a vehicle?

1. Description
2. License number
3. Direction of travel

C. Suspect descriptions:

1. How many?
2. Direction of travel?
3. Physical description:
   Sex:
   Age:
   Race:
   Height:
   Weight:
   Hair:
   Eyes:
   Beard:
   Hat :
   Glasses:
   Complexion:

Shirt:	Type and color
Jacket:	Type and color
Pants:	Type and color
Shoes:	Type and color

Cooperate fully with the police.

Press charges when your attacker is caught.

Be a good witness—remember the attacker's description, height, weight, age, hair color, eyes, marks or scars, mannerisms, language, vehicle description, license number, and direction of escape.

You should consider your responsibility to report the crime to the police. If not for yourself, then for the others who may become victims if the perpetrator is allowed to continue to operate. Many suspects remain in general areas. Most of them use the same

Continued on next page

Private Troubles   Public Issues

methods of operation that could help the police identify a suspect. It is important to tell the police as much as you can; no fact is too trivial.

What Is Suspicious?

Suspicious Persons

- Going Door-to-Door in Residential Area
  Especially suspicious if, after a few houses are visited, one or more of the subjects go into a back or side yard. More suspicious if another remains in the front when this occurs. *Possible significance:* "Casing" for a house to burglarize, burglary in progress, soliciting violation, or trespass.

- Waiting in Front of a House or Business
  Particularly suspicious if owners are absent, or—if it's a business—the establishment is closed. *Possible significance:* Lookout for a burglary in progress inside.

- Forcing Entrance to or Tampering with a Residence, Vehicle, etc.
  Suspicious under almost any circumstances. *Possible significance:* Burglary, theft, malicious mischief, or trespass in progress.

- Nonresident Going into Back or Side Yard of House
  Suspicious under almost any circumstances. *Possible significance:* Possible burglary or trespass in progress.

Drugs and the History of Minority Oppression

An additional form of social harm related to the war on drugs concerns the enforcement of drug laws. Many legal experts have remarked that one of the first casualties of the war on drugs may be the civil liberties guaranteed Americans in the U.S. Constitution (Wisotsky, 1993:17). The sordid history of America's antinarcotics laws has always been "closely tied to the social control (repression of the rights of) minority groups" (Michalowski, 1985:307).

The first narcotics laws in the United States were the antiopium laws of the 1870s. These were a direct attack on the working-class Chinese immigrants of the West and East Coasts, many of whom participated in the building of the American railroads. In 1914, the Harrison Act outlawed cocaine in the United States. Cocaine was a very popular drug among middle-class people. It was an ingredient in Coca-Cola, and Sears even sold it by mail order. But American racists convinced the federal government that blacks, high on

- Carrying Property
  Suspicious, depending upon the circumstances. For example, if at an unusual hour or in an unusual place, and if the property is not wrapped as if just purchased. *Possible significance:* Subject leaving the scene of a robbery, burglary, or theft.

Other Unusual Situations

- Property in Homes, Private Garages, Storage Areas, etc.
  Suspicious if accumulations are large or otherwise unusual (such as several TV sets in a garage) and if the items are in good condition, but are not in use. *Possible significance:* Stolen property.

- Much Human Traffic to and from a Certain Residence
  Not suspicious unless it occurs on a daily or very regular basis, especially during late or unusual hours. *Possible significance:* Vice or narcotic activities, or "fence" operation.

- Unusual Noises, etc.
  Gunshots, screaming, sounds of combat, abnormally barking dogs—anything suggestive of foul play, danger, illegal activity. *Call the police immediately!*

Source: San Diego, California, Police Department.

cocaine, were busily committing violence and sexual assaults, and it was partially for this reason that it was outlawed.

In 1919, liquor was outlawed (until 1932) because white Protestant middle-class reformers feared that the newly arrived urban, Catholic, working class would use the neighborhood bar to plan disorder or revolution. The reformers did not understand that saloons were an important meeting place in the social lives of ethnics from Southern Europe. In 1937, the Marijuana Tax Act outlawed marijuana. That law was the outcome of a campaign by people convinced that marijuana was primarily used by lazy Mexican workers. Since the 1960s, these antidrug laws have been used against young middle-class whites and others whose alternative lifestyles are a threat to an economic system based on the "work ethic," with its stress on punctuality, stability, and conformity. Thousands of members of these groups have been arrested and/or deported from the United States under these laws. Today, this same pattern of minority oppression continues. African Americans make up 14 percent of drug users, yet account for almost 50 percent of all persons arrested for drugs (Walker, 1994:234). Clearly, blacks are being singled out through the drug policy.

The current war on drugs is likewise a threat to the civil rights of millions of Americans, both in their homes and in the workplace.

- Each state in the Union has laws punishing cocaine possession, but the penalties vary widely. One young woman was arrested in Texas in 1987 for speeding and running red lights. Three vials of crack were found in her purse. The penalty for first-offense cocaine possession in Texas carries a twenty-year maximum sentence. The same offense in Virginia, the woman's home state, could have resulted in her being released with a mere warning (Berger, 1987:83–84).

- Beginning in August, 1987, federal workers in sensitive jobs had to undergo mandatory drug testing. This policy has been upheld by courts and by 1992 meant that an estimated 22 million workers inside and outside government were subject to drug testing. Almost immediately, an underground "clean urine" industry sprang up whereby people could buy samples of clean urine to pass such tests. The temptation to do so may not be confined just to drug users. The urine tests are not always reliable, and may show "false positives" if the tested urine's owners have eaten such foods as poppy seeds. False positives can occur in 3 to 5 percent of cases (Harris, 1991:167–168). Urine tests can not tell when someone has taken a drug, or if the drug has affected his or her job performance. Marijuana can be detected as long as three weeks after ingestion.

During the 1920s, the United States tried to stem alcohol consumption by prohibiting its manufacture and sale. Prohibition was in large measure a great failure—one that resulted in the huge growth of organized criminal syndicates from the sale of illegal liquor. Thus, America has a long history of trying to prevent the use of drugs by making them illegal. Each attempt at limiting drug consumption has made drug problems only worse.

Residents of minority areas frequently complain that their neighborhoods are subject to sweeps by the police, especially when law enforcement personnel are in pursuit of drug addicts and pushers. There have been numerous incidents of civil rights violations by police in such areas. Such cases have involved illegal searches and seizures. Moreover, almost 90 percent of those serving time for crack possession are black.

Perhaps the most serious threats to civil rights involve recent search and seizure (Fourth Amendment) issues.

- In 1989, police, unannounced, entered the home of a machine worker at five A.M. on a tip given them almost two years earlier. The man awoke and began to get out of bed to resist the unknown intruders. The police shot and killed him. A single marijuana cigarette was found in his house (Sterling, 1989:36).

- Police sweeps in black ghettos are common in large cities. Bush administration drug czar William Bennett ordered sixty low-income residents of a Washington, DC, public housing project evicted for *reported drug use in their apartments* (D'Amato, 1990:80).

- In Key West, Florida, a shrimp fisherman's boat was seized by the Coast Guard when three grams of cannabis seeds and stems were found. Under the law, the boat can be taken whether or not the owner was responsible for the drugs being on board (Wisotsky, 1993:20).

Aside from these harms, the American drug abuse problem also symbolizes widespread forms of alienation.

Alienation Among Underclass, Blue-Collar, and 'Yuppie' Drug Abusers

Recent analyses have noted the presence of despair and class envy within the under (lower) class, which is largely African-American and Hispanic (Harris, 1987: 116–140; Wilson, 1988). It is claimed that the underclass not only suffers from the ill effects of poverty and profound dehumanization, but they are highly susceptible to the constant harangue of advertising and mass consumption. Designer sneakers and gold chains are so coveted in some neighborhoods that possessors of these items have been murdered by desperate perpetrators.

Some sociological analyses on the drug-using portion of the underclass (Wilson, 1988; Duster, 1988; Kasarda & Williams, 1989; Jackson, 1988) have stressed, not only the effects of the loss of traditional manufacturing (factory) jobs, but the significant migration from the central cities of the black middle class and small business owners, leading not only to unemployment among lower-class African Americans, but a lack of legitimate role models as well.

Such socioeconomic trends have contributed to a subcultural alienation among the underclass' hard-core disadvantaged, a group of approximately 2.5 million people, mostly between ages sixteen and twenty-four (Kasarda & Williams, 1989:16), now heavily engaged in drug abuse, drug selling, and a significant proportion (40–50 percent) of the felony offenses (Walker, 1990; Graham, 1987:2; Gropper, 1987:11). This group's high school dropout rate has soared from 12 percent in the 1970s to 43 percent in the 1990s among black males. Likewise, the rates of youth unemployment in central cities often ranges between 60 and 75 percent (Shapiro, 1987:21–22). Scholars are just beginning to appreciate the subcultural alienation suffered by this particular group as manifested by their disproportionately high rates of illegitimate births, violent rages, and mental illness.

Working-Class Alienation

Within the blue-collar community, drug abuse relates to work alienation and economic insecurity. Work alienation (self-dehumanization) stems from dull, repetitive, specialized tasks, coupled with the uncertainty of being fired or laid off. Studies demonstrate a link between factory work and substance abuse, absenteeism, and other forms of deviance in the workplace (Lindquist, 1990:A-1; M. Harris, 1987:17–59). Drugs commonly abused by working-class people include prescription and illegal stimulants and depressants. Many members of this class have also borne the brunt of the economic dislocations of the 1970s and 1980s. Between 1974 and 1984, 11.5 million Americans lost their jobs due to plant relocations and shutdowns. Only 60 percent of those rendered unemployed during this

Many blue-collar workers suffer from work-related stress. Their work is often boring and repetitive, and they suffer from the inability to concentrate. Some of these workers take stimulants in order to heighten their energy levels. Moreover, each social class has its favorite drugs of abuse.

period were able to obtain new jobs, and nearly half of those who found new jobs resorted to work paying less than they had previously earned (Ehrenreich, 1989:206–207). Brenner (1973) has demonstrated the link between sustained unemployment and alcohol abuse. It would likewise be no surprise if the same relationship existed between increased unemployment and increased rates of substance abuse.

The working-class subculture legitimizes drugs as an escape from intolerable economic and working conditions. The frequent result is the consumption of escapist drugs (especially amphetamines) as a response to stress both at work and at home (Rubin, 1977). Working-class males also have heavy rates of alcohol abuse. They form a substantial portion of the 20 percent of the nation's beer drinkers that consume 80 percent of all the beer. Within the working class are ethnic subcultures (e.g., the Irish) who have historically showed a high rate of alcohol consumption. These consumption patterns are reinforced by the dominant culture's advertising of alcohol aimed at working-class males. This is why beer is so heavily advertised on sports programs. These inauthentic, puffery messages (Simon & Eitzen, 1993: Chapter 3) legitimize drug use within alienated members of the working class.

The Yuppies

A *yuppie* is defined as a young, upper-middle-class professional person whose gross income exceeds $40,000 annually, and who usually resides in a large metropolitan area (Ehrenreich,

1989). On the surface, much so-called "yuppie" cocaine abuse appears due to personality-related factors. One study of 430 successful professionals who snort cocaine found that the typical abuser is "a certifiable narcissist who has an undeveloped sense of identity and a profound despair, and an inability to express rage toward one or both parents" (Andersen, 1983:25). This result closely parallels the literature on narcissism in American culture (Lasch, 1978, 1984). The narcissism of certain yuppies is probably better thought of as an extreme version of what is a widespread trait within the American social character, namely extreme individualism, materialism, and status seeking.

Yuppie drug taking also represents a response to an inability to form committed bonds, a lack of affect manifesting itself in emotional emptiness (Bellah et al., 1986). Ultimately, upper-middle-class drug abuse is legitimated in part because of the drug-taking mentality fostered by advertising, and further reinforced by the "hippie" drug experimentation mentality of the 1960s. It is estimated by former New York City police commissioner Patrick Murphy that "middle class recreational users generate more than 80% of the $150 billion cocaine traffic" (*Ethics,* 1990:1), meaning cocaine is widely available to this subculture. Thus drug abuse is socially patterned within different social classes and subcultures.

Moreover, these various forms of alienation, as well as the realities of the crime-drug nexus, and its crime factory, discussed earlier in this chapter, are nowhere addressed in policies related to the war on drugs. The drug war of the 1980s and 1990s marks the third time in this century that the American government has declared a war on drugs. While the ongoing drug war has become a more or less permanent feature of America's political landscape, there is hardly ever a report of victory in the drug war. What exists instead is a massive policy failure.

Policy Failure:
The Disastrous Nonwar on Drugs

The government has always insisted on perceiving drug abuse as a crime, rather than a disease or a public health problem (as in other industrial democracies). The result is an actual worsening of both the crime and the drug problems. Aside from being a major cause of political corruption and violations of civil liberties, policies associated with the drug war have produced almost no significant results. Since 1981, thousands of new Border Patrol and Customs agents have been added to stations along the U.S.–Mexican border to intercept drugs and arms shipments. U-2 spy planes were used in Oregon, California, and other states to spot marijuana growth at a cost of $200,000. In 1990, there were more arrests for marijuana possession in the United States (330,000) than for vehicle theft, yet no evidence exists that the supply or use of marijuana has declined (McCaghy & Capron, 1994:377). In fact, drug use among American young people was increasing in 1993 according to the results of the University of Michigan's annual survey of American junior high and high school students, including a sharp rise in marijuana use throughout the country at all grade levels, as well as an increase in the use of stimulants, LSD, and inhalants. Aside from failing to reduce the supply of drugs, the drug war has filled prisons and jails with inmates.

There were more people in federal prison on drug charges when Ronald Reagan left office in 1989 then there were people in federal prison when he took office in 1981. But the flow of drugs and rates of crime had both increased. These failed policies have, at times, reached illogical extremes. A 1983 Arizona law required illicit drug dealers to buy a $100 business license and costly tax stamps to attach to the drugs they sold. Those failing to comply with this law were subject to criminal penalties and additional taxes. If they did obey the law, they were still subject to prosecution for drug dealing. Very few prosecutors used the law which, quite possibly, violated the constitutional right against self-incrimination (Bennett, 1989:280). Such irrational acts demonstrate how desperate legislators are to try almost anything, no matter how ineffective, to curb the supply of drugs. However, even by the most optimistic estimates, only 10 to 15 percent of illegal drug shipments imported into the United States are seized by law enforcement officials. In a 1988 *National Law Journal* poll of 181 prosecutors, two-thirds of those interviewed stated they are having little or no impact against illegal narcotics (Reiman, 1990:28).

Policies that criminalize addicts, and seek to confiscate illegal drug supplies do not work because they do not address the causes of crime and drug abuse in America. The United States' drug policy emphasizes punishment and seizing supplies over treatment. Both of these policies have managed to make things only worse. Hundreds of thousands of prisoners convicted of largely property and drug crimes are now crowded into dehumanizing human warehouses wherein they are increasingly isolated and alienated from outside society, and embittered towards it. As of 1990, prisons nationwide were overcrowded by a factor of almost 30 percent. Many were under court order to reduce their overcrowded conditions (Irwin & Austin, 1994:65–66, 69). Adding hundreds of new U.S. Customs and Border Patrol officers in the early 1990s has not made even a dent in the supply of drugs being smuggled into the United States. Each year in the United States about 800,000 addicts undergo some kind of treatment, but there are an additional 1 million addicts for whom treatment is unavailable. These are abusers who want to get off drugs (Malcolm, 1989). Medicalizing the drug problem (not wholesale legalization) appears to offer the best hope for taking the profit out of the drug trade and reducing the number of addicts through treatment.

There are plenty of models around of successful medicalization policies. Other modern democracies, like Holland, make maintenance doses of drugs available to addicts. Holland's government also offers treatment for those who want to be drug free. Between 1982, when the policy went into effect, and 1986, the number of addicts requesting drug-free treatment for their abuse has doubled (Eglesman, 1989:45). Under this policy 60 to 80 percent of all Holland's addicts are being given some kind of assistance, and the number of cocaine and heroin addicts appears stable.

Summary

Crime in all its forms and drug abuse in all its forms are two of the most serious social problems facing American society. Street crime costs about 25,000 lives each year, and accounts for about $20 billion in property losses. Drug abuse costs about 500,000 lives per year (including deaths from alcohol and tobacco) and probably tolls around $200 billion in financial harm from medical bills, lost work productivity, and expenditures of the criminal justice system.

Crime and drug abuse are intimately interrelated social problems. The vast majority of street, property, and violent crime are now drug related. Drug abuse is also related to every other major form of crime in America and internationally as well. The $750 billion annual drug trade is widely shared by street gangs that distribute illegal drugs to street users. Organized criminal syndicates on all inhabited continents manufacture illegal drugs and sell them to street gangs for distribution. Individual white-collar criminals sometimes put up finance capital for drug shipments. Such individuals also launder drug profits. Some large corporate banks and investment firms have been involved in multimillion-dollar money-laundering schemes, and have even provided security for money launderers. Organized criminal syndicates are also a major source of corruption of law enforcement personnel and politicians. The CIA and other government agencies have demonstrated a surprising willingness to aid organized criminal syndicates in the establishment of drug territories in the name of foreign policy objectives. Thus the crime problem in America is more like a crime-producing (crimogenic) department store wherein all floors (types of crime) are interconnected with dark stairways (secret arrangements).

The causes of crime and drug abuse are somewhat complex, but among the most important factors are a society characterized by extreme inequalities of wealth and power, and a set of cultural values that contain a surprising admiration of successful criminals, and many inducements to use drugs to solve personal and social problems. One of the saddest aspects of the drug problem is that other modern democracies, like Holland, have brought drug abuse under control by viewing the solution in pragmatic, medical terms. Meanwhile, the United States still insists on viewing drug abuse as a crime, and this policy has failed.

Suggested Readings

Victor Kappeler et al. (1993) *The Mythology of Crime and Criminal Justice* (Prospect Heights, IL: Waveland). This book explores myths about various types of crime and drug abuse that are created by the mass media and reinforced by the simplistic promises of politicians.

Nathan Miller (1992) *Stealing from America* (New York: Paragon House). Miller's discussion of the history of corruption on the federal level in America is the best book of its kind. He clearly demonstrates that America was founded on corruption and that corruption is widespread in America today.

Samuel Walker (1994) *Sense and Nonsense about Crime and Drugs: A Policy Guide,* 3d ed. (Belmont, CA: Wadsworth). This is an important discussion of the myths on which American crime policy is based. The book also contains dramatic evidence that the assumptions behind much of the "lock 'em up and throw the key away" policy are wrong.

Exercises

Critical Thinking Exercise 8.1	**Fear of Crime: A Survey**

Do a survey involving the fear of crime on your campus. Ask a random sample of students questions like the following:

1. Have you ever been the victim of a crime? Which crime?
2. Have you ever known anyone who was a homicide victim?
3. Do you feel safe on the campus at night?
4. Do you know students who regularly use drugs?
5. Do you know people who regularly use alcohol?

Please provide the following information:

Your age _____

Year in School _____ (Fr So Jr Sr Grad Student)

Major _____

Sex _____

Which students are most fearful of crime? Is crime on your campus more, less, or about the same frequency as in American society in general? (About 40 percent of Americans report being crime victims.)

Critical Thinking Exercise 8.2	**Crime Coverage**

Do a content analysis of crime coverage in local newspapers. Kappeler et al. (1993:10–19) report that coverage in newspapers is often characterized by:

- the creation of crime waves; if there are two to four sex crimes, for example, in a two-week period, the press will claim a sex-crime wave is underway.
- sensationalism. The crimes covered in newspapers are violent or of lurid interest (e.g., mass murders, bank robberies, rapes). Most crimes are actually household burglaries, however, and are rarely mentioned.
- a failure to address risk and prevention techniques the public can use.

Continued on next page

Exercise 8.2 Continued

- targeting of certain groups as criminals (e.g., youths, minorities), to the point of underreporting crimes by other groups (e.g., whites).
- portraying victims as innocent, good people, whose victimization represents a genuine loss to the community. (Many times victims of crimes could just as easily be perpetrators.)

Use the above themes as categories. Analyze about fifty articles from recent issues of your local paper.

The Medical-Industrial Complex: Problems of Health and Mental Health

Chapter • Chapter • Chapter • Chapter • Chapter

9

The Medical-Industrial
Complex and Its Contradictions

Just as there is a military-industrial complex, there is also a medical-industrial complex. America's medical-industrial complex receives over four times more money than the military-industrial complex. (Compare the $1 trillion spent on health care in the United States with the $230 billion spent on defense.) The medical-industrial complex is not a conspiracy. It is a combination of interests that includes approximately five hundred private corporations and their allies in Congress, and the mass media (Konner, 1993:50ff; Wohl, 1984). Among its most influential institutions are:

For-Profit Hospital Chains: One reason for the astronomical increases in medical costs since 1965 is the emergence of for-profit hospitals in the 1970s. Some of these chains have experienced tremendous growth.

- The Hospital Corporation of America (HCA) increased the number of hospitals it owned from twenty-three in 1970 to 7300 in 1981.

- The Humana Corporation grew from a $4.8 million Kentucky nursing home company in 1970 to a national chain of hospitals worth $1.4 billion in 1980 (Konner, 1993:48).

- Corporations supplying goods and services to the health care industry (Eli Lilly, Johnson & Johnson, Upjohn, DuPont, Dow Chemical, IBM, American Hospital Supply, Hewlett-Packard) all provide either medical supplies or computer and other services used by health care facilities.

Private hospitals are an important part of America's medical–industrial complex. Such hospital chains typically charge more for their services than public hospitals. The result is an increase in medical care costs for all (due to rising health insurance rates).

The American Medical Association and Physicians

In Florida alone, 40 percent of doctors have a financial interest in medical labs, and physician-owned labs do more tests and charge more for them. Costs at labs not owned by doctors are 46 percent lower than at physician-owned labs, and the quality of procedure is lower at such labs. Indeed, diagnostic procedures at doctor-owned labs are done four to four and one-half times more often. It is estimated that such labs waste $500 million in Florida alone. Many states have recently outlawed the practice of doctors referring patients to labs in which they have a financial stake (Keyser, 1993:47).

In 1941, the average physician's income was three times that of the average wage earner in America. By 1990, physicians as a group earned an average of $164,300, six times the income of the average American. The average Canadian doctor earns only $97,000. In general, nonprimary care physicians (specialists) earn 50 to 100 percent more than primary care doctors (general practitioners).

Medical Insurance Companies

Private medical insurance is a $150 billion-a-year industry in America. Some seven hundred insurance firms possess over $116 billion in assets. The top ten firms provide about 17 percent of the commercial health insurance policies and include firms with assets ranging from $30 billion (Travelers) to $94 billion (Metropolitan Life) (Bodenheimer, 1992a:51–52).

Private insurance firms make only a tiny percentage of their net profits from medical insurance, but this statistic is somewhat misleading. An amazing 33.5 cents of every dollar of private insurance goes to pay the salaries of administrators, marketing personnel, and related expenses. The top-heavy insurance firms spend fourteen times as much as Medicaid and eleven times as much as Canada just to administer policies (Brandon et al., 1992:73).

The Pharmaceutical Industry

The prescription drug industry has one of the highest profit margins of any American industry (see below), and it has a powerful lobby in Washington, DC. The pharmaceutical associations spend $32 million per year just to lobby Congress, and the industry has been handsomely rewarded for its efforts. In 1990, Congress passed a law giving tax breaks to any drug company that opened a manufacturing plant in Puerto Rico. Today drugs manufactured in Puerto Rico are four times more profitable than those made stateside. From 1993 to 1997, this tax deduction will cost the federal treasury $15 billion as more drug firms establish plants in Puerto Rico (Drake & Uhlman, 1993:47). Several pharmaceutical firms, like Squibb, Merck, Lilly, and others, are found among the largest five hundred American corporations, and they are major forces in both health care and drug development policies. The political activity of the insurance, pharmaceutical, and medical care institutions is an important aspect of the medical-industrial complex.

Members of Congress
Serving on Committees
Overseeing Health Care Policy

The medical-industrial complex remains profitable by being a powerful political force in Washington, DC, and in state capitals throughout the nation. As of 1990, there were 783 medical trade membership and health care–related political action committees (PACs) at all levels of American government (Brightbill, 1992:123–126).

In 1992, health care and insurance industry interests donated $41.4 million to Senate and House campaigns, a 31 percent increase over their 1990 contributions, and largely to conservative Democrats and Republicans (*U.S. News & World Report*, 1993:29).

Politicians who sit on congressional committees responsible for health care policy have become very adept at securing such funds. In 1992, two U.S. Democratic senators held a seminar for two hundred Washington lobbyists. The senators charged the lobbyists $5000 apiece to attend, raising $1 million for their reelection campaigns in a single day. The event is symbolic of the relationship between the health care industry and the members of Congress on committees that make health care policy. Since 1979, the health insurance industry has given $153 million to congressional campaigns, $34 million in 1992 alone (a 20 percent increase over 1990).

In 1992, Senator David Prior, an Arkansas Democrat, sponsored a bill that would link a huge tax break for establishing factories in Puerto Rico with stable prices for prescription drugs. Nine of the top ten recipients of drug PAC money from 1981 to 1991 voted for tabling (thus killing) this unfavorable legislation (Drake & Uhlman, 1993:41). Health care PACs thus do receive a good deal for their millions in campaign contributions. The relationship between health care lobbies and Congress members involved in health care legislation is a chief reason why the United States is the only industrial democracy that lacks some form of national health insurance (White House Domestic Policy Council, 1993:3–8).

Malpractice Lawyers

Medical malpractice lawyers have had an enormous effect on the cost and quality of medical care in recent years. Malpractice claims are filed for only one in every eight cases of negligence, and negligence occurs in less than one of every 1000 cases. The vast majority of malpractice claims are without merit, and result in small settlements. However, those few suits that result in settlements are enormous, amounting to 2.5 percent of the United States' gross national product (five times the Canadian level for malpractice suits). Only 43 percent of the monies awarded in such suits go to plaintiffs. Fifty-seven percent of such awards go for lawyers' fees, court costs, and related expenses (Keyser, 1993:54). Lawsuits against doctors and hospitals increased 300 percent between 1970 and 1993. By 1991, malpractice insurance premiums cost physicians and hospitals $30 billion per year. Fear of malpractice suits also drives up the cost of medical care. Billions of dollars worth of unnecessary tests and other procedures are performed in order to avert malpractice suits. These events, and all additional health care concerns, are relayed to the public by the mainstream news media, another important member of the medical-industrial complex.

The Establishment Press and Health Care News

The press is not just an objective bystander in the nation's health care debate, but is an active force with ties to major health care corporations. Thus New York *Times'* board of directors, for example, includes four individuals who also have seats on the boards of some of the nation's largest medical insurance companies. One member also sits on the board of one of America's largest drug firms, Bristol, Meyers, Squibb. The press has consistently exaggerated the weaknesses of the national health insurance plans enjoyed by other modern democracies, especially those with single-payer systems in which the national government acts as a single insurance company that pays doctors and hospitals. Taken together, these institutions have generated the contradictions that plague the American health care system.

In the name of rugged individualism and free market efficiency, the American health care system has become the most expensive in the entire world. Yet, the more money spent on medical care, the fewer the number of people covered by medical insurance. Ironically,

Middle-class people may be deprived of health insurance in the future. Many companies are laying off full-time workers and replacing them with part-time employees in part to avoid providing benefits, like health insurance.

between 1980 and 1994, the proportion of gross domestic product spent on health care has increased from 9 to 14 percent. The amount spent on health care during these years increased from around $500 billion to $1 trillion, and spending on health care by corporations rose from 8.4 percent of after-tax profits in 1965 to 56.4 in 1989 (Judis, 1992:14).

The number of people lacking health insurance between 1980 and 1994 nearly doubled, from 19 million to 37 million. An additional 19 million who are medically underinsured lack the insurance necessary to pay for so-called catastrophic illnesses costing as much as $1 million or more, as well as other vital services. Among the 37 million Americans lacking health insurance in 1994 were 9.5 million children. Incredibly, 85.5 percent of these children come from families in which at least one adult is employed full-time. Moreover, at least 2.2 million people lose their health insurance coverage for some period of time each year. An additional 100,000 people per month are expected to lose their insurance coverage for good between 1995 and 2000 (unless reforms are made). Thus corporate greed (cutting health benefits saves billions) and a deteriorating economy have resulted in a dramatic increase in the number of American families without health insurance. More health care expenditures accompanied by many fewer people having access to affordable health care make up a major contradiction of this system. Additionally, the wealth and political power of medical-industrial institutions result in a health care system riddled with great harms, one of which involves substandard care for those lacking the means to purchase health care.

The Double Standard
of Health Care

The quality of care for the 56 million Americans lacking adequate insurance is often substandard. Consider the following individual examples:

- A medically uninsured janitor was admitted to a coronary care unit with rheumatic heart disease. His bill totaled $26,000. In order to pay his expenses he sold his car, which was used to commute to work. After selling the automobile, he lost his job, and was forced onto the welfare rolls.

- A thirty-five-year-old employed black man was admitted to a hospital emergency room with cough and fever. He had delayed seeking treatment due to lack of health insurance. He was diagnosed as suffering from acute leukemia, treatable with chemotherapy. Because of delay in treatment, the illness was too far advanced and the man died within several months.

- Two neurosurgeons at a private hospital refused to treat a young uninsured man who was lapsing into a coma after being severely beaten on his head. The man died shortly after being transferred to a public hospital (Bodenheimer, 1992b:1–92).

What is true for these individuals is also the case for the uninsured as a whole:

- A New York study concluded that the uninsured are twice as likely as privately insured patients to be victimized by substandard care in medical facilities.

Nationally, there are 300,000 injuries and deaths in the nation's hospitals annually (Konner, 1993:37)

- One study of 4750 women with breast cancer demonstrated that uninsured women were 66 percent more likely to die from the disease than insured women. Women with Medicaid insurance were 40 percent more likely to die from breast cancer than privately insured women (*Wall Street Journal*, 1992:B-1).

- Over 25 percent of pregnant women, mostly poor, have no maternity coverage, and get no prenatal or neonatal care for their babies. This is a major reason why poor people have much higher infant and maternal mortality rates, and higher rates of birth defects than middle- and upper-class people.

Just as the nonaffluent often receive substandard treatment, the rich and famous often receive preferential treatment. For instance, the national median waiting period for patients in need of a new liver is 142 days. Many Americans were accordingly surprised in 1995 when ailing baseball great Mickey Mantle received a life-saving new liver in only two days. Likewise, Pennsylvania Governor Bob Casey received a new liver and a new heart after only one day. (The median waiting time for a new heart in the United States is 208 days.) Other famous people, like singer David Crosby and actor Jim Nabors, have received their new livers in only about three weeks (*Time*, 1995:14).

Gigantic increases in health care costs and fewer and fewer Americans with medical insurance are merely the tip of a dirty iceberg. The medical-industrial complex has managed to institutionalize greed, while endangering the health of the nonaffluent. The United States ranks:

- twenty-first in infant mortality, last among industrialized nations;

- seventeenth in male life expectancy;

- sixteenth in female life expectancy;

- seventeenth in maternal mortality (mothers who die in childbirth); and

- last among industrialized nations in the percentage of people who are satisfied with their health care.

Moreover, each sector of the medical complex exhibits its own form of harm:

For-Profit Hospitals

A number of studies demonstrate that for-profit hospitals have:

- 20 to 47 percent higher admissions costs,
- 6 to 58 percent higher prices for surgical procedures than public hospitals, and
- 46 to 56 percent of vacant hospital bed spaces (Dallek, 1990:296).

In addition to higher costs, for-profit hospitals take fewer uninsured people than public hospitals. In one Florida study, the for-profit hospitals accounted for 32 percent of total occupancy, but treated only 4 percent of charity cases. Texas for-profit hospitals accounted for nearly 20 percent of hospital beds, but treated only 1 percent of charity cases. These figures are supported over and over in national statistics. Nationally, for-profit hospitals handle under 5 percent of the charity cases (uninsured patients), for which hospitals pay the bills. One harmful result of private hospital refusal to take charity cases is that public hospitals treat a much larger proportion of the uninsured and end up saddled with a disproportionate share of charity case costs.

These costs increase the indebtedness of state and local governments while acting as something of a subsidy to for-profit hospitals. The costs of the uninsured which for-profit hospitals might otherwise help bear are transferred to the taxpayers.

Additionally, uninsured patients are frequently placed in harm's way by the refusal of for-profit hospitals to treat them. Over 250,000 people in need of treatment are turned away from hospitals each year. In 87 percent of such cases, patients are rejected for lack of means. The results are scandalous:

Consider Mrs. Palmer, who was nine months pregnant, and suffering from excruciating abdominal pain. She went to the hospital nearest her home. The for-profit hospital refused to admit her and turned her away. The woman and her baby died before receiving medical care.

Finally, in a 1990 study of 277 public hospitals, it was found that 37 percent of patients are kept in emergency rooms overnight due to lack of hospital bed space. Moreover, 40 percent of these hospitals had to turn away ambulances due to overcrowding (*Consumer Reports*, 1993).

While many for-profit hospitals exhibit greed, so do some doctors.

Greedy Physicians

The vast majority of physicians are ethical and honorable professionals, who work very hard and perform a vital service. However, a minority of members of this profession cause a great deal of physical and financial harm.

For example, there is an estimated $80 billion in medical fraud committed every year, primarily by doctors and medical laboratories. Fraud consumes twelve cents of every health care dollar. A medical lab can charge $10,000 for a single visit, depending on how many tests are prescribed. In 1991, one Bronx laboratory submitted $3.7 million in false claims to Medicare (Crenshaw, 1992:232–234).

The trend toward specialization has increased health care costs in a number of ways. First, the number of specialists has dramatically increased since 1965. Between 1965 and 1980 the number of medical school graduates doubled in the United States. During these years the number of surgeons increased seven times more rapidly than the population of the nation. By 1993, two-thirds of the nation's doctors were specialists, and by 2000, 75 percent of physicians will be specialists (Keyser, 1993:18, 32).

Specialists not only charge more for their services and perform more tests, they also do more surgery, much of which is thought unnecessary by critics. Two million of the 25 million surgical procedures performed each year may be unnecessary (Keyser, 1993: 19–22). Of the nearly $1 trillion spent on health care in the United States in 1993, at least $200 billion is wasted on these useless, sometimes harmful, treatments. They include:

- 50 percent of cesarean sections (a childbirth procedure)
- 27 percent of hysterectomies
- 14 percent of laminectomies (back surgery)

- 32 percent of atherscopic plaque removals in arteries
- 14 percent of expensive (about $14,000) coronary bypass surgeries
- 20 percent of pacemaker installations (which regulate heartbeats)
- 27 percent of carpal tunnel operations (nerves in wrists)
- 60 percent of all preoperation lab tests
- 30 percent of gastrointestinal X-rays
- 40 percent of angiograms.

These trends have also spread moral harm among the public. Seventy percent of the public believes that doctors are overpaid (Woodhandler & Hemmelstein, 1993:21), but this will not stop doctors from specializing. As one Ohio physician stated, "Why bother with 60- to 70-hour work weeks, constant phone calls, . . . demanding patients, the need for instant, exact decisions when you can specialize in one organ, get paid $500 for a 15-minute procedure, and need only to know a dozen drugs and side effects, and work part-time?" (*Consumer Reports*, 1993:34).

Moreover, the greed of hospitals and physicians is also shared by insurance companies.

Medical Insurance Companies

Consumer Reports believes that $70 billion per year is wasted on administrative inefficiency by hospitals and insurance companies. Indeed, between 1970 and 1991, the number of medical administrative personnel in the United States increased 697 percent, whereas all other health care personnel increased only 129 percent. Just streamlining the administrative procedures of private insurance companies would save an estimated $13 billion per year (Woodhandler & Hemmelstein, 1993:20).

The private medical insurance firms are an important cause of inadequate health care in America. The nation's private insurers have blacklisted about forty different high-risk occupations. These jobs carry with them high risk of accidents, AIDS, or alcoholism, and people in these posts have been declared medically uninsurable (Bodenheimer, 1992b:94). One study concluded that a national health care plan would save 47,000 to 100,000 such lives in America each year, a 17 percent drop in the national death rate. Add to that, such a plan would cost $10 billion less than our current health care system (Woodhandler & Hemmelstein, 1993:18).

Another important institution in the medical-industrial complex responsible for high health care costs is the pharmaceutical industry.

The American Way of (Prescription) Drugging

The drug industry is the most profitable industry in the United States. Between 1983 and 1993, prescription prices increased 147 percent, while the overall cost of living increased only 50 percent. Americans paid 54 percent more for prescriptions for the same drugs sold in Europe in 1989, 32 percent more than Canadians. The United States is one of the few nations in the world that does not control drug prices, and this causes real-life tragedies for many people:

Consider Mary Nathan, who suffers from a rare condition called Gaucher's disease, which is potentially fatal. The drugs she takes for it cost $270,000 per year. She worries about what will happen when she reaches the maximum amount her insurance will pay. Her experiences with drug costs are representative of the problems that stem from this $77 billion-per-year industry.

When drug prices in the United States increased 81 percent between 1980 and 1985, the Drug Manufacturers Association told Congress that the increases were merely temporary, but during the following six years (1986–1992) drug prices increased another 66 percent. In 1993, the average prescription drug costs $22.50 (versus $6.62 in 1980). In the 1990s, prescription prices have increased almost 9 percent per year, far exceeding inflation in other costs (Drake & Uhlman, 1993:3,8,21–22).

Why are Americans charged so much for prescriptions? The drug companies claim it costs $231 million on average to bring a new drug to market, and they are merely recuperating their investment costs. Yet, consider the case of Premarin, made from a hormone found in horse's urine. The drug has been used for over fifty years, and all research and development costs on the drug were recovered long ago. Since 1985, however, the cost of the drug has increased 75 percent (from 20 cents to 35 cents for a daily dose). The real reason for this great price increase is profit margins.

Moreover, the drug industry peddles its wares with 45,000 representatives at a cost of $36 billion. Another $500 million is spent on ads in medical journals. A 1992 study by the Department of Health and Human Services rated the information in such ads. The conclusion: 60 percent of these ads were rated poor or unreliable concerning the information they contained, and three-fourths were described as aimed squarely at physicians, most of whom are acquainted with only a fraction of the 2500 prescription drugs on the market. There is strong evidence that these ads influence doctors' decisions about prescribing drugs, and much of the information in the ads is misleading.

A 1992 study, wherein 150 health professionals examined 109 full-page ads for drugs in medical journals, found that more than 90 percent of the ads violated the Food and Drug Administration's standards in some way (Konner, 1993:54). Moreover, such misleading and manipulative efforts are not limited to medical journal ads.

For example, in 1988, sixteen drug companies sponsored some 34,000 symposia for doctors at a cost of $89.5 million. These events are held in expensive locations, and are little more than long commercials designed to get doctors to prescribe various drugs. The meetings often present misleading claims about various drugs, and are not subject to oversight by the Food and Drug Administration due to their private nature (Konner, 1993: 54–55).

There is no question that such efforts at persuasion pay off. The American pharmaceutical industry made $10 billion in profits on $76 billion in sales in 1992, a 13 percent profit margin. This is the highest profit margin of any legal industry in the country. And for all their carping about the costs of developing new drugs, the drug industry never mentions the rewards its pays its top executives. In 1991, the chief executive officer (CEO) of Eli Lilly made $10.1 million ($2.2 million in salary and $7.89 million in stock options). He was the twelfth-highest-paid CEO in America. Number thirteen was the CEO of another drug firm (Merck). The top executives of large drug firms earn from $1.9 million to $13 million per year, and the nation is the poorer and less healthy for the actions of this industry.

Moreover, sometimes the prescription drug industry causes serious physical harms as well. Dr. Sidney Wolfe of the Public Interest Research Group claims that 104 of the 287 most frequently prescribed drugs are too dangerous to use. Their side effects can cause death in some cases. This is especially true with regard to elderly citizens, over 70,000 of whom die each year from dangerous prescription drugs. Along with private hospitals, greedy doctors and insurers, and the drug industry, malpractice lawsuits are a major source of financial harm.

Serious as these problems are, the practices of the medical-industrial complex are not the only reasons for the ill health of the American people. There are additional sociological factors that also contribute to these harms, a major one of which is alienation.

Ill Health, American Culture, and Alienation

Perhaps the greatest tragedy concerning the health of Americans is that many of the health problems afflicting them are preventable. In 1993, Dr. J. Michael McGinnis, head of the Office of Disease Prevention of the Department of Health and Human Services, and his colleagues conducted a first-of-its-kind study on the causes of death in America. Their conclusions, published in the *Journal of the American Medical Association, (JAMA)*, were startling. The researchers found that half of the 2.148 million deaths in 1990 "could have been prevented" by simple behavioral changes (Los Angeles *Times*, 1993:A-6). Tobacco use was singled out as the leading cause of the nation's two leading killers, heart disease and cancer.

The researchers found that smoking was responsible for 400,000 deaths in 1990, (426,000 in 1993), more deaths than were caused by drug addiction, auto accidents, firearms, and sexually transmitted diseases combined. Most important, even national health insurance will do little to stem America's growing medical costs (now estimated at $14,000 for a family of four). Real reductions in medical bills will come only when people begin living according to healthy lifestyles—and dealing with cigarette addiction is a must.

Smoking is related not only to heart attack, stroke, and other coronary diseases. It is the leading cause of the leading cancer. Over 90 percent of all lung cancer cases are caused by cigarettes. Lung cancer often spreads and causes brain cancer and other cancers as well. Think of it: There would probably be no pulmonary (lung) disease units in American hospitals were it not for smoking.

The ills associated with smoking do not end here. Smoking is a leading cause of emphysema, a deadly lung disease, and it causes shortness of breath in children living with smokers. Cigarettes are also a cause of birth defects (low birth weight babies), as well as osteoporosis, a disease that causes bones to become brittle from calcium loss. Osteoporosis kills 25,000 women per year over age forty-five. Smoking is America's quiet holocaust, causing perhaps 16 million deaths in the last four decades (the period during which tobacco firms knew of smoking's hazards, but refused to make them public). This may be the most detrimental cover-up in American history.

Much of the focus of health and illness research in sociology has been on the poor health and health care of lower-class individuals and other minorities. While there are very serious harms that surround these issues, America's attitudes about health cut across all social groups. Moreover, the lower classes and minorities are not the only groups who suffer health problems that are caused by sociological factors.

Consider Victor Fuchs' (1994) interesting study of two states, Utah and Nevada. Utah, a state with a largely Mormon population, has the lowest rate of alcohol and cigarette consumption in the nation. Nevada, on the other hand, has the fourth-highest per capita rate of cigarette consumption and the highest rate of per person alcohol consumption in America. Residents of Nevada are two to six times more likely to die from lung cancer and cirrhosis of the liver than residents of Utah (Fuchs, 1994). There is no population in Nevada whose religious or other beliefs inhibit them from engaging in unhealthy habits.

Dr. John Knowles (1994) has argued that 99 percent of the illnesses and conditions that cause death in the United States are the result of individuals not acting responsibly to protect their own health. If people would cease smoking, and drinking, wear seat belts, exercise, and eat properly, the death rate in America from heart disease, cancer, and auto accidents would decline substantially. However, individuals, no matter how responsible, can

---

Private Troubles	Public Issues

Nutrition, Habits, and Your Health

One of the most important aspects of good health and long life concerns your habits concerning diet and exercise. Many diseases are associated with poor nutrition and poor eating habits, as is a lack of energy, stamina, and strength.

Nutrition is a fascinating topic, and, until recently, one sorely neglected by the American medical system. There are some nutrition essentials that most people fail to appreciate:

- Water is one of the most important nutrients. Just going thirsty for awhile can decrease your energy level by about 30 percent. It is advised by health experts that people drink six to eight eight-ounce glasses of water per day. Water is also critical for flushing toxins out of your system.

- Vitamins and minerals are important in good health, but there is a tremendous amount of misinformation concerning what amounts of these substances humans require. Vitamins are really enzymes, chemicals required for digesting food properly. Vitamins also serve other important functions in preventing diseases and promoting healing when you are ill. There are two kinds of vitamins.

1. *Fat-soluble vitamins* are stored in the body's fatty tissue. These include vitamins A, D, E, and K. Because these substances are stored by your body, you should not exceed the recommended daily doses for A, D, and E. (Vitamin K is found in so many foods that it is not usually placed in vitamin and mineral supplements.) Exceeding the recommended doses of fat-soluble vitamins can cause the same symptoms as deficiencies do. This may even include death in rare instances. Vitamins A and D are placed in milk by law, and vitamin E is readily available in multivitamin supplements and capsules.

not bear this burden alone. The tobacco companies withheld information concerning the dangers of smoking for forty years. Meanwhile Americans were encouraged in ads and movies to smoke for a variety of reasons. The American Tobacco Institute has yet to admit that smoking is in any way dangerous to smokers and vehemently denies that secondhand smoke is a health hazard to nonsmokers (ABC Television, 1994).

There is good evidence to support part of Dr. Knowles' contention. In one study, 7000 people followed a few simple rules for fifty-five years. These rules included: eating three meals a day, not smoking, getting moderate exercise two to three times per week, getting adequate sleep (seven–eight hours per night), maintaining normal weight, consuming little or no alcohol, and eating breakfast every day.

The results of the study were profound. Men forty-five years of age who followed three or less of these rules lived 21.5 years longer (to age sixty-seven). Those following four or five rules lived twenty-eight additional years (to age seventy-three). Finally, those following six or seven of the rules lived an additional thirty-three years (to age seventy-eight).

2. *Water-soluble vitamins* are substances not capable of being stored by the body. Your body gets rid of these through your urine. Consequently, these vitamins must be replaced on a daily basis. Many people take these substances in mega (very large) doses, and doing so makes sense for people who must cope with the stresses of modern life. Many substances hasten the exit of water-soluble vitamins from your body, especially caffeine and alcohol. Water-soluble vitamins include all B-complex substances (especially B_1 through B_{12}). These enzymes are essential for energy because they are involved in carbohydrate digestion. Vitamin C is the other water-soluble enzyme. This acid is important in making collagen, the substance from which body cells are made. Vitamin C is also critical in preventing infections and, along with vitamin E, is part of a group of chemicals called antioxidants.

3. *Antioxidants* are various molecules including vitamins E, C, and beta carotene (a preform of vitamin A). Antioxidants are thought to prevent the formation of so-called "free radical" molecules in the body. These free radicals are thought important in causing cancer and cholesterol buildup in arteries, a major cause of heart disease and stroke.

4. *Minerals* are chemicals that occur naturally, and are essential in making vital bodily substances, promoting healing, and preventing cancer and possibly heart disease. Minerals are not washed from the body daily, and, consequently, are essential in only small doses (often in micrograms rather than milligrams). Two mineral shortages that commonly affect women are iron and calcium. Lack of

Continued on next page

Private Troubles **Public Issues**

iron can cause anemia, a disease wherein the body can not make red blood cells that carry oxygen. Anemia causes pale skin, fatigue, and low resistance to disease. Calcium is critical in making bone tissue. Calcium, like other vitamins and minerals, is essential in extra amounts in women who are pregnant, over forty-five, or who smoke.

5. *Other nutrients* have also been found to enhance human health. One of these is garlic. Garlic, a wonderful flavor enhancer in many Mediterranean dishes, is a blood purifier. It also kills mold and fights viruses. Onions are also very healthful, and can even reduce blood cholesterol. These are strong substances, and most people prefer to eat them well cooked. Garlic is also available in odorless tablets. These are worth taking as a good amount of garlic is required to receive its health benefits (Worthington-Roberts, 1981:102–103).

Aside from vitamins and minerals, your body also requires a sufficient number of calories found in foods. A calorie is a unit of energy. There are 3500 calories in a pound, as most dieters know. Associated with each type of calorie are potential problems and unfortunate myths. There are three types of these energy-containing substances that make up all foods: carbohydrates, fats, and proteins.

1. *Carbohydrates* are simple and complex sugars that contain four calories per gram. These molecules are easily digested (in part by your body's saliva) and provide quick increases in energy level. This is why athletes engage in complex carbohydrate "loading" before sporting events and marathons. In advanced societies, many people get much of their carbohydrate intake from processed sugars, such as those found in candy and desserts. Excess consumption of processed sugars causes tooth decay, obesity, and is associated with adult onset diabetes. The best sources of carbohydrates are whole grains, fresh fruits, and vegetables (devoid of pesticide residues). These substances also contain fiber (cellulose), a nonnutritive material necessary for proper digestion, as well as prevention of cancer and other intestinal problems.

2. *Fats* are acidic substances that contain nine calories per gram (more than double the caloric content of proteins and carbohydrates). Fats are found in all foods, but in amounts that vary greatly. There are two types of fats, unsaturated and saturated. Unsaturated fats have spaces between their molecules. In saturated fats, the spaces between molecules are filled with hydrogen atoms. Saturated fats are used by the body to make "bad" cholesterol, a waxy substance that clogs arteries with layers of plaque. Excess fat intake is also associated with intestinal and other cancers.

In the United States, people get about 40 percent of their calories from fatty foods. Government studies recommend that no more than 20 percent of total calories come from fat. Fat also makes people fat because these foods are metabolized differently than carbohydrates and proteins. Fats are stored in cells by the body, whereas carbohydrates are burned as fuel immediately. Fats are essential for making hormones in the body, so it is not advisable to neglect these substances entirely. The best source of fat is found in so-called "cold pressed" oils. These fats are unsaturated and are liquid at room temperature. Monounsaturated fats, such as peanut oil and olive oil, and polyunsaturated fat, especially canola oil, are excellent sources of fats thought to produce "good" cholesterol.

3. *Proteins* are made of chemicals called amino acids. There are two types of protein, essential and nonessential. Nonessential proteins are produced in your body, thus you do not need these in your diet. Essential proteins cannot be made by your body, and, consequently, you need to eat foods containing these amino acids each day. Not getting enough protein in infancy can result in brain damage (called *kwashiorkor*, a syndrome prevalent in Third World nations). You also need protein for making muscle tissue, skin, and hair cells. However, most Americans eat too much protein, and they often obtain proteins from foods containing high amounts of saturated fats (especially beef and pork products). The average American needs only 40 grams of protein per day (Bender, 1985:3ff). The best sources of essential proteins ("best" meaning most usable by your body) are egg whites and milk, followed by fish, poultry, and animal meat.

There are some unfortunate myths about protein. Eating large amounts of it will not increase your sex drive, muscle size, or strength. Only exercise can do that. (There is some evidence that taking chromium picolinate, a mineral, will slightly increase muscle mass.) Your muscle tissue will decrease only if your body is starving (termed *marasmus*). People between ages eighteen and sixty need .8 of a gram of protein per kilogram (2.2 pounds) of body weight. Thus if you weigh 140 pounds, you need only about sixty-six grams of protein per day. This is the amount found in about two ounces of tuna fish. While protein is important in a healthy diet, it is not a magical or medicinal substance. Excess protein intake is associated with high cholesterol. Protein also requires large amounts of water to digest, and can cause dehydration. So drink plenty of fluid when ingesting protein. Finally, millions of Americans have allergies, and all allergic substances are protein based. The best way not to become allergic to foods is to rotate them, eat them only every four days.

Continued on next page

Private Troubles   Public Issues

Habits

Good nutrition is essential to good health, but nutrition is affected by your lifestyle. Some of the factors that influence nutrients include:

1. *Alcohol:* Drinking alcohol depletes your body of water, vitamin B_1, and other B vitamins. If you drink one beer or a glass of wine, you should drink two glasses of water to replace the lost fluid. You should also take extra vitamin B_1 (thiamine) if you drink.

2. *Smoking:* Cigarettes deplete your body of many nutrients, especially B vitamins. This is made worse by the fact that almost everyone who drinks heavily also smokes (but not everyone who smokes also drinks). Smoking is a death-causing addiction, one that will shorten your life and the lives of others around you. If you smoke, you are paying the ruling elite of this society for the opportunity of causing a painful, early death. That may sound extreme, but it is not incorrect. It is hard to quit smoking without help, especially for women. Ninety percent of people who smoke say they want to quit. It will take ten years for the effects of smoking to completely reverse themselves in your body. The sooner you quit, the sooner your health will improve. Otherwise, you stand a good chance of dying about a decade earlier than necessary, and probably from a horribly painful disease such as lung cancer.

3. *Regular exercise,* three times per week for just twenty minutes, can cause a dramatic improvement in your appearance and energy level, reduce emotional and physical stress, and increase your feeling of well-being. Regular exercise can also strengthen your heart and reduce "bad" cholesterol levels (when combined with proper nutrition). Exercise also burns calories and can increase your weight loss rate by 25 percent (if you are on a diet). Your body requires 1 percent fewer calories per year after age twenty-five. In other words, by age fifty your caloric requirements are only one-fourth of what they were at age twenty-five.

While it would be beneficial for Americans to pursue these regimens, our health problems are intimately associated with other social problems:

Food

The best-selling books in America are books about dieting and cooking. The mass media through advertising encourage people both to consume their favorite foods, and then lose

4. *Stress:* Modern life, especially life in a depressed and unstable economy, is stressful for many people. Holmes and Masuda (1967) developed a useful index of "life events" relative to the amount of stress inflicted upon individuals. The most stressful events are characterized by separation from others by death, divorce, or estrangement (such as incarceration in jail or prison). Important as well is the realization that not all stressful episodes are "negative" in quality. Getting married, starting school, seeing a child leave home following graduation, and even vacations are stressful. Many economic role changes, like losing your job, a spouse starting working, sudden increase or decrease in income, changing working conditions, or unsatisfying relations with a boss, increase stress levels. Holmes and Masuda found that if one experiences three hundred or more "life crisis units" within a two-year period, the chances of suffering a serious illness are eight in ten. In short, stress causes both physical and mental illness.

   If you feel under stress, and I am always amazed at the number of students who do, it is dangerous to keep it inside you. All of the following are useful in reducing stress levels:

- Regular exercise

- Meditation and biofeedback

- Taking walks in a beautiful setting

- Reading for pleasure, and listening to music.

   If none of these measures do you much good, you might benefit from some therapy, or even need a tranquilizing drug. Do not hesitate to use your school's health and counseling services. The problem here is that many colleges are experiencing a cut in these services. If these services are not available on your campus, call the nearest mental health association referral service. The good news about stress is that it is treatable, but it does need to be treated.

the pounds they gain by going on magical diets. Estimates are that over 64 million Americans are overweight, half of them obese, meaning they are more than 20 percent above their normal weight. The annual cost of obesity is enormous, $120 billion in health costs alone (New York *Times*, 1994:A-7). Obesity is associated with a host of illnesses including hypertension, diabetes, and heart disease. Ninety-five percent of people who lose weight on diets gain it back within a year. This means that billions of dollars are wasted on diets each year.

Gunshot Wounds and Homicide

There are currently 25,000 murders in the United States each year, and about one hundred reported assaults for every murder reported by hospital emergency rooms. These assaults result in some 45,000 spinal cord injuries, costing $800,000 over a lifetime if the injury is quadriplegic. Gunshot wounds have become a major public health problem in the United States with each wound costing over $40,000 to treat—about $200 billion per year, much of it at taxpayers' expense (Rich, 1992; Boroughs, 1994).

Drug-Exposed Babies

The United States has 375,000 drug-exposed babies. Each infant born addicted to a substance costs $63,000 to treat.

Environmental Hazards

Exposure to hazardous substances in air, water, and the food supply is a serious public health problem in America. Air pollution may be responsible for 30 percent of the nation's cancer cases. Environmental hazards are found in the 1500 potentially cancer-causing food additives that have never been tested, and in the carcinogenic substances to which 1.7 million workers are exposed each year, accounting for 23 to 38 percent of all yearly cancer deaths (Simon & Eitzen, 1993:131–141). There are ten pesticides used in food production that have been proven carcinogenic and leave residues in raw and processed food and in breast milk (Winter, 1991:1).

Children are at risk for lead poisoning from eating paint chips off floors. Lead affects 17 percent of preschool children in Illinois, for example, and children who live in old housing (built before 1978) are especially at risk. This is most true among lower-class minority children in America's inner cities (Millichap, 1993:18–24).

Alcoholism

Alcohol abuse is a major public health problem in the United States, killing over 120,000 Americans each year (as discussed in Chapter 3). There is evidence that the more heavily alcohol is advertised in a culture, the higher the per capita consumption. Liquor companies spend billions each year advertising their products on television (wine and beer) and in magazines.

There are currently an estimated 18.5 million alcoholics in the United States. The cost of a liver transplant alone is $250,000. Total costs to society from alcohol abuse, counting medical bills, lost workdays, and alcohol-related crimes, exceed $120 billion per year (Simon & Eitzen, 1993:290).

While these pathological factors in American culture greatly contribute to ill health, no disease is as controversial as acquired immunodeficiency syndrome (AIDS).

AIDS and
the Sociological Imagination

Acquired immunodeficiency syndrome (AIDS) is a modern-day plague. The virus that causes AIDS destroys the body's immune system, making victims prey to several

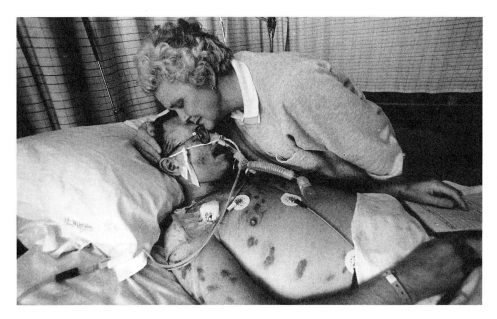

This patient has one of the many serious diseases associated with AIDS. In the United States, the at-risk population for AIDS typically includes homosexual males, drug addicts (who share needles), prostitutes (especially those who are drug addicted), and those people who receive transfusions with AIDS-tainted blood.

microorganisms that cause serious infections. This horrible disease is often characterized by weight loss, chronic fatigue, and neurological complications caused by damaged brain cells. There is frequently a high incidence of certain rare cancers, especially Kaposi's sarcoma and a form of pneumonia involving parasites, as well.

AIDS is commonly transmitted by intimate sexual contact, blood-contaminated needles used by drug addicts, from AIDS-infected mothers to their babies in the uterus (and perhaps through infected mother's milk), and, rarely, through transfusions of contaminated blood. The virus thought to cause AIDS, called HIV, is a retrovirus, one which may take up to ten years to develop symptoms. The virus appears to constantly change its genetic makeup and, thus, the human immune system cannot make antibodies necessary to fight it. It has also made developing a vaccine against the virus very difficult (Brown, 1994).

Sociologically, AIDS constitutes a major source of physical, financial, and, at times, moral harm. Since the first case of AIDS was diagnosed in New York in 1979, over 200,000 Americans have died from the disease.

Worldwide, however, North America accounts for only 10 percent of total AIDS cases, 70 percent of which are found in sub-Saharan Africa (a region south of North Africa's vast desert). There, some 9 million people are infected, including 1 million children (Farrington, 1994:10). Worldwide, more than 75 percent of reported AIDS cases take place through heterosexual contact, often from prostitutes who are drug users. In the United States, most AIDS cases involve white males, who contract the disease through homosexual contact, but that trend has begun to change.

Thus the U.S. Department of Health and Human Services reported over 328,000 American AIDS cases in 1993 (four times the rate in Canada). AIDS is the eighth-largest cause of death in America, currently claiming about 17,000 lives per year. The number of AIDS-related deaths has increased since 1985, from 6700 to over 285,000 (in 1993). Of the over 328,000 American AIDS cases, over 285,000 are males. Of the males with AIDS, nearly 181,500 of them contracted the disease through homosexual contact with other gays. Another nearly 56,000 cases of male AIDS were contracted through use of dirty needles, largely by heroin addicts.

The pattern of AIDS transmission in American women is almost the exact opposite of what it is in men. Of the nearly 39,000 females cases of AIDS in 1993, nearly 20,000 were attributed to use of contaminated needles, and another 7500 were caused by heterosexual contact. In addition, nearly 5000 AIDS cases among children twelve years of age or younger were reported in 1993. Over 60 percent of these children are African Americans (who comprise only 12 percent of the population), and 20 percent are Hispanic (who comprise only 3 percent of the population). Children contract AIDS largely from their infected mothers (National Center for Health Statistics, 1994).

Officials at the Centers for Disease Control (CDC) noted that 80,691 new AIDS cases were reported in 1994, down from 106,618 the previous year. This was the first decline in the number of AIDS cases since statistics were begun in 1985 (New York Times, 1995:A-1). A central reason for this decline is needle exchange programs for drug addicts. In New York City, a two-year evaluation of 2500 participants in clean needle programs showed an HIV infection rate of 2 percent a year, compared with 4 to 7 percent for high-frequency intravenous drug users not enrolled in needle exchange programs (Lee, 1994a:A-1). Likewise, according to a 1995 survey, nearly one-third of Americans have changed their sexual habits in an effort to avoid getting AIDS. Even those people who are at low risk for getting the disease have changed their behaviors by becoming monogamous and using condoms (Jet, 1995:10). This has especially been the case among gay men. According to the CDC, gay men accounted for fewer than half of the United States' new AIDS cases in 1993 (Newsweek, 1994:70).

However, the disease is spreading among women. A 1994 CDC report noted that 14,081 of the 79,674 persons aged thirteen and over reported with AIDS were women. This figure represents a nearly threefold rise in the proportion of women reported with AIDS in 1985. Heterosexual contact is the most rapidly increasing transmission category for women (Journal of the American Medical Association, 1995). In addition, AIDS now tops accidents as the leading killer of young American adults twenty-five to forty-four years old. AIDS took the lives of 28,090 young adults in 1993, exceeding deaths from accidents (25,960) for the first time (American Medical News, 1995:20).

Globally, by the year 2000 some 30 to 40 million people are expected to be infected with AIDS, 95 percent of these from Third World nations. This will result in staggering medical costs, as well as the loss of many productive young workers. Up to two-thirds of the entire medical budgets in certain Third World nations may soon go toward treating AIDS cases (McCarthy, 1995:1628). Additionally, these deaths will produce some 10 million orphaned children in sub-Saharan Africa alone (United Nations, 1994:150–151). In the United States estimates are that as many as 125,000 children will lose their mothers to AIDS by the year 2000. In 1992, there were 865,000 children under eighteen being reared by their grandparents; in 1993, that number jumped to over one million (Lee, 1994a: A-1).

AIDS is also an American public health crisis. Nearly 60 percent of AIDS patients have their medical bills paid for by the government because they lack medical insurance or are on Medicaid. Medical bills from AIDS total nearly $9 billion per year, plus millions more for research. The typical AIDS case costs well over $100,000 to treat (Bateson, M. & R. Goldsly, 1991:362). Medical institutions have major problems because of AIDS. Morale among medical workers suffers out of fear of contracting the disease, and from seeing young people die without being able to help them.

There is a great deal of ignorance about how AIDS is transmitted, and this naivete is likely to lead to further social problems.

- Fundamentalist clergy have maintained that AIDS is God's revenge against gays for their sinful sexual orientation, thus increasing the already severe prejudice against homosexuals in the United States.

- A plurality of American teens are afraid to go to doctors and dentists because of their belief that medical personnel have HIV.

- Many people with HIV are discriminated against in their pursuit of health care. Insurance companies have tried to set benefit limits on the amount of money they will spend on AIDS cases, limits that are different from the limits on other kinds of illnesses. In 1994, a federal appeals court ruled this a violation of the Americans with Disabilities Act of 1992 (Quint, 1994).

- A study of fifty nursing homes located in the five U.S. cities with the highest AIDS incidence found that 48.2 percent of the facilities had been approached about admitting a person with AIDS; only 15.4 percent had admitted AIDS patients (Gentry et al., 1994).

The main reason for all these problems is that the United States has long stuck its head in the sand concerning AIDS. According to the *Journal of the American Medical Association*, the United States is among the most backward of nations when it comes to AIDS prevention. Much of the foot dragging that has characterized the American response to AIDS stems from the disease's prevalence among homosexuals and drug addicts, nonelite and oppressed populations that lack power and media access. In the 1980s, for example, the Reagan administration refused to even fund money for AIDS research until Reagan's friend Rock Hudson died from the disease. President Reagan stated that he had never even heard of AIDS until Hudson's death in 1985. This collective denial of AIDS is a chief reason why there is no vaccine, and no effective treatment for those with AIDS.

Likewise, needle exchange programs for addicts, though effective, face the criticism of encouraging drug addiction, a charge for which there is no evidence. The media have been content merely to report AIDS-related news, rather than educate the public concerning the true facts about AIDS transmission and prevention (Rich, 1995:15).

In short, decisions about what a person does with his or her life are not just a matter of individual preferences. In Chapter 2, Max Weber's notion of life chances was discussed. One's chances of physical and mental well-being are dramatically affected by one's social class, gender, race, ethnicity, place of residence (urban versus rural), and age. Above all, social class, both within one's society and within the class structure of nations, has a major impact on health. While the rich in virtually all nations are physically and mentally healthier than the poor, it is not money alone that causes good health. Internationally, citizens in affluent nations live longer because of what is done with their money. Accordingly, though citizens of richer countries tend to live longer, it is not wealth per se that brings longevity, but rather the services wealth can buy. Rich or poor, the countries that have higher longevity rates are generally those that use the money they do have to provide sanitation, nutrition, immunizations, education, and other basic services. When countries spend more money on other expenses, such as building up their military operations, their national longevity rates reflect the void of social programs (Kane, 1993:32).

While it is true that money is correlated with good health and long life, being rich does not guarantee longevity. Sammy Davis, Jr., made $50 million during his lifetime, and died at age sixty-four from throat cancer (due to cigarette smoking). Mr. Davis, a greatly talented man, was, unfortunately, unable to control his spending impulses. He spent every penny of the $50 million he made, some of it on illegal drugs, experienced run-ins with the Internal Revenue Service, and left his widow heavily in debt.

Money can potentially contribute to longevity by affording the rich access to the best medical care, and by greatly reducing the mental stress associated with poverty. However, many rich people, like Mr. Davis, have been unable adequately to take advantage of such resources. Moreover, Mr. Davis was a very insecure man, with low self-esteem and a terribly fragile sense of self. What Sammy Davis, Jr.'s tragic early death also demonstrates is the strong relationship between mental and physical health.

The Mental Health–
Physical Health Link

There is an important relationship between mental and physical well-being. Strong evidence shows that mental stress is a major cause of both mental and physical illness. Stress affects a person's entire body, not just his or her mind. Mental stress is highly detrimental to both the cardiovascular and digestive system. Stress is highly correlated with hypertension, heart attacks, strokes, angina, arrhythmia, migraine headaches, allergies, ulcers, arthritis, backaches, elevated blood cholesterol levels, and infections (French & Caplan, 1970: 383–397; Roberts, 1978).

There are two types of stress that act on the entire human body. One is called subjective stress overload. Subjective overload is found within the personality of the individual, is characterized by chronic worry, and can result in mental breakdown from reaching one's breaking point. Objective stress overload stems from stressful stimuli in one's environment, such as war, earthquake, economic dislocation (job loss), or the death of a close friend or relative (McQuaile & Kerman, 1974).

There are certain groups in American life that suffer more objective kinds of stress than others, and, therefore, are prone to more mental and physical illness. The most stress-prone groups are found within the more vulnerable classes socioeconomically, whether as to gender, marital status, or race, sexual orientation, and ethnicity.

Consider mental illness. The American Psychiatric Association (1987) (APA) currently classifies the following as mental illnesses:

1. Disorders usually first evident in infancy, childhood, or adolescence such as stuttering, anorexia nervosa, and mental retardation.

2. Organic mental illness including genetic brain diseases like Huntington's chorea, Alzheimer's disease, and brain damage.

3. Substance use disorders of alcohol and/or other substances.

4. Schizophrenic disorders that include withdrawal from daily social interaction and hallucinations.

5. Paranoid disorders involving constant delusions of being persecuted by outside forces and delusions of grandeur (like imagining one is Jesus Christ).

6. Mood disorders including depression and bipolar conditions wherein one's mood radically swings between maniacal highs and deep depressive lows.

7. Anxiety disorders like phobic reactions, panic attacks, extreme anxiousness and worry, and stress stemming from traumatic experiences.

8. Somatoform disorders, psychologically caused physical symptoms like hypochondria (imaginary illnesses).

9. Dissociative disorders, wherein one's personality is separated from the self. These include episodes of amnesia (memory loss) or multiple personality.

10. Sexual disorder, including transsexualism, sexual inhibition (frigidity in women, premature ejaculation in men), and exhibitionism (flashing in public).

11. Sleep disorders, especially insomnia.

12. Impulse control disorders, the inability to control undesirable impulses (like compulsive gambling, stealing, sexual gratification, and eating).

13. Adjustment reactions, wherein one suffers temporary stressful changes in reaction to divorce, unemployment, or other trauma (such as criminal victimization, or loss due to natural disaster).

These current labels are, of course, subject to revision. The definition of mental disorder is inherently social in nature and subject to changes in values, medical discoveries, and other historical events. Certain behaviors that were formerly classified as mental illnesses, such as being homosexual, are no longer classified as such by the APA.

Mental illness is extremely widespread in America. Until 1994, it was consistently estimated that 25 to 30 percent of the population would develop symptoms of mental illness serious enough to require treatment sometime during their lives. More recent estimates now put this figure closer to 50 percent. This makes mental illness the most common disease in America.

The most prevalent mental illness among American adults is depression, the so-called common cold of mental illness. Incidents of depression are not equally divided among all groups. Women are more than twice as likely to suffer depression than are men. Why? In 1990, the American Psychological Association sponsored the first-ever study that linked depression to cultural causes (Mann, 1993:246–247). The study concluded that women suffer twice the rate of depression as do men because women suffer systematic patterns of victimization in American life. Cultural causes of women's depression include:

- economic insecurity due to unemployment and underemployment in the workplace,
- physical abuse at home from violent husbands and significant others,
- being routinely raped on college campuses and on urban streets, and
- bearing the burdens of child care.

Concerning economic insecurity, 8.5 million women live in poverty in the United States, that is, 15 percent of the adult female population. As is evident, women's depression is intimately linked to social class. Concerning abuse and rape, at least 37 percent of the female population is either sexually and/or physically abused before age twenty-one. The real figure may be as high as 50 percent (Mann, 1993:247). This means that a disturbingly high percentage of women suffer with posttraumatic stress disorder as a legacy of such abuse.

Concerning child care, the American Psychological Association study discovered that employed women who find adequate child care and whose husbands share child care responsibilities had significantly lower rates of depression than working women who had all the child care responsibilities. This study also found a high suicide rate among professional women who were employed in male-dominated occupations (such as engineering, law, and accounting).

There are also ethnic factors in women's depression.

The study also found that causes of women's depression are routinely misdiagnosed 30 to 50 percent of the time by psychiatrists, and antidepressant drugs are misprescribed in 70 percent of cases. Prescribing such drugs for conditions with cultural causes is another instance of what has been termed "the Medicalization of deviance," wherein social problems are redefined as medical problems (Conrad & Schneider, 1980). In this way medicalization becomes a way to socially control victimized groups who might otherwise do something to bring about meaningful social change in a society that oppresses them.

Given the victimization patterns among women, it should come as no surprise that women are twice as likely to suffer from anxiety disorders as men. Women are made anxious and fearful by all of the environmental stressors discussed above, plus the realization that there is more pressure on women to be physically attractive. This is why anorexia is almost exclusively a female disease in America. Anorexia nervosa is an eating disorder characterized by weight loss that dips 25 percent or more below normal body weight. Anorexia is a serious disease that can result in heart failure and death, as it did in the case of singer Karen Carpenter in 1983. Between 5 and 15 percent of U.S. women may be anorexic at some time in their lives (Brumberg, 1994:110).

Again, it is not just gender, but social class and age that play a role in this disease. Ninety to 95 percent of anorexics are upper-middle- and upper-class young women, largely of traditional college age (eighteen to twenty-two). Up to 20 percent of the women on large college campuses may be anorexic. Anorexia is a disease typically caused by the link between a women's self-esteem and her body weight. Anorexics typically perceive themselves as overweight and unlovable, and believe that a thinner body will result in male attention. This is an extreme reaction to a culture that treats women's bodies as objects of desire. The link between anorexia and alienation from one's body is sad and apparent.

Finally, there is a double standard concerning mental illness among women. In one study, male and female psychologists were asked to describe the character traits of men and women. These traits were classified into three different groups: competent males, competent

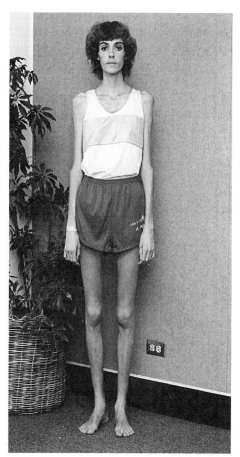 

Anorexia is an eating disorder that primarily affects young, upper-middle-class women. With so much emphasis placed on appearance in postmodern societies—especially on the appearances of women's bodies—many young women always see themselves as overweight, even when they are not. Sometimes the effects of anorexia can result in serious illness and even death. These photos represent a young woman before and after treatment for anorexia nervosa.

females, and competent adults. Competent females were viewed as more passive, gullible, less competitive, more anxious, emotional, less objective, and less able to handle stress than males. Competent males were described in exactly the opposite terms (more competitive, objective, and so on). When it came to describing the traits of a normal adult, more male traits were described as ideal, while female traits were deemed less positive. Accordingly, even when female traits are stated in their most positive light—like loyal, affectionate, understanding, and compassionate—such traits are still deemed less desirable.

All of this means that women are in a double bind (contradiction) when it comes to societal approval. If they are "normal," such normality is viewed as less desirable than male characteristics. If women take on the male role by acting more competitively, they are viewed as deviant (pushy, aggressive, bitchy, and the like) (Broverman et al., 1970; Cockerham, 1992).

This situation puts both men and women at a disadvantage in American society. It means that women's bizarre behavior is more tolerated by society because males are supposed to be more competent, and they are under more pressure to achieve. As a result, mentally retarded males are more often hospitalized than mentally retarded females (Tudor et al., 1979).

Does all this mean that women are more mentally and physically ill than men? Absolutely not. Women and men tend to suffer about the same rates of mental illness, but they do suffer from different forms of mental disturbance. Freudian psychology teaches that depression is caused by anger that is kept inside (repressed). One reason Lorena Bobbitt drew so much attention for cutting off her husband's penis in 1993 is that she is an exceptional woman. She released her rage at being sexually and physically abused, and acted it out.

Men are much more likely than women to release their stress rather than keep it inside (Cockerham, 1992). Thus the most common mental disorders among men are

- alcohol and drug abuse, and
- personality disorders that involve lying, stealing, and cheating. All of these disorders have the fact that they are behaviors that are acted out, not just symptoms characterized by uncomfortable feelings, in common (Riche, 1987). Thus more male mental illness is associated with criminal and deviant behavior than is female mental disorder.

There are other important sociological variables associated with stress and mental illness:

- Mental health is better among married persons. Over half of mental hospital admissions in 1980 were of persons who had never married. Never marrieds often lack the competence and social skill to form stable relationships. Persons who are separated or divorced have the second-highest rate of mental hospital admission.
- Married women suffer more mental illness than married men, and this is especially the case for lower-class married women. Indeed, being married offers some protection for male mental health, but not for the mental health of wives.
- Depression is more common in rural areas. Rural people may be less flexible in attitude, more isolated, fatalistic in outlook, and authoritarian (rigid) in relating to other people. Schizophrenia is more common in urban areas (especially among members of the lower class). Slum dwellers are often more mercenary, distrustful, selfish, and cynical than middle-class urban residents, and are subject to greater objective stress and, because of their distrust of others, more likely to withdraw inward (become schizophrenic) in reaction to stress.

An interesting exception to this finding concerns the mental health of Hispanic Americans. One of the poorest ethnic groups is the Mexican-American population. They have about the same mental illness rates as the white population, and Mexican-American housewives do not suffer the same distress that non-Mexican housewives endure. The low stress level among this Hispanic group is thought due to their strong personal attachment to family members, and strong sense of community ties (Cockerham, 1992:188–198).

Gender, Class, and Health

Regarding gender and physical health, there is evidence that males are born with some disadvantage. Male death rates exceed female rates at all ages. More male babies die at both prenatal (before birth) and neonatal (infancy) stages. This constitutes good preliminary evidence that men are the weaker sex when it comes to the ability to survive (Conrad & Kern, 1994).

However, most male deaths in adulthood are heavily influenced by sociological factors. Death rates among males exceed those of females for every leading cause of death: heart disease, stroke, cancer, accidents, and infections. Heart disease is the number one killer of women after age sixty-six, but it is the number one killer for men after age thirty-nine. However, heart attacks in men under age fifty are rare, *unless cigarette smoking is involved.*

Men in American culture are more alienated from their bodies than women, and suffer a great deal more illness because of this alienation. The most important manifestation of this bodily neglect is that men go to doctors much less than women do, and it is this lack of medical attention, not genetic differences, that is primarily responsible for women living longer than men. Men go to doctors less often because of cultural values that encourage men to "bite the bullet"; (be tough, endure pain, and not express emotions). Women suffer more acute and chronic diseases, but go to physicians more often for digestive problems, infections, hypertension, diabetes, and arthritis (Cockerham, 1992).

For many males going to doctors is a sign of weakness. In consequence, there are twice as many women in America as men over age seventy-five, but this does not hold true cross-culturally. A study in India, for example, between 1970 and 1972, found that Indian men lived three years longer than Indian women on average (Waldron, 1994:43).

Men also engage in more risk-taking behavior than women. Men are primarily the ones who drive taxis (the occupation with the highest homicide rate), fight wars, engage in drunk driving, and work jobs with environmental hazards (e.g., mining, factory work, law enforcement, and fire fighting). Males also have higher suicide rates than women, primarily because male access to guns is so much higher than it is for women (Waldron, 1994:43).

However, male and female health is intimately related to social class. As Syme and Berkman (1994:29) note, white males with low levels of education have mortality rates 64 percent higher than white males with higher educational experience (college). Moreover, white women with low educational levels have mortality rates 105 percent higher than white females with higher educational backgrounds. These differences regarding social class and health are found the world over, and have not changed since they were first observed in 1900.

Race, Class, and Health

On the surface, there appears to be a clear relationship between being African American and being at risk for serious forms of mental and physical diseases. Mortality rates from twelve preventable diseases among blacks are 4.5 times higher than among whites. African Americans suffer:

- 6.5 times more high blood pressure,

- 2.8 times more rheumatic heart disease,

- 3.8 times more bronchitis and pneumonia,

- 1.3 times more influenza,

- 4.4 times more asthma,

- 3.2 times more appendicitis, and

- 2.6 times more cervical cancer and 40 percent more prostate cancer than whites (Colburn, 1993:224; Washington, 1994:32).

Sadly, although blacks comprise 12 percent of the American population, they suffer 31 percent of all AIDS cases, largely due to drug addiction and passing the AIDS virus through dirty hypodermic needles. Black males live 7.4 fewer years than white males, and black females live 5.5 fewer years than white females (Washington, 1994:32).

Moreover, only 3 percent of American doctors are black, and they earn significantly less money and have higher medical school debt than white physicians.

Likewise, Hispanic Americans, primarily Mexican Americans, suffer

- four times more tuberculosis,

- three times more diabetes,

- two to four times more cancer, and

- two times more high blood pressure than white Americans (Blendon, 1989).

Hispanic children also have higher rates of lead poisoning (from poor environments) and measles. Finally, Native Americans suffer from a 20 percent greater suicide rate than whites.

Indeed, the higher stress levels among black and Hispanic Americans mean that they suffer much more hypertension. More high blood pressure means much more heart attack, stroke, and kidney disease.

However, most of these differences are due to class and not to race. In fact, middle-class blacks and Hispanics enjoy the same good health as white middle-class people do. However, black Americans account for 12 percent of the population, and nearly 22 percent of the medically uninsured (Washington, 1994:34).

African Americans are also plagued by a host of additional problems. Consider violent crime. African Americans account for half of all homicide victims in the United States. Ninety-four percent of all homicides committed by blacks victimize other blacks (ABC News, 1994). Deaths from violent crime and illegal drugs doubled in the United States between 1982 and 1992, and young black males have suffered the bulk of this increase (Males, 1993:18).

Consider poor black neighborhoods like New York City's Harlem. In 1990, two doctors studied Harlem's death rate and came to some shocking conclusions. The death rate in Harlem for males over age forty was greater than for males in Bangladesh, one of the poorest nations in the world. Moreover, Harlem is only a symbol of what takes place in poor neighborhoods. In New York City alone, there are fifty-four unhealthy neighborhoods that are home to some 650,000 people, and these areas annually suffer twice as many deaths as white neighborhoods.

In Harlem, the number of primary care physicians is 74 percent less than in the rest of New York City, but hospital admission rates are 26 percent higher, emergency room use is 73 percent higher, and use of outpatient facilities 134 percent higher than in other areas of the city (McCord & Freeman, 1991:427–428). Moreover, 83 percent of 181 patients discharged from Harlem Hospital with tuberculosis in 1988 were never rechecked, and failed to continue treatment.

The Harlem study paints a dismal picture of health in a poor neighborhood, one afflicted by crime and other social problems. The data used in the study were largely from the early 1980s, and did not include the recent outbreak of AIDS and drug addiction to crack-cocaine. Conditions have probably gotten worse.

Being poor not only causes ill health, it also keeps people from working. In consequence, 26 percent of poor people are disabled, compared with 8 percent of Americans with incomes over $35,000 (Coser et al., 1990).

To illustrate, 30 million people in the United States in 1994 were so poor they could not feed themselves properly. Poor nutrition is associated with a host of diseases including blindness (from vitamin A deficiency), mental retardation, anemia, and respiratory infections. The poor are much more likely to suffer from serious mental illness than are the nonpoor. Numerous studies have found much higher rates of schizophrenia and other psychoses among the poor (Cockerham, 1992:159):

- In 1939, Faris and Dunham studied a representative sample of residents of Chicago, and found the greatest concentration of schizophrenics among residents of the city's central business district, Chicago's poorest neighborhood. In 1973, Levy and Rovitz did a replication of the Faris and Dunham study and found the same results.

- In the 1950's, Hollingshead and Redlich divided New Haven, Connecticut, into five social class zones, ranging from upper class to lower class. Again, it was found that in lower-class people schizophrenia was the most common mental illness.

- In 1962, Leo Srole and his associates interviewed 1660 residents of Manhattan at random, and found that serious mental illness was most prevalent among lower-class people. Srole et al. also found that stress is a major factor in causing this disease.

The stress suffered by lower-class people differs somewhat from the stress suffered by middle- and upper-class people in general. Lower-class people tend to suffer from multiple stressful events of the kind described by Holmes and Masuda (1967). The case of one poor woman is instructive. A complicated pregnancy ended in the death of her unborn baby. Her husband lost his job, decimating the family's meager resources. The woman's husband left home to stay with his mistress, a constant source of stress between the couple. The woman's sister lived with her, but was so impaired herself that she could not help with any of the housework. The woman's child (born earlier) became sick and soon died. Overwhelmed by the stress of these related events, the woman became schizophrenic (Rogler & Hollingshead, 1965).

These examples of poor mental health, as well as our discussion of the ills of the health care system, point to a massive policy failure in the world's richest democracy.

Policy Failure: Reforming Health Care

National health care was first proposed in the United States in 1937 when 430 doctors proposed it in a letter to the New York *Times*. The health care professionals proposed a sweeping reform of the medical system that included preventive care, public funding of care for indigent people, medical research funds, and medical training of more doctors.

The American Medical Association, which controls the training and certification of physicians, campaigned against universal health insurance. The ideal of national health care was not raised again in the United States until President Truman proposed it after World War II. Meanwhile, in the 1940s and 1950s, virtually all other industrial democracies enacted national health care systems, providing medical insurance or government-provided health care for all their citizens.

This combination of interests evolved from a structure created by the health care reforms of the 1960s. Medicare (a federal program administered through Social Security, which insures people sixty-two and over) and Medicaid, (a federal and state program for reimbursing hospitals and doctors who treat people who are disabled or who live below the poverty line) were enacted into law in 1965. "It is only a slight exaggeration to say these programs wrote the medical profession a blank check" (Bassis et al., 1982:434). This came about because the Medicare law provided that physicians could set their own fees on a "usual and customary basis" (Crenshaw, 1993:235–236). The result was that doctors and hospitals could charge the government, and later private insurance companies, increasing prices without limits. In 1992, for the first time, largely through Medicare and Medicaid, the federal government paid over 50 percent of the nation's medical bills. Medicaid and Medicare now account for almost 15 percent of the entire federal budget of the United States, and the sizes of proposed cuts in these programs are currently part of an ongoing debate between Republicans and Democrats (Schaffer & Wellstone, 1994:152).

Meanwhile, the American Medical Association eased its opposition to all forms of medical insurance, and private insurance companies began issuing health policies whereby bills were determined by usual and customary fees. This was fine with the insurance companies because they could raise medical insurance premiums faster than doctors raised their fees. The result was that the medical profession got to set its own prices, and the cost of medical care skyrocketed. Before Medicare's enactment (1950–1965), health care prices rose about 7 to 8 percent annually. Between 1965 and 1980, medical care costs rose 10 to 12 percent per year. Less than a year after the passage of Medicare, the federal government had to raise Social Security taxes by 25 percent. Since 1970, the total cost of American health care has risen nearly 3000 percent, from $39 billion to about $1 trillion (in 1994), far outpacing inflation in all other areas of the economy.

The medical-industrial complex is primarily interested in profits and the political power necessary to ensure that their profits continue or increase. Meanwhile, as discussed, 56 million citizens remain medically uninsured or underinsured.

Summary

Just as there is a military-industrial complex, there is also a medical-industrial complex. The medical-industrial complex is a combination of interests that includes approximately five hundred private corporations and their allies in Congress, and the mass media. Among its most influential institutions:

FOR-PROFIT HOSPITAL CHAINS

Nationally, for-profit hospitals handle under 5 percent of the charity cases (uninsured patients), thus the costs of the uninsured, which for-profit hospitals might otherwise help bear, are transferred to the taxpayers. Moreover, uninsured patients are frequently placed in harm's way by the refusal of for-profit hospitals to treat them.

THE AMERICAN MEDICAL ASSOCIATION (AMA) AND PHYSICIANS

The AMA has encouraged doctors to specialize for about three decades now. The trend toward specialization has increased health care costs.

MEDICAL INSURANCE COMPANIES

The private medical insurance firms are an important cause of inadequate health care in America. Thus $70 billion per year is wasted on administrative inefficiency by hospitals and insurance companies each year.

THE PHARMACEUTICAL INDUSTRY

The drug industry is the most profitable industry in the United States. It spends billions per year to lobby Congress, have its representatives visit physicians, and place ads in medical journals. Sometimes the prescription drug industry causes serious physical harms as well, including illness and death.

MEMBERS OF CONGRESS SERVING ON COMMITTEES OVERSEEING HEALTH CARE POLICY

These politicians receive millions in campaign contributions from the institutions within the medical-industrial complex, and in return sponsor largely favorable legislation for the medical industry. The political influence of the medical-industrial complex is a chief reason why the United States is the only industrial democracy without a national health care system.

MALPRACTICE LAWYERS

Malpractice lawyers increase medical costs by winning occasional large sums in lawsuits, thus upping doctors' malpractice premiums, the costs of which are passed along to insurance companies in the form of higher physicians' fees.

THE ESTABLISHMENT PRESS AND HEALTH CARE NEWS

It is largely reported that the United States medical system is efficient and works relatively well, save for those with no medical insurance. Press coverage of the medical system thus serves to preserve the status quo.

Perhaps the greatest tragedies contributing to many Americans' health problems are: tobacco use, alcohol abuse, artery-clogging, high-fat diets, gunshot wounds, homicide, drug-exposed babies, environmental hazards, alcoholism, and acquired immune deficiency syndrome (AIDS). All of these stem from preventable social problems.

The stress associated with the lives of the poorest and most alienated of citizens also takes its toll in the form of mental illness. The definition of mental illness is inherently social in nature and is subject to changes in values, medical discoveries, and other historical events. Currently mental disorders are classified into categories related to biogenetic versus environmental causes, and range from disorders usually first evident in infancy, childhood, or adolescence (stuttering, anorexia nervosa, and mental retardation) to schizophrenic and paranoid disorders involving loss of touch with reality.

The most prevalent mental illness among American adults is depression—the so-called common cold of mental illness—and primarily affects women. The most common mental disorders among men are behaviors that are acted out. There are other important sociological variables associated with stress and mental illness, such as marital status, being female, social class, and place of residence (rural versus urban).

Men in American culture are more alienated from their bodies than women, and suffer a great deal more illness because of this alienation. However, male and female health is intimately related to social class. Thus African Americans are at risk for serious forms of mental and physical diseases, as are Hispanic Americans.

Health care in America has also been a disastrous policy failure. National health care was first proposed in the United States in 1937. However, the medical-industrial complex is primarily interested in profits and the political power necessary to ensure that its profits continue or increase. Meanwhile, as discussed, 56 million citizens remain medically uninsured or underinsured.

Suggested Readings

D. Drake and M. Uhlman (1993) *Making Drugs Making Money* (Kansas City, MO: Andrews & McMeel). This is a wonderful exposé of the structure and deviant practices within the American pharmaceutical industry by two Philadelphia *Inquirer* reporters.

P. Conrad and R. Kern (eds.) (1994) *The Sociology of Health and Illness*, 4th ed. (New York: St. Martin's). An excellent collection of current and important articles about health and the health care system from a critical sociological perspective.

Consumer Reports (1993) *How to Resolve the Health Care Crisis* (Yonkers, NY: Consumer Reports Books), M. Konner (1993) *Dear America* (Reading, MA: Addison Wesley), and H. Keyser (1993) *Prescription for Disaster: Health Care in America* (Austin: Eakin Press). These three books on the ills of the American health care system are passionate in tone, interesting in fact, and thoughtful in their proposals.

B. Worthington-Roberts (1981) *Contemporary Developments in Nutrition* (St. Louis: Mosby). Although a bit dated, this is a fascinating book about all aspects of nutritional knowledge. It is informative without being overly technical.

Exercises

Critical Thinking Exercise 9.1	**Medical News and the Media**

Compare a medical journal article with a news report about the article. What are the differences? What are the similarities?

Critical Thinking Exercise 9.2	**Health Care Policy Debate:** **Myths About Canada's Single-Payer System**

Canada's single-payer system is affordable, provides universal coverage, can be moved from one job or geographic location to another, covers all medically necessary treatment, and is publicly run and publicly accountable. Doctors work for themselves, have their own offices (the system is not "socialistic"), patients can choose any physicians they like, and fees are negotiated and set by the Ministry of Health and the doctors themselves (*Consumer Reports,* 1994:499–502).

Yet both conservative and liberal media and politicians in the United States criticize the Canadian system. Do a content analysis of newspaper editorials and news coverage about what American politicians have said regarding the Canadian system. Use outlets like the New York *Times,* Washington *Post, Wall Street Journal,* and weekly news magazines. The *Readers Guide, Proquest, Infotrack,* and other databases should provide you with a readymade sample of writings. What criticisms do American news media and political leaders have of Canada's health care system? Do these criticisms jibe with the facts presented in the *Consumer Reports* article cited above?

Part
THREE

The Sociology of Oppression: Problems of Inequality and Alienation

● ● ● ● ●

Poverty and the Underclass: Global and National Inequality

Structural Inequality:
Global and National

Inequality of wealth and income is a major structural characteristic in almost all nations, outside of Western Europe, Canada, and Japan. Nowhere is this more true than in the Third World nations of Asia, Africa, and Latin America. A 1990 report by the United Nations concluded:

- More than 1.2 billion people, most in the Third World, live in absolute poverty, unable to afford the basic food, clothing, and shelter necessary to sustain life. This is an increase of 200 million people in poverty over the 1980 figure, and is expected to reach 1.5 billion by the year 2000 (Sells, 1993:15). Between 184 and 300 million of these people live in sub-Saharan Africa alone. Nearly 900 million are illiterate, 1.75 billion lack access to safe drinking water, 150 million under age five are malnourished, and 14 million of these will die before their fifth birthday (Perdue, 1993:270).

- One hundred million people around the world are homeless, and 400 million are so malnourished they are likely to suffer stunted growth, retardation, and death (Durning, 1992:274).

- Between 1950 and 1980, world income per person doubled, but almost all of this increase has gone to people in First World nations.

- In most of the world's nations, between 60 and 70 percent of the population earn less than half the national average income.

- The debt of the Third World nations stands at over $1.2 trillion, costing poor nations $50 billion per year in interest and principal payments that inhibit economic development. The poorest 40 percent of Third World nations receive less aid now than they did in 1970 (Sells, 1993:15).

Concerning poverty both worldwide and in the United States, many of the same structural forces are at work. In most Third World nations the richest 3 percent of the population typically owns between 60 and 90 percent of all the wealth, and receives about two-thirds of all annual income. This is partially described in Table 10.1.

It is also important to understand what causes the great inequalities of wealth and income in Third World nations. Multinational corporations are headquartered in the First World economies of the United States, Western Europe, and Japan. Together these giant MNCs control about half of all world trade (Braun, 1993:121). Initially, MNCs enter Third World nations in search of cheap labor, which (with unemployment rates averaging 30 percent in such nations) is plentiful. Bornschier et al. (1978) studied the effects of MNCs penetrating (buying stock in domestically owned companies) in 103 nations between 1965 and 1977. They found that as the degree of foreign ownership increases, the economic growth in such nations decreases.

A second consequence of penetration by MNCs is increased indebtedness by Third World nations. Indebtedness increases because MNCs eat up local investment capital through loans, tax benefits, and repressed wages, all of which prevent the start-up of local

Table 10.1

World vs. U.S. Income Inequality (in percent)

	POOREST 20 PERCENT	TOP 20	RICHEST 10
Amount of Wealth Owned:			
All Nations	5.3	48.2	32.4
United States (1990)	1.0	80	23.4
Other Industrial Democracies	6.6	39.8	24.3
Third World	4.2	55.1	39.0

Sources: Babbie, 1993:126; Braun, 1993:75–76.

industries (George, 1993). A number of studies indicate that the entry of MNCs into a poor nation is highly associated with increased indebtedness. Accordingly, Third World nations with little MNC ownership of domestic industries have only half as much debt and half the percentage of gross domestic product (GDP) devoted to repaying international debt as poor nations that are economically dominated by multinational corporations (Braun, 1993:124).[1] There is some interesting evidence demonstrating that as Third World nations of the semi-periphery and periphery of the capitalist world system undergo economic development, the distribution of income in those nations actually increases. This paradoxical situation is in large measure explained by the policies of multinational corporations (MNCs).

Moreover, if one divides the world's poorest nations into those with per person annual incomes below $730 and those above $730, a clearer picture of the economic dominance of transnational corporations emerges. MNC penetration reduces the average per person income growth, despite high levels of foreign investment capital, high savings rates, a large domestic labor market, and high exports by eighty-eight poor nations between 1965 and 1985 (Braun, 1993:126). The key factor in poor nations improving economically is domestic investment, which decreases dramatically upon economic penetration by MNCs.

Consider the example of Brazil, a nation highly penetrated by MNCs, and South Korea, a nation among the lowest in MNC dominance. Between 1968 and 1973, both of these nations experienced real economic growth of between 8 and 9 percent. Then a world

---

[1]The following discussion is based on this excellent source.

recession hit. Brazil faltered badly and ceased growing, whereas South Korea continued to boom. Curiously, it does not matter if MNCs economically dominate manufacturing, mining, or agriculture. Economic growth stagnates regardless of the area of MNC investment.

Moreover, MNC penetration is also highly correlated with increased income inequality, and this inequality is greater in poor nations. Even if the GDP of a poor nation increases after transnationals become economically dominant, income inequality tends to increase. Even if exports increase in economically dominated poor nations, income inequality still increases. As evidence, between 1960 and 1986, exports in forty-six Third World nations increased, but so did inequality of income. In fact, Braun (1993:129) concludes, economic investment by transnational corporations had a six-times greater effect on income inequality than indebtedness did!

Another study by London and Williams (1988) concluded that the more MNCs economically dominate a nation, the less basic human needs are met in that nation. Thus, increased investment by transnationals is associated with lower caloric intake and increased malnutrition, decreased amounts spent on benefits for the poor, increased infant mortality, a lack of medical doctors, and decreased school attendance.

In many respects, multinational economic domination is a form of doom that resembles what ancient Roman legions used to do to their colonies in a past era. MNCs saddle poor nations with huge debts that can not possibly be repaid and impose hidden taxes on already weak economies. Moreover, protection of the investments and properties owned by MNCs is usually accomplished by terrorism, intimidation, repression, torture, and outright

These Shining Path rebels from Peru represent members of a local rebel movement. Like most Third World rebels, they join together in response to grinding poverty (and frequent government oppression), and represent the ultimate stage in the war between the haves and have-nots now being fought throughout much of the world.

warfare by Third World governments against their own people (Braun, 1993:134). As a result, economic domination of Third World economies is highly associated with increased malnutrition and political violence, violence that often spawns revolutionary movements and civil wars.

When affluent nations are economically dominated by their own transnational corporations, some of the same patterns of inequality emerge (albeit for slightly different reasons). In advanced industrial nations, domination by MNCs has a negative effect on the international trade balance (balance of payments). Accordingly a higher percentage of a nation's gross domestic product is needed to pay its international trade deficit. The United States currently has a per person trade balance of minus-$586 while West Germany's stands at plus-$613 and Japan's is plus-$706 per person (Braun, 1993:131). Economically advanced nations spend only about 2.4 percent of their GDP to pay their trade deficit, while poor nations pay an average 2.8 percent to pay their indebtedness.

Increasing Inequality in America

One of the great American myths is that the United States is an overwhelmingly middle-class nation wherein wealth and income are fairly distributed within a vast middle class. This cherished self-image is contradicted by the fact that the United States is now the most economically stratified of all industrial democracies. Even England, long considered a class society, has greater economic equality than does America. In Great Britain, the richest 1 percent of the population own 18 percent of the wealth (down from 59 percent in the early 1920s). By contrast, the richest 1 percent of Americans own nearly 40 percent of the nation's wealth as of 1990 (the latest figures available), and the wealthiest 20 percent of Americans own 80 percent of all the privately held wealth in the United States (Bradsher, 1995:A-1, A-9).

Likewise, as Table 10.2 demonstrates, the figures for income are just as unequal. The poorest 20 percent of income recipients in the United States received only 1 percent of the national income of the United States in 1990, 4.2 times less than even the poorest of the world's nations, and 6.6 times less than the poorest income earners in other industrial democracies. To be sure, per capita income in the United States is much higher than in the world's poorest nations (about $18,000 in the United States versus $1573 in the poorest nations) (Braun, 1993:55–57), but that is not the point. Income inequality in the United States is now more unequal than even Third World nations, and this inequality in and of itself is a major cause of poverty. While it may seem obvious, a major reason the poor remain poor is that their lack of resources prevents them from acquiring the education, political power, and economic wherewithal necessary to escape poverty.

Conservatives are fond of telling the poor how fortunate they are to be poor in America instead of a Third World nation. The reality is that the reference point for America's poor is other people in their own society, not some Third World nation. The lifestyles of affluent people are paraded in front of poor people in a host of television shows about the "rich and famous." The result is a form of class envy that is almost certain to cause social problems in the future.

| Table 10.2 | | | | |
| Trends in U.S. Income Inequality, 1980–1990 Income (in dollars) | | | | |
POPULATION SEGMENT	1980	1990	$ CHANGE	% CHANGE
Poorest 10%	$5134	$695	−$439	−8.6
Poorest 20%	8031	7725	−306	−3.8
Next Poorest 20%	19,088	19,348	260	1.4
Middle 20%	30,047	30,964	917	3.1
Second 20%	41,640	44,908	3268	7.8
Richest 20%	81,041	105,209	24,168	29.8
Richest 5%	142,306	206,162	63,856	44.9
Richest 1%	313,206	548,969	235,763	75.3

Source: Congressional Budget Office.

Poverty in America

The poor in America have grown poorer in recent years, and their numbers are increasing. This is demonstrated in Table 10.2. Between 1980 and 1990, the great increases in incomes were all at the top of the American income scale. The nation's richest income groups increased their incomes by between 30 and 75 percent during the 1980s. Yet the poor were unable to increase their incomes at anywhere near that rate. In fact, the poorest 20 percent of households lost between 4 and 9 percent of their incomes during the 1980s (Greenstein et al., 1993:299–300).[2]

Not only did the income of the poor not increase in the same fashion as the rich, the poorest 20 percent of Americans saw their federal taxes increase by 16.7 percent. Further, the percentage of federal taxes paid by the richest 20 percent declined by 6 percent, and by 1990, the top 20 percent of American households had as much income as the bottom 80 percent (Greenstein et al., 1993:301)!

The result of all these changes is dramatic. In 1980, the middle 60 percent of households had 12 percent more income than the richest 20 percent. In 1990, the middle 60 percent of income earners had 8 percent less income than the richest 20 percent of households. It is important to remember that one important reason for poverty is not the poor's

[2]The following discussion is based on this source.

Over two-thirds of Americans live their lives from paycheck to paycheck, and millions of them have trouble paying their bills each month. Some 40 million Americans are members of what is termed "the working poor." They are employed, but work in either part-time jobs, or full-time only part of the year.

unwillingness to work as much as it is the government's unwillingness to adopt policies that will lift the poor out of poverty. This fact flies in the face of the many myths and stereotypes about America's poor.

Contradictions
That Cause Poverty

Aside from the gross structural inequality of wealth and income, there is probably no problem about which American culture is so contradictory as poverty. As a culture, Americans have always viewed the poor as both worthy of their pity and of their anger. As Salerno et al. (1984:4) relate, social welfare in the United States has always been an unruly alliance between the warring attitudes of pity and contempt toward the disabled and dependent. Welfare has been stigmatized as a characteristic of the undeserving poor whose poverty is deemed of their own making.

The pitiable or deserving poor are labeled charity cases. During the Thanksgiving and Christmas holidays, almost all of the poor are viewed as people who need to eat. Each year at holiday time, the New York *Times* profiles the city's "one hundred neediest cases." Such symbolic gestures are functional in that the nonpoor can view themselves as giving people. The other 363 days of the year, the poor are viewed in terms of a contemptuous stereotype. This stereotype is steeped in myths about both poverty and the poor.

- *Myth:* Poor women on welfare keep having children in order to receive more money.
- *Fact:* There are no economic incentives for having additional children. The average per person amount of welfare grants decreases as the number of children in a household increases. As a result, having more babies simply makes a family poorer. In 1990, the average per person welfare payment was as follows:

NUMBER PERSONS IN HOUSEHOLD	MONTHLY PER PERSON WELFARE PAYMENT
1	$326.90
2	185.38
3	150.23
4	128.06

The most typical family on welfare is a mother and one child, and 73 percent of all welfare households have two or fewer children (Funiciello, 1993:56–57).

- *Myth:* The welfare problem is based primarily in the fact that teenage mothers have illegitimate babies.
- *Fact:* Teenage mothers, as of 1992, made up only 7.6 percent of the total Aid to Families with Dependent Children (AFDC) budget (Hacker, 1995:93). This is down from a record 8.3 percent in 1975. Only one in three teen mothers ever goes on welfare. Most of the rise in illegitimacy comes from a drop in the marriage rate among teen mothers. Teens do have sex earlier and more often than they did two decades ago. However, they also have many more abortions, some choosing to use abortion as a form of birth control. This is a health problem, not a part of welfare policy. Moreover, teenage girls are most frequently impregnated by adult males. Statutory rape laws are rarely enforced. It's the girl who is punished by American culture.
- *Myth:* Welfare dependency is passed from one generation to the next.
- *Fact:* Most children who grow up on welfare do not receive welfare as adults. In fact, 75 percent of first-time welfare recipients originate in the creation of single-parent households. Most of these families are made up of previously married women who are separated or divorced. If a woman gives birth and has no income from a job or a partner, she will probably go on AFDC, whether her parents were on welfare or not.
- *Myth:* Most people who go on welfare stay on it for life.
- *Fact:* Only 8 percent of welfare recipients are on welfare for eight or more years. One of every four American citizens is on welfare at some time during a decade, but only one in fifty receives half or more of his or her income from welfare for eight years or longer. Over two-thirds are off AFDC within three years or less. Most families defined as long-term welfare recipients are large, and owe their penury to the fact that the father has deserted the family or a divorce has occurred. When children begin to leave the family, the parents get off welfare voluntarily or are ineligible.

- *Myth:* Most welfare recipients cheat the system.

- *Fact:* There is an unconscionable level of fraud in all areas of American life. The welfare fraud charges levied on the poor by manipulative politicians and right-wing commentators are an interesting piece of projection. That is, most fraud is the product of middle- and upper-class people, corporations, and political organizations, not the poor. More specifically, most welfare and food stamp fraud is committed by welfare workers. A recent Department of Health and Human Services study found that only 2.6 percent of petty fraud investigations are worthy of further study. Even fewer are labeled as true fraud by investigators. Most overpayments were welfare department errors (Funiciello, 1993:60).

- *Myth*: Most poor people are able-bodied black adults, who are too lazy to get a job, and enjoy being on welfare.

- *Fact:* In 1992, approximately 36 million Americans lived below the federally defined poverty level. Two-thirds of them were white. Second, half of the poor are either under eighteen or over sixty-five years of age. Less than a third of the poor ever go on any kind of public assistance (Gilbert & Kahl, 1993:279).

- *Myth*: The vast majority of the poor live in the ghettos of America's central cities.

- *Fact:* About 60 percent of the poor live either in suburbs or in small urban or rural areas (Kirp, 1993:4). Even in America's inner cities, the total number of whites in poverty (8.3 million) is larger than the number of poor blacks (6.1 million) (Jones, 1994:15–16). In fact, more poor blacks live outside America's central cities (11 million) than in central city areas (6.1 million) (Jones, 1994:16).

The poor outside America's ghettos are largely ignored by the media because they are not exciting to write about. The media tend to pander to our perverse fascination with guns, sex, and drug abuse, providing details of what some observers call the violent and sensational breakdown of family organization and community standards. The mundane, everyday strivings of the vast majority of poor people (regardless of race) make for dull copy (Jones, 1994:17).

- *Myth*: Public assistance pays enough in money and services to lift people out of poverty without working.

- *Fact:* The United States spends less on public assistance than any industrialized nation. Since the founding of the republic to the present day, the United States has spent less on welfare than it has to pay off the costs of the savings and loan scandal (Vidal, 1994). U.S. public policies lift fewer people out of poverty—through taxes and transfer payments—than in any other advanced industrial nation (Amott, 1994:170).

Perhaps most important, the welfare payments received by the poor are part of what has been described as a dual welfare system in the United States (Simon & Eitzen, 1993: Chapter 2). What the poor receive is called welfare, but the subsidies, tax deductions, government loans, and grants received by middle- and upper-class people and corporations from government are called other things, labels that do not bear the stigma of welfare. In 1994, the total welfare budget in the United States was $25 billion. The poor actually receive only 16 percent of the American welfare budget. The remainder goes to wealthy individuals and corporations, and totaled over $650 billion in 1990 (Katz, 1990:460).

This last point is symbolic of an entire range of behaviors engaged in by both poor and nonpoor alike. What we have here is a series of double standards. Consider the following:

- If nonpoor people invest in the stock market or play the state lottery, it is called a gamble. If a poor person is caught shooting craps in a back alley or playing a numbers game, it is called a crime.

- If a professional woman has a child out of wedlock, it is viewed in some circles as an act of liberation. If a poor unmarried teenager bears a child, it is termed illegitimacy.

- If nonpoor people have sex outside marriage, it is often termed sexual freedom. If the poor have intercourse without marriage, it is called promiscuity, the inability to delay gratification, or irresponsibility.

What all this demonstrates is that poor people lack the power to define their station in life and their behavior as respectable or legitimate. There is no more solid proof of the poor's lack of power to define values as the definition of poverty itself.

Defining and Measuring Poverty

In 1994, the Clinton administration issued a report on homelessness in America. The Bush administration had claimed that 600,000 people were homeless on a given night in the United States. The Clinton report claimed that there were 7 million homeless in the United States (San Francisco *Chronicle*, 1994:A-1). The problem involved in counting the homeless is symbolic of all measures relating to the poor.

The concept of poverty itself is largely political (ideological). The definition of poverty used by the federal government is criticized by both conservatives and liberals (for different reasons). In the 1960s, the Kennedy administration defined poverty as the cost of a nutritious diet, plus the proportion of income a family spends on food. It was estimated that the average family spends one-third of its income on food. Accordingly, multiplying the price of food times three became the nation's official measure of poverty level income. In 1992, it was estimated that a family of four spent $4400 on food in a year. The poverty level was then set at $13,600 (Gilbert & Kahl, 1993:269).

There are a number of criticisms of this definition. Many researchers feel that it is much too low for a number of reasons:

- The poor usually pay more for food than the nonpoor because grocery stores in poor neighborhoods are usually more expensive than stores in nonpoor areas.

- The cost of other items beside food is also expensive, and these are not even included in the government's concept of poverty. In the 1990s, poor people spent an average of 70 percent of their incomes just on rent. If one figures the other 30 percent will be spent on food, this leaves no money at all for necessities like clothes, medical care, transportation, insurance, appliances, and so on.

- Using this definition grossly undercounts the actual number of poor people, if being poor means being unable to afford basic necessities. Schwartz and Volgy have rightly argued that for a family of four to afford the true basic necessities of American life, including food, clothes, shelter, medical care, and a car that runs, would cost $21,600 in 1992. This figure is 155 percent of the federally defined poverty level (which, remember, assumes all of life's basics are affordable with an income three times one's annual food budget). Using the basic necessities concept of poverty, Schwartz and Volgy (1993:92) estimate that an additional 10 million American adults, and millions of additional children, were in poverty in 1992.

Using the basic necessities measure of poverty, an astounding 38 to 40 percent of the American people were poor in 1992. Most critically, this included 13 million people, two-thirds of whom possessed high school or college educations, who worked in full-time jobs! As we can see, one of the dirty little secrets of American poverty is that some 13 million full-time jobs do not pay enough to lift a family of three out of poverty.

There are two important implications of this research. First, a major cause of poverty is that many full-time jobs pay wages and salaries below the federally defined poverty level, and, second, there are many more hungry and poor people in America than any presidential administration has thus far been willing to admit.

Conservatives have their own view of poverty, one that sharply contrasts with either the official or necessities definitions given above. Conservatives are fond of arguing that even the official definition of poverty actually overestimates the number of poor people. This is because people tend to underestimate their incomes when giving such information to the federal government. Moreover, the annual income survey that measures poverty is estimated on the basis of *money income only*. Since poverty measures were first established, conservatives claim, there has been a substantial increase in *in-kind income benefits* (food stamps, Medicaid, and subsidized housing). Nor are gifts, wealth holdings (stocks and bonds), durable goods (e.g., computers), and barter (I'll baby-sit for you, if you mend my dress), and income off-the-books counted in official measures of poverty (Haveman, 1993:25).

One problem with this argument is that it assumes all poor people receive welfare benefits, and this is simply untrue. Six million of the people with incomes below the officially defined poverty level receive no food stamps at all (Dority, 1993:28). This is partially because it takes a long time to begin receiving welfare benefits (at least thirty days in most states) (Funiciello, 1993:60). More importantly, most poor people believe in American values about individualism as strongly as the nonpoor. They believe they would feel a great loss of independence, self-respect, and dignity if they went on welfare. They are painfully aware that being on welfare is considered deviant in America. Finally, many poor people are unaware that they are eligible for in-kind benefits, and, hence, never bother to apply for them.

The conservatives would have a valid argument when it comes to food stamps, which are like cash, if most of the poor received them, but they do not. Second, the right-wing view overlooks the fact that since the 1960s, when many of these programs were initiated, there has been a dramatic increase in the taxes paid by the poor, especially sales and payroll taxes (Phillips, 1993:107–114). However, taxes are not even recorded in official poverty surveys or reflected in the official poverty statistics (Gilbert & Kahl, 1993:277).

Given these various views of poverty, what is the true number of poor people in America, and is the situation getting better or worse? First, taking any measure you care to use, it is no exaggeration to say that most Americans are only one paycheck away from being poor (Dority, 1993:28). This is because the vast majority of Americans own no substantial wealth (property that generates an income, like stocks, bonds, and land). Nor do many people in America possess a large savings account. The United States has the lowest rate of savings of any industrial nation, about 3 percent of net income. Moreover, the average U.S. household not only possesses little savings, but is up to its neck in debt. Private household debt in the United States soared from $1.3 trillion in 1980 to $3.4 trillion in 1990. Families now pay an average of 14 percent of their disposable incomes just to pay the interest on their debts. Moreover, the wealth of the average American household has actually decreased over $5000 in value since 1984, and is now below $32,000 (Phillips, 1993:178–179).

Second, poverty in the United States is bad and getting worse:

- Over 3 million people were added to the poverty rolls between 1990 and 1992.

- The percentage of children living in poverty increased 50 percent between 1980 and 1990. One of every five American children now lives in poverty, including one-half of all black children and one-third of all Hispanic children (compared to 16 percent of all white children) (Brill, 1993:35). Currently, a child is born into poverty every thirty seconds in the United States (Lavelle et al., 1995:32).

Moreover, as of 1992, the adult poverty rate in the United States was 11 percent. The percentage of children living in poverty was 21 percent, the highest percentage of poor children since 1965. These rates are higher than in any other Western democracy (Males, 1994:18). In fact, as of 1994, American children were twice as likely to live in poverty as Canadian children, three times as likely to be poor as British children, and four to thirteen times more likely to live in poverty than French, German, Dutch, or Swedish children (Lavelle et al., 1995:38).

- The percentage of black households headed by a woman increased from 23 percent in 1959 to 55 percent in 1991. Three-fourths of children born out of wedlock in the United States are born into poverty (Becnel, 1993:92).

- The number of homeless poor has increased from around 3 million in the 1980s to about 7 million in 1994. If present policies persist, the number of American homeless could reach 19 million by 2003 (Dority, 1993:28).

As psychiatrist Norman Brill (1993:4) has written, at no time during the last seventy-five years has the United States experienced the amount of poverty and related ills (urban crime, substance abuse, out-of-wedlock births, family disintegration, and homelessness) now taking place.

The Harms of Poverty

There is overwhelming evidence that poverty is extremely harmful in every sense—physically, economically, and morally/psychologically. Concerning physical harm, the poor are at terrible risk for shortened lifespans, diseases that nonpoor people do not contract, and life-threatening victimizations:

- There are 33 million Americans who go hungry each day, including 12 million children under age eighteen (Lavelle et al., 1995:36). A recent hospital survey of 11,000 poor people found that often their choices were between having heat and having food, but they could not afford both (*Jet*, 1993) Most of these people live in families of the working poor. Their incomes are just over $10,000 per year, and, therefore, they are not poor enough to qualify for food stamps or Aid to Families with Dependent Children (AFDC, a.k.a. welfare) (Kaitschuck, 1992:22).

- One American child dies every fifty-three minutes from the effects of poverty. One of every five American children lives below the federally defined poverty level (McWilliams, 1993:8).

- Since the mid-1970s, 30 million women worldwide have been forcibly sold into prostitution. Many of these women end up serving as hostesses in sex clubs frequented by affluent business executives in Asian nations (Hornblower, 1993).

- Ninety percent of the nation's homicides are committed by poor minorities, and 94 percent of their victims are other poor minorities. As of 1993, a young black male in Detroit had a greater chance of dying of murder than a World War II infantryman had of dying in combat. In one four-month period in 1992, 102 youngsters in Detroit, aged sixteen or younger, were shot by stray bullets (Brill, 1993:4).

  Almost three-fourths of poor children who suffer child abuse go on to commit crimes, and currently 80 to 90 percent of state and federal prison inmates claim they were physically abused as children (Brill, 1993:20).

  Concerning financial harm, the poor are ripe for all manner of exploitation. They are often gullible victims of a wide variety of rip-offs. Low-income people are often victims of price gouging from a variety of landlords, merchants, finance companies, banks, and other businesses.

- Food chains claim it costs 2 or 3 percent more to operate stores in poor areas, yet charge the poor 5 to 10 percent more for groceries than is paid by consumers in middle-class areas.

- Many ghetto merchants raise prices on goods on the first and fifteenth of each month because those are the dates when welfare checks are received.

- Banks justify higher interest rates being charged to poor customers on the grounds that the poor are a bad credit risk, lacking collateral for loans. Many banks refuse to lend money to poor people, leaving them to deal with loan-sharks who charge illegally high rates of interest.

- Jewelry stores in poor areas often charge poor customers double the markup charged to middle-class people. A ring selling for $50 wholesale will sell for $100 in a middle-class neighborhood and $300 in a poor one (Simon & Eitzen, 1993:104–105).

Being unorganized as consumers, the poor lack access to the powerful, who might be able otherwise to aid them with consumer protection legislation.

Moreover, the poor do not have powerful lobbies in Washington and state legislatures, and, consequently, do not influence the writing of tax legislation. The poor pay a higher percentage of their incomes in state and federal taxes than the nonpoor. They also tend to suffer severe alienation from themselves, each other, and their society.

Poverty and Alienation

The poor are much more often the sufferers of some of the worst forms of alienation. The lower down in the class system people are located, the more people feel powerless to change the conditions of their lives. The poor feel their station in life is due to bad luck or other circumstances beyond their control.

This sense of fatalism, along with their economic desperation, helps explain why the poor gamble their meager holdings with great frequency. Nationwide, 2 percent of lottery players account for 65 percent of wagers. The vast majority of wagers are made by poor black and Hispanic Americans. Currently there are 4.2 million gambling addicts in the

The vast majority of people arrested for violent "street" crimes come from America's poor neighborhoods. Their victims tend to be other poor people, and slightly over 90 percent of their criminal acts involve efforts to obtain money or property that can be exchanged for money.

United States. Sixty percent of so-called compulsive gamblers have incomes below $25,000 and 43 percent of them are nonwhite (McClory, 1992:60).

Finally, poverty seriously contributes to the alienation that influences a wide variety of other social problems. As detailed in Chapter 8, the leading concern of the American public at present is crime. However, the American fear of crime is really a fear of street (i.e., violent) crime. Violent criminal acts are, as we have seen, largely committed by the poor against the poor. Indeed, in one study of a Baltimore public clinic (which serves the poor), 24 percent of 168 teen visitors to the clinic had personally witnessed a murder, and 72 percent personally knew someone who had been shot (Brill, 1993:4). Even though street crime primarily victimizes the poor, it is the middle class that is demanding political action to deal with it, arming itself with guns, and installing security alarm systems.

The entire ideology of street crime promotes moral harm because of what it functions to do. The public has been convinced by the media, corporations, and politicians that street crime alone makes up the American crime problem, having had their attention focused on lower-class criminals. This is morally harmful for two important reasons: First, focusing attention and financial resources on street criminals means that attention is diverted from the activities of corporate and political criminals, whose activities cost far more money and many more lives than street criminals do (Simon & Eitzen, 1993:294–295).

Second, emphasizing only violent crime in public policy also functions to hide the many important links between street crime, organized crime, and the elite criminality of corporations and political organizations. As discussed in Chapter 8, there are many relationships, both symbolic and financial, between the various types of criminality that make up America's entire crime problem. Focusing on only one at a time keeps the public from seeing these interrelationships, and permits middle- and upper-class criminality to flourish with relative impunity.

To cite an example, the Smith family[3] is a symbol of the shortcoming of the current definition of poverty. This family of four has an annual income of $19,700, well above the $13,920 poverty level income for a family of four. Yet this family can not afford a telephone, must skip meals occasionally, and can not afford to fix their fourteen-year-old car. The Smiths are an example of what have been termed the working poor (Schwartz & Volgy, 1993:192).

What all of these Americans have in common is that they are poor. It may sound silly to demonstrate that poverty is a harmful condition, but a surprising number of writers claim that poverty is a freely chosen, even enjoyable condition. Conservative Edward C. Banfield (1993) insists that the urban poor are thrill seekers who riot, commit crimes for fun, and constantly want to be where the action is. *Action* refers to uninhibited sexual conduct, drug abuse, alcoholism, and violent activity. Moreover, Banfield believes that the needs of lower-class people for sex and their taste for action take precedence over everything else—certainly over any work routine. The poor drift from job to job not wanting much success. What the poor enjoy is the slum because it is a place of excitement (where the action is), a congenial place for people who live in the present. The slum is fun because it is a place of opportunity for vice and a host of illegal goods and services. It is also a place to conceal one's criminal identity from the police. Moreover, in the slum one can beat

---

[3]The name is fictitious, and is used by the writers cited to protect the family's identity.

While over 33 million Americans are officially counted as poor, and some 40 million more constitute the near poor, a few thousand celebrities, sports heroes, and executives earn tens of millions of dollars per year, as well as the admiration of millions of people.

one's children, lie drunk in the gutter, or go to jail without attracting any special notice (Banfield, 1993:61). Indeed, claims Banfield (1993:214), many young poor people enjoy rioting as excitement, action (fun)—as rampage-destruction for the sake of destruction and fighting for the sake of fighting.

Some leftist commentators have also remarked on the fun aspects of being poor. Liberal Herbert Gans (1991:266) claims that the nonpoor believe the poor are having fun, and, are, therefore, fun to watch. Gans argues that the poor offer vicarious participation to the nonpoor. In other words, the uninhibited sexual, alcoholic, and narcotic behavior of the poor is free of middle-class moral constraints. Consequently, the poor are thought to enjoy such behavior more often than do the envious middle classes, who find the poor fun to watch because the poor do deviant things the middle classes would like to do. Moreover, the poor create a culture that often becomes part of the lifestyles of the broader society. Many types of popular music, including the blues, spirituals, country, and rap, began with urban or southern poor people. There are also many books, movies, and television shows that portray the poor as homeless, hobos, prostitutes, and Robin Hood–like crooks with hearts of gold. The poor are thus at times viewed as heroic, and poverty appears as a builder of character.

Finally, poor neighborhoods have historically provided many of the nation's gifted athletes, especially its boxers, baseball, and basketball players. In keeping with this image, poor areas are sometimes viewed as low-cost athletic training camps and sports become celebrated as vehicles of social mobility and the American Dream. The problem, of course, is that for every Frank Thomas or Michael Jordan, there are 54,000 poor males who do not become professional athletes. However, the poor in the 1990s not only suffer from a lack of upward mobility but a tragic form of downward mobility: homelessness.

Homelessness: "More Fun"

One of the most recent developments in the nature of American poverty is the presence of homeless people on the street of every major and many medium-size cities. The homeless in America are viewed with the same mixture of pity and contempt as are the rest of the nation's poor. Michael Katz has admirably summarized the contradictions of having a homeless population in the richest, most technologically advanced nation on earth:

> The homeless embody the contradictions of the (postmodern society). Huddled over steam vents, in doorways, on the benches of subway and train stations, they remind us daily that economic recovery has not lessened poverty or tempered inequality. They bear the most visible cost of the transformation of American cities by urban renewal . . . of the dismantling of the old industrial economy; and of the government's war on welfare. They show us that the richest and most powerful nation in the world can not provide all its citizens with a decent secure place to live. They tell us that the billions of dollars poured into urban reform have not yet rendered archaic (American poverty). The growing number of families among them drive home the awful fact that among industrialized countries, only in America is childhood the age of greatest poverty. (Katz, 1989:186)

Like the poor in general, there are negative stereotypes and myths about the homeless:

- *Myth:* Homeless people choose to be homeless. Again, it is thought to be an adventurous, exciting life, free of the responsibilities and moral restraints that so frustrate middle-class people.

- *Fact:* Most homeless people are homeless for only a short time, but they move in and out of homelessness on a periodic basis. Fifty percent of homeless people have been homeless more than one year, but only 20 percent of the homeless have been in that condition for four or more years. Sixty percent of homeless people have lived in the same city for ten or more years, and 75 percent have resided in the same location for at least a year. Unlike earlier eras, the homeless of the 1990s are not hobos (drifters) who ride the nation's rails in search of employment (Baum & Barnes, 1993:27). The vast majority are people who would love to have a home (National Alliance to End Homelessness, 1991:12).

- *Myth:* The majority of homeless people are mentally ill.

- *Fact:* The majority of homeless people in 1990s America are a diverse group: 4 percent are unaccompanied youths, 35 percent are veterans; families with children are the fastest growing homeless population, and the explosion in America's homeless population, which began in the 1980s, has far surpassed government's ability to deal with the problem. While it is very difficult to count accurately the homeless because they drift into and out of homelessness with great rapidity, it does appear that the number of homeless has grown substantially. Between 1984 and 1994, the number of American homeless grew from about 3 million to around 7 million. (For a discussion of what you can do to help, see this chapter's "Private Troubles/Public Issues.")

Profile of the Homeless

The homeless are different than the nonhomeless poor in some important respects. What the homeless represent is not only the poorest of the poor, but, more importantly, the most alienated and disconnected of the nation's lower classes.

Most important, the homeless are not just like us. In fact, the homeless are not even like other poor people. The vast majority of homeless people lack the web of friends and other supports that keep other poor people from becoming homeless. In one study, 75

Private Troubles   **Public Issues**

What Can You Do to Help the Homeless?

The problems of the poor and homeless in America are serious, but they are not impossible to resolve. In fact, poverty is one of the few social problems that can be resolved within the current economic and political structure of American society. Your own life could be dramatically enriched by helping the homeless. These efforts may not end homelessness, but they can ease the suffering of those affected, and aid in creating one form of community that is sadly lacking in America today.

What You Can Do

Here are some things you can do to bring joy to homeless children. It's usually best to go through an established social service agency.

1. Get your club or church—or just some friends—together and see if you can arrange to take homeless children from a local family shelter on field trips one Saturday or Sunday a month. You can take them to such things as:

   - Baseball or basketball games
   - The zoo
   - Children's theater matinees
   - The movies
   - Museums
   - Bowling
   - Special events like fireworks or parades

percent of the homeless people who were interviewed said there were no family members, relatives, or friends on whom they could depend for assistance. Three-fourths of pregnant homeless women do not choose to return to their families because they say their families do not want them back (Baum & Barnes, 1993:15). Emotionally, the homeless are fearful of close contacts with other people. They are extreme outcomes of America's pathological fascination with rugged individualism. In other words, it not merely the absence of housing that causes their homelessness, but their lack of bonds with other people and societal institutions.

Baum and Barnes (1993a:13–29) have assembled a tragic profile of America's homeless:

- Homeless people tend to die twenty years before the average American adult. Sixteen percent of deaths among the homeless are directly attributable to alcohol abuse and another 16 percent are caused by other substances. One-fourth of

- Ice skating

- The aquarium.

2. Coach homeless kids in baseball, soccer, volleyball, or other sports on weekends.

3. Collect a load of children's books from your friends, acquaintances, coworkers, and your own attic, and donate them to your local family shelter.

4. Volunteer to pay for a homeless child to go to summer camp. Make sure to contribute enough to buy the clothes and equipment he or she will need.

5. Become a Big Brother or Big Sister and request to be assigned to a homeless child.

Remember that it's important to honor any commitment you make to the children—whether it's a one-time trip or a regular monthly outing. Homeless children have had their faith and trust shaken. What you're trying to do is show them that you care and that you respect them enough to fulfill your promises to them.

"It's like feeding birds," comments Havelock Hewes, a teacher who worked at the Children's Storefront School in Harlem, New York City. "You have to keep feeding them all winter because they come to rely on it. If you don't feed them they'll die.

"We had volunteers who came to the Storefront, spent time with the kids, took them to ball games, then stopped coming. Our kids got depressed and angry. Volunteers need to maintain commitment."

Maintaining your connection to homeless children is easier if you make your program as accessible to them as possible. Provide transportation to and from events. Plan events requiring parents' signatures—such as summer camp—far in advance so you have plenty of time to secure permission for children to participate.

Continued on next page

Private Troubles   **Public Issues**

Christmas

Christmas is a magic time for children. No matter how squalid the circumstances, how jaded the child, come Christmas, all children dare to hope that they will find coziness, presents, good cheer, loving parents—and a secure home. You may not be able to bring a child a home or an intact family, but you can work on the rest of the wish list.

Invite everyone at your office, church, or other group to donate a Christmas-wrapped toy for a homeless child and bring the presents to family shelters.

Arrange for your club or office or other group to hold a holiday party for homeless children.

When you help kids feel good, their joy is contagious—it makes you feel good.

While Christmas is a rewarding time to help, many programs are inundated with help then and receive little at other times of the year. Think about having Christmas in July— and spreading the cheer to another season.

What You Can Do

1. Go through your home and find any household items in good condition that you no longer need or use. (Remember to set aside usable discards *whenever* you're cleaning out your closets or the attic.) Call the Salvation Army or look through the Yellow Pages for local organizations that accept donations for the homeless, and arrange to drop off your donations or have them picked up. By passing your unneeded things on to resettled families instead of to the dump, you'll help others, get a significant tax deduction, and benefit the environment, too.

    Your donation of the following used items can help displaced people settle into new homes:

    Furniture, such as beds, dressers, tables, sofas, chairs, desks, cribs, wardrobes, bookshelves

    Appliances, such as lamps, clocks, vacuum cleaners, televisions, radios, telephones, dishwashers, refrigerators, washer/dryers

    Household essentials, such as dishes, glassware, flatware, pots and pans, kitchen utensils, brooms, mops, buckets, tools, rugs, sheets, towels, curtains, window-shades

    Gas stoves and cooking devices such as toaster ovens, microwaves, and hot plates (since many apartments do not provide stoves).

2. Donate your time and skills to a furniture collection drive. If you own a van or truck you can pick up and deliver items; if you're handy around the house you can fix, refinish, or clean donations. And anyone can help keep track of inventory. Lending a hand can be fun: You'll meet new people and really feel good about yourself.

3. Start a furniture collection program of your own at your church, school, or club. Get in touch with a group that resettles homeless families and coordinate your efforts with theirs. Members who drive vans, pickups, or station wagons can provide transportation; donations can be stored in a spare classroom, basement, or meeting space. In order to attract donations, you can publicize your program through fliers and newspaper advertising. Ask donors to bring small items in, but arrange to pick up large items from them. Before storing donated items, inspect, sort, and record them, and clean or repair anything that needs attention. In conjunction with your partner agency, set up one day a week when resettled families can come look over the donations and choose what they need. After that, all you need do is deliver the items to their new address.

Contact

The Sponsorship Program for
Homeless People

P.O. Box 54555

Atlanta, GA 30308-0555

(404) 892-6404

Contact: Annette Allyn Day

Contact your local homeless coalition, homeless service program, or Salvation Army for information about what's needed.

What You Can Do

1. Call homelessness groups and other charitable organizations to find out if they are operating a literacy program, and ask how you can get involved.

Continued on next page

Private Troubles   Public Issues

2. Arrange for your church, club, business, or school to contribute services or supplies to a literacy program. Your club or church can donate space or transportation; your business can offer paper, pencils, refreshments, or the use of a van; your school can supply tutors. Any group can raise funds to support a literacy program, through bake sales, raffles, or car washes. Perhaps your group will want to make volunteering for a literacy program part of its regular schedule of activities.

3. Once plans have been made, you'll need the help of at least one qualified teacher to oversee the program. A shelter or a church can provide a space in which to conduct the program.

Contacts

Literacy Volunteers of America

5795 Widewaters Parkway

Syracuse, NY 13214-1846

(315) 445-8000

Push Literacy Action Now (PLAN)

1332 G Street, SE

Washington, DC 20003

(202) 547-8903

homeless people have AIDS. Homeless people have tuberculosis at a rate two hundred times greater than that of the general population, and their death rate is three times higher than the general population.

• The average homeless American is in his or her mid-thirties. Over 80 percent of homeless adults are single males, many of whom are veterans of the Vietnam War. In fact, 33 percent of the homeless are Vietnam veterans.

• Sixty-five to 80 percent of homeless people are either chronic alcoholics, drug addicts, or suffer from severe mental illness, especially schizophrenia. About 40 percent of the homeless, including 52 percent of homeless men and 17 percent

What You Can Do

Teenage runaways generally cannot stay in adult shelters, and few places have shelter space specifically for youngsters.

1. Find out if such space is adequate in your community. If not, write to your mayor and the media, and encourage them to investigate the problem.

2. If you know of youngsters who are in danger of leaving home or being forced out (throwaways), help them by finding out where they can get professional assistance.

3. Contact your local school to see if it has counseling for runaways. If not, encourage the school to develop special programs.

Contacts

The National Runaway Hotline
(800) 231-6946

Covenant House
(800) 999-9999

Or contact your local shelter to see if they need volunteers to work with at-risk teenagers.

Source: The National Alliance to End Homelessness (1991): 24–25, 44, 46–48, 61.

of homeless women, are chronic alcoholics (compared to only about 11 percent of the general population), and many have lost jobs because of their drinking. Homeless alcoholics have extremely high rates of tuberculosis, infections, malnutrition, sexually transmitted diseases, AIDS, and hypothermia (loss of body heat in cold weather). Alcoholic homeless people also suffer from higher rates of arrest, violent criminal victimization, and fights than nonalcoholic homeless people.

• About 80 percent of the homeless in men's shelters and 29 percent of homeless in family shelters test positive for drugs. Homeless female heads of families are four times more likely to use drugs than nonhomeless poor women, and drug trafficking is a major problem in welfare hotels and homeless shelters. Crack-cocaine is the drug of choice among the homeless, especially among homeless women, because it is cheap and it does not require injection. Among the drug-abusing homeless, those over forty years of age tend to use alcohol, while those under forty use drugs and alcohol.

Many of these conditions are treatable, but the nation has not decided to commit the resources necessary to alleviate these problems. Sadly, only about one-third of homeless people ever make use of what public benefits do exist. This is because they are so alienated from other people and from social welfare institutions that they are deeply suspicious of such efforts.

Finally, as Dority (1993:28) has noted, the homeless are often deprived of civil rights by the criminal justice system. Their right to due process under the Fourth Amendment is often violated simply because there are no interpreters at benefit hearings for the Hispanic homeless. In 1993, Miami Court Judge Clyde Atkins ruled that the homeless have a consti-tutional right to eat, sleep, and bathe on public property, and that arresting them for these acts is discriminatory because they are homeless. Judge Atkins ordered safety zones created for Miami's homeless population, where they are not to be arrested, harassed, or abused by law enforcement officials. In general, the homeless do suffer cruel and unusual punishment at the hands of police, and it is hoped that the Miami ruling will become a model for other cities around the country.

Many major cities have cracked down on the homeless. In San Francisco, New York, and elsewhere, laws have been passed against sleeping in the streets.

- One-third of the homeless exhibit chronic mental illness, such as schizophrenia. Further, the homeless suffer mental retardation at rates two to three times high-er than the general population.

- About one-third of the nation's homeless are families, and 15 percent of the homeless are children. Ninety percent of homeless households are composed of one-parent families.

- Many homeless teenagers are the products of multigenerational child abuse, and teen runaways often prefer the violence of the streets to their home environ-ments. Once on the streets, they are likely to turn to prostitution, drugs, alco-hol, and crime as coping mechanisms. Homeless teens are almost certain to become the next generation of homeless adults. A very high percentage of homeless children over age twelve abuse drugs. Those who do have very high rates of hepatitis, AIDS, and sexually transmitted diseases (STDs).

- The homeless are unemployed for longer periods than other poor people, many of whom work full- or part-time at low-paying jobs. One-third of homeless people have been unemployed for over two years, 60 percent for over one year. Only 5 percent have steady, full-time jobs. Those who work part-time are over-whelmingly unskilled or semiskilled workers.

What has caused the dramatic increase in homelessness? Most experts agree that four major sociological forces are at work. These include:

1. The loss of affordable housing: About 2.5 million people are involuntarily displaced each year through eviction, unaffordable rent increases, and so-called revitalization projects (e.g., gentrification)—designed to encourage affluent people to remain in the central cities. In the 1980s, rents in the United States increased over twice as fast as renter income. Rents increased 30 percent for people with incomes under $3000, half of whom paid more than 70 percent of their incomes for rent, leaving about $71 per month for all other expenses (Salarno et al., 1984:7).

2. *Unemployment*: About 40 percent of the homeless seek shelter because they have lost a job. Between 1972 and 1992, over 8 million manufacturing jobs were taken out of America's central cities and transferred either to the suburbs, overseas, or to the "sunbelt" (western and southern United States). Between 1972 and 1982, alone, Chicago lost 47 percent of its manufacturing jobs. Between 1987 and 1990, Los Angeles lost 327,000 jobs, half of which were in manufacturing. Between 1978 and 1988 the poorest 20 percent of Americans became 8 percent poorer. The poverty rate in black communities in inner cities increased from 32 percent in 1980 to 44 percent in 1989. The current rate of poverty among inner-city blacks is 50 percent (Walters, 1993:3–4).

3. *Cutbacks in federal programs to aid the poor*: Federal housing programs were cut 70 percent in the 1980s and early 1990s, a total of $12 billion reductions between 1980 and 1992 (Dority, 1993:28). Employment training and welfare programs were slashed by $600 billion from 1980 to 1990 (Walters, 1993:4; National Alliance to End Homelessness, 1991:12).

4. Deinstitutionalization: In the 1950s, there were 550,000 mental patients housed in state mental hospitals. During the 1960s and 1970s a policy was instituted whereby the hospitalized mentally ill were released to welfare hotels and other facilities. During the 1980s, budgets for these programs were slashed, turning those people onto the streets. In 1991, there were less than 150,000 people in state mental hospitals and other facilities, leaving hundreds of thousands of mentally ill people to fend for themselves (National Alliance to End Homelessness, 1991:12).

While the homeless are a significant social problem in their own right, they are part of a much larger condition that characterizes the poorest of America's poor. These lowest elements of the lower class are now described as the American *underclass*. There is currently a raging debate over the composition and causes of the underclass.

The Underclass

Time magazine (1977:14–28) ran a cover story exposing the existence of an underclass composed of hopeless poor Americans, people who had been untouched by all efforts on the part of government to end American poverty. The underclass was described as a diverse group of people made up of somewhere between 7 and 10 million people who included discouraged workers and unemployed people who had given up looking for jobs and were no longer counted as unemployed in official statistics; some 2.4 million Americans who had been on welfare for longer than one year; people who were chronically unemployed; 2 million children living in poverty; and some 4.4 million disabled people, unable to work.

Time's article was immediately denounced by the Social Security Administration, which claimed that the underclass numbered no more than 500,000 to 4.4 million, less than half of the *Time* estimate. The debate over the size of the underclass has continued ever since. Ken Auletta (1982) wrote one of the first books on the underclass. He included in their number the passive poor—long-term welfare recipients; hostile, lower-class street criminals, largely school dropouts and drug addicts; hustlers—people who make their living in the unreported income sources of the "underground economy" by selling drugs, fencing stolen goods, prostitution, and other property-related, nonviolent crimes; traumatized poor people—including alcoholics, drifters, homeless bag ladies, and former mental patients.

The underclass is thought of as the permanent poor, a consequence of the increase in poverty and the concentration of poverty in inner cities. It is impossible to count their real numbers. The U.S. Census Bureau tracks samples of poor people for two years at a time, reporting that only 25 percent of people who are poor one year are poor the next. The underclass makes up approximately 8 percent of all welfare recipients (Gilbert & Kahl, 1993:285; Wilson, 1987).

The Nature of the Underclass

Are the permanent poor really the underclass? That depends on how the underclass is defined. If the underclass is viewed as people without access to jobs that will lift them out of poverty, then the above profile fits this economic notion of the underclass. However, if the underclass is perceived as people with flawed moral characteristics, high school dropouts, single mothers, welfare dependents, and unemployed persons who live in inner-city neighborhoods with high rates of such deviance, then there were about 7 million underclass people in 1992.

Given that few writers agree on a definition of the underclass, it is impossible to measure their exact numbers. The definitions given thus far are reminiscent of the definitions of art or pornography. People claim to know it when they see it. However, this has not stopped anyone who has written about these concepts from analyzing what causes underclassness or poverty in general.

Poverty and Policy Failure

Both conservatives and liberals have had their turn in creating American social welfare policy for over a century. Both have failed miserably. The conservatives in both Europe and the United States have always displayed a great contempt for the poor, and have, since the French Revolution of 1789, seen them as a criminal, "dangerous" class (Krisberg, 1975:

The character "Two Face," played by Tommy Lee Jones in the *Batman Forever* film, is typical of the stereotype of early Hollywood villains, suggesting that evil people were also physically unattractive.

151). By 1800, European society was largely convinced by the work of Franz Joseph Gaul (1776–1832) that the lower class has different skull shapes than the rich, and that these abnormal skulls are a reflection of abnormal brains. Doctors who treated the poor in public hospitals soon discovered "wolf-man" and "lion-man" head shapes. They assembled charts that were used to classify prisoners well into the twentieth century.

Artists began portraying the poor as physically ugly public drunks, ragpickers, and hunchbacks. This association of the poor and violent criminals with physically ugly features carried over into comic strips like "Dick Tracy," and in movies from the 1920s to the 1950s villains were portrayed as physically grotesque. Physically deformed villains also appear in 1990s movies like Jim Carey's *The Mask*, and the 1995 blockbuster *Batman Forever* (Tommy Lee Jones' "Two Face" character).

One of the leading voices in this effort was that of Sir Francis Galton, Charles Darwin's cousin. Darwin's work, *The Origin of Species* (1859), had argued that life on earth survived by an evolutionary process based on the survival of the fittest. Darwin wrote about a struggle for survival between animal species, and why different species become extinct. However, Darwin's notions were soon distorted and applied to human behavior.

Galton concluded that white people were by far the superior racial group in the world, and that if people were bred in the correct manner, the white race would produce even more superior beings (mentally and morally). His method for producing this superior race was termed eugenics and involved breeding people as if they were dogs or horses.

In the United States, Darwin's theory was embraced by the upper classes, who, at the time, were a group of wealthy capitalists known as the Robber Barons. These men had engaged in bribery, theft, murder, sabotage, and violence against factory and railway workers in order to establish the corporate monopolies that ultimately became today's transnational conglomerates.

Conservative Policy Failure

Early conservative policy toward the poor was predicated, not on public welfare, but on the notion that the poor, being biologically (if not racially) inferior, had no business reproducing themselves. The vice-president of the Boy Scouts of America advocated that the Boy Scout movement be used to breed a superior human being. At many county fairs in the Midwest blue ribbons were presented to families who had produced what were judged the best pedigrees, and such awards were given along with those for prize cows and pigs.

Meanwhile, eugenicists in the United States began lobbying for passage of sterilization laws. Favorite targets of sterilization included criminals, epileptics, people who scored low on newly created intelligence tests, and newly arrived immigrant group members, "beer smelling Germans, ignorant Bohemians, uncouth Poles, and wild-eyed Russians," as the New York *Times* called them (Howard & Rifkin, 1977). By 1931, more than thirty American states had passed laws allowing for the surgical removal of the sex organs of deviants ranging from chicken stealers and bomb throwers to auto thieves.

What proved the undoing of the eugenics movement was the Great Depression of 1929 and its aftermath. With America's financial elite going broke and committing suicide and middle-class professionals and academics standing in unemployment lines alongside poor immigrants and blacks, the myth that certain groups were biologically superior lost credibility (Rifkin & Howard, 1977:21).

Unfortunately, the "biology is destiny" thinking has reappeared. The director of the federal Alcohol, Drug Abuse, and Mental Health Administration, Frederick Goodwin, told an advisory panel that only half of male monkeys reach adulthood because they are killed by other monkeys. Violence is the "natural" way for monkeys to kill each other and the monkeys who kill, like lower-class males, are also hypersexual. Perhaps calling some areas of the inner cities of America *jungles* is justified because they represent a retreat to a more natural evolutionary state.

Conservative views of the poor have centered on the notion that class is defined by culture, not economic position in society. In the 1970s, conservatives embraced the notion of the culture of poverty, a coping mechanism for those in chronic poverty. They suggested that poverty was caused by the values embraced by the poor, the inability to delay gratification, unstable family life, infidelity, and child abandonment (Muwakkil, 1994:22). This view holds that poverty is freely chosen, and accordingly the poor are to be blamed for their destitution.

Most recently, the culture-of-poverty thesis was updated during the Reagan-Bush years. The Reagan conservatives argued that the civil rights laws and antipoverty programs of the 1960s (which many conservatives opposed at the time) gave blacks legal access to American prosperity, almost completely eliminating poverty. They also claimed that the poor were overcounted due to a definition of poverty that was too liberal. However, conservatives claimed that liberal antipoverty legislation had also created welfare dependency, reduced the desirability of marriage, and increased benefits for unwed mothers with children (which, as noted earlier in this chapter, is untrue). Consequently, the attractiveness of low-status jobs (e.g., washing dishes for the minimum wage) declined, and, as a result, the poor did not want to work. Thus the work ethic had been undermined, and the poor demoralized by welfare (Katz, 1989:139).

The conservative solution to this problem is basically to motivate the poor by cutting welfare benefits, and making it harder to qualify for welfare. The Reagan administration eliminated the CETA job training program, a major source of jobs and job training for the poorest of the poor. AFDC and food stamps were slashed, and overall social welfare expenditures were cut 9 percent during the Reagan-Bush years. After 1981, any income that welfare recipients earned from jobs was deducted from welfare payments, making it virtually impossible to rise above poverty while on welfare. By 1984, there was a 30 percent increase in the number of people who lived in severe poverty, less than 50 percent of the officially defined poverty income level (Gilbert & Kahl, 1993:300).

Liberal Policy Failure

To their detriment, liberals have not been able to do better than conservatives in developing a workable social policy. When President Kennedy took office in 1961, there was a confidence among liberals that poverty in America could be ended. Poverty was not thought to exist during most of the 1950s, only to be "rediscovered" in 1958 with the publication of John Kenneth Galbraith's *The Affluent Society*. Galbraith argued that two types of poverty existed alongside of middle-class comfort. One category consisted of people who were poor because of personal conditions beyond their control: the handicapped, blind, those in poor health, and the mentally retarded. A second group of poor people lived in "islands of poverty" that remained unaffected by the economic prosperity of postwar America. Places like the Appalachian Mountains, rural America, and the inner cities were suddenly the targets of the attention of policy makers. However, none of Galbraith's views suggest a class of undeserving poor; nor did the other book that influenced the Kennedy administration's poverty program, Michael Harrington's *The Other America* (1962). Harrington, a democratic socialist, claimed there were 40 million poor people in the United States, and they were poor because of unemployment. The technological progress of the 1950s had actually made many people poor because of the lack of available jobs for people without many skills.

However, the Kennedy administration ignored Harrington's analysis of the causes of poverty, and simply prescribed a tax cut which was hoped would stimulate economic growth for everyone. For those in need, programs such as Medicare and Medicaid, food stamps, and Headstart were added during the Johnson years. Spending on all social welfare programs increased fourfold between 1960 and 1976. The effort became known as the War on Poverty.

The liberal attempt to end poverty allowed Reagan–Bush conservatives to declare that the program had worked and could now be scaled back. However, the problem of unemployment as a cause of poverty persists.

The Clinton administration has accepted many of the conservative precepts about poverty and welfare and has demonstrated little of the sympathy or optimism of the liberal administrations of the 1960s. Indeed, the culture of poverty theory has been accepted as fact, and the goal of policy has once again become to make the poor morally responsible rather than getting them out of poverty. President Clinton has vowed "to end welfare as we know it" (Amott, 1994:175). Consequently, the president proposed (and it is now a law), that welfare recipients should be allowed a maximum of only two years of benefits, after which they should be forced to take a job. This policy is called "workfare." Along with health benefits from a national health plan, education, job training and placement, the poor will be provided tax deductions, day care, and transportation. To be created as well is a "deadbeat databank," designed to rigorously enforce child support laws, although no one expects that getting fathers to pay child support will lift a substantial number of people out of poverty.

The great contradiction in this proposal is that it fails to provide a means of creating jobs that would enable the poor who are supposed to get off welfare. Workfare experiments are politically popular because they appeal to people's wish to end welfare dependency and encourage the work ethic. Yet no workfare program has yet lifted welfare mothers more than $2,000 above the welfare grant level (which is still below the officially defined poverty level)(Cloward & Piven, 1993:693). The most successful of these have raised employment rates and lowered welfare rolls by a paltry 7 percent (Gueron, 1993:40).

The Clinton policy would throw between 1.5 and 2 million people into a labor market where there are already between 10 and 12 million unemployed people (Amott, 1994:176; Cloward & Piven, 1993). In 1989, 11 million people, one of every seven workers, worked full-time jobs with incomes below the federally defined poverty level for a family of four. This certainly does not allow even full-time workers to be "self-sufficient."

Some experts estimate that AFDC mothers working at minimum-wage jobs, the only kind most of them qualify for, would have to be given $5000 worth of "free" medical care and other resources each year to supplement their incomes. This would cost $50 billion annually, an amount that Congress is most unlikely to spend (Cloward & Piven, 1993:694).

Summary

Defining poverty as a social problem means that its causes are located in the social structure of society, and therein is where its solution is located. As William Julius Wilson notes, joblessness in the ghetto has increased for a number of factors:

1. The loss of over 2 million manufacturing jobs has dramatically increased unemployment among black males. There are now few skilled and semiskilled blue-collar positions in big cities where blacks live.

2. The two-parent black family is disappearing because male joblessness had made marriage less attractive.

3. Both single-parent families and male unemployment have also increased among ghetto blacks because the black middle class has left the inner cities. Consequently, black inner-city schools have deteriorated, ghetto businesses have gone under, the police have less community support in fighting crime, job seekers have fewer people they can turn to help find employment, and there are no longer many role models for young black males (Wilson, 1987; Jencks, 1992:122).

In addition to these factors, Douglas Massey claims that residential segregation is a major reason for urban poverty. America's black neighborhoods are 77 percent segregated. Blacks are discriminated against when applying for mortgage loans, and lack opportunities to build home equity, live close to better jobs, occupy safe neighborhoods, and go to good schools. Segregation has resulted in increased social problems, especially crime and drug abuse, and a growing underclass (Moeberg, 1994:22–23).

There have been some studies testing these theories, and the results may be summarized as follows:

1. Black males do not suffer from a culture of poverty. What black males want are jobs and wages comparable to those of whites. The reluctance of black males to take low-status, dead-end jobs lengthens their periods of unemployment. Yet, black males are more willing to take dead-end jobs. The problem here is not a lack of aspirations, but blocked opportunities that prevent blacks from aspiring to the same success that nearly all Americans share: a good job with security, home ownership, and opportunities for their children.

2. Black youth often do not live near jobs for which they qualify, although the exact importance of this fact in black unemployment is not clearly understood at present. Moreover, black males have been substituted for by black females in manufacturing jobs. Black males also lack references for jobs.

3. Church attendance is also an important factor in escaping from poverty. However, the number of parents in a family is not. What is important is whether or not there are parents in the family who work. Taken together these studies demonstrate that the crisis of black youth is a function of a depressed labor market and racial discrimination (Katz, 1989:211–213).

The great problem with poverty is not poverty itself. The United States could easily solve its poverty and unemployment problems by making full employment, a decent job for all who wish to work, a national priority (Ellwood, 1988). This could effectively eliminate welfare for all able-bodied people. The odds of this happening are almost nil. Why? Because, as Herbert Gans (1991) and others have noted, poverty is useful for too many powerful interests in the United States.

1. Having a large pool of unemployed labor available keeps wages low, and assures that "dirty" work (low-status jobs) that otherwise would not be filled are occupied.

2. The poor, as this chapter has explored, are a dumping ground for the pathologies of American individualism. The poor are a measuring rod for status, they provide middle- and upper-class people with someone to look down upon.

This is very important in a society of equals where, in reality, no one wants to be just like everybody else. The poor provide a valuable scapegoat for the ills of society. The poor and their crime distract attention from deviance and crime in high places, and from other ills of the social structure. Politically right-wing politicians use the undeserving poor to promise simplistic solutions to complex problems, and, thereby, get elected. Crime is resolved by building more prisons and putting poor street criminals in them. Liberals can win the votes of the poor and those sympathetic to them by promising to reform welfare and end poverty.

3. The poor provide jobs for a wide range of occupations, from welfare workers to incompetent doctors, lawyers, and dentists. They are a market for second-hand goods and day-old foods. Much of the employment provided by the criminal justice system is about arresting, adjudicating, and incarcerating poor criminals. In these ways, the poor aid in the upward mobility of the nonpoor.

4. The poor help the nonpoor justify their position in society by being the recipients of charity. The charity work done by the upper class demonstrates their altruism and hence their superiority over others who engage only in money-making. The rich tend to become especially charitable after corporate or personal scandals when they want the public to think well of them. In other words, their charity sometimes serves as an inauthentic façade behind which deviance may go unpunished or continue.

5. The poor absorb a good deal of the social costs of "progress," often being displaced from their houses for the sake of freeways, urban renewal projects, mass transit, the expansion of hospitals, universities, and civic centers. The poor also provide the foot soldiers of the armed forces and are more likely to be drafted and die in war than the nonpoor. This was especially the case during the Vietnam conflict when middle-class college students could obtain draft deferments while the poor were drafted in large numbers.

6. Ending poverty is a real threat to the political power structure as well. People with income levels above the poverty line tend to vote in much larger numbers than do the poor. Providing poor people with good jobs would end the stereotype concerning the poor's unwillingness to work. This would also reveal the inequities in the American political economy, and might lead to widespread demands for a greater equalization of income, wealth, and power in America.

Of all of these functions, notes Gans, the hardest to do without concerns the poor's service as a class for all others to look down on. Poverty would not cost much to effectively eliminate. In fact, just using what is spent on social programs now to create decent jobs with a stable future would probably do the trick. This will probably not happen as long as the poor do not become too "dysfunctional" for the nonpoor. Thus if the poor become so destructive of their own or nonpoor people's neighborhoods, or begin victimizing the rich and powerful in great numbers, something meaningful may be done. The other circumstance that may lead to a sincere effort to end poverty is an outbreak of affluence for the nonpoor, as occurred in the 1960s. Barring these extremes, the poor will continue to be "with us," but we will not be "with them."

The other possibility of ending poverty could stem from a dramatic change in how Americans perceive their poor. A number of philosophers and religious leaders in recent years have emphasized that permitting poverty to exist in this country is immoral, and that being poor is inconsistent with basic human rights to which all people should be entitled (Katz, 1989). As the National Conference of Catholic Bishops notes, ending poverty is a matter of social justice. "The right to have a share of earthly goods sufficient for oneself and one's family belongs to everyone . . . Minimum material resources are an absolute necessity for human life. If persons are to be recognized as members of the human community, the community has an obligation to help fulfill these basic needs . . ." (Catholic Bishops of the United States, 1986:578–579).

Moreover, modern poverty researchers in Europe have criticized American ideologies for neglecting economic resources and political power as major causes of poverty. Americans may yet develop a sense of moral outrage at the persistence of hunger, homelessness, inadequate medical care, and other forms of deprivation. "[T]he substitution of human dignity, community, and the realization of democracy in place of classification" (Katz, 1989:238–239) of the poor into deserving and undeserving categories would be a humane step forward. This would require a major change of our vocabulary concerning the poor. We would no longer refer to "them" but "us" in a way that expands the American conception of citizens of a democracy with both economic and political rights. The goal of human rights would be to ensure that all citizens are encouraged to engage in enjoyable work and participate in their political system.

Perhaps the saddest reality concerning the suffering of the poor is that most of it could be ended quickly, if it were decided that, as President Clinton stated, "we cannot afford to leave anybody behind" as America progresses. This rhetoric has yet to be matched by reality.

Suggested Readings

Michael B. Katz (1989) *The Undeserving Poor: From the War on Poverty to the War on Welfare* (New York: Pantheon). A passionate, clearly written analysis of the contradictions regarding America's view of the poor and policies designed to help them.

The National Alliance to End Homelessness (1991) *What You Can Do to End Homelessness* (New York: Simon & Schuster). An inspiring work offering concrete suggestions on what any concerned citizen can do to personally help homeless Americans.

William Julius Wilson (1987) *The Truly Disadvantaged* (Chicago: University of Chicago Press). This is the most influential and sociologically oriented work on the nature of the inner-city underclass in America. This book won the C. Wright Mills Award given by The Society for the Study of Social Problems.

Exercises

Critical Thinking Exercise 10.1	Media Coverage of the Homeless

How are stories about the homeless covered in your local newspapers? This is an important question because, as the discussion in this chapter demonstrates, American society is highly conflicted about the homeless problem. We can't seem to make up our minds whether the homeless are worthy of our pity or our contempt. Stories that portray the homeless with pity might involve the following themes:

- There are not enough shelters to house the homeless in cold weather.
- The homeless are featured as victims of crime.
- The civil rights of the homeless are being abused.
- The homeless are suffering from a variety of illnesses (physical and mental).
- The homeless are hungry, out of work, and in need.

Stories that portray the homeless with contempt might include the following themes:

- The homeless are an irritant because they bother people by panhandling. Merchants believe the homeless keep customers away.
- The homeless are responsible for a good deal of criminal activity.
- The homeless are largely made up of people who are mentally unstable and/or addicted to drugs or alcohol.

Code each story using the above categories, and construct a table summarizing your results. Each article may contain more than one theme, and some may mix pity and contempt themes.

Select a sample of articles from your local paper. If your city has more than one paper, you might want to select articles so you can compare orientations. For brief in-class exercises, three to five articles should suffice. If this is to be a term project, between twenty-five and fifty articles per paper is desirable. Your instructor will let you know what constitutes an acceptable sample size.

Critical Thinking Exercise 10.2	Media Coverage of the Homeless

Students may also wish to compare the orientation of their local papers with those of the New York *Times,* Washington *Post, Wall Street Journal, USA Today,* or other large-circulation newspapers, or compare the orientations of news magazines, like *Time, Newsweek,* and/or *U.S. News & World Report,* or news magazines and newspapers.

A sample coding sheet is provided on the next page, as well as a sample table. What is the dominant orientation of the local papers?

Coding Sheet: Homeless Articles

Newspaper:

Date:

Article Number:

Pity Themes:

- There are not enough shelters to house the homeless in cold weather.
- The homeless are featured as victims of crime.
- The civil rights of the homeless are being abused.
- The homeless are suffering from a variety of illnesses (physical and mental).
- The homeless are hungry, out of work, and in need.

Contempt Themes:

- The homeless are an irritant because they bother people by panhandling. Merchants believe the homeless keep customers away.
- The homeless are responsible for a good deal of criminal activity.
- The homeless are largely made up of people who are mentally unstable and/or addicted to drugs or alcohol.

Number of Pity Themes:

Number of Contempt Themes:

Overall Rating of Article:

Pity: Contempt: *Mixed/Other:

*Mixed articles are those with an equal number of pity and contempt themes, or articles whose orientations do not fit into either of the above categories.

Coding Sheet: The Homeless

Newspaper:

Story #:

Date:

Pity:

Contempt:

Continued on next page

Exercise 10 Continued

Table 1
Results of Newspaper Article Ratings

NEWSPAPERS

"Pity"-Oriented Stories:	65
"Contempt"-Oriented Stories:	30
Mixed/Other:	5
	100
	★(N = 25)

*N indicates the actual number of cases, as opposed to percentages.

The Sociology of Oppression: Problems of Race and Ethnicity

Chapter · Chapter · Chapter · Chapter · Chapter · 11

Oppression and
the Sociological Imagination

Within the sociological imagination paradigm a central focus is the conflict between the world's haves and have-nots. Many of the world's have-nots tend to be members of racial and ethnic minority groups. The mechanism by which the have-not status of minorities is maintained is called oppression. Otherwise defined, **oppression** is a process that takes place over time, and involves one or more groups within a culture systematically and successfully preventing other groups within that culture from attaining the scarce and valued resources (Turner et al., 1984:1–2). These resources include:

- **Material resources**—property, income, and the educational opportunities and employment necessary to achieve material gain.

- **Political power**—access to political office, and the processes necessary to gain political power (like voting, campaigning, and running for office).

- **Positive cultural values**—the access to means of communication and persuasion necessary for the group to gain equal opportunity to acquire material resources and political power. Such values include recognition of the oppressed group's contributions to society and the development of a positive sense of self-esteem among its members.

From a sociological imagination viewpoint, oppression is about acts of physical, financial, and moral harm that function to keep oppressed groups from acquiring the scarce resources involved in the conflict between the haves and the have-nots. Perceived this way, oppression is a harmful form of social stratification. Oppressed groups are prevented from gaining access to opportunities that would allow them to move up the social class ladder on the basis of characteristics that have little to do with class (Miller, 1992:73). Oppression is also related to status.

The pioneer sociologist Max Weber pointed out that much of oppression is about status groups. A **status group** is one whose members share certain qualities to which positive or negative honor is attached. Members of status groups are singled out for unusual treatment, which may be either positive (receiving social rewards) or negative (receiving social control and denied social rewards). Positive status groups include celebrities like those who appear in *People* magazine, or on "Lifestyles of the Rich and Famous." Positive groups can also include members of specific professions, like doctors and lawyers. These are the people who succeed in America (Walton, 1993:179). This chapter is not about the celebrities among us. It is about those groups singled out for negative treatment.

Typically, groups singled out for negative status include:

- **Racial groups**—A race is a population with a distinct set of identifiable physical characteristics. Races are usually set apart by their skin color, the shape of their eyelids, noses, or other features. Sociologically, race is important only because a given society believes that it is, and often treats members of racial groups based on certain beliefs about that race. In other words, race is not a biological concept, but an ideological one used to oppress nondominant peoples (Hacker, 1992: Chapter 1).

African Americans own only .5 of 1 percent of America's wealth. Most is owned by white Anglo–Saxon Protestants like Donald Trump. In the past twenty years, it has become fashionable to make showy displays of one's riches, contributing to the envy of those on the bottom of society.

Many Americans think that nonwhite minorities form a majority of the American poor. In truth, two-thirds of Americans in poverty are white, and many live in dilapidated rural housing, like the family pictured here.

- **Ethnic groups**—an ethnic group, like Jewish Americans, Irish Americans, Puerto Rican Americans, and so on, is a subgroup in a larger society that has a common set of cultural traits and values. Accordingly, members of an ethnic group are usually of the same religion, eat distinct foods, and have their own festivals and holidays. There is a sense of community and identity with a common heritage and history, as well as a feeling of uniqueness among group members. Ethnicity is an ascribed status; one is born and raised within an ethnic culture (Marger, 1994:34–35).
- **Gender groups**—especially women.
- **Age groups**—the young and the old.
- **Sexual orientation groups**—especially male homosexuals and lesbians.
- **The physically and/or mentally impaired.**

While it is these characteristics that will concern us in this chapter and the next, any characteristic can serve as a basis for being singled out by society. The persecuted have included people who practice witchcraft, people who believe in flying saucers, prostitutes, drug addicts, criminals, people who once attended meetings of left-wing groups, and so on. What is important is not the groups' physical or cultural characteristics, but society's response to them.

The harms of oppression begin when a group, due to its physical or cultural characteristics, is singled out for differential and unequal treatment. Those groups that are so differentiated are called **minorities.** Minorities are not necessarily defined as small numbers of people. For example, women comprise 52 percent of the American population, yet are victimized in employment, lack political power, and live in fear of being raped and otherwise socially controlled by male-dominated institutions. Blacks in South Africa outnumber whites nearly four to one, but for decades could not vote, were victimized by police atrocities, and lacked access to all manner of educational and job opportunities.

The Techniques of Oppression: Prejudice and Stereotypes

Oppression is made up of a variety of techniques that function to maintain the domination of one group over another. These techniques begin with **prejudice,** preconceived judgments about an entire group made without being tested against reality. These are emotional biases, usually involving generalized favorable judgments about the positive and negative moral and intellectual capacities of one's own group and the negative moral and intellectual capacities of other groups (Pettigrew, 1980; Allport, 1988). Often prejudice is based on erroneous images called **stereotypes** that function to reinforce the negative values and beliefs users have about minority groups. Once these beliefs are learned, individual members of minority groups are judged according to generalized stereotypes. The mass media, especially television and movies, spread such negative images throughout mass societies. As C. Wright Mills noted "the members of the masses . . . know one another only as fractions in specialized (environments): the man who fixes the car, the girl who serves your lunch, the saleslady, the women who take care of your child at school during the day. Prejudgement and stereotype flourish when people meet in such ways. The human reality of others does not, can not come through. . . . It is for people in such a narrow (environment) that the mass media can create a pseudo-world" (Mills, 1956:320–321) filled with the stereotypes that separate and alienate people in mass societies.

Stereotypes become part of the culture of an entire society, an important element of the social character of both the dominant and minority groups. Almost everyone learns them through the mass media. What minorities lack is the power to counter the creation of stereotypes. The first study of oppression, done in 1933 at Princeton University, involved a sample of one hundred Princeton students. This elite group held many stereotypes about minorities. Most thought Jews were shrewd, mercenary, and ambitious. They saw blacks as superstitious, happy-go-lucky (not serious), and lazy (Marger, 1994:80ff).

The results of this study tell us some important things about stereotypes. Nearly any characteristic can be viewed positively or negatively. Being ambitious is generally considered a precondition for success in America, unless a minority group displays it. Then ambition becomes associated with greed, scheming, secrecy, and a host of additional unfavorable traits. Also, being thrifty is good, but if thrift is associated with a minority, it is called miserliness. Generosity degenerates into being a spendthrift. Intelligence becomes manipulation and deceit. There is no end to which traits and behaviors can become part of a stereotype.

One of the most interesting features of stereotypes concerns how and why they change over time. Initially oppressed groups, like African slaves and women, are often stereotyped as innocent, childlike, and even infantile. The stereotype of the minority group member as a child lasts as long as the oppressed group stays in its place, and does not cause problems for dominant groups.

Likewise, the childlike stereotype of the black slave was like the character Prissy from Margaret Mitchell's *Gone with the Wind,* a black child who was not competent to function without the help of her white master. In fact, slavery was originally justified as critical to the very survival of blacks.

As long as oppressed groups accept being stereotyped as incompetent, they are not violently oppressed most of the time. After all, if one is a child, one should not be killed for one's misbehavior, but rather disciplined. Infantile treatment is directly related to a group's docile behavior.

However, if a group's behavior becomes uppity, rebellious, or protest oriented, the stereotype of that group rapidly changes. Instead of being infantile, the group is now dehumanized, and labeled subhuman. Usually the dehumanized stereotype takes the form of an animal, a witch, or a devil. Since wild animals and devils are threats, they can be killed.

All this means that the oppressed are in a **double bind**; no matter how they behave, it is wrong. Marilyn Frye (1992:54) has perceptively argued that the root of the word *oppression* is press, as to be pressed into military service, or to press a pair of pants. "Presses are used to mold things or flatten them, or reduce them in bulk. . . . Something is pressed when it is caught between or among forces and barriers which are so related to each other that jointly they restrain, restrict, or prevent the thing's motion or mobility. Thus oppressed peoples are caught in the middle of forces that offer them few choices, any one of which expose the oppressed to penalties, deprivation, or censure. Whether treated like children or dehumanized as beasts, devils, or witches," the oppressed are never viewed as equals, and this is the essence of the double bind described by Frye.

They are supposed to smile and be cheerful, docile, and invisible to those in power. Anything but the sunniest of dispositions results in oppressed peoples being labeled as mean, difficult, dangerous, which can result in rape, arrest, beating, and murder.

Television and movies are full of role models of minority stereotypes, and these images change over time. Once blacks began to be featured in television programs, they were almost always presented as poor and disadvantaged. There are now numerous studies of virtually every oppressed minority's treatment by the media, and the results are not encouraging:

To illustrate, for decades, American Indians were portrayed in movies as savage barbarians, and no distinctions were made between the various tribes. Until films like Kevin Costner's *Dances with Wolves* (1990), Native Americans were constantly portrayed as vicious, lazy, cruel drunks who were lazy, stupid, and uncommunicative (except for grunts).

Similarly, Arabs are customarily pictured as wealthy barbarians, sex maniacs with a lust for white women and a love of terrorism (Shaheen, 1984).

Stereotypes serve an extremely valuable function for oppression. The U.S. Constitution and the Declaration of Independence guarantee equal rights to all Americans, regardless of any status characteristics. However, stereotypes are crucial in that they allow dominant groups to oppress minorities, despite the notion of political equality under law. Otherwise stated, stereotypes are part of an ideology that justifies the great contradiction that causes oppression, namely, unequal treatment in an egalitarian society.

One of the most disturbing aspects of contemporary stereotypes is that they are now such an accepted aspect of American popular culture. Minorities, women, gays, and lesbians are the favorite targets of entire segments of show business. For example, in heavy metal music, 20 percent of the lyrics mention forced oral sex at gunpoint, ice pick murders of minorities, forced anal penetration, and satanic murders. Moreover, women in these and many rap songs are referred to as "bitches" and "whores" (Levin & McDevitt, 1993:36–38). Political figures have also played on stereotypical views of minorities in recent years. Right-wing Senator Jesse Helms of North Carolina, during his 1990 reelection campaign, ran a series of ads showing a white hand crumpling up a job rejection notice, implying that a minority was given the position due to affirmative action. George Bush's 1988 presidential campaign ran a series of ads showing black parolee Willie Horton, and exaggerated the types and number of crimes committed by Horton after being furloughed from prison. The ads probably perpetuated the stereotype of blacks as violent, and helped convince white voters that Bush's opponent, Michael Dukakis, was "soft" on crime.

Whatever characteristic is selected as the basis of negative special treatment, all differential treatment of minorities is justified by an ideology. One of the most important ideologies in modern America is racism. **Racism** is an ideology, belief system, designed to justify or rationalize the unequal treatment of members of socially defined racial groups. Racial groups are physically different, and they are also perceived as possessing different (inferior) personalities, behaviors, and intelligence levels than dominant groups. The ideology of racism is actually a recent development in history. Race as a social category strongly emerged only about 250 years ago during Europe's founding of colonies. At that time nonwhites and European whites came into direct contact with each other for the first time. Europeans and American colonists conquered and exploited Africans, many of whom (about 20 million) were kidnapped and brought to America as slaves.

Once nonwhites were enslaved, racial categories were invented by whites and given pseudoscientific validity by whites. For example, a slave who attempted to run away was considered mentally ill. Blacks and many other groups were often judged mentally retarded or unintelligent because they could not pass intelligence tests created by English-speaking whites. Most of the time, the minority groups tested neither spoke nor read English, and thus could not even understand such tests (Duster, 1990).

The stereotypes and ideologies created to justify negative treatment of minorities result in minorities becoming **inferiorized,** defined as of poorer quality than dominant groups. Inferiorization is in and of itself a serious form of moral harm. Once a minority group can be portrayed as morally or intellectually inferior through stereotyping, that group is dehumanized, or viewed as less than human. Once a group is dehumanized, almost any sort of special handling can be justified. Dehumanization of minorities opens the way for two interrelated types of physical, financial, and moral harms to occur. These include discrimination, and a complex of negative reactionary responses by minorities to the oppression caused by discrimination.

Discrimination

Discrimination consists of the acts evidenced in the negative special treatment of minorities. These are the forms of social harm that maintain the domination of one group over another. Acts of discrimination consist of acts of physical, financial, and/or moral harm committed by prejudiced individuals or institutions. There are a wide variety of these acts (Pettigrew, 1980):

1. **Slur language** is used to describe minorities. Jews are kikes, blacks are niggers, and the like. Derogatory slurs can also include pejorative references. In business one can Jew someone down, or be gyped (from *gypsy*), or be an Indian giver (untrustworthy, take back what one has given or promised).

2. **Social distance** involves degrees of avoidance of minorities. Social distance is a measure of intimacy that people are prepared to maintain in their relationships with others. It involves feelings of unwillingness to accept or approve a given degree of intimacy in interaction with members of a minority (Williams, 1964:29). A scale designed to measure the social distance between various American groups was developed in the 1920s by sociologist Emory Bogardus, and has been used ever since. The scale involves asking people about their willingness to interact with members of particular groups under specific circumstances (Marger, 1994:83).

   • Are you willing to permit (name minority) to live in your country?
   • Are you willing to permit (name minority) to live in your community?
   • Are you willing to permit (name minority) to live in your neighborhood?
   • Are you willing to permit (name minority) to live next door to you?
   • Are you willing to permit your child to marry a (name minority) (Babbie, 1989:407)?

   Each question presents an increasing degree of intimacy, and each answer is usually assigned a numerical value. Social distance studies from the 1920s to the 1970s in the United States have shown more or less stable scores regarding different minority (ethnic and racial) groups (Marger, 1994:83–86). White Anglo-Saxon Protestants (WASPS) are the most tolerated, racial-ethnic minorities such as Jews, blacks, Asian Americans, and Native Americans the least tolerated.

3. **Segregation, denial of opportunities,** and **economic exploitation**—these forms of discrimination are interrelated, and frequently used together. They are the usual mechanisms by which minorities are kept in their place by dominant groups. These are the most prevalent forms of institutional discrimination today, and are discussed throughout this chapter. Historically, virtually every ethnic and racial group immigrating to America in the nineteenth century was victimized by segregation, occupational discrimination, and exploited as a source of cheap labor. Usually ethnic immigrants were confined to white ghettos in urban areas, and allowed to work only as factory workers and domestics. As noted below, many of these practices continue today.

4. **Threat** or **physical attack** is a sadly frequent form of discrimination in America. There has been a sharp increase in so-called hate crimes, criminal acts motivated by prejudice, by individuals against African Americans, gays, Jews, and Hispanics, in the last few years. Between 1984 and 1989 the number of hate crimes reported to the New York City Gay and Lesbian Task Force

increased 300 percent, and the number of such crimes continues to increase. Synagogues have been painted with swastikas; civil rights organizations' headquarters firebombed; gays and African Americans set on fire, shot, kicked to death, and assaulted (Leonard, 1990:9-A). These crimes are not motivated by economic gain, drugs, passion, or provocation. They are committed for no reason but hated of other people's skin color, religion, sex, or sexual orientation.

Types of Discrimination

There are two basic types of discrimination. They are: (1) **individual discrimination**— discriminatory actions of individuals or groups of individuals in response to feelings engendered by prejudice; and (2) **institutional discrimination**—the systematic exclusion of people from equal access to and participation in a particular institution or institutions because of their minority status (Kornblum, 1993:455). Most of the time, institutional discrimination arises from established ways of doing things, from customary routines, rules, and procedures in organizations. The U.S. Commission on Civil Rights (1981:11) identified a number of institutionalized forms of discrimination:

- Unnecessary height and weight requirements geared to the physiques of white males, which exclude females and certain minorities from certain jobs.

- Seniority rules applied to positions historically held by white males make more recently hired women and minorities subject to layoffs—the last hired, first fired syndrome—and also make them less eligible for advancement.

- Restrictive leave policies, along with limitations on part-time jobs or denial of fringe benefits to part-time workers, make it difficult for heads of single-parent families (largely women) to obtain and keep positions and take care of their families.

- Using standardized academic tests or criteria, geared to middle-class and/or white male culture. Often these tests are not reliable indicators of job success.

- Bank and lending institution credit policies denying mortgage loans to married women and minorities previously denied the opportunity to establish good credit ratings in their own names.

Institutional discrimination can be intended or unintended. If a corporation has an unwritten but explicitly understood policy not to hire African Americans, this is intended institutional discrimination. However, if a corporation chooses to shut down a factory in an inner-city ghetto and relocate to suburbs or overseas, denying African Americans access to job opportunities, this is unintended institutional discrimination. Either way the discriminatory actions of *institutions* result in denying minorities valued rewards. Individual discrimination is almost always intentional, and relates to the implementation of prejudicial attitudes. A family may refuse to sell its home to an African-American couple because the neighbors are afraid integration may bring a decline in property values. If this attitude is widespread enough, a segregated society results.

By contrast, institutional discrimination over time can result in what has been termed **interinstitutional practices** that maintain an overall pattern of oppression (Blaunner,

A surprisingly large number of Americans (about 25 percent) believe that America should be reserved for white Christians, and that all those who are different do not constitute "real" Americans. Many of these prejudiced people display the characteristics associated with the authoritarian personality, part of which includes the belief that those who are racially different are biologically inferior to whites.

1972:185). This is a complex form of institutional discrimination that results in minorities being treated like they are members of colonized populations. The riot that followed the acquittal of the four Los Angeles police officers in the Rodney King beating in 1992 probably stemmed from the African Americans in south central Los Angeles feeling trapped in self-perpetuating circumstances caused by a long history of discrimination and poverty (Blaunner, 1989).

A lack of educational opportunities means that minorities end up with low skilled jobs, which, when combined with employment discrimination, limits incomes. Low incomes and discrimination in housing ensure that African Americans will end up in heavily segregated ghettos, sometimes with inadequate public services like mass transit, making it difficult to look for work. In minority neighborhoods, schools rarely motivate students, especially those from dysfunctional family lives. Dropout rates are higher than in more affluent neighborhoods, setting the stage for the next generation to continue living in poverty. Young people in these neighborhoods often exhibit low self-esteem and little attachment to their neighbors and/or the dominant society. They may join gangs and be perceived by the outside world as innately violent. The police typically patrol ghetto neighborhoods, often harassing young African-American men, who not infrequently face police brutality (as in Rodney King's case) (Chambliss, 1994). These circumstances combined with frequent arrests can result in the type of riot that occurred in 1992.

Alienation, Social Character, and the Fruits of Oppression

Stereotyping constitutes a major form of dehumanization. Oppressed minorities are frequently viewed as less than human by their oppressors. People who are viewed as less than human by the dominant culture react to being systematically alienated in a variety of ways. In other words, being dehumanized is perceived by oppressed groups with different attitudes, and these various attitudes influence reactions to oppression by the oppressed.

Psychologist Gordon Allport relates that every form of ego defense may be found among members of every persecuted group. "Some handle their minority group membership easily, with surprisingly little evidence in their personalities that this membership is of any concern to them. Others will show a mixture of desirable and undesirable compensations. Some will be so rebellious . . . that they will develop many ugly defenses" (Allport, 1988:140). These negative responses may include any or all of the following:

1. Oppressed groups may suffer **mental illness** from the anxiety, fear, suspicion, and insecurity caused by aggressive acts of dominant groups. Jews, for centuries, were the subjects of European pogroms in which they were frequently kidnapped, murdered, or otherwise exploited. The fear of such episodes sometimes caused Jewish mothers to overprotect their children. Jewish women lived in a state of constant anxiety regarding the threat of aggression.

2. **Denial,** by oneself and others, concerning actual membership in the minority group is common. Thus many gays are still afraid to come out of the closet, that is, publicly acknowledge their own sexual orientation. Many Jews converted to Christianity and changed their names so as not to appear Jewish. Light-skinned blacks frequently rejoice in the option of being able to pass for white in racist cultures.

3. **Social withdrawal** and **passivity** are a frequent response to oppression. Severely alienated members of oppressed groups learn to act passively in the face of oppression. They become fatalistic, convinced they have no chance of making it in the white man's world. Withdrawal into alcohol and/or drugs sometimes follows. Drug addiction becomes an escape from feelings of inferiority and fatalism so that there are no chances of becoming successful in a world dominated by those who hate you.

4. **Clowning, acting like the court jester** in order to be accepted by the dominant group, is frequently seen. American blacks have historically adopted a happy-go-lucky mask designed to convince whites that they will not cause trouble that might result in their being lynched. This functional defense mechanism allowed many blacks to survive life in the American South between the end of the Civil War and the passage of the Civil Rights Acts of the 1960s. Blacks who acted funny and simpleminded were stereotyped as dumb—an image that allowed them to survive in a threatening society.

5. **Slyness** and **cunning**—Members of oppressed minorities sometimes become thieves and con artists in order to get back at dominant group members and merely survive economically.

6. **Identification with the aggressor**—Not only do dominant groups believe the stereotypes about minorities, much of the time, so do the minorities themselves. By identifying with the dominant groups, members of minorities come to believe in their inferiorization and, consequently, resent themselves and members of their own group. For example, it is not unusual for a Jew to be prejudiced against other Jews, believing them to be selfish, deceitful, and so on.

7. **Blaming the victim** is an extremely destructive form of identifying with the dominant group. Self-hatred is turned against members of one's own group by committing violent acts against them. Most of the victims of minority crime, including homicide and rapes, in the United States are other minorities.

8. **Discriminating against other minorities**—Minority oppression frequently sets one minority group against another, and this is used by the dominant majority as a technique of domination. Tension between African Americans and Jews has been high in the United States for nearly two decades now. In Palm Springs, California, black and Mexican-American gangs war with each other over the struggle to become kings of the bottom of Palm Springs society. They disrespect each other and refuse to come to a truce over territorial considerations.

9. **Excessive neuroticism** is especially common among homosexuals and lesbians. Homosexuality can be denied, hidden, regretted, or accepted, but rarely can it simply be ignored. Gays frequently come to believe there is something morally and/or physically wrong with them. They are frequently deeply ashamed of their own sexuality, and become severely depressed, anxious, obsessed, and tortured by it.

10. **The self-fulfilling prophecy** involves believing in and acting out the very stereotypes created by dominant groups, and is one of the most serious moral harms stemming from oppression. The self-fulfilling prophecy operates in many areas of social life. Such prophecies begin with false premises that are made true by the actions stemming from the belief in them. During the Great Depression of 1929 and the ensuing years, rumors would frequently start that local banks were going to fail, and depositors would not be able to withdraw their money. These rumors would cause a run on the bank whereby large numbers of depositors would try to withdraw their funds. Unable to pay off everyone, the banks would then go out of business. Much the same logic operates among oppressed groups.

Minority groups who are treated like second-class citizens soon begin to act like their stereotypes. Denying African Americans unsegregated housing, decent schools, and well-paying jobs frequently causes them to give up hope, become extremely angry, and alienated from both the dominant group and

Thanks to the Civil Rights Acts of the 1960s, and other laws that have fostered increased equal opportunity for all Americans, there is now a sizable and growing African–American middle class, with good educations, incomes, and increased opportunity to gain political power.

their own group. The result is crime, prostitution, drug addiction, race riots, teen pregnancy, school dropouts, and host of other illegal and deviant behaviors. Accordingly, blacks fulfill the stereotype of being dishonest, untrustworthy, unintelligent, and violent.

11. **Excessive status striving**—Some minority members attempt to overcome the inferiority they feel by becoming workaholics. Once dehumanized by society, they dehumanize themselves by becoming compulsive workaholics. They strive so hard for success in competition with members of the dominant culture to substitute for the inferiority they feel. One problem here is that no matter how much they succeed, most can never shake the perceptions held by dominant groups. Successful blacks in America are nearly always referred to as black doctors (instead of just doctors, like whites), black authors, black athletes, and so on. Moreover, minorities who succeed in professions are often viewed with disdain by their own members. Successful minorities are sometimes viewed as having sold out to the dominant system, a perception that puts them in a no-win situation. Even success brings them dehumanized status.

Oppression can drastically affect the social character and feelings of alienation experienced by oppressed groups. It is, however, important to understand that those doing the oppressing frequently possess their own unique social character and forms of alienation.

The Authoritarian Social Character and Hate Crimes

Why is it that some people more than others are apt to hold prejudicial attitudes and exhibit discriminatory behavior? There are three interrelated theories that seem to explain this:

Frustration–aggression theory was developed by psychologists Dollard, Miller, and Doob (1939); this theory suggests that prejudice originates with the buildup of frustration. When frustration can not be released on its intended target, individuals experience a free-floating hostility that may be released against an available target, or scapegoat. For example, laid-off American auto workers begin smashing Japanese cars in public and even attacking Japanese-American citizens. They can not vent their anger against American auto executives who laid them off, so the Japanese American becomes an available target, especially when prejudiced individuals believe the stereotype of Japanese as sneaky, greedy, and manipulative businesspeople, who are threatening to buy up American business and land.

Projection is the process whereby people (minorities in this case) are accused of behaviors that prejudiced people can not accept in themselves. For example, African-American males have historically been accused by white southern males of uninhibited, even uncontrollable sexual behavior. Projection theory explains this claim as white male attraction to African-American females, an attraction that was frowned upon in southern society. So white males projected their own sexual feelings toward black females on to black males.

The authoritarian personality makes for a more specific explanation of prejudice than frustration and projection. The authoritarian personality is actually a type of social character that was developed in pre-Nazi Germany by psychiatrist Erich Fromm (1944), and later tested in the United States in a much-maligned study by Theodor Adorno and his colleagues (1950). Both studies found a consistent relationship (correlation) between prejudice against Jews and other minorities and a set of characteristics termed authoritarian. Authoritarian individuals are typified by:

- A blind, unquestioning obedience to people in positions of authority (submission) and a wish to dominate (hold authority over) others.
- A great fear of self-examination and inner thought (introspection).
- A tendency to project (blame problems on) minorities, who are regarded as inferior.
- A rigid belief in conventional sexual norms (virginity, heterosexuality, and post-marital sex).

- A fatalistic, paranoid attitude regarding a lack of personal power in the world and the existence of all manner of conspiracies based in minority groups, like Jewish bankers, homosexual recruitment of children, ecologists out to destroy capitalism, and so on.

- An aggressive ethnocentric posture toward all out-groups regarded as inferior. Ethnocentrism is a generalized distrust and resentment of groups that are different than one's own. Many authoritarians are thus prejudiced against any and all out-groups: blacks, Latinos, Jews, Asians, women, gays, and lesbians are the favorite targets of authoritarian prejudice and discrimination today.

- The frequent use of physical punishment in disciplining children, usually based upon frequent punishment at the hands of their own parents (Kornblum, 1994:449).

The authoritarian personality concept has been criticized for failing to tell us "how . . . prejudice and discrimination arise in the first place" (Marger, 1994:95). Moreover, the focus of the early authoritarian personality studies was on the most extremely prejudiced populations, like Ku Klux Klan members. In reality, prejudice and discrimination are usually more complex and less intense, not to mention characteristic of people whom we would not think of as extremists. Fromm (1944) found in his study of Hitler supporters that only about one-fourth of the German population could be characterized as authoritarian, and that many of Hitler's supporters were not particularly anti-Semitic.

However, in studies of authoritarianism between 1960 and 1990, a consistent pattern of authoritarianism has emerged along with some fundamental causes. Other studies have discovered an association between authoritarian attitudes and economic insecurity, low levels of education, lack of participation in political organizations, little reading, and physical punishment within the family (Dye & Zeigler, 1993:123; Lipset, 1963:87). The further down the class system one descends, the more one is likely to find a lack of acceptance of free speech, civil rights for minorities, religious freedom, due process, and homosexuality (McClosky and Brill, 1983).

Within this constellation of factors are the causes of prejudice. The poorest and least-educated members of both dominant groups (whites) and nonwhite minorities are more likely to experience scarcity of valued resources within their own lives. Accordingly, authoritarianism is most prevalent among the most deprived and oppressed members of nonminorities. Authoritarianism is highly associated with lower-middle- and lower-class status, belief in a fundamentalist religion, and an educational level below high school. Even among working-class people, those with high school educations or those with some college are significantly more tolerant of minorities, more supportive of civil rights, and more supportive of democracy in general (Kornhauser, 1959:33, 174). Moreover, people with authoritarian attitudes are usually politically apathetic (they don't vote). They also tend to be uninformed about political matters, but can be politically mobilized by extremist demagogues, such as David Duke or Jesse Helms, who appeal to their prejudices by blaming the nation's troubles on minorities. Being alienated from the culture's dominant institutions, they project their own failures onto scapegoats and away from the members of dominant groups who tend to rule the nation.

There is emerging evidence that this analysis is correct. Levin and McDevitt (1993) have provided an interesting analysis of hate criminals and their deeds. They point out that authoritarian personalities possess only a superficial attachment to their parents, who show them little love and a good deal of punishment, and, therefore, have likewise been dehumanized. Such people tend to treat other people like their parents treated them, and authoritarians tend to resent weakness displayed by oppressed groups, and resent the fact that minorities were helped by the social programs of the 1960s.

In the 1990s, out-groups are resented not only because they are being helped, they are also resented for being increasingly visible. There are more women in college, the workplace, and in important and powerful governmental jobs. Gays and lesbians have come out of the closet and lobbied heavily for funds for AIDS research. The demographic progress of blacks, Latinos, and other minorities is carefully monitored in government reports. Meanwhile, a shrinking economy has led to downward mobility for many former members of the white middle class, who increasingly perceive that minorities have taken jobs from them.

As a result of the scarcity of good jobs and the perception that the oppressed have been unfairly helped by government programs, authoritarian segments of the population have borne resentment against oppressed minorities. This resentment and authoritarianism are also associated with the explosive increase in hate crimes against minorities. **Hate crimes** are illegal acts of intimidation and violence committed against minority group members attributable to prejudice on the part of the perpetrator. Hate crimes are committed against people on the basis of their race, ethnicity, gender, religion, or sexual orientation (Sheffield, 1992:395). Hate crimes include all crimes classified by the FBI as violent crimes (murder, assault, nonnegligent manslaughter, forcible rape, and arson) as well as vandalism, destruction or damage of property, and intimidation of minorities. So numerous have these crimes become in the last decade that in 1990 President George Bush signed the Federal Hate Crimes Statistics Act, which requires the Justice Department to undertake a five-year statistical study on such crimes. Below are some reasons why such a study is needed. Between 1980 and 1986 the number of such reported crimes reached 3000 per year. In 1988, thirty state attorneys general reported that such crimes had dramatically increased in their states.

The Anti-Defamation League of the B'nai B'rith reported that the number of anti-Semitic hate crimes, ranging from desecration to murder, reached their highest point, in 1989, since the organization began collecting data in 1979.

Various hate crimes were reported on 130 college campuses in 1986–1987, a dramatic increase over prior years. The hate crimes reported to police tend to have other distinct characteristics:

- They are excessively brutal. Half of all hate crimes in one study involved physical assault (versus 7 percent of all other crimes nationally). Of these, almost 75 percent of hate crimes resulted in serious injury to the victim (versus just 29 percent of nonhate crimes). Thus the force involved in such crimes is beyond what is necessary to make victims comply.

- Victims tend to be randomly selected strangers. Over 80 percent of victims are unknown to their assailants (nationally, 61 percent of violent crimes are stranger-on-stranger episodes).

- They tend to be committed by multiple-offenders. Nearly two-thirds of hate crimes (versus one-fourth of all violent crimes) are committed by two or more people. This is dangerous because members of such groups are often young males who feel the need to prove themselves to each other, hence, the tendency for the violence involved to escalate.

Moreover, while all hate crimes share a common basis of resentment of minorities, there are different types and degrees of hateful acts (Levin & McDevitt, 1993:65–99). These include the following:

- Thrill hate crimes are usually committed by young men twenty years of age and under. This is a type of wilding in which sadistic young people look for vulnerable would-be victims in order to vent their aggression. In thrill crimes, which range from assault and rape to murder, minorities are frequently viewed as interchangeable. That is, if there are no niggers around a spic will do. If it is a rape, any white woman may serve as victim. Hate crimes for the young serve not only as fun, but also as a way to be accepted by a group who meets the emotional needs not fulfilled by their unloving, authoritarian parents. Moreover, today's young people are often profoundly confused, and easily persuaded, and, consequently, will do things as teens that they would not do as adults.

- **Personal threat hate crimes** are usually committed by adults who feel that minorities are invading their neighborhoods, taking their jobs, seducing their women, and so on. Personal threat hate crimes are committed as protection from encroachment by minorities, usually after a stern warning (racial slur) is perceived to have been ignored.

  To cite an example, in Galveston, Texas fishermen asked the Ku Klux Klan for help after some Vietnamese immigrants began to compete with them in the local fishing industry.

  And in Newark, Delaware, a black engineer attempted to move into an all-white neighborhood, only to find signs with "KKK" posted on his front door.

  About half of all violent crimes occur as a reaction to blacks and other racial minorities attempting to move into previously all-white working-class neighborhoods.

- **Mission hate crimes** are committed by individuals or organized groups that are out to rid the entire world of evil minorities who are threatening their way of life. Many of these individuals are psychotics, or paranoid individuals convinced they are receiving instructions from a leader. Mission hate crimes are committed out of a conspiratorial belief about the intentions of out-groups. The mission of these hate criminals is often suicidal.

  For example, in 1989, Patrick Purdy took his AK-47 rifle into a Stockton, California, schoolyard and opened fire on the children there. Purdy killed five children and wounded thirty others in an effort to rid his community of Asian immigrants.

Hate crimes are a serious social problem in the United States, and their effects on victims and would-be victims are explored in the "Private Troubles/Public Issues" forum on the following page.

Private Troubles   Public Issues

Hate Crimes on Campus

Hate crimes are on the rise on American college campuses, high schools, and even elementary and secondary schools, and, thus far, relatively little is being done about it. A 1990 Harris poll of 1865 high school students in public, parochial, and private institutions found some disturbing statistics. One-half of American high school students claim they have personally witnessed a racial confrontation, and one-fourth of those polled stated they have been targets of such attacks. Only one-third of the students claimed they were prepared to help the victims of hate attacks, but one-half claimed they would join in hate incidents, or agree that those being attacked deserve it.

Likewise, a 1991 Los Angeles *Times* poll of local elementary and high school students found that 37 percent of students had personally witnessed incidents of racial hatred within the last year (including 34 percent of elementary school students). The students reported that a wide variety of groups had been singled out as targets, including Arabs, blacks, Latinos, Asians, Jews, gays and lesbians. In 95 percent of cases, no organized hate groups, like the KKK, were involved. The acts were committed by prejudiced individuals.

These developments parallel the rise of hate crimes on college campuses as well. Between 1986 and 1989, 160 college campuses reported the occurrence of hate incidents. It is now estimated that 20 percent of all minority college students in the United States have either been verbally or physically harassed. The number of anti-Semitic incidents recently increased 30 percent in a single year.

- The Jewish student center at the University of Arizona was fired upon.
- Statements from Hitler's *Mein Kampf* appeared in the Dartmouth University student paper.
- The Hillel Foundation at Rutgers University was defaced with swastikas.
- A group claiming the Holocaust never happened took out an ad in a City University of New York student paper, although an editorial challenging the ad appeared in the same issue of the paper (CBS "60 Minutes," March, 20 1994).
- In some cases, college students have been victims of noncollege youths. One Vietnamese premed student was kicked to death by eight eighteen-to twenty-two-year-olds, none of whom were in college.
- During the 1991 Gulf War, a large number of Arab and Jewish students were targets of hate crimes.
- Chinese student reporters at the University of California at Davis received threatening phone calls after an effort failed by some student government members to cut off the funding of the campus' minority-oriented newspaper, *The Third World*.

Continued on next page

Private Troubles | Public Issues

There have been a disturbing number of bigotry incidents in college fraternities around the nation:

- Members of the Zeta Beta Tau fraternity at the University of Wisconsin put on a mock slave auction for which they painted their faces black, wore Afro wigs, and lip-synched Jackson Five tunes.

- At Oklahoma State University, one fraternity put on a plantation party during which members dressed as slaves and sang songs to sorority members.

- At the University of Cincinnati, one fraternity held a Martin Luther King trash party, where guests were asked to wear KKK hoods, carry boom boxes and welfare checks, and to bring your father, if you know who he is.

- One fraternity at Brown University issued party invitations announcing that only heterosexuals could attend.

- At Arizona State University, one fraternity forced its Jewish pledges to say: "My number is 6 million. That's how many Jews were killed, and I should have been one of them, sir."

- At Syracuse University, some fraternity members gave away T-shirts stating "Club faggots not seals!" and "Homophobic and proud of it."

The most frequent targets of campus hate crimes are gays and lesbians, in part because perpetrators believe homosexuals are so ashamed of who they are that they will not report such victimizations.

There are some things you can do to promote tolerance and understanding on your campus. Some of the most useful include the following:

The existence of minority organizations on college campuses is deemed essential by many social scientists. If you are a member of any of the minorities targeted for victimization on your campus, joining a support group composed of like-minded students is a solid idea. If one does not exist, why not start one? Perhaps you could be given credit for doing so as an exercise in sociology or some related class.

The Media Role in Authoritarianism

The mass media are not owned or controlled by working-class authoritarian personalities. Yet, it is the media that perpetuate stereotypes about all minorities. We maintain that the media elites display, not authoritarian traits, but *inauthentic* traits. **Inauthenticity,** in this sense, indicates, not a lack of prejudice, but no prejudices at all. Media elites project

Another useful form of collegiate organization concerns fraternities and sororities that are based on diversity, rather than sameness. If you are already a member of one of these organizations, you might inform your brother or sister members of the importance of diversity within your organizations. You also might want to start speaking out against racial and ethnic slurs, and derogatory songs that have become alarmingly popular within some Greek organizations. Likewise, if your fraternity brothers talk about women as objects of conquest, you might want to invite a speaker to discuss date rape in your fraternity.

Finally, it is very important that campus faculty and administrators do everything possible to promote a tolerant atmosphere on campus. The same is true for state and local political elites. Community leaders have supported the B'nai B'rith–sponsored program to reduce prejudice on some college campuses. You might want to get campus and community officials to support such events on your campus. The Anti-Defamation League has offices in most major metropolitan areas, and should be listed in your local phone book.

The mayor of Burlington, Vermont, led a tolerance rally on the University of Vermont campus after one fraternity kicked a discovered gay member out of its ranks. After finding the fraternity had discriminated against the gay student, a campus judicial board ordered the fraternity to apologize to the student, return his initiation fee, and hold educational programs for its members. The mayor also got a housing discrimination ordinance amended in 1990 prohibiting college fraternities from discriminating on the basis of sexual orientation.

At Brandeis University, students boycotted the college bookstore after black customers complained that they were carefully watched by store clerks. The boycott, which was supported by over seven hundred white students, succeeded in replacing the bookstore manager; additionally, a new system for handling complaints was instituted, more black students were hired, and a training program in racial sensitivity begun.

There are numerous civil rights organizations, like the NAACP, Urban League, ACLU, and National Gay and Lesbian Task Force, that will be happy to assist you in establishing programs for reducing prejudice on your campus.

Source: Levin & McDevitt, 1993:115–137, 228–229.

whatever images they believe will increase their profits, be they tolerant or racist images. As Robert Merton (1948) noted almost five decades ago, there are people who are not prejudiced, but who discriminate because they believe it is expected of them. In fact, during the 1950s, African Americans were hardly allowed on television at all because network executives were afraid of offending white southern audiences—not because they were racist.

In this sense, the social characters of some elites are amoral (without morals), when they assume their institutional roles. This amorality is precisely what makes elites so untrustworthy.

Oppression in America

The types and nature of both individual and institutional discrimination to which different minorities are subjected are varied and subject to changing historical conditions. In other words, not all minorities are oppressed in the same ways, nor to the same degree, nor at the same time. For example, African Americans frequently live in segregated neighborhoods, but women, unless members of a segregated minority group, may not. African Americans are no longer the victims of systematic institutional discrimination in the American South. For almost a century after the Civil War, African Americans were unable to drink from the same drinking fountains as whites, ride in the fronts of buses, eat in white restaurants, stay in all-white hotels, or attend all-white schools and colleges. The Civil Rights Act of 1964 and Voting Rights Act of 1965 remedied many of these conditions.

One way to measure the degree of oppression currently experienced by American minorities is to compare their annual incomes relative to those of American white males (arguably, America's dominant group). As Table 11.1 describes, there are vast differences in the incomes of American minorities relative to those of white males.

Table 11.1		
Median Annual Incomes of American Minorities Relative to White American Males		
YEAR	**1970**	**1992**
White Americans	$30,000	38,909
African Americans	18,260	21,645
Hispanic Americans	21,484	22,691★
Native Americans	N/A	13,678★

Source: U.S. Census Bureau (1993:457).
★Figure for 1989.

Two important facts are revealed in this table. First, the median incomes of minorities are about $10,000 less than those of white Americans. Second, over the last twenty years, the gap has not closed at all. In fact, the incomes of African Americans have fallen even further behind (from $11,740 dollars less in 1970 to $12,762 less in 1990). The gap between Hispanic Americans and whites has also increased (from $8516 less in 1970 to $8878 less than white median income in 1990). Moreover, the gap between Native Americans and whites is greatest of all, nearly $18,000 below the white family median income! Native Americans are indeed the poorest of the poor in America, and this fact is directly reflected in the rates from which they suffer from other social problems.

It is important to remember that the median income indicates the midpoint in income distribution, which means that half of African-American families live on less than $18,807, half of Hispanic-American families live on less than $22,691, and half of all Native-American families on less than $13,678. In other words, a substantial portion of families in these groups live below or near the federally defined poverty level. It also means that such groups suffer from high unemployment and underemployment rates. These facts are confirmed in Table 11.2.

Table 11.2

Poverty and Unemployment Rates Among Selected Minorities, 1992

GROUP	PERCENTAGE OF FAMILIES IN POVERTY	PERCENT UNEMPLOYED
White	7.1	6.5
African Americans	31.9	11.3
Native Americans	23.7	13.0★
Hispanic Americans	26.5	11.3

★Native-American figures are for 1989.

Table 11.2 reveals that poverty rates among minority families are at least three times higher than the poverty rate among white families. Poverty among African-American families is over four times higher than among white families, and Hispanic-American family poverty rates are nearly four times greater than that of white families. Likewise, if we use the standard of 10 percent unemployment as a beginning for economic depression, substantial numbers of the minority families described in Table 11.2 live in a state of economic calamity.

Native Americans: A Nearly Genocidal Existence

About 1500 A.D. there were 5 to 10 million members of Indian tribes living on the American continent. By 1900, there were fewer than 250,000. The native population had been the victims of violence by both white settlers and the U.S. government. In 1829, Congress passed, and President Jackson signed, an Indian removal law. In 1831, 13,000 Choctaw Indians were forcibly relocated from their Mississippi homes to points across the

Mississippi River. The government hired private contractors to oversee the relocation. The contractors charged the government as much as possible, but provided the Indians with as little as possible. Thousands died from pneumonia and cholera (Zinn, 1980:137–138). In many other instances, Indian lands were taken without compensation, treaties broken, and Indian women raped by white settlers. If the Indians fought back, as the Florida Seminoles did in the 1830s, they were arrested by the thousands (after signing peace treaties that ended the long Seminole War). In 1838, the U.S. Army enforced the Indian Removal Act of 1830 by rounding up 16,000 Cherokee Indians in the southern United States. The Cherokees were first forced into disease-ridden camps, then forcibly relocated to Oklahoma Territory. Some 4000 died on the way in the march. Three chiefs who signed the treaty allowing for the removal were found dead.

Finally, in 1887, the Dawes Act was passed. This made the Indians American citizens, and placed them under the protection of the U.S. government, which promptly segregated most of them on Indian reservations, where tribal lands were broken up and given to individual tribal members (Hagan, 1961). All in all, every treaty ever signed with Native Americans was broken, and American Indians were almost the victims of **genocide,** the systematic extermination of an entire group of people.

After nearly a century and a half of steady decline the Native-American population actually began to increase in the last five decades of this century. Between 1980 and 1990, the number of American Indians increased by 38 percent, to about 2 million (U.S. Census Bureau, 1993). Despite this increase, the world into which most Native Americans are born differs greatly from that of the white middle-class American. American Indians are the only minority that still has a separate agency of the U.S. government, the Bureau of Indian Affairs, that exclusively governs their lives. They are also the only minority over half of whose population (51 percent) is located in rural areas. Further, a number of studies indicate that many Native Americans living in urban and suburban areas would prefer to return to rural reservations which to them are home (Snipp, 1989).

The geographic isolation of Native Americans hides many of their worst social problems:

- Native Americans earn incomes substantially lower than those of other groups. Unemployment rates on Indian reservations average around 40 percent, and represent a major economic depression. Poverty rates range from 50 to 75 percent on reservations, and off reservations, Native-American poverty rates are significantly higher than those of whites, and are exceeded only by those among African Americans and Hispanic Americans (see Table 11.2).

- Native-American students have the highest school dropout rates of any ethno-racial minority in the United States. Their levels of educational achievement are among the lowest of any minority group. Only 7.7 percent of Native Americans have graduated from college (compared to 16.2 percent of the total population). Native Americans constitute only .76 of college enrollments and 53 percent of Indian-American college students in 1990 were enrolled in junior colleges, not four-year colleges (American Council on Education, 1991).

- The life span of the average Navaho is only forty-two years (compared to seventy-five years for the average American). One reason for this is that there are only ninety-six doctors and 251 nurses for every 100,000 Indians on reservations (compared to 208 doctors and 672 nurses per 100,000 white Americans). Rates of suicide and alcoholism on reservations are several times higher than the national average. Rates of infant mortality are at least three times higher than in the general population on reservations like Pine Ridge in South Dakota (Worsnop, 1992; Kilborn, 1992).

The social character of American Indians has been dramatically shaped by the poverty and hopelessness that stem from reservation life. Their living conditions and psychological outlook resemble those of previously conquered Third World peoples. Over two-thirds of housing on reservations is so dilapidated that it is beyond renovation, and nearly 15 percent of reservation dwellers lack proper sanitation and sewage and in-home water facilities (Harvey et al., 1990).

Federal programs designed to give Native Americans self-determination were cut drastically in the 1980s. Government assistance to Indian colleges was cut $200 per student, even though the costs of education rose 75 percent during these years. Most housing programs and appropriations for the Indian Health Service were either substantially reduced or totally eliminated.

Most reservation sites were established on unwanted lands that whites believed were worthless for farming, grazing, and other commercially profitable activities (Marger, 1994). America's 270 Indian reservations contain 5 percent of the natural gas and oil reserves, one-third of the low-sulfur coal, and half of all the privately held uranium in the United States. Native Americans on these lands live in fear that they will be cheated out of the ownership of these minerals, and there is much in American history that lends support to this suspicion.

African Americans

From the time the first ship came to America in 1619 carrying black slaves, blacks have always been singled out for differential treatment. They have been kidnapped and sold into slavery, and were unable to resist their own enslavement. Blacks, as slaves, are the only racial group that was forbidden to marry, to own books, to learn to read and write, and to inherit money. They are the only status group whose dehumanization was deliberately mentioned in the U.S. Constitution. For purposes of political compromise, each slave was counted as three-fifths of a person in the U.S. census.

In the United States, slavery was a calculated economic choice. Southern landowners had cheap agricultural labor in the black slaves. In the American North, slavery interfered with industrialization, and was abolished by 1800 in most places. The master-slave relationship was firmly established as a father-child dependency. Most slaves were used as field hands, and most were kept at a great social distance from whites, except for the relative few who were used as household servants, mammies (who raised white children), and concubines for male slave owners.

Post–Civil War Oppression

After the Civil War, African-American inferiority was viewed first as a product of slavery's legacy, and soon thereafter as a biological matter. Black cranial size (allegedly blacks had smaller brains than whites) was used to explain why blacks were of low intelligence and had failed to develop a civilized (Christian, sexually repressed) culture. In the North, many whites, including Abraham Lincoln, advocated that a separate black colony be established in Africa or the Caribbean (Marger, 1994:237).

Between 1865 and 1964, African Americans were rigidly segregated in both the North and South. In many places they were not allowed to vote, hold political office, attend white schools and colleges, or intermarry with whites. The system of rigged segregation in housing, education, employment, and politics began to crack somewhat during World War II. African Americans fought alongside white Americans in a war in which racial superiority was a major issue. The contradiction between America's guarantee of equality of rights and its treatment of its African-American population could no longer be ignored. In 1947, President Truman integrated the U.S. Army, and in the 1954 *Brown* v. (Topeka) *Board of Education* decision, the U.S. Supreme Court declared that separate schools for whites and African Americans were inherently unequal.

While little has been done to integrate most American public schools since the *Brown* v. *Board of Education* decision, it did mark the first time that the American justice system sided with African Americans on an important issue. The decision provided the motivation for the black civil rights movements to press for equality in accommodations, voting rights, and employment. After years of political struggle, the Civil Rights Act of 1964 and Voting Rights Act of 1965 made some of the worst forms of discrimination illegal (Polenberg, 1980:189–191).

The Post-Protest Era in Race Relations

Although since 1965 there has been a noticeable decline in the influence of the Ku Klux Klan and other extremist vigilante groups, African Americans still suffer many forms of oppression, some of which are difficult for whites to comprehend. For example, when white ethnic groups migrated to American cities in the late nineteenth centuries, there was a real need for manual and unskilled workers, especially male workers. This meant that two or more people from an immigrant family could obtain unskilled or factory positions, and make enough money to live. Many families even saved money for college educations for their children. In the America of the 1990s, even white-collar executives are being laid off in large numbers, and the need for unskilled labor is almost nonexistent. Moreover, unskilled workers are paid at rates below the poverty level. As a result,

- African-American incomes since 1955 have fluctuated between 58 and 66 percent of white incomes, with no trend toward greater improvement. Indeed, one of the most difficult aspects of life among African-Americans concerns the differences in economic opportunities for African-American men and women. The incomes of African-American women are higher than those of African-American men.

- There is strong evidence that, between 1965 and 1993, many African Americans were steered into segregated neighborhoods by Realtors who feared white flight to the suburbs. Moreover, many urban banks discriminated against blacks in mortgage lending practices. As Table 11.4 shows, African Americans are rejected by banks much more often than whites. In fact, even whites with incomes below the poverty level obtain mortgage loans more easily than well-to-do African Americans (69 percent approval for poor whites versus only 65.5 percent for nonpoor African Americans). Overall, blacks are rejected four times more often than whites (Knight, 1993:129). Many banks made no mortgage loans where property values were declining. Older homes deteriorated and were converted into multiple-occupancy rental units. Minority home buyers were ignored, and banks invested heavily in suburbs, where businesses and industries that left central cities were relocating.

- African Americans continue to lag behind whites in educational achievement. While rates of graduation from high school have dramatically improved among

Table 11.3

White and Minority Female Income Compared to White Male Income, 1970–1990

	1970	DIFFERENCE	1990	DIFFERENCE
White Males	$29,517		$28,541	
White Females	$17,157	−$12,400	$18,922	−$9,619
Black Females	$13,545	−$15,972	$17,389	−$11,152
Hispanic Females	$15,207	−$14,310	$15,662	−$12,879

Source: U.S. Census Bureau, and Ries & Stone (Eds.), 1993:353.

Table 11.4

Mortgage Loan Rejection Rates in Nineteen Major Cities, 1991

	CONVENTIONAL MORTGAGES	FHA-VA
Whites	14.4%	12.1%
African Americans	33.9%	26.3%
Hispanic Americans	21.4%	18.4%
Asian Americans	12.9%	12.8%

Source: Knight, 1993.

African Americans since 1960, the percentage of blacks graduating from college has shown no improvement for the past decade. In consequence, 82 percent of blacks and 87 percent of whites between twenty-five and thirty-four years of age have now graduated from high school. However, only 12 percent of African Americans, compared to 25 percent of white Americans, have graduated from college (U.S. Census Bureau, 1992). Moreover, the high school dropout rate among African Americans under eighteen is much higher than the dropout rate for whites of the same age groups. Conservatives continue to blame the lack of African-American educational achievement on genetic factors (Jensen, 1969, 1973), while liberals and some radicals see the entire educational system as inherently racist (Hacker, 1992; Bowles & Gintis, 1976).

- African-American children, especially those in poverty, face serious risks to their health. Almost 70 percent of African-American children from families with incomes below the poverty level have lead poisoning (compared with 38 percent of black children from families with incomes above poverty levels) (Weisskopf, 1993). Moreover, 46 percent of African-American children and 56 percent of Hispanic children are regularly exposed to toxic levels of carbon monoxide.

African Americans have a long history of discrimination within the American criminal justice system. Blacks have long complained that they are more watched by the police, more subject to police harassment, forced confessions, and miscommunications with police than any other group. Ghetto riots have been triggered over an initial incident with the police:

- In 1965, a highway patrol officer stopped a black motorist in the Watts section of Los Angeles. A small crowd of onlookers misinterpreted the reason the driver was pulled over, and a riot broke out that resulted in thirty-four deaths, 4000 arrests, and $35 million in property damage (Levin & McDevitt, 1993:160).

- The 1991 Los Angeles riot also started with a police incident, as an all-white jury acquitted four white police officers in the Rodney King beating. The Christopher Commission, established by L.A. Mayor Tom Bradley after the King beating to investigate the police department, found a pattern of institutional discrimination against blacks in Los Angeles. Radio calls and police computers sometimes described incidents with black citizens as "monkey slapping time," and "gorillas in the mist" (Levin & McDevitt, 1993:162).

- Police mistreatment of blacks is found in every section of the United States. Between 1956 and 1983, over half of the citizens killed by police in Miami were African American, yet blacks represented only about 8 percent of the Miami population during these years. In 1994, a black Boston minister died of a heart attack brought on by fright when a SWAT team mistakenly burst into his apartment, threw him to the floor, and slapped handcuffs on him (San Francisco *Chronicle,* March 31, 1994:A-11). A similar incident happened in New York City several years earlier when twenty-five police mistakenly entered the apartment of four black males, and proceeded to attack them (Levin & McDevitt, 1993:160).

- African-Americans are frequent victims of hate crimes. In September, 1993, two black men were set on fire, one in Palm Beach, Florida, another in Cincinnati. In the Cincinnati incident, a thirty-year-old black man had stopped to help two stranded motorists. After he brought them a can of gasoline, they used it to set him on fire (New York *Times,* September 4, 1993:A-3, and September 23, 1993:A-9).

Along with Native Americans and African Americans, Hispanic Americans represent the poorest of the oppressed minority groups.

Hispanic Americans

The term *Hispanic American* is somewhat misleading because Hispanic peoples in America are actually made up of a number of subgroups, including Mexican Americans, Puerto Rican Americans, Cuban Americans, and others. Most Mexican peoples are actually products of Mestizo Indians and European white unions, and most Puerto Ricans stem from unions between Europeans, Africans, and some Indians. Almost 75 percent of Hispanic Americans are either of Mexican (62.6 percent) or Puerto Rican (11.1 percent) heritage. These are not only the most numerous Hispanic groups, they are also the most oppressed.

The American railroads of the nineteenth century were built largely with the labor of blacks, Chinese, and other minorities. Many of these groups found their ability to immigrate severely restricted when their labor was no longer needed by white employers.

Mexican Americans have suffered from a brutal heritage of European conquest and colonialization that lasted from the 1500s to 1810. Although the Treaty of Guadalupe-Hidalgo extended the rights of U.S. citizens to Mexican Americans, still, the properties of these peoples were taken forcibly and fraudulently by white American settlers, and Mexicans became a colonized workforce without political rights.

From 1810 to 1865, Mexican labor was used to build America's railroad, agricultural, and mining industries. Mexican immigrants were paid much less in wages than white workers, and were frequently kept indebted by their employers. Mexicans were segregated in the least desirable unskilled occupations and often used as strikebreakers by antiunion employers.

The educational levels of Hispanic Americans are disturbingly low and serve to aggravate other social problems:

- Only 45.2 percent of Mexican Americans over age twenty-five have graduated high school, compared with 60.5 percent of Puerto Rican Americans, and 62.1 percent of Cuban Americans. Hispanic Americans drop out of high school at rates twice as high as African Americans and three times higher than white Americans.

- Moreover, the vast majority of Hispanic Americans have entered the labor force since 1950, most in the least-skilled and lowest-paying jobs. Frequently they have been the last hired and first fired workers, especially when the need for cheap unskilled labor ebbs. Here again, there is a minority group whose skills resemble those of early white immigrants, but whose skills are no longer needed by what is now a postindustrial economy. A great need in coming years for minorities will be higher education to remedy the lack of highly skilled technicians in such careers as computer repair.

- The more dark complexioned Hispanic Americans are, the more they are likely to be perceived as African American, and suffer the same kinds of discrimination to which blacks are subject. Puerto Rican Americans are frequently stereotyped as dirty, crime-prone drunks, who are childlike, lazy, and hypersexual. Reagan appointee J. Peter Grace, for example, believed that most Puerto Rican Americans lived on food stamps.

- Hispanic Americans have a long history of oppression by the police. In 1943, two hundred servicemen on leave in Los Angeles went on a rampage in a Mexican-American neighborhood. The police did little to help, and often arrested the victims of the riot. Murder, destruction of property, and vandalism continued for a week before the military police were called in to quell the riot.

- While there is less residential segregation of Hispanics than of African Americans, there is still discrimination in mortgage lending (see Table 11.4). Moreover, African Americans and Hispanic Americans now frequently live in the same neighborhoods, but in distinct patterns. Puerto Ricans are much less segregated from African Americans than are Cuban Americans and Mexican Americans. Sadly, Puerto Ricans and Mexican Americans have joined blacks as part of the underclass, so many of whom lack hope for a better future.

Latinos continue to be the object of a good deal of hate crime violence, especially by neo-Nazi skinheads and, in cities like Miami:

To cite an example, there have been six riots in Miami since 1981 primarily due to racial tension between blacks and Cuban Americans. Many Miami blacks perceive that Cuban immigrants are treated more leniently by the government than rejected black-Haitian immigrants have been. Cubans have also replaced blacks in menial jobs in the tourist trade. In just one incident, blacks killed a Latino Miami police officer, and went on a rampage that resulted in two hundred arrests.

Also, in 1991, a black Washington, DC, police officer shot a Salvadoran immigrant. A riot began in which two hundred arrests were made.

Tension between blacks and Latinos will probably increase in years to come due to increasing Latino immigration and the shrinking job base in American urban centers.

Asian Americans

Chinese and Japanese immigrants began arriving in the United States around 1820, but the Vietnamese, Cambodians, and Thai did not enter America in large numbers until after the end of the Vietnam War (1975). Between 1980 and 1990, the Asian population of the United States increased by 108 percent. Today, 80 to 90 percent of Asian Americans are first-generation immigrants, and Asians are the fastest-growing American minority group. By 2000, there may be 12 million Asian Americans, and by 2050, perhaps as many as 41 million (Marger, 1994; Worsnop, 1992).

Longtime Asian-American residents are one of the most economically successful groups ever to come to America. Generally their incomes are nearly twice as high as newly arrived immigrants, and a few thousand dollars higher than the incomes of white Americans.

The Chinese arrived in the 1840s, after the California gold rush began. They helped build the western railroads, where their willingness to work for low wages was perceived as a threat by white workers. When the need for their labor dried up, the Chinese Exclusion Act was passed in 1882, barring Chinese immigration for ten years. By 1960, their ranks had declined from 125,000 to 70,000, the vast majority of which were male. A new immigration law passed in 1965 resulted in an increase in Chinese immigrants, including women.

Japanese immigrants share a similar history. They settled mostly in California after 1820, and worked at menial jobs. They were so frugal that they were able to send money home to their families. In 1908, a gentlemen's agreement was signed with Japan that effectively stopped all Japanese immigration to the United States until the 1960s. Today, Japanese Americans comprise 11.7 percent of the Asian-American population.

Both Chinese and Japanese immigrants have long been stereotyped as barbarian invaders, the Yellow Peril. They were tolerated as long as they were in demand as cheap labor. With the bombing of Pearl Harbor, in 1941, Japanese-American stereotypes of sneaky Asians flourished, and 120,000 loyal Japanese-American citizens were forcibly locked up in West Coast detention camps, their homes and possessions confiscated, their life's savings lost. The Army general in charge of the project termed them the enemy race.

Today, Asian Americans are subject to both hate crimes and certain forms of institutional discrimination. Elite colleges have established quotas for the number of Asian students they will admit. Hate crimes against Asians are socially patterned in black neighborhoods,

Much of the economic success of Asian Americans stems from family-owned businesses in which each family member works long hours to support the family. Some of these small businesses are located in non-Asian minority areas, and have, at times, contributed to the racial tension between Asians and other minorities.

and white working-class neighborhoods, where the success of Asian Americans is sometimes perceived as unfair. This is especially true in neighborhoods where Koreans and other Asian-American minorities have opened grocery stores.

- A number of Korean-owned grocery stores were looted and burned during the 1991 Los Angeles riot in south central Los Angeles.

- Chinese-American engineer Vincent Chin was murdered in Detroit by two white auto workers, one of whom was unemployed at the time. Chin was mistaken for a Japanese, who were blamed for the layoff of auto workers. Mr. Chin's attackers were fined $3780 and given three-year probation terms. Many Asian Americans were outraged over the leniency of the punishment.

- An assault against a Laotian man in Ft. Dodge, Iowa, resulted in a six-month suspended sentence. The attacker was ordered to pay the victim's medical expenses and write a twenty-five word essay about the incident.

- In Jersey City, New Jersey, Asian Indians have been victimized by constant harassment by black, Hispanic, and white youth.

- In 1986, twenty-eight Cambodians were burned out of their homes on Christmas Eve in Revere, Massachusetts, when their homes were torched by white arsonists (Marger, 1994:354–355).

During World War II, Japanese Americans were placed in internment camps on the West Coast. Because they were of Japanese descent, many were automatically suspected of siding with America's enemies. Many of these families had their property taken away without due process of law. It was not until fifty years later that the survivors of these families were reimbursed by the government for this confiscation.

As of April, 1994, three Japanese visitors had been murdered in California alone. The number of hate crimes against Asians has increased dramatically since 1980, and may well be underreported due to language problems, distrust of the criminal justice system, and the shame that comes with being victimized (U.S. Commission on Civil Rights, 1992).

A Word About Anti-Semitism

Anti-Semitism is one of the oldest derogatory ideologies in the world. Anti-Jewish hatred probably began about the year 300 A.D. when the Jews refused to accept the missionary zeal of the Roman Catholic Church's attempts to covert them to Christianity. In response to Jewish stubbornness, the church issued the Synod of Elvira in 306, prohibiting Jews and Christians from eating meals together, having sex, or intermarrying. In 535, Jews were prohibited by the church from holding political office, and, in 538, from employing Christians as servants. It was the Italians who created the first Jewish ghetto (Mason, 1993:222).

Some notions from this period are still much alive. In 1980, the president of the Southern Baptist Convention told an evangelical audience that "God Almighty does not hear the prayer of a Jew, for how in the world can God hear the prayer of a man who says that Jesus Christ is not the true Messiah?" (Hall, 1993:ix). On the other hand, the Jews for centuries have been blamed for crucifying Jesus, as Christ killers. "This one charge against the Jews has been responsible for centuries of massacres and persecutions, pogroms and expulsions . . . and the depredations of the (Spanish) Inquisition (of the 1400s), laying the groundwork for the unspeakable horrors of the Holocaust" (Ostling, 1994:72).

The Jews fared little better with the coming of the Protestant Reformation. Martin Luther's *The Jews and Their Lies* described Jews as bloodthirsty hounds and murderers of all Christendom (Mason, 1993:223). Jews were stereotyped as poisoners of gentile water and wells, and murderers of Christian children. By 1895, Europe's Jews were labeled beasts of prey, parasites, and cholera germs. The Nazis picked up on these themes in the 1920s, calling the Jews vermin, lice, and cancer.

The most persistent theme in anti-Semitism, however, is money. The Jews have long been stereotyped as materialistic, miserly, business cheats, and economically powerful beyond what is fair. It is this stereotype that rages among American hate groups today. Jews, especially Jewish bankers, are viewed as part of a plot to take over America and the world. This conspiracy was first described by the Russian secret police in their nineteenth-century tract *Elders of Zion,* which helped form the basis for the Nazis' ideology.

Today American Jews are among the most successful non-WASP groups in America. Representing only about 2 percent of the population, American Jews account for about one-quarter of American Nobel Prize winners. They are especially well represented in academia, science, medicine, and the movie and entertainment industries. Over 50 percent of American Jews over age eighteen have college degrees (versus just 19 percent of the general population). The average income of American Jews is well above the national average ($48,700 in 1986, versus about $31,000 for the average American), exceeding even that of Asian Americans. Indeed, the very success of the Jews has fanned the flames of prejudice and discrimination against them.

With the economic recessions of the 1980s and 1990s have come a host of anti-Semitic incidents that have included all manner of hate crimes. While it is an exaggeration to say that American anti-Semitism is worse today than in the past, there is plenty of evidence that hate crimes against Jewish people and property are increasing. Some anti-Jewish beliefs are more widespread than ever, especially the notion that Jews are constantly stirring up trouble with their ideas, have too much business power, and are more loyal to Israel than to the United States (Levin & McDevitt, 1993:24). Hate crimes against Jewish people and property in the 1980s and 1990s have grown out of a belief that the Jews have more than their fair share of scarce resources.

Some of these hate crimes are the result of serious incidents between Jews and blacks. Relations between these former allies in the civil rights struggles of the 1960s have sadly degenerated into episodes of scapegoating in mixed neighborhoods. This is because in places like Brooklyn, New York, some Jews own property in or near black areas, and are viewed as the closest and most visible symbol of the white power structure.

To illustrate, a seven-year-old black child, Calvin Cato, and another black were struck by a Jewish motorist in Brooklyn's Crown Heights section in 1991. After rumors began that the Jewish ambulance company at the scene refused to treat injured blacks, a rampage followed in which black rioters killed a twenty-nine-year-old rabbinical student, and Jewish stores were looted.

Tension between blacks and Jews remains uneasy, thanks in part to the utterings of extremists like Reverend Farrakhan, who claims that Jews are responsible for the enslavement of blacks in the New World. Actually, Jews brought less than 2 percent of African slaves to America (Levin & McDevitt, 1993:139).

The continuing prejudice and discrimination against Native Americans, African Americans, Hispanic Americans and Asian Americans, as well as Jewish Americans, are also a symptom of the policy failures of conservative and liberal efforts to overcome minority oppression in America.

Policy Failures in Race and Minority Relations

The policies enacted to protect the rights of racial and ethnic minorities have been minimally successful at best. Nearly thirty years after the civil and voting rights acts, there is still much institutional discrimination against African Americans and Latinos. Individual acts of discrimination in the form of hate crimes are an increasingly serious problem in the United States.

The formula that worked so well for most white ethnic groups at the turn of the century now has serious limitations. No longer can two or more family members be employed in low-skill or manufacturing positions that pay below poverty level wages and expect to rise out of poverty. Today, even people with a college education frequently have problems finding and keeping a job. Second, those well educated immigrants who do come to the United States and find work or go into their own businesses immediately are frequently the victims of hate crimes, many committed by minority group members that remain on the bottom of America's social class ladder.

Despite all this, American public policy continues to be based on the premise that equal opportunity exists for today's racial minorities. Rapidly, however, it is becoming an equal opportunity to beg in the streets and sleep under bridges, as writer Anatole France once remarked. Dominant groups and threatened white ethnics already feel that enough has been done to help today's most oppressed minorities. Affirmative action, a policy designed to allow qualified minorities to gain access to jobs and admission to graduate, law, and medical schools, is now under serious attack by both the U.S. Supreme Court and a host of state and federal legislators. The University of California has already voted to end an admissions policy that used race as a category, and to end hiring people for positions on the basis of race, gender, or other minority status (*USA Today*, 1995: A-1). Other universities are expected to follow suit.

In the meantime, neither liberals nor conservatives have offered any meaningful solutions to deal with these problems. Enterprise zones, designed to bring businesses to poor neighborhoods, have failed almost everywhere they have been attempted. Civil rights legislation has helped put more minorities in office and into a small middle class, but the crushing poverty that still haunts minority Americans shows no signs of abating and every sign of increasing.

The issue behind oppression of all groups is scarcity. Affirmative action failed, not only because it gave rise to charges of quotas and reverse discrimination, but because its effects did not touch the millions of minority underclass members who are steeped in poverty, homeless, often drop out of school completely, and frequently lack the skills to compete for jobs that pay enough to end their poverty. Making resources more equitably available to all groups is something America does less of than any other industrial democracy in the world. This same scarcity also applies to women, gays and lesbians, and the elderly and disabled, the subjects of our next two chapters.

Summary

Within the sociological imagination paradigm, the mechanism by which the have-not status of minorities is maintained is called oppression. Oppression involves one or more groups within a culture systematically and successfully preventing other groups within that culture from attaining the scarce and valued resources. These resources include material resources, political power, and positive cultural values.

- **Material resources**—property, income, and the educational opportunities and employment necessary to achieve material gain.
- **Political power**—access to political office, and the processes necessary to gain political power (like voting, campaigning, and running for office).
- **Positive cultural values**—the access to means of communication and persuasion necessary for the group to gain equal opportunity to acquire material resources and political power. Such values include recognition of the oppressed group's contributions to society and the development of a positive sense of self-esteem among its members.

The lack of these scarce resources results in a wide variety of physical, financial, and moral harm to oppressed groups, and, ultimately, to the groups that oppress them.

Typically, groups singled out for negative treatment constitute what Max Weber termed status groups, groups that have unique physical or cultural characteristics. Such groups include racial groups and ethnic groups. Collectively they are called minorities.

- **Racial groups**—A race is a population with a distinct set of identifiable physical characteristics. Races are usually set apart by their skin color, the shape of their eyelids, noses, or other features. Sociologically, race is important only because a given society believes that it is, and often treats members of racial groups based on certain beliefs about that race.
- **Ethnic groups**—An ethnic group, like Jewish Americans, Irish Americans, Puerto Rican Americans, and so on, is a subgroup in a larger society that has a common set of cultural traits and values.

Those groups that are so differentiated are called **minorities.**

Oppression is made up of a variety of techniques that function to maintain the domination of one group over another. These techniques begin with prejudice, preconceived judgments about an entire group made without being tested against reality. Often prejudice is based on erroneous images called stereotypes, which function to reinforce the negative values and beliefs users have about minority groups. Stereotypes become part of the culture of an entire society, an important element of the social character of both the dominant and minority groups.

Stereotypes become a basis for prejudicial attitudes against minorities, and these prejudices give rise to harmful actions called discrimination. Discriminatory acts include a variety of physical and financial harms that range from the use of slurs and socially distant behaviors, to segregation, economic exploitation, and physical attack. Discriminatory acts can be committed by both individuals and groups, as well as institutions. Institutional discrimination is often subtle, such as height and weight requirements for jobs that end up excluding women, when compared to the discriminatory acts of individuals.

Oppression is also firmly linked to alienation. The reactions of oppressed people to their dehumanization include a variety of attitudes and behaviors that sometime shape their social character. These reactions vary from certain forms of mental illness to becoming prejudiced against their own ethnic and racial groups. Likewise, the social character of oppressor groups is also characterized by alienation. The authoritarian personality syndrome involves projecting characteristics oppressors do not like about themselves onto scapegoated minorities, who thereby become blamed for whatever failure is experienced by the least well-off members of dominant groups. In contemporary American life, economic dislocations are often blamed on minorities and such scapegoating frequently takes the form of hate crimes. Hate crimes are illegal acts of intimidation and violence committed against minority group members attributable to prejudice on the part of the perpetrator. Hate crimes are committed against people on the basis of their race, ethnicity, gender, religion, or sexual orientation.

There is a long history of racial and minority oppression in the United States. Native Americans were viewed as savages by the original settlers, their lands taken away, and their entire population nearly wiped out. Today Native Americans are found on reservations in a few geographically isolated areas. They suffer from high rates of poverty, unemployment, alcoholism, and other harms.

The racial group that has experienced the most severe oppression is blacks. Brought to America as kidnapped slaves beginning in 1619, African Americans were forcibly bred by their owners, their families frequently broken up, and they were prohibited from being educated. After their liberation at the end of the American Civil War, a wide variety of discriminatory tactics were employed to keep African Americans from achieving equality with whites. Today, despite the gains of the Civil Rights Acts of the 1960s, and affirmative action programs, black America is as segregated, poor, unemployed, and reeling from social problems, such as crime, drug abuse, and ill treatment within the criminal justice system, as ever.

Hispanic Americans have endured a long history of oppression in America. Mexicans came here as laborers in the nineteenth century after centuries of colonial oppression, and built railroads or contributed agricultural production. Hispanic Americans are today a diverse group, but the poorest of them suffer from lack of education, poverty, unemployment, discrimination in housing, and are still relegated to the poorest-paying jobs requiring the least skills, such as agricultural migrant work.

Likewise, Asian Americans, especially Chinese and Japanese immigrants, have suffered unique forms of discrimination in the United States. Originally brought to America in the

1820s to build the railroads, when economic times turned sour, a wide variety of discriminatory acts were taken against both groups. Asians were deported and barred from entering the United States due to the passage of exclusionary acts. During World War II, Japanese Americans were placed in internment camps and their property confiscated. Today, newly arrived Asian immigrant groups, especially those from Southeast Asia, are subject to discriminatory acts, including quotas by elite colleges and hate crimes by various individuals and groups.

Jews constitute a uniquely oppressed minority. They have been extremely successful within the dominant culture. Yet their great economic success has been used against them as a symbol of their greed, manipulation, and hatred of non-Jews. Hate crimes against Jews are a common feature of American life, some of them committed by blacks.

The oppression suffered by these various minorities also symbolizes the failure of conservative and liberal policies designed to bring equal opportunity to America. Not the civil rights laws, Great Society programs, enterprise zone proposals, or other attempted remedies have gotten to the root causes of oppression.

Suggested Readings

Martin Marger (1994) *Race and Ethnic Relations: An International Perspective* (Belmont, CA: Wadsworth). An excellent treatment of the nature of oppression and its effects both in the United States and in selected societies around the world, especially Ireland and South Africa.

Jack Levin and Jack McDevitt (1993) *Hate Crimes: The Rising Tide of Bigotry and Bloodshed* (New York: Plenum). A very readable and provocative discussion of the nature and consequences of the hate violence currently so widespread in American life.

Paula Rosenblatt (1992) *Class, Race, and Gender: An Integrated Approach,* 2nd ed. (New York: St. Martin's). An excellent discussion of all aspects of oppression of women and minorities from many perspectives.

Exercises

Critical Thinking Exercise 11.1	Stereotypes

This exercise can be done either in class or as a group project. One measure of how important a given culture thinks something is concerns the number of words it has in its language for that phenomenon. For example, Eskimos have about one hundred words to describe different types of snow. Using the same logic, it could be argued that a measure of the intensity with which a minority group is oppressed is reflected in the number of derogatory words a culture uses to refer to that group.

Divide a piece of paper into columns and place the name of a different minority group at the head of each column, as depicted below. If you are doing this in class, it may be done in one of the following ways:

1. Each student in the class should write down as many slur terms for each minority as he or she can think of on the coding sheet given below. Alternatively, students may be divided into six groups with each group being responsible for writing down the slur names of one of the minorities listed in the coding sheet. The instructor can then lead a discussion in which a list of such names can be placed on the blackboard, using the same format as in the coding sheet below.

2. Students may form groups and do the exercise outside of class in a week's time. For those not familiar with slur names, a slang dictionary may be consulted. Results may be presented in class. If there are enough students for six groups, each group can be assigned one minority.

Which racial or ethnic group has the most names used by the American culture? Which has the least?

Coding Sheet for Exercise 11.1	The Degrees of Oppression				
BLACKS	HISPANICS	ASIANS	NATIVE AM.	JEWS	ITALIANS
1. Nigger	Spic	Gook	Redskin	Kike	Dago
2.					
3.					
4.					
5.					
6.					
7.					
8.					
9.					
10.					
11.					
12.					
13.					

Continued on next page

Exercise 11.1 Continued

BLACKS	HISPANICS	ASIANS	NATIVE AM.	JEWS	ITALIANS
14.					
15.					
16.					

Critical Thinking Exercise 11.2	Hate Crime Watch

Using databases in your college library, collect a year's worth of stories about hate crimes from newspapers around the nation. Do a content analysis of these stories using the *Thrill, Personal Threat,* and *Mission* hate crime categories defined below. Which type of hate crime is the most numerous? Did you notice any additional sociological patterns in your analysis, like region of the nation, the kinds of minorities most likely to be targeted, and the types of crimes most frequently committed (intimidation, assault, arson, murder, and the like)? A sample coding sheet is given below. You may reproduce the coding sheet, and use one sheet for each article you read. You may also use additional categories that you find important in various articles.

Definitions

- **Thrill hate crimes** are usually committed by young men twenty years of age and under. This is a type of wilding in which sadistic young people look for vulnerable would-be victims in order to vent their aggression.

- **Personal threat hate crimes** are usually committed by adults who feel that minorities are invading their neighborhoods, taking their jobs, seducing their women, and so on. Personal threat hate crimes are committed as protection from encroachment by minorities, usually after a stern warning (racial slur) is perceived to have been ignored.

- **Mission hate crimes** are committed by individuals or organized groups that are out to rid the entire world of evil minorities who are threatening their way of life. Many of these individuals are psychotics, or paranoid individuals convinced they are being given instructions from a leader. Mission hate crimes are committed out of a conspiratorial belief about the intentions of out-groups. The mission of these hate criminals is often suicidal.

In tabulating your results, use the same categories, along with a total column. Which types of crimes are the most prevalent in these stories? Which group(s) is most often targeted?

Coding Sheet for Exercise 11.2	Hate Crimes		
TYPE OF CRIME	# OF REPORTS	REGION	TARGET GROUP
		East/NW/S/W	*Jews/Af Am Hispanics/Asians*
Thrill Crime			
Personal Threat Crime			
Mission Crime			

The Sociology of Oppression, Gender, and Orientation

Gender Oppression
and Alienation

Gender roles constitute the cultural and institutional expectations that are linked to a person's sex. They are referred to as masculinity (attributes appropriate for males) and femininity (attributes appropriate for females) (Thompson & Hickey, 1994:259). C. Wright Mills once maintained that gender roles, for both males and females, constituted a trap for both sexes. **Gender roles** are the social expectations a society has for boys and girls, men and women, and involve definitions of masculinity and femininity, that is, appropriate behavior for men and women. In America, thought Mills, neither men nor women are free to shape the concepts of masculinity and femininity. Both concepts are stereotypes, and both limit the human being (Mills, 1963:343–344). Men are limited in their capacity for intimacy in many ways, not the least of which is that they are taught to view women as sexual objects. Women, on the other hand, are taught to use their beauty and sexuality as a vehicle for social mobility. They are socialized to view men as success objects and to marry up in the class system. As a result, both genders approach each other through a lens of dehumanizing stereotypes. People are not judged as individuals, but as stereotyped categories.

Stereotypes about men and women exist in every area of daily life, and at every stage of the life cycle. These stereotypes give rise to a wide variety of prejudice and discrimination against women, men, gays, and lesbians. Such prejudices and discriminatory behavior also give rise to some bizarre contradictions.

For example, at least one branch of the U.S. military allows convicted rapists and child molesters to remain on active duty (under a rehabilitation program), but immediately discharges homosexual military personnel! Prejudice against gays runs deep in our nation's armed forces, a policy that is merely a reflection of America's values about gender and homosexuality.

In many cultures, it is customary for males to kiss and hug each other as a greeting. In fact, much research demonstrates that such physical affection is healthy for human beings.

The stereotypes of men and women stem in part from the notion of **sex,** a biological category or division defined on the basis of male and female anatomical, hormonal, and chromosomal differences. Accordingly, while men and women have obvious physical and sexual differences, it is the sociological meaning that is attached to these differences that becomes gender roles.

There is a tendency to think that male and female roles are the same in all cultures. Actually, roles vary greatly depending on the culture and historical period. For example, in the United States it is considered unmanly for men to kiss each other, but many cultures in Europe and the Third World have no such restrictions. In some societies, a woman is considered unclean or irrational during the time she is having her menses. Indeed, in preindustrial societies, women are often required to go into physical and social isolation in special huts, and not allowed contact with other members of the society until the menses is over. In other societies, no special importance is attached to a woman's period, and women function in their gender roles as workers, wives, mothers, and so on.

Changing of the Guard

To the extent that one has acknowledged and internalized (accepted) the rules, values, and behaviors associated with one's gender roles, one possesses a gender identification. However, accepting such an identification carries with it the burden of playing a particular role at a certain point in a society's historical development. Above all, gender roles are about social character, about which traits are encouraged or discouraged in men and women.

In the postmodern era, there is serious confusion over what it means to be a man or a woman. Take an apparently simple act—dating, for example. Until the 1960s, there was little doubt about appropriate role behavior for the two genders. Men were expected to ask women on dates (thereby risking rejection) and to pay for whatever activities were undertaken. Many women were socialized to believe that when their dates paid for dinner and a movie, they were sexually obligated to that date.

Dating has now become a much more complicated affair. It is no longer clear to either sex who is supposed to initiate contact. This has the advantage of giving both genders the freedom to do so, but in some quarters there is a double standard. If a woman asks a man out, she is stereotyped as both liberated and aggressive (pushy). If a man asks a woman for a date, he is still just being a man. Further, most couples have at least one conversation about who pays. There is no confusion, however, about the fact that gender oppression is both widespread and demonstrably harmful to both men and women.

This chapter examines the harms from which both genders generally suffer. Collectively these harms constitute evidence of a coherent system of gender stratification, "male domination," designed to keep women in second-class status regarding economic resources, political power, and the ability to define values and gender roles.

Discrimination in Religion

A major contributing force to the dehumanization of both women and homosexuals (discussed below) has been the world's major religions. Judaism, Christianity, Islam, and

Hinduism, all of which are patriarchal (male dominated), have always viewed men as spiritually superior to women, a view that has endured to this day. In the Bible God is referred to as He, and man is created in his image. For millennia in Judaism, Christianity, and Islam, women have been viewed as evil temptresses who prevent men from attaining spiritual salvation. In the Old Testament, women were created largely because men were lonely, and soon after Eve's creation, from Adam's rib, she tempts him into evil. This manipulation results in their both being expelled from paradise. As punishment, men are forced to go to work, and women are to experience the pain of their menses.

The New Testament makes clear that women were created for men's sake, and wives are instructed to be submissive to their husband in all matters (Ephesians 5:22–23). All the important biblical prophets are males, and prophets are the only biblical figures who had a close relationship with God (Schwartz, 1994). Women are portrayed as either obedient spouses and nurturers or as prostitutes and temptresses, responsible for hideous acts like the beheading of John the Baptist.

This Madonna (good woman)–whore (bad woman) contradiction has existed down through the ages, and been used historically to control women socially (Lemoncheck, 1985:54ff). Throughout history women have been confined to the role of docile housewife. Throughout the late nineteenth and early twentieth century women were viewed as "daddy's girls," and were encouraged to remain at home (in the kitchen and the bedroom). Their childlike subservience was perpetuated by fashions such as bobbed hair, baby-doll nightgowns, and little girl dresses. The corsets in which women dressed to show off their girlish figures caused many severe back pain, and some actual physical disabilities. If women exhibited the slightest independence, as by remaining unmarried, they were often labeled as witches, had their property taken away from them, and were burned at the stake. In fact, between the fifteenth and eighteenth centuries, millions of European and colonial women were murdered because they were labeled witches. They were single (without a man's protection), and most of them owned property. In some places it was illegal for women to own property and inheritance laws did not permit property to be passed on to a female. Accordingly, burning women as witches was a legal way for men to take the property owned by women. This stereotype of out-of-control, evil women has also been used to label women as insane. It survives today among physicians who perceive women as in need of being tranquilized.

In the Catholic church all popes, bishops, priests, and other major decision makers are exclusively male. In most religions, women are relegated to subordinate roles as Sunday school instructors, or choir members. Only recently have women been admitted to the clergy in the Anglican, Methodist, and Episcopal churches, and then only after a great deal of resistance.

Within other Protestant churches, especially fundamentalist denominations, women remain subordinated. Fundamentalists in America have historically opposed any expression of female independence. For example, fundamentalists have

- opposed female suffrage on grounds that it would threaten home life;
- opposed ordination of women on the grounds that giving women power over men would disrupt God and nature's natural state;
- opposed women dressing in short skirts and tight clothing on the grounds that they would cause men to have impure thoughts; and

- opposed birth control in the 1800s and abortion in the 1900s (French, 1992:56–59).

Marilyn French (1992) has convincingly argued that the point at which fundamentalists became most concerned about the relations between the sexes was exactly at the time (1840–1880) when women began to enter the workforce, have premarital sex, attend college, and demand political power (such as the right to vote). Women were also in the forefront of the movement to abolish slavery, another threatening symbol of female independence. The most dehumanizing institution concerning the stereotyping of both men and women today is no longer religion, but the mass media.

Media Stereotypes and the Victimization of Females

Women have long been negatively stereotyped in movies, magazines, advertising, music, and books, most frequently as sexual objects. Women's sexual attraction is used by those doing the objectifying (male-dominated corporations and advertising firms) as a vehicle for treating women as deserving less of the rights or none of the rights to well-being and freedom that other persons enjoy (Lemoncheck, 1985:2). Treating women as sexual objects converts them into sexual commodities. Once objectified, their needs and desires or interests become subordinated, manipulated, and subverted to satisfy the needs of those who are victimizing them. Accordingly, women are defined by men in terms of their sexual attractiveness to men. This is one reason why so many women suffer feelings of inferiority concerning the shape of their bodies, why eating disorders like anorexia and bulimia are so much more common among women than among men. The ideal standard of beauty in America media is still a young, fair-skinned, blond woman with large breasts and curvaceous hips. The fact is that only 2 or 3 percent of American women are built this way. Moreover, since most pictures of women in magazines are airbrushed photos, not even the women in the ads actually look as well as their pictures.

None of this, of course, prevents media sources from trying to persuade women that they must achieve this impossible standard of beauty. (By the way, most men, at least most mature men, are quite happy to settle for a woman who is less than a Marilyn Monroe lookalike.) However, this fact has not stopped the media from trying to convince women they need to buy $19 billion worth of cosmetics each year; or spend great amounts of money on clothes; or surgically enlarge their breasts, fix their noses, enlarge their lips, and so on.

The female image of the flawless, young, and beautiful sex object is found over and over again in advertising. Synnott's (1991) content analysis of gender presentations in the New York *Times Magazine* revealed that youth and beauty in ads were essential for women, but not for men. Men were often given names in ads, whereas women never were featured with names, implying they were not real. Women were severely dehumanized, so much so that in many ads only certain parts of the female anatomy were shown (e.g., hands, breasts, buttocks, feet, faces, thighs, and so on). Women were much more often featured in a state of semi-undress—in panties, bras, and swimsuits. The emphasis on the female body "affirms the greater role of the body in social life for women rather than for men" (Synnott, 1991:340). This stereotype of woman as a collection of erotic body parts was not the only female image discovered by Synnott.

Women in the New York *Times Magazine* were featured with strange expressions on their faces, implying that they were crazy. Men were never pictured in awkward or strange poses. Men were portrayed as working and physically active, women were almost never working in ads. Women were also pictured in ads in subservient positions to men, looking up at them, implying an inequality of power between the sexes. Finally, ageism and racism were implied themes in the ads. Virtually no African Americans or elderly people were shown.

The mass media shape some key sexual traits, including the link between sex and violence. Recent studies of media advertising and sexual portrayals contain a number of disturbing conclusions:

- Eroticization (assigning of sexual symbols) pervades postmodern culture. Sexual symbols are now attached to virtually every product and service that is the subject of media advertising. Sex has become a commodity in itself, and in ads is associated with youth, power, and success. Even children in ads have become sexual beings "thrusting their pelvises in suggestive ways to sell jeans, kiddie cosmetics," and even women's underwear (Davis & Stasz, 1990:251).
- Studies of movies and television, men's magazines, and pornography all indicate "increased depictions of violence against women" (Malamuth, 1984; Davis & Stasz, 1990:251). The main effect of such presentations is a public desensitization (an immunity) to the link between sex and violence. Such images also reinforce myths about women and rape (e.g., they like it and want it, or they deserve it). Over half of rape victims are under eighteen years old. One-fifth of rape victims under twelve are raped by their fathers, reflecting the sexualization of children by the media, as well as the power realities within families in which abuse takes place (San Francisco *Chronicle*, 1994: A-3).

Ultraconservative talk show magnate Rush Limbaugh daily refers to feminists as "femi-Nazis." Slasher films typically portray the most sadistic kind of violence against women. In *Boxing Helena* a woman's arms and legs are cut off, and she is placed in a box. In *Tool Box Murders* a woman is nailed to a wall. In *I Spit on Your Grave* a brutal gang rape is depicted. Such films send the message to young men that sexual pleasure and violence against women go hand in hand.

Sociologist Diana Russell has devoted her professional life to studying violence against women. Her findings demonstrate the powerful effect media images can have on behavior. Dr. Russell defines pornography as material that combines sex or/and exposure of genitals with the degradation or abuse of women in a way that appears to encourage, condone, or endorse such behavior. This definition is important, because it specifically incorporates the maltreatment of women, thus giving it a focus lacked by many other views. It is important to have a clear definition because the U.S. Supreme Court has left the definition of pornography up to local communities, thus refusing to provide any firm guidelines about what is pornographic.

There is a group of scholars who believe that there is a link between pornography and rape. They claim that males who are predisposed to commit violence against women will do so after being exposed to pornographic material. Dr. Russell, however, has discovered that pornographic material can similarly motivate even those males with no predisposition to rape. While most men do not act out their desire to rape women, there are important lessons here: (1) Many American men find the notion of raping a woman "sexually exciting" (Beneke, 1994:18), and (2) pornography increases the likelihood that men will act on their desire to rape women by reinforcing the common myth that women want to be sexually assaulted, and that women enjoy being raped. Even so-called "soft core" pornography that depicts women merely as sexual objects can encourage rape. In soft porn women are presented as mere commodities, less than human, thus encouraging men to treat women in dehumanized ways.

Much of the content of the media's sexual presentations is mirrored in the sex crime statistics:

To illustrate, the United States has twenty times more reported rapes than Japan, Spain, and England combined. Moreover, 20 percent of American women report being victims of date rape (Patterson & Kim, 1991:120, 129). Using a conservative definition of rape as forced intercourse under threat of physical violence, or intercourse when a person is unable to give consent due to physical helplessness (like being asleep or unconscious), Diana Russell found that 44 percent of women have been victims of rape or attempted rape (Beneke, 1994:11).

Women are frequent victims of hate crimes. The following examples demonstrate some of the types of violent resentment towards women:

- Marc Lepine, a man who had been rejected from engineering school, walked into an engineering class at the University of Montreal in 1989 with a semiautomatic rifle and killed fourteen women. He claimed the feminists had stolen his place in the school. He then killed himself.
- In 1991, George Henard drove his pickup truck into the front window of Luby's cafeteria in Killeen, Texas, and opened fire as he cursed women. Twenty-two people were killed including fourteen women. Henard expressed his hatred for Anita Hill, who, he felt, had harassed Supreme Court nominee Clarence Thomas. Henard's mission was to rid the world of all "white women."

Judith Lorber (1994:75–79) recently studied gender discrimination and came to some shocking conclusions concerning the use of rape as a mechanism of social control. Men who are most likely to rape women had emotionally distant relationships with their fathers, yet want to be like their fathers, suggesting that rapists are emotionally alienated from themselves. Studies of rapists reveal a generalized hostility towards women, an insistence that women be sexually faithful to men, and a perception that men should be tough, athletic, conquerors of women. Rapists also believe that women's own provocative behavior causes rape (they want it and enjoy it). About three-fourths of rapists had been drinking at the time they raped, and 80 percent cite a stressful event as precipitating the rape, especially being let down in some way by a wife or girlfriend. Revenge is thus a common motivation among rapists, many of whom admit they got pleasure from humiliating and degrading their victims. Rapists also mention gaining sexual access to an unavailable or unwilling woman, impersonal sex, feeling powerful, and receiving a "bonus" during the commission of another crime as reasons for rapes (Lorber, 1994:77–78).

Most important, *in societies where rape is virtually nonexistent women are respected for their abilities to reproduce children and to work as equals with men.* There is also a balance of political power between men and women and very little personal violence between the genders. In other words, in societies where rape is rare, women are viewed as valuable human beings, and traits associated with being female are encouraged.

Other Media Images of Women

When women are not being sexually dehumanized, or made to look mentally ill by the media, they are being trivialized, neglected, and ignored. This image of the unimportant, nearly invisible woman pervades the news media:

To cite examples, a content analysis of twenty major American newspapers indicated that only 14 percent of the quotes in major news stories came from women. Likewise, only 32 percent of front page photographs were of women. A study of major news weeklies, *Time, Newsweek,* and *U.S. News & World Report,* had similar results. Only 13 percent of the references in their stories were from female sources, as were a mere 27 percent of the photographs accompanying major stories (Curran & Renzetti, 1993:108).

One major reason women's activities are so underreported is that male reporters and male opinions dominate the news media. This was brought home to me when I attended a lecture given by ABC News "Nightline" media correspondent Jeff Greenfield. In a question-and-answer session following his lecture, my wife asked why there were so few females on the "Nightline" program. Greenfield's sexist answer was that the show was very short and, therefore, commentators had to be succinct in their remarks (implying that the world of television journalism suffers from a lack of succinct female reporters).

Feminist Naomi Wolf recently captured the import of such thought. In 1992, there were fifty-five female guests on CNN's "Crossfire," compared to 440 male guests. During the same year, only 13 percent of the Washington *Post's* op-ed pieces were authored by women. Women wrote only 14 percent of *The New Republic's* articles, comprised less than 20 percent of *Harpers'* contributors, 23 percent of *The Nation's* contributors, and 33 percent of the *Atlantic Monthly's* (Wolf, 1993:20). The pattern of male dominance was the same for every periodical of elite social criticism in this study.

Why this pattern? First, there is an institutionalized bias against women writing about "important" social issues. Women are frequently accused of writing too much about their feelings and their bodies. When men write about male experiences, it is termed important and pioneering. When women write about their experiences, it is termed too subjective.

In fact, even women's magazines treat women's social character as a trivial exercise in self-absorption. Ferguson studied British women's magazines published between 1949 and 1980, and found them obsessed with the same themes, no matter what the decade. The emphasis was overwhelmingly on personal goals: staying attractive, losing weight, getting a good job, romance, a happy family, or cooking well (Ferguson, 1983). Research on American women's magazines has demonstrated that the same narcissistic themes are present (Cantor, 1987). You can easily confirm these results just by looking at the covers of women's magazines that line the checkout stands in the nation's supermarkets.

Confinement to the Private Sphere

Women in many societies are confined to the home, the sphere of physical and social reproduction. In some societies, they are literally not permitted to enter the public space. This is especially the case in Muslim countries. During the Gulf War of 1991, American

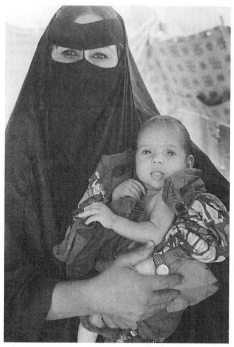

During the Persian Gulf War of 1991, female military personnel operated the same heavy equipment as did male soldiers. Modern technology has done much to erase any physical differences between the sexes. Nevertheless, women in these fields still do not always receive equal treatment.

In most Moslem societies, women are required to have their faces covered in public. In such societies, men have almost complete control over the married and reproductive lives of women. During the 1991 Gulf War, even America's female military personnel stationed in Moslem countries were not allowed to have their faces showing in public.

men and women fought and died to liberate Kuwait, an Islamic nation where women are not allowed to vote, drive cars, or go out in public without their husband's permission. When Kuwaiti women do appear in public, they are required to wear veils.

This treatment of women in Kuwait produced some interesting contradictions during the war. American servicewomen made up 6 percent of all military personnel serving the Persian Gulf (35,000 of 541,425), but American women made up 10 percent of those killed. Yet, when American servicewomen went off base they were required to wear long sleeves, be accompanied by a man, have the man pay for whatever they purchased, and use the back doors of gyms and other public facilities (Lorber, 1994:10).

The Economic
Exploitation of Women

The economic discrimination against women is found worldwide. In advanced societies like the United States, women are occupationally segregated in a dual or split labor market, often in lower-paid or less-valued work. In many nations, including the United States, they are paid lower wages, even if they do the same work as men. The segmented labor market means that there are two sets of jobs in America. One class of positions is characterized by job security, on-the-job training, high pay, good benefits, and promotions. These positions are characteristic of posts held by corporate managers, engineers, and professional workers (like doctors, professors, psychologists, and lawyers). A second set of jobs is characterized by poor pay, a lack of job security, frequent layoffs, few raises, and little hope of promotion. These posts are overwhelmingly held by women, especially women who labor in low-level service sector positions. The financial harms involved are staggering:

- "Of the 100 million women 16 and older in the U.S., 58 million were labor force participants (working or looking for work) during 1992. Women accounted for 60 percent of labor force growth between 1982 and 1992" (French, 1992:39). Despite these increases, women still account for less than one-half of 1 percent of the jobs in the highest echelons of corporate management. Only 3 percent of the top five positions below corporate chief executive officer in the largest 1000 corporations are occupied by women.

- Only 49 percent of teenage women (ages sixteen to nineteen) were in the labor force, compared with 58 percent of adult women. However, the unemployment rate among teenage women is three times higher than that of adult women—18.5 percent and 6.3 percent, respectively. The unemployment rate for all females was 6.9 percent in 1992. Unemployment rates among teenage black and Hispanic women are very high—37.2 percent and 26.4 percent, respectively (*World Almanac and Book of Facts,* 1993:123).

- "Of the 54 million employed women in the United States in 1992, 40 million worked full time (35 or more hours per week); nearly 14 million, or 25 percent of all women workers, held part-time jobs. Two-thirds (66 percent) of all part-time workers were women" (*World Almanac and Book of Facts,* 1993:123).

- Women continue to be overrepresented in low-paying jobs. Forty-four percent of employed women work in technical, sales, and administrative support jobs (clerical and secretarial workers). Even though the earnings gap between men and women is slowly closing, women earn only seventy-five cents for every dollar earned by men when comparing 1992 median weekly earnings of full-time workers ($381 for women and $505 for men) (*World Almanac and Book of Facts,* 1993:123).

- The median earnings for women high school graduates (with no college) working full-time, all year (1991) were less than those of full-time employed males who were high school dropouts—$18,042 and $20,944, respectively. "In addition, men with an associate's degree working year-round, full time earned nearly the same as similarly employed women with a master's degree—$32,221 and $33,122, respectively!"(*World Almanac and Book of Facts,* 1993:123.)

The effects of this economic exploitation result in devastating poverty. Of the 67 million families living in poverty in the United States in 1992, 12 million (18 percent) were headed by women. Forty-seven percent of black families are headed by women; in Hispanic families, 24 percent; and in white families, 14 percent. The median weekly earnings of families maintained by women in 1992 was $385, compared with $779 for married-couple families and $519 for families maintained by men. In 1991 women represented 63 percent of all persons eighteen years old and over who were living below the poverty level. The poverty rate for families maintained by women with no husband present was six times as high as for married-couple families—35.6 percent and 6.0 percent, respectively. Women maintained 54 percent of all poor families in 1991. Women maintained 78 percent of poor black families, about 46 percent of poor Hispanic families, and 44 percent of poor white families. Indeed, families headed by women are 5.5 times more likely to live below the poverty level than families where a man is present. Families headed by black women are 10.5 more likely to live in poverty as families headed by white men (French, 1992:40).

Many of the devastating physical, financial, and moral wrongs generated by poverty were discussed in previous chapters. The economic future of the poor in America, especially poor families headed by women, is bleak. There are 12 million children in the United States without medical coverage, and 5 million are now on the brink of homelessness, thanks in large part to the entitlement cuts of the 1980s, two-thirds of which were made in programs for the poor (French, 1992:40).

One reason for these tragic realities points to women's place in the structure of the postindustrial (service) economy. Nearly two-thirds of all temporary workers are women, and 27 percent of all employed women (versus 11 percent of all employed males) are part-time workers, most of whom lack benefits like medical insurance (McClure, 1994:23).

Around the world, women fare even worse economically than in the United States economically. Millions of women toil for pennies a day in Third World factories owned by First World multinational corporations. These women face a variety of physical hazards—from radiation exposure from cathode ray tubes (computer screens) to poisonous chemicals and toxic waste in the factories and landfills surrounding their meager homes.

Moreover, women have often relied on bizarre methods to obtain and keep jobs in male-dominated fields. Billy Tipton (1914–1974) was a professional jazz musician, who played piano, saxophone, and performed with a number of famous bands. In the 1950s, Billy formed the Billy Tipton Trio and appeared in clubs throughout the western United States for ten years. When Billy died in 1974, the director of the Ball and Dodd funeral home in Spokane, Washington, discovered that Billy Tipton was actually a woman. Billy had spent her entire career posing as a man in order to improve her chances of getting jobs with jazz bands (New York *Times,* 1989:A-1).

A related form of discrimination against women involves their roles as consumers. Women and minorities are especially prone to be victims of white-collar crimes. A recent study undertaken by a Northwestern University Law School professor illustrates how women, especially minority women, are subject to rip-offs. Six males and six females, including a black male and a black female, were given training in body language and learned the same script concerning how to shop for a car. The twelve then collectively visited ninety car dealerships in the greater Chicago area, inquiring about the prices of automobiles.

In nearly every case, white males were given the best deals on car purchases. Even in instances where the salespeople were minorities or women, white males still were charged less for the cars. Moreover, those perceived as most able to afford the cars were always charged significantly less. White women, on average, were charged $150 more than white men for the same automobile. African-American males were charged $400 more than white males, and African-American women were charged the most, $900 more than white males. This case sadly demonstrates the additive effects of gender and racial discrimination (French, 1992:43).

Recent literature has acknowledged that women have been victims of white-collar crime. The Dalkon Shield intrauterine birth control device, which caused sterilization, infections, and death in some women, was a scandal that victimized women, as was the withholding of information about Ovulen, an oral contraceptive, by its manufacturer, Searle. Women also suffered from the use of silicone breast implants, which were found to cause toxic reactions and other serious diseases. The same is true for conditions related to the use of video display terminals in offices, which can cause a variety of neck, back, and shoulder problems, as well as eyestrain and carpal tunnel syndrome. Carpal tunnel syndrome (a condition caused by continuous pressure on the median nerve in the wrist) primarily affects female assembly line workers and typists.

Women make up from 62 to 89 percent of the workers in the textile industry who are in danger of contracting "brown lung" disease from exposure to cotton dust (Gerber & Weeks, 1992:325–340). All these examples point to the fact that the most powerless people in American society and around the world are the leading victims of elite deviance of all kinds, and part of their ongoing victimization includes a lack of attention to exactly this elite deviance and related social problems.

Women's "Second Shift"

When women take jobs in the "real" labor force, they are expected to work a "second shift" (Hochschild, 1990), that is, doing most of the housework and child care. The housework issue is a typical example of how personal troubles are experienced as alienating conditions in everyday settings. Just trying to mesh family and work (or student) roles is no small challenge for many people, but it is particularly tough on women.

Arlie Hochschild (1990) has documented a profound change in the relationship between the sexes. The rise of the service economy, coupled with galloping inflation and increasing numbers of married women in the workplace, has redefined marital happiness for women. Marital contentment for wives now, in part, revolves around the willingness of husbands to do housework.

However, the role of homemaker continues to be devalued in American society, and working couples often try to pass it on to low-paid domestic help. Otherwise it is still the woman who does most of it. Men tend to regard most housework done by women as beneath them because women have done it for so long (Lorber, 1994). In fact, women work an average of fifteen more hours per week at home than do their male counterparts. Even when husbands share some of the housework, it is still the wives who *feel* more responsible for it. Women also feel more responsible for checking on the children's safety while at work. Moreover, men have more power over the housework they do perform, such as changing the oil in the car or repairing appliances. Husbands tend to do fewer of the least desirable tasks associated with housework, such as scrubbing the toilet. Some polls indicate that a majority of men claim they believe they should help with housework, but opinions in this case are not related to actual behavior. In fact, Hochschild's study of 600 couples documented that men's failure to help with household chores was the second most common reason for divorce (Hochschild, 1990:68).

The housework issue is also reflected in each gender's view of marriage itself. A 1993 national poll revealed that almost half of America's single women do not want to get married. Many of these women have become disillusioned by the high divorce rate.

Sexism and the Law

In many cultures, women suffer the effects of legal discrimination, even those holding jobs within the legal profession. In 1994, *Redbook* magazine described the behavior of what is termed America's most sexist judges. Most of the judges mentioned were white males who were over fifty years old. Their sexism in at least one case extended to the treatment of one judge's own wife:

- In 1993, a seventy-one-year-old South Carolina judge kidnapped his own wife and her mother. He proceeded to tie them both up with duct tape and administer electric shocks to his wife with a cattle prod. The judge in his case gave the defendant five years probation and sixty months of house arrest.

- A Baltimore county judge gave a forty-four-year-old man a sentence of probation after he raped his eighteen-year-old female employee. The woman had become drunk and then passed out on her boss' bed.

- One judge allowed a trial delay of three months for a male lawyer who was going on a fishing vacation, but refused to allow a delay for a female lawyer who had gone into premature labor.

- A judge in South Carolina was convicted of sexually harassing several female defendants who appeared in his own court. The charges ranged from breast fondling to ordering one woman to kiss his penis. The defendant pleaded no contest to the charges, which were punishable with a maximum thirty-six-year prison term. The judge trying the case gave his judicial colleague a mere three-year suspended sentence, four hundred hours of community service, a $500 fine, and mandatory mental health counseling, noting that the defendant's wife was an invalid and that the man was needed at home (Weller, 1994:83–88)!

- During the 1994 major league baseball strike, multimillionaire slugger Barry Bonds pleaded hardship and persuaded a local domestic relations court judge to cut by half his spousal and child support payments. After granting Bonds' request, the starstruck judge then promptly turned to Bonds and asked for his autograph (San Francisco *Chronicle,* 1994:A-1).

Women are sentenced to prison terms for behaviors men can never engage in. Judges all over America sentence women to use birth control for the remainder of their reproductive lives, for example when women abandon their babies, or abuse their children. Pregnant women who drink during pregnancy are threatened with manslaughter charges if they miscarry, or are arrested in their hospital beds if their babies test positive for illegal drugs (French, 1992:143ff).

The number of women serving prison terms has tripled since the 1980s. Almost two-thirds of female prisoners are in prison for using drugs. The number of women on death row, contrary to myth, is now proportional to the number of males awaiting execution. Forty percent of females who murder kill men who have abused them. Only recently have women whose abuse drove them to kill their abusers begun to be paroled.

Violence and the law frequently function to socially control women. Rape and domestic abuse, and the threat of these activities, are often used to maintain male dominance. These crimes, while illegal in many societies, are not effectively prosecuted. Instead such acts function to intimidate women into passively accepting their abuse, limit their sexual freedom, and keep them out of public life opportunities.

Sexism in Education

Women lack equal access to educational opportunity at every level of schooling. Important differences in socialization are established in the earliest grades. Girls are told to act like "little ladies," which usually means sit still and be quiet. Boys, in contrast, are permitted to wrestle on the floor with each other. Recent studies in the United States, Germany, and England demonstrate that sexism in education is institutionalized in Eurocentric culture. In all three nations:

- Boys were called on in class two-thirds of the time, and were praised or criticized much more often than girls, receiving the vast majority of teacher attention and encouragement. Boys are far more often praised for the intellectual content of their work, while girls receive praise for neatness.

- Both male and female teachers described boys as "intelligent, interested, and creative." Girls were described as "conscientious, clean, orderly and diligent," thereby stereotyping both sexes, and labeling females as unscholarly.

- Boys in all three nations interrupt girls, criticize their classroom remarks, and make fun of them. Boys are seldom upbraided for calling out answers in class, but girls who do the same thing are criticized for being rude. Sexual harassment of female students is widely tolerated in many high schools.

This behavior has a negative effect on the confidence and self-esteem of female students. Girls attending all-female classes, especially in math and science, have more confidence and participate more often than girls in coed classes (Schmidt, 1992:50). Unfortunately, girls who attend college, even if they get better grades than boys (which is frequently the case), suffer from lower self-confidence about their possibilities for success in college and lower aspirations regarding their career goals. Tragically, girls are less likely to reach their potential in life than are boys, and sexism in schools is one major reason.

A 1992 study by the American Association of University Women (AAUW) found that "sexism may be the most widespread and serious form of bias in the classroom" (Kantrowitz et al., 1992:62). To illustrate,

- Boys who frequently need help with reading are regularly offered remedial classes, but girls, who just as often need help with math, find no such remedial classes offered.

- Studies indicate that boys learn better in competitive environments and girls function better in cooperative ones. Most schools operate on the competitive model.

- Science and math classes are where the differences between the genders are most pronounced. In fact, boys are often perceived by teachers as better in science and math than girls (Felson & Trudeau, 1991), and there are very few women to serve as role models in these fields. The vast majority of female science and math majors come from all-girl high schools or all-female colleges, not from coed schools. A recent Canadian study found that only 2 percent of Canadian engineering faculty are female (fifty-four out of 2438). The reasons given for this great underrepresentation point to the lack of female role models, gender stereotyping by parents and teachers, "and systematic discrimination in universities and in the workplace" against women (Powell, 1992:607).

- More than two-thirds of the nation's teachers are women, yet even female teachers are likely to treat students according to gender stereotypes. Asked to remember their favorite students, both male and female teachers mention the boys who were assertive. Students least liked are assertive females. Studies reveal that when women are administrators of educational institutions, such schools are much less likely to adhere to gender stereotypes. Yet women constitute only 10 percent of college presidents, and women of color only 1.4 percent (Ries & Stone, 1992:303).

- Textbooks have been studied extensively and found to reinforce traditional gender stereotypes. Females in primary and secondary school texts are depicted in traditional female roles, as nurses, teachers, secretaries, or homemakers, whereas men are presented as middle-class professionals, especially doctors, lawyers, and scientists (Richmond-Abbott, 1986).

- Girls are less likely to attend primary and secondary schools than are boys in most cultures (even with mandatory attendance laws), and less likely to go to college or graduate education.

Women's Health

Women's physical health and mental health until quite recently were given second-class status. For decades, women's health issues had been excluded in medical research:

- Virtually all studies involving cholesterol were based on male samples, as were studies of the relationship between taking aspirin and preventing second heart attacks.

Before abortion became legal in the United States, many women died from "back alley" abortions performed by incompetent amateurs. Many people fear a return to such days if abortion rights are abolished. Others insist that the goal of the antiabortion movement is in reality an attempt to control the sex lives of American women.

- Women are the fastest-growing population to develop AIDS, but as of 1992, no studies of the effects of AIDS therapies on women had been performed.

- The incidence of breast cancer has doubled in the United States since 1960, yet until 1992, the vast majority of cancer research involved cancers that affect both sexes. Collectively, only 13 percent of the research funds spent by the National Institutes of Health involved research on women's health issues (French, 1992: 133).

- In some cultures, girls suffer higher death rates due to malnutrition or neglect. Worldwide, some 100 million female fetuses have been selectively aborted and female infants murdered because the culture requires a dowry for a bride. As a result, men now outnumber women in dowry-practicing cultures like India, Pakistan, and the United Arab Emirates (French, 1992:125ff).

Reproduction and
Discrimination Against Women

Control over reproduction is in large measure about the control of women's sexual activity. Yet men set the policies in contraception, sterilization, abortion, and access to child care, while women are held responsible for getting pregnant or for not raising children properly. The head of the antiabortion group Operation Rescue, Randal Terry, has remarked on several occasions that his real goal in the "right to life" movement is control over the circumstances under which women are allowed to conceive and bear children. His preference is that children be born only inside marriages characterized as monogamous, heterosexual marriages, preferably where the wife is a full-time homemaker. Terry has also remarked that if doctors can be prevented from performing abortions, it makes no differences whether or not abortion is legal (Sydell, 1993:26).

Men, but not women, are viewed as sexually autonomous and entitled to receive sexual pleasure. Women are defined as the sexual servants of men. Moreover, women are frequently exploited as providers of "intimate" sexual and reproductive services, especially prostitution and surrogate mothering. Women become commodities as providers of such services, but have little control over the rules governing such exchanges.

One of the most blatant forms of this sexual discrimination is sexploitation or sex-tourism. This involves sex tours for men, many of whom are affluent corporate executives from First World countries like Japan. These men visit brothels in Third World nations like Thailand and the Philippines. The brothels are staffed by young women—many just girls—who have been sold into virtual slavery by their poor peasant fathers. The sexploitation industry was first proposed as an economic development strategy by international foreign aid agencies like the World Bank, International Monetary Fund, and the U.S. Agency for International Development. Worldwide, there are an estimated 14 million women who have become prostitutes involved in the multinational sex-tourism industry. There is also a thriving mail-order bride business that operates out of the former West Germany. Brochures advertise young Asian and Latin American women brides as "submissive, non-emancipated, and docile" (French, 1992:35–36). Both the sex-tourism and wife-selling industries are supported and maintained by a web of multinational corporations in the airline, resort, and hotel industries.

Sexual Harassment of Women

Sexual harassment is defined as sexual behavior or attention that is unwanted, unsolicited, and nonreciprocated. Sexual harassment was hardly ever discussed in public until the 1970s, and women had learned to expect such behavior from males at work, in marriage, and in public settings (Lott, 1994:258). It was not until 1980 that the federal Equal Employment Opportunity Commission (EEOC) interpreted Title VII of the 1964 Civil Rights Act to include sex discrimination. The EEOC guidelines came in response to the Working Women's Institute claim that "sexual harassment is the single most widespread occupational hazard faced by women in the workforce" (Lott, 1994:258). These guidelines now make it illegal for engaging in sexual acts to be made as a condition of work assignment, employment, or for sexual conduct to interfere with an employee's work performance or to create a hostile environment. More than three-fourths of workplace sexual harassment victimizes women, is usually perpetrated by older married men, and frequently goes unreported. Indeed, following the 1992 Senate hearing of Justice Clarence Thomas' Supreme Court nomination, and the testimony of Anita Hill, complaints of sexual harassment filed with the EEOC increased from 6883 in 1991 to over 10,500 in 1992 (in Lott, 1994:258).

Sexual harassment is encountered frequently in male-dominated areas that women have begun to enter, such as the U.S. military:

To illustrate, a 1993 Defense Department report found that eighty-three women and seven men were assaulted during the 1991 Tailhook Association convention at the Las Vegas Hilton. (The association's members are present and former Navy fliers.) The three hundred–page report was based on more than 2900 interviews, and it stated that victims were "groped, pinched, fondled" and "bitten" by their assailants and that the oral sex and sexual intercourse performed in front of others contributed to a "general atmosphere of debauchery" (*World Almanac and Book of Facts,* 1994:52). Ultimately, Navy Secretary John Dalton asked for the removal of Admiral Frank Kelso, chief of naval operations, and three

The U.S. Navy was rocked in the early 1990s by the Tailhook Scandal in which many female naval personnel were sexually harassed and physically injured by male naval pilots in a Las Vegas hotel. The harassment had been taking place for years. As a result of the scandal, naval operations chief Kelso, pictured here, was forced to retire.

other admirals were censured. Twenty-eight other admirals and one marine general received letters of caution (New York *Times,* October 2, 1993: A-1, A-8). None of the officers involved ever went to prison.

The Tailhook Scandal is symbolic of a much more widespread condition. In March, 1994, four women serving in the military told a House committee that sexual harassment in the military is very common and that complaints about it often go unheeded. Indeed, nearly two-thirds of women questioned by Defense Department investigators felt they had been sexually harassed (Kantrowitz et al., 1991). While stronger harassment rules have been issued by all branches of the armed services, and sensitivity training initiated, female personnel claim that complaints of sexual harassment are met with disdain, ostracism, and in some cases they are transferred to a dead-end job.

Sexual harassment in male-dominated professions is certainly not limited to the armed services. Studies in the 1980s and 1990s of women conclude that nearly one-third of female doctors and medical students, 60 percent of 3000 high-ranking female lawyers, and 53 percent of female business executives report being sexually harassed sometime during their careers (Lott, 1994:259). A 1992 study conducted by the U.S. federal courts found that 60 percent of the female lawyers practicing in the federal judiciary complained of being sexually harassed by male lawyers or judges within the last five years. Forty percent of women lawyers stated they were harassed by their male clients (Hansen, 1992:50).

The problem of sexual harassment is even worse in traditional male working-class occupations. A California commission was established in 1991 to investigate why so few construction workers are female. The commission found a work environment characterized by constant warfare between the sexes. Men frequently urinated beside female workers, and hung lewd photos in women's restrooms. One woman electrician was doused with water while working on a ladder with live electrical wires (French, 1992:131).

The Hooters restaurant chain, which hires large-busted women, recently published a calendar with the months out of order. Hooters claims it was designed by their female employees, implying that the women they hire are so dumb they can not even get the months of the year straight. A group of former Hooters employees is currently suing the company for sexual harassment (NBC "Dateline," 1994).

Female Lack of Political Power

Women suffer from underrepresentation in virtually all the world's political systems, political parties, elective offices, international agencies, courts, and administrative agencies. Under the U.S. Constitution, women were excluded from voting, and did not receive the vote until 1920. A major reason they were granted it then was that the Republicans nominated Warren Harding that year, and the GOP thought women would vote for Harding because he was handsome.

Between 1920 and 1960, very few women were elected to public office. The three women governors who were elected during this period were put into office to succeed their husbands, either because these men were ineligible to run for additional terms, or because they were ill and could no longer continue in office.

Today, only six of one hundred U.S. senators are women, and four of the six weren't elected until 1992. In the House of Representatives, forty-three of 435 members are female, and twenty-four of these women weren't elected until 1992. In 1990, a larger percentage of women held office in India's Parliament than in the U.S. House of Representatives (7.9 versus 6.4 percent, respectively) (French, 1992:45). In the United States, the supposed bastion of women's liberation, women have less voice in government than in Third World nations. Only 17.9 percent of U.S. state cabinet posts are female occupied, and only four of fifty governors are women (*World Almanac and Book of Facts,* 1994:88).

When women do get elected to public office, or become America's First Lady, they are subject to attacks never leveled at male politicians. If a First Lady seems to influence the president's decision making, she is derided for being domineering and manipulative. Hillary Clinton has been attacked for playing an active role in shaping health care policy, for speaking out in favor of retaining funds for the Public Broadcasting System, and for other positions she has taken on issues.

In Third World nations women occupy only about 6 percent of government posts, and in most European democracies, between 5 and 11 percent of government positions are held by women. Worldwide, only 12.7 percent of elected legislators are female (down from 14.6 percent in 1988). The situation is even worse in the newly emerging democracies of Eastern Europe. Nearly all the top government posts in Romania and Hungary are male occupied, and in Poland President Lech Walesa has yet to appoint a single woman to his cabinet (French, 1992:46).

Mutilation of Men and Women

Both sexes are victims of mutilation of their sexual organs, but the effects are more detrimental to women. Worldwide, some 20 million women have had their external vaginal areas altered without their consent. About 80 percent of Islamic nations, most in Africa, engage in such practices.

The mutilation takes various forms, but the most common include placing a large ring through the large genital lips, sealing the vaginal opening to prevent intercourse. In other cases, the vaginal opening is sewn up. Some cultures practice clitorectomy, cutting away the entire clitoris and the small lips surrounding the vagina, denying women any pleasure from sexual activity. In some places, the sealed flesh which keeps the vagina closed is cut open to allow penetration of the penis after marriage. These vaginal alterations make women more vulnerable to serious infections, hemorrhaging during childbirth, and painful urination (French, 1992).

Warren Farrell (1993) has noted that the circumcision of the male penis is also a form of mutilation. The removal of the foreskin of the penis has now been rejected by most medically advanced nations (except the United States). There is no question that circumcision performed without anesthetic is a painful experience for male babies, and there is simply no evidence that the procedure enhances either the health or sexuality of males.

Sexism Against Men

Men are dehumanized by the mate selection process in Western culture, and in the work roles of American life. Men work more than working women do, eight hours more per week on average, to be exact (Farrell, 1991:82). Women still marry men who make more money than they do. Men still feel responsible for the family finances in the same way that women feel more responsible for the family housework. Farrell's point is that if women are sex objects and darling little slaves, then men are success objects, chosen, not for their humanity, but for their material potential.

One of the most interesting studies of the self-alienation (self-directed dehumanization) experienced by successful American males was reported by psychologist Jan Halper in her book *Quiet Desperation* (1988). Dr. Halper interviewed 4126 *Fortune* 500 executives, middle managers, and other professionals. She also conducted in-depth interviews and provided free therapy to a subsample of executives. These men told her that in order to advance in their firms, they had to go along, make "sacrifices" for the sake of their careers. Many of these successful men were self-estranged, that is, cut off from their feelings, wishes, wants, and needs. Their socialization both within their families and at work has taught them to deny their feelings, and conform to the demands of job and family, according to Halper.

The distinguished psychologist, Rollo May (1953), noted that the most common problem of the postmodern era is emotional emptiness. Many people are so self-estranged that they don't know what they want, and often they do not know what they feel. Most often, successful men deny their unhappiness at work and home by rationalizing their feelings away. Their disappointments and feelings of emptiness and isolation are shrouded in excuses: "I was loyal. I did my duty. You can't fight the system. You've got to go along to get along." Many of these executives and professionals are so disconnected from their feelings because "no one ever taught them how to find out what is important to them" (Halper, 1988:29).

Many of these men suffer the ill effects of not knowing who they are. They confuse the roles they play with who they are as people. Often they see themselves as a group of titles: "hero, breadwinner, lover, husband, father, warrior, empire builder, or mover-and-shaker" (Halper, 1988:66). Relinquishing a role or two, through dismissal, retirement, or divorce, often leads to an identity crisis in which they feel they are nothing without their roles. Stress reactions such as depression and feeling out of control are not uncommon. Some even commit suicide.

Because men are not supposed to have emotional needs, they rarely bond with each other by sharing their feelings. If men do have other male friends, they are often accused of being irresponsible, neglecting their wives and children. Spending time with friends is viewed as time wasted, time not spent to get to the top of their profession. Consequently, what few male friendships American men do have are superficial relationships undertaken for business purposes or purposes of conveniences (Leitch, 1991).

Is it any wonder that men and women have a difficult time communicating with each other? Deborah Tannen has discovered that men and women not only communicate in different ways; they actually have different expectations concerning the outcome of the communication process, as the accompanying "Private Troubles/Public Issues" points out.

Private Troubles   Public Issues

Why Is It So Hard for Men and Women to Talk to Each Other?

—Deborah Tannen

For women, as for girls, intimacy is the fabric of relationships, and talk is the thread from which it is woven. Little girls create and maintain friendships by exchanging secrets; similarly, women regard conversation as the cornerstone of friendship. So a woman expects her husband to be a new and improved version of a best friend. What is important is not the individual subjects that are discussed but the sense of closeness, of a life shared, that emerges when people tell their thoughts, feelings, and impressions.

Bonds between boys can be as intense as girls', but they are based less on talking, more on doing things together. Since they don't assume talk is the cement that binds a relationship, men don't know what kind of talk women want, and they don't miss it when it isn't there.

Boys' groups are larger, more inclusive, and more hierarchical, so boys must struggle to avoid the subordinate position in the group. This may play a role in women's complaints that men don't listen to them. Some men really don't like to listen, because being the listener makes them feel one-down, like a child listening to adults or an employee to a boss.

But often when women tell men, "You aren't listening," and the men protest "I am," the men are right. The impression of not listening results from misalignments in the mechanics of conversation. The misalignment begins as soon as a man and a woman take physical positions. This became clear when I studied videotapes made by psychologist Bruce Dorval of children and adults talking to their same-sex best friends. I found that at every age, the girls and women faced each other directly, their eyes anchored on each other's faces. At every age, the boys and men sat at angles to each other and looked elsewhere in the room, periodically glancing at each other. They were obviously attuned to each other, often mirroring each other's movements. But the tendency of men to face away can give women the impression they aren't listening even when they are. A young woman in college was frustrated: Whenever she told her boyfriend she wanted to talk to him, he would lie down on the floor, close his eyes, and put his arm over his face. This signaled to her, "He's taking a nap." But he insisted he was listening extra hard. Normally, he looks around the room, so he is easily distracted. Lying down and covering his eyes helped him concentrate on what she was saying. . . .

Women's conversational habits are as frustrating to men as men's are to women. Men who expect silent attention interpret a stream of listener noise as overreaction or impatience. Also, when women talk to each other in a close, comfortable setting, they often overlap, finish each other's sentences and anticipate what the other is about to say. This practice, which I call "participatory listenership," is often perceived by men as interruption, intrusion and lack of attention. . . .

The Sounds of Silence

These differences begin to clarify why women and men have such different expectations about communication in marriage. For women, talk creates intimacy. Marriage is an orgy of closeness: you can tell your feelings and thoughts, and still be loved. Their greatest fear is being pushed away. But men live in a hierarchical world, where talk maintains independence and status. They are on guard to protect themselves from being put down and pushed around.

This explains the paradox of the talkative man who said of his silent wife, "She's the talker." In the public setting of a guest lecture, he felt challenged to show his intelligence and display his understanding of the lecture. But at home, where he has nothing to prove and no one to defend against, he is free to remain silent. For his wife, being home means she is free from the worry that something she says might offend someone, or spark disagreement, or appear to be showing off; at home she is free to talk.

The communication problems that endanger marriage can't be fixed by mechanical engineering. They require a new conceptual framework about the role of talk in human relationships. Many of the psychological explanations that have become second nature may not be helpful, because they tend to blame either women (for not being assertive enough) or men (for not being in touch with their feelings). A sociolinguistic approach by which male-female conversation is seen as cross-cultural communication allows us to understand the problem and forge solutions without blaming either party.

Once the problem is understood, improvement comes naturally, as it did to the young woman and her boyfriend who seemed to go to sleep when she wanted to talk. Previously, she had accused him of not listening, and he had refused to change his behavior, since that would be admitting fault. But then she learned about and explained to him the differences in women's and men's habitual ways of aligning themselves in conversation. The next time she told him she wanted to talk, he began, as usual, by lying down and covering his eyes. When the familiar negative reaction bubbled up, she reassured herself that he really was listening. But then he sat up and looked at her. Thrilled, she asked why. He said, "You like me to look at you when we talk, so I'll try to do it." Once he saw their differences as cross-cultural rather than right and wrong, he independently altered his behavior.

Women who feel abandoned and deprived when their husbands won't listen to or report daily news may be happy to discover their husbands trying to adapt once they

Continued on next page

Private Troubles	Public Issues

Continued

understand the place of small talk in women's relationships. But if their husbands don't adapt, the women may still be comforted that for men, this is not a failure of intimacy. Accepting the difference, the wives may look to their friends or family for that kind of talk. And husbands who can't provide it shouldn't feel their wives have made unreasonable demands. Some couples will still decide to divorce, but at least their decisions will be based on realistic expectations.

In these times of resurgent ethnic conflicts, the world desperately needs cross-cultural understanding. Like charity, successful cross-cultural communication should begin at home.

Deborah Tannen, professor of linguistics at Georgetown University, is the author of *You Just Don't Understand: Women and Men in Conversation,* published by William Morrow.

Source: The Washington Post Writer's Group (ed.) (1993):158–162.

The Oppression of Gays and Lesbians

Homosexuals are severely oppressed in almost all of the world's nations. Like all other forms of oppression, there are important stereotypes about gays and lesbians that contribute to being oppressed. These stereotypes survive despite much scientific evidence to the contrary, and despite efforts to educate the public concerning the realities of gay and lesbian life.

Among the most durable stereotypes concerning homosexuals are:

• Gay teachers desire to molest their students, especially children, and "convert" them to homosexuality. An accompanying notion holds that gays, especially gay men, are obsessed with sex. Both of these notions are patent untruths. For one thing, child abusers are primarily heterosexual. In fact, over 90 percent of all child abuse is committed by heterosexuals. Scapegoating is very functional in that blaming child abuse on gays prevents society from examining the real source of most abuse: the venerated American family. It colors the family with a false glow of innocence as regards not only child abuse, but wife battering and incest as well. A second fallacious stereotype holds that a person can be talked into (converted to) homosexuality. The most recent evidence strongly suggests a biologically inherited (genetic) component to homosexuality.

- Lesbians are really women who want to be men. Whatever function served by this confusing notion, the truth is that lesbians are women who are sexually attracted to other women. The most masculine-looking and -acting lesbian women tend to get noticed; however, there are many lesbian women who are not demonstrably masculine.

- Gay men are "swishy," effeminate in their behavior, including speaking with a lisp, and affecting effeminate mannerisms. There are some gays who act this way, but there are many others who do not. Many gay men are truck drivers, weight lifters, and members of the military, who are indistinguishable from their heterosexual counterparts. Many gays who do adopt effeminate mannerisms do so to rebel against the heterosexual world's persecution of them.

- Gays are exclusively members of certain "feminine" occupations, such as hair dressing, interior decorating, and fashion designing. Gays may be attracted to these professions because they are jobs that require caring sensitivity and, typically, involve working with women, who are more tolerant of gays than men. However, gays and lesbians choose the same professions as do heterosexuals. In fact, many fields that are male dominated (like the military, police, and firefighters) attract some gays precisely because there are a lot of eligible males. When someone in one of these professions is found out to be gay, heterosexual males, who often enter such jobs to "prove" their masculinity, are extremely angered by gays' presence, or frightened that a gay person may make a pass at them.

Discriminating Against Gays and Lesbians

Discrimination against homosexuals has a theological basis dating back about 6000 years. The Old Testament, New Testament, and Koran all contain passages describing homosexuality as an "abomination," and "a mortal sin." These proscriptions against same-sex relations perhaps had their origins in the desire of religious groups to increase their numbers. Whatever the reason for the proscription, homosexuals have been persecuted ever since.

In many ways gay and lesbian oppression is hardest to measure. Even if efforts were made to do so, many homosexuals are secretive about their sexual preference, so that measuring abuses of their rights constitutes a formidable task. Nevertheless, some distinct patterns of discrimination are clear:

Gays and lesbians have long been subject to acts of discrimination by homophobic individuals. The National Gay and Lesbian Task Force reported a 142 percent increase from 1985 to 1986 and a 42 percent increase in 1987 in incidents of anti-gay violence. In 1988, there were seventy gay-related murders in the United States (Sheffield, 1992:390). One recent study by the National Gay and Lesbian Task Force found that 90 percent of gays and lesbians had been victimized in some way on the basis of their sexual orientation (Mohr, 1992a:355).

Institutional Discrimination
Against Gays and Lesbians

Homosexuals have been victimized by a wide variety of acts of institutional discrimination, not the least of which involve their treatment by the U.S. military.

For example, a recent investigation by the American Civil Liberties Union of Southern California found that the navy's treatment of gays was harsher than its treatment of heterosexual child molesters and rapists. For example, a navy dentist who was convicted of committing sodomy with his sixteen-year-old son was permitted to remain on duty because of a new rehabilitation program for sex offenders. Homosexual officers and enlisted personnel engaging in adult consensual sex are ordered discharged immediately (Los Angeles *Times,* 1994: A-1).

Only in 1994, for the first time in American history, a gay man was granted political asylum under the Refugee Act of 1980. The gay man was an illegal immigrant who had been in the United States for fourteen years. He claimed that were he to return to his native Mexico, he would face certain death because of his homosexuality. Forty other gays and lesbians from several Latin American nations, Iran, Russia, and Algeria have also filed for political asylum, indicating that hatred of gays takes place on nearly all continents (Doyle, 1994: A-1, A-12).

Richard Mohr (1992b:5) has aptly remarked that "gays in America have fewer rights than do barnyard animals in Sweden." Title VII of the 1964 Civil Rights Act promotes equal employment opportunities, and prohibits discrimination on the basis of "race, color, religion, sex, and national origin" (Lee & Brown, 1993:46), but not sexual orientation. Attempts to include sexual orientation under the law date back to 1981, but have been unsuccessful. Gays are not included in the Civil Rights Act of 1991, nor do they have a right to privacy under the Fifth and Fourteenth Amendments. In *Bowers* v. *Hardwick* (1986) the U.S. Supreme Court ruled that gays having consensual adult sex were in violation of a Georgia sodomy law, and a ten-year prison sentence for having homosexual sex in the privacy of a gay man's home was allowed to stand!

There are fifty-nine cities and four states (Connecticut, Hawaii, Wisconsin, and Massachusetts) in America that do have local civil rights laws, but a national gay civil rights law has yet to be passed. Further, the U.S. Commission on Civil Rights and the U.S. Census Bureau regularly collect information on racial, ethnic, and gender minorities under various civil rights laws. However, there is no comparable information collected on gay and lesbian citizens. Being officially invisible in this way in and of itself constitutes a subtle form of institutional oppression.

The military blatantly discriminates against gays, having discharged about 1400 gays per month before the Clinton "don't ask—don't tell" policy went into effect (Weisberg, 1990:20; Duke, 1993:164). After the Clinton policy went into effect (July 1993), there were actually *more* discharges of gays than before the policy went into effect (Rosin, 1994:12), because gays were being informed upon by private third parties. One lesbian woman protested the military's policy in a case that could have far-reaching repercussions. In *Doe* v. *Rosa,* a judge ordered military recruiters off a college campus because an admitted lesbian law student was refused an interview by the Judge Advocate General's office (*ABA Journal,* 1994:32). It is unclear whether or not ROTC programs will also be removed from college campuses as a result, but if they are, the result could be devastating. Other forms of discrimination against gays are common:

- Most health insurance plans do not allow gays to insure their partners. Only 143 major corporations (out of 2 million) do have policies that protect gays against discrimination. Gay marriage is still illegal in all states, except Minnesota, California, and Hawaii. Gay couples do not qualify as married persons for the purpose of adopting children. Gays also remain unprotected by laws involving discrimination in housing, inheritance, immigration, security clearances, public accommodation, and police protection (Blumfield & Raymond, 1993:252).

- Most Christian denominations, Orthodox Judaism, and other major religions (Islam) do not allow gays to become members of clergy. Fundamentalist Christians believe that AIDS is a plague brought against homosexuals by God for their sin of being gay (McSpadden, 1993:91ff). In the field of education, surveys indicate that about 15 percent of lesbians and one-third of gay men had been discriminated against because of their sexual orientation. Only about half of gays in education have disclosed their identities to coworkers due to fear of discrimination (Fassinger, 1993:121).

- In medicine, U.S. courts have upheld the rights of hospitals to fire workers who refuse to disclose results of HIV tests, and a number of surveys indicate that workers do not want HIV positive workers around them, even when they know the chances of contracting AIDS is minimal (Roth & Carman, 1993: 173–183). Studies of public opinion concerning gays with AIDS report that homosexual patients are perceived as being "more responsible for and more deserving of, their illness, more deserving of employment loss, and less deserving of sympathy and even medical care" than nonhomosexuals with other diseases (Norton & Bunch, 1993:189). About two-thirds of 2000 workers in this same study don't even want to use the same bathrooms as people with AIDS (Norton & Bunch, 1993:194). Only 4 to 10 percent of businesses have written insurance policies for people who test HIV positive, at a time when people diagnosed with HIV are living longer than ever before. Only twenty-four states include AIDS as a disability.

- In many hospitals, gays and lesbians are often denied visitation rights because policy dictates that only blood relatives or spouses are allowed visitation. Gays and lesbians have frequently been denied license to practice medicine as well.

- The U.S. Postal Service used to provide employers with a list of patrons receiving gay and lesbian literature. This practice was ordered stopped in 1966.

- The criminal justice system has discriminated against gays for decades. Police commonly make sweeps of areas suspected of containing gay prostitutes, and "queer bashing" (beating up gays) has been reported for years. Police commonly enter gay bars under the guise of inspecting for possible code violations only to intimidate gay patrons. Gays are commonly arrested for jaywalking and other minor offenses as they leave gay bars. It is not uncommon for police departments to draw up lists of suspected and known gays, and proceed to arrest them on a variety of trumped-up charges: lewd conduct, vagrancy, or public nuisance laws (Blumfield & Raymond, 1993:253).

- In court, gay and lesbian crime victims are often viewed as having provoked the criminal behavior. People who commit assaults against gays and lesbians (which are disturbingly common) are often given light sentences or acquitted.

- In jails and prisons, homosexuals are frequently harassed, sexually assaulted, and sometimes murdered.

What all of these forms of discrimination demonstrate collectively is that gays and lesbians are perceived as dehumanized "queer" creatures, who deserve the evils that befall them. It is small wonder that so many gay people suffer a low self-esteem born of constant rejection and the shame that comes with having to keep secret one's very identity as a person.

Summary

Discrimination against women, men, and gays is all-pervasive in a society plagued by dehumanization of various racial, ethnic, gender, religious, and homosexual groups. The social character traits associated with being female are not just not valued, they are actively repressed. Women are stereotyped as irrational sex objects whose activities, be they at work or home, are trivial and of less value than those of men.

Women are discriminated against in virtually every area of their lives. In many nations around the world, women are kept at home, where their primary role is one of reproduction and nurturing. When in the paid labor force, women are also expected to perform a "second shift" of home domestic chores, without much help from their male partners. Further, women are heavily segregated into certain occupations, usually those involving lower-paying and less-valued jobs and are often paid lower wages and salaries, even if they are in the same occupations as men. They are less likely to be promoted into executive and managerial positions, and even more rarely into positions involving the supervision of males. When they do gain access to managerial and professional positions, they frequently encounter a "glass ceiling" beyond which they can not be promoted.

Women are often socially controlled by legal discrimination. In some societies, their right to own property is extremely limited. They are sometimes forbidden from obtaining divorces, testifying in court, and partaking of many other rights enjoyed by men.

Violence also frequently functions as a means of social control of women. Domestic violence and rape serve to maintain male domination. While many of these acts are technically illegal, many remain unreported by intimidated women, and are ineffectively prosecuted.

Women continue to suffer discrimination in education. They are less likely to be called on by teachers, less likely to be encouraged to major in "serious subjects" like math and science," and their athletic programs are grossly underfunded, compared to male sports. Despite laws mandating school attendance, women are less likely to attend or finish primary and secondary schools, less likely to attend college.

Women's physical and mental health and general well-being are not a major societal priority. In many developing societies, women's rates of mortality and malnutrition are higher than men's. Moreover, in developing nations, family health issues are underfunded.

Frequently women are denied participation in decisions concerning reproduction. Their needs for abortion, contraception, access to child care, and sterilization are rarely taken into account.

Women are victimized by a sexual double standard that does not allow them to experience sexual pleasure and independence. Female sexuality is consistently controlled either by male family members or the state. Women are underrepresented in political institutions. They are excluded from party organizations, elective office, the judiciary, international agencies, administrative posts in governmental bureaucracies in almost every nation and international political organization.

Gay men and women are nearly invisible in American society because their rights are not included under the various civil rights laws passed since 1964. Discrimination against gays is blatant in the military, the workplace, antihomosexual religions, and in the criminal justice system. Being gay is considered a deviant status in American life, and, as a consequence, the social character of gay people is associated with hidden identities, shame, and low self-esteem.

Finally, all of this has a great spillover effect on the social character of males in America. Men are dehumanized as success objects, and sexually manipulated by women for their potential as providers. Second, men are taught to repress the side of their character associated with the feminine—behavior such as expressing and being in touch with their own feelings, being intimate and vulnerable, and exhibiting compassion. The repression of these traits by males results in an inability to be emotionally intimate, and a fear of showing vulnerability. Consequently, by repressing traits associated with being a woman or a gay, men end up repressing part of themselves, and being emotionally cut off from themselves in the process.

Suggested Readings

Warren Farrell (1993) *The Myth of Male Power* (New York: Simon & Schuster). Dr. Farrell is a San Diego psychologist who has been in the forefront of the men's liberation movement. His book is a valuable balancing mechanism that is useful in pointing out that both men and women suffer from sexism in Western culture.

Marilyn French (1992) *The War Against Women* (New York: Summit). Ms. French's book is a brief but comprehensive catalog of ills concerning the most dramatic examples of discrimination against women. It is passionately written, and broad in scope. It is valuable to read this book with Professor Lorber's book (cited below).

Judith Lorber (1994) *The Paradoxes of Gender* (New Haven, CT: Yale University Press). This is one of the best sociological discussions of the meaning of gender and the types of discrimination experienced by women. Dr. Lorber's liberal feminist approach to this important topic provides a valuable counterargument to recent extreme feminist notions that all sex is rape.

Exercises

Critical Thinking Exercise 12.1	Communication Between Genders: The Fishbowl

This is an in-class observation exercise. It begins with a "fishbowl." All the women in the class sit in a circle, with all of the males sitting in a second circle surrounding the female students. Only one gender is to speak at a time. For twenty minutes, the female students should discuss what most annoys them about the behavior of men. After the initial period, the males sit on the inside of the two circles, and women change to the outside. The males are then given twenty minutes to discuss what annoys them about women. The instructor may write the complaints of both genders on the blackboard or a piece of paper.

Following the exercise, write a brief paper (three–five pages) concerning the sociological significance of each gender's complaints about the other. Do the complaints fall into any clear patterns? If so, how do these patterns relate to the social character of each gender?

Critical Thinking Exercise 12.2	Male Oppression: Reactions to Farrell's *The Myth of Male Power*

Look up book reviews of Warren Farrell's *The Myth of Male Power* in the *Book Review Digest, Reader's Guide to Periodical Literature,* or other databases (e.g., *Psychological Abstracts, Sociological Abstracts*). Do a content analysis of twenty-five to fifty of the reviews. Of those reviewers who agreed with Farrell's arguments, why did they agree? For those reviewers disagreeing with Farrell's claims, what were their disagreements? Use a coding sheet like the one below to analyze each review.

Coding Sheet for Exercise 12.2	Reasons for Agreeing with Farrell's Arguments

PART 1

1.
2.
3.
4.
5.

Coding Sheet for Exercise 12.2	Reasons for Disagreeing with Farrell's Arguments

PART 2

1.
2.
3.
4.
5.

Give each review an overall rating of either "agreeing" or "disagreeing" with Farrell's perspective. Show your results in a table like the one below.

Reviews "agreeing" are those showing agreement with Farrell's perspective over 50 percent of the points cited in each review. Those disagreeing with Farrell disagree with over 50 percent of points cited in each review. Code as "mixed" reviews those that both agree and disagree with Farrell's points on a 50/50 basis.

Which periodicals primarily agree with Farrell's views, and which primarily disagree? Write a term paper discussing your analysis and its results.

Table 1	Results of Analysis of Reviews of *The Myth of Male Power*

Agreeing: 60
Disagreeing: 30
Mixed: 10

The Sociology of Oppression: The Paradox of Ageism

Chapter · Chapter · Chapter · Chapter · Chapter

13

Ageism and Alienation

Ageism is one of the newer forms of oppression in Western societies. It is defined as age-related prejudice and discrimination. In the United States, ageism is generally associated with "old age," however ageism involves the young as well as the old. There are three causes of age discrimination: social construction of social roles, fundamentalist religion, and the Social Security Act of 1935.

Social Construction
of Social Ideas

Stages of life, like childhood and old age, are social roles that are socially constructed and defined. Reaching old age was regarded as a special status just two hundred years ago in the United States. In fact, evidence exists in the 1776 U.S. Census that many Americans told census takers they were actually older than they were (Fisher, 1978:82–86). In part, they did this because elders were respected as there were so few of them, and so living to an old age was considered a great accomplishment (Cherlin, 1983:7). Today, being old, which is legally defined as age sixty-five or older, is increasingly common, however, reaching a venerable age is no longer regarded with the respect it used to receive.

The number and percentage of elderly persons in the United States and in other nations are growing dramatically. According to the U.S. Census Bureau,

- America is an aging society. In colonial America, 50 percent of the population was age sixteen or younger; in 1990, less than one-fourth of Americans were under age sixteen, and a half were thirty-three or older; and by 2050, at least half could be thirty-nine or older. Thus, older people cannot easily be accurately perceived as a numerical minority. Their numbers are growing, as is their political influence. Millions of people belong to groups like the American Association of Retired Persons (AARP), a powerful Washington lobby group that is influential in policy matters affecting elderly people: Social Security reform, health care reform, and tax laws relevant to retired persons.

- In 1900, only 3 million people were sixty-five or older, but the 1990 census recorded 31.1 million Americans age sixty-five or older, 12.5 percent of the population. Eighteen million elderly citizens were sixty-five to seventy-four, 10 million were seventy-five to eighty-four, and 3 million were eighty-five or older. This elderly population increased by 22 percent between 1980 and 1989, and between 2010 and 2030, the Census Bureau predicts that elderly population will increase an additional 76 percent, more than ten times the expected growth of the population under sixty-five.

- 6.9 million Americans were age eighty or older in 1990, and that population may increase to more than 29 million by 2050. One in thirty-five Americans was eighty or older in 1990; by 2050, at least one in thirteen may be eighty or

The activism of elderly citizens has also helped dispel many of the myths about inactivity and old age. Many elderly citizens maintain a very active lifestyle well into their eighties and nineties. There are also more Americans living to be one hundred or older than ever before.

older. From 1980 to 1990, Americans eighty-five years and older increased almost 38 percent.

- Centenarians, people one hundred years or older, numbered 35,808 in 1990. The number of centenarians more than doubled during the 1980s. This group is 80 percent white and 79 percent female.

- The elderly population is increasingly racially diverse. In 1990, 10 percent of elderly persons were nonwhite. About 20 percent of the elderly may be non-white by 2050.

The first paradox of aging in America is that the elderly are more numerous than ever before in American history, but are often anything but respected.

Respect for elderly people is common in agricultural societies, but declines dramatically when societies industrialize. In agricultural economies where status is heavily dependent on land ownership, old people often own a good deal of land. Moreover, in such societies the elderly are a source of oral history and other traditions, making elders a unique resource. In industrial societies, in contrast, status is more a function of the job one holds, and one's ability to be a productive member of the economy. Similarly, in modern societies, history is kept by written record, as opposed to relying on the unique knowledge held by the elderly. Rather than being respected, the elderly are often viewed as nonproductive, and in a state of deterioration. Therefore, if you are a sixty-five-year-old advertising art executive, you are considered creatively over the hill. If you are fifty and female, you are sexually disenfranchised (Secunda, 1984:1–2), because society believes you no longer have a sex drive, and if you do, you are viewed as perverted.

Ageism really was not evident in America until industrialization began, shortly after the Civil War. By 1900, the elderly were frequently viewed as physically and mentally degenerated because the medical profession concluded that older people suffered from diseases specifically related to aging, like hardening of the arteries. These diseases were thought to be incurable and, thus, resulted in many elderly people being placed in nursing homes. This view reached its zenith when a 1907 veterans law declared that *all people over age sixty-two,* regardless of their actual state of health, *were disabled.*

Ageism and Religion

The second cause of age discrimination is fundamentalist religion. Fundamentalist Christianity defined older people as morally degenerate as well as physically degenerate. Because of their diminished moral capacity, older people were viewed as sinners, incapable of attaining salvation. This, of course, was a form of emotional blackmail against the elderly, who often converted to "born again" Christianity in order to save themselves. This created a lively market for Bible-thumping preachers who pitched their revival tents all over America after 1865.

Social Security

Another probable cause of age discrimination against the elderly was the Social Security Act of 1935. Ironically, the law was designed to help older people enjoy their "golden years" by providing them with a guaranteed, although meager, pension. Unfortunately the law had the effect of forcing many older Americans out of the labor force after age sixty-five, a practice not made illegal until 1967 with the passage of the Federal Age Discrimination Act.

What most people who are not old feel about older people is ambivalence. On the one hand, the elderly are perceived as dependent, rigidly conservative, and asexual. On the other hand, the public perceives older people as trustworthy, friendly, and knowledgeable. Studies demonstrate that people are more likely to offer help to elderly citizens because of these positive qualities.

The great paradox of ageism is that everyone alive starts out young, and, if they are fortunate, they become old. Putting prejudiced people in contact with any repressed minority tends to reduce levels of prejudice in all but one case: the elderly. The great paradox, of course, is that this is the only minority group (and there is considerable debate concerning whether the elderly are a minority) that all will become a member of if they are lucky enough to reach old age.

The prejudice of ageism is so unyielding in part because the United States is a youth-obsessed culture. The fear of aging is a common neurosis in American life. Americans of almost every age, except the very young, possess a terror of being older than they are. This makes the United States the most age-conscious society in the world (Secunda, 1984:1–2). This obsession with youth is a major trait of the American social character, with millions of Americans spending billions of dollars on pills and elixirs to retard the aging process, and undergoing plastic surgery to retain a youthful appearance. "We lap up books that promise to make us forever young. We say we are seventy-two years young" (Secunda, 1984:3).

Ageism and the Media

One reason for our aging phobia concerns the way the mass media virtually ignores the elderly or portrays them in negative ways. Betty Friedan (1993:37–56) uncovered some key aspects of the media's view of the elderly, an important element of which is their near invisibility:

- A study of 290 faces in ads in *Vogue* magazine depicted only one woman who might have been over sixty—a small snapshot of a young woman and her grandmother, among thirty-eight pictures in a double-spaced ad. There were four older men including Gene Autry and former President Reagan and two white-haired men.

- Of 116 faces in *Vanity Fair* magazine only two women over sixty were pictured—Imelda Marcos and the Queen Mother, neither one of whom is associated with the problems of the elderly.

- In *Ladies Home Journal,* seventy-two photos featured only two people who might have been in their sixties—President and Nancy Reagan, Queen Elizabeth, and a movie actor dead of AIDS, Rock Hudson.

The men's magazines exhibit the same invisibility and denial of the elderly:

- Of 201 *Esquire* magazine ads, only three faces pictured were potentially sixty or older. In *Fortune,* only three of forty-nine faces were conceivably sixty or older, and these included Walter Cronkite, and a drawing of a symphony conductor. Even in the *Fortune* articles, only eleven of 129 males were sixty or older, including four Supreme Court justices, and retired business gurus brought out of retirement as consultants.

- In *Psychology Today,* only two of sixty-six pictures featured people with white hair, and in *Time,* no faces over sixty were depicted in ads. In *Time's* news photos, twelve of 125 people were over sixty, mostly world leaders.

Because the elderly are largely invisible in the mass media and because their lifestyles and social problems are ignored, stereotypes about their physical, mental, and moral conditions abound. Some of these stereotypes are products of media creations. The movies are obsessed with showing that the elderly love to enjoy a second childhood as they age. As Friedan (1993:56–57) observes,

- The late geriatric actress Ruth Gordon, in the film *Harold and Maude,* plays a childlike old lady, who marries a teen dropout who is rebelling against authority.

- McDonald's senior citizens birthday party ad offers party favors, a cake, and paper hats for the "birthday kid" who is "young at heart." Studies of television programs from the 1960s to the 1980s confirm that only about 5 percent of the characters on prime-time shows were elderly people.

A section of the Boston *Globe* offers a guide to August activities for children and senior citizens. The "Kiddies Menu" of a Massachusetts ice cream chain pictures a white-haired elderly man and a little boy, and features items "for all kids under 10 and over 65."

Myths About Aging

Treating oppressed minorities in childlike fashion is nothing new, as we explored in Chapter 10. However, there are other stereotypes about the elderly that are equally damaging. There are a number of negative myths about the aged:

- *Myth:* The elderly are senile, mentally ill, or suffer from declining intelligence.

  Fact: Most elderly people are not mentally ill or senile. Many world leaders in their seventies and eighties function quite well. Most elderly people can learn quite well, as long as they are encouraged to see themselves as vibrant, alive, and physically active. In 1990, of the 30 million people who were aged sixty-five and older, only 4.4 million, less than one in seven, experienced some sort of impairment in their daily activity level (which includes eating, bathing, dressing, walking, or using the bathroom) (U.S. Senate Committee on Aging, 1991: 144). Unfortunately, mental deterioration among the elderly is something of a self-fulfilling prophecy: Many assume they cannot learn or be active, and, therefore, take no steps to do so.

- *Myth:* The aged are lonely and unhappy to the point of being miserable.

  Fact: There is no evidence that most elderly people are lonely and miserable. There are millions of nonelderly Americans who are lonely and unhappy, and much of their misery gets projected onto this stereotyped minority. While a large proportion of older people live alone, which presents other problems, there is no evidence they are particularly lonely.

  According to a Harris poll taken in 1965 and repeated in 1981, most people aged eighteen to sixty-four believe that people over sixty-five are lonely, and about half of the people over sixty-five thought older Americans suffer from loneliness. However, loneliness was not among the problems reported personally experienced by those over sixty-five. Indeed, most older Americans describe themselves as satisfied with their lives (Friedan, 1993:62).

- *Myth:* The elderly are chronically sick.

  Fact: Most people over sixty-five do not suffer from chronic illness that limits their ability to work or engage in most other satisfying activities. However, because the stereotype of the elderly as sick and tired is so popular, it results in discrimination against them in the workplace. The assumption made by many employers is that older people will simply not be as dependable as their younger counterparts. This is not only untrue, but tends to mask the fact that older people are even more dependable than many younger workers. Likewise, there is evidence that the intelligence of elderly people does not decline with age. Indeed, a type of intelligence called crystallized intelligence systematically increases with age in most elderly people (Baltes & Schaie, 1974).

The increased physical activity among many older Americans is also helping to dispel other myths about old age as well. Many people now manage to maintain satisfying sexual lives together throughout their lives.

- *Myth:* The aged are unable to live by themselves.

  Fact: It is untrue that most elderly citizens live in institutions. A whopping 90 percent of older males and 81 percent of older females live with their spouse or by themselves. Most people over sixty-five report an understandable desire to live near their children and grandchildren.

- *Myth:* The elderly become ill upon retirement.

  Fact: There is no evidence that deterioration and illness follow immediately upon retirement. It is true that retirement requires a major psychological adjustment, and for most people it takes time to make the transition (Friedan, 1993:201). The crucial variables of retirement are a person's economic, physical, and mental state, and not retirement, per se.

- *Myth:* Most of the aged are poor.

  Fact: The vast majority of older Americans do not live in poverty, but there are a large number of elderly people in poverty and their economic plight does cause them serious problems. Only about 5 percent of elderly males live in poverty, as do 14 percent of elderly females. Two-thirds of the elderly poor are widows. Older people who live alone are five times more likely to be poor than couples, and four-fifths of the elderly people living alone are widows. By the year 2020, it is predicted that nearly all poverty among the elderly will be confined almost exclusively to women living alone (Colburn: 1993:207). Moreover, it is the most elderly of the elderly who are poor, often due to the devastating effect of retirement on working- and lower-class elderly. Thus social class, gender, and ethnicity are as important as age in determining income level in later life.

However, many elderly Americans do live near the poverty level, with nearly two-thirds of Americans over age sixty-five receiving over half of their income from Social Security. Social Security tends to be detrimental to the economic well-being of the elderly in a number of ways:

People on Social Security are permitted to keep only $1 of every $2 they earn over $5000. Couples are treated as a unit under this law. Consequently, there are a large number of elderly living together out of wedlock just so both of them can collect meager monthly payments, and no one is sure how many elderly couples feel forced to divorce for the same reason. Social Security was never meant to provide a comfortable retirement. It was created when there were relatively few elderly people in America, and life expectancy was shorter than it is today. Today people over sixty-five have a lower median income than people age twenty-five to sixty-four in the United States, and minority elderly (blacks, Hispanics, and other minorities) have lower median incomes than non-minority elderly. Moreover, most private pension plans do not have payments adjusted for inflation, and workers who work part-time, change jobs, or have not worked enough consecutive years often do not qualify for private plan benefits.

It is estimated that a modest increase in the Supplemental Security Income program (SSI) of $4.4 billion per year would all but end poverty among poor elderly women living alone (Colburn, 1993:210).

- *Myth:* Older people are asexual and uninterested in sex.

Fact: Asexuality is one of the most interesting stereotypes about the elderly. The idea that many Americans believe older people incapable of sex is really our sexually repressed society's way of letting older people know we disapprove of them even thinking about sex "at their age." In nursing homes and other institutions, if older people are "caught" having sex, they are viewed as immoral or naughty children. As we can see, there is a contradiction concerning the sexuality of the elderly. If they refrain from sexual activity, they are viewed as physically deteriorating. If they engage in sex, they are often viewed as morally deteriorating. Either way, they can't win.

The fact is: The human body has a lifelong potential for sexual enjoyment. One study of 244 married couples, average age seventy-two, found that two-thirds were still sexually active on a weekly basis (Ade-Ridder, 1990).

- *Myth:* Most of the elderly live in nursing homes and other long-term care institutions (Eshelman et al., 1993:275ff; Bassis et al., 1982:405–408).

Fact: Only about 5 percent of older Americans live in institutional settings. Because these institutions are sometimes featured in the mass media, especially on holidays like Thanksgiving, the stereotype is perpetuated that most older Americans live in them. While there are major wrongs promoted in some of these places (discussed below), they are largely a symbol of how the elderly are segregated from everyone else in society, especially the young. This is probably a cause of the high suicide rate among elderly persons. The older the person, the more likely he or she is to be alone, and, thus, to commit suicide.

The suicide rate among elderly people age eighty-five and over is 22.5 per 100,000 compared with a rate of eighteen per 100,000 for people aged sixty-five to seventy-four (Astroth, 1994: 412). These rates are 2.5 times higher than the suicide rates for young people aged ten to nineteen, but there is much more concern about suicide rates among the young.

Although many of the negative images concerning older Americans are myths, the elderly do indeed suffer from serious social problems. Among the most serious of these are economic discrimination in work and consumption, criminal victimization, inadequate housing, and abuse and neglect.

Employment Discrimination and Age

A federal law passed in the 1960s prohibits discrimination against the elderly in the job arena. Another paradox of ageism in America, however, is that the number of job discrimination suits filed by elderly persons has reached an all-time high. Between 1981 and 1990, the number of age-related employment discrimination cases filed with the Equal Employment Opportunity Commission increased by 21 percent (Baig, 1992:59). The sagging American economy has moved corporations to lay off workers in larger numbers, and between 1983 and 1992, the unemployment rate among workers aged fifty-five and older tripled in New York City alone (Webb, 1993:68). Most of the cases filed concern older workers forced into retirement against their will, or firing them in the name of a general reduction in a company's number of workers.

Age discrimination is a particular problem for blue-collar workers employed in declining industries, such as automobiles and aerospace. At General Motors, for example, only 2 percent of blue-collar workers continue to work until the normal retirement age (Levin & Levin, 1980:123).

One discrimination case involved Thomas Taggart, a printer with thirty years' experience who lost his job when his employers went out of business. The parent firm, owned by Time, Inc. promised to help displaced workers find new jobs. Taggart applied for thirty openings and was not offered a single post. His employer told him that he was overqualified, and Mr. Taggart filed suit in a case that went to the U.S. Supreme Court. The Court ruled that employers cannot refuse to hire workers who are termed *overqualified* because the word is often used as a euphemism that masks age discrimination.

Since 1990, cases of forced retirement and outright firing have been filed on behalf of older workers in a broad variety of fields, like real estate, television news broadcasting, and investment. The bitter truth is that older workers are frequently at the top of the pay structure within most companies, and forcing them out, while retaining younger, less costly workers, is a deviously rational act in an age of restructuring and downsizing. Of the 10 million workers who lost their jobs between 1983 and 1988, the most likely target of layoffs was the older employee (Fritz, 1990). It appears that as long as the economy is unstable, older workers will continue to present an inviting target for reducing labor costs.

Criminal Victimization
and the Elderly

A survey conducted in the 1980s suggested that older people fear criminal victimization more than any other problem, even health care, lack of money, and loneliness (Cox, 1984:291). Yet official statistics reflect the fact that the rate of victimization among elderly citizens is among the lowest of American age groups. Research also shows that elderly women fear crime more than elderly men, but this might have been due to the reluctance of males to admit their fear.

Older Americans have a greater fear of crime than other groups because many older people live alone, are isolated in their own neighborhoods, and unlikely to belong to various community groups (Cox, 1984:296). Moreover, the elderly who live alone fear crime more than those who do not, and those older persons most likely to live alone (widowed, never married, divorced, or separated) suffer much higher rates of violence and theft than do married older people. How realistic are the elderly's fears? Well, the problem is complex. Some criminologists insist that the elderly underreport criminal victimization—in fact one-half to two-thirds of all crime against all age groups goes unreported. While the official data show the elderly the least likely of all adult groups to be victimized by street crime, robbery and larceny are the two most common crimes against elderly people, especially pickpocketing and purse snatching, and rates of theft are higher among the elderly than for any other group in America. The most likely victims among the elderly are:

1. The urban poor, who have the highest rates of violent crimes (robbery and assault).
2. The nonpoor elderly, who suffer the highest rates of larceny.
3. The black elderly, who suffer the highest rates of assault and robbery.

The fear of crime expressed in polls by elderly people is justified. They are more likely to be assaulted or shoved around, and for them being victimized is more of a direct threat to their personal safety. They have fewer personal or financial resources with which to protect themselves, or to recover losses.

The elderly are most likely to be assaulted in their own neighborhoods, a violation of their own immediate physical space and sense of well-being. Their losses are more devastating due to their own meager resources. Many elderly people, especially following criminal victimization, take precautionary measures. Among these are staying in at night, adding locks to doors and windows, keeping lights on when away, and marking personal property with crime prevention identification. The most likely group to take precautionary measures is elderly men who feel territorial about their possessions (Patterson, 1977). The least likely older people to engage in such precautions are those who live alone, or do not have a territorial attitude about their property.

Finally, the elderly suffer very high rates of victimization from white-collar crimes, especially scams (confidence games) and frauds. Amazingly, nine of ten fraud victims do not report crimes against them to the police, largely due to personal embarrassment or the smallness of the loss.

To cite examples, over 10,000 elderly residents of Arizona alone are victims of fraudulent auto repairs and other consumer frauds, and the same is true nationwide ("60 Minutes," July 10, 1994). Additionally, the elderly are among those vulnerable to cons by televangelist hucksters. In 1990, Reverend Jim Bakker received a forty-five-year prison sentence for mail fraud and related offenses when he misappropriated monies supposedly raised to support his PTL (Praise the Lord) ministries. Bakker's $150 million-a-year church was well connected to the Reagan and Bush administrations and large corporations. One firm, Wedtech (later bankrupted in a scandal involving defense contracting fraud), paid thousands to silence Jessica Hahn, a secretary who was forced to engage in sex with Bakker and an associate. Many of the people who mailed money to Bakker were elderly people, who may have gone without heat during the winter, and whose only incomes were their Social Security checks (Simon & Eitzen, 1993:2). The elderly's cost of living continues to rise faster than that of other consumers. This is because the elderly spend a greater proportion of their incomes on medical care and shelter than do other groups. Throughout the 1980s, a consumer price index (CPI) specific to the elderly rose 19.5 percent compared with an 18.2 percent CPI rise for nonelderly persons living in urban areas (Rich, 1993:205).

Inadequate Housing and Abuse

The abuse of elderly people in America is a recently discovered and serious social problem that includes several forms of maltreatment. Physical abuse can include everything from pushing and shoving to rape and assault. Psychological abuse consists of threats, verbal intimidation, and isolation. Many elderly also suffer from neglect, deprivation, inadequate medical care, poor nutrition, and other essential goods and services. Finally, the elderly are also prone to financial exploitation, wherein their money is mismanaged, misused, squandered, or stolen (Thompson & Hickey, 1994:307).

In 1989, the New York *Times* featured an article titled "Granny Bashing." The article claimed there are over 500,000 elderly people who have suffered from physical abuse in the United States at the hands of their own children (Russell et al., 1989:133). If verbal and financial exploitation are included in definitions of elder abuse, the estimates climb to between 700 thousand and 2.5 million cases per year (Pillemer & Finkelhor, 1988:51–57).

While the true extent of all forms of elderly abuse is impossible to measure because they are easily covered up and the definitions defy precise measurement, there are some important findings that have recently emerged. Passive neglect is the most common form of elder abuse. This includes of cutting off of food, medical care, and being left alone. Active neglect is also common, and involves tying elderly persons to a bed or a chair, or locking them in a room while the caregiver goes out. Most elderly Americans suffering from abuse are older women. Their abusers tend to be dependent children (whom the older person supports financially), or a mentally or physically disabled spouse, who suffers from great stress and frustration. The most likely abuser is a son or daughter characterized by alcoholism or drug abuse, and, frequently, marital or financial problems. A recent study by the University of New Hampshire's Family Research Laboratory found that children of elderly parents were abusers in 23 percent of cases, but spouses were abusers in 58 percent of cases (Steitfeld, 1993:212).

Part of the abuse problem is related to the living situations of the elderly. Some 40 percent of elderly Americans live with their spouses, while 10 percent live with their children. Accordingly, spouses have much more opportunity to engage in abuse than do children of the elderly. There are some 4 to 6 million older Americans (20 to 30 percent of elderly people) who live in inadequate structures. These include dwelling units that lack indoor flush toilets, hot running water, sufficient heat, and/or are in disrepair. The most likely targets of abuse are the older elderly (seventy-five and above) (Pillemer, 1985).

Finally, there are serious problematic conditions in the nation's nursing home system. While there are many fine nursing residence units in the United States, a minority of these institutions have been involved in scandals that have caused the public to distrust all nursing homes. These unfortunate conditions are symbolized by the experience of a former nursing home worker, Sue Harang (Beck, 1992:58).

Ms. Harang, a nursing home worker turned reformer, has had firsthand experience with nursing home scandal. When she first started working in nursing homes in the late 1970s, the patients used to show her their bruises from being handled roughly at night. When she complained, her bosses told her that such treatment was standard in the industry. She then quit her job, vowing not to work in the industry again. She did return years later when her husband, a personal injury attorney, asked her advice about a case.

A client of her husband's claimed her mother was being unnecessarily restrained, oversedated, and beaten in a home owned by Beverly Enterprises, Inc., the nation's largest nursing home chain. Ms. Harang reviewed the evidence and subsequently brought nineteen separate lawsuits against Beverly, two of which were settled out of court in 1990 for modest amounts ($50,000 for leaving a patient in her own feces and $15,000 for failing to bathe a patient).

Since 1990, Sue and her husband have filed suits on behalf of seventy-five families, and won all four that have gone to trial. In May, 1992, someone slipped into the Harangs' bunkhouse while their daughter and a friend of hers were asleep, and set the place on fire. The FBI suspects Medico Healthcare Systems, Inc. might be responsible. Whatever the truth, what the Harangs' uncovered in their investigations is symptomatic of a much more widespread condition. In addition to these abusive practices, negligence and careless conduct result in injury or violations of a person's rights that can have dire consequences:

- A can of liquid Drano was left next to a patient's bed in a California home. Some of it was consumed by mistake, but no treatment was administered for eight hours. Emergency surgery was performed, but the patient died a week later.

- In a Chicago nursing home, a patient's swollen foot went unattended, despite pleas from the patient's daughter. The woman's foot became gangrenous, and had to be amputated.

- One patient was allowed to drink and smoke by herself. After falling asleep, liquor accidentally spilled in her lap, and was set afire by her still-burning cigarette.

- A paralyzed patient in New York City was given a bath by an aide, who used scalding hot water. The patient died a week later.

Sometimes physical injury is deliberately inflicted:

- A Washington, D.C., nursing home administrator murdered a patient and then forged the patient's name on civil service retirement checks. The administrator was later charged with and convicted of murder.

- A ninety-three-year-old woman with a heart condition was struck in the face by an aide for spilling water, and died.

Some nursing homes suffer from notoriously unsanitary conditions:

- Fecal matter is left on stairs.

- Dirty laundry is carried through kitchens when food is about to be served.

- Patients are allowed to sit on their beds in their own waste.

- One nursing home patient in Minnesota testified that he had to walk in urine with his bandaged foot. He had an orderly bring him a bunch of rags just so he could clear a trail between urine and feces in the bathroom when he needed to use it.

A number of nursing homes have had problems with poor food preparation and inadequate nutrition. Nursing home worker Jill Frawley (1991:30) described feeding in her place of employment: "Aides fed the helpless two spoonfuls of pureed stuff, dripping down chins; no time to wait for them to swallow. It gets charted: 'Residents didn't eat much tonight.' She loses weight; she gets more frail as each day passes. . . . Slow starvation is hard to get used to."

A very harmful problem in nursing homes concerns the misuse of drugs. Often, inadequate medication records are kept. Patients are given medicine that has not been prescribed for them, and sometimes, unqualified personnel, even patients themselves, can obtain access to narcotics and other drugs. Other times drugs that have been prescribed by a doctor are not dispensed. Other problems include the use of outdated drugs, or drugs are being dispensed with unsterile needles (Moss & Halamanduris, 1977:30–31).

While adults sixty and over comprise 17 percent of the nursing home population, more than one-third of the antipsychotic drugs are written for this population, often with dire consequences. Persons sixty and over account for more than half of the deaths resulting from drug reactions. Almost 2 million of the nearly 11 million elderly admitted to hospitals each year are there because of drug reactions. In 4 percent of these cases, an estimated 76,000 elderly citizens die annually. This translates to two hundred older Americans dying every day from drug reactions. This exceeds all American lives lost in Vietnam (58,000) (Bibeau, 1994:45).

Nursing homes also suffer from physically unsafe conditions. Air conditioners break down during heatwaves, causing patients to suffer from heat exhaustion or strokes. Fires often kill frail residents due to smoke inhalation. Conditions like lice and tuberculosis sometimes erupt, requiring some patients to be quarantined in their rooms. This isolation, if prolonged, sometimes produces mental instability.

Nursing homes also suffer from a host of related problems, such as the cruel use of unauthorized restraints, including handcuffs and straightjackets; forced tranquilizing of patients; and reprisals against patients who complain about conditions and maltreatment. One relative complained that her mother was not being helped with breakfast and dinner, whereupon, staff stopped feeding the patient lunch. Other relatives feel compelled to tell staff how "wonderful" conditions are in the home for fear of reprisals if complaints are filed.

A final and serious problem with nursing homes concerns their costs to the elderly and their families. According to a report in *Dollars and Sense* (1993:76–77), there were

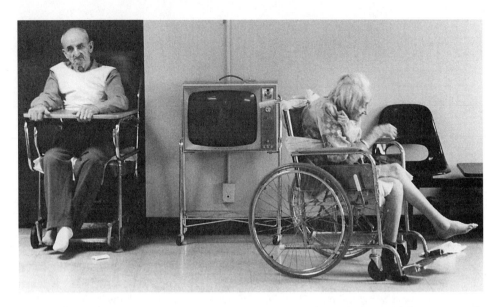

Millions of Americans now live out their final days in nursing home facilities. While most provide good care, some feature shameful conditions in which patients are neglected, abused, or even killed.

19,000 nursing homes in the United States in 1990, with revenues totaling $38 billion. Most were operated by large corporate chains, who charged an average of $100 a day, $25 to $40 thousand per year, only one hundred days of which is usually paid for by Medicaid insurance. Medicaid payments are on average 15 to 20 percent lower than those provided by private insurers. This gives nursing homes strong motive to discriminate against those on public assistance, and they frequently do.

No government insurance program pays for a major portion of home care services. About 15 percent of the elderly living at home receive some care from home care providers, and 60 percent of those receiving home care pay the entire bill themselves.

What all of the examples in this section about the elderly indicate is how much victimization can take place when a group is perceived (stereotyped) as useless and rendered invisible to the rest of society. The tragic truth is that in our society the elderly do not have a meaningful place in the social order, are alienated from other groups, and, as a consequence, their victimization tends to go unnoticed. Much the same is also true of America's youth.

The Social Problems of Youth and the "Family Values" Debate

Childhood became a socially defined and acceptable stage of life only about four hundred years ago during the Enlightenment period (1700s). Prior to that children were treated like little adults. Children and adults ate, slept, and worked together. There were no stories, games, toys, or special social events just for children. Children worked side by side with adults in factories, and frequently were injured or killed from working with danger-ous machines, or breathing coal dust while sweeping (Postman, 1983).

In America, a child-saving movement flourished between 1880 and 1914. Begun by upper- and middle-class reformers, the child savers worried over the health of children, as well as the perceived delinquent tendencies among newly arrived immigrant children (who were arriving in America by the millions) (Takanishi, 1978). Public schools were expanded and attendance was made mandatory. Juvenile courts were established to rehabil-itate (not punish) those children running afoul of the law, and crusades were launched for pasteurized milk, and sending kids to summer camp so they could breathe clean air. Child labor was banned. New professions that serviced troubled children were created: pediatrics, social work, day care centers, child psychiatrists, and psychologists.

Adolescence

Adolescence is an "in-limbo" place in American life. Teenagers are no longer children, nor are they fully adults. Life for teens is in many ways a no-win situation. If they begin to act like adults, insisting on adult rights and freedoms, they are often admonished to be mindful of their elders. If they persist in self-centered fun and irresponsibility, they are told to grow up. Not being taken seriously is a special problem for young girls, and is often devastating to their self-esteem. A unique study cosponsored by the American Association of University Women and a Harvard University Project on the Psychology of Women and the Development of Girls revealed surprising results. Girls aged nine to eleven tend to have much higher self-esteem than girls aged twelve to thirteen. The rea-son: Girls approaching puberty begin to understand the message that the culture doesn't value their experience; it literally doesn't want to listen to what they have to say (Larsen, 1992:20).

The mass media also play a part in this problem. Female characters on television out-number males only in the under-thirteen age group. There are no teen girls featured at the center of most shows about the young who can serve as role models for them. Moreover, as we have seen, girls' opinions are given second-class status when they are in classes with boys.

This problem has been recently underscored in a sensitive study of a San Francisco middle school by journalist Peggy Orenstein (1994). Ms. Orenstein spent a year observing relationships between young teens. She discovered that girls who find themselves having normal sexual thoughts and desires learn quickly to convert their wishes into feelings of disgust, and to perceive other girls who express such wishes as sluts (Orenstein, 1994:55). The terrible truth is that teen girls are in a no-win situation concerning their sexuality. Most boys their age are free to express their sexual needs, indeed girls rapidly perceive that sex is the main reason most boys are interested in them. However, if a girl does consent to being sexual with a boy, he feels free to brag about his experience with her. The result: Sex enhances boys' reputations, but ruins the reputations of girls. The result is tragic; neither boys nor girls develop a healthy sense of their own sexuality and emotional intimacy with the opposite sex. Such is the price of dehumanization in a world where boys are perceived as studs and girls as sluts.

Private Troubles   Public Issues

Date Rape Among Youth

When you hear the word "rape," what do you think of? If you imagine a stranger jumping out of the bushes on a dark night and attacking someone, you are only partly right—because most rapes are not committed by strangers but by men who know their victims, who often have gone out with them previously and are supposedly their friends. This phenomenon is called "acquaintance" or "date" rape.

Acquaintance rape is forced, unwanted intercourse with a person you know. It is a violation of your body and your trust. It is an act of violence. It can be with someone you have just met, or dated a few times, or even with someone to whom you are engaged. The force involved can come from threats or tone of voice, as well as from physical force or weapons. Experts estimate that as many as 90 percent of all rapes are never reported; in those that are reported, about 60 percent of the victims know their assailants. In one study by the National Center for the Prevention and Control of Rape, 92 percent of adolescent rape victims said they were acquainted with their attackers (*Newsweek,* April 9, 1984). Of these, women fifteen to twenty-five years old are the majority of victims (McDermott, 1979:131).

A 1985 survey of approximately 7000 students on thirty-two campuses on behalf of *Ms.* magazine found that one in eight women was the victim of rape. One in every twelve men admitted to having forced a woman to have intercourse or tried to force a woman to have intercourse through physical force or coercion, that is, admitted to raping or attempting to rape a woman. Virtually none of these men, however, identified themselves as rapists. Similarly, only 57 percent of the women who had been raped labeled their experience as rape; the other 43 percent had not even acknowledged to themselves that they had been raped (Sweet, 1985:56).

Date rape occurs on virtually all campuses, small or large, private or public, rural or urban. Unfortunately, it cannot always be prevented. The more you know about it, however, the more likely it is that you can avoid being put in a situation where it could occur. You can learn the early warning signs and how to react to them. The majority of men are not rapists but some are. We hope to show you what to watch out for, why it occurs, and what to do should it happen to you or a friend. Thinking and talking about acquaintance rape and what you might do if you find yourself in a bad situation can increase your chances of avoiding rape.

How Does Date Rape Usually Occur?

Date rapes typically occur when a woman is alone with a man. If you go to a man's room or apartment or even get into his car alone, you are vulnerable. Date rapes can occur when others are relatively close by; for example, they can take place in an upstairs bedroom while fifty people are attending a party on the first floor.

Alcohol and drugs are sometimes a significant factor in date rape. Many victims say later that they drank too much or took too many drugs to realize what was going on. Others may believe that if a woman is sexually active, she will willingly have sex with anyone, including them.

Acquaintance rape, however, is not simply a crime of passion, or merely a result of miscommunication. It is, instead, often an attempt to assert power and anger. Some men are sexually aggressive because they are basically insecure. Forcing sex on another person makes them feel strong because it makes someone else feel weak. Rape is violence against a woman. It is an issue that strikes at the heart of the personal relationship between a man and a woman, how they treat each other, and how they respect each other's wishes. People who respect others do not coerce others to do things they do not want to do.

Seduction v. Rape

One of the key questions in the issue of date rape is the difference between seduction and rape: The man feels he has merely seduced a woman; the woman feels that she was raped. A useful distinction to keep in mind is that seduction involves no force, implied or otherwise. Seduction occurs when a woman is manipulated or cajoled into agreeing to have sex; the key word is "agreeing." Acquaintance rape often occurs when seduction fails and the man goes ahead and has sex with the woman anyway, despite any protests and without her agreement.

Avoiding Situations That Might Lead to Date Rape

You can't always avoid date rape. Nevertheless, there are some things you can do to minimize your chances of being raped.

1. *Examine your feelings about sex.* Many women have been socialized to believe that sex means that they will be swept away with the emotion of the moment or that they can "make out" and then decide whether to say "yes" or "no" to sex later. The problem with this kind of thinking is that it gives too much control to the other person.

Continued on next page

Private Troubles | Public Issues

Continued

2. *Set sexual limits.* It is your body, and no one has the right to force you to do anything you do not want to do. If you do not want someone to touch you or kiss you, for example, you can say "Take your hands off me," or "Don't touch me," or "If you don't respect my wishes right now, I'm leaving." Stopping sexual activity doesn't mean that anything is wrong with you, or that you're not a "real" woman.

3. *Decide early if you would like to have sex.* The sooner you communicate firmly and clearly your sexual intentions the easier it will be for your partner to hear and accept your decision.

4. *Do not give mixed messages; be clear.* Say "yes" when you mean "yes" and say "no" when you mean "no." (The ability to be assertive can be developed by training and practice, and there are many good books on the subject in the self-help section of most large bookstores and public libraries.)

5. *Be alert to other unconscious messages you may be giving.* Men may interpret your behavior differently from what you intended. Often women and men send strong nonverbal signs of willingness to enter a sexual relationship and unintentional signals that might conflict with their words, and thereby contribute to sexual assault. Be aware of signals you send with your posture, clothing, tone of voice, gestures, and eye contact.

Families and Children: The Weakest Links

A primary explanation for the problems of youth and family crises lies in the contradiction between America's professed value of the traditional family and the actual value of the family as an institution in relation to other American institutions, especially the political economy. A moment's reflection will soon make you aware that the family is the weakest of all institutions, and the young are the primary victims of its instability.

America probably leads the world in the number of politicians who claim the family is an important institution, but it is actually woefully neglectful of families and children. The United States remains the only modern democracy without national health insurance, without subsidized day care, and without paid family leave. People who work with children receive only two-thirds as much as bartenders in the United States (Messner & Rosenfeld, 1994:78–81).

Moreover, the family is in many ways an invisible institution in the American power structure. Symbolically, the nation sets aside only one day each to honor mothers and fathers, but there is no day to honor children. There are no powerful Washington lobbies and political action committees with the kind of influence enjoyed by business lobbies in the United States. Where other postmodern nations provide protection and support, such as paid family leave, American families are prone to disruption:

- The American divorce rate for first-time marriages increased from 25 percent in the 1950s to 50 percent in the 1990s, and has remained steady. Moreover, since the late 1980s, about two-thirds of all marriages have ended in separation or divorce (Glenn, 1993:26).

- Poverty is also a cause of family breakup. The U.S. Census Bureau found that between 1982 and 1992, 12 percent of all poor families broke up, compared to 21 percent of all poor black families (Hernandez, 1993:28). Moreover, in 1993, poor two-parent families were almost twice as likely to break up as families with above poverty level incomes.

- Today 30 percent of American children have only one parent, an increase of 20 percent since 1980. Eighty percent of white children have two parents compared to 50 percent of black children. Children from one-parent homes have a much greater chance of using drugs, getting in trouble with the law, and dropping out of school. It is a problem that can follow them all of their lives.

- Twenty-eight percent of babies in the United States are now born to unmarried parents.

It is no longer unusual to see high school students having their own children, sometimes well before graduation. Most teen mothers are impregnated by young adult males, not other teenagers.

- One-half million teenagers in the United States give birth each year. Most of these teenage parents are from poor families, costing America $19 billion a year in health care and social services. America's teen birthrate (eighty-three teen births for every 1000 births) is the highest in the industrialized world (Wattleton, 1989:138). Moreover, 25 percent of all pregnant women, many of them poor teens, get no prenatal care at all, increasing the chances for birth defects.

- Ten million children in the United States (42 percent of all American children between five and nine years old, and 77 percent of children between ages ten and eighteen) are now described as "latchkey" kids. Latchkey children are defined as children lacking adult supervision on an occasional or frequent basis (Willwerth, 1993:46).

Young children also face other serious risks both inside and outside the family:

- The United States has the highest rate of infant mortality in the industrial world (9.1 deaths for every 1000 babies born in 1992). Black American infants die at a rate of 17.6 per 1000 births, compared to 8.5 per 1000 births for white children. Much of this death rate for both races is due to drug and alcohol abuse, including the effects of cigarette smoking (responsible for 10 percent of infant deaths).

- Over 3 million American children (one in six under age seven) have dangerous levels of lead in their bodies from paint chips and dust. Each year, gunshots, drownings, and bicycle and motorcycle injuries kill 8000 American children and permanently disable 50,000. Many of the injuries could be prevented by proper safety measures, such as helmets (Cowley, 1993:25–26).

Children are the least powerful and most unprotected members of families. About one in every six children in America is a victim of incest, physical and/or psychological abuse. One-third of the victims of physical abuse in the United States are babies (San Francisco Chronicle, 1994: A-3)! At least 5000 children die from child abuse each year (Elias, 1986:64).

Within the family, children are most vulnerable to child abuse at frighteningly young ages: from birth to five years of age. They are most vulnerable to sexual abuse between ages nine to fifteen, but sexual abuse cases of children five years of age and younger have been reported. Dislocated joints, sprains, internal bleeding and twists are the most frequent injuries in children from birth to age two. Cuts, welts, and bruises are most common in children aged three to five, although girls sustain these injuries most frequently between ages fifteen and seventeen (Wilson et al., 1981).

Child neglect can sometimes be worse than abuse. One case involved a twenty-three-year-old mother from Philadelphia who was charged with third-degree murder after her three-year-old daughter starved to death from being locked in a bedroom. The child's body was found kneeling next to her bed in a mummified state (Voigt et al., 1994:106).

Children face abuse not only from inside the family but outside as well. The most recent notorious examples concern sexual abuse by Catholic clergy and day care center personnel. For example, between 1984 and 1993, the American Catholic Church paid out $400 million in settlements for child molestation incidents by priests. Over four hundred priests were accused of sexual acts with children during this period (Oakland Tribune, 1993:A-8).

This great harm was, in many instances, aided and abetted by the church itself, which often knew of such incidents but refused to report them or discipline those responsible.

Between 1964 and 1987, at least thirty-six students in a Catholic school in Santa Barbara, California, were molested by eleven friars. One priest molested sixteen different boys and girls from fourteen to sixteen years of age. In a number of these incidents, church officials were aware of the problem, but let them continue for fear of scandal. The students waited until they became adults to lodge the complaints because they were convinced that they would not be believed over the word of clergy (Myadans, 1993: A-1). Such abuse is a major cause of a new social problem—attachment disorder.

One New Jersey day care center operator, Margaret Michaels, was sentenced to a forty-year prison term for 115 sex crimes committed against nineteen preschool children. However, despite the sensationalism that sometimes accompanies sexual abuse in institutions outside the family, there is a great deal more abuse of children that takes place within families.

The harms perpetrated by child abuse, incest, and neglect are staggering, and in many ways incalculable. Take, for example, what is termed "attachment disorder," a condition that affects 30 million children in America (Keogh, 1993:53). Attachment disorder begins in the first three years of life. It is estimated that all children eligible for adoption in the United States have some degree of this syndrome, as do most of the almost 500,000 children living with foster parents, which represents a doubling of the number of children not living with either parent between 1987 and 1991 (Chira, 1994: A-12).

These children are the victims of incest, abuse, and neglect. These harms leave them unable to bond—to become attached to—other human beings. As children they often strangle animals, start fires, try to drown their playmates, steal, lie, and inflict physical damage on other people's belongings.

The symptoms associated with attachment disorder involve severe forms of inauthenticity and dehumanization. Disordered children do not treat themselves or other people as human beings with need for love and recognition. Consequently, their symptoms reflect extreme forms of alienation. These symptoms include:

- *Self-destructiveness:* Disordered children often stab themselves with knives, and exhibit no fear of dangerous heights or other risky situations (like reckless driving or robbing convenience stores).

- *Phoniness* (personal inauthenticity): Attachment-disordered children have no idea how to relate to other people. Consequently, they tend to behave insincerely when expressing love, or other emotions. They tend to be perceived as untrustworthy, and come across as manipulators. One parent of an attachment-disordered child remarked that it was like living with a "robot" (Keogh, 1993:56).

- *Stealing, hoarding, and gorging of food and possessions* are common among attachment-disordered children. Not knowing how to form attachments to other people, disordered children experience severe unmet emotional needs. As a substitute for needs involving love and human contact, disordered children often steal and hoard items like food, even if they are not hungry.

- *Conning behavior:* Acts of deception take place in both childhood and adulthood. As children, disordered persons often feign helplessness, act loving or cute, smart or beguiling, whatever suits their need at the time to obtain what they want. In adulthood, such behavior may manifest itself as fraud or a con game.

- A final symptom of attachment disorder involves what is termed *"crazy lying"* (Keogh, 1993:55). Such children lie even under the most extreme circumstances, especially when they are caught directly in the act of misbehaving. Crazy lying means lies will be told even when it is obvious that a lie is being told. The "me-first" attitude demonstrated by some parents, so noticed by social critics of the last two decades, is being passed onto their children, sometimes with devastating results. In adulthood, these people become the salespeople who sell unsafe used cars, the bosses who steal their subordinates' ideas, the consumers who fail to pay their debts, or the serial killers (like Ted Bundy or Charles Manson). Attachment disorder is associated with the most serious social problems of youth, including runaways, delinquency, drug abuse, and, most harmful perhaps, criminal victimization, and suicide.

Runaways, Criminals, and Victims

Each year an estimated 1.3 million children run away from home. A growing number (around 10 percent) are "pushouts" who leave because their parents refuse to let them live at home, but most leave home without parental permission. The number of runaways is evenly divided between girls and boys, and cuts across all social class lines (Touhy, 1993:20). While most go less than ten miles away, and return home within three weeks, about three-fourths of runaways are escaping from parental abuse or rejection, or alienation from school. According to Olsen (1980), many former runaways were "labeled" stupid or lazy by teachers at an early age and reacted by being truant, not doing homework, or becoming detached from or hostile to school. Less than half of former runaways are regularly employed, and middle-class runaways usually possess a deep feeling of failure as well as major problems in getting along with parents. Indeed, they tend to trace running away to the conflicts they have with parents over school performance. Nearly all former runaways had problems with the law for offenses ranging from public drunkenness to assault and battery. At least 50 percent of homeless children were physically or sexually abused before leaving home, and "pushout" runaways report more violence and conflict with parents than children who left without parental permission (Touhy, 1993:22).

Moreover, both crime and criminal victimization are serious problems for runaway children. Many teenage girls turn to prostitution, experience drug abuse, are rape victims, and both runaway boys and girls are frequent targets of robberies and assaults. One study of 576 runaways found that 44 percent were school dropouts, 14 percent had been arrested, 10 percent had destroyed property, and 8 percent were gang members (Rotherham-Boris, 1993:150). Over 50 percent reported they were in some kind of trouble with the law at home before running away. One recent study (Touhy, 1993) reports that runaways who stay on the streets two or more weeks have a 75 to 90 percent chance of becoming involved in illegal activity.

Runaways are also frequent victims of both other runaways and various youthful criminals, a large percentage of whom (50 to 80 percent) are seeking money to support a drug addiction.

Suicide Among Adolescents

Runaways have the highest suicide rate of any adolescent group. The suicide rates among all teens rose 300 percent between 1968 and 1993. All tolled, about 500,000 adolescents attempt suicide each year, and about 5000 actually kill themselves. Today, 60 percent of high school students know someone who has attempted suicide and 15 percent say they have considered it themselves. The leading causes of suicide among the young concern problems with grades in school, confusion over career choices they are often pressured to make, and problems in getting along with parents. Of those who attempt suicide, 87 percent report being influenced to do so by peer group members, 57 percent claim they were influenced by their parents, and 47 percent were influenced by conditions at school (Ackerman, 1993:183). The picture for runaways is even bleaker. One study of 576 teens in a New York City runaway shelter found that 37 percent of runaways had attempted suicide within the last month (Rotherham-Boris, 1993:103). All of these tragic numbers indicate a strong link between suicidal behavior and a profound alienation from the institutions of everyday life. Adolescents are also prone to criminal victimization.

Adolescents and Crime

Slightly over half of all street crimes of violence and crimes against property are committed by young people aged fourteen to twenty-four. Juveniles between ages fourteen and twenty account for over 25 percent of all arrests, and almost 40 percent of arrests for the most serious street crimes (homicide, rape, burglary, robbery, larceny, aggravated assault, vehicle theft, and arson). Between 1987 and 1991, the number of juveniles arrested for serious crimes (murder, rape, robbery, and assault) rose by almost 50 percent, according to the FBI (*CQ Researcher,* 1994:5). Much delinquency stems from the fact that American society does not have a meaningful role for the young. Their unemployment rates are much higher than those of adults, and teen unemployment is highly correlated with property crimes by juveniles. Accordingly, the higher the teen unemployment rate, the more property crime is committed by the young (Britt, 1994). Most frightening perhaps, 90 percent of all young people murdered in industrialized nations are killed in the United States! The homicide rate for youths ages fifteen to twenty-four is five times higher than that of Canada, the second-highest country for youth homicide. Another serious problem for American youth is drug abuse.

Drug Abuse

Drug abuse and its problematic consequences (including alcohol abuse) are a major social problem in the lives of millions of American adolescents:

- A 1992 survey by the Department of Health and Human Services found that 8 million high school students, out of 20.7 million (nearly 40 percent!) are weekly users of alcohol, including 454,000 "binge" drinkers, those who consume an average fifteen drinks per week. Estimates are that 5.4 million students have binged at least once and that more than 3 million have binged within the last month (Isikoff, 1993a:319).

- It is also estimated that 6.9 million teens, some as young as thirteen, have no trouble obtaining alcohol, despite laws in all fifty states making the legal drinking age twenty-one.

- Drug abuse of all types is highest among young people aged twelve to twenty-five, except for crack-cocaine users. According to the National Institute on Drug Abuse's (NIDA) 1991 National Household Survey, 75.4 million (37 percent of) Americans aged twelve and older reported some use of an illegal substance at least once during their lifetimes. For people age twenty-five and under, an estimated 2.5 million reported using cocaine (including crack), and 9 million reported using marijuana at least once within the previous year.

- Cigarette smoking is high among three grade levels: 16 percent of eighth graders, 22 percent of tenth graders, and 28 percent of twelfth graders reported having smoked during the month before being interviewed. Nearly 31 percent of the college students used some illicit drugs at least once in the prior twelve months of the survey. One in every eight college students (13 percent) reported using an illicit drug other than marijuana: 6.8 percent reported using hallucinogens. LSD use accounted for most or all of this increase, rising from 3.4 percent to 5.7 percent between 1989 and 1992. Crack, stimulants, barbiturates, tranquilizers, inhalants, heroin, opiates other than heroine, and other illicit drugs showed little or no further decline in active use among college students in 1992, although a number of them had been declining previously.

A 1993 survey of 32,000 sixth to twelfth graders found that drug use is associated with a number of problems. Drug users are:

- twice as likely to get into fights as nonusers;
- three times more likely to be truant from school;
- twice as likely to have trouble concentrating in class; and
- four times more likely than nonusers to vandalize property (Schroeder, 1993:75).

Youth Unemployment

Nothing quite attests to the fact that America has no real place for its youth as much as the unemployment rate among teens, versus that of adults. The unemployment rate for young men and women (sixteen to nineteen years old) averages just over 19 percent in the United States, a rise from 15.3 in 1988 (Vogel, 1994:56). Unemployment rates are just over

6 percent for adults twenty and over, just one-third of the teen unemployment rate. For poor and minority teens, the picture is even bleaker. Poor teens suffer unemployment rates averaging just over 30 percent, compared to rates of 11.2 percent for poor adult males and 10.5 percent for poor adult females. In May, 1994, the unemployment rate for black teenagers stood at over 40 percent (Pearlstein & Brown, 1994: A-1).

The central cause of teen unemployment concerns a changing economy. Most teens, especially high school dropouts, lack the necessary arithmetic, reading, and writing skills, and do not receive on-the-job training. The larger society has refused to provide the additional help needed to master these skills. In 1987, The New York Telephone Company administered a basic level math test to 57,000 applicants of various ages. It was flunked by 54,900 (over 90 percent) (Whitman et al., 1989:47). Most corporations, including New York Telephone, have decided that the more a worker needs training, the less they are able to provide it.

The jobs available to teens are largely minimum wage posts in fast-food and other restaurants, as well as menial jobs in nonfood companies (like delivery and mail sorting). Most of these jobs pay minimum wage, and below. They lack essential benefits such as health insurance, leave, and retirement, and many of them are merely part-time posts. Thus teens are denied the basic benefits associated with full-time "adult" jobs.

Summary

Both old age and youth are sociologically defined stages of life. Ageism is a condition that affects both the old and the young in American life. Both elderly and young Americans share some important sociological characteristics. Young and old alike are stereotyped by the mass media as being less than human, and both are nearly invisible in television and movies. The elderly are perceived as frail, miserable, lonely, and physically and mentally ill. The young are often perceived as rebellious, irresponsible, and confused.

Both groups are substantially isolated from working adults, and both are considered nonproductive in American economic life. Teens and the elderly face serious discrimination in areas like employment. Both groups are frequent victims of physical and psychological abuse by family members, and criminal victimization by society at large.

Finally, both young and old have been victims of the declining fortunes of the American family in an age of self-centeredness and dehumanization. Thousands of runaway youths face multiple problems such as suicide, drug abuse, criminal victimization, or arrest. Thousands of elderly are victims of nursing home abuses and death from being improperly medicated. Young and old face abandonment and neglect by affluent and marginally affluent parents and children who feel economic pressures to make ends meet and engage, when possible, in lifestyles based on material consumption. At the bottom of the social-class ladder, old and young suffer the highest rates of unemployment and all forms of victimization.

Suggested Readings

Betty Friedan (1993) *The Fountain of Age* (New York: Simon & Schuster). This is a book by a founder of the modern American feminist movement that dispels many of the destructive myths about aging, and takes an in-depth look at the positive aspects of later life.

Peggy Orenstein (1994) *School Girls* (New York: Doubleday). A first-rate journalistic study of alienation and social problems among young teen girls in a San Francisco Bay Area middle school. The author's sensitive and passionate concerns for the suffering of these young people are movingly revealed on each page.

Leonard Hayflick (1994) *How and Why We Age* (New York: Ballantine). Aging is such a taboo topic in youth-obsessed America that even its biology has been long neglected. Dr. Hayflick is an outstanding microbiologist, who takes a fascinating look at the causes of aging and death, and recommends concrete solutions to the physical problems of aging.

Exercises

Critical Thinking Exercises 13.1 and 13.2	Youth and the Elderly and the Mass Media

Collect twenty ads from current issues of popular magazines such as: *Seventeen, Reader's Digest, Rolling Stone,* and various women's and men's periodicals recommended by your instructor.

Ten of the ads should picture young people (teens and young adults) and the other ten should picture elderly people. Do a content analysis of the ads centered around the following categories:

1. What products are advertised by the young in these ads?
2. What products are advertised by the elderly in these ads?
3. What social roles do the ads picture young people playing?
4. What social roles do the ads picture the elderly playing?

Finally, when you write up your results, comment on what these ads tell us about the places held by both youth and the elderly in American culture. For those students or instructors wishing to make a term project of this exercise, expand the sample of ads to at least one hundred, evenly divided between ads picturing youth and elderly persons.

The Nature of Postmodern Alienation: The Sociological Problems of Everyday Life

Chapter • Chapter • Chapter • Chapter • Chapter • Chapter

14

The crises of daily life are made of seemingly personal troubles encountered in immediate environments of family and neighborhood, work, school, and religion. The feelings of alienation caused by alienating conditions motivate individuals to commit deviant acts. A family is dissolved by divorce caused by adultery. A postal worker kills his manager after being subjected to years of stressful oversight. Drugs are sold on campus. A student is murdered by another student.

Religious institutions increasingly suffer the traumas of deviance. The local priest is charged with molesting children. A rabbi is convicted of money laundering. The minister has an affair with a member of the congregation. It is learned that in all these cases officials knew what was happening but preferred to cover it up. Why do these episodes take place? What is it about the structure of modern life that regularly produces contradictions in the form of deviant behavior? From the viewpoint of the sociological imagination, what is the link between seemingly personal troubles and institutional contradictions?

Dehumanization and inauthenticity are the dominant alienating conditions of modern life, but each elicits different feelings of alienation in individuals. Dehumanization is closely linked to powerlessness, loneliness, meaninglessness, and feelings of isolation (as explored below). Dehumanization often motivates angry reactions against specific targets, like sabotage at work, strikes by unions, or revolutionary movements against repressive governments. Inauthenticity, in contrast, is likely to result in a state of confusion, unspecified anger, and many forms of deviant behavior (from drug abuse and con games to homicide)(Simon & Eitzen, 1993).

Erich Fromm's classic works, *Escape from Freedom* (1941) and *The Sane Society* (1955), first analyzed the roots of modern dehumanization and inauthenticity. Fromm studied the rise of individualism in Western cultures. During the Middle Ages, he argued, there was no such thing as freedom or individualism. A person's identity was identical with the social role he or she played. One was a knight, a peasant, or an artisan (skilled worker). One's entire life was spent in work, family, and religious roles. Marriages were usually arranged, often before the bride and groom were even born. God was portrayed as unconditionally loving and forgiving, and the church provided people with a sense of security and belonging. People were born, lived, and died in the same place, surrounded by extended family relatives.

With the rise of capitalism came the rise of individualism. People for the first time regarded themselves as psychologically and physically separate from other people. With individualism came the advent of freedom. The ideology of individual freedom was based on the idea that individuals could be masters of their own fate, could make their own decisions concerning work, marriage, and the form of government under which they would live. The great problem with individual freedom was that the ties that had provided people with security and a sense of belonging had also disappeared. The rise of capitalism also witnessed the rise of a wealthy elite along with a shapeless mass of propertyless people. There was no unemployment or health insurance, no welfare state, and there were no social supports that could provide a basis for an individualism rooted in security. All workers became potential competitors for factory jobs. The individual was free, but also alone, isolated, and "overwhelmed by a sense of individual nothingness and helplessness" (Fromm, 1941:62–63). Feelings associated with dehumanization—especially insecurity, loneliness, powerlessness, and anxiety—became widespread. Labor, under capitalism, became a freely

One of the most important institutions of everyday life concerns the "rating, dating, and mating" complex that usually leads to marriage and family life. With half of all first-time marriages ending in divorce, there is little evidence that mate selection based on romantic love is a particularly good way to choose a marital partner.

regulated commodity. No longer were people linked to guilds of workers, or tied to communities. Labor, like the sense of self, became individualistic, and atomistic (alone and isolated) (Josephson & Josephson, 1962:21). People lost control over both the conditions and fruits of their labor. It was now the factory owners who determined virtually all conditions of work: quality of product, wages, and pace and circumstances of the work process itself. Work rapidly became an empty experience, merely a means to an end (making money in order to survive).

Bureaucracy became the dominant form of social organization, and also exerted its grasp over individuals. Conduct became subject to rules, regulations, hierarchies of power, and most important, emotional detachment. In factories, bureaucratic procedures meant that work became broken down into minute tasks, monotonous, repetitive, and requiring little skill. For white-collar workers, the challenge became one of "selling themselves on the personality market" (Mills, 1953; Fromm, 1941, 1955), putting on phony masks in order to manipulate workers and customers, what Mills termed the "cheerful robot." This, coupled with the growth of consumer advertising, marked the birth of inauthenticity. These changes in the structure of the workplace meant that work became something people were at best indifferent to and, at worst, hostile towards. Fromm believes the alienation experienced at work spills over into all areas of daily life, including family relations, religion, and education (Fromm, 1955). Let us review the evidence for alienation in the various institutions in which daily life is spent.

Work Alienation:
Dehumanization and Inauthenticity

There is a good deal of evidence confirming the powerlessness felt by workers, especially shop floor and manufacturing workers. This is because these employees traditionally have the least control over their working conditions. Robert Blauner's early study of blue-collar workers of different professions found that workers with the least control over their working conditions experienced alienation as powerlessness, meaninglessness, isolation, and self-estrangement. Blauner (1964) found that even among working-class workers, those who viewed their job as a craft, such as printers, felt a sense of control and involvement with their work that assembly line workers and miners lacked. Powerlessness within organizations is caused by hierarchical rule from the top (with employees having little input in managerial decisions). Meaninglessness grows when work is divided up into minute tasks, fragmented, so that the worker is alienated from the overall product and from the work process as well. Finally, a sense of isolation is frequently found among assembly line workers, who perform monotonous, routine tasks working alone (Gintis, 1986:141–142). As one worker told Lilian Rubin (1976:124) "God, I hate the assembly line . . . I used to fall asleep on the job standing up and still keep on doing my work. There's nothing more boring, more repetitious in the world. On top of it, the machine is running you, you're not running it."

The American Workplace:
Blue-Collar Workers

Sociologist Kai Erikson (1990:19–21) has noted that the modern workplace is so characterized by worker separation from product and process that many workers never see raw materials that enter into the production cycle. Instead of making products, workers perceive that they are producing "stuff" (Schleuning, 1990:3). Creativity is nonexistent, and the mentality of the worker is described as "lobotomized," made mentally dull and uncreative (Braverman, 1975:25). People who do not like their jobs, who feel they have no control over their working conditions, often experience declining physical and mental health, family instability, disillusionment with the political system, increased risk of alcohol and drug addiction, and violent forms of aggression (including insubordination and/or sabotage at work)(Edwards et al., 1986:138).

As might be expected, at the very bottom of the bureaucratic system are unskilled and shop floor workers, who are often members of the working poor. The resentment of this group of repressive bosses has sometimes spilled over in extreme forms of workplace deviance. For example, murder in the American workplace was virtually unheard of from 1980 to 1988. Since 1988, there have been nearly twenty murders per year in the United States, and some of the largest corporations and government agencies, such as the U.S. Postal Service, have been affected. The most frequent motive given for workers killing their bosses and coworkers is resentment over having been laid off. Workplace murders are but one symptom of the changing conditions in the America of the 1990s, especially job insecurity due to layoffs, and the explosive growth of part-time jobs with no security.

Subsequent studies by Melvin Kohn and his colleagues have established a firm link between the effects of work and a sense of self-esteem. Lower self-esteem is associated with low rank in organizational hierarchies, a lack of self-direction in working conditions, low complexity of job tasks, closeness of supervision, job-related stress (especially time pressures, dirtiness of working conditions, and the number of hours worked in an average week)(Kohn, 1990:41). Kohn notes that these job conditions are intimately bound up with "the class and stratification system of industrial society" (1990:43). Accordingly, the lower down one is in the class system one is, the more one's job is likely to contribute to low self-esteem. A major goal of bureaucratic authority is control of the worker and of productivity. With computers has come a new, more complete, form of control over the work process and the worker. Computers not only completely monitor the work process, but the worker as well. Computers can be used to "count and measure, and time virtually everything its operator does, and it can be used to keep a record of performance for as long a stretch of time as the most curious manager could ask. Once computers are linked, anyone who touches the keyboard is automatically reporting on himself" (Garson, 1988:205).

The Modern Workplace: White-Collar Workers

White-collar workers exhibit somewhat different, yet related forms of alienation. Middle- and upper-middle-class workers generally experience their work as cheerful robots, involving a constant sale of the self in the personality market. Pretending to be interested in others, either customers or work mates, their real purpose is one of manipulation for personal gain.

The white-collar worker is often alienated from him- or herself and other people. Personal relationships come to resemble work relationships, where the sexes manipulate each other for purposes of sex and money. Boston University Professors Donald Kanter and Philip Mirvis have substantiated that such attitudes are surprisingly widespread in America. About half of their national sample agree with the statement that "most people are only out for themselves and that you are better off zapping them before they do it to you" (Kanter & Mirvis, 1989:34). Among their most important findings are that many people in America take a cynical approach to the work they do, and that this cynicism extends from the very top to the lowly bottom of the American occupational structure.

At the zenith of corporate America are so-called "command cynics." These are senior managers who see themselves in a corporate jungle. They believe that their advancement was an outcome of Darwinian logic, which holds that since they are on top, those beneath them must be "weak, naive, inept, or just plain dumb." Command cynics also hold that everyone has his or her price, and everyone can be had.

Beneath the "command cynics" are the "administrative side liners," middle managers and upper-level government bureaucrats who view human nature as being cold and uncaring, and who have no genuine concern for people, except as means for their own ends. Next is a group of young game players, self-absorbed professionals who became visible symbols of the greed and narcissism of the 1980s. What these self-centered people have in common is willingness to do whatever it takes to move up the bureaucratic ladder. Kanter and Mirvis referred to them as "porcupine quills," people who take pleasure in putting others down as they climb to the top of the corporate or government hierarchies.

At work, many people report they are expected to put on "false fronts" for coworkers and the public. Polls indicate that 90 percent of Americans dislike their jobs, and a sizable percentage do not trust their coworkers or bosses.

In the middle levels of the bureaucratic layers of business and government sit so-called "squeezed cynics," usually the sons and daughters of skilled factory workers and working-class clericals. This once upwardly mobile working-class group has been made cynical by the loss of manufacturing jobs and the decline of heavy industry. The job they once expected to give them security has been sent overseas, automated, or completely eliminated. They are now downwardly mobile Americans, and have lost faith in the American Dream, and their cynicism stems from a belief that their careers have reached a dead end. These sad people are hard-bitten cynics, who believe they can not trust anyone at work or in business, and that "expecting anyone to help you makes you a damn fool."

The Part-Time Explosion

The contemporary workplace is increasingly characterized by fewer and fewer full-time workers, and large numbers of increasingly alienated part-time employees, especially among white-collar workers at all bureaucratic levels. Since 1982, temporary employment in the United States has increased nearly 250 percent, while all employment grew only 20 percent. As a result, these workers suffer the increased stress that comes with a lack of job security and benefits, and their numbers are increasing. As a result, over 60 percent of the jobs created in 1993 were for "temps," and *any* type of worker, even bosses, may now be hired part-time (Castro, 1993:47). Many temporary workers complain of feeling like dehumanized objects, mere "fixtures," borrowed things who don't belong where they are (Castro, 1993:44). Sadly, temporary employees have become attractive to companies precisely because they lack the rights enjoyed by full-time workers. If Fromm's analysis is correct, we would expect that white-collar workers suffer from self-estrangement and other ills associated with inauthenticity. Jan Halper's book *Quiet Desperation* (1988) found that professionals and executives believe that America is a society that tries to quantify everything. Accordingly, white-collar professionals often act as if subjective reasoning—one's preferences, desires, values, and beliefs—has no place in decision making or behavior. However, Halper found that what these executives told her about their rationality and their actual behavior was contradictory. Many of the individuals she interviewed did use their intuition and preferences as a basis for decision making, but were reluctant to admit it.

Halper found that a large portion of these men, almost two-thirds, are tired of being dutiful, loyal employees, with no control over their jobs. Most of them also suffer from numerous contradictions. One of the most common among the executives is that they feel forced to demonstrate that they are both tough and nice guys at the same time. She found that 57 percent of managers don't delegate authority because they fear giving up control over decisions. As a result, many feel great stress over being constantly responsible for what takes place inside their firms.

Related to this control over decision making is the fact that many corporate executives Halper interviewed find it difficult to trust their fellow employees. There is a good deal of hostility and resentment, as well as a fear of betrayal in coworker relationships. The sad result of this distrust is that few male workers over age thirty have any male friends. Despite their considerable accomplishments in many cases, a large number of these professionals suffer from low self-esteem. Many of them also confessed that their personal lives were dull, unfulfilling, and alienating. Frustrated at work, not intimately related to their wives, many of these men lead rich fantasy lives, preferring to see themselves as who they want to be, rather than who they really are. No matter how successful they are, many feel that they've failed to achieve success. Many suffer from reactions to denying their feelings for so long. Depression, feeling out of control, and other stress reactions are common. Some commit suicide.

Contemporary Workplace

The distrust between workers has increased in the 1990s. This is because of the massive layoffs that have taken place in recent years in corporate America. No job seems safe anymore. Frequently, those not laid off feel the guilt, irritability, fatigue, and stress that come with being left on a job that requires more effort. Moreover, this situation is likely to worsen in coming years. In the United States, corporations now eliminate some 2 million full-time jobs per year, and most newly created jobs are located in the low-wage service sector, so-called McDonald's-type positions.

The fact is that capitalist economies are in the early stages of a long-term shift from a mass (manufacturing) to an elite (highly educated) labor force:

In 1933, one-third of the labor force was involved in manufacturing. By 1990, only 17 percent were so engaged. By 2005, a mere 12 percent of the American labor force will manufacture anything.

Between 30 and 40 percent of all banking jobs will be eliminated by 2002. New jobs are likely to be in science, engineering, management, consulting, teaching, media, entertainment, and a few additional highly complex fields (Rifkin, 1995:53–55).

Workers who remain on the job are increasingly likely to experience clinical depression as a response to increased stress. The alienation felt by unemployed workers is even more profound. Studies reveal that unemployment for white-collar workers is an exceptionally traumatic event, accompanied by worry over finances, and lowered self-esteem. The increase in workplace stress has resulted in a dramatic increase in stress-related illnesses, and an increasing number of employees are now suing and being compensated for work-related mental disabilities. Many factors are contributing to increased feelings of powerlessness by workers who feel they are being robbed of control over how to do their jobs (Nielsen, 1993:45).

A related problem concerns unemployment among white-collar workers. During the recession of the 1990s, nearly 30 percent of laid-off employees were white-collar professionals (Desir, 1993:77). Many unemployed white-collar workers report feeling the alienation associated with inauthenticity. These workers were implicitly promised careers, and the long-term job security that comes with a profession. Once fired, the dismissed employees are likely to feel the resentment that comes with feeling betrayed.

Job security, long a part of the American Dream, has all but disappeared for many middle-class white-collar workers. During the early 1990s, 40 percent of those losing their jobs in the recession were white-collar executives and professionals.

Many former white-collar workers report that their needs for security and justice were violated by former employers.

There are now 34 million "contingent workers" in the United States, and only 10 percent of the *Fortune* 500 corporations is now composed of full-time employees (Castro, 1993:43). Most temporary workers have no sense of security or identity, no health insurance, vacation, or retirement benefits, in a workforce that has become "fluid, flexible, and disposable" (Morrow, 1993:41). One-third of the entire American workforce is now part-time.

Alienation and Religion: Authoritarianism and Dehumanization

Religion has undergone great changes in modern Western societies since the Middle Ages. The concept of God has become a form of reification in Fromm's (1941) eyes. Reification takes place when human beings invest powers and magical qualities in what are really human creations. These artificial creations are then worshipped as if they were real. The religious term for this is *idolatry,* the worship of idols.

The writings of Martin Luther and John Calvin appealed to the urban middle class and the poor for whom freedom had become so problematic. What the new Protestant doctrines offered was relief from the loneliness and anxiety brought about by the rise of industrial capitalism. Luther envisioned a religion in which human nature was considered sinful, and freedom something that humans were not capable of handling. People were viewed as powerless in a world dominated by sin and temptation. Instead of being loving and forgiving, God became an all-powerful force that required complete submission. What Lutheran and Calvinian theology did was to make people dependent on sources outside themselves for salvation and security. What began as a wish to have freedom came to represent a wish to escape from freedom.

Today such complete submission is a sign of religious extremism. Extreme religious sects, and fundamentalists of all types, constitute a major source of social harm. In the United States, fundamentalist Christians have formed a base of support for the Republican Party since 1980, and there is considerable evidence that their views mirror those described by Fromm.

Gilbert Menendez studied the leading textbooks used in fundamentalist Christian schools in the United States, and found some interesting patterns. He found the books promoted religious intolerance, anti-intellectualism, and a disdain for science (if it contradicts the Bible). Humans are viewed as imperfectable until Christ returns during the last days of the earth. God, not people, is viewed as the source of all good. The Devil is seen as in control of the physical world. War is viewed as necessary in a world corrupted by evil. Darwinism and evolution are viewed as causing a breakdown of morality because they are "Godless" notions.

Most significantly, Menendez found that the fundamentalist texts are not against slavery. The claim is that slavery is not specifically condemned by the Bible. Native Americans are viewed as immoral heathens; the civil rights movement of the 1960s is

Religion used to be among the most trusted of American institutions, but no longer. Scandals like those involving the Reverend Jim Bakker have given televangelism and other aspects of America's religious institutions a negative reputation.

labeled as "militant," and all Democratic administrations in American history are labeled "socialistic" (Menendez, 1993:35). All other religions except fundamentalist Christianity are labeled as cults and idol worshipers. The Jews are specifically blamed for Jesus' crucifixion, and Catholics are resented as intrusive immigrants. The texts also claim that most Americans have rejected God, despite great evidence to the contrary.

Menendez's findings are reflective of the views of fundamentalist Christians in general. Clide Wilcox (1992) has gathered evidence that indicates that fundamentalists tend to fit the profile of authoritarian personalities. A number of recent studies (Lipset & Raab, 1987; Wald et al., 1989; Wilcox, 1992) have all found that fundamentalist Christians feel threatened by open expressions of any values and lifestyles that counter their own. They are especially intolerant of feminists, pro-choice advocates, and gays and lesbians. A number of fundamentalists have been convicted of bombing abortion clinics, and murdering doctors who perform abortions, thus underscoring the lengths to which some of their members will go in opposing people whose views are contrary to theirs.

Sociologically, fundamentalist Christians perceive that their status (degree of honor, respect, and deference) in mass society is declining, and their reaction is to support extremist clergy and political candidates who feel the way they do (Wilcox, 1992). Members of fundamentalist sects tend to feel that morality in America is declining as a result of a secular conspiracy made up of liberal intellectuals, homosexuals, and other deviant groups. The success of this conspiracy has made it difficult to successfully socialize their children to embrace fundamentalist values.

The extreme opinions and values held by Christian fundamentalists result in some interesting contradictions. Because of the extremeness of their ideology and the unquestioning way in which it is held, fundamentalists are prone to be victimized by those willing to manipulate and defraud them for personal gain.

For example, in 1990, Reverend Jim Bakker received a forty-five-year prison sentence for mail fraud and related offenses when he misappropriated monies supposedly raised to support his PTL ("Praise the Lord") ministries. Bakker's $150 million-a-year "church" was well connected to the Reagan and Bush administrations, and large corporations. One of these corporations, Wedtech (later bankrupted in a scandal involving defense contracting fraud), paid thousands of dollars to silence Jessica Hahn, a secretary who was forced to engage in sex with Bakker and an associate.

The PTL scandal was followed by other incidents that discredited the world of fundamentalist televangelism. Reverend Jimmy Swaggert, after being secretly photographed by a rival minister's son, confessed on television to hiring prostitutes to disrobe in front of him while he masturbated. Another fundamentalist, Oral Roberts, whose "ministry" is worth $500 million, told his television viewers in 1989 that God would "call him home" (cause his death), if his followers did not send in $4.5 million immediately (Simon & Eitzen, 1993:2).

Some of the people who gave money to these preachers were elderly people whose only support was Social Security. Some went without heat in the winter for a time in order to send money to these "churches."

Besides extremism, a second harmful condition troubling some religions these days is child molestation. Between 1984 and 1993, the American Catholic church paid out $400 million in settlements of child molestation incidents by priests. Over four hundred priests were accused of acts with children during this period (Oakland *Tribune*, 1993:A–8). This great harm was, in many instances, aided and abetted by the church itself.

Crises of Family Life: Structure and Contradiction

There is a good deal of talk these days about family values, and the family as the backbone of American life. Everyone from the fictional Murphy Brown to the fictional Addams Family has expressed concern for the crisis of the American family. A great contradiction arises when the family is examined in relation to the other institutions of American life. A moment's reflection will soon make you aware that the family is the weakest of all institutions. Families in America are most often begun by mothers and fathers, although, thanks to modern technology, two parents are no longer a requirement for starting a family. Because families are begun by only two people, who nowadays do not live near their relatives, they are vulnerable to destruction. It takes very little to tear families apart: the death of a parent, a divorce, a war, or a crippling disease.

The percentage of children not living with either natural parent doubled in the United States between 1987 and 1991. As a result, there are now almost 500,000 children living with foster parents (Chira, 1994: A–12).

As of 1989, 3.6 million men and women with children under age fifteen also took care of a disabled parent. Nearly one-third of married women in America with children under age fifteen also gave care to both an elderly parent and to children (Vobejda, 1993: 186). This extension of care represents an enormous source of psychological stress, as working women try to balance work and family roles.

The family is probably the most violent institution in American life. Each year, an estimated 4 million women are battered by their husbands or lovers, and some four thousand are beaten to death. Familial abuse is more injurious to women than all the rapes, muggings, and auto accidents combined that take place outside the home (Rouner, 1993:195). Moreover, familial abuse is a very underreported crime, and most doctors are not sensitized to spot these occurrences. Sadly, there has been a significant increase in reported abuse cases since 1990, and it is thought that most of this increase is real, not merely the product of encouraging abuse victims to come forward. The increase in abuse cases is attributed to increased unemployment, especially among men, as well as an increase in drug and alcohol abuse (which, in turn, is linked to worsening economic conditions).

There are millions of American children who are now products of divorced families, and the studies done on children of divorce suggest lasting harmful effects. A study of 699 families in thirty-eight states found that children of divorce are significantly more likely than children from intact families to engage in drug abuse, violence, suicide, and out-of-wedlock childbirth.

One reason why family crises occur is that many people view family life through an inauthentic cloud of misunderstandings and myths. Since the 1950s, television programs such as "Ozzie and Harriet," "Father Knows Best," "Leave It to Beaver," "The Waltons," "The Brady Bunch," and "Little House on the Prairie," have presented a portrait of family life that has never really existed.

The perfect family of the 1950s was a middle-class unit consisting of an employed father and a full-time mother/homemaker. While there were such families in the 1950s, they were the great exception in American familial history. The United States had the world's highest divorce rate in 1889, and has had the highest rate ever since. Even in the idealized 1950s, about one in four American marriages ended in divorce. Today's divorce rate for first-time marriages is 50 percent (Taylor, 1993:64). In the 1950s, one-third of American children lived in poverty, hardly evidence supporting notions of an affluent society. Divorce was considered uncommon and shameful, and was rarely discussed in public. The same is true for such problems as wife beating, incest, and child abuse, behaviors that today are the subject of television talk shows, and daily newspaper accounts.

Perhaps the most idealized notion stemming from the 1950s myths concerns the idea that married women, especially mothers, did not work outside the home. Fewer women had careers during the 1950s because many were forced out of jobs they had held during World War II. Returning servicemen were given preference over working women. Nevertheless, by 1959's end, 40 percent of women over age sixteen had full-time jobs. Between 1940 and 1960, there was a 400 percent growth in the number of working mothers, and by 1960 women with children under eighteen accounted for nearly one-

Hedda Nussbaum (pictured) was involved in a famous case in which not only was she abused by her husband, but he also killed her child. Many studies indicate that the family is one of the most violent and dangerous institutions in American life, especially for women and children. Estimates are that one in every six children suffers some sort of abuse and that one-third of homicides in the United States take place between spouses or significant others.

third of women workers (Coontz, 1992:160). This trend in female employment continued into the mid-1990s. As of 1993, 60 percent of mothers with children under six years of age and 75 percent of mothers with children between six and twelve years old had jobs (Hulbert, 1993:26). Today, only 4 percent of American families feature the father as the lone breadwinner and mother as a full-time homemaker.

Why all the concern about women working outside the home? The reason is largely ideological. Conservatives supporting "traditional" family values claim that full-time motherhood is essential for raising emotionally healthy children, as are two-parent families. Not only does this place most of the blame for family ills on women, it is also largely wrong. However, there is no evidence that employed mothers produce children with more emotional problems than full-time homemakers do. Nor is there much evidence that two-parent families are necessary for raising emotionally healthy children.

What seems to have happened is that mothers began working outside the home just as numerous other socioeconomic changes were taking place in the United States. Vietnam, Watergate, and the scandals of the 1970s and 1980s created a great distrust of government, economic institutions, and adult authority in general. Galloping inflation during the 1970s and 1980s literally forced large numbers of women into the workplace. The unemployment rate has increased from about 3 percent in the 1950s to 7 percent in the 1990s. Violent crime rates, drug abuse, and rates of mental illness all dramatically increased between 1960 and 1990, as we have seen. Sexual mores also underwent a profound change, beginning with the invention of the birth control pill in the 1960s (Harris, 1986). Thus there are many disturbing trends that have contributed to the problems of the American family, but the decline of motherhood is not one of them.

The United States is the only industrial nation that does not provide paid family leave of four months or a year at 80 to 90 percent pay, as well as ten weeks parental leave, subsidized day care, free preschool, and public day care centers (Moberg, 1993:20). In France, each family receives a $1100 yearly child care allowance. Therefore, there is no truth whatever that the family is treated as the backbone of American institutions by either our economic or political system.

Alienation, Courtship, and Marriage

Relations between the sexes are also characterized by dehumanization and inauthenticity. These forms of alienation figure directly in divorce statistics. One problem is that both men and women are taught to perceive each other as objects, albeit, different kinds of objects. C. Wright Mills (1959) believed that women were socialized to be "darling little slaves" (unpaid domestic workers), and, unfortunately, there is evidence confirming that this situation has not changed.

Arlie Hochschild (1990) has documented a profound change in the relationship between the sexes. The rise of the service economy, coupled with severe inflation and increasing numbers of married women in the workplace, have redefined marital happiness for women. Marital contentment for wives now, in part, revolves around the willingness of husbands to do housework. One study of six hundred couples documented that men's failure to help with household chores was the second most common reason for divorce (Hochschild, 1990:68). As a result, the role of homemaker continues to be devalued in American society, and working couples often try to pass it on to low-paid domestic help. Otherwise it is still the woman who gets stuck doing most of it. In fact, women work an average of fifteen more hours per week at home than do their male counterparts. Even when husbands share some of the housework, it is still the wives who feel more responsible for it, especially for checking on the children's safety while she is at work. Moreover, men have more power over the housework they do perform, such as changing the oil in the car or repairing appliances. Husbands tend to do fewer of the least desirable tasks associated with housework, such as scrubbing the toilet.

The housework issue, which makes women into unpaid commodities, is also reflected in each gender's view of marriage itself. A 1993 national poll revealed that almost half of America's single women do not want to get married. Many of these women have become disillusioned by the high divorce rate. Men, on the other hand, are significantly more likely to want marriage. Two-thirds of unmarried men are seeking wives, and single men are twice as likely as single women to believe that people who live alone are unhappy (Hargrove & Stempel, 1993: C–1, C–9), again reflecting the fact that men have few close male friends.

Men are also dehumanized in the mate selection process, and in the work roles they play in American life. Women still marry men who make more money than they do. If women work more at home, it is also true that men work more than working women do—at their jobs (Farrell, 1991:82). Men still feel responsible for the family finances in the same way that women feel more responsible for the family housework. Farrell's point is that if women are sex objects and darling little slaves, then men are success objects, chosen, not for their humanity, but for their material potential. (The following "Private Troubles/ Public Issues" addresses the important issue of satisfying love relationships.)

Private Troubles | Public Issues

Safisfying Love Relationships

One of the most alienating aspects of American culture involves the values about sex and sexual behavior. Americans are the unfortunate heirs of puritanical and Victorian traditions. These influences provide the idea that sex is not to be enjoyed, that it is sinful and should be used primarily for reproduction. It is certainly not to be discussed in public, and often it is not discussed in private either. The upshot of this legacy is one of America's great cultural contradictions.

Because sexuality was repressed for so long in America (until the 1960s), sex has taken on exaggerated importance. America is a nation of addicted voyeurs. Americans love to watch sexual stimuli. They are constantly titillated by seductive ads, and sexual portrayals in movies and television fare. The repression of sex and sexuality has produced an intensive, obsessive curiosity about sex. Yet, when it comes to sexual behavior, there is an embarrassing ineptness. Over half of the couples in America report a sexual dysfunction in their relationship. Such dysfunctions include premature ejaculation in men and the inability to achieve orgasm in women.

This history of sexual repression has given us some important lessons. One destructive myth is that large sexual organs are required for optimum function and satisfaction. In fact, quite the opposite may be true. Large breasts, for example, are less sensitive than small breasts. Moreover, penis size is totally unrelated to orgasm in women. In addition, most penises are about the same size once they are erect.

The most important sex organ you have is your brain. Your attitude about sex and your sexuality has more to do with sexual satisfaction than any physical attribute. Sex is most satisfying when it is an expression of intimacy between two people who care about pleasing each other and themselves. This means that to be truly enjoyable, sexual intercourse must be devoid of the inauthenticity and dehumanization so common in American life.

Sex and the Mass Media

Sex is used as a means to an end in mass media, and manipulative people use it for similar purposes in private life. Consider for a moment the sexual slang terms you know. To be

Continued on next page

Private Troubles   Public Issues

"screwed" or "fucked" doesn't just mean to have sex. These words also mean to be taken advantage of, exploited, victimized. Often they mean to have your money or property stolen. These meanings speak volumes about America's distrust of sex and its consequences.

You can observe these alienating aspects of sex any day of the week. Simply go to a bar with a reputation as a "meat market" (another dehumanizing term). Sex that begins with pickups in bars is usually short-lived (a "one-night stand") and usually very alienating. This is not the stuff of which stable relationships are made.

Sexual alienation almost always involves dehumanization. There are many men whose only wish is to "score," and who actively keep tabs on how many women they have seduced. Such men usually refer to women in nonhuman terms (like "broad," "chick," "pussy," and other terms with which you are, no doubt, familiar). These dehumanizing terms are used because such men are insecure around women, and labeling them as less than human makes them seem less threatening. They are threatening because, as initiators of sexual contact, men always risk, and fear, being rejected. This dehumanization is also a major cause of widespread sexual harassment of women in American society. It is no accident that among the occupations with the highest rates of harassment of women are those that are traditionally male dominated, especially medicine, law, and law enforcement (Richman et al., 1993). Men resent the intrusion by the sex they fear into their previously private enclaves, and harassment becomes a form of retaliation. The truth is that everyone rejects and everyone is rejected somewhere along the relationship trail. Rejection is part of life, one that can lead to real growth and maturity, if properly perceived.

What all this indicates is that sex is no mere physical act. It is the most intimate of experiences, one that can dramatically affect your self-esteem. It is, therefore, an excellent idea to approach sex with the following in mind:

1. Be honest about how you feel about sex. Do not let anyone talk you into bed with promises or compliments. If you do not trust what is going on, listen to your feelings. They are the best guide to decision making. The great problem with intuition is that more people do not listen to it.

2. Love is not about words or sex. It's about action designed to meet one's own needs and the needs of another person. It is important to know your preferences about arousal and the sexual act itself. Know what you like and what you do not want. This includes what you want your partner to do to you, and what you want to do to your partner.

3. The great contradiction of sexual relations is that women are supposed to express their feelings everywhere in social life except in bed. Likewise, men are

supposed to be stoic in social life except in bed (Rubin, 1977). This often makes sexual communication difficult, especially for women. This is why trust is such an important ingredient in intimacy.

4. Sex and relationships in general need to be fun to be satisfying. Sex as fun resembles a dance. It's most enjoyable when there are feelings of freedom, experimentation, and anticipation involved. If sex is not fun, it is often perceived as work, an obligation, or as part of some kind of deal. This makes sex an alienating and emotionally empty experience.

5. It is most important that you really get to know the people you date. How can you increase your chances of having a contented relationship? The following have been recommended by self-help experts:

(a) Wait awhile, at least a few weeks, to engage in sexual intercourse. If one of the partners insists on not waiting, this may be an important signal about that person's lack of caring about the partner.

(b) There is much evidence that having a courtship of at least two years before marriage dramatically increases one's chances of a contented relationship.

(c) Most self-help experts recommend that the chances for a satisfying relationship increase when the partners are sociologically similar (are of the same social class, race and ethnicity, religion, and political ideology), and psychologically opposite (extroverted versus introverted). It also helps to become friends first, and to share some important interests and activities in common. It is extremely important that two people learn to have fun together.

(d) Another important variable in relationships is power. Power in relationships refers to the ability to make decisions about the relationship, including:

- Where you will live.

- Finances.

- Which doctors, dentists, attorneys, tax preparers, and other professionals you will utilize.

- What social activities you will do together (Blood & Wolfe, 1960: 5–6).

The nature of interpersonal power is complex. If, for example, one partner insists that the other make certain decisions, which one has the power? (It's probably the one who insists the other make the decisions.) There is evidence that there are sociological patterns of power in relationships. Decisions tend to be made in ways that are either:

Continued on next page

Private Troubles | Public Issues

Continued

1. male dominated, made primarily by the male

2. female dominated, made primarily by the female

3. democratically made jointly by both partners.

These patterns are associated to some extent with ethnicity. Asian-American couples are among the most male dominated, and African-American and Jewish couples are among the most female dominated. Most other ethnic groups tend toward male domination or the democratic model.

Most crucial, power in relationships is related to satisfaction within relationships. Respondents indicate that democratic or male-dominated power structures give the most satisfaction, and that female-dominated relationships are the least contented.

People learn about power in relationships largely from their parents and other family members. If you did not like the way your parents related to each other, or to you, it will take some deliberate effort on your part to change such patterns within yourself. Therapy with a qualified social worker or psychologist may be useful in such an undertaking.

In addition, sometimes relationships end when one of the partners wants to change the distribution of power. The theory is that power relationships are usually not discussed, but are part of what is termed a *subterranean (hidden) contract* that lets couples know which partner is to be dominant and which is to be submissive. This will give you some idea how important it is to discuss issues of decision making early on in relationships. Finally, as you have probably concluded, relationships are complicated matters, and need to be approached with patience and commitment.

Alienation and Education

A great deal has been written concerning both the manifest and latent (hidden) functions of education in the United States. Such functions are important to understand as causes of alienation. The great contradictions of American education stem from the fact that schools do much more than just impart facts. They also shape the personalities in ways that are antidemocratic.

Take, for example, the simple procedures necessary to secure order in the classroom. From their first days in school, students are taught to stand in line without speaking, to raise their hands when they want to question or make a comment, to take turns at the chalkboard, and to ask permission to engage in the most natural bodily functions. Students are increasingly socialized to take one standardized, objective test (true/false, multiple choice) test after another.

At first glance, these do not seem like character-shaping activities, but think again. Is not "the hidden lesson of such (rules) to obey teachers (and other authority figures) and to follow rules without question" (Inciardi & Rothman, 1990:411)? As Richard Flacks states, "can people be capable of self-government if most of their daily lives is spent in situations of submissive authority and most of the authority they encounter is not legitimately accountable to them" (Flacks, 1973:18)?

Another crucial aspect of education concerns the ideology of capitalism and especially competition. Alfie Kohn (1986) has written what is perhaps the definitive book concerning the evils of competition in America. Reviewing hundreds of scholarly studies, Kohn makes an eloquent argument concerning the idea that competition is intimately related to self-esteem. One of his conclusions is that most highly competitive people suffer from low self-esteem. Such people feel the need not only to "win," but to put down those they defeat in the process. Another conclusion reached by Kohn is that competitive people's self-esteem is always on the line in competitive situations. If they win, self-esteem increases, but if they "lose" their self-esteem declines. Sadly, such people never understand that "losing" can be an important learning experience, one that can help one win the next time around. Unfortunately, American education is based on individual competition for grades, scholarships, and admission to graduate, law, medical, and business schools.

The educational institution has undergone a dramatic shift in recent years. As women have pressed for equality with men, many schools and colleges have been forced to devote more resources to women's athletics. Most female coeds, like most male students, do not possess the physical ability to play on such teams. Thus, educational institutions continue to reward only the few possessing special talents.

Finally, Kohn (1986:96–131) cites dozens of studies that confirm that cooperation works much more effectively in building self-esteem, friendships, productivity, and reducing aggression than does competition. Unfortunately, American schools stress competition on tests, in sports, and in many other facets of the educational experience.

Critics of education have long held that schools at all levels of society function to do two things, (1) act as a gate-keeper of the social class system, and (2) engage in various forms of political socialization designed to get students to accept inequality. Thus, despite Head Start and other programs designed to help poor minorities obtain equal educational opportunities, 33.5 percent of white children aged three and four attend preschool classes, compared with only 27.1 percent of black children and 20.3 percent of preschool Hispanic children. Moreover, 80 percent of black and white children attend kindergarten, compared to only 76.6 percent of Hispanic children (National Center of Education Statistics, 1990:54).

The gate-keeping theory of schools is supported by a great deal of evidence both observational and statistical in nature:

- James Coleman and Thomas Hoffer (1987) found that students at private schools score higher on standard achievement tests than do students at public schools. Private schools feature more demanding college preparatory curricula, smaller classes, and stricter codes of discipline than public schools. Due to high costs, especially for tuition, private schools are much too expensive for poor, working-class, and many middle-class families.

- In 1966, James Coleman studied nearly 650,000 students in over 4000 American schools. His report noted that the public schools receiving the most funding—the best equipped—had smaller classes, better libraries, and laboratories, more extracurricular activities, and were predominately white. Yet both Coleman's report and another study by Jenks et al. (1972) confirmed that it is not the amount of money per se that determines the amount of educational opportunities, but that social class variables affect the amount of educational aspirations students have. These variables include the number of books in students' homes, the social class of their parents, and their parents' attitude regarding education.

- Summarizing a number of studies on the subject, Herbert Gintis and Samuel Bowles (1986:235) note that children whose parents are at the top of the occupational structure in the United States get more education than working-class and lower-class children. These unequal educational levels are a function of expectations on the parts of teachers and parents, and student responses to institutionalized patterns of teaching and control. One such pattern is known as tracking. Tracking consists of "placing students perceived to have similar intelligence and academic abilities in the same classroom" (Thompson & Hickey, 1994:351). These patterns are reinforced by the differential amounts of financial resources different social classes are able to devote to educational expenditures. Thus working-class children are over two and one-half times less likely to go to college than are middle- and upper-class children (Gintis & Bowles, 1986:236).

These mechanisms that assure that children at the upper levels of the social class system go on to college, while those at the bottom of the class ladder do not are both intentional and unintentional. Intentionally, studies of school guidance personnel reveal that children of working-class parents are expected to do poorly in school, terminate school early, and follow in their parent's footsteps by ending up in similar jobs (Gintis & Bowles, 1986:237). Consequently, students are labeled as potentially "successful" or "unsuccessful" concerning their chances for furthering their education according to their social class, and, once labeled, they are treated in accordance with such expectations.

Numerous additional studies have confirmed that the tracking system is heavily influenced by the dehumanization so widespread in bureaucratic institutions. In this case, studies confirm the existence of racial, class, and gender stereotypes among teachers at elementary, secondary, and university educational levels (Becker, 1952; Kozol, 1968, 1991; Nettles, 1990; Steele, 1992). Even more sadly, the tracking system is also aided and abetted by patterns of institutional segregation that have nothing to do with teacher expectations. Forty years after the landmark U.S. Supreme Court *Brown* v. *Board of Education* decision (1954), which held that separate and unequal schools are inherently unequal, segregation in U.S. schools is even worse. A 1993 study by the Harvard Educational Project found that 66 percent of all black students and 74.3 percent of all Hispanic students attending public schools in 1991–1992 attended schools whose student populations were at least 50 percent minority students (Celis, 1993:A–1). As a result of this study and others, civil rights organizations in twenty-eight states have filed lawsuits over the financing of public schools in minority areas.

High school students these days face forms of alienation not found in earlier years of the post–World War II period. Brent Collins is a high school teacher in Milwaukee who teaches creative writing. After over a decade of teaching, Collins (1990) has concluded that a great problem faced by students is apathy. Some students simply do not care about learning due to several important factors. Many hold part-time jobs after school, and studies have shown the more time students spend engaged in outside work, the lower their grade point averages. Collins relates that over two-thirds of the students in his classes never even bothered to turn in their homework assignments. Most of these students are not products of dysfunctional families, nor do they possess special learning disabilities. These indifferent boys and girls tend to be average students from average families. It is because they are average that they do not receive the special attention that is heaped upon the gifted and the learning disabled, who are literally "programmed for success" (Collins, 1990:68). It is this forgotten majority of students in the middle that is losing interest in school and losing ground in their grades. What these students lack is any pressure to succeed either from parents or peers.

Indeed, one study of 58,000 high school students revealed that 88 percent of "A" students report a high degree of parental supervision in their schoolwork, and that 80 percent of them come from two-parent families. Likewise, only 66 percent of "D" students report a high degree of parental involvement in their schoolwork (Lean & Eaton, 1990:41).

Aside from a lack of parental involvement, students also suffer from declining standards in teacher quality. For example, one-half of junior and senior high school English teachers did not major in English in college. A study by the Educational Testing Service (ETS), based on student papers corrected by ETS, found that the average English teacher is "barely literate" (Lean & Eaton, 1990:29).

Another recent study of 140,000 fourth-, eighth-, and twelfth-grade students found that one-fourth of high school seniors have not achieved even the most basic level of reading comprehension, and that two-thirds of all students do not have more than a superficial understanding of what they read. The same study also found that the more television students watch, the worse they read (Asimov, 1993a:A–5). Most students watch a lot of TV, about fifty-five hours per week in most cases. Ironically, before compulsory education laws were passed in the United States (in the 1950s), the nation's literacy rate stood at 98 percent. It has never again reached this height (Gatto, 1990:74).

Some parents are so disgusted with public schools that 1.5 million of their children are now being educated at home. More surprisingly, the average student receiving a home-based education is five to ten years ahead of his or her public school counterparts (Gatto, 1990:73).

Award-winning teacher John Gatto has concluded that the great problem with high schools is simply that they have become irrelevant. Schools no longer teach the kinds of science, math, and language skills necessary for success in the global service economy of the 1990s. The United States has long been an anti-intellectual nation, one suspicious of ideas and attracted to practicality and money making. Thus, the relatively few people who read, write, and do math well do not get much respect. A 1993 study of nineteen industrial democracies found that the United States spends less of its gross domestic product on teachers than all but two other nations (Norway and Italy). American teachers also work harder and play less than teachers in other nations. American teachers spend an average of thirty hours per week in the classroom, versus just eighteen hours per week in Japan and twenty-one per week in Germany. America's high school teachers average four years of higher education, versus five to six years of education training in European countries (Asimov, 1993b:A–6).

Alienation and the University

Alienation within universities is no less than the alienation found in other segments of education. A basic reason for these alienating conditions is the same bureaucratic processes that affect other forms of education. As Lean & Eaton (1990:55) state, "the structure of the modern university with its departmental separations and its total lack of order among its specialized disciplines represents perfectly the disunity and chaos of modern culture."

The nation's junior colleges reflect this alienation. Community colleges have long been criticized for their "cooling-out" functions. This refers to the lowering of community college students' aspirations from four-year degrees to terminal vocational degrees (in sub-jects like computer programming). This cooling-out function is part of the class-based tracking system that channels working-class community college students into low-prestige majors and relatively low-paying jobs. Such tracking also preserves elite colleges for more highly educated students from more affluent families. Currently there is a debate concern-ing whether community colleges deliberately undertook this role under pressure from cor-porate America (Vaughan, 1992).

There is little doubt, however, that contemporary junior colleges continue to cool out students by channeling those from transfer programs (to four-year colleges) to vocational education (Vaughan, 1992:107–111). There is also evidence that students at community colleges are highly alienated from their teachers. Studies of junior college faculty confirm that most students are virtual strangers to their teachers. This is primarily due to large classes and heavy teaching loads at community colleges (Vaughan, 1992:110–117).

College students at large universities frequently complain of feeling dehumanized ("like a number"). Many never see their departments' most famous professors. These faculty have made their names through their research and publication, not with their teaching. In many large universities, it is not uncommon for one-half to two-thirds of all undergraduate courses to be taught by part-time faculty and graduate teaching assistants (Lean & Eaton, 1990). Professors in most universities are primarily rewarded for their publications and for the research grants they bring into the university, not for their ability to teach students (Roche, 1992:74).

Alienation in the university is further increased by the glut of journals established to ensure that professors receive tenure. In sociology alone, the *New Republic* estimated in 1991, there are over 14,400 articles, books, and reviews published each year, and that's just in the United States. The "print explosion," as it is called, has, of course, stimulated a flood of articles and books criticizing professors for writing too much and writing about trivial things (Sykes, 1988; Smith, 1990).

However, as long as tenure, promotion, royalties, and grant funds are dependent on publication, there is little chance these priorities will change anytime soon. This also means that teaching in many universities will continue to receive a lower priority than research and writing.

Summary

The crises of daily life are made up of seemingly personal troubles encountered in the immediate environments of family and neighborhood, work, school, and religion. The feelings of alienation caused by the alienating conditions of inauthenticity and dehumanization motivate individuals to commit deviant acts. Each of these conditions elicits different feelings of alienation in individuals. Dehumanization is closely linked to powerlessness, loneliness, meaninglessness, and feelings of isolation. Dehumanization often motivates angry reactions against specific targets, like sabotage at work, strikes by unions, or revolutionary movements against repressive governments. Inauthenticity, in contrast, is likely to result in a state of confusion, unspecified anger, and many forms of deviant behavior (from drug abuse and con games to homicide).

Much evidence confirms the presence of such alienation within the institutions of everyday life. In the workplace, manufacturing workers experience high levels of alienation due to feelings of powerlessness over their working conditions. White-collar workers are likewise dehumanized, often feeling unable to talk about the stresses they are under. People at all levels of the work hierarchy have become cynical about their workplaces, distrustful of bosses and coworkers alike. The workplace is evolving into a world in which only the most highly skilled and educated workers will occupy well-paying positions, while the unskilled will be relegated to part-time work or the unemployment line.

Within the modern religious institution, alienating conditions are frequently present. Fundamentalist religions typically view people as the source of all evil, condemn gays, lesbians, and feminists, and advocate authoritarian political measures. The Catholic church in America has experienced a wave of child molestation by its clergy, and some televangelist ministers have been convicted of defrauding their contributors and other scandalous behaviors. Religion is often used as a front behind which a great deal of deviance takes place.

The crises of the contemporary family include high rates of divorce, child and spousal abuse, teen pregnancy, and poverty among single-parent families. Conservative politicians have tried to scapegoat working mothers for these problems, but the evidence shows that many other causes, especially changing economic and cultural conditions, are responsible. Both men and women often dehumanize each other in their relationships, with men viewing women as sex objects and women still viewing men as success objects. Children are frequently treated in a dehumanized manner as well. Some 30 million of them suffer from detachment disorder, which is characterized by an inability to bond emotionally with other people, and contributes to serious forms of deviant and criminal behavior in both childhood and later life.

Finally, the educational institution is characterized by various forms of alienation. Primary and secondary schools often function as bureaucratic factories where social control and gate-keeping take precedence over learning. Lower-class students and minorities are likely to be labeled as problem students, and their schools are often rigidly segregated. Many studies confirm that high school students rarely do homework, watch too much television, and suffer from high rates of functional illiteracy. Teachers must spend much of their time just keeping order, and the quality of teachers is declining.

At the college and university levels, junior colleges now function as tracking institutions, devoid of the joy of learning and characterized by a profound alienation between teacher and student. At the university level, professors often prefer to spend their efforts seeking research grants and/or writing for publication. It is in these competitive areas that the greatest professional rewards are found. Good teaching is often demeaned and sometimes treated as deviant behavior. Numerous studies confirm that the testing and competition on which the entire educational system is based often inhibit rather than promote learning.

In short, inauthenticity and dehumanization pervade the institutions of everyday life, and the result is a great deal of harmful deviant behavior at all levels of American life.

Suggested Readings

S. Coontz (1992) *The Way We Never Were: American Families and the Nostalgia Trap* (New York: Basic Books). This very readable book exposes many destructive myths concerning the idealized families in America's past. It also contains many useful commentaries on today's families.

Erich Fromm (1941) *Escape from Freedom* (New York: Holt, Rinehart and Winston).

————(1955) *The Sane Society* (New York: Fawcett).

These two volumes present a readable and logical case for the dehumanization and inauthenticity that have become the hallmarks of our age. They are required reading for anyone interested in the problem of alienation.

Alfie Kohn (1986) *No Contest: The Case Against Competition* (Boston: Houghton Mifflin). This volume presents strong evidence that America's version of individualistic competition has negative effects on the self-esteem of many Americans. Kohn also presents numerous interesting examples and proofs for the benefits of cooperation.

Arthur Lean and William Eaton (1990) *Education or Catastrophe?* (Wolfboro, NH: Longwood Academic). This brief work is an excellent introduction to the problems of education in America. It is beautifully written by two humanistic and passionate educators.

Exercises

Critical Thinking Exercise 14.1	**The Television Family in the 1990s**

Watch one week's worth of episodes of current network television shows about family life. Next, those students with access, watch the cable reruns of family shows from earlier decades, like "Leave It to Beaver," "Father Knows Best," "The Brady Bunch," and the like. Compare the shows from the two eras on the following issues:

What problems do the children in these shows share with each other or their parents? How do the problems from earlier eras compare with those presented in current shows?

What is the father's/husband's role in current shows versus those from earlier decades? Do you detect changes in the definition of masculinity between the two eras?

What is the mother's/wife's role in current shows versus those from earlier decades? Do you detect changes in the definition of femininity between the two eras?

Critical Thinking Exercise 14.2	**Alienation and College Students**

With the help of your instructor, construct a questionnaire to administer to a sample of one hundred students in different majors at your college. Use a Likert scale, which requires people to score an item using a range of numbers (e.g., 0 to 4), like the one provided on p. 462, as a way to score answers. Feel free to add additional questions concerning specific issues at your school.

A. Independent Variables

Major: _____

Year In School: _____

Age: _____

Gender: _____

Continued on next page

Exercise 14.2 Continued

Other variables of interest to class members (e.g., political ideology, religion, social class of parents, race/ethnicity):

B. Dependent variables: For each of the following, please circle one of the following (each answer gets the number of points indicated):

0. Don't Know
1. Very Satisfied
2. Satisfied
3. Somewhat Dissatisfied
4. Very Dissatisfied

(This is the Likert scale mentioned on p. 461.)

1. How satisfied are you with your choice of major?

    0   1   2   3   4

2. How satisfied are you with the overall quality of your professors' classroom teaching?

    0   1   2   3   4

3. How satisfied are you with the teaching of part-time instructors and teaching assistants in your classes?

    0   1   2   3   4

4. How satisfied are you with your professors as advisors?

    0   1   2   3   4

5. How satisfied are you concerning your college's counseling services?

    0   1   2   3   4

6. How satisfied are you with your college's financial aid programs?

    0   1   2   3   4

7. How satisfied are you with your college's student benefits (e.g., health insurance, recreational facilities, athletic programs, sponsored social events, and the like)?

    0   1   2   3   4

8. Please describe other aspects of college life that are important to you. How satisfied are you with these aspects of your college experience?

    0   1   2   3   4

Freedom, Reason, and the Sociological Imagination: Social Change and Personal Transformation

Epilogue

Our examination of the social problems plaguing America and much of the world has not shown an unconnected group of disparate conditions adrift in a chaotic world. Rather, our investigation indicates that the problems of the postmodern era are interrelated in complex ways, and exist within a culture and social structure whose values and institutions are a major cause of the ills of the postmodern world. This Epilogue is both a summary of the major findings of our inquiry, as well as an identification of directions (main drifts and master trends) in which America and the world are heading.

On Valentine's Day, 1929, four Chicago gangsters dressed as police officers killed seven members of a rival crime family. The incident, known as the St. Valentine's Day Massacre, sparked outrage all over the nation. A "better government association" was formed in Chicago and federal agents, under the direction of Elliot Ness, began an investigation that eventually brought down the leader of one Chicago syndicate, Al Capone. The incident also resulted in the eventual repeal of Prohibition, which had become associated, not only with illegal alcohol, but gang warfare as well.

In the 1990s, there has been at least one incident similar to the St. Valentine's Day massacre every weekend in most major American cities, but there is no corresponding outrage. In fact, an astonishing amount of deviance is now tolerated as "normal" in American life:

- Junk bond king Michael Milken swindled billions of dollars in the 1980s, and was hired to teach business ethics at UCLA in 1993.

- Ronald Reagan's administration was characterized by more corruption than any in American history. Over 120 of his appointees resigned from office under ethical clouds. The Bush administration that followed was basically a continuation of the "grab it while you can" ethic that began during the Reagan years.

- In 1960, one in every forty white babies and one in five black infants were born out of wedlock. In 1993, one of every five whites and two of every three blacks were born out of wedlock (Moynihan, 1993:17).

- In 1987, a poll was taken of 200,000 college freshmen by the American Council on Education. Of those polled, 76 percent said that it was very important to be financially well off. Twenty years earlier, only 44 percent of freshmen held such materialistic views. In 1976, 83 percent of respondents felt it important to develop a philosophy of life. In 1987, only 39 percent of students expressed such a credo (Shames, 1989:43). A 1990 report by the Carnegie Foundation for the Advancement of Teaching complained of a breakdown of civility on the nation's college campuses. Especially alarming were an epidemic of cheating by students, racial attacks, hate crimes, and rapes on campus. Studies at the University of Tennessee and Indiana University found a majority of students at each campus admitted to submitting papers that were written by others, or copying large sections of friends' papers (Derber, 1992:101).

- Family life in America is increasingly filled with considerable risk and uncertainty. The divorce rate has stabilized at twice what it was between 1950 and 1964, three times the rate of 1920–1930. The U.S. divorce rate is the highest among advanced capitalist nations, four times that of Japan, three times that of England and France, and twice that of Denmark and Sweden. The number of single-parent American households is likewise four times the Japanese rate, three times the Swedish rate, and twice the English rate (Derber, 1992:116).

These examples are symptomatic of socially patterned problems. The problem has many names: "social breakdown" (Dissent, 1991), "social disintegration," the rise of "the morally loose individual" (Nisbet, 1988), instrumental and expressive "wilding" (Derber, 1992), "defining deviancy down" (Moynihan, 1993), or as referred to throughout this book, the antisocial social character. Whatever one chooses to call it, the problem is a tragically measurable aspect of contemporary American life.

The rise of this antisocial social character may be termed a "master trend" of the postmodern society (Mills, 1959:7ff). **Master trends,** or **"main drifts,"** are fundamental mechanisms by which social change takes place. In addition to changes in America's moral climate, we have discussed other trends that promise to bring more unwanted changes, unless something is done to reverse them. These trends include:

- Increasing inequalities of wealth and political power are the causes of the numerous macro- and micro-level problems (unemployment, recession/depression, corporate crimes and political corruption, and related woes).

- The emergence of postmodern culture with its emphasis on sex, violence, and materialism, and lack of humane values. Contained within this new lifestyle is a set of behaviors that will mark our era and its social problems for decades to come. Postmodern culture emphasizes themes that reinforce a host of alienating tendencies in capitalist societies, especially inauthenticity and commodification (making virtually everything into a salable commodity).

- A decline of optimism about the future that was once the hallmark of the American character. There is currently a widespread belief that political and business leaders can not be trusted by the public, that the best days of America as an economic and military power are over, and that life will not be as good for future generations.

- Within the United States, the great structural change of time has been the increased commingling of political, economic, and military institutions, complete with their control over modern technology's weapons of mass destruction and social control of civilian populations; and the institutionalization of the higher immorality among the national power elite.

- The end of the Cold War has also meant the end of massive military budgets, and severe increases in unemployment are possible because of the absence of economic conversion plans. Southern California alone lost 96,000 jobs in the aerospace industry between 1987 and 1993. Hundreds of thousands of workers will need to be retrained if the middle class is to stave off further decline. Retraining will cost billions, and perhaps increase budget deficits, taxes, or both.

- Internationally, there is a crisis of uncontrolled population growth, especially in nations in Asia, Africa, and Latin America. This growth could send the world population soaring from about 5.5 billion people in 1992 to 10 billion in 2050 (Hertsgaard, 1993:23).

Nearly two-thirds of Americans now feel that political candidates represent the interests of wealthy and powerful people and organizations. They feel alienated from political processes like televised debates, which are really not debates at all, but lengthy news conferences.

This chapter deals with the nature and ramifications of these trends, and what needs to be done about them. For example, the doubling of the world population in less than sixty years would have immense negative consequences for numerous social problems, including poverty and immigration, crime and pollution, famine and war, the repression of human rights, and declining standards of living in First World nations. Poverty and destitution, especially in the Third World, already cause tremendous suffering.

The Third World is a place where

- the average child does not see a doctor before age five,
- 1 billion people (30 percent) are unemployed,
- between 60 and 90 percent of the wealth in most nations is owned by 3 to 20 percent of the population,
- massive famines and starvation already kill over 30 million people per year (Simon & Eitzen, 1993:203–204), and
- more than 700 million Third World adults are unable to read, and half of all school-age children are not yet in school (Simon & Eitzen, 1993:203–204).

One result of this immense suffering is political instability. A war or revolution has occurred in the Third World about once per month since 1945, and there is little sign of peace breaking out any time soon. These wars and revolutions influence First World nations in the forms of international terrorism and military involvement (such as America's involvement in Vietnam, 1963–1975).

The Third World is also a place where military dictatorships brutally repress human rights while seeking aid from democratic nations like the United States (Simon & Eitzen, 1993:194–202). In the name of anticommunism, the United States has been all too willing to support noncommunist dictatorships. This has served American multinational corporations' needs for cheap labor, new markets, and access to raw materials (see Part II). Exploitation by multinationals results in much resentment by Third World peoples toward First World nations, especially the United States.

Inequalities of Wealth and Resources

Domestically, the "main drift" of the postmodern era, the one from which virtually all other patterns flow, has been the unprecedented accumulation of economic and political power in the hands of a small group of elites. The nature of this power elite was explained in Chapter 2. The exact scope and ramifications of these interacting groups are of interest. Let us begin with an examination of the distribution of wealth.

Table 15.1 reflects the following sad realities of American life:

1. Between 1982 and 1992, the percentage of wealth owned by the wealthiest 1 percent of Americans increased from 31 to 37 percent, an all-time high. More important, it is now estimated that the top 10 percent of wealth holders own as much wealth as the bottom 90 percent of the population (Phillips, 1993).

2. Income distribution has also become more concentrated since the 1970s. During the twenty years between 1970 and 1990, only the top 20 percent of income earners saw their earnings increase. The other 80 percent of families lost ground, and by 1995, fully 90 percent of income earners would experience no real growth or experience a decline in income (Phillips, 1993).

3. The heart of a democratic society rests with its middle class, and the American middle class is shrinking dramatically. Between 1969 and 1990, the percentage of families earning middle-class incomes declined by 15 percent, the largest such drop in American history.

   The decline of the middle class is a master trend that will spawn other serious social problems:

   a) Increased numbers of people will not be able to afford basic health insurance.

   b) There will be increased long-term unemployment. Studies in the 1970s (Brenner, 1974) indicated that for each 1.5 percent increase in unemployment lasting at least eighteen months, there are significant increases in rates of other major social problems. This suggests that any significant rise in the unemployment rate will result in increased rates of homicide, admissions to state mental hospitals and prisons; a rise in death rates due to alcohol, suicide, and perhaps, drug abuse. Jails and prisons, already overcrowded in over thirty states, will become more so.

Table 15.1
The Increasing Concentration in Ownership of Wealth and Income, 1960s–1990s

YEARS	PERCENTAGE OF WEALTH HELD BY TOP 1 PERCENT
1962–1982	31
1982–1992	37

Trends in American Income Distribution, 1960–1990

YEAR	AMOUNT EARNED BY TOP 4 PERCENT	BOTTOM 35 PERCENT
1959	$31 Billion	$31 Billion
	TOP 4 PERCENT	BOTTOM 51 PERCENT
1989	$452 Billion	$452 Billion

American Income Distribution by Fifths, 1970s–1990s (in percent)

	1950s	1970s	1990s
Top 20	43	45.6	51.4
Second 20	24	22.9	21.7

Finally, sustained unemployment also spawns more homelessness, and increases in monies spent on government social programs (which in turn result in more government debt, borrowing, and probably increased taxes. Nonelites may believe that government does not function on their behalf, which will result in increasing political alienation. Such alienation may result in dramatic decreases in voter participation, increased votes for extremist candidates, and/or the disintegration of the Republican and Democratic parties as we know them.

Dangers of Mass Behavior

The working and lower classes may also react to the decline of the quality of American life. We may see more urban riots, hate crimes, and other outbreaks of mass deviance. This will result in an increasingly fearful society characterized by conflict between the haves and have-nots. Elites often respond to mass disorder by increases in propaganda, often involving

	1950s	1970s	1990s
Third 20	17	16.3	14.7
Fourth 20	12	10.8	9.2
Lowest Fifth	5	4.7	3.6

Percentage of Families Earning Middle-Class Incomes

YEAR	PERCENT
1969	71.2
1990	63.3

Projected Income Data, 1985–1995

PERCENT OF U.S. FAMILIES	PERCENT OF GAIN (ADJUSTED FOR INFLATION)
Top 1	50–75
Top 5	25
Remaining 94	0 or a decline in income

Source: Adapted from Phillips, 1993: 22–31.
Phillips states that middle-class incomes begin at about $28,000 per family and end at about $200,000 per family.

appeals to patriotism, and the creation of scapegoats. If these measures fail, ruling classes are not averse to calling in riot police, National Guard, and, if all else fails, the U.S. military. The result may be a new American civil war, slow, painful, and guerrilla in nature.

Indeed, this war may have already begun. The 1993 bombing of New York's World Trade Center and the apparent attempt to assassinate former President Bush reflect this tension on an international level. Nationally, there have been recent incidents identified as guerrilla warfare. Fanatical white supremacists had planned to attack several key African-American targets in hopes of starting a race war. Today the distinction between war and terrorism has become blurred. The proliferation of weapons capable of immediate mass destruction has allowed small groups of disenfranchised people to become important political actors in the postmodern world order. New forms of terrorism involving bombings of innocent civilians in large American cities, drug-financed weapons caches, and airplane hijackings are all with us, and likely to increase before they stop.

The Militarized Economy and American Economic Decline

The enrichment of the upper class and the decline of the middle class are the result of political and economic changes that have taken place since World War II. At war's end, the United States did not dismantle the military establishment it had used to overcome fascism. Instead the National Security Act of 1947 created three military services and a host of governmental intelligence organizations. National security became the measure of foreign and defense policy as the Cold War against Communism began. Between 1947 and 1992, the United States spent about $4 trillion on defense, and entered into alliances with nations on all continents. The economic results were devastating. By 1988, over two-thirds of all funds spent in the United States for R & D were spent for military purposes. Less than 1 percent was spent to develop products used in the civilian sector of the economy (Kennedy, 1993). As a result, the U.S. economy became noncompetitive with other capitalist nations, especially Japan and countries of Western Europe. Manufacturing of any kind was relinquished to other nations. Fully 68 percent of U.S. jobs and 71 percent of U.S. national income were based on service sector jobs (Kennedy, 1993). Other economic traumas also haunted America:

- Between 1980 and 1990 the United States went from having the world's largest surplus from international trade to become the world's largest debtor nation in international commerce.

- Between 1980 and 1992, U.S. national debt increased from $1 trillion to over $4 trillion, the largest such increase in the shortest amount of time in world history. Much of this increase is due to the Reagan administration's $2 trillion defense spending and $750 billion in corporate tax relief.

Ever since the end of World War II, government, especially the federal government, has been an intimate part of the American economic system. Government has been the focus of an economic contradiction. On the one hand, politically influential corporations press demands for state assistance in capital accumulation (profit expansion) by requesting tax relief, lucrative government contracts, subsidies, loans, and loan guarantees. For example, a 1993 study by the General Accounting Office found that 41 percent of the largest 2000 American corporations (with assets of $250 million or more) paid either no federal income taxes or less than $100,000 in taxes in 1989. These companies had total receipts of $544 billion in that same year (San Diego *Times-Union*, 1993:A-1). Corporations also receive military protection of their overseas markets and investments. On the other hand, in order for its legitimacy to be maintained, the state must meet the demands placed on it for public assistance. These are social programs designed to aid those suffering from poverty, unemployment, homelessness, mental illness and retardation, drug addiction, and other social problems arising in modern capitalist societies (O'Conner, 1975).

The result is that the state suffers from competing demands for corporate favors versus social programs. Expenditures consistently exceed state revenues, resulting in a dramatic decline in U.S. middle-class living standards, a dramatic increase in homelessness, and the worsening of numerous social problems (including crime victimization, court and prison overcrowding, government deficits, and cuts in government services).

Elite Power and
the Higher Immorality

Corporate crime and deviance also play a role in the prostitution of the American econo-my. Harold Barnet (1981) has argued that the marketing of unsafe products, the polluting of the environment, and violations of health, safety, and labor laws all increase corporate profits by transferring various costs to either consumers, workers, or the public in general. Moreover, the appalling lack of enforcement of corporate crime laws and the lenient sen-tences handed down in such cases serve further to support the notion that the state func-tions largely to encourage capital accumulation, rather than discourage elite wrongdoing. At the elite level, such deviance is part of a higher immorality. C. Wright Mills (1956: Chapter 13) used the term "higher immorality" to refer to an institutionalized set of values and practices among the nation's corporate and political elite. Mills believed that America's upper class loves money, has mediocre cultural tastes, and, most important, possesses a moral insensibility that allows for the commission of various criminal and deviant acts (Simon, 1996: Chapter 2). The acts comprising the higher immorality were discussed in Chapter 2.

Since Mills wrote in 1956 about the higher immorality, the nation has experienced unprecedented forms of corruption. No longer are American scandals simply about politi-cians taking bribes from corporate elites seeking political favors; organized criminal syndi-cates have become active players in scandalous situations. As discussed in Chapters 2, 5, and 6, today these practices run the gamut from material self-enrichment and corrupt acts of acquiring political power (as in Watergate) to deception of public opinion, to sexual per-version. What Mills perceived about American political power in the 1950s was the begin-ning of "the secret government" (Moyers, 1988).

The Military and
the Secret Government

The Constitution grants Congress the power to declare war. Although war has not been officially declared since 1941, the United States has fought dozens of secret wars between 1954 and 1993, often without the knowledge of Congress or the American peo-ple. Abroad, the government has secretly backed corrupt military dictatorships and death squads. At home, the CIA has violated the civil rights of millions of Americans by collect-ing dossiers, opening mail, and enlisting the FBI to burglarize the headquarters of organi-zations who merely oppose U.S. government policies.

The effects of the secret government have devastated the trust of the American people in their government and American prestige in many Third World nations. Beginning with the overthrow of the duly elected government of Iran (1953), the CIA has repeatedly destabilized democracies unfriendly to U.S. multinational corporations. American military intervention has gone hand-in-hand with the militarization of the economy, and increasing secrecy in the making of defense and foreign policy.

Within the United States, the effects of the secret government have been evident in scandal after unprecedented scandal. Beginning with the assassination of President

Kennedy and the investigation thereof (Simon, 1993), the United States has experienced a continual barrage of scandals at the federal level. The crimes associated with these incidents have been seriously harmful.

The secret government will stake out a new role for itself in the coming "new world order." CIA director Robert Gates has already stated that the CIA needs to insure corporate security as well as governmental security. The CIA is stressing the need for domestic counterterrorism, involvement in the drug war, and "crisis management" of low-intensity conflicts around the world. The CIA and its sister intelligence agencies are doing this with a classified budget of about $35 billion (Baker, 1992:81). Such practices tend to have antidemocratic effects at home as well.

Deviance and crime among many segments of the nation's economic, political, and military elites are frequent practices. Moreover, the deviance within the elite differs markedly from that of other social classes because it involves so much more money, power, and resources than those to which people in other strata have access.

Links Between Various Types of Crime

Corporate crime and political scandal interrelate, not only to each other, but to other types of crime and deviance as well, most obviously organized crime. The American drug problem is a classic example. Drugs are smuggled into the United States only with the cooperation of banks (which launder drug money) and political elites both here and in the countries of origin who accept payoffs. The drugs are distributed to street gangs and peddlers by organized criminal syndicates, one of whom is the Italo-American Mafia.

At its lowest level, the American drug problem is tied to the vast majority of property crime committed by "street" criminals, who seek money to support drug habits. Crime at all levels of American life is now interrelated.

Postmodern Culture and America's Main Drift

Many people perceive that we live in a dangerous world. Everyday life is loaded with concerns that a generation ago never entered the consciousness of most middle-class families:

- Is my job safe or will a worsening economy result in layoffs?

- Are children practicing unsafe sex? Are they using drugs? Are they at risk for AIDS? Will they be victims of gang violence?

- When does discipline turn into abuse?

- Will my marriage last? Do I want it to?

The problems and concerns of daily life have created a desire for solution and/or escape that has resulted in the emergence of a postmodern culture. The themes of postmodern culture now dominate the mass media and advertising.

a) preoccupation with the self and neglect of the larger social good,

b) preoccupation with sex and the separation of sex and love,

c) increasing reliance on violence as a solution to conflict, and

d) commodification of virtually every human impulse, moral principle, and sacred belief into a product that is capable of being advertised.

These themes and the creation of products and commodities occurred through the use of inauthenticity and dehumanization in advertising. The result is a decline of traditional values (see Chapter 3).

Social Character in an Age of Confusion

Social character remains the great dependent variable, shaped by both the political economy and the dominant culture. The master trend in American social character revolves around identity confusion and uncertainty about the future of the nation and its values. Since 1945, the social character literature has come "full circle" (Wilkinson, 1988; Wilkinson, ed., 1992). The social critics of the 1940s and 1950s complained that Americans were too conformist and insecure. The American people were described as "cheerful robots" (Mills, 1953), "other-directed" (Riesman, 1950), and overly receptive to the opinions of other people. In short, the fear of the 1950s was that the population had lost its independence under the pressures of bureaucratic and suburban life.

There followed in the 1960s and 1970s a cultural revolution that encouraged "doing your own thing." An entire self-help movement sprang up that stressed consciousness expansion, sexual freedom, and experimentation. Many members of the middle classes, products of the civil rights, antiwar, and feminist movements of the 1960s, eagerly adopted lifestyles based on self-awareness and self-fulfillment. No sooner had these seemingly independent streaks emerged than did the literature of the day begin to criticize Americans for their narcissism (selfishness and self-concern), and neglect of the common good.

By the time the "yuppies" emerged in the 1980s, social critics had become alarmed over the new lifestyle "enclaves" based solely on material gratification, designer drugs, and greed. Robert Bellah and his colleagues (Bellah et al., 1986) noted with alarm the inability of new members of the upper middle class to form emotional bonds of any kind. Even conservative social critics, like Charles Sykes (1992), complain that Americans have tried to pass themselves off as victims so they can scam their way into lucrative lawsuits.

Thus in the literature, at least, one notes conflicting trends from one decade to the next. Perhaps the greatest change during the past forty years has been a virtual end to the affluence the generation of the 1950s took as a birthright. Critics like Christopher Lasch (1984) noted the rise of a survival mentality among middle-class victims of inflation and unemployment.

As economic conditions become worse for many Americans, there is often a search for scapegoats who are frequently capitalized on by extremist candidates like right-wing populist Pat Buchanan. Favorite scapegoats of the extreme right these days are illegal immigrants, welfare mothers, and "greedy" elderly people who want the government to pay for their Medicare. In fact, the deterioration of the American economy has been brought about by numerous structural changes, such as corporate downsizing and mergers, the transference of well-paying jobs to areas with cheap labor, the militarization of the American economy and resultant uncompetitiveness in the world market, and the global shift from industrial to service industries in First World nations.

One can point to a new and more problematic aspect of the American character, namely, uncertainty and confusion. Many Americans now possess conflicting values or no values at all regarding faith in their most basic institutions. They are fearful about the nation's future, but haven't a clue about what will solve the nation's problems. There is no longer a basic faith in any political ideology or political figure. Business executives are every bit as distrusted as politicians. The "main drift" of the American character is one of cynicism and alienation.

Much of this alienation stems from the inauthenticity and dehumanization that are the hallmarks of postmodern culture. This means that Americans live in a world where it is increasingly difficult to separate fiction from fantasy, form from substance, and lasting values from fad. The result of these influences on social character is an unprecedented confusion about life's most basic questions. Such confusion serves to spread a diffuse anger toward American institutions. Thus, Americans will remain hostile to politics and big business for a long time to come. Such hostility is usually met with slick new forms of propaganda and advertising. These efforts serve to raise up candidates, who, shortly after their election, demonstrate an ineffectual leadership, and corrupt practices of various kinds (related to the higher immorality described above).

The public reacts by turning away from politics or searching for a new, and probably dangerous, candidate (like Ross Perot), promising simplistic answers to complex structural problems. As a result, we live at a dangerous moment in public life. Declines in economic well-being often trigger extremist political movements and the scapegoating of minorities (like gays, or newly arrived nonwhite immigrants). The result could conceivably be some ugly moments in America's future where civil rights are repressed, hate crimes increase, and many people fall victim to demagogic appeals of irresponsible powerseekers. Such events will have profound consequences for the social character of the scapegoated groups.

The Changing American Way of Life

There are other dramatic changes contributing to the uncertainty and confusion of American life. The family, often touted as the backbone of the nation, has undergone dramatic change in the last forty years. Women no longer stay home and take care of children while men go off to work. Today, over 60 percent of married women work outside the home (Ries & Stone, eds., 1992:306), and there are unprecedented numbers of unmarried women who work and raise children alone. The divorce rate has doubled since the 1950s, from 25 percent to 50 percent of first-time marriages (Glenn, 1994). Conflict over the custody of children is more complicated than ever, with some children now choosing to divorce their parents. All this means that trust and stability of families are on the decline, as is the self-esteem of children of divorce (Smelser, 1988).

There have also been dramatic changes in American economic life. Physical labor was valued when the United States possessed a manufacturing and agriculturally based economy. The changes in technology and the coming of the service economy have seriously decreased the value of manual labor. Today, only about 20 percent of the American workforce produces products, and there are now more college students than farmers in the United States. This means that those who lack the skills derived from higher education are often unable to obtain work. High unemployment and attendant social problems result. While an unemployment rate of 3 percent or less was considered normal in the 1960s, the normal unemployment rate is placed at 7 percent in the 1990s, and this may soon rise.

Taken together, these changes have altered the perceptions of both children and adults. Adults often remember when conditions appeared more prosperous and there were fewer social problems that resulted in traumas of daily life and national crisis. Children growing up in postmodern America live in the present, devoid of a sense of past. Often they must find their way through a confusing thicket of media messages, parental admonitions, and peer pressures. The results have been dramatic increases in teen suicide rates, drug addiction, and pregnancies (over 1 million per year). Taken together, these trends have contributed to America's loss of optimism concerning the future.

The Changing Self in a Changing Society

As argued from the beginning of this book, the sociological imagination teaches that what often appear as personal troubles are merely symptoms of more widespread harmful conditions, like divorce, drug and child abuse, mental illness, unemployment, and crime. One may try to deny the truth of the environment's impact on daily life, or even escape from it for a time, but such efforts will work only until the realities of our age come crashing through such barriers.

There are a host of personal issues that Americans confront. Many Americans are experiencing identity confusion over what values to believe in, what it means to be a man or woman in contemporary life, and how to cultivate a positive sense of self in a society steeped in dehumanization and inauthenticity. The sociological imagination, as a worldview, offers a promise of therapeutic transformation for those in need of meaningful self-help.

America's view of extreme individualism and intense competition for scarce rewards and values (money, recognition, and power) creates a society where relatively few people become great successes. Consequently, many people in America feel they have "failed," and their self-esteem suffers. Knowledge about America's reward system and the American sense of individualism is a useful form of self-help. Studying the attitudes and experiences of others, their biographies (as Mills would call them), can be a liberating experience in a society that encourages self-blame; appearances over realities; and materialism over caring, concern, and emotional intimacy. Studying these dynamics can give you an important lesson in what is really important and lasting in life, and it can aid you in developing a sense of self-worth. Self-esteem is a crucial aspect of one's well-being, and ability to love and be loved in returned. The American social character is experiencing unmet needs for love, recognition, and identity. These issues are social problems. The sociological imagination is an ideal paradigm for their analysis. Accordingly, why not combine sociological analysis and self-help in what we may call "sociotherapy," the unity of the sociological and psychological. Sociotherapy is about the relationship between collective psychic crises and the crises of your own personal life.

Studying the typical psychological problems experienced by members of American culture will teach you a great deal about the problems of your own life. It will also teach you some important truths about the contradictions of American culture and society. You should be able to learn to "blame yourself" less and focus on the sociological causes of personal problems. This does not mean that you'll be able to escape personal responsibility for your actions, or violate the norms of society at will, but it does mean that you'll acquire a greater appreciation for the sociological nature of seemingly personal problems.

The Local Community and Social Change

While government has a role to play in positive social change, it has become clear since the 1960s that no government can be made to positively change society on its own. Today, there is a quiet revolution taking place in the United States. Social change that will ultimately end poverty, hunger, and unemployment is taking place in thousands of voluntary organizations. In Milwaukee, Esperanza Unida run businesses through which young people receive job training and jobs. In Ohio, Open Shelter operates a nonprofit auto repair shop that teaches young people how to repair vehicles, rehabilitates houses using carpenter trainees, trains welders, and places trainees into paying positions within the community.

Former President Jimmy Carter demonstrates one of the most important yet neglected aspects of solving social problems—human cooperation. The emergence of a caring and charitable spirit in America would do much to transform our society from one based on individualism and greed to one based on the welfare of all citizens and the common good.

Habitat for Humanity, Jimmy Carter's favorite charity, builds houses for the poor with volunteer labor. Other groups feed and shelter the homeless; grow food in their own urban gardens; recycle bottles, cans, and newspapers; comfort victims of AIDS; operate neighborhood crime watch programs; and perform countless other necessary tasks (Garr, 1995). There is a growing body of opinion that argues that such groups are much more creative than government bureaucracies, have much more community support, and provide services more efficiently in many cases. Their supporters argue that government funding for these nongovernmental organizations (NGOs) will not only promote positive solutions to problems, it will also allow these nonprofit groups to provide many jobs which will be sorely needed as corporations and government at all levels continue painful downsizing and restructuring processes (Rifkin, 1995; Osborne, 1995). Other suggestions for positive social change include:

1. Reorganize large corporations democratically to meet human needs: Multinational corporations are a primary barrier to progressive change. They possess no local or national loyalties, and are unconcerned with their role in causing inflation, unemployment, pollution, and the perpetuation of gross inequalities, inequalities that inherently corrupt democracy. One of the best ways to extend democracy and community responsibility to corporations is to have workers invest their pension funds in them until they own a majority of the companys' stock. This would not only ensure worker ownership and control, but would

take away the layers of secrecy, from which so much corporate scandal grows. Worker-owned companies are much less likely to experience strikes and the problems that accompany worker alienation, especially drug abuse, absenteeism, and sabotage.

2. Reduce government's size: In the United States it is a near political and economic impossibility. For most Americans, the greatest problems represented by government concern deficit spending, high taxes, unfair welfare programs, and gridlock. The system now in place has degenerated into government by special (business) interests, with reelection campaigns of politicians financed by such groups. Overcoming these problems is a complex task, but it is not impossible.

   The writers of the American Constitution never dreamed there would be a class of professional politicians, who make being in office a life's work. The Constitution says nothing about political parties. Our current pathologies suggest the need for (1) campaign finance reform (federally financed congressional elections); (2) term limitations for senators and representatives; and (3) the abolition of "welfare" for able-bodied people of working age. Perhaps the best way to reduce the debt and the deficit is to pare down all possible expenditures, including welfare and corporate subsidies, and increase government receipts without raising taxes on working people. Full employment is the best medicine for our economic woes.

3. Bring about full employment: This may require issuing new tax write-offs to employee-owned corporations to expand factories and jobs here in the United States. It may also require making government the employer of last resort if not enough corporate sector jobs are available. There is no question that government is capable of playing such a role, as Roosevelt's New Deal demonstrated with the Works Progress Administration (WPA), Civilian Conservation Corps (CCC), and similar programs. Moreover, attached to every job ought to be cradle-to-grave benefits: health and dental insurance, life insurance, and family leave, and some system of day care for children of employees. Day care centers go back at least as far as World War II in America, and there is no reason why such facilities at job sites could not experience a rebirth. Why not finance these benefits through a combination of government sponsorship, employer contribution, and employee payroll deduction? The vast majority of other industrial democracies already sponsor such programs as paid family leave and national health care. Are Americans any less valuable than citizens of other democracies?

   The financing of such programs could also take place through increased taxes on those Americans who possess the greatest wealth and who earn the greatest income. It is now the case that the richest 2.5 million Americans earn more income than the poorest 100 million. Clearly this situation is incompatible with the growth of democracy in a nation where money buys access and influence. The framers of the Constitution assumed that America would be an upper-middle-class society and Jefferson, himself, warned that if the United States became an urban, manufacturing nation, class conflict and the growth of a few rich and many poor would follow. "He believed that almost all Americans should continue farming to avert social ills, class distinctions, and

Many of America's social problems, such as providing educational opportunities for poor minorities are solvable, but they often require government action. The notion that government programs can be used to resolve social issues has fallen into disfavor in recent decades. Yet, some programs, like Head Start, have had a positive effect on those enrolled in them.

social conflict" (Etzkowitz, ed., 1980:3). Jefferson said all this decades before Karl Marx was born. As historian Charles A. Beard once noted, one does not have to be a Marxist to know that wealth and power go hand in hand. Americans have always believed in the unlimited accumulation of wealth. It is part of the American Dream, as well as part of our conception of individualism. The notion that a few ought to fairly sacrifice for the benefit of all has not become part of the American character. Would there be much harm to Americans' motivation if their wealth was limited to $100 million? One billion? For 98 percent of the population, such a limitation would be of no consequence. A national debate on such limits ought to begin soon.

4. A program of social reconstruction: Rarely has there been such unmet need in America. Trillions of dollars worth of streets, roads, and bridges are in disrepair. Millions of first-time home buyers can not afford a home. There is a need for better schools and smaller classes, more family doctors (and fewer specialists), more nurses, teachers, computers in education and in homes, police and fire personnel, libraries, and drug treatment facilities (to name just a few). What seems reasonable is a domestic Marshall Plan for America, one similar to the one that rehabilitated the economic stability of European nations after World War II.

The question is, of course, how to pay for these programs. Aside from the tax programs discussed above, there is a need to reduce spending on defense weapons systems drastically, and engage in economic conversion to meet these needs. Many corporations can convert their plants to engage in badly needed peacetime activity: manufacturing mass transit systems, prefabricated housing units, and development of future technology (like interactive video and virtual reality systems).

While economic democracy is a necessity in America, government also suffers from concentrated power within organizations. Secretive organizations can lead the nation into war without a congressional declaration. This is proof enough of democracy's erosion in America. Many proposals exist for extending democracy in America. Dr. Michael Lerner has advocated making extensive use of legislative initiatives (proposals for law or changes therein that come from citizens and appear on ballots after the proper number of petition signatures has been collected). People then vote the proposal(s) up or down in the next general election. Lerner also advocates more extensive use of the recall, where a majority of voters can vote a politician out of office. One of Lerner's more provocative notions concerns the use of television to extend democracy. Voters express their preferences through voting devices attached to their television sets. They would vote after an electronic town hall meeting that debated the issue(s) in question. Representatives would consider the results of the vote (Lerner, 1973). Lerner's ideas are not the last word concerning how to expand democracy in America. The need to do so, however, remains paramount.

Foreign Policy and Population Crisis

Because we live in an interdependent world, whatever happens elsewhere is a matter of concern everywhere. The United States has political and economic relations and commitments everywhere. Consequently America's true interest and moral principles lie in promoting peace, democracy, and prosperity/full employment wherever possible.

The United States is, after all, only one nation in a world composed of nearly 150 nations. America can, nevertheless, do more than it is doing now. One valuable policy the United States could promote is to have as many Third World nations as possible coalesce into Common Market trading partners. Such arrangements can serve indirectly to promote freedom of travel and other human rights. The arrangement has worked so well in Europe that much of that continent is on the verge of a forming a united, super-economic power complete with multiple citizen privileges, a common currency, and many additional advantageous features.

Given the depth of the global crisis population and environmental crises, organized groups of people must engage in nonviolent action to oppose shortsighted corporate and governmental environmental policies.

Why Change Must Come

The reforms we have considered are not merely utopian. If we look at the history of progressive social change in America, we will soon discover a central trend. All the progressive reform of the nineteenth or twentieth century, such as the abolition of slavery, the right to vote for women, the eight-hour work day, the right to collective bargaining, the civil rights acts, or the voting rights act, are the outcome of protracted struggle by collective social movements. Such movements were products of marches and demonstrations by groups of people who aided each other. Despite all the American folklore about the importance of individual heroes, it is collectivities that produce progressive social change.

Possessing a sociological imagination involves the realization that positive social change in America has come about, not so much through acts of individual heroism, as through the episodes of collective action. These movements involve groups of people who share a genuine concern for each other's well-being and human rights. This is what Americans call "teamwork." If you wish to extend democratic life in this society, you must be willing to work for worthy causes. This means creatively participating in democratic social movements, and joining worthwhile groups. The need for people to work for social change has rarely been greater, and the number of groups looking for dedicated volunteers and paid employees is astounding. Pick a cause: helping the poor, improving the environment, extending human rights here and overseas, ending hunger and malnutrition, gun control, befriending parentless children, world peace. The list is almost limitless. Such lists appear in nearly every issue of the *Utne Reader*. Part of developing a sociological imagination can mean experience in such organizations.

Second, working for social change also means staying informed about the issues of the day. One of the assumptions made by many of the writers of the Constitution was that the American citizenry would consist of people who took an active interest in public issues, who would stay informed and engage in ongoing public debate. Our democracy has degenerated into a place where ten-second sound bites and meaningless political slogans have nearly replaced serious debate about complex issues.

Summary

Society's "main drift" is an important topic, if for no other reason than that citizens' perception of their society's future profoundly affects their attitudes and behaviors on a daily basis:

1. Increasing inequalities of wealth and political power will worsen the numerous macro- and micro- level problems that have been the subject of this book (unemployment, recession/depression, corporate crimes and political corruption, and related woes).

2. There are disturbing trends in postmodern culture and social character that have been evolving since the late 1940s.

3. Partially as a result of these trends, the social character of our age suffers from a lack of and yearning for stable moral values that will serve as a guide to decision making in daily life. Given the constant social changes concerning economic conditions; cultural fads; technological breakthroughs in birth control devices, medicine, and invasive technology, stable values seem a long way off at best. Moreover, there is every reason to believe that the current mass disrespect

for political and economic elites will continue, perhaps culminating in collective social movements that will result in the basic structural reforms necessary to resolve the great social problems of our age.

From a sociological imagination perspective, solutions to the problems of our age must take place on the individual, community, and societal levels. Along with a humane transformation in social character, masses of people must be encouraged to engage in collective action that will extend both economic and political democracy.

Suggested Readings

D.L. Bartlett and J.B. Steele (1992) *America: What Went Wrong?* (Kansas City, MO: Andrews and McNeel). This is an award-winning analysis of the ills of the American economy. It is interesting, passionate, and essential for those seeking an understanding of America's economic decline.

P.C. Kennedy (1987) *The Rise and Fall of Great Powers* (New York: Random House).

——— (1993) *Preparing for the Twenty-First Century* (New York: Random House).

Dr. Kennedy is a history professor at Yale University. He has written two of the most important works of comparative history concerning global master trends. His work is very rich with facts and is also compassionate and interesting.

Exercises

Critical Thinking Exercise Epilogue 1	Studying Master Trends in Mass Media Coverage

Most major American newspapers contain a trends section. The Los Angeles *Times*, New York *Times*, Washington *Post*, and other major large city dailies are especially good sources for such material. These sections are rarely called "Trends," and are more likely titled "Lifestyles," "Living," "Cues," "Modern Living," and the like. More often than not, they are the same section of the paper in which movie and television listings, as well as advice columns (like "Dear Abby," and "Ann Landers"), are located. Weekly news magazines also devote some space to various cultural, political, or economic trends.

A master trends in mass media coverage study may be done individually or in research teams. Research teams might select three major dailies. Study the trends section of each newspaper for one month. Compare and contrast trend articles from each paper with an eye on answering the following questions:

1. What are the topics of these articles?

2. Which newspapers pay attention to the types of trends discussed in this chapter (trends that are causing or will cause major social problems)?

3. Which newspapers pay attention to only lifestyle trends (fads, popular culture) and ignore social problems completely?

4. Which newspapers have a mix of articles devoted to both social problems topics and pop culture trends?

Those seeking an alternative sampling method may compare trend articles from major newspapers with trend articles from weekly news magazines. Since newspapers are published daily and the magazines are weeklies, it is a good idea to use several months' worth of weeklies to compare with one month's worth of newspaper articles.

Those wishing a structured set of topics to look for may use the major trends described in this text:

(a) increasing inequality of wealth and power,

(b) activities of the secret government and threats to democracy,

(c) the overpopulation crisis and its consequences, and

(d) elements of postmodern culture (advertising's increase, violence and sex in media).

The results of this exercise should yield a great deal of information concerning which publications possess something of a sociological imagination in their approach to reporting. I know that many sociologists will probably not expect to find any evidence of such an approach in journalism, but C. Wright Mills thought otherwise and so do we. By the way, I've noticed that many major papers also analyze trends by running a series of articles on major social problems. Such series frequently appear on the paper's front page. These items would make excellent samples as well. For those instructors wishing an alternative to this exercise, please see Exercise Epilogue 2 below.

Critical Thinking Exercise Epilogue 2	Studying "Main Drifts" in Social Criticism

If there is a group of people who consistently write about the "main drift" in modern mass society, it is social critics (Simon, 1977). The world of social critics is a fascinating and unique one, and its study can yield important information concerning, not only the views of various ideological groups on the future, but trend-setting policy proposals as well.

As an introduction to the study of social criticism, I suggest that students be assigned one of the periodicals on the list given in Exercise 5.2 and asked to do an analysis of "main drifts" using the coding sheet that follows. If students are assigned to work in teams, two or more periodicals may be compared. I suggest that students study each periodical's last full year of publication, and analyze the first article of each issue for weekly or semi-weekly publications. If monthlies or quarterlies are assigned, more articles should be chosen

Continued on next page

Exercise Epilogue 2 Continued

at random. The number of articles in the sample can be tailored to the needs of each class. I have students select a dozen pieces initially. Use larger samples for examining social criticism in a term paper or an independent study.

Predictions concerning the consequences of a given social problem often take one of the following forms:

1. *Benign*—no consequence will befall society, and, therefore, no action need be taken in solving the problem.

2. A *worsening* of the problem—the numbers of people or degree of severity of the problem will increase unless something is done soon.

3. A *catastrophe* is possible—averting catastrophe usually involves declaring a crisis. Examples of catastrophes often given by American social critics include:

    (a) a racial civil war, urban riots, etc.,

    (b) possible ecological destruction of the earth, either slowly or relatively quickly,

    (c) economic depression,

    (d) nuclear war—limited or global,

    (e) a coup d'état in America—the establishment of a dictatorship and ending of democracy as we know it,

    (f) other catastrophic possibilities—the decline of America as a world economic, political, and/or military power, shrinking of the middle class, America being overrun by illegal immigrants, etc.

Each of the above themes is a category in this exercise.

It is possible to have more than one catastrophe predicted in a single article.

A separate coding sheet, like the following one, should be used for each article.

The results of the analysis should be presented in a table.

Coding Sheet for Articles of Social Criticism	Master Trends

ARTICLES OF SOCIAL CRITICISM

1. *Periodical Name*: (See list in Exercise Epilogue 1.)

2. *Article #*: (This is a number assigned to each article by the coder. If twelve articles are coded, they should be numbered 1–12, and so on.)

3. *Topic(s)*: Social problem topic(s) of each article, usually reflected in article title.

4. *Prediction Code(s)*:

   1. *benign*—no consequence will befall society, and, therefore, no action need be taken in solving the problem.

   2. a *worsening* of the problem—the numbers of people or degree of severity of the problem will increase unless something is done soon.

   3. a *catastrophe* is possible—averting catastrophe usually involves declaring a crisis. Examples of catastrophes often given by American social critics include:

      (a) a racial civil war, urban riots, etc.,

      (b) possible ecological destruction of the earth, either slowly or relatively quickly,

      (c) economic depression,

      (d) nuclear war—limited or global,

      (e) coup d'état in America—the establishment of a dictatorship and ending of democracy as we know it,

      (f) other catastrophic possibilities—the decline of America as world economic, political, and/or military power, shrinking of the middle class, America being overrun by illegal immigrants, etc.

Results of this analysis can yield interesting data on which periodicals are the most optimistic or pessimistic regarding the possibility of resolving specific social problems.

Glossary

Acid rain—caused by emissions of sulfur dioxide and nitrogen oxides from metal foundries and power plants, as well as from heating systems and vehicles. These particles are carried by the wind over long distances.

Alienation—characterized by feelings of estrangement from either society or from oneself, often from both.

Anomie—a lack of norms concerning how a goal is to be achieved; a social situation where norms are unclear.

Biodepletion—the mass extinction of species throughout the globe.

Biography, or **social character**—personality traits and behaviors that are widely shared by members of a culture. Social character stems from the values that are widely shared within a culture.

Collectivized sense of self—conceiving of one's self as part of a group, like one's family (or ancestors), clan, tribe, or nation.

Contradictions—permanent conflicts within the structure of society that are a frequent cause of social problems.

Corporate elite—part of the national power elite, made up of the largest 100 to 200 industrial corporations in the nation and the insurance companies, banks, and other financial entities (such as mutual funds) that own stock in them.

Cultural estrangement (value isolation)—a condition under which one rejects widely shared societal values, such as wealth and success.

Deconstruction—a criticism of other paradigms or ideologies, especially their contradictions.

Deinstitutionalization—a policy instituted in the 1970s whereby the hospitalized mentally ill were released to welfare hotels and other facilities.

Discrimination—the acts involved in the negative special treatment of minorities.

Double bind—A method of treating minorities by which no matter how they behave, it is wrong. For example, blacks are stereotyped as either harmless "Sambos," who behave like simple-minded children, or as explosively violent.

Ecopsychology—a field of study devoted to mass consumption and its relationship to environmental concerns.

Environmental racism—a term used to describe the victimization of people of color by corporate polluters. Various studies have established that minorities in the United States, are at considerable risk from such victimization.

Ethnic group—any group, such as Jewish Americans, Irish Americans, Puerto Rican Americans, and so on, that is a subgroup in the larger society and has a common set of cultural traits and values.

Ethnocentric—having a general distrust and resentment of groups that are different than one's own.

Eugenics—the notion that the poor, being biologically (if not racially) inferior, have no business reproducing themselves.

Federal Trade Commission Act (1914)—the determination which made it unlawful to restrict competition and to engage in unfair and deceptive trade practices. However, the power of the FTC is limited to issuing cease-and-desist orders, which it can do only upon securing the permission of a federal court. The FTC can recommend prosecution of criminal cases, but the Justice Department is specifically charged with this task.

Frustration-Aggression Theory—the theory suggesting that prejudice originates in the buildup of frustration. When frustration can not be released on its intended target, individuals experience a free-floating hostility that may be released against some other available target, or scapegoat.

Gender roles—the social expectations a society has for boys and girls, men and women, involving definitions of masculinity and femininity, that is, appropriate behavior for men and women.

Genocide—the systematic extermination of an entire group of people.

Global warming—a potential threat to the sustainability of life on earth in the form of the average surface temperature rising three to eight degrees. The increase in temperature might result in the melting of polar ice caps, and sharp changes in weather patterns.

Hate crimes—illegal acts of intimidation and violence committed against minority group members and that are attributable to prejudice on the part of the perpetrator.

In-kind income benefits—nonmonetary entitlements such as food stamps, Medicaid, and subsidized housing.

Inauthenticity—an important alienating condition characterized by the presence of *positive overt appearances* coupled with *negative underlying (hidden) realities.*

Individual discrimination—actions of individuals or groups of individuals in response to feelings engendered by prejudice.

Inferiorized—defined as inferior to dominant groups.

Institutional discrimination—the systematic exclusion of people from equal access to and participation in a particular institution or institutions because of their minority status.

Institutions—collections of social roles, norms, and social organizations that are organized to meet particular societal needs.

Laissez-faire capitalism—a vision of the world where numerous businesses in the same industry, without government regulation, compete for consumer loyalty by producing the amount of product in demand at the price consumers are willing to pay.

Loneliness—feelings of estrangement from and rejection by others that results from a lack of social acceptance by people within one's environment.

Mass society—a modern industrial society in which small, intimate (primary) groups, such as extended families and communities, have lost their substance, and interaction in the social world is impersonal.

Master trends, or **main drifts**—fundamental mechanisms by which social change takes place within the social structure.

Meaninglessness—confusion or vagueness about what one ought to believe or about the criteria for making important decisions.

Medical-industrial complex—a combination of medical interests that includes approximately five hundred private corporations and their allies in Congress, and the mass media.

Medicalization—the treatment of drug addiction by qualified medical professionals. This model allows for the prescription of controlled substances as part of a treatment regimen.

Military component (of the military-industrial complex)—the major branches of the military services (army, navy, and air force), as well as the nation's intelligence community (the National Security Council, the Central Intelligence Agency, the Defense Intelligence Agency, and the intelligence arms of the various branches of the military).

Minorities—a group that, by virtue of its physical or cultural characteristics, is singled out for differential and unequal treatment.

Mission hate crimes—those crimes committed by individuals or organized groups who are out to rid the entire world of "evil" minorities who are threatening their way of life.

Normlessness (anomie)—a social situation according to which people strive to achieve culturally prescribed goals (e.g., becoming "successful" by acquiring money and status) but without norms influencing their behavior.

Object-directed dehumanization—an alienating condition of the social structure that occurs when people are labeled less than human for purposes of profit, exploitation, and manipulation.

Objective stress overload—a condition that stems from stressful stimuli in one's environment, such as war, earthquake, economic dislocation (job loss), or the death of close friend or relative.

Oppression—one or more groups within a culture systematically and successfully preventing other groups within that culture from attaining the scarce and valued resources.

Organized crime—a criminal syndicate consisting of an organized hierarchy (an organization) making profits through criminal activity (criminal enterprise), using the threat of or actual use of force, engaging in corruption of public officials (law enforcement and politicians), providing illegal goods and services that are in high public demand (e.g., drugs, prostitution, illegal gambling, loan sharking, dumping illegal toxic waste, arson, securities fraud, and so on). Taken together these attributes constitute a definition of organized crime as an ongoing criminal enterprise engaged in profit making from illegal activities that are in high demand.

Overpopulation—a perception that the world's resources are being pushed to new limits due to ever increasing population growth. It is extremely relative to a nation's ability—and most important its willingness—to devote resources to meeting survival needs and establishing humane policies of population control.

Personal threat hate crimes—crimes usually committed by adults who feel that minorities are invading their neighborhoods, taking their jobs, seducing their women, and so on.

Political alienation—a special form of moral harm involving cynicism about and distrust of government.

Political sector (of the military-industrial complex)—defense contracting lobbies, members of Congress who sit on the appropriations committees of the U.S. Senate and House of Representatives, the Joint Chiefs of Staff, and the civilian administrators (the secretary of defense and the secretaries of the various armed services) who oversee the nation's military establishment.

Poly drug users—those addicted to more than one drug, some of which, like sedatives, are legal substances.

Postmodern—a term which describes a variety of institutional and cultural phenomena characterizing the current historical epoch. Postmodern is four things at the same time. First, it describes a sequence of historical moments from World War II to the present. Second, the postmodern references the multinational forms of *late capitalism* which have introduced new cultural logics and new forms of communication and representation into the world economic and cultural systems. Third, it describes a movement in the visual arts, architecture, cinema, popular music, and social theory which goes against the grain of classic realist and modernist formations. Fourth, it refers to a form of theorizing and writing about the social. Postmodern theorizing is preoccupied with the visual society, its representations, cultural logic, and the new types of personal troubles (AIDS, homelessness, drug addiction, family and public violence) and public problems that define the current age.

Power elite or **military-industrial complex**—collectively the people who head the institutions of great power (large corporations, the executive branch of the government, and the military apparatus).

Powerlessness—people's expectation or belief that their behavior will not determine or affect their future.

Prejudice—preconceived judgments about an entire group made without being tested against reality.

Projection—the process whereby people (minorities in this case) are accused of behaviors that prejudiced people can not accept in themselves.

Racial group—a population with a distinct set of identifiable physical characteristics. Races are usually set apart by their skin color, the shape of their eye lids, noses, or other features.

Racism—an ideology, or belief system, designed to justify or rationalize the unequal treatment of members of socially defined racial groups.

Regulatory capture—a situation wherein regulatory agencies become dominated by the very industries they are supposed to be regulating.

Segregating, denial of opportunities, and **economic exploitation**—the usual mechanisms of discrimination by which minorities are kept in place by dominant groups. These are the most prevalent forms of institutional discrimination today.

Self-alienation—a condition in which one feels powerlessness, meaninglessness, loneliness, isolation, normlessness, and estrangement from oneself, from other people and from society at large.

Self-directed dehumanization—a form of self-alienation. It involves turning oneself into a "cog in a wheel," a dehumanized machine.

Self-estrangement—experiencing of oneself as alien, with resultant feelings of resentment and confusion.

Sex—a biological category or division defined according to male and female anatomical, hormonal, and chromosomal differences.

Social constructions—widely agreed-upon definitions of wrongful conditions within society.

Social disorganizationists—an early school of thought about social problems dominated by the belief that society's smooth functioning was made possible by agreed-upon rules (norms) that provided guidelines for appropriate behavior for people in the performance of their various social roles (family members, workers, teachers, clergy, students, and so on). Social problems were caused by deviations from these rules.

Social distance—a term referring to the degrees of avoidance of minorities.

Social pathologists—An early group of straightforward moralists, staunch supporters of the virtues of thrift, hard work, sexual purity, and personal discipline. This school of thought put forth a social problems paradigm that concentrated on the "social pathology" of the lower ("dangerous") classes, whose *personal* defects, either biological or moral, caused their poverty, sexual deviance, drug and alcohol abuse, crime, delinquency, mental illness, and suicide.

Social problem—a socially patterned condition involving widespread physical, financial, and/or moral harm that is caused by contradictions (permanent conflicts) stemming from the institutional arrangement of a given society. Such harms exist whether or not they have gained the attention of the mass media, and politicians.

Social structure—an interrelated set of societal institutions.

Sociological imagination—an ability (quality of mind) to see the interrelationship of one's own life and the historical period and institutional arrangement (society) in which one lives.

Status group—one whose members share certain qualities to which positive or negative honor is attached.

Stereotypes—negative generalizations about entire groups' characteristics that function to reinforce the negative values and beliefs users have about minority groups. Once learned, individual members of minority groups are judged according to generalized stereotypes.

Subjective stress overload—a condition observed in the personality of the individual, and characterized by chronic worry that can result in mental breakdown from reaching one's breaking point.

Sustainability—the efforts that meet the needs of the present generation without compromising the needs of future generations.

The Higher Immorality—an institutionalized set of deviant and criminal practices that take place within corporate and governmental institutions. These practices involve deception and manipulation of the public, corruption, corporate crime, and, occasionally, cooperation with organized criminal syndicates. All the practices associated with the higher immorality are in and of themselves major social problems and they, in turn, cause further problems.

Terrorism industry—those governmental and economic organizations and activities that are related to terrorism. Its comprehension is essential to understanding both social problems, and how the overall political economy of the nation functions.

Thrill hate crimes—those acts usually committed by young men twenty years of age and under. The perpetrators are often sadistic young people looking for vulnerable victims as an outlet for their aggression. In thrill crimes, which range from assault and rape to murder, minorities are frequently viewed as interchangeable.

Underclass—the lowliest members of the lower class, described as a diverse group of somewhere between seven and ten million people that have included: discouraged workers, unemployed people who have given up looking for jobs and are no longer counted as unemployed in official statistics; some 2.4 million Americans who have been on welfare for longer than one year; people who are chronically unemployed; two million children living in poverty; and some 4.4 million disabled people, unable to work.

Workfare—a welfare policy which limits welfare recipients to a maximum of two years of benefits, after which they are required to take a job.

Yuppie—a young, urban professional whose gross income exceeds $40,000 annually, and usually resides in a large metropolitan area.

Bibliography

Abadinsky, H. (1989). *Drug Abuse.* Chicago: Nelson-Hall.

Abadinsky, H. (1990). *Organized Crime* (3rd ed.). Chicago: Nelson-Hall.

ABA Journal (1994) (February): 32.

ABC News. (1988). Sons of Scarface: The new Mafia (Documentary).

ABC Television. (1994). 20/20 Segment. (13 January).

Ackerman, G. (1993). A congressional view of youth suicide, *American Psychologist* (February): 183–84.

Adams, J. R. (1929). *Our business civilization.* New York: Holmes & Meier.

Ade-Ridder, L. 1990. Sexuality and marital quality in older married couples, in T. H. Brubaker (Ed.), *Family Relationships in Later Life.* (2nd. ed.) Newbury Park, CA: Sage.

Adorno, T. (1974). The stars down to earth, *Telos 19* (Spring): 13–91.

Albanese, J. (1989). *Organized crime in America.* (2nd ed.). Cincinnati: Anderson.

Albanese, J. (1995). *White-collar Crime in America.* Englewood Cliffs, NJ: Prentice-Hall.

Albanese, Jay & Pursley, R. (1993). *Crime in America: Some emerging issues.* Englewood Cliffs, NJ: Prentice-Hall.

Allaby, Michael. (1989). *Dictionary of the environment* (3rd ed.). New York: New York University Press.

Allport, G. (1988). *The nature of prejudice.* Garden City, NY: Doubleday.

Alper, J. (1992). A crowded planet. Los Angeles *Times, 13,* 15.

American Council on Education. (1991). *Minorities in higher education.* Washington, DC: American Council on Education.

American Medical News. (1995) (27 February): 20.

American Psychiatric Association. (1987). *Diagnostic and statistical manual of mental disorders* (3rd ed., rev.). Washington, DC: American Psychiatric Association.

Amott, T. (1994). Eliminating poverty. In R. Caplan & J. Feffer (Eds.) *State of the union 1994* (pp. 166–183), Boulder: Westview.

Anderson J. & Spear J. (1988a). Witness tells of CIA plot to kill Castro. Washington *Post* (1 November): C-19.

Anderson, J. (1985). LBJ sought to quell conspiracy talk. Washington *Post* (1 April): B-13.

Anderson, J. & Van Atta D. (1988). Death in Dallas: A plot that backfired. Washington *Post* (2 November): E-15.

Anderson, W. (1990). *Reality isn't what it used to be.* San Francisco: Harper.

Asimov, N. (1993a). Alarming report on U.S. students reading skills, San Francisco *Chronicle* (16 September): A-5. (1993b) U.S. teachers pay ranks low in study of developed nations. San Francisco *Chronicle* (9 July): A-6.

Astroth, K. (1994). Beyond ephebiphobia: problem adults or problem youths? *Phi Delta Kappan* (January): 411–13.

Auletta, K. (1982). *The underclass* (5th ed.). New York: Vintage.

Babbie, E. (1989). *The practice of social research.* Belmont, CA: Wadsworth.

Babbie, E. (1994). *The Sociological Spirit.* Belmont, CA: Wadsworth.

Babcock, C. R. & Devroy A. (1992). The uncertain intersection: Politics & private interests. In The Washington Post Writer's Group (Ed.) *Society in crisis: The Washington Post social problems companion* (pp. 34–39). Boston: Allyn & Bacon.

Bagdikian, B. (1991). Statement to the Federal Trade Commission. In A. A. Berger, *Media U.S.A.* (2nd ed.). New York: Longman.

Banfield, E. (1974). *The unheavenly city revisited.* Boston: Little Brown.

Barnet, H. (1981). Corporate capitalism, corporate crime. *Crime & Delinquency, 27* (January): 4–23.

Barnet, H. (1994). *Toxic debts and the superfund dilemma.* Chapel Hill, NC: University of North Carolina Press.

Barnet, R. J. & Cavanagh J. (1994). *Global dreams: Imperial corporations and the new world order.* New York: Touchstone.

Barnet, R. J. (1993). The end of jobs. *Harpers* (October): 47–52.

Bartlett, D. L. & Steele, J. (1992). *America: What went wrong?* Kansas City, MO: Andrews & McMeel.

Bassis, M., Gelles, R. J., & Levine, A. (1982). *Social problems.* New York: Harcourt, Brace.

Bateson, M. & Goldsly, R. (1991). AIDS: The epidemic and the society. In J. Skolnick & E. Currie, (Eds.) *Crisis in Amercan Institutions* (8th ed.). (pp. 433–466). New York: Harper Collins.

Baum, A. & Barnes, D. (1993). *A nation in denial: The truth about homelessness.* Boulder: Westview Press.

Beaty, J. & Gwynne, S. C. (1991). The dirtiest bank of all. *Time.* (July 29): 42–47.

Beck, M. (1992). The flames of a crusader. *Newsweek* (19 October): 58.

Becker, H. (1952). The career of a chicago public school teacher. *American Journal of Sociology, 57* (March): 470–477.

Becnel, B. C. (1993). Poverty as policy. *Essence* (December): 92–94.

Berlin, D. (1988). *Final Disclosure.* New York: Scribners.

Bell, D. (1993). Downfall of the business giants. *Dissent, 40* (Summer): 316–323.

Bellah, Robert et al. (1986). *Habits of the heart.* New York: Harper & Row.

Bender, A. (1985). *Health or hoax?: The truth about food and diets.* New York: Prometheus.

Beneke, Timothy (1994). The intimate war. *The East Bay Express 16.* (July 22): 1, 11–21.

Benoit, E. (1989). The case for legalization. *Financial World* (October 3): 32–35.

Bequai, A. (1978). *White-collar crime: A 20th century crisis.* Lexington, MA: D.C. Heath.

Bequette, F. (1993). The right to clean air. *UNESCO Courier* (March): 23–24.

Berger, A. A. (Ed.). (1991). *Media U.S.A.* (2nd ed.). New York: Longman.

Berger, G. (1987). *Crack: The new epidemic.* New York: Franklin Watts.

Bernard, V. P. et al. (1971). Dehumanization: A composite psychological defense mechanism in relation to modern war. In R. Perrucci & M. Pilisuk, (Eds.) *The triple revolution emerging: Social problems in depth.* (1994). (pp. 16–30). Boston: Little, Brown.

Bernstein, D. & Howard, L. (1994) Reagan aid linked to drug running says former DEA agent. *San Francisco Weekly* (18 May): 6.

Bischak, G. (1994). Investing in our future. In R. Caplan & J. Feffer (Eds.). *The State of the Union, 1994* (pp. 88–101). Boulder: Westview.

Black, R. F. & Grant, L. (1995). Getting business off the dole. *U.S. News & World Report* (10 April): 38.

Blauner, R. (1964). *Alienation and Freedom.* Chicago: University of Chicago Press.

Bluestone, B. & Harrison, B. (1982). *The deindustrialization of America.* New York: Basic Books.

Bodenheimer, T. (1992a). Should we abolish the private health insurance industry? In V. Navarro (Ed.), *Why the United States doesn't have a national health care program.* (pp. 51–72). (Amityville, NY: Baywood)

——— (1992b). Private insurance reform in the 1990s: Can it solve the health care crisis. In V. Navarro (Ed.). *Why the United States doesn't have a national health care program.* (pp. 91–110). Amityville, NY: Baywood.

Bornschier, V. et al. (1978). Cross national evidence of the effects of foreign investment and aid on economic growth and inequality: A survey of findings and a reanalysis. *American Journal of Sociology, 84,* 651–683.

Borosage, R. (1994). Meeting real security needs. In R. Caplan & J. Feffer (Eds.). *The state of the union 1994* (pp. 63–77). Boulder: Westview.

Boroughs, D. (1994). Cost of crime: $674 billion. *U.S. News & World Report* (17 January): 40–44.

Bradsher, K. (1995). Rich getting richer in U.S., studies find. San Francisco *Chronicle* (17 April): A-1, A-9.

Brandon, R. et al. (1992). Premiums without benefits. In V. Navarro (Ed.). *Why the United States does not have a national health program.* (pp. 73–90). Amityville, NY: Baywood.

Braun, D. (1993). *The rich get richer.* Chicago: Nelson-Hall.

Breed, W. (1971). *The self-guiding society.* New York: Free Press.

Brenner, H. (1973). *Mental illness and the economy.* Cambridge: Harvard University Press.

Brightbill, T. (1992). Political action committees: How much influence will $7.7 million buy?" In P. Navarro (Ed.) *Why the United States does not have a national health program* (pp. 123–128). Amityville, NY: Baywood.

Brill, N. Q. (1993). *America's psychic malignancy.* Springfield, IL: Charles C. Thomas.

Britt, C. (1994). Crime and unemployment among youths in the united states, 1958–1990. *American Journal of Economics and Sociology, 53* (January): 99–109.

Brooks, J. (1988). Waste dumpers turning to West Africa. New York *Times* (17 July): 1.

Broverman, I. K. et al. (1970). Sex role stereotypes and clinical judgments in mental health. *Journal of Consulting and Clinical Psychology, 34:* 1–7.

Brown, Lester, McGrath, P. L. & Stokes, B. Twenty-two dimensions of the population problem. *Worldwatch paper, 5* Washington, DC: Worldwatch Institute, 1976.

Brown, P. (1994). Fear and denial as infections soar.

Brumberg, J. (1994). Anorexia nervosa in context. In P. Conrad & R. Kern (Eds.). *The sociology of health and illness: A critical approach* (4th ed.). (pp. 101–124). New York: St. Martins.

Buder, L. (1988). Hertz admits use of fraud in bills for auto repair. New York *Times* (5 August): A-1; A-10.

Budiansky, S. (1994). 10 billion for dinner, please. *U.S. News & World Report* (12 September): 57–60.

Bullard, R. D. (Ed.). (1994). *Unequal protection: Environmental justice and communities of color.* San Francisco: Sierra Club Books.

Buncher, J. F. (1977). Excerpts from the final act of the 1975 Helsinki Conference. In *Human rights and*

American diplomacy: 1975–1977. New York: Facts On File: 11–17.

Cable News Network (CNN). (1994). Headline News (13 January).

Cable News Network (CNN). (1995) Headline News (26 June).

Calabrese, R. (1987). Adolescence: A growth period conducive to alienation. *Adolescence, 88* (Winter): 929–938.

Caldicott, H. (1992). *If you love this planet: A plan to heal the earth.* New York: Norton.

———— (1984). *Missile envy.* New York: Morrow.

Cantor, M. G. (1987). Popular culture and the portrayal of women: content and control. In B. B. Hess and M. M. Ferree (Eds.) *Analyzing Gender.* (pp. 190–214) Newbury Park, CA: Sage.

Caplan, R. & J. Feffer (Eds.). (1994). *The State of the Union, 1994.* Boulder: Westview: 63–77.

Cass, V. (1994). The international toxic waste trade: Who gets left holding the toxic trash bag? Presented at the 1994 Meeting of the American Society of Criminology.

Cavanagh, J., et al. (1994). Forging a global new deal. In R. Caplan & J. Feffer (Eds.) *The State of the Union 1994* (pp. 29–45). Boulder: Westview.

Celis, W. (1993). Study finds rising concentration of black and hispanic students. The New York *Times.* (14 December): A-1; A-11.

Cherlin, A. (1983). A sense of history: recent trends on aging and the family. In M. W. Riley et al (Eds.). *Aging in society: Selected Reviews of Recent Research.* (pp. 5–23) Hillsdale, NJ: Erlbaum.

Chira, S. (1993). Surprising survey on kids and guns—40% know a victim. San Francisco *Chronicle* (July 20): A-10.

Chromsky, N. & Herman E. S. (1978). U.S. vs. human rights in the third world." *Monthly Review, 29* (July/August): 30–35.

Chomsky, N. (1992). *What Uncle Sam really wants.* Berkeley: Odonian.

Clinard, M. (1979). *Illegal corporate behavior.* Washington, DC: U.S. Department of Justice.

Cloward, R. & Piven, F. F. (1993). The fraud of workfare. *The Nation* (24 May): 693–696.

Cochran, T. et al. (1990). The U.S. nuclear warhead production complex. In A. H. Erlich & J. W. Bircks, (Eds.) *Hidden dangers: The environmental consequences of preparing for war.* (pp. 3–17). San Francisco: Sierra Club Books.

Cohen, S. (1990). The war on drugs is racist. In N. Bernards (ed.). *War on drugs: Opposing viewpoints.* (pp. 76–82). San Diego: Greenhaven Press.

Colburn, D. (1993). Needless deaths from treatable diseases. In The Washington Post Writers Group, (Ed.). *Society in crisis* (pp. 224–227). Needham Heights, MA: Allyn & Bacon.

Colburn, Don (1993). The woes of widows in America. In The Washington Post Writers Group (Ed.). *Society in Crisis* (pp. 207-211) (Needham Heights, MA: Allyn & Bacon).

Coleman, J. S. (1992). The asymmetric society. In M. David Ermann and Richard J. Lundman, (Eds.). *Corporate and governmental deviance,* (4th ed.) (95–106). New York: Oxford University Press.

Coleman, J. W. (1994). *The criminal elite: The sociology of white collar crime* (3rd ed.). New York: St. Martins.

Coleman, J. and Hoffer, T. (1987). *Public and private high schools: The impact of communities.* New York: Basic Books.

Coleman, J. et al. (1966). *Equality of educational opportunity (The Coleman Report).* Washington, D.C.: U.S. Department of Health Education, & Welfare.

Collins, B. (1990). Student indifference erodes the public schools. *UTNE Reader* (September/October): pp. 68–69.

Commoner, B. (1994). Achieving sustainability. In R. Caplan & J. Feffer, (Eds.) *State of the union, 1994* (pp. 134–150). Boulder, CO: Westview.

Conrad, P. & Kern, R. (Eds.). (1994). *The sociology of health and illness* (4th ed.). New York: St. Martins.

Consumer Reports. (1994). Health care in crisis: Does Canada have the answer? In J. Skolnick & E. Currie (Eds.) *Crisis in American Institutions* (9th ed.). (pp. 499–509). New York: Harper Collins.

Coontz, S. (1992). *The way we never were: American families and the nostalgia trap.* New York: Basic.

———— (1993). *How to resolve the health care crisis.* Yonkers, NY: Consumer Reports Books.

Corn, D. (1988). The same old dirty tricks. *The Nation.* (27 August): 158.

Coser, L. et al. (1990). *Introduction to Sociology* (3rd ed.). New York: Harcourt Brace.

Cotton, P. (1994). U.S. sticks its head in the sand on AIDS prevention. *Journal of the American Medical Association, 272* (14 September): 756–757.

Cowley, G. (1993). Children in peril. In Harold Widdison (Ed.). *Social Problems 93/94.* (pp. 25–27) Sluice Dock, CN: Dushkin.

Cox, G. W. (1992). *Conservation ecology—Biosphere and biosurvival.* Dubuque, IA: Wm. C. Brown Publishers.

Cox, H. (1984). *Later life: The realities of aging.* Englewood Cliffs, NJ: Prentice-Hall.

CQ *Researcher.* (1994). Juvenile justice, (February): 5.

Craig, S. (1993). *The malevolent leaders: Popular discontent in America.* Boulder, CO: Westview.

Crenshaw, A. (1993). Diagnosing medical fraud. In The Washington Post Writer's Group (Ed.). *Society in crisis.* (pp. 232–234). Needham Heights, MA: Allyn & Bacon.

Cunningham, W. P. & Saigo, B. W. (1992). *Environmental science—A global concern.* Dubuque, IA: Wm. C. Brown Publishers.

Curran, D. & Renzetti, C. (1993). *Women, men, and society.* Needham Heights, MA: Allyn & Bacon.

Curran, R. (1995). Too hot to handle. San Francisco Bay *Guardian* (29 March–4 April): 15–17.

Curie, E. (1991). The market society, *Dissent* (Spring): 255–258.

D'Amato, P. (1990). An attack on civil liberties. In N. Bernards, (Ed.). *War on drugs: Opposing viewpoints.* San Diego: Greenhaven.

Davis, J. H. (1984). *The Kennedys: Dynasty and disaster, 1848–1984.* New York: Bantam.

——— (1989). *Mafia kingfish: Carlos Marcello and the assassination of John F. Kennedy.* New York: Signet.

Davis, N. & Stasz, C. (1990). *Social control of deviance: A critical perspective.* New York: McGraw-Hill.

Dees, M. (1994). Letter. (pp 1–5). Montgomery, AL: Southern Poverty Law Center.

Derber, C. (1992). *Money, murder, and the American dream: Wilding from Wall Street to Main Street.* Boston: Farber & Farber.

Desir, M. (1993) Strategies for coping with workplace depression. *Black Enterprise.* (September): pp. 77–79.

Diamant, L. (Ed.) (1993). *Homosexual issues in the workplace.* New York: Taylor & Francis.

Dionne, E. J. (1991). *Why Americans hate politics.* New York: Simon and Schuster.

Dissent (Spring 1991): 3–33.

Dollars and Sense. (1993). Who cares for our elders. In H. Widdison (Ed.). *Social Problems 93/94.* (pp. 76–77) Sluice Dock, CN: Dushkin.

Domhoff, G. W. (1967). *Who rules America?* Englewood Cliffs, NJ: Prentice-Hall.

——— . (1974). *The bohemian grove and other retreats.* New York: Harper & Row.

———. (1990). *The power elite and the state.* New York: Aldine-DeGruyter.

Dominguez, J. & Robin, V. (1990). *Your money or your life: Transforming your relationship with money and achieving financial independence.* New York: Penguin.

Donahue, J. (1992). The missing rapsheet: Government records of corporate abuses. *Multinational Monitor.* (December): 17–19.

Donlan, T. G. (1995). Editorial commentary. *Barron's* (27 March): 50.

Dority, B. (1993). The right to a decent life. *The Humanist* (May/June): 28–30.

Dowd, D. (1993). *Capitalist development since 1776.* New York: M. E. Sharpe.

Doyle, J. (1994). Political asylum granted to gay from Mexico. San Francisco *Chronicle* (25 March): A-1, A-12.

Drake, D. & Uhlman, M. (1993). *Making drugs making money.* Kansas City, MO: Andrews & McMeel.

Duke, L. (1993). Military's last social taboo. In The Washington Post Writer's Group (Ed.). *Society in crisis: The Washington Post social problems companion.* (pp. 164–69) Needham Heights, MA: Allyn & Bacon.

Durkheim, E. (1960). *Suicide: A study in sociology.* New York: The Free Press.

Durning, A. (1992). *How much is enough?* New York: Norton.

Duster, T. (1990). *Back door to eugenics.* New York: Routledge.

Duster, Troy (1988). Social implications of the new black underclass. *Black Scholar 19* (May/June): 2–10.

Dye, T. & Zeigler, H. (1993). *The irony of democracy: An uncommon introduction to American government* (8th ed.). Pacific Grove, CA: Brooks/Cole.

Dye, T. (1990). *Who's running America?: The Bush years.* Englewood Cliffs, NJ: Prentice-Hall.

Eckholm, E. (1993). Introduction. In The White House Domestic Policy Council. *The president's health security plan.* (pp. i–xiii). New York: Random House.

Eckstein, H. (1984). Civic inclusion and its discontents. *Daedalus, 113* (Fall).

Edwards, R. C. et al. (1986). Alienation and labor. In R. C. Edwards et al (Eds.). *The capitalist system.* (3rd ed.). (pp.138–140). Englewood Cliffs, NJ: Prentice-Hall.

Ehrenreich, B. (1989). *Fear of Falling.* New York: Pantheon.

Ehrhart, W. D. (1993). On the virtues of dishonesty. San Francisco *Examiner* (March, 19): A-23.

Elias, R. (1986). *The politics of victimization.* New York: Oxford University Press.

Ellwood, D. (1988). *Poor support: Poverty in the American family.* New York: Basic Books.

Epstein, R. (1994). Ranking the heavy emitters. *The Nation* (5 December): 688–694.

Erikson, K. (1990). On work alienation. In Erikson, K., and Vallas, P. (Eds.). *The Nature of Work.* (pp.19-35) New Haven: Yale University Press.

Eshelman, J. et al. (1993). *Sociology: an introduction*. (4th ed.). New York: Harper/Collins.

Ethics, E. Z. (1990). Wreck-reation. *Student Lifelines 4* (April), 1, 6.

Etzioni, A. (1977). The neoconservatives. *Partisan Review, 4* (Autumn): 1–15.

——— (1990). Is corporate crime worth the time? *Business and Society Review, 36* (Winter): 33–36.

Etzkowitz, H. (Ed.) *Is America possible?* (2nd ed.). St. Paul: West.

Evans, D. (1993). We arm the world. *In These Times* (November 15–18): 14–18.

Famighetti, Robert (1993). *World almanac and book of facts*. Mahwah, NJ: Funk & Wagnalls.

Faris, R. & Dunham, H. W. (1939). *Mental disorders in urban areas*. Chicago: University of Chicago Press.

Farnham, A. (1990). The S & L felons. *Fortune* (November 5): 90–108.

Farrell, W. (1986). *Why men are the way they are*. New York: McGraw-Hill.

——— (1991). Men as success objects. *UTNE Reader* (May/June): pp. 81–84.

——— (1993). *The myth of male power*. New York: Simon & Schuster.

Farrington, J. (1994). Epidemics: A historic timeline. *Current Health* (November): 6–11.

Fassinger, R. (1993). And gladly teach: Lesbian and gay issues in education, pp. 119–142 in Louis Diamant (Ed.).

Fearnside, P. M. (1989). Extractive reserves in Brazilian Amazonia. *Bioscience, 39*: 387–389.

Felson, R. B. & Trudau L. (1991). Gender differences in mathematics performance, *Social Psychology Quarterly, 54* (June): 113–126.

Ferguson, M. (1983). *Forever female: Women's magazines and the cult of femininity*. London: Heinemann.

Ferrante, J. (1992). *Sociology: A multicultural perspective* Belmont, CA: Wadsworth.

Fisher, D. (1978). *Growing old in America*. New York: Oxford University Press.

Fisher, M. (1992). Health insurance industry campaign donations surge. *National Underwriters Life* (19 October): 3.

Flacks, R. (1973). *Conformity, resistence, and self-determination*. Boston: Little Brown.

Forbes (1994). (10 October): 94.

Fortune Magazine (1993). (9 August): p. 12.

Foster, J. (1993). Let them eat pollution. *Monthly Review* (January): 10–20.

Fox, K. & Lutgen, T. (1992). Today on the planet. Los Angeles *Times* (May 25): H6–H7.

Frank, N. & Lynch, M. (1992). *Corporate crime corporate violence: A primer*. New York: Harrow & Heston.

Frawley, J. (1991). Inside the home. *Mother Jones* (March/April): 30; 70.

Freeman, A. (1994). Bad chemistry at EPA. *Multinational Monitor* (July/August): 5.

Freitag, P. (1975). The cabinet and big business. *Social Problems, 23*: 137–152.

French, H. F. (1990). Clearing the Air. In L. Starke (Ed.). *State of the world 1990*. (pp. 98–118). New York: W. W. Norton.

French, J. R. & Caplan, R. (1970). Stress and Disease. *Industrial Medicine*.

French, M. (1992). *The war against women*. New York: Summit.

Freund, C. P. (1988). How the Kennedy killing drove America crazy. Washington *Post* (November 13): C-1; C-4-5.

Frieden, B. (1993). *The fountain of age*. New York: Simon & Schuster.

Fritz, B. (1990). Layoffs and the older worker. *Aging* (March): 70.

Fromm, E. (1944). *Escape from Freedom*. New York: Avon.

Fromm, E. (1955). *The sane society*. New York: Holt, Rinehart, & Winston.

Frye, M. (1992). Oppression. In P. Rothenberg, (Ed.). *Race, Class, and Gender: An integrated approach*. (2nd ed.) (pp. 54–57). New York: St. Martins.

Fuchs, V. (1994). A tale of two states. pp. 55–57. In P. Conrad & R. Kern, (Eds.).

Fukuyama, F. (1992). *The end of history and the last man*. New York: Avon.

Funiciello, T. (1993). *Tyranny of kindness*. New York: Atlantic Monthly Press.

Funkhouser, R. (1973). The issues of the sixties: An exploratory study in the dynamics of public opinion. *Public Opinion Quarterly, 37* (Spring): 62–75.

Galbraith, J. (1958). *The Affluent Society*. Boston: Houghton Mifflin.

Galbraith, J. K. (1977). Crime and no punishment. *Esquire* (December): 102–106.

——— (1992). *The Culture of Contentment*. Boston: Houghton Mifflin.

Garment, S. (1991). *Scandal*. New York: Anchor.

Garner, R. (1995). *Social Movements and Ideologies* New York: McGraw-Hill.

Garr, R. (1995). *Reinvesting in America*. Reading, MA: Addison Wesley.

Garson, B. (1988). *The electronic sweatshop*. New York: Simon & Schuster.

Geertz, C. (1964). Ideology as a culture system, In D. Apter, (Ed.). *Ideology and discontent*. New York: Free Press.

Geis, G. (1974). Upperworld crime. In A. S. Blumberg (Ed.). *Current perspectives in criminal behavior.* (pp. 114–137). New York: Knopf.

Gentry, D. et al. (1994). *AIDS Patient Care, 8* (June): 130–137.

Gerber, J. & Weeks, S. (1992). Women as victims of corporate crime: A call for research on a neglected topic. *Deviant Behavior 13*: 325–347.

Gerbner, G. (1995). Television violence: The power and the peril. In G. Dines & J. M. Humez (Eds.). *Gender, race, and class in media: A text reader.* Newbury Park, CA: Sage.

Gergen, K. (1991). *The saturated self.* New York: Basic Books.

Gerth, H. & Mills, C. Wright. (1953). *Character and social structure.* New York: Harcourt, Brace, & World.

Gibbons, D. C. & Garabedian, P. (1974). Conservative, liberal, and radical criminology: Some trends and observations, In C. Reasons, (Ed.). *The criminologist: Crime and the criminal* (pp. 51–63). Pacific Palisades: Goodyear.

Gilbert, D. & Kahl J. (1993). *The American class structure: A new synthesis* (4th ed.). Belmont, CA: Wadsworth.

Gintis, H. & Bowles S. (1986). Schooling and inequality. In R. C. Edwards et al. (Eds.). *The Capitalist System* (3rd ed.). (pp. 235-247). Englewood Cliffs, NJ: Prentice-Hall.

Gintis, H. (1986a). Alienation and Capitalism. In R. C. Edwards et al (Eds.). *The Capitalist System.* (3rd ed.). (pp. 141-49). Englewood Cliffs, NJ: Prentice-Hall.

Gitlin, T. (1988). *The sixties.* New York: Random House.

Glassman, J. (1990a). The great bank robbery: Deconstructing the S & L crisis. *New republic* (October 6): 16–21.

——— (1990b). Looking for new S & L culprits. *Newsweek* (November 26): 55–56.

Glenn, N. (1993). What's happening to american marriage, *USA Today* (May): pp. 26–28.

Gomes, M. (1995). The ecopsychology of consumerism. Presented at The Environmental Spirit Conference (April 14), University of California, Berkeley.

Goode, E. (Ed.). (1993). *Drugs, society, and behavior* (8th ed.). Guilford, CT: Dushkin.

Goodgame, D. (1994). Reigning in the rich. *Time* (19 December): 35–37.

Gore, A. (1993). *From red tape to results: Creating a government that works better and costs less.* Washington, DC: U.S. Government Printing Office.

Gornick, V. (1976). For the rest of our days things can only get worse. *Village Voice* (24 May): 32 ff.

Gozan, J. (1992). Wealth for the few. *Multinational Monitor* (December): 6.

——— (1993). The tortures lobby. *Multinational Monitor* (April): 6–7.

Graham, M. G. (1987). Controlling drug abuse and crime: A research update. *NIJ Reports, 202* (March/April): 2–7.

Greenberg, D. (1993). Delinquency and the age structure of society. In David Greenberg (Ed.). *Crime and Capitalism.* Philadelphia: Temple University Press.

Greenberg, E. S. (1985). *Capitalism and the American politican ideal.* New York: M. E. Sharpe.

Greenwald, J. (1991). Feeling the heat. *Time* (August 5): 44–46.

Greider, W. (1992). *Who will tell the people?* New York: Simon and Schuster.

Griswold, W. (1994). *Cultures and societies in a changing world.* Thousand Oaks, CA: Pine Forge.

Groden, C. and Livingston, H. (1990). *High treason.* New York: Berkeley.

Gropper, B. A. (1987). Probing the links between drugs and crime.

Gross, M. L. (1992). *The government racket: Washington waste from A to Z.* New York: Bantam.

Grunwald, L. (1991). JFK: Why do we still care? *Life, 14* (December): 35–46.

Gueron, J. (1993). Work for people on welfare. *Public Welfare* (Winter): 39–41.

Gusfield, J. (1984). On the side: Practical action and social constructionism in social problems theory. In J. Kitsuse & J. W. Schneider, (Eds.). *Studies in the sociology of social problems.* (pp. 31–51). New Jersey: Ablex.

Hacker, A. (1992). *Two nations: One black, one white.* New York: Ballantine.

Hacker, A. (1995). *Two nations.* (Rev. ed.). New York: Ballantine.

Hagan, F. & Simon, D. R. (1994). Crimes of the Bush era. Presented at the Meeting of the American Society of Criminology (November) (Miami, FL.).

Hagan, W. (1961). *American Indians.* Chicago: University of Chicago Press.

Hall, S. G. (1993). *Christian Anti-Semitism and Paul's Theology.* Minneapolis, MN: Fortress Press.

Halper, J. (1988). *Quiet desperation: the truth about successful men.* New York: Warner.

Hansen, G. (1992). 9th Circuit Studies Gender Bias, *ABA Journal 78* (November): 50.

Hargrove, T. & Stempel, G. (1993). Here comes the groom, San Francisco *Examiner* (29 July): C-1; C-9.

Harrington, M. (1962). *The Other America.* New York: Macmillan.

Harris, A. & Harris T., (1985). *Staying O.K.* New York: HarperCollins.

Harris, L. (1989). *Inside America.* New York: Vintage.

Harris, M. (1987). *Why Nothing Works.* New York: Simon and Schuster.

Harris, R. (1991). *Drugged America.* New York: Macmillan.

Harvey, K. D. et al. (1990). *Teaching about native Americans.* Washington, D.C.: National Council for Social Studies.

Haveman, R. (1993). Who are the nation's truly poor? *The Brookings Review* (Winter): 24–27.

Hedges, S. & Witkin G. (1990). The bulletproof villains. *U.S. news & world report* (July 23): 18.

Hellinger, D., & Judd, D. (1991). *The Democratic Facade.* Belmont, CA: Wadsworth.

Hemmelstein, H. (1984). *Understanding television.* New York: Praeger.

Henderson, J. & Simon, D. R. (1994). *Crimes of the Criminal Justice System.* Cincinnati: Anderson.

Herbert, B. (1993). No job, no dream. . . . Oakland *Tribune* (10 September): A-15.

Hernandez, D. (1993). Jobs, poverty, and family breakup, *USA Today* (November): 28–9.

Hernstein, R. J. & Murray, C. (1994). *The bell curve.* New York: The Free Press.

Hertsgaard, M. (1993). Still ticking. . . . *Mother Jones* (March/April): 20–23, 68–74.

Hewitt, J. (1991). Building media empires. In A. A. Berger, (Ed.). *Media U.S.A.* (2nd ed.). (pp. 363–403). New York: Longman.

Hilts, P. J. (1993). 50,000 deaths a year blamed on soot in air. San Francisco *Chronicle* (19 July): A-1, A-15.

Hochschild, A. (1983). *The managed heart.* Berkeley: University of California Press.

Hochschild, A. (1990). The second shift. *UTNE reader* (March): 66–81.

Hollingshead, A. & Redlich, F. (1958). *Social class and mental illness.* New York: Wiley.

Hopkins, J. (1993). How the cold war ended: Defeat for everybody. San Francisco *Examiner* (September 5), A-16.

Horney, K. (1938). *The neurotic personality of our time.* New York: W. W. Norton.

Horton, J. (1968). Order and conflict theories of social problems. In F. Lindenfield (Ed.). *Radical perspectives on social problems.* (pp. 590–602). New York: Free Press.

Howe, I. (1991). By way of a beginning. *Dissent, 38* (Spring): 165–169.

Hulbert, A. (1993). Home repairs. *The new republic* (16 August): pp. 26–32.

in Boaz, D. (ed.). *The crisis in drug prohibition.* San Francisco: Laissez Faire Books.

Inciardi, J. & Rothman, T. (1990). *Sociology.* New York: Harcourt Brace.

Inciardi, J. (1986). *The War on Drugs.* Palo Alto, CA: Mayfield.

Irwin, J. & Austin, J. (1994). *It's about time: America's imprisonment binge.* Belmont, CA: Brooks Cole.

Isikoff, M. (1993a). Teen alcohol use heavy, survey finds. In The Washington Post Writers Group (Ed.). *Society in crisis.* (pp. 319–20) Boston: Allyn & Bacon. (1993b). Cocaine use on upswing. In The Washington Post Writers Group (Ed.). *Society in crisis.* (pp. 321–22). Boston: Allyn & Bacon.

Israel, J. (1971). *Alilenation: An integrated approach.* Boston: Allyn & Bacon.

Jencks, C. (1992). *Rethinking social policy: Race, poverty, and the underclass.* New York: HarperCollins.

Jencks, C. et al. (1972). *Inequality: A reassessment of the effect of family and schooling in America.* New York: Basic Books.

Jensen, C. (1993). *Censored: The news that didn't make it—and why.* Chapel Hill, NC: Shelburne.

Jensen, C. & Project Censored (1994). The U.S. is killing its young, *Censored: the 1994 Project Censored Yearbook.* New York: Four Walls, Eight Windows: 50–52.

Jerome, L. E. (1975). Astrology: Magic or science? *The Humanist, 35* (September): 10–15.

Jet (1995). (6 March): 10.

Johnson, B. et al. (1993). Whatever happened to Central America? *Propaganda Review, 10* (Summer): 10–13, 53–55.

Johnson, H. (1987). Casey circumvented the CIA in '85 assassination attempt. Washington *Post* (26 September): A-1.

Jones, J. (1994). American others. *In these times* (7 February): 14–17.

Josephson, E. & Josephson, M. (Eds.) (1962). *Man alone: Alienation in modern society.* New York: Dell.

Journal of the American Medical Association. (1995). Update: AIDS among women—United States, 1994. *273* (8 Mar): 767–768.

Joyce, J. A. (1978). The international bill of rights. In *The New Politics of Human Rights.* (p. 239). New York: St. Martins.

Kaiser, D. E. (1983). Did Oswald act alone? Washington *Post* (November 20): F1–F4.

Kaitschuck, G. (1992). Combating hunger in the USA. *Current Health.* (December): 22–24.

Kane, H. (1993). Can money alone buy a longer life? *World Watch* (November–December): 32–34.

Kanter, D. & Mirvis, P. (1989). *The cynical Americans.* San Francisco: Jossey-Bass.

Kantrowitz, B. et al. (1992). Sexism in the schoolhouse, *Newsweek* (24 February): p. 62.

Kantrowitz, et al. (1991). Striking a nerve. *Newsweek* (21 October): 34–40.

Kanungo, R. A. (1982). *Work Alienation: An integrated approach.* New York: Praeger.

Kappeler, V. et al. (1993). *The mythology of crime and criminal justice* Prospect Heights, IL: Waveland.

Kassarda, J. & Williams, T. (1989). Drugs and the dream deferred. *New Viewpoints* (Summer): 16–26.

Katz, M. (1989). *The undeserving poor: From the war on poverty to the war on welfare.* New York: Pantheon.

Katz, M. (1993). Reframing the debate. In M. Katz, (Ed.). *The underclass debate* (pp. 440–477). Princeton: Princeton University Press.

Kellner, D. (1990). Advertising and consumer culture. In John Downing et al. (Eds.). *Questioning the media: A critical introduction.* (pp. 242–254). Newbury Park, CA: Sage).

Kelly, M. (1993). Free trade and the politics of toxic waste. *Multinational Monitor* (October), 13–17.

Keniston, K. (1965). *The uncommitted.* New York: Dell.

Kennedy, P. C. (1987). *The rise and fall of great powers.* New York: Random House.

——— (1993). *Preparing for the twenty-first century.* New York: Random House.

Kerbo, H. (1993). Upper class power. In M. E. Olsen & M. N. Marger, (Eds.). *Power in modern societies.* (pp. 223–237). Boulder, CO: Westview Press.

Keyser, H. (1993). *Prescription for disaster: Health care in America.* Austin: Eakin Press.

Kilborn, P. T. (1992). Sad distinction for Sioux: Homeland is no. 1 in poverty. New York *Times.* (20 September): A-1, A-14.

Kirp, D. (1993). A sedan is not a home. *Commonweal* (12 February): 4–5.

Kitsuse and Schneider, J. W. (Eds.). *Studies in the sociology of social problems.* New Jersey: Ablex.

Klare, M. (1991). One, two, many Iraqs. *The Progressive.* (April): 20–23.

Knapp, P. & Spector, A. (1991). *Crisis and change: Basic questions of Marxist sociology* (Chicago: Nelson Hall).

Knight, J. (1993). Race factor in mortgage lending seen. In The Washington Post Writer's Group. *Society in crisis* (pp. 127–129). Needham Heights, MA: Allyn & Bacon.

Knowles, J. (1994). The responsibility of the individual. In P. Conrad & R. Kern (Eds.).

Kobler, J. (1971). *Capone: The life and world of Al Capone.* New York: Fawcett.

Kohn, A. (1986). *No contest: The case against competition.* Boston: Houghton Mifflin.

Kohn, M. (1990). Unresolved issues in the relationship between work and personality. In Kai Erikson and Peter Vallas, (Eds.). *The Nature of Work.* (pp. 36–68). New Haven: Yale University Press.

Konner, M. (1993). *Dear America.* Reading, MA: Addison Wesley.

Korb, L. (1990). 36 billion dollars worth of secrets. New York *Times Book Review* (16 September): 28.

Kornblum, W. (1994). *Sociology in a changing world.* (3rd ed.) New York: Harcourt Brace.

Kornhauser, W. (1959). *The politics of mass society.* New York: Free Press.

Kovic, R. (1976). *Born on the fourth of July.* New York: McGraw-Hill.

Kozol, J. (1991). *Savage inequalities: Children in America's Schools.* New York: Crown (1968).

——— (1968). *Death at an Early Age.* New York: Bantam.

Krisberg, B. (1975). *Crime and privilege: Toward a new criminology.* Englewood Cliffs, NJ: Prentice-Hall.

Krulak, V. H. (1993). Time to get tough on terrorists. San Diego *Times Union* (13 July): B-6.

Kurtis, B. (1993). *The men who killed Kennedy.* Aired September/October on the Arts & Entertainment Network.

Kwitney, J. (1984). *Endless Enemies.* New York: Cogdon/Weed.

Kwitney, J. (1987). Crimes of patriots. *Mother Jones, 6* (August/September): 15–23.

Ladd, E. C. (1986). *American ideologies.* Washington, DC: University Press of America.

Landers, R. K. (1988). Living with hazardous wastes. *Congressional Quarterly Editorial Research Reports* (July, 29): 378–386.

Lane, M. (1991). *Plausible Denial.* New York: Thunder's Mouth Press.

Lardner, G. (1991). . . . Or just a sloppy mess. Washington *Post* (June 2): D-2.

Larsen, E. (1992). The great teen girl self-esteem robbery, *UTNE Reader, 49* (January/February), pp. 20–21.

Lasch, C. (1978). *The culture of narcissism.* New York: W. W. Norton.

——— (1984). *The Minimal self: Psychic survival in troubled times.* New York: W. W. Norton.

Lavelle, R. et al. (Eds.). (1995). *The new war on poverty* San Francisco: KQED Books.

Lazare, D. (1990). The drug war is killing us. *Village Voice* (23 January): 22–29.

Lean, A. and Eaton, W. (1990). *Education or catastrophe?* Wolfboro, NH: Longwood Academic.

Lee, F. R. (1994). Needle exchange programs shown to slow HIV rates.

Lee, J. A. & Brown, R. (1993). Hiring, firing, and promoting, in Louis Diamant (Ed.). *Homosexual issues in the workplace.* (pp. 45–64). New York: Taylor & Francis.

Leitch, L. (1991). Do you know who your friends are? *UTNE Reader* (May/June): pp. 85–87.

Lens, S. (1977). *The promise and pitfalls of revolution.* Philadelphia: Pilgrim Press.

Leonard, A. (1994). Dumping Pepsi's toxic waste. *Multinational Monitor* (September): 7–10.

Leonard, B. (1990). Stein holds hearing on hate crime. New York *Times* (13 May): A-9.

Leonard, B. (1990). Stein holds hearing on hate crime. New York *Times* (13 May): A-9.

Lerner, M. (1973). *The new socialist revolution.* New York: Delacorte.

Levin, J. & McDevitt, J. (1993). *Hate crimes: The rising tide of bigotry and bloodshed.* New York: Plenum.

Levin, J. & Levin, W. C. (1980). *Ageism: prejudice and discrimination against the elderly:* Belmont: CA: Wadsworth.

Levine, A. (1990). America's addiction to addictions. *U.S. News, 108* (Feb. 5): 62–64.

Levy, L. & Rowitz, L. (1973). *The ecology of mental disorder.* New York: Behavioral Publications.

Lewis, A. (1992). Bush may have squandered great chance to nurture democracy in eastern bloc. St. Paul *Pioneer Press* (19 February): 8-A.

Liazos, A. (1993). Nuts, sluts, and perverts': The poverty of the sociology of deviance. In H. Pontell (Ed.) *Social deviance: Readings in theory and research* (pp. 164–179).

Englewood Cliffs, NJ: Prentice-Hall.

Lifton, D. (1988). *Best evidence.* New York: Carroll & Graf.

Light, P. C. (1988). *The babyboomers.* New York: Norton.

Lindquist, D. (1988). Drugs said rampant in every industry. San Diego *Times-Union* (March 25): B-1ff.

Linklater, M. (1984). *The Nazi legacy.* New York: Holt, Rinehart, & Winston.

Lipset, S. M. & Raab, E. (1987). *The politics of unreason.* Chicago: University of Chicago Press.

Lipset, S. M. (1963). *Political man: The social basis of politics.* Garden City, NY: Doubleday.

London, B. & Williams, B. (1988). Multinational corporate penetration, protest, and basic human needs provision in non-core nations: A cross-national analysis. *Social Forces, 66* (March): 747–773.

Long, G. (1993). Homosexual relationships in a unique setting: The male prison, pp. 143–159 in L. Diamant (Ed.).

Lorber, J. (1994). *Paradoxes of gender.* New Haven, CN: Yale University Press.

Lord, W. (1955). *A night to remember.* New York: Henry Holt).

Los Angeles *Times* (1993). Study: Tobacco no. 1 cause of death in U.S. Oakland *Tribune* (10 November): A-6.

Los Angeles *Times* (1993). Study: Tobacco No. 1 Cause of Death in U.S.

Lott, B. (1994). *Women's Lives: Themes and variations in gender learning.* (2nd ed.). Monterey, CA: Brooks Cole.

Lupsha, P. (1981). American values and organized crime: Suckers and wiseguys. In B. Girgus (Ed.). *The American self* (pp. 144–155)

Albuquerque, New Mexico: University of New Mexico Press.

Lutz, W. (1989). *Doublespeak.* New York: HarperCollins.

MaFarquhar, E. (1994). Population Wars. *U.S. News & World Report* (12 September): 54–57.

Magdoff, H. (1992). Globalization—To what end. In R. Miliband & L. Panitch. (Eds.). *The Socialist Register, 1992: New World Order?* London: Merlin Press.

Magnuson, E. (1988). Did the mob kill JFK? *Time* (November 28): 42–44.

Malamuth, N. M. (1984). Aggression against women: Cultural and individual causes. In N. Malamuth & E. Donnerstein, (Eds.). *Pornography and sexual aggression.* New York: Academic Press.

Males, M. (1994). The real generation gap. *In These Times* (7 February): 18–19.

———— (1993). Infantile arguments. *In These Times* (August) 9: 18–20.

Manegold, K. (1995). A woman's obsession pays off—At a cost. New York *Times* (26 March), Section 4, p. 1 & 4.

Manis, J. (1974). Assessing the seriousness of social problems. *Social Problems, 22* (Fall): 1–15.

Manis, J. (1974). Reassessing the seriousness of social problems. *Social Problems, 21* (Fall): 1–14.

Mann, J. (1993). Our culture as a cause of depression. In The Washington Post Writer's Group (Ed.). *Society in crisis* (pp. 246–247).

Marger, M. (1994). *Race and ethnic relations: An international perspective* (3rd ed.). Belmont, CA: Wadsworth.

Marrs, J. (1989). *Crossfire: The plot that killed Kennedy.* New York: Carroll & Graf.

Marshall, G. (1994). *A concise dictionary of sociology.* New York: Oxford University Press.

Marx, G. T. (1988). Fraudulent identification, and biography. Paper delivered at a seminar of the Department of Sociology, San Diego State University (February).

Masuda, M. and Holmes, T. H. (1967). Magnitude estimations of social readjustments. *Journal of Psychosomatic Research, 2:* 219–225.

Mattox, W. (1993). America's family time famine." In H. Widdison (Ed.). *Social Problems, 1993/1994.* (pp. 16–20). Sluice Dock, CN: Dushkin.

May, R. (1953). *Man's search for himself.* New York: Dell.

McCaghy, C. & Capron, T. (1994). *Deviant behavior: Crime, conflict, and interest groups.* (3rd ed.). New York: Macmillan.

McCarthy, M. (1994). World Bank warns of AIDS economic threat. *The Lancet, 344* (10 December): 1628.

McClory, R. (1992). Gambling's easy money. *UTNE Reader* (Sept./Oct.):60.

McClosky, H. & Brill A. (1983). *Dimensions of Tolerance.* New York: Russell Sage Foundation.

McClure, L. (1994). Working the risk shift. *The progressive* (February): 23–27.

McCord, C. & Freeman, H. (1991). Excess mortality in Harlem. In J. Skolnick & E. Currie (Eds.). *Crisis in American institutions.* (8th ed.) (pp. 426–432). New York: HarperCollins.

McCoy, A. (1991a). The CIA Connection. *The Progressive* (July): 20–26.

————— (1991b). The Afghanistan drug lords. *Convergence* (Fall): 11–12, 14.

McDermott, J. (1979). Rape victimization in 26 American cities. Washington, DC: U.S. Dept. of Justice. Cited in Pauline H. Ban and Patricia H. O'Brien, *Stopping rape.* New York: Pergamon Press.

McGinnis, J. & Fogel, M. (1993). Actual causes of death in the U.S. *journal of the American Medical Association* (10 November): 2207–2211.

McQuale, W. & Ackerman, A. (1974). *Stress.* New York: Dutton.

McWilliams, M. (1993). Standing up for the powerless. *ABA Journal* (February): 8.

Mecca, A. M. et al. (Eds.). (1989). *The social importance of self-esteem.* Berkeley: University of California Press.

Melanson, P. (1990). *Spy saga.* Boulder: Westview.

Merrian-Webster (1986). *Webster's Third International Dictionary.* Springfield, MA: Merriam-Webster.

Merton, R. K. (1948). Discrimination and the American creed. In R. K. MacIver (Ed.). *Discrimination and national welfare.* New York: Harper.

Messner, S. & Richard R. (1994). *Crime and the American dream.* Belmont, CA: Wadsworth.

Miller, E. & Miller, R. (1991). *Environmental hazards: Toxic waste and hazardous material.* Santa Barbara: ABC-CLIO.

Miller, J. B. (1992). Domination and subordination. In P. Rothenberg (Ed.). *Race, class and gender in the United States: An integrated approach.* (2nd ed) (pp. 20–26). New York: St. Martins.

Miller, N. (1992). *Stealing from America.* New York: Paragon House.

Miller, W. (1974). Ideology and criminal justice policy: Some current issues. In C. Reasons (Ed.). *Criminology.* Pacific Palisades: Good Year.

Millichap, J. (1993). *Environmental poisons in our food.* Chicago: PNB.

Mills, C. W. (1951). *White-collar.* New York: Oxford University Press.

————— (1956). *The power elite.* New York: Oxford University Press.

————— (1958). *The causes of world war III.* New York: Simon and Schuster.

————— (1959). *The sociological imagination.* New York: Oxford University Press.

————— (Ed.). (1960). *Images of man: The classic tradition in sociological theory.* New York: Braziller.

————— (1962). *The marxists.* New York: Dell.

————— (1963). IBM plus humanism = sociology. In Irving Louis Horowitz (Ed.). *Power, politics, and people: The collected essays of C. Wright Mills.* (pp. 568–576). New York: Ballantine.

————— (1943). The professional ideology of social pathologists. *American Journal of Sociology, 49* (September): 165–180.

Mills, J. (1986). *The underground empire.* New York: Dell.

Moberg, D. (1994). Can we save the inner city? *In These Times* (7 February):20–25.

Moberg, D. (1993). All in the family, *In These Times.* (22 February): 18–21.

Mohr, R. (1992a). Anti-gay stereotypes. In P. Rothenberg (Ed.). *Race, class and gender in the United States: An integrated approach.* (2nd ed.). (pp. 351-57). New York: St. Martins.

————— (1992b). *Gay ideas.* Boston: Beacon Press.

Mokhiber, R. (1993). Corporate crime and violence: The ten worst corporations of 1991. In C. Jensen, (Ed.). *Censored: The news that didn't make it—And why.* (pp. 115–124). Chapel Hill, NC: Shelburne.

Moldea, D. (1986). *Dark victory: Ronald Reagan, MCA, and the mob.* New York: Viking.

Montagu, A. & Matson, F. (1985). *The dehumanization of man.* New York: McGraw-Hill.

Moore, J. (1990). *A conspiracy of one.* Fort Worth, TX: The Summit Group.

Morganthau, T. & Miller, M. (1990). Tougher law enforcement will win the war on drugs. In N. Bernards (Ed.). (pp. 207–213).

Morley, J. (1991). A political Rorschach test. Los Angeles *Times* (8 December): M1–M2.

Morrow, L. (1993). The tempting of America, *Time* (29 March): 40–41.

Mother Jones (1993). (January): Pull Out Section.

Moyers, B. (1988). *The secret government.* Berkeley: Seven Locks Press.

Moynihan, D. P. (1993). Defining deviancy down. *American Scholar* (Autumn): 1–16.

Muwakkil, S. (1994). Urban poverty theory comes full circle. *In These Times* (7 February): 22.

Myadans, S. (1993). 11 friars at California seminary molested students, inquiry finds, The New York *Times.* (1 December): A-1, A-12.

Myers, N. (1988). Tropical deforestation and climatic change. *Environmental Conservation, 15:* 293–298.

———— (1994a). The big squeeze. *San Diego earth times* (February/March): 6–7.

———— (1994b). What ails the globe. *San Diego Earth Times* (April/May): 5, 13, 23, 25, 29.

Nader, R. (1985). Speech at the University of North Florida.

National Center of Education Statistics (1990). *Digest of Education Statistics, (1989).* (25th ed.). U.S. Department of Education: Washington, D.C.: U.S. Government Printing Office.

NBC Dateline, Aired 16 March, 1994.

Neier, A. and Brown, C. (1987). Pinochet's way *New York Review of Books,* (June, 25): 17–20.

Neilsen, P. (1993). Enemy in the workplace. *Monthly Labor Review,* (April): 45.

Nettles, M. (1990). Success in doctoral programs: Experiences of minorities and white students, *American Journal of Education 98* (August): 494–522.

New Scientist, 143 (17 September): 4–5.

New York *Times* (1993). (11 November): C-1.

———— (1994). (29 April): C-2.

Newsweek (1984) (9 April).

Newsweek (1986) (27 January): 46.

Newsweek (1988) (7 November): 66–68.

Newsweek (1994) Danger signs (21 March): 70.

NIJ Reports, 202 (March/April): 11.

Nisbet, R. (1988). *The present age.* New York: HarperCollins.

Nixon, W. (1994). Crowded out. *In These Times* (5 September): 14–18.

Nocera, J. (1990). How the middle class has helped ruin public schools. *UTNE Reader* (September/October): 66–72.

Norton, S. & Bunch, K. (1993). Human resources: policies and practices. In Louis Diamant (Ed.). (pp. 187–202).

Nossiter, N. (1991). Sand dolars. *The Progressive* (April): 26.

O'Conner, C. (1994). The waste goes on—and on and on. *The Nation* (24 April): 350–351.

O'Conner, J. (1973). *The fiscal crisis of the state.* New York: St. Martins.

Oakland Tribune (1993) The Church confronts unholy behavior. (7 December): A-8.

Oakland Tribune (10 November): A-6.

Olsen, M. E., & Marger, M. E. (Eds.). (1993). *Power in modern societies.* Boulder, CO: Westview.

Omar, S. (1993). Astrological forecast. Los Angeles *Times* (March 26): E-11.

Orenstein, P. (1994). *School girls.* New York: Doubleday.

Osborne, D. (1995). Forward. In R. Garr. *Reinvesting in America.* (pp. viii–x). Reading, MA: Wesley.

Ostling, R. (1994). Why was Christ crucified? *Time* (4 April): 72–74.

Oswalt, W. (1986). *Life cycles and lifeways: an introduction to cultural anthropology.* Palo Alto, CA: Mayfield.

Packard, V. (1960). *The waste makers.* New York: David McKay.

Papson, S. (1985). Bureaucratic discourse and the presentation of self as spectacle. *Humanity and Society, 9* (August): 223–236.

Parenti, M. (1991). *Make believe media.* New York: St. Martins.

Parenti, M. (1995). *Democracy for the few* (6th ed.). New York: St. Martins.

Patterson, J. & Kim, P. (1991). *The day America told the truth.* New York: Prentice-Hall Press.

———— (1989). *People* (March 15).

Pearce, F. (1976) *Crimes of the powerful.* London: Pluto Press.

Pearlstein, S. (1992). This time, a different kind of downturn. In The Washington Post Writer's Group, (Ed.) *Society in crisis.*

Pearlstein, S. and Brown, D. (1994). Blacks facing worse jobs prospects, The Washington *Post.* (4 June): A–1.

Peele, S. (1978). *Love and addiction.* New York: Bantam.

———— (1990). A value approach to addiction: Drug policy that is moral rather than moralistic. *Journal of Drug Issues, 20* (Fall): 639–645.

People. 1989 (March 15).

Perdue, W. D. (1993). *Systematic crises: Problems in society, politics, and world order.* New York: Harcourt Brace.

Perot, R. & Choate, P. (1993). *Save your job, save our country.* New York: Hyperion.

Perot, R. (1993). *Not for sale at any price: How can we save America for our children.* New York: Hyperion.

Pettigrew, T. (1980). Prejudice. In S. Thernstrom (Ed.). *Harvard Encyclopedia of American Ethnics.* (pp. 820–829). Cambridge, MA: Harvard University Press.

Phillips, K. (1990). *The Politics of rich and poor.* New York: Random House.

Pillemer, K. & Finkelhor, D. (1988). The Prevalence of elder abuse: A random sample survey, *The Gerontologist 28:* 51–57.

Pillemer, K. (1985). The dangers of dependency: new findings on domestic violence against the elderly. *Social Problems 33* (December): 146–158.

——— (1993). *Boiling Point: Democrats, Republicans, and the decline of middle class prosperity.* New York: Random House.

Pizzo, S., & Muolo, P. (1993). Take the money and run. New York *Times Magazine* (10 May): 56–61.

Podolsky, D. et al. (1991). Hype-free food labels. *U.S. News & World Report* (3 June): 67–70.

Polenberg, R. (1980). *One nation divided: Class, race, and ethnicity in the United States since 1938.* New York: Penguin.

Posner, G. (1988). *Warlords of crime, Chinese secret societies: The new mafia.* New York: Penguin.

Posner, G. (1993). *Case Closed: Lee Harvey Oswald and the Assassination of JFK.* New York: Random House.

Poveda, T. (1990). *The FBI in transition.* Monterey, CA: Brooks/Cole.

Powell, D. (1992). Women in engineering, *Science:* 607.

Preston, I. (1975). *The great American blow-up: Puffery in advertising and selling.* Madison, WI: University of Wisconsin Press.

The Progressive (1994). (October): 8.

Quint, M. (1994). Court says employer insurance plans cannot limit AIDS. (???)

Raskin, M. (1994). Dismantling the national security state, In R. Caplan & J. Feffer (Eds.): 78–87.

Rebovich, D. J. (1992). *Dangerous ground: The world of hazardous waste crime.* New Brunswick, NJ: Transaction.

Reich, C. (1970). The Greening of America. New York: Random House.

Reich, R. (1987). *Tales of a new America.* New York: Vintage.

Reiman, J. (1990). *The rich get richer and the poor get prison.* (3rd ed.). New York: Macmillan.

Rich, F. (1995). A bigger splash. New York *Times* (12 March): 15.

——— (1992). Tracing medical costs to social problems: U.S. paying dearly in comparison. In The Washington Post Writer's Group (Ed.). *Seeing ourselves and others: The Washington Post sociology companion.* (pp. 261–262). Needham Heights, MA: Allyn & Bacon.

Richman, J., et al. (1993). Workplace abusive experiences and problem drinking among physicians: Broadening the stress/alienation paradigm. Paper presented at the 1993 Meeting of the American Sociological Association.

Richmond-Abbott, J. (1986). *Sex roles over the life cycle.* New York: Random House.

Riddell, T. (1988). The political economy of military spending. In R. Cherry, (Ed.). *The imperiled economy,* Vol. 2 (pp. 227–235). New

York: Union For Radical Political Economics.

Ries, P. & Stone A. (Eds.). *The American women, 1992–1993.* New York: W. W. Norton.

Riesman, D. (1950). *The lonely crowd.* New Haven: Yale University Press.

Rifkin, J. & Howard, J. (1977). Who shall play God? *The Progressive, 41* (December): 21–24.

Ritzer, G. (1980). *Sociology: A multiple paradigm science.* Boston: Allyn & Bacon.

Ritzer, G. (1993). *The McDonaldization of society.* Thousand Oaks, CA: Pine Forge Press.

Roberts, R. (1978). *Social problems: Human possibilities.* St. Louis: Mosby.

Rodriguez, Cecilia. (1991). The world's most polluted city. Los Angeles *Times* (April 21): M-1.

Rogler, L. & Hollingshead, A. (1975). Trapped: Families and schizophrenia. New York: Wiley.

Rose, A. (1957). Theory for the study of social problems. *Social Problems, 4* (January): 190–205.

Rosen, R. (1994). Who gets polluted? The movement for environmental justice. *Dissent* (Spring): 223–230.

Rosenau, P. M. (1992). *Postmodernism and the social sciences: Insights, inroads, and intrusions.* Princeton: Princeton University Press.

Rosenfeld, M. (1993). Broken children, broken homes. In the Washington Post Writer's Group (Ed.). *Society in Crisis.* (pp. 190-94) Needham Heights, MA: Allyn & Bacon.

Rosin, H. (1994). The ban plays on. *New Republic,* (24 May): 12.

Rotfeld, H. J. & Preston I. L. (1981). The potential impact of research on advertising law. *Journal of Advertising Research, 21* (1981): 9–16.

Rotfeld, H. J. & Rotzall, K. B. (1980). Is advertising puffery believed? *Journal of advertising, 9:* 16–20.

Roth, N. & Carman J. (1993). Risk Perception and HIV Legal Issues in the Workplace. In Louis Diamant, (Ed.). (pp. 173–186).

Rouner, S. (1993). Battered Wives: Centuries of silence. In The Washington Post Writer's Group, (Ed.) *Society in crisis.* (pp. 195–197). Needham Heights, MA: Allyn & Bacon.

Rubin, L. (1977). *Worlds of pain.* New York: Basic Books.

——— (1993). San Diego *Times Union* (20 July): A-1.

Russell, J. W. (1992). *Introduction to macrosociology.* Englewood Cliffs, NJ: Prentice Hall.

San Diego *Times Union* (12 April, 1991): A-21.

San Diego *Times Union* (1993) 20 July): A-1.

San Francisco *Chronicle* (1993). (29 September): A-7.

San Francisco *Chronicle* (1993). Classroom paddling reported on rise, (23 September): A-15.

——— (1994). (17 July): C-1, C-4.

San Francisco *Chronicle* (20 August, 1994): A-1; A-15.

——— (15 February): A-1.

Sargent, L. T. (1992). *Contemporary political ideologies* (9th ed.). Belmont, CA: Wadsworth.

Saunders, D. (1995). Sex, video, and the single 7-year-old. San Francisco *Chronicle* (12 May): A-25.

Scanlan, D. (1994). Sterilized banana workers sue. San Francisco *Chronicle* (15 March, 1994), A-1, A-8.

Schaef, A. W. (1988). *When society becomes an addict.* New York: HarperCollins.

Schaffer, E. R. & Wellstone, P. (1994). Health care: Providing

comprehensive coverage. In R. Caplan & J. Feller, (Eds.). *State of the union 1994* (pp. 151–165). Boulder: Westview.

Scheim, D. (1988). The Mafia killed President Kennedy. London: Allen. Published in the U.S. as *Contract on America.* New York: Kensington.

Schmidt, P. (1992). Boys and girls apart, *World Press Review* (September): 50.

Schmidt, R. (1983). *Alienation and class.* Cambridge, MA: Schenkman.

Schmoke, K. (1990). Remarks to U.S. conference of mayors (1988).

Schrager, L. & Short, J. F. (1978). *Towards a sociology of organizational.*

Schrank, J. (1977). *Snap, crackle, and popular taste.* New York: Dell.

Schroeder, K. (1993). Student Drug Use, *Education Digest 59* (December): 75.

Schwartz, H. (1994). *God's phallus.* Boston: Beacon Press.

Schwartz, J. & Volgy, T. (1993). Above the poverty line—But poor. *The Nation* (15 February): 291–292.

Scimecca, J. (1995). *Society and freedom: An introduction to humanist sociology* (2nd ed). Chicago: Nelson-Hall.

——— 1977. *The sociological theory of C. Wright Mills.* Port Washington, NY: Kennikat Press.

Scott, P. D. (1988). Beyond Irangate. *Crime and Social Justice, 6.* (Summer): 25–46.

Seeman, M. (1961). On the meaning of alienation. *American Sociological Review, 26:* 753–758.

Select Committee on Assassinations, U.S. House of Representatives (1979). Investigation of the Assassination of President John F. Kennedy. Volume 4. Washington, DC: U.S. Government Printing Office.

Sells, S. (1993). Always with us? *New Statesman and Society* (26 March): 15.

Shames, L. (1989). *The hunger for more.* New York: Times Books.

Shaw, D. (1993). Distrustful public views media as them—not us. Los Angeles *Times* (April 1): A-1, A-18–19.

Sheffield, C. (1992). Hate-violence. In P. Rothenberg, (Ed.)

Shenon, P. (1988). FBI papers show wide surveillance of Reagan critics. New York *Times* (28 January): A-1; A-8.

Sherrill, R. (1988). White-collar thuggery. *The Nation* (28 November): 573.

Shira, S. (1994). Study confirms worst fears on US children, The New York *Times* (12 April): A-12.

Shrader, W. (1992). *Media blight and the dehumanizing of America.* New York: Praeger.

Simon, D. R. (1986). Alienation and alcohol abuse, *The Journal of Drug Abuse:* 44–56.

Simon, D. R. & Eitzen, D. S. (1993). *Elite deviance* (4th ed.). Needham Heights, MA: Allyn & Bacon.

——— (1992). Watergate and the Nixon presidency. In Leon Friedman & William Levantrosser (Eds.). *Watergate and afterward—The legacy of Richard M. Nixon* (pp. 5 22). Westport, CT: Greenwood.

——— (1986). Alienation and alcohol abuse. *Journal of Drug issues, 3* (Summer): 35–46.

——— (1990). Dominant forms of alienation. Paper presented at the 1990 Meeting of the Society For the Study of Social Problems (August) Washington, DC.

——— (1975). *Ideology and sociology: Perspectives on contemporary social criticism.* Ph.D. Dissertation, Rutgers University.

——— (1977a). *Ideology and sociology: Perspectives on contemporary social criticism.* Washington, DC: University Press of America.

——— (1977b). The ideologies of American social critics. *Journal of Communication, 25* (Summer): 44–55.

——— (1981). Exercise in ideological context analysis. *Teaching Political Science, 10* (July): 488–492.

——— (1993). Criminology and the Kennedy assassination. *Quarterly Journal of Ideology, 15* (Autumn): 33–45.

——— (1995). *Social problems and the sociological imagination* New York: McGraw-Hill.

——— (1996). *Elite deviance* (5th ed.). Needham Heights, MA: Allyn & Bacon.

Sixty Minutes (1994). (10 July), First Segment.

Skolnick, J., & Currie, E. (1994). *Crisis in American institutions.* (8th ed). New York: HarperCollins.

Skolnick, J. (1995). What not to do about crime. *Criminology, 33* (February): 1–16.

Slater, P. (1970). *The pursuit of loneliness.* Boston: Beacon Press.

Sloyan, P. (1995). Defense merger bonuses to cost U.S. $31 million. *West County Times* (17 March): 2B.

Smelser, N. J. (1989). Self-esteem and social problems: An introduction. In A. M. Mecca et al. (Eds.) *The social importance of self-esteem.* Berkeley: University of California Press.

Smith, D. (1975). *Mafia mystique.* New York: Basic Books.

Smothers, R. (1994). Principal causes furor on mixed-race couples. *New York Times* (16 March): A-10.

Spector, M. & Kituse, J. (1973). Social problems: A reformulation. *Social Problems, 21* (Fall): 145–59.

Srole, L. et al. (1962). *Mental health in the metropolis: The midtown*

Manhattan study, Vols. 1 & 2 (Revised). New York: Harper & Row.

Steel, R. (1978). Beneath the Panama Canal. *New York Review of Books, 23* (March): 23.

Steele, C. (1992). Race and the schooling of black americans, *Atlantic Monthly* (April): 68–78.

Sterling, E. (1991). Trashing the Bill of Rights. *The Progressive, 17* (29 June): 34–37.

Stevens, W. K. (1992). Global warming threatens to undo decades of conservation efforts. *New York Times* (25 February): C4.

Stone, O. (1991). JFK: A higher truth. *Washington Post* (June 2): D-1–3.

Streitfeld, D. (1993). Abuse of the elderly-often its the spouse. In The Washington Post Writer's Group (Ed.) *Society in crisis: The Washington Post social problems companion.* (pp. 212-213). Needham Heights, MA: Allyn & Bacon.

Strickland, D. E. et al. (1982a). A content analysis of beverage alcohol advertising: Magazine advertising. *Journal of Studies on Alcohol, 7:* 655–682.

——— (1982b). A content analysis of beverage advertising II: Television advertising. *Journal of Studies on Alcohol, 9:* Westport, CT: Greenwood: 964–987.

Stubbing, R. and Mendel, R. (1989). How to save $50 billion a year. *The Atlantic* (June): 55–58.

Suplee, C. (1995). U.S. graded D for violence. San Francisco *Chronicle* (14 June): A-10.

Sweet, E. (1985). Date rape. The story of an epidemic and those who deny it. *Ms.* (October): 56.

Sydell, L. (1993). The right to life rampage, *The Progressive* (August): 24–7.

Sykes, C. J. (1992). *A nation of victims.* New York: St. Martins.

Szasz, A. (1986). The process and significance of political scandals: A comparison of Watergate and the "Sewergate" episode at the Environmental Protection Agency. *Social Problems, 33* (February): 200–217.

National Alliance to End Homelessness (1991). *What you can do to end home homelessness.* New York: Simon and Schuster.

New York Times (Nov 26): A-1.

——— (1994b). AIDS toll on elderly: Dying grandchildren. (November 21): A-1.

——— (1989). (2 February): 1.

——— (19??) October): A-20.

——— (1993). (24 October): D-1.

——— (1993). (9 September): A-1.

——— (1993). (15 January): A-3.

——— (1992). (24 October): B-1.

——— (1992). (9 October): B-11.

——— (1992). (31 July): B-1.

——— (1992). (10 January): A-12.

——— (1991). (9 October): B-4.

——— (1991). (24 September): A-1.

——— (1991). (23 March): I-40.

——— (1990). (28 December): A-4.

——— (1990). (11 December): B-3.

——— (1990). (22 November): A-25.

——— (1990). (17 August): A-15.

——— (1990). (23 July): A-1.

——— (1995). (13 February): A-1.

——— (1994). (10 January): A-7.

——— (1993). (29 January): A-10.

Wall Street Journal (1992). (19 June): B-1.

Wall Street Journal (1994). (11 February): B-6.

Washington Post (1992a) (25 Jan.): A-18.

——— (1992b). (28 Feb.): A-18.

——— (1993a). (30 September): D-11.

——— (1993b). (23 December): D-10.

White House Domestic Policy Council. (1993). *Health security: The president's report to the American people.* New York: Simon and Schuster.

World almanac & book of facts. (1995).

World almanac of U.S. politics, 1993–1995 edition (1993). Mahwah, NJ: Funk & Wagnalls.

Thio, A. (1988). *Deviant behavior: An integrated approach* (3rd ed). New York: Harper & Row.

Thomas, R. (1990). Feast of the S & L vultures. *Newsweek* (July 30): 40.

Thompson, W. & Hickey, J. (1994). *Society in focus: An introduction to sociology.* New York: HarperCollins.

Time (Year?). (19 June): 14.

——— (1991). (23 December): 52.

——— (1977). The American underclass (29 August): 14–27.

Touhy, J. (1993). There's no such thing as childhood on the streets. *U.S. Catholic* (March): 18–25.

Traub, J. (1988). Into the mouths of babes. New York *Times Magazine* (24 July): 18–20, 51.

Tudor, W. (1979). The effect of sex role differences on the social reaction to. (???)

Turner, R. et al. (1984). *Oppression: A socio-history of black-white relations in America.* Chicago: Nelson-Hall.

U.S. Commission on Civil Rights (1981). *Affirmative action in the 1980s: Dismantling the process of discrimination (a proposed statement).* Clearinghouse Publication 65.

——— (1992). *Civil rights issues facing Asian Americans in the 1990s.* Washington, DC: US Government Printing Office.

U.S. House of Representatives, Select Committee on Assassinations (1979). *Investigation of the Assasination of President John F. Kennedy.* Volume 9. Washington, D.C.: U.S. Government Printing Office.

U.S. News & World Report (1993). Money, Congress, and Health Care. (May 24): 29–34.

U.S. Senate Committee On Aging et al. (1991). *Aging America: Trends and projections.* Washington, D.C.: U.S. Government Printing Office.

United Nations (1994). *World social situations in the 1990s.* New York: United Nations.

USA Today (1995). (21 July): A-1.

Vancise, J. (1979). *The federal antitrust laws* (3rd ed., rev). Washington, DC: The American Enterprise Institute.

Vidal, G. (1994). Speech at University of California, Berkeley. (14 February).

Vobejda, B. (1993). Caring for three generations. In The Washington Post Writer's Group (Ed.) *Society in crisis.* (pp. 186–189). Needham Heights, MA: Allyn & Bacon.

Vogel, J. (1994). Throw away the key, *UTNE reader* (July/August): 56–60.

Voigt, L. et al (1994). *Criminology and justice* New York: McGraw-Hill.

Wald, K. (1989). Evangelical politics and status issues. *Journal for the Scientific Study of Religion. 28:* 1–16.

Walker, S. (1994). *Sense and nonsense about crime and drugs: A policy guide.* (3rd ed). Belmont, CA: Wadsworth.

Walters, R. (1993). A strategy for redeveloping the black community. *The Black Scholar, 23:* 2–10.

Walton, J. (1993). *Sociology and critical inquiry* (3rd ed) Belmont, CA: Wadsworth.

Wattleton, F. (1989). The Case For National Action. *The Nation* (July 24/31): 138–141.

Webb, H. (1993). Too old! *New York* (29 March): 68–71.

Weber, M. (1946). Bureaucracy. In C. Wright Mills, (Ed.) *Images of man: The classic tradition in sociological*

thinking (pp. 149–191). New York: Braziller.

World almanac and book of facts. (1993).

Weberman, A. & Canfield, M. (1992). *Coup d'etat in America.* San Francisco: Quick American Archives.

Weiner, T. (1990). *Blank check: The Pentagon's secret budget.* New York: Simon and Schuster.

——— (1994). Blowback from the Afghan battlefield. New York *Times Magazine* (13 March): 53.

——— (1995). A Guatemalan officer and the CIA. New York *Times* (26 March): A-6.

Whitman, D. (1990). The streets are filled with crack. *U.S. news, 108* (March 5): 24–6.

Whitman, D. et al. (1989). The forgotten half. *U.S. News and World Report* (26 June): 45–53.

Wilcox, C. (1992). *God's warriors: The christian right in twentieth century America.* Baltimore: Johns Hopkins university Press.

Wilkinson, R. (1988). *In search of the American character.* New York: HarperCollins.

Wilkinson, R. (Ed.) (1992). *American social character.* New York: HarperCollins.

Willwerth, J. (1993). Hello? I'm home alone. *Time* (1 March): 46–7.

Williams, R. (1964). *Strangers next door: Ethnic relations in American communities.* Englewood Cliifs, NJ: Prentice-Hall.

Wilson, M. I. et al. (1981). Differential maltreatment of girls and boys. *Victimology* 6:249–261.

Wilson, W. J. (1988). The ghetto underclass and the social transformation of the inner city. *Black scholar, 19* (May/June): 10–17.

——— (1987). *The truly disadvantaged.* Chicago: University of Chicago Press.

—— (1994). The political economy and urban racial tensions. *The American Economist, 39* (Spring): 1–12.

—— (1995). The 'new poverty:' Social policy and the growing inequality in industrial democracies. Joanna Jackson Memorial Lecture, Library of Congress (30 March) Washington, DC.

Winter, R. (1991). *Poisons in your food.* New York: Crown.

Winters, L. (1988). Does it pay to advertise to hostile groups with corporate advertising. *Journal of Advertising Research, 3* (June): 1–15.

Wise, D. (1976). *The American police state.* New York: Vintage.

Wisotsky, S. (1993). A society of suspects: The war on drugs and civil liberties. *USA Today, 122* (July): 17–21.

Witkin, G. & Griffin, J. (1994). The new opium wars. *U.S. News & World Report* (10 October): 39–44.

Witkin, G. (1991). The men who created crack. *U.S. News & World Report* (19 August): 44–53.

Wohl, S. (1984). *The medical industrial complex.* New York: Harmony.

Wolkomir, R. (1994). Hot on the trail of toxic dumpers and other eco-outlaws, Texas style. *Smithsonian* (May): 26–37.

Woodhandler, S. & Hemmelstein, D. (1993). Socialized medicine is good business. *In These Times* (25 January–7 February): 18–21.

Workman, B. (1993). Stanford to lose millions for research, San Francisco *Chronicle* (29 July): A-4.

Worsley, P. (1982). *Marx and Marxism.* London: Tavistock.

Worsnop, R. (1991). Asian Americans. *CQ Researcher, 1* (3 December): 385–408.

—— (1992). Native-Americans. *CQ Researcher, 2* (8 May): 945–68.

Worthington-Roberts, B. (1981). *Contemporary developments in nutrition.* St. Louis: Mosby.

Wyckham, R. (1987). Implied superiority claims. *Journal of Advertising Research, 27* (Feb./March): 54–63.

Yoachum, S. (1993). The problem with gun control laws. San Francisco *Chronicle.* (13 July): A-1.

Zinn, H. (1980). *A people's history of the United States.* New York: Harper Perennial.

—— (1988b). Ask: Who killed JFK. Washington *Post* (17 November): C-13.

Picture Credits

Name Index

Subject Index